NAPOLEON'S M...
edited by SOMERSE...

Napoleon Bonaparte, the Emper... unexpectedly in a Corsican drawing ... Assumption of 1769. He was born, he claimed, 'on an old carpet, on which were worked large designs.' He climbed rapidly in the French Revolutionary Armies and by 1796, aged 27, he commanded the Army of Italy which he led to victory against Austria. In 1798 he conquered Egypt but was thwarted in his hopes of destroying British Power in India by Nelson's naval victory at Aboukir Bay. In 1799 Napoleon took advantage of a political crisis in Paris to return there. His popularity was still high and he engineered the *coup d'etat du 18 Brumaire* from which he emerged as First Consul, effectively a dictator. In 1802 he was elected consul for life and was constituted emperor by the *senatus-consulte* of 18 May 1804, confirmed by plebiscite. He and his wife Josephine were crowned at Notre-Dame in the presence of Pope Pius VII.

He had no children by Josephine, and divorced her in 1809 to marry the archduchess Marie-Louise of Austria, who bore him a son. He restored order and civil unity to France and reconstructed the financial, educational, judicial, executive and legislative systems. At the same time he ruthlessly suppressed conspiracies and destroyed the freedom of the press. By 1810 his empire covered most of Europe, excluding Russia, but following his disastrous Russian campaign (1812) and defeat at Leipzig (1813) the allies invaded France in 1814. Napoleon abdicated unconditionally, and was granted sovereignty of Elba, a small island to which he was confined off the Mediterranean coast. Ten months later he escaped on the brig *L'Inconstant* and landed with 700 soldiers at Juan les Pins. Louis XVIII fled to Belgium and Napoleon made his way to Paris amidst scenes of exultation. The allied coalition regathered in order to destroy him, and he was narrowly defeated at Waterloo (1815). He abdicated for a second time and considered sailing for America, but finally gave himself up to the British government. He spent the rest of his life interned on the Atlantic Island of St Helena, where he dictated and corrected his memoirs. He died in 1821, probably of stomach cancer, but possibly of Arsenic poisoning.

Somerset de Chair (1911–) was a member of the House of Commons (1935–45, 50–51) and parliamentary private secretary to the Minister for Production (1942–44). During the war he served in the British Army in the Middle East in the Royal Horse Guards (1938–42). He is an author and poet.

BONAPARTE

From the miniature of Napoleon wearing the uniform of the Institute painted by Jean Baptiste Paulin Guerin, not later than 1799.

NAPOLEON BONAPARTE

MEMOIRS

DICTATED BY THE EMPEROR AT ST HELENA
TO THE GENERALS WHO SHARED HIS CAPTIVITY

EDITED BY SOMERSET DE CHAIR
WITH A PREFACE BY MICHAEL FOOT

HISTORY

PUBLISHED BY THE SOHO BOOK COMPANY
1 BREWER STREET   LONDON W1

MCMLXXXVI

Published by
THE SOHO BOOK COMPANY
1/3 Brewer Street, London W1R 3FN
1986
Originally published by the Golden Cockerel Press in 1945
Republished by Faber and Faber in 1948
© Somerset de Chair 1945, 1986
Preface © Rt Hon Michael Foot 1986

British Library Cataloguing in Publication Data

Napoleon I, *Emperor of the French*
    Napoleon's Memoirs.
    1. Napoleon I, *Emperor of the French*
    2. France—Kings and Rulers—
        Biography
    I. Title II. De Chair, Somerset
    944.05′092′4   DC203

ISBN 0-948166-10-X

OTHER BOOKS BY SOMERSET DE CHAIR

Historical Fiction: Enter Napoleon; The Story of a Lifetime (Limited Edition, 100 copies only); Bring Back the Gods; Friends, Romans, Concubines; The Star of the Wind; Legend of The Yellow River (1979)
Contemporary Fiction: Red Tie in the Morning (Satire); The Teetotalitarian State (Satire); The Dome of the Rock
1939–45 War: The Golden Carpet (Limited Edition); The Silver Crescent (Limited Edition) (Published jointly in the public edition as The Golden Carpet); A Mind on the March
Historical: (As Editor and Translator)
The First Crusade (Limited Edition only); Napoleon's Memoirs (Limited and Public Editions); Supper at Beaucaire (Limited and Public Editions); Julius Caesar's Commentaries (Limited Edition only)
Biographical: (as editor)
The Sea is Strong; The Naval Memoirs of Admiral Sir Dudley de Chair, KCB, KCMG, MVO
Political: The Impending Storm; Divided Europe
Drama: Peter Public
Poetry: The Millennium; Collected Verse

Printed and bound in Great Britain
by Redwood Burn Ltd, Trowbridge, Wilts
Cover design, title page and introductory material
© THE SOHO BOOK COMPANY LTD 1986
Designed by Sally McKay at Graham Rawle Designs

The Glittering Legend
Preface by Michael Foot

"God was bored with him," said Victor Hugo. God, perhaps; but man, never. Many more books have been written about Napoleon, I imagine, than about any other figure of the last two centuries. The libraries are stacked with biographies, monographs, volumes of memoirs and detailed examinations of particular incidents. All the more surprising is it, therefore, that no one before had hit upon the brilliant idea of Mr. Somerset de Chair of compiling from all the scattered recollections dictated by Napoleon himself a coherent and consecutive autobiography. The idea has turned out to be a thrilling success. For some tastes, the slightly stereotyped descriptions of the battles may be tedious. But, for the rest, all the glamour and the glitter and the grandeur of the Napoleonic legend shine again in these pages, and who indeed can be bored with such a story?

Not merely do the books about Napoleon and his Marshals and his mistresses and his codes and his idiosyncrasies still pour from the presses. The arguments about him still rage. Some very great men, from Tolstoy to H. G. Wells, have sought to reduce his stature to human proportions, to expose his shameless arrogance, and to puncture the legend. Wells did it better than any.

"Since his time," he says in the *Outline of History*, "his name has been one of the utmost reassurance to great multitudes of doubting men; to the business man hesitating over a more than shady transaction, to the clerk fingering a carelessly written cheque that could so easily be altered, to the trustee in want of ready money, to the manufacturer meditating the pros and cons of an adulteration, to thousands of such people the word 'Napoleonic' has come with an effect of decisive relief. We live in a world full of would-be Napoleons of finance, of the press, of the turf; half the cells in our jails and many in our mad houses are St. Helenas. He was the embodiment of that sound, clear, self-centred commonsense, without sentiment or scruples or reflection, that struggles with our feebler better nature, that may ultimately destroy mankind.... The cultivation of the Napoleonic legend seems to offer a kind of refuge. From salvation."

No doubt that indictment of the "saturnine egotist" is true. Napoleon was no better than Hitler in his love of power, his lust for adulation, his colossal self-conceit. Yet there are many witnesses on the other side. Chateaubriand said: "Napoleon's grey greatcoat and hat hoisted on a stick, on the coast of Brest, would set all Europe in arms." His reception when he returned to Paris from Italy, from Egypt, from Elba, and on so many other occasions, proved that the devotion to him was real. Wells says it was "not him that they idolised, but a carefully fostered legend of an incredibly clever, recklessly brave little man, a little pet of a man, who was devoted to France and to them." No doubt that is also true. No doubt the scenes in Paris were re-staged for Hitler in Berlin. And yet it is also true that it was the lingering sentiments of the Revolution which hung round his name and which he knew so well how to incite that helped form the legend and the chief part of his glamour.

Napoleon called himself "the liberator of Italy," and the claim is not really disputable. He was, in fact, the precursor of Garibaldi and Cavour and Victor Emmanuel. He foresaw the unity of Italy more clearly than any of his contemporaries, and it is very hard to read his own descriptions of the Italian campaigns and believe that his constant appeals to the ideals of liberty and equality were entirely cynical. Cynical or not, they prove him to have been the best exponent of political warfare who ever lived. He understood the meaning of the Revolution, whatever his private reservations. "I knew," he said, "when and how to use the talisman, the magic word of liberty, and, above all, of national independence."

Something similar happened in Germany, and Heinrich Heine—no bad witness—has described his emotions when he saw the Emperor ride by: "A smile warming and calming all hearts played about his lips—and yet all knew that those lips had but to whistle *et la Prusse n'existait plus*; those lips had but to whistle and the entire clergy had tinkled its last; those lips had but to whistle for the whole Holy Roman Empire to dance. And those lips were smiling, and the eye, too, was smiling. It was an eye clear as the sky; it could read the hearts of men: it saw all things in this world at a glance, while we others see them only one after the other, and see only coloured shadows. The brow was not so clear; the spectres of future battles were nesting there; and at times flashes crossed that brow and they were the creative thoughts, the great seven-league-boots ideas, with which the Emperor's spirit invisibly strode over the world—and I think that each of those thoughts would have provided a German author with material to write about all their lives." No doubt powerful treatises could be written, tearing such exaggerated, romantic outbursts to tatters, and exposing such hero-worship as a dangerous illusion. But this is what Napoleon, the child of the Revolution, "Robespierre on horseback," meant to so many millions of people in the Europe of that age. So great was the liberating impulse felt at the downfall of feudalism. So great was the business started on that day when the Bastille was overthrown.

The same mood crossed the Channel and was even felt in England, where Napoleon was pictured as a hobgoblin to frighten the children or as a fiend who really did frighten the aristocracy. William Hazlitt—again, no bad witness—could not join the national rejoicing over the news of Waterloo. He saw the re-emergence of the Bourbons, the revival of "the old hag, Legitimacy," the strengthening of all those forces of evil which were strangling English freedom. And William Cobbett—an excellent witness—had felt the impact of those seven-league-boots ideas and understood what had been happening in Europe so much better than the rulers of that time and most of the historians who have written since. He wrote:

"The bridge of Jena, the column of Austerlitz, all the memorials of French triumph, brought from Amsterdam, Naples, Vienna, Rome, Turin, Madrid, Munich, Berlin, Moscow, and dearest *Hanover*: all these may be destroyed; but never will the whole world, combined in arms, be able to destroy the effect of those principles which sent the conquerors forth, which first warmed their hearts with enthusiasm, and which are now become part of the settled possessions of their minds."

Such sentiments helped to form at least part of the Napoleonic legend. The ugly fascination which Wells describes accounts for less than half the secret. And those who find themselves unable to read these enthralling memoirs without a sneaking admiration for the boastful hero may comfort themselves with the knowledge that Heine, Hazlitt and Cobbett are good enough company for any man.

*This book is dedicated by the editor
to*
OLIVER LYTTELTON

INTRODUCTION

The world has had to wait more than a century for Napoleon's autobiography, because no one could so describe the curious assortment of papers published under the disjointed editorship of Gourgaud and de Montholon as 'Memoirs of the History of France during the reign of Napoleon, dictated by the Emperor at Sainte-Helena to the generals who shared his captivity and published from the original manuscripts corrected by himself'.

Yet Napoleon spent most of the six years which elapsed between his Abdication and his death in writing his memoirs. His book was dictated to the separate members of his staff—Bertrand, Las Cases, Gourgaud, and de Montholon; he would dictate at odd moments, and when one of them was exhausted the other would take his place. Nearly every one at Longwood seems to have been roped in. Las Cases records Napoleon as saying at dinner on Tuesday, 4 June, 1816, 'I have been severely scolded to-day over my laziness; I am therefore going to start work again, attacking several points at the same time. Each one shall have his bit. Did not Herodotus, I think, give the name of the Muses to his books? Very well. I want each of mine to bear one of yours. There will be no one, down to little Emmanuel, who will not have his own. I am going to start on the Consulate with Montholon; Gourgaud will have some other epoch or some individual battles, and little Emmanuel will prepare the facts and materials of the epoch of the Coronation.'

The narrative, as it came from Napoleon, was reasonably complete up to 1800, but those portions of it recorded in the notebooks of the separate recipients were necessarily haphazard. Yet, when Gourgaud and de Montholon finally came to collaborate in editing the completed memoirs, they preferred to publish as isolated volumes those sections which each had recorded separately. One might as well take the manuscript of an exciting novel and publish the 1st, 3rd, 5th and 7th chapters in one volume, the 2nd, 4th, 6th and the 8th in the next, and so on. The result would be quite unintelligible. Thus Volume I, published from Gourgaud's script, begins with a chapter on Toulon and

INTRODUCTION

jumps to Brumaire, while we must wait until Volume III for the intervening chapters dictated to de Montholon.

Furthermore, a pathetic loyalty to their master caused these misguided followers to include in the publication every audible whisper uttered by Napoleon, and, as he was in the habit, when dictating his memoirs, of launching out into voluble digressions on any topic that arrested his attention, the narrative is continually interrupted while the Emperor gives his opinions on different technical subjects. To each volume they added pages of appendices, and, to crown all, they decided to include in the actual memoirs all the observations which Napoleon dictated on the books of the day with which he was supplied at St Helena. They had the grace to add these as separate volumes, but they were part of the completed set, and the reader who wanted four volumes of Napoleon's Memoirs had to pay for an extra three volumes on what the editors described as 'Historical Miscellanies'. Vol. III of these Miscellanies is a complete treatise in itself on the Wars of Marshal Turenne in eighteen chapters and of Frederic the Great in nine chapters.

If they had wished to silence for ever the voice of their master, they could have hit upon no more ingenious expedient than the slavish reproduction of his every word.

This weird publication first appeared in England in 1823, and it is not surprising that it was never published again. Obscurity has enveloped Napoleon's one great book. As Editor of this book, I have done no more than present the self-portrait scientifically cleaned and hung in a good light; a treatment which has long been considered justified in the presentation of lost masterpieces.

People have listened eagerly to every whisper of gossip, from the Tuileries, from Malmaison, Fontainebleau and Longwood. But the voice of the giant himself has been muted until now.

If Napoleon had been alive when the book was being published he would surely have rearranged the material in the most attractive, most arresting form. He who had always been content to appeal to the million, who was the originator of the modern dictatorship by plebiscite, would have wished his book to become a best-seller. I have surely done what he would have wished and, if the appearance of Napoleon's autobiography from the shadows of the tomb has something of the awe-inspiring surprise of a miracle about it, Napoleon, the master of surprise, the Man of Miracles, would rub his hands and chuckle at the astonishment of a world which imagined him silenced for ever, just as he chuckled on the eve of Austerlitz when he heard the Russians moving down to Sokolnitz.

It is a pity that Napoleon did not live long enough at St Helena to carry his memoirs, as a consecutive narrative, beyond the battle of Marengo, when

INTRODUCTION

he was First Consul. But he has described—what interests us most—his incredible rise to the first place in France, seized uneasily at Brumaire, but fixed beyond hazard at Marengo.

Half of Napoleon is worth two of Hitler, and, in an age of *ersatz* Napoleons, the authentic voice is arresting. He need not fear comparisons. What Napoleon Bonaparte failed to achieve, Adolf Hitler need not have attempted. Napoleon was the last example in the expanding field of War of a general who could, at one and the same time, successfully direct the strategy of a nation and lead its decisive armies in the field.

I have not added to the script, as dictated by Napoleon and scored with corrections in his own almost indecipherable handwriting. I have merely removed overlapping and obviously irrelevant asides; and arranged the narrative in its proper sequence.

I have taken one liberty only, and, since a translation must necessarily have a somewhat different ring from the original in another language, I think the change would meet with his approval. In dictating to his friends, he used the third person—in imitation of Caesar, possibly for convenience or to avoid embarrassment. But the use of the third person tends to obscure the fact that it is Napoleon himself who is the author; and what is in reality a vivid revelation of his personality tends to assume the character of an account by some other personality, aloof and remote. I have no doubt that many readers of the original papers imagined that the continual references to 'Napoleon' were the observations of Gourgaud or de Montholon, and thought that they were reading a biography of their master by these two, and not, as is virtually the case, his own extremely vivid autobiography.

I have retained the translation of 1823 throughout, partly to facilitate comparison between this edition and that, but especially because the contemporary translation seems to retain in a way which no modern translation could, the atmosphere of the period which Napoleon describes.

There remains the question as to how much, if anything, of Las Cases' 'Mémorial de Sainte-Hélène ou Journal, où se trouve consigné, jour par jour, ce qu'a dit et fait Napoléon durant dix-huit mois' can be accepted as part of Napoleon's Memoirs. For the present I have decided to use none of it; and for the following reasons.

It is purely a diary in which Las Cases records from day to day Napoleon's opinions on various matters, but it was not taken down to dictation, nor does it pretend to present a consecutive narrative of Napoleon's life. The only part of it which does so is the rough draft of the Italian Campaign which Napoleon was dictating to Las Cases before the latter left St Helena. But Las Cases himself puts this material forward purely as a rough draft offered in advance of the official memoirs, corrected and finally revised by Napoleon, which Las Cases knew would be published eventually.

INTRODUCTION

This is what Las Cases says in the Journal about Napoleon's work on the Memoirs, Vol. II, p. 173 (Brussels edition. P. J. de Mat. 1828.):

'Cependant l'Empereur continuait régulièrement ses campagnes d'Egypte avec le Grand-Maréchal. Ma campagne d'Italie était au bout depuis long-temps; nous la touchions et retouchions sans cesse, quant à sa forme typographique, à la contexture des chapitres et à la coupe des paragraphs, etc. On en verra, dans le courant de cet ouvrage, le peu qui m'en est resté dans les mains.

'De temps à autre il dictait des parties séparées à MM. Gourgaud et Montholon.'

But Las Cases then adds a note (p. 176):

'N.B. J'ai dit plus haut que je donnerais les fragmens de la campagne d'Italie demeurés en mes mains. Me voilà à la fin d'un mois; j'en vais placer quelques chapitres.

'A mon retour en France, par la funeste circonstance qui m'a rendu à moi-même, les motifs de garder pour moi seul les fragmens de la campagne d'Italie, que je possédais du consentement de l'Empereur, n'existant plus, et la privation de mes papiers par le ministère anglais ne me laissant pas l'occasion de rien publier sur Sainte-Hélène, je distribuai quelques-uns de ces fragmens, ne mettant d'autre condition à leur publicité que de bien spécifier qu'ils étaient de simples brouillons, de premières dictées qui auront reçu sans doute, par la suite, de grandes altérations. Aujourd'hui que la restitution de mes papiers m'a mis à même de publier le Mémorial de Sainte-Hélène, j'ai eu la pensée d'y réunir tous ces fragmens de la campagne d'Italie, imaginant qu'ils ne seront pas sans intérêt pour ceux qui aimeront à comparer ce premier jet avec les idées arrêtées: d'autant plus que, tenant des dépositaires mêmes du manuscrit de ces campagnes que la volonté de l'Empereur a été que le tout fût publié avec luxe, cartes, plans, etc., et dédié à son fils, j'ai tout lieu de croire qu'on sera long-temps encore avant de jouir de cette publication. J'insérerai donc le peu que je possède, 7 chapitres sur 22, soit à la fin des mois, soit dans le cours même du journal, quand il viendra à languir.'

From all this it is clear that Las Cases can contribute nothing to the account of the period covered by the Memoirs finally revised by the Emperor. Those Memoirs, as edited by Gourgaud and de Montholon, included the approved version of such parts of the narrative as were dictated in the first instance to Las Cases and Bertrand. I have rested on the manuscripts of the Memoirs dictated by Napoleon as such and corrected in his own handwriting. Although it imposes some strain on the autobiographical theme, I have decided to add to this edition the chapter (XXXIV) 'Of Neutral Powers', which includes Napoleon's account of Nelson's battle at Copenhagen and the murder of the Czar Paul. It also includes Napoleon's reactions to the news of George Washington's death.

INTRODUCTION

Napoleon's Memoirs of the Waterloo campaign, which I translated for the Golden Cockerel Press as a companion volume, are included in this volume as Part II. Dictated to Baron Gourgaud at St Helena, and smuggled to Europe, they were first published in 1820. An English translation by Barry O'Meara, who had volunteered to go to St Helena as Napoleon's British surgeon, was published in February, 1820, under the title *Historical Memoirs of Napoleon,* 1815, and French editions from the original were published in the same year both in Paris (chez Barrois l'aîné) and Brussels (chez H. Remy), under the title *Mémoires pour servir à l'Histoire de France en* 1815. In the English edition O'Meara made it clear that the account was by Napoleon himself. 'It is Napoleon himself who speaks,' he emphasizes in the preface. In the first French editions the Memoirs of 1815 were published anonymously.

At this time, 1820, while Napoleon was still living, a very strict censorship was imposed on any attempt by the ex-Emperor to address public opinion in Europe; and some doubt at first existed as to whether the Memoirs of 1815, translated by O'Meara, were in fact authentic. They certainly are; and in the second French edition of the complete memoirs, published by Bossange et Cie, Paris, in 1830, they were duly included as Volume IX. They are not to be confused with the spurious *Manuscript Venu de Ste-Hélène d'une Manière inconnue* which was published soon after Napoleon was sent into exile.

If any corroboration were needed of the authenticity of Napoleon's Memoirs of 1815, Las Cases supplies it in his *Mémorial de Sainte-Hélène,* in which he describes the day-to-day life of Napoleon's exile. Writing of Monday, 26 August, 1816 (fourth edition, published by P. J. De Mat, Brussels, 1828, page 377, Vol. V) Las Cases records:

'L'Empereur fait lire ce qu'il avait dicté de la bataille de Waterloo au Général Gourgaud. Quelles pages! . . Elles font mal. . . . Les destinées de la France ont tenu à si peu de chose!! . .

'N.B. Cette production a été publiée en Europe, en 1820. [Footnote: "Mémoires pour servir à l'Histoire de France en 1815." Bruxelles, chez H. Remy 1820.] On était venu à bout de la faire sortir furtivement de Ste-Hélène, en dépit de toute vigilance. Dès que cette relation de Waterloo parut dans le monde, personne ne se trompa sur son auteur. On s'est écrié: Napoléon seul pouvait la décrire de la sorte; et l'on assure que c'est précisément ainsi que s'est exprimé son antagoniste lui-même. Quels beaux chapitres! . . . Il serait impossible d'en essayer une analyse, ou de prétendre à les faire juger dignement; il faut lire l'original. Toutefois nous transcrivons littéralement ici, les dernières pages, contenant, en forme de résumé, neuf observations de Napoléon, sur les fautes qu'on lui a reprochées dans cette campagne.

'Ce sont des points qui demeureront classiques et nous avons pensé qu'on ne serait pas fâché de retrouver ici des objets qui deviennent toutes les fois que l'occasion s'en présente, le sujet de vives et importantes discussions.

INTRODUCTION

'Nous ferons précéder ces observations, et toujours de la dictée de Napoléon, du tableau des ressources qui restaient encore à la France, après la perte de la bataille.

' "La position de la France était critique après la bataille de Waterloo, mais non désespérée, etc., etc." '

The passage, which he proceeds to quote, will be found on page 540 of this translation.

No English translation or edition has been published since O'Meara's translation appeared in 1820; and the 1820 edition is to-day so rare, that I have only been able to find copies in the British Museum and the Bodleian Library at Oxford.

In editing Napoleon's Memoirs, it seemed best to keep the consecutive narrative of events from Corsica to Marengo separate from the isolated campaign of 1815.

The extensive rearrangement of the 1823 translation made it advisable to retain the wording of that translation in Part I if it were to be checked easily against the original. There is, however, no need to rearrange the sequence of the 1815 Memoir and, at the close of another war between England and a continental dictator, there is something to be said for presenting Napoleon's explanation of his downfall in the idiom of the present day.

I must thank Captain J. H. F. McEwen, for a valuable coup d'œil; Mr. F. A. Taylor (Modern Language tutor at Christ Church, Oxford) for help with technical passages in Chapter II; and Miss Caroline Senator for generally ironing the wrinkles out of my translation.

As in the earlier Memoirs, Napoleon dictated his narrative in the third person, usually (in the 1815 Memoir) referring to himself as 'L'Empereur', occasionally as 'ce Prince' or 'Napoléon'. As in the Corsica-Marengo part, I have taken the liberty of putting the words back into Napoleon's own mouth—but, except for the tables and footnotes, it has not been necessary to edit the record in any other respect. Whereas in the earlier memoirs all was chaos to be rearranged and sifted, here the narrative, after a certain amount of factual exposition in the early chapters, flows clearly and inexorably towards its sombre close.

Indeed there is something of the inevitability of a Greek tragedy in these pages, and one has the feeling that Napoleon saw it all as a drama, with himself, naturally, as the tragic hero. In describing the Battle of Waterloo he writes (page 525), 'A battle is a dramatic action, which has its beginning, its middle and its end.' We need not accept Napoleon's judgment of Wellington, nor concur in his opinion that the victor of Waterloo committed every blunder imaginable; but it is clear from the facts given by Napoleon that, though the outcome was decisive, the margin between victory and defeat was extremely narrow.

INTRODUCTION

The frontispiece is from a miniature of Napoleon by Guérin, which is generally accepted as the most authentic likeness of him before he became First Consul.

I have been able, thanks to the kindness of the Trustees of the present Lord Bathurst, to preface the Waterloo Campaign with a reproduction of the Canova bust of Napoleon, as Emperor, brought back from France after the Treaty of Paris by Lord Bathurst, the Colonial Secretary.

I have visited all the principal battlefields, scattered from Toulon to Saint-Jean d'Acre, which Napoleon describes.

The emphasis of his narrative is on the Italian campaigns; and it was in the high summer of 1933 that I climbed through the Ligurian foothills to that ridge commanding the valleys of the Bormida where Napoleon won his first and perhaps most brilliant battles between Montenotte and Millesimo.

I drifted lazily across the plain of Lombardy—visiting Marengo, Lodi, Arcola, Rivoli, Castiglione. It is easy to pin-point the origin of the Napoleonic legend: I found it in a little village drowsing in the hot Lombardy sunshine, where a narrow, rusted iron bridge spans a dyke with precipitous grass sides. On the further bank was a square grey house, from the windows of which Austrian guns in 1796 swept a little stone bridge with grape-shot, as Napoleon fought shoulder to shoulder with the bravest in the Army of Italy to get across it. We can picture him, a tiny figure in general's uniform, his skin still pale and taut from the poverty and illness of Paris before Vendémiaire, his brown hair hanging down to his shoulders, the hard glitter of ambition in his eyes. Napoleon describes the incident on page 119 of these Memoirs:

'I determined to try a last effort in person. I seized a flag, rushed on the bridge, and there planted it; the column I commanded had reached the middle of the bridge, when the flanking fire and the arrival of a division of the enemy frustrated the attack; the grenadiers at the head of the column, finding themselves abandoned by the rear, hesitated, but being hurried away in the flight, they persisted in keeping possession of their general; they seized me by my arms and by my clothes, and dragged me along with them amidst the dead, the dying, and the smoke; I was precipitated into a morass in which I sunk up to the middle, surrounded by the enemy. The grenadiers perceived that their general was in danger; a cry was heard of "Forward, soldiers, to save the general!" These brave men immediately turned back, ran upon the enemy, drove him beyond the bridge, and I was saved. This was the day of military devotedness. Lannes, who had been wounded at Governolo, had hastened from Milan; he was still suffering; he threw himself between the enemy and myself, covering me with his body, and received three wounds, determined never to abandon me.'

Napoleon was twenty-seven years old.

INTRODUCTION

As I looked over the bridge into the dyke where Napoleon was swept with the repulse of his charge, the little urchins of Fascist Italy gathered around me, pointing to the small obelisk monument which still commemorates the battle of Arcole. And one of them said proudly of his little village, 'Piccola, ma grande'—for there the Napoleonic legend was born.

SOMERSET DE CHAIR

Chilham Castle, Kent
  21 May, 1946

CONTENTS

PART I: CORSICA TO MARENGO

I. CORSICA

Biographical Notice. Topographical description of Corsica. Pascal Paoli. French administration. Effects of the Revolution of 1789. The King of England assumes the title of King of Corsica. *page* 3

II. TOULON

Remarks on the state of parties in France in 1793. Expedition against Sardinia. Toulon delivered to the English. Plan of attack adopted against Toulon. Siege and taking of the place. Consequences of the reduction of Toulon by the troops of the Convention. My appointment to the command of the artillery of the Army of Italy. *page* 12

III. THE WAR OF ITALY

Fortifying of the shores of the Mediterranean. Taking of Saorgio. Positions of the French Army. Accused. Action of Cairo. I direct the army in the Campaign of 1794. Taking of Saorgio, Oneglio, the Col di Tende and all the upper chain of the Alps (April 1794). I appease general insurrections in Toulon. I quit the Army of Italy and arrive in Paris (June 1795). Kellerman, being defeated, rallies in the lines of Borghetto (July 1795). Battle of Loano (December 1796). *page* 26

IV. THE THIRTEENTH OF VENDEMIAIRE

Constitution of the Year III. Additional Laws. The Sections of Paris take up arms in resistance. Dispositions for the attack and defence of the Tuileries.

CONTENTS

Action of the 13 Vendemiaire. Commander in chief of the Army of the Interior. *page* 36

V. DESCRIPTION OF ITALY

Italy. The Alps. The Apennines. The great plain of Italy. The Valley of the Po, and the Valleys, the waters of which fall into the Adriatic, north and south of the Po. Frontiers of Italy on the land side. Lines which cover the Valley of the Po. Capitals of Italy. Her maritime resources. *page* 45

VI. BATTLE OF MONTENOTTE

Plan of the Campaign. State of the Armies. I arrive at Nice towards the end of March, 1796. Battle of Montenotte (12 April). Battle of Millesimo (14 April). Action of Dego (15 April). Action of Saint-Michel (20 April). Action of Mondovi (22 April). Armistice of Cherasco (28 April). Examination of the expediency of passing the Po, and proceeding farther from France. *page* 50

VII. BATTLE OF LODI

Passage of the Po (7 May). Action of Fombio (8 May). Armistice granted to the Duke of Parma (9 May). Battle of Lodi (10 May). Entrance into Milan (14 May). Armistice granted to the Duke of Modena (2 May). Berthier. Massena. Augereau. Serrurier. *page* 64

VIII. REVOLT OF PAVIA

The army quits its cantonments to take up the line of the Adige. Revolt of Pavia (24 May). Taking and sack of Pavia (26 May). Causes of this revolt. The army enters the territories of the Republic of Venice (28 May). Battle of Borghetto; passage of the Mincio (30 May). The army arrives on the Adige (3 June). Description of Mantua. Blockade of Mantua (4 June). Armistice with Naples (5 June). *page* 74

IX. MARCH ON THE RIGHT BANK OF THE PO

Motives of the march of the French Army on the Apennines. Insurrection of the Imperial Fiefs. Entrance into Bologna and Ferrara (19 June). Armistice granted to the Pope (23 June). Entrance into Leghorn (29 June). At Florence. Revolt of Lugo. Opening of the trenches before Mantua (18 July). Favourable posture of affairs in Piedmont and Lombardy. *page* 83

CONTENTS
X. BATTLE OF CASTIGLIONE
Marshal Wurmser arrives in Italy at the head of a new army. Situation of the French Army. Plan of the Campaign. Wurmser debouches in three columns (29 July), the right by the road of the Chiesa, the centre on Montebaldo, between the Adige and the lake of Garda, and the left by the valley of the Adige. Prompt resolution taken by me. Action of Salo. Action of Lonato (31 July). Battle of Lonato (3 August). Surrender of the three divisions of the enemy's right, and of part of his centre. Battle of Castiglione (5 August). Second blockade of Mantua (end of August). Conduct of the different nations of Italy, on the news of the success of the Austrians. *page* 91

XI. MANOEUVRES AND ACTIONS BETWEEN THE MINCIO AND THE BRENTA (SEPTEMBER)
Position of the Austrian army in the Tyrol, on 1 Sept. Battle of Roveredo (4 Sept.). Wurmser descends into the plains of the Bassanese. Actions of Primolano, Covolo, and Cismone (7 Sept.). The French army forces the defiles of the Brenta. Action of Verona (7 Sept.). Battle of Bassano (8 Sept.). Wurmser passes the Adige by the bridge of Porto Legnago (11 Sept.). Battle of Saint-George (19 Sept.). Wurmser is shut up in Mantua (18 Sept.). Third blockade of Mantua. *page* 102

XII. BATTLE OF ARCOLE
Marshal Alvinzi arrives in Italy at the head of a third army. Good condition of the French army; all the nations of Italy confident of its success. Battle of the Brenta (5 Nov.); Vaubois evacuates the Tyrol in disorder. Battle of Caldiero (12 Nov.). Murmurs and various sentiments of the French soldiers. Nocturnal march of the army on Ronco, where the troops pass the Adige over a bridge of boats (14 Nov.). The army re-enters Verona in triumph, by the Venetian gate, on the right bank (18 Nov.). *page* 111

XIII. NEGOTIATIONS IN 1796
1: With the Republic of Genoa. 2: With the King of Sardinia. 3: With the Duke of Parma. 4: With the Duke of Modena. 5: With the Court of Rome. 6: With the Grand Duke of Tuscany. 7: With the King of Naples. 8: With the Emperor of Germany. 9: Congress of Lombardy. Cispadan Republic.
page 124

CONTENTS

XIV. BATTLE OF RIVOLI

Affair of Rome. Situation of the Austrian army. Situation of the French army. Plan of operations adopted by the Court of Vienna. Action of Saint-Michel (12 Jan.). Battle of Rivoli (14 Jan.). Passage of the Adige by General Provera; and his march on Mantua (14 Jan.). Battle of la Favorite (16 Jan.). Capitulation of Mantua (2 Feb.). *page* 137

XV. TOLENTINO

Rupture of the armistice with the Court of Rome. Army of the Holy See. Action of the Senio; submission of Romagna. The prisoners taken at the action of the Senio sent home. Action of Ancona; taking of that place. Our Lady of Loretto. Mission of the General of the Camaldolites to Pope Pius VI. Treaty of Tolentino. Mantua. Arrival of two divisions of the armies of the Sambre and Meuse, and Rhine, in Italy. *page* 147

XVI. THE TAGLIAMENTO

Plan of the Campaign for 1797. Passage of the Piave (12 March). Battle of the Tagliamento (16th March). Retreat of Prince Charles. Action of Gradisca (19 March). Passage of the Julian Alps and the Drave (29 March). Actions in the Tyrol. *page* 159

XVII. LEOBEN

The Imperial Court leaves Vienna. Overtures of Peace. Action of Neumarck (1 April). Action of Unzmark. Armistice of Judenburg (8 April). Junction of the divisions of the Tyrol, Carniola and Carinthia. Preliminaries of peace of Leoben (18 April). Motives which actuated the French. Of the Armies of the Rhine and Sambre and Meuse; they commence hostilities on 18 April, the very day of the signature of the preliminaries of peace. *page* 170

XVIII. OBSERVATIONS

On Field-Marshal Beaulieu. On my manoeuvres against Field-Marshal Beaulieu. On Field-Marshal Wurmser. On my manoeuvres against Field-Marshal Wurmser. On Field-Marshal Alvinzi. On my manoeuvres against Field-Marshal Alvinzi. On the march against the army of the Holy See. On the Archduke Charles. On my manoeuvres against the Archduke Charles.

page 180

CONTENTS
XIX. VENICE

Description of Venice. The Senate. Conduct of the Proveditores Mocenigo and Foscarelli. Factions; Brescia; Bergamo. Difficulties attending the affairs of Venice. Conferences of Goritz, on 20 March. Verona. Mission of the Aide-de-camp Junot to the Senate; Declaration of war of Palma-Nuova. Entrance of Venice by the French; Revolution of that capital. Revolution of the Terra-Firma States; the colours taken from the Venetians and in the last days of the campaign forwarded to Paris. *page* 202

XX. NEGOTIATIONS IN 1797

1: Head-quarters at Montebello. 2: Negotiations with the Republic of Genoa. 3: With the King of Sardinia. 4: With the Pope. 5: With Naples. 6: The Cispadan and Transpadan Republics; they form the Cisalpine Republic. 7: Negotiations with the Grisons and the Valteline. *page* 217

XXI. THE EIGHTEENTH OF FRUCTIDOR

Of the Executive Directory. Public spirit. Religious affairs. New system of weights and measures. The Factions which divide the Republic. Conspiracy against the Republic, headed by Pichegru. I defeat this conspiracy. 18 Fructidor. Law of 19 Fructidor. *page* 235

XXII. PEACE OF CAMPO-FORMIO

Exchange of the ratifications of the preliminaries of Leoben (24 May). Conferences of Montebello; conferences of Udine previous to 18 Fructidor. Conferences of Passeriano. After 18 Fructidor, the French government is no longer desirous of peace. Motives which determine me as French plenipotentiary to sign the treaty of peace. My interest and policy. Extravagant pretensions of the Imperial plenipotentiaries; threats, movements of the armies. Signature of the treaty of peace of Campo-Formio (17 Oct.). Of General Desaix and General Hoche. I leave Italy and proceed to Paris, passing through Rastadt. *page* 251

XXIII. PARIS

My arrival at Paris. Affairs of Switzerland. Affairs of Rome. Bernadotte, the ambassador of the Republic at Vienna, is insulted by the populace. Plan of an expedition into the East. 21 January. *page* 267

CONTENTS

XXIV. NAVAL BATTLE OF ABOUKIR

Reports at London respecting the expedition preparing in the ports of France. Movement of the English squadrons in the Mediterranean, in May, June, and July. Chances for and against the French and English naval armaments, if they had met on the way. The French squadron receives orders to enter the old port of Alexandria. It moors in Aboukir roads. I learn that it remains at Aboukir. My astonishment. The French squadron is reconnoitred at its moorings by an English frigate. Battle of Aboukir. *page 278*

XXV. EGYPT

Alexandria. The Nile and its inundations. Ancient and modern population. Division and productions of Egypt. Commerce. Alexander. Of the different races by which Egypt is inhabited. The Desert and its inhabitants. Government and importance of Egypt. Army Policy. *page 292*

XXVI. EGYPT: BATTLE OF THE PYRAMIDS

March of the army on Cairo. Despondency and complaints of the soldiers. Position and forces of the enemy. Manoeuvres of the French army. Impetuous charge of Murad-Bey repulsed. Taking of the intrenched camp. French headquarters at Gizeh. Taking of the Isle of Rodah. Surrender of Cairo. Description of the city. *page 305*

XXVII. EGYPT: RELIGION

Of Christianity. Of Islamism. Of the difference in the spirit of these two religions. Hatred of the Caliphs against Libraries. Of the duration of Empires in Asia. Polygamy. Slavery. Religious Ceremonies. Feast of the Prophet.
page 314

XXVIII. EGYPT: CUSTOMS, SCIENCES AND ARTS

Women; Children. Marriages. Clothing of the men and women. Harness of Horses. Houses; Harems. Arts and Sciences. Navigation of the Nile and canals. Carriage, Camels, Dromedaries, Asses, and Horses. Institute of Egypt. Labours of the Scientific Commission. Hospitals; different diseases, etc. Plague. Works executed at Cairo. Anecdote. *page 321*

XXIX. SYRIA

Motives of the Expedition into Syria. The Siege of Saint-Jean d'Acre.
page 330

CONTENTS
XXX. EGYPT: MARCH, APRIL, AND MAY, 1799. BATTLE OF ABOUKIR

Insurrection against the French. Murad-Bey leaves the desert of Nubia, and advances into Lower Egypt. Mustapha-Pacha lands at Aboukir, and takes the fort. Movements of the French army. I advance to Alexandria. Junction of the army at Birketh; I march against the Turkish army. Battle of Aboukir, 25 July, 1799. *page* 340

XXXI. EGYPT

Objects of the Expedition to Egypt. Project to convert the French Army to Islam. Arrival of English newspapers. My return to France. Events in Egypt after my departure. Résumé of the Egyptian campaign. Comparison with Saint Louis' campaign of 1250. *page* 350

XXXII. THE EIGHTEENTH OF BRUMAIRE (9 NOVEMBER, 1799)

My arrival in France. Sensation produced by that event. At Paris. The directors, Roger Ducos, Moulins, Gohier, Sieyes. My Conduct. Roederer, Lucien and Joseph, Talleyrand, Fouché, Réal. State of the different parties. They all make proposals to me. Barras. I coalesce with Sieyes. State of feeling among the troops in the Capital. Measures arranged for 18 Brumaire. Proceedings of that day. Decree of the Council of the Ancients, which transfers the seat of the Legislative Body to Saint-Cloud. My speech to the Council of the Ancients. Tumultuous sitting at Saint-Cloud. Adjournment of the Councils for three months. *page* 361

XXXIII. PROVISIONAL CONSULS

State of the Capital. My Proclamation. First sitting of the Consuls; myself president. Ministry; changes therein. Maret, Dubois-Crancé, Robert-Lindet, Gaudin, Reinhart, Forfait, Laplace. First acts of the Consuls. Funeral honours paid to the Pope. Shipwrecked emigrants at Calais. Nappertandy, Blackwell. Suppression of the festival of 21 January. Interview of two royalist agents with me. La Vendée, Chatillon, Bernier, D'Autichamp, Georges. Pacification. Discussion on the Constitution. The opinions of Sieyes and myself. Daunou. The Constitution. Nomination of the Consuls Cambaceres and Lebrun. *page* 380

CONTENTS
XXXIV. OF NEUTRAL POWERS

Of the law of Nations observed by belligerent states in war by land; and of that which is observed by them in maritime war. Of the principles of the maritime rights of neutral powers. Of the armed neutrality of 1780, the principles of which, being those of France, Spain, Holland, Russia, Prussia, Denmark, and Sweden, were in opposition to the claims of the English at that period. New claims of England successively brought forward during the war of the Revolution, from 1793 to 1800. America acknowledges these pretensions; consequent discussions with France. Opposition to these claims on the part of Russia, Sweden, Denmark, and Prussia. Ensuing events. Convention of Copenhagen, in which, notwithstanding the presence of an English Fleet of superior force, Denmark acknowledges none of the pretensions of England, the discussion thereof being adjourned. Treaty of Paris between the French Republic and the United States of America, by which the differences which had arisen between the two powers, in consequence of the submission of the Americans to the claims of England, are terminated. France and America solemnly proclaim the principles of the maritime rights of neutrals. Causes of the Emperor Paul's dissatisfaction with England. Russia, Denmark, Sweden and Prussia, proclaim the principles acknowledged by the treaty of the 30th September between France and America. The Convention, called the Armed Neutrality, signed on the 16th December, 1800. War between England, on one side, and Russia, Denmark, Sweden, and Prussia, on the other; which proves that these powers were as far from acknowledging the claims of the English, as France, Holland, America, or Spain. Battle of Copenhagen, April 2nd, 1801. Assassination of the Emperor Paul I. Russia, Sweden and Denmark desist from the principles of the armed neutrality. New principles of the rights of neutrals acknowledged by these powers. Treaty of June 17, 1801, signed by Lord St. Helens. These new principles binding only on the powers who have acknowledged them by treaty. *page* 402

XXXV. ULM. MOREAU

Defects of the plans of the campaigns of 1795, 1796, 1797. Position of the French armies in 1800. Position of the Austrian armies. My plan. My dispositions. Opening of the campaign. Armistice of Pahrsdorf, 15 July, 1800. Critical remarks. *page* 432

XXXVI. GENOA. MASSENA. 1800

Respective positions of the Armies of Italy. Genoa. Melas intersects the French army. Massena endeavours ineffectually to re-establish his communications with his left. He is invested in Genoa. Blockade of Genoa. Melas

CONTENTS

marches upon the Var; Suchet abandons Nice. Massena attempts to raise the blockade. Pressed by famine, Massena negotiates. Surrender of Genoa. The Austrians recross the Alps in order to advance to meet the Army of reserve. Suchet pursues them. Consequences of the victory of Marengo. Suchet takes possession of Genoa. Critical remarks. *page* 440

XXXVII. MARENGO

Army of Reserve. My departure. Review at Dijon. Head-quarters at Geneva. Lausanne. Passage of the Saint-Bernard. The French army passes the Sesia and the Trebbia. Entry into Milan. Position of the French army at the moment of receiving intelligence of the taking of Genoa. Action of Montebello. Arrival of General Desaix at head-quarters. Battle of Marengo. Armistice of Marengo. Genoa restored to the French. My return to France. *page* 451

PART II: THE WATERLOO CAMPAIGN

XXXVIII. RETURN FROM THE ISLAND OF ELBA

The Imperial Eagle flies from steeple to steeple until it reaches the towers of Notre Dame at Paris. The Bourbons leave France. Secret convention concluded at the end of 1814 between Austria, France and England against Russia and Prussia. The King of Naples declares war on Austria on 22 March. The Congress of Vienna in March, 1815. *page* 475

XXXIX. MILITARY STATE OF FRANCE

State of the Army on 1 March, 1815. Organization of an Army of 800,000 men. Armament, clothing, re-mounts, finance. State of the Army on 1 June, 1815. Paris. Lyons. *page* 482

XL. PLAN OF CAMPAIGN

Could the French Army begin hostilities on 1 April? Three plans of campaign. First project: remain on the defensive and draw the enemy armies upon Paris and Lyons. Second project: take the offensive on 15 June and, in the event of not being successful, draw the enemies on Paris and Lyons. I adopt this plan of operations. *page* 494

CONTENTS

XLI. OPENING OF THE CAMPAIGN, JUNE, 1815

State and position of the French army on the evening of 14 June. State and position of the Anglo-Dutch and Prusso-Saxon armies. Manoeuvres and fighting during the day of the 15th. Position of the belligerent armies during the night of the 15th to 16th. *page* 500

XLII. THE BATTLE OF LIGNY

Marches made by the French army to give battle to the Prusso-Saxon army. Battle of Ligny, 16 June. Engagement at Quatre-Bras, 16 June. Position of the armies during the night of the 16th to 17th. Their manoeuvres during the day of the 17th. Their positions during the night of 17 to 18 June. *page* 508

XLIII. BATTLE OF MONT-SAINT-JEAN (WATERLOO)

The Anglo-Dutch army's line of battle. The French army's line of battle. My aims; attack on Hougoumont. General Bülow arrives on the battlefield with 30,000 men, which brings the Duke of Wellington's army up to 120,000 men. Attack on la Haie-Sainte by the First Corps. General Bülow is repulsed. Cavalry charge on the plateau. Marshal Grouchy's movements. Marshal Blücher's movements, which brought the enemy on the battlefield to 150,000 men. Movements of the Imperial Guard. *page* 519

XLIV. THE RALLYING

Rallying of the army at Laon. Marshal Grouchy's retreat. Resources remaining to France. Effects of my abdication. *page* 538

XLV. OBSERVATIONS *page* 543

APPENDIXES

A. TABLES *page* 555

B. SUPPER AT BEAUCAIRE *page* 565

INDEX *page* 577

PART ONE

CORSICA TO MARENGO

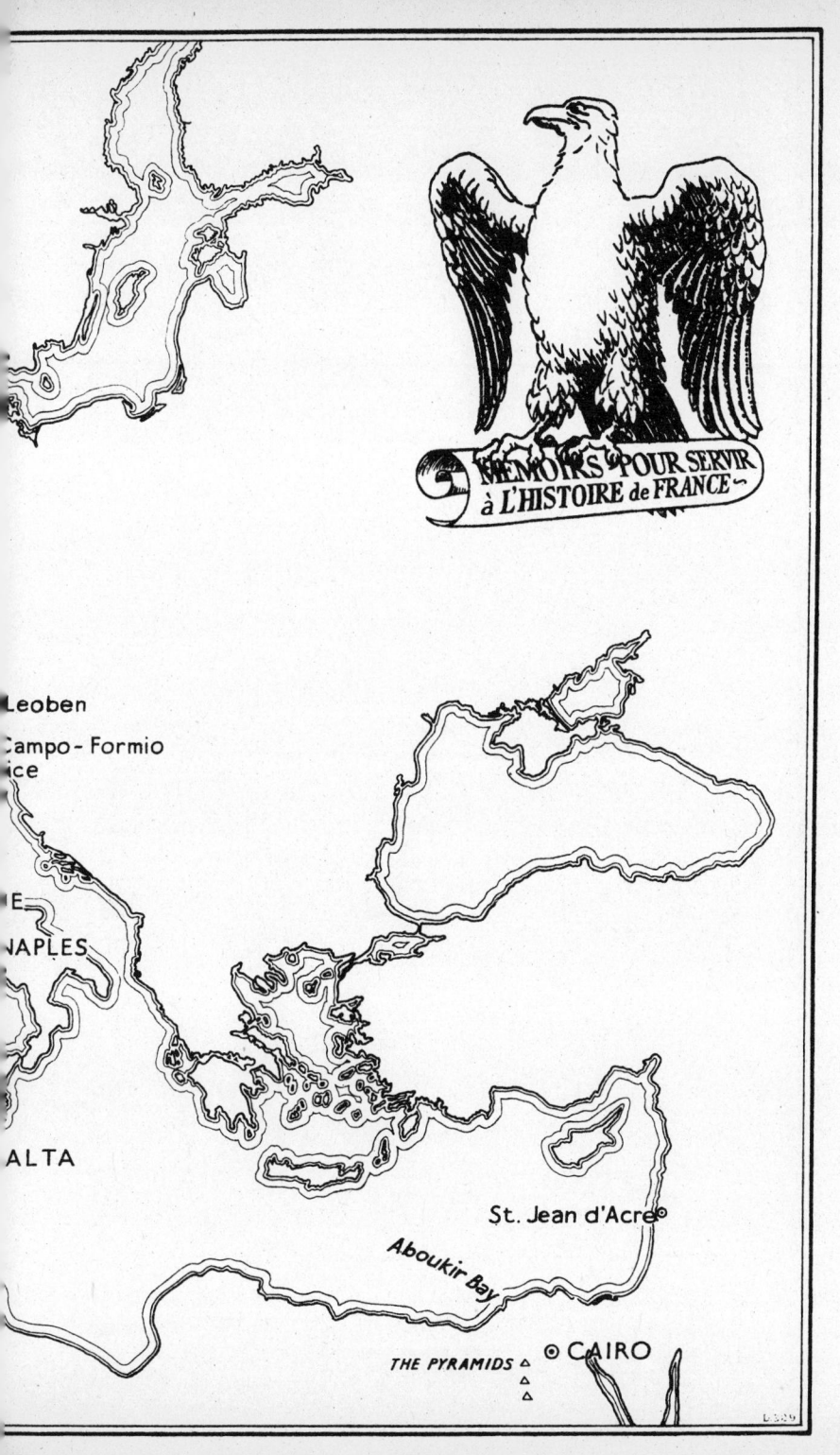

Chapter I

CORSICA

Biographical Notice. Topographical description of Corsica. Pascal Paoli. French administration. Effects of the Revolution of 1789. The King of England assumes the title of King of Corsica.

I have commenced my memoirs with the siege of Toulon. I did not consider my actions previous to that date as belonging to history; but public curiosity requiring information respecting the origin and progressive elevation of a man who has played so large a part on the theatre of life, it is therefore conceived that some notice of his family, his early years, and the commencement of his distinguished career, will not be misplaced here.

The Bonapartes are of Tuscan origin. In the middle ages they figured as senators of the republics of Florence, San Miniato, Bologna, Sarzana, and Treviso, and as prelates attached to the court of Rome. They were allied to the Medici, the Orsini and Lomellini families. Several of them were engaged in the public affairs of their native states; whilst others employed themselves in literary pursuits at the period of the revival of letters in Italy. Giuseppe Bonaparte published one of the first regular comedies of that age, entitled *The Widow*; copies of which exist in the libraries of Italy, and in the Royal Library at Paris, where is also preserved the History of the Siege of Rome by the Constable de Bourbon of which Nicolo Bonaparte, a Roman prelate, is the author. This narrative is highly esteemed. In 1797, literary men, whom no coincidence escapes, remarked the circumstance, that since the time of Charlemagne Rome had been twice menaced by great foreign armies; at the head of one of which was the Constable de Bourbon, and at the head of the other, one of the remote descendants of the family of his historian.

When the French Army entered Bologna, the Senate took care to have

CORSICA

their *Golden Book* presented to me by Counts Marescalchi and Caprara, to draw my attention to the names of several of my ancestors, inscribed amongst those of the senators who had contributed to the honour of their city.

In the fifteenth century, a younger branch of the Bonaparte family settled in Corsica. At the time of the campaign of Italy, there was no one left of all the Italian branches, but the Abbé Gregorio Bonaparte, Knight of Saint Stephen, and Canon of San Miniato. He was an old man of great respectability and wealth. In my march on Leghorn, I stopped at San Miniato and was received with my whole staff at the house of my relation. During supper, the conversation turned entirely on a Capuchin, a member of the family, who had been beatified a century before; and the canon solicited my interest to procure his canonization. This proposal was several times made to me as Emperor after the *Concordat*: but less importance was attached to these pious honours at Paris than at Rome.

Those who are well acquainted with the Italian language know that it is optional to write *Buona* or *Bona*. The members of the Bonaparte family have used both these modes of orthography indiscriminately: of two brothers it has happened that one has written his name with the *u*, and the other without it. It seems that the suppression of this letter was common in very ancient times: in the church of Saint Francis, belonging to the Minor Friars in the town of San Miniato, on the right of the principal altar is a tomb with this inscription:

> CLARISSIMO SUAE AETATIS ET PATRIAE VIRO
> JOANNI JACOBI MOCCII DE BONAPARTE
> QUI OBIIT ANNO M. CCCCXXXXI. DIE XXV.
> SEPTEMBRIS NICOLAUS DE BONAPARTE
> APOSTOLICAE CAMERAE CLERICUS FECIT
> GENITORI BENEMERENTI ET POSTERIS.

The Christian name of *Napoleon* has also been the subject of much discussion. It was usual in the Orsini and Lomellini families, from whom it was adopted by that of Bonaparte. The manner of writing it has been disputed in Italy. Some pretended that it was derived from the Greek, and signified *Lion of the desert*; others that it was derived from the Latin. The correct way of writing it is *Napoleone*. This name is not found in the Roman calendar. From the searches made in the martyrologies at Rome, at the period of the *Concordat*, it appears that Saint Napoleone was a Greek martyr.

My great grandfather had three sons, Joseph, Napoleon, and Lucien. The first of these left only one son, whose name was Charles; the second left only a daughter, named Elizabeth, who was married to the head of the Ornano family; the third was a priest, and died in 1791, aged eighty years; he was archdeacon of the chapter of Ajaccio. Charles, who thus became the only heir

CORSICA

to his father, was my father. He was educated at Rome and Pisa, where he took his degree of Doctor of Laws. At a very early age he married Letitia Ramolino, a lady of a very good family of the country, descended from that of Colalto of Naples. By her he had five sons and three daughters. Charles Bonaparte was twenty years of age at the breaking out of the war of 1768; he was a warm friend to Paoli, and a most zealous defender of the independence of his country. The town of Ajaccio being occupied at the commencement of hostilities, by the French troops, he removed with his family to Corte in the centre of the island. His young wife, then pregnant with me, followed Paoli's head-quarters and the army of the Corsican patriots, in the campaign of 1769, across the mountains, and resided a long time on the summit of Monte Rotondo, in the parish of Niolo. But her pregnancy advancing, she obtained from Marshal Devaux a safe conduct to return to her house at Ajaccio. I was born on 15 August, being the Feast of Assumption.

Charles Bonaparte followed Paoli, on his retirement, as far as Porto Vecchio, and wished to have embarked with him; but the entreaties of his family, his attachment to his children and his affection for his young wife, retained him.

Corsica is situated at a distance of twenty leagues* from the coast of Tuscany, forty from that of Provence, and sixty from that of Spain. It belongs, geographically, to Italy; but as that peninsula does not constitute a power, Corsica naturally becomes an integral part of France. The surface of the island is five hundred square leagues in extent; it contains four maritime towns, Bastia, Ajaccio, Calvi and Bonifacio; sixty-three pieves or valleys; four hundred and fifty villages or hamlets, and three great roads capable of containing the largest fleets; that is to say, San Fiorenzo, Ajaccio, and Porto Vecchio. The island is mountainous; a chain of lofty granite mountains runs through it from the north-west to the south-east, dividing it into two parts; the highest peaks of this range are perpetually covered with snow. The three principal rivers are the Golo, the Liamone, and the Tavignano. Rivers and torrents gush from the high mountains, and fall into the sea in all directions; towards their mouths there are little plains of a league or two in circuit. The coast towards Italy, from Bastia to Aleria, is a plain twenty leagues in length, and from three to four in width.

The isle is woody; the plains and hills are or may be covered with olives, mulberry, orange, lemon and other fruit-trees. The sides of the mountains are clothed with chestnut-trees, amidst which there are villages naturally fortified by their position. On the tops of the mountains are forests of pines, firs and evergreen oaks; the olive-trees are as large as those of the Levant; the chestnut-trees are enormous, and of the largest species; the pines and firs are not inferior to those of Russia in height and bulk; but as top-masts they will not

* One league equals approximately three miles. S. de C.

CORSICA

last above three or four years, becoming dry and brittle after that time; whereas the Russian pine always retains its elasticity and pliancy. Oil, wine, silk, and timber are four great branches of exportation proper to enrich this island. The population is under one hundred and eighty thousand souls; it might be five hundred thousand. The country would supply the corn, chestnuts, and sheep necessary to feed them. Before the invasion of the Saracens, all the sea-shore was peopled. Aleria and Mariana, two Roman colonies, were great cities of sixty thousand souls; but the incursions of the Musulmans in the seventh and eighth centuries, and afterwards those of the Barbary powers, drove the whole population into the mountains. Hence the plains became uninhabited, and of course unhealthy.

Corsica is a beautiful country in the months of January and February; but in the dog-days it becomes dry; water grows scarce, especially in the plains; the inhabitants are then very fond of taking up their residences on the sides of the hills, whence they descend into the low grounds in winter, either to graze their flocks, or to cultivate the plains.

The French government appointed provincial states in Corsica, and continued the magistracy of the twelve nobles, who, like the Burgundian deputies, governed the country. Charles Bonaparte, who was very popular in the island, formed part of this magistracy. He was attached as counsellor to the tribunal of Ajaccio; this was an intermediate step for getting into the supreme council of the country. In 1779 the states appointed him deputy for the nobles to Paris. The clergy chose the bishop of Nebbio, and the third estate a Casabianca. Charles Bonaparte took with him his two sons, Joseph and myself, the one aged eleven years, the other ten; he placed the former in the boarding-school at Autun, and I entered the military school at Brienne as a pupil.

I remained six years at that school. In 1783, Field-Marshal the Chevalier Kergariou, inspector of the military schools, selected me to pass the following year to the military school at Paris, to which three of the best scholars, chosen by the inspector, were annually sent from each of the twelve provincial schools. I remained only eight months at Paris. In the month of August, 1785, I was examined by the Academician Laplace, and received the brevet of a second lieutenant of artillery in the regiment of La Fère; I was then sixteen years of age. Phelippeaux, Pecaduc, and Demasis passed at the same examination: they all three emigrated at the commencement of the Revolution. The first defended Saint Jean D'Acre, where he evinced much talent, and where he died; the second was a Breton, and attained the rank of major in the Austrian army; the third, who returned to France during the consulate, was appointed administrator of the crown moveables, and chamberlain.

The regiment of La Fère was at Valence, in Dauphiny, where I kept garrison for the first time. Some commotions having taken place in the town

CORSICA

of Lyons, I was sent thither with my battalion. This regiment afterwards passed to Douay in Flanders, and to Auxonne in Burgundy. In 1791 I was made a captain in the regiment of artillery of Grenoble, then in garrison at Valence, whither I returned. The revolutionary ideas began to prevail. Part of the officers emigrated. Gouvion, Vaubois, Galbo Dufour and I were the four captains who, having preserved the good opinion of the soldiers, kept them within the limits of order.

I was in Corsica for six months in 1792. I took the earliest opportunity of waiting on Paoli, with whom my father had been intimate. Paoli received me in a very friendly manner, and did all in his power to retain me, and keep me out of the way of the disturbances with which the mother-country was threatened.

In January and February, 1793, I was intrusted with a counter attack on the North of Sardinia, whilst Admiral Truguet was operating against Cagliari. The expedition not having succeeded, I brought my troops safely back to Bonifacio. This was my first military achievement, and obtained me testimonials of the attachment of the soldiers, and a local reputation.

A few months after, Paoli, against whom an accusation had been decreed by the senate, threw off the mask and revolted. Previously to declaring himself, he communicated his scheme to the young artillery officer (myself) of whom he used frequently to say 'You see that youth; he is a man for a Plutarch's biography'. But all the persuasions and influence of this venerable old man were unavailing. I agreed with him that France was in a frightful state, but reminded him that nothing that is violent can last long; and that as he had an immense influence over the inhabitants, and was master of the places of strength and of the troops, he ought to maintain tranquillity in Corsica, and let the fury of the moment pass away in France; that the island ought not to be torn from its natural connexion on account of a momentary disorder; that it had everything to lose in such a convulsion; that it belonged geographically either to France or Italy; that it never could be English; and that as Italy was not a single undivided power Corsica ought constantly to remain French. The old general could not controvert all this, but he persisted in his plans. I quitted the convent of Rostino, where this conference was held, two hours afterwards. Affairs grew worse; Corte openly revolted, bodies of insurgents from all quarters advanced on Ajaccio, where there were no troops of the line or means of resistance proportioned to the attack.

In the course of twenty years, from 1769 to 1789, the island of Corsica was greatly improved. But all these benefits had no effect on the hearts of the inhabitants, who were anything but French at the time of the revolution. A lieutenant-general of infantry, who was crossing the mountains, entered into conversation with a shepherd respecting the ingratitude of his countrymen. He enumerated the benefits of the French administration. 'In your

CORSICA

Paoli's time you paid double what you pay now.'—'That is true, Signor; but then we gave it, and now you take it.' The native wit of these islanders appears on every occasion. Thousands of their repartees might be mentioned; we will take one at random:—Several titled officers who were travelling in Niolo, were saying one evening to their host, one of the poorest inhabitants of the pieve, 'What a difference there is between us Frenchmen and you Corsicans; see how we are clothed and maintained.' The peasant rose, looked at them attentively, and asked each of them his name. One was a marquis, another a baron, and the third a chevalier. 'Pooh!' said the peasant, 'I should like to be dressed as you are, I own; but pray are all the French marquisses, barons, and chevaliers?'

The Revolution altered the disposition of these islanders; they became French in 1790. Paoli then left England, where he lived on a pension allowed him by Parliament, which he abandoned. He was well received by the Constituent Assembly, by the National Guard of Paris, and even by Louis XVI. His arrival in the island produced a general rejoicing; the whole population flocked to Bastia to see him. His memory was wonderful; he knew the names of all the families, and had been acquainted with the late heads of them. In a few days he obtained a greater influence over the people than he had ever possessed. The Executive Council appointed him a general of division, and gave him the command of the troops of the line in the island. The National Guards had chosen him to command them. The Electoral Assembly nominated him as president. He thus combined in himself every kind of power. This conduct of the Executive Council was not politic, but it must be ascribed to the spirit of that period. However this may be, Paoli faithfully served the Revolution until the tenth of August. The death of Louis XVI, completed his dissatisfaction. He was denounced by the popular societies of Provence; and the Convention, which never hesitated for any consideration whatever, summoned him to its bar. He was nearly eighty years of age. This was a mere invitation to lay down his head on the scaffold. He had no resource but to appeal to his countrymen; and he prevailed on the whole island to revolt against the Convention. The representatives of the people, commissioned to carry the decree into execution, arrived, under these circumstances. All they could do was to preserve the fortified places of Bastia and Calvi, by the aid of a few battalions. If the determination of the measures to be adopted by Corsica had depended on an assembly of the principal families, Paoli would not have succeeded. The excesses which had been committed in France were generally blamed; but it was thought that they would prove transient, and that it would not be expedient, in order to avoid the inconvenience of the moment, to separate from a country which alone could secure the welfare and tranquillity of the island. Paoli was astonished at the little attention he obtained in private conferences. Many of those very individuals

CORSICA

who had followed him to England, where they had spent twenty years in cursing France, were now the most refractory. But amongst the mass of the people there was but one cry when their ancient leader called upon them. The banner of the death's head was instantly hoisted on every steeple, and Corsica ceased to be French. A few months afterwards the English occupied Toulon. After they were forced to evacuate that place, Admiral Hood anchored at San Fiorenzo; he landed 12,000 men, whom he placed under the command of Nelson. Paoli joined them with 6,000 men. They surrounded Bastia. La Combe, Saint-Michel and Gentili defended the town with the greatest intrepidity, and it did not capitulate until after a siege of four months. Calvi resisted forty days after the opening of the trenches. General Dundas, who commanded an English corps of 4,000 men, and was encamped at San Fiorenzo, refused to take part in the siege of Bastia, not choosing to compromise his troops without the special orders of his government.

An extraordinary event now took place. The King of England placed the crown of Corsica upon his head, where it was strangely associated with the crown of Fingal. In June, 1794, the Council of Corsica, of which Paoli was president, proclaimed that its political connexion with France was for ever broken off; and that the crown of Corsica should be offered to the King of England. A deputation, of which Galeazzi was president, and Filippo of Vescovato, Negroni of Bastia, and Cesari Rocca of La Rocca, members, proceeded to London; and the king accepted the crown. He appointed Sir Gilbert Elliot* viceroy. The Council had at the same time decreed a constitution, to secure the liberties and privileges of the country: it was modelled on that of England. Elliot was a man of merit; he was appointed governor-general of India in 1806; but he soon quarrelled with Paoli. The old man had retired amongst the mountains, where he disapproved of the conduct of the Viceroy, who was influenced by two young men, Pozzo di Borgo and Colonna; one of whom was in his service as a secretary, and the other as an aide-de-camp. Paoli was accused of being of a restless character, of not being able to make up his mind to live as a private individual, and of always wanting to act the part of master of the island. Still the influence he possessed there, which was undisputed, the services which he had rendered to England on this occasion, and the respectability of his character and conduct, induced the English ministers to treat him with great indulgence. He had several conferences with the viceroy and the secretary of state; in one of which, piqued by several of the observations that were made, he said, 'This is my kingdom; I carried on war against the King of France for two years; I expelled the republicans: if you violate the privileges and rights of the country, I can still more easily expel your troops'. A few months afterwards the King of England wrote him a suitable letter, in which he recommended him, from the interest he felt for

*Baron Minto.

his tranquillity and happiness, to go and end his days in a country in which he was respected and had been happy. The secretary of state took this letter to him at Ponte-Lechio. Paoli felt that it was an order; he hesitated: but there were then no signs of the termination of the reign of terror in France. The army of Italy was still in the county of Nice. In declaring war against the English, Paoli would have exposed himself to the hostility of two great belligerent powers. He submitted to fate, and went to London, where he died in 1807. It is due to his memory to state, that in all his letters from England, during the last eight years of his life, he constantly advised his countrymen never to separate from France; but to share the fortune, good or bad, of that great nation. He left by his will considerable sums to establish a university at Corte.

Had the English wished to preserve their influence in Corsica, they should have acknowledged the independence of the country, established Paoli's power, and granted a few trifling subsidies, in order to preserve a kind of supremacy, as well as privileges of anchorage for their squadrons in the principal roads, especially that of San Fiorenzo. They would then have possessed a point of *appui* in the Mediterranean; they might, in case of need, have raised an auxiliary corps of five or six thousand brave men for service in this sea; and the ports of Corsica would have been at their command. The numerous refugees who were in France would gradually have rallied to a national government; and France herself, at the peace, would readily have sanctioned a state of affairs which public opinion had suggested to Choiseul.

The Corsicans were extremely dissatisfied with the English governors; they neither understood their language, their habitual gloom, nor their manner of living. Men who were continually at table, almost always intoxicated, and of uncommunicative dispositions, exhibited a remarkable contrast to their manners. The difference of religion was also a cause of dislike. This was the first time, since the origin of Christianity, that their territory had been profaned by an heretical worship; and every thing they saw confirmed them in their prejudices against the Protestant religion. Its unceremonious worship, and its naked, dismal temples, could not affect southern imaginations to which the pomp and splendour of the Catholic religion, its beautiful churches, adorned with pictures and frescoes, and its imposing ceremonies, are so highly agreeable. The English scattered gold profusely; the inhabitants accepted it, but without feeling any gratitude towards the givers.

The Bonaparte family retired to Nice, and afterwards into Provence; our property was devastated; our house, after being pillaged, was long used as barracks by an English battalion. On reaching Nice, I was preparing to join my regiment, when General Dugear, who commanded the artillery of the Army of Italy, required my services, and employed me in the most delicate operations. A few months after, Marseilles revolted; the Marseillese army got possession of Avignon; the communications of the Army of Italy were cut off; there was a want of ammunition; a convoy of powder was intercepted; and the general-in-chief was greatly embarrassed by these circumstances. General Dugear sent me to the Marseillese insurgents, to try to induce them to let the convoys pass, and at the same time to take all necessary measures to secure and accelerate their passage. I went to Marseilles and Avignon, had interviews with the leaders of the insurgents, convinced them that it was their own interest not to excite the resentment of the Army of Italy, and got the convoys forwarded.

During these proceedings Toulon had surrendered to the English: I, now a lieutenant-colonel (chef de bataillon), was ordered on service to the siege of Toulon, on the proposal of the committee of artillery. I joined the besieging army on 12 September, 1793.

During my residence at Marseilles, when sent to the insurgents, having an opportunity of observing all the weakness and incoherence of their means of resistance, I drew up a little pamphlet, which I published before I left that city. I endeavoured to open the eyes of these frantic people and predicted that the only result of their revolt would be to furnish a pretext to the men of blood of the day, for sending the principal persons amongst them to the scaffold. This pamphlet produced a powerful effect, and contributed to calm the agitation which prevailed.*

*See Appendix B.   S. de C.

Chapter II

TOULON

Remarks on the state of parties in France in 1793. Expedition against Sardinia. Toulon delivered to the English. Plan of attack adopted against Toulon. Siege and taking of the place. Consequences of the reduction of Toulon by the troops of the Convention. My appointment to the command of the artillery of the Army of Italy.

The Constituent Assembly went in some respects too far, and in others did too little. It was composed of men endowed with distinguished talents, but devoid of experience. It committed two errors, which might have produced the total ruin of the nation: the first was the establishment of a constitution at variance with the experience of all ages and states, and the mechanism of which was contrived, not for the purpose of strengthening social order and promoting national prosperity, but of restricting and annulling the public power, which is that of government. Great as this error was, it was less flagrant and had less deplorable consequences than that of persisting in re-establishing Louis XVI on the throne after the affair of Varennes. What then ought the Assembly to have done? It ought to have sent commissioners extraordinary to Varennes, not to bring the King back to Paris, but to clear the way for him, and to conduct him safely beyond the frontiers; to have decreed, by virtue of the Constitution, that he had abdicated; proclaimed Louis XVII King; created a regency, confided the care of the King, during his minority, to a Princess of the House of Condé, and composed the council of regency and the ministry of the principal members of the Constituent Assembly. A government so conformable to principle, and so national, would have found means to remedy the disadvantages of the Constitution;

TOULON

the force of events would soon have led to the adoption of the necessary modifications. It is probable that France would have triumphed over all her enemies, domestic and foreign, and would have experienced neither anarchy nor revolutionary government. By the period of the King's majority, the Revolution would have been so well rooted that it might have defied every attack. To act otherwise was intrusting the steering of the vessel, during a most tremendous storm, to a pilot no longer capable of conducting her; it was calling the crew to insurrection and revolt in the name of public safety; it was invoking anarchy.

The royalists formed the right side of the Constituent Assembly; the constitutionals took the left side, placing themselves at the head of the people. But in the Legislative Assembly the constitutionals formed the right side, and the *Girondins* the left. In the Convention, the latter in their turn composed the right side, and the faction called that of the Mountain, formed the left side, directing the popular party. In the Constituent Assembly the constitutionals demanded the expulsion of the troops of the line, proclaiming the principle that the assembly ought to be guarded by the national guard. In the Legislative Assembly they maintained a contrary opinion, and loudly clamoured for troops of the line; but the *Girondins* indignantly rejected the employment of any hired army against the majority of the people. The *Gironde* party, in its turn, claimed the protection of an army of the line against the popular party. Thus did the different parties alternately change their opinions according to circumstances.

The factions of the Gironde and the Mountain were too violent in their mutual animosity. Had they both continued to exist, the proceedings of administration would have been encumbered with so many impediments, that the Republic could not have maintained the contest against the combination of all Europe. The good of the country required the triumph of one of these parties. On 31 May, the Gironde fell, and the Mountain thenceforth governed without opposition. The consequence is known: the campaigns of 1793 and 1794 delivered France from foreign invasion.

Would the result have been the same if the Gironde party had gained the day, and the Mountain had been sacrificed on 31 May? I think it would not. The Mountain party, although checked, would always have possessed great influence, in France, in the popular societies and armies, and would have essentially diminished the energies of the nation, the whole of which were necessary at that crisis. There was undoubtedly more talent in the Gironde than in the Mountain; but the Gironde was composed of more speculative men, with less resolution and decision of will; they would have governed more mildly, and it is probable that under their reign only part of the excesses which the revolutionary government of the Mountain committed would have taken place. The Gironde prevailed in the towns of Lyons, Marseilles,

TOULON

Toulon, Montpellier, Nîmes, Bordeaux, and Brest, and in several provinces. The home of the Mountain was the capital, and it was supported by all the Jacobins in France. On 31 May it triumphed; twenty-two deputies, the leaders of the Gironde, were proscribed.

At the commencement of the winter of 1793, the Army of Italy had experienced a check: the first maritime expedition that the republic attempted, the expedition against Sardinia, covered us with shame. Never, indeed, was an expedition planned with such want of forethought and so little talent.

Admiral Truguet, who commanded the squadron, was master of the sea. He had attacked and burnt the little town of Oneglia, which belonged to the King of Sardinia, and the outrages committed on that occasion by his men had filled all Italy with horror.

Some thought that the expedition against Sardinia was proposed by this Admiral; others that it was by the Executive Council; but in either case he was charged with its management and direction.

The General of the Army of Italy was to furnish him with troops: he did not choose to give him those that passed the Var; he therefore placed at his disposal 4 or 5,000 men from the Marseillese phalanx, who were still at Marseilles. General Paoli, who commanded in Corsica, furnished also three battalions of troops of the line, which were in that island. The Marseillese phalanx was as undisciplined as it was cowardly; the officers were no better than the men; and they carried along with them all sorts of revolutionary disorder and excess. Nothing could be expected from such rabble; but the three battalions drawn out of the twenty-third division were chosen troops.

In the course of February, 1793, the French troops landed, in spite of the fire of the batteries which defended the shores of Cagliari. The next morning, by break of day, a regiment of Sardinian dragoons charged the Marseillese advanced posts, who, instead of meeting them, took to flight, crying 'Treason': they massacred an excellent officer of the line, who had been chosen to conduct them. This dragoon regiment would have cut off all the Marseillese phalanx, had not the three battalions of the line from Corsica stopped the charge, and given the Admiral time to re-embark his troops without further loss. He then returned to Toulon, after having lost many other vessels, which were burnt by his own orders, on the shores of Cagliari.

There was, in reality, no object whatsoever in this expedition: its pretended aim was to facilitate the arrival of corn from Africa into Provence, where it was much wanted; and even to procure it in the island of Corsica, so fertile in grain. But in that case the Executive Council ought to have made choice of a general officer fitted for the command, and have given him artillery-officers and engineers of sufficient ability, with several troops of cavalry and horse-artillery. Instead of mere revolutionary levies, the troops ought to have consisted of 15,000 effective men. The blame was afterwards laid upon the general who commanded the Army of Italy, but that was unjust; this general disapproved the expedition, and studied the interest of the Republic in reserving the troops of the line to defend the frontier and the county of Nice. He was tried and perished on the scaffold, under the pretext of his having been guilty of treason, both in Sardinia and Toulon; he was, however, innocent of it in either place.

The squadron was composed of good vessels, completely manned with able seamen; but they were undisciplined and riotous like the Marseillese troops; forming themselves into clubs and popular assemblies, and deliberating on the affairs of the nation. Whenever they arrived in port they endeavoured to hang some of the citizens, under pretence of their being nobles or priests, and diffused terror wherever they went.

In consequence of the events which took place in Paris on 31 May, Marseilles revolted, raised several battalions, and sent them to the assistance of Lyons. General Carteaux, who was detached from the Army of the Alps with 2,000 men, beat the Marseillese at Orange, drove them out of Avignon, and entered Marseilles on 24 August, 1793. Toulon had shared in the insurrection of Marseilles, she received the principal Marseillese sectionaries within her walls, and in concert with them the inhabitants summoned the English and gave up the place to them—a place of the utmost importance to us. We had there from twenty to twenty-five ships of the line, besides noble establishments and immense stores. On hearing of it, General Lapoype set out from Nice with 4,000 men, accompanied by the Representatives of the People, Freron and Barras: he advanced on Saulnier, observing the redoubts of Cape Brun, which the enemy occupied with a part of the garrison of Fort la Malgue; the rideau of the forts of Pharaon, and the line comprised between Cape Brun and Fort Pharaon.

On the other side General Carteaux, with the Representatives of the People, Albitte, Gasparin, and Salicetti, advanced on Beausset, and observed the passes of Ollioules, which were in possession of the enemy. The combined troops, English, Spanish, Neapolitans, Sardinians, etc., collected from all quarters, were not only in possession of the place itself, but also of all the defiles and avenues for six miles round the town.

On 10 September, General Carteaux made an attack upon the passes of Ollioules, and gained possession of them. His advanced posts arrived within sight of Toulon, and of the sea.

Twelve or fifteen days after the taking of the passes of Ollioules, I, at that time chief of a battalion of artillery, arrived from Paris, being sent by the Committee of Public Safety to command the besieging artillery. The non-commissioned officers and ensigns had been promoted, through the Revolution, to the superior ranks of the artillery. A great number of them were capable of making good generals in that department of the arm; but many had neither the capacity nor the information necessary for the elevated rank, to which their seniority and the spirit of the times had promoted them.

On my arrival, I found the headquarters at Beausset. They were busy making preparations to burn the Allied squadrons in the road of Toulon; and the next day I went with the General-in-Chief to visit the batteries. What was my surprise to find a battery of six twenty-four pounders planted a quarter of a league from the passes of Ollioules, at three gun-shots from the English vessels and two from the shore; and all the volunteers of the Côte d'Or and the soldiers of the regiment of Burgundy occupied with heating the balls at all the *bastides*! (A name given in the South of France to a sort of country-houses.) I did not conceal my astonishment.

My first care as Commandant of the artillery was to get together a great number of officers in that department, whom the circumstances of the Revolution had removed. At the end of six weeks, I was enabled to assemble, organize, and supply a park of two hundred pieces of artillery. Colonel Gassendi was placed at the head of the arsenal of constructions at Marseilles. The batteries were advanced, and placed on the most advantageous points of the shore; and their effect was such, that some large vessels were dismasted, several smaller ones sunk, and the enemy were forced to abandon that part of the road.

During the time that the preparations for the siege were completing, the army was considerably increased. The Committee of Public Safety sent plans and instructions relative to the conduct of the siege. They had been drawn up in the Committee of Fortifications by General D'Arçon of the engineers, an officer of great merit. The chief of battalion, Marescot, and many brigades of engineer officers arrived. All appeared to be in readiness to commence. A council was called, of which Gasparin, a representative, was president: he was a sensible and well-informed man, who had himself been in the service. The instructions from Paris were read: they detailed at great length the operations necessary to recover Toulon by a regular siege.

For the space of a month I had been carefully reconnoitring the ground, and had made myself perfectly acquainted with all its localities. I proposed the plan of attack which occasioned the reduction of Toulon. I regarded all the propositions of the Committee of Fortifications as totally useless, under the circumstances of the case; and it was my opinion, that a regular siege was not at all necessary. In fact, supposing a position could be gained, which, with from fifteen to twenty mortars, thirty or forty pieces of cannon, and furnaces for red-hot balls, would keep up a fire upon every point of the great and lesser roads, it was evident that the combined squadron would be obliged to abandon them; and the garrison would then be placed in a state of blockade, not being able to communicate with the squadron, which would be forced to stand out to sea. On this hypothesis I had laid it down as a principle, that the combined forces would prefer drawing off the garrison, and burning the French vessels and magazines, rather than leave 15 or 20,000 men in the fortress, who sooner or later would be obliged to surrender, without having anything in their power to destroy, so as to ensure terms of capitulation for themselves.

In a word, I declared that it was not necessary to march against the place at all, but only to occupy the position proposed; and which was to be found at the extreme point of the promontory of Balagnier and l'Eguillette; that I had discovered this position a month before, and had pointed it out to the General-in-Chief, assuring him that if he would occupy it with three battalions, he would take Toulon in four days; that the English had become, since I first observed it, so sensible of its importance, that they had disembarked 4,000 men there, had cut down all the wood that covered the promontory of Cair, which commanded the whole position, and had employed all the resources of Toulon, even the galley-slaves, in order to intrench themselves there; making of it, as they expressed themselves, 'a little Gibraltar'. But that the point, which a month ago might have been seized and occupied without opposition, now required a serious attack; that it would not be advisable to risk an assault, but to form batteries, mounted with twenty-four pounders and mortars, in order to destroy the epaulments, which were constructed of wood, to break down the palisades, and throw a shower of shells into the interior of the fort; and that then, after a vigorous fire for eight-and-forty hours, the work should be stormed by picked troops. Two days after this fort should be taken I gave it as my opinion that Toulon would belong to the Republic. This plan of attack was much discussed; and the engineer officers who were present at the council were of opinion that my project was a necessary preliminary to regular sieges, the first principle of all sieges being the establishment of a strict blockade.

From this time there was unanimity of opinion: the enemy constructed two redoubts under the two hillocks, one of which immediately commands l'Eguillette and the other Balagnier. These redoubts flanked Little Gibraltar, and played on the two sides of the promontory.

In conformity to the plan adopted, the French raised five or six batteries against Little Gibraltar, and constructed platforms for fifteen mortars. A battery had also been raised of eight twenty-four pounders and four mortars against Fort Malbosquet, the construction of which was a profound secret to the enemy, as the men who were employed on the work were entirely concealed from observation by a plantation of olives. It was intended that this battery should not be unmasked till the moment of marching against Little Gibraltar; but on 20 November the Representatives of the People went to inspect it, when they were informed by the cannoneers that it had been completed eight days, and that no use had yet been made of it, though it was supposed the effect produced by it would be very important. Without further explanation, the Representatives ordered them to open a fire, and accordingly the cannoneers with great joy immediately opened an alternate fire from the battery.

General O'Hara, who commanded the Allied Army at Toulon, was greatly surprised at the erection of so considerable a battery close to a fort of such importance as Malbosquet, and gave orders that a sortie should be made at break of day. The battery was situated in the centre of the left of the army: the troops in that part consisted of about 6,000 men; occupying the line from Fort Rouge to Malbosquet, and so disposed as to prevent all individual communication, though too much scattered to make an effectual resistance in any given point.

An hour before day, General O'Hara sallied out of the garrison with 6,000 men; and, meeting with no obstacle, his skirmishers only being engaged, spiked the guns of the battery.

In the meanwhile, the drums beat the generale at headquarters, and Dugommier with all haste rallied his troops: I posted myself on a little hillock behind the battery, on which I had previously established a depot of arms. A communication from this point of the battery had been effected, by means of a boyau which was substituted for the trench. Perceiving from this point that the enemy had formed to the right and left of the battery, I conceived the idea of leading a battalion which was stationed near me through the boyau. By this plan I succeeded in coming out unperceived among the brambles close to the battery, and immediately commenced a brisk fire upon the English, whose surprise was such, that they imagined it was their own troops on the right, who through some mistake were firing on those on the left. General O'Hara hastened towards the French to rectify the supposed mistake, when he was wounded in the hand by a musket-ball, and a serjeant seized and dragged him prisoner into the boyau; the disappearance of the English General was so sudden, that his own troops did not know what had become of him.

In the mean time, Dugommier, with the troops he had rallied, placed himself between the town and the battery: this movement disconcerted the enemy, who forthwith commenced their retreat. They were hotly pursued as far as the gates of the fortress, which they entered in the greatest disorder and without being able to ascertain the fate of their General. Dugommier was slightly wounded in this affair. A battalion of volunteers from the Isere distinguished itself during the day.

General Carteaux had conducted the siege at its commencement; but the Committee of Public Safety had found it necessary to deprive him of the command. This man, originally a painter, had become an adjutant in the Parisian corps; he was afterwards employed in the army; and, having been successful against the Marseillese, the deputies of the Mountain had in the same day obtained him the appointments of Brigadier-General and General of division. He was extremely ignorant, and had nothing military about him; otherwise he was not ill-disposed, and committed no excesses at Marseilles on the taking of that city.

General Doppet succeeded Carteaux: he was a Savoyard, a physician, and an unprincipled man: he was entirely governed by interested motives. He was a decided enemy to all who possessed talent. He had no idea of war, and was anything but brave. This Doppet nevertheless, by a singular chance, in forty-eight hours after his arrival had very nearly taken Toulon. A battalion of the Côte d'Or and a battalion of the regiment of Burgundy, being on duty in the trenches before Little Gibraltar, had one of their men taken by a Spanish company on guard at the redoubt: they saw their companion ill-treated and beaten, and at the same time the Spaniards offered them every insult by shouts and indecent gestures. The French, enraged, ran to their arms, commenced a brisk fire, and marched against the redoubt.

I immediately hastened to the General-in-Chief, who was ignorant of what was going on. We galloped to the scene of action, and there perceiving how the matter stood, I persuaded the General to support the attack, with the assurance that it would not be productive of greater loss to advance than to retire. The General, therefore, ordered the different corps of reserve to be put in motion: all were quickly on the alert, and I marched at their head. Unfortunately, an aide-de-camp was killed by the side of the General-in-chief. Doppet was panic-struck; and ordering the drums in all directions to beat a retreat, recalled his soldiers at the very moment when the grenadiers, having repulsed the skirmishers of the enemy, had reached the gorge of the redoubt, and were about to take it. The troops were highly indignant, and complained that painters and physicians were sent to command them. The Committee of Public Safety recalled Doppet, and at length perceived the necessity of employing a real military man: they accordingly sent Dugommier, an officer who had seen fifty years of service, who was covered with scars, and who was as dauntless as the weapon he wore.

The enemy were every day receiving reinforcements: the public watched with anxiety the direction of the operations of the siege. They could not conceive why every effort should be directed against Little Gibraltar, quite in an opposite direction to the town. 'There has not been any thing done yet,' it was said all over the country, 'but laying siege to a fort which has nothing to do with the permanent fortifications of the place. They will afterwards have to take Malbosquet, and open trenches against the town.' All the popular societies made denunciation after denunciation on this subject. Provence complained of the long duration of the siege. A scarcity began to prevail, and increased to such a degree that Freron and Barras, having lost all hopes of the

TOULON

prompt reduction of Toulon, wrote in great alarm from Marseilles to the Convention, to persuade them to take into consideration whether it would not be better that the army should raise the siege and repass the Durance—a manoeuvre which had been planned by Francis the First at the time of the invasion of Charles the Fifth. He retired behind the Durance, while the enemy laid Provence waste; and when famine compelled them to retreat, he then attacked them with fresh vigour. The Representatives urged, that, if our troops should evacuate Provence, the English would be obliged to find provisions for its support, and that after the harvest, offensive operations might be renewed with considerable advantage by an army complete in itself and invigorated by rest. This measure was, they said, absolutely necessary; for as yet, after four months' operations, Toulon had not even been attacked; and as the enemy were perpetually receiving reinforcements, it was to be apprehended that we should in the end be obliged to do precipitately and in confusion, what at the present moment might be effected with regularity and order. However, in a few days after the letter had been received by the Convention, Toulon was taken. The letter was now disowned by the Representatives as a forgery. This was ill-judged; for it was genuine, and gave a just idea of the opinion that existed at the time of its being written, respecting the issue of the siege, and of the difficulties that prevailed in Provence.

Dugommier determined that a decisive attack should be made upon Little Gibraltar: I accordingly threw 7 or 8,000 shells into the fort, while 30 twenty-four pounders battered the works.

On 18 December, at four in the afternoon, the troops left their camps and marched towards the village of Seine: the plan was to attack at midnight, in order to avoid the fire of the fort and the intermediate redoubts. At the instant when every thing was ready, the Representatives of the People held a council to deliberate whether the attack should be put in execution or not: it is probable they either feared the issue of it, and were desirous to throw all the responsibility of the affair upon General Dugommier, or they were influenced by the opinion entertained by many officers, who conceived success impossible, chiefly on account of the dreadful weather; the rain was falling in torrents.

Dugommier and I ridiculed these fears: two columns were formed, and marched against the enemy.

The Allied troops, to avoid the effect of the shells and balls, which showered upon the fort, were accustomed to occupy a station at a small distance in the rear of it. The French had great hopes of reaching the works before them; but the enemy had placed a line of skirmishers in front of the fort, and as the musquetry commenced firing at the very foot of the hill, the Allied troops hastened to the defence of the fort, whence a very brisk fire was immediately opened. Case-shot showered all around. At length, after a most furious

TOULON

attack, Dugommier, who according to his usual custom headed the leading column, was obliged to give way; and in the utmost despair he cried out 'I am a lost man'. Success was in every way important in those days, for the want of it usually conducted the unfortunate General to the scaffold.

The fire of the cannonading and musquetry continued. Captain Muiron of the artillery, a young man full of bravery and resources, who was my adjoint, was detached with a battalion of light infantry, and supported by the second column, which followed them at the distance of a musquet-shot. He was perfectly acquainted with the position; and he availed himself so well of the windings of the ascent, that he conducted his troops up the mountain without sustaining any loss. He debouched at the foot of the fort: he rushed through an embrasure: his soldiers followed him—and the fort was taken. The English and Spanish cannoneers were all killed at their guns, and Muiron himself was dangerously wounded by a thrust from the pike of an English soldier.

As soon as they were masters of the fort, the French immediately turned the cannon against the enemy.

By the time that Dugommier had been three hours in the redoubt, the Representatives of the People came with their drawn swords in their hands to load the troops which occupied it with eulogiums. (This positively contradicts the accounts of that time, which incorrectly state that the Representatives marched at the head of the columns.)

At break of day the French marched on Balagnier and l'Eguillette: the enemy had already evacuated those positions. The twenty-four pounders and the mortars were brought to mount these batteries, whence they hoped to cannonade the combined fleets before noon; but I deemed it impossible to fix them there. They were of stone, and the engineers who had constructed them had committed an error, in placing a large tower of masonry just at their entrance, so near the platforms that whatever balls might have struck them would have rebounded on the gunners, besides the splinter and rubbish. They therefore planted pieces of cannon on the heights behind the batteries. They could not open their fire until the next day; but no sooner did Lord Hood, the English Admiral, see that the French had possessed themselves of these positions, than he made signal to weigh anchor and get out of the roads.

He then went to Toulon to make it known that there was not a moment to be lost in getting out to sea directly. The weather was dark and cloudy, and every thing announced the approach of the Libeccio wind (called also Lebeche; a south-west wind in the Mediterranean), so terrible at this season. The council of the combined forces immediately met; and, after mature deliberation, they unanimously agreed that Toulon was no longer tenable. They accordingly proceeded to take measures as well for the embarkation of the troops, as for burning and sinking such French vessels as they could not carry away with them, and setting fire to the marine establishments: they

TOULON

likewise gave notice to all the inhabitants, that those who wished to leave the place might embark on board the English and Spanish fleets.

When these disastrous tidings were spread abroad, a scene of confusion took place which it would be difficult to describe; any more than the disorder and astonishment of the garrison, and of the unfortunate inhabitants, who, only a few hours before, calculating on the great distance of the besiegers from the place, the slow progress of the siege during four months, and the expected arrival of reinforcements, not only hoped to effect the raising of the siege, but even to become masters of Provence.

In the night, Fort Poné was blown up by the English, and an hour afterwards, a part of the French squadron was set on fire. Nine 74-gun ships and four frigates or corvettes became a prey to the flames.

The fire and smoke from the Arsenal resembled the eruption of a volcano, and the thirteen vessels which were burning in the road were like so many magnificent displays of fireworks. The masts and forms of the vessels were distinctly marked by the blaze, which lasted many hours, and formed an unparalleled spectacle. It was a heart-rending sight to the French to see such grand resources, and so much wealth consumed within so short a period. They feared, at first, that the English would blow up Fort La Malgue, but it appeared that they had not time to do so.

I then went to Malbosquet. The fort was already evacuated. I ordered the field-pieces to sweep the ramparts of the town, and heighten the confusion by throwing shells from the howitzers into the port, until the mortars, which were upon the road with their carriages, could be planted in the batteries, and shells thrown from them in the same direction.

General Lapoype took possession of Fort Pharaon, which was evacuated by the enemy. During all this time the batteries of l'Eguillette and Balagnier kept up an incessant fire on the vessels in the road. Many of the English ships were much damaged, and a great number of transports with troops on board were sunk. The batteries continued their fire all the night, and at the break of day the English fleet was seen out at sea. By nine o'clock in the morning a high Libeccio wind got up, and the English ships were forced to put into the Hyeres.

Many thousands of the families of Toulon had followed the English; so that the revolutionary tribunals found but few of the guilty in the place: all the parties most deeply implicated had left it. Nevertheless above a hundred unfortunate wretches were shot within the first fortnight.

Orders afterwards arrived from the Convention for demolishing the houses of Toulon: the absurdity of this measure did not impede the execution of it, and many houses were pulled down, which were obliged subsequently to be built up again.

On 18 December, at ten o'clock at night, Colonel Cervoni broke down a

TOULON

gate and entered the city at the head of a patrol of 200 men. He traversed the whole town: the deepest silence prevailed. The port was crowded with baggage which the inhabitants had not had time to put on board. A report prevailed that matches were lighted for the purpose of blowing up the powder-magazines; piquets of cannoneers were accordingly sent to secure them. Immediately after, the troops intended to guard the city entered. Excessive confusion prevailed at the naval arsenal, where 8 or 900 galley slaves were making the most strenuous exertions to extinguish the fire. These convicts had rendered the greatest services, having overawed the English officer, Sir Sidney Smith, who had orders to burn the ships and the arsenal, and performed his task very ill. The Republic was indebted to him for all the valuable treasures recovered. I proceeded to the spot with all the disposable cannoneers and workmen, and succeeded, in the course of a few days, in extinguishing the fire and preserving the arsenal. The loss which the navy had suffered was considerable, but it still retained immense resources; all the magazines were saved except the general one. There were thirty-one ships of war at Toulon at the time of its treacherous surrender; four sail had been employed in carrying 5,000 soldiers to Brest and Rochefort; the combined troops burned nine in the roads, they left thirteen dismantled in the basins, and carried off four, one of which was burnt at Leghorn. Fears had been entertained that they would blow up the basin and several of the jetties, but they had not time enough for that purpose. The wrecks of the thirteen ships and frigates which were burnt and sunk in the roads contracted the channel; many attempts were made to remove them in the course of the ten following years; at length, some Neapolitan divers succeeded in getting the whole out, piece by piece, by sawing the hulls. The army entered Toulon on the 19th, the troops had been seventy-two hours under arms amidst mud and rain; they abandoned themselves, on entering the town, to some excesses, which seemed authorized by the promises made to the soldiers during the siege.

The General-in-Chief restored order by declaring that all effects in Toulon were the property of the army; he had the contents of the private warehouses and the furniture of the deserted houses collected in central magazines. The Republic afterwards seized the whole, allowing only the gratification of a year's pay to every officer and soldier. The emigration from Toulon was very considerable, the refugees crowded the English, Neapolitan and Spanish ships, which were consequently obliged to anchor in the roads of Hyeres, and to make the emigrants encamp in the isles of Porquerolles and the Levant. It is said that the number of these emigrants amounted to 14,000. Dugommier gave orders to leave the white flag hoisted on all the forts and bastions of the roads, by which means a great number of ships of war and merchantmen bringing men or supplies intended for the enemy were deceived. During the first thirty days succeeding the taking of the city, vessels richly laden were

TOULON

daily captured. An English frigate, on one occasion had cast anchor under the great tower, carrying supplies to the amount of several millions; she was considered as taken, and two naval officers in a small boat boarded her accordingly, declaring to the captain that they took possession of the frigate as their prize. The captain clapped them into the hold, cut his cables, and was lucky enough to escape without farther loss. One evening, towards the end of December, being on the quay, about eight o'clock, I saw an English skiff come ashore, from which an officer landed, and asked me for Lord Hood's lodgings. This was the captain of a fine brig which brought despatches and announced the approach of reinforcements. The brig was taken, and the despatches read.

The Representatives established a revolutionary tribunal, according to the laws of that period; but all the guilty had escaped and followed the enemy; all who had resolved to stay, were conscious of their innocence. Nevertheless this tribunal caused several persons to be arrested who had been prevented from following the enemy by various accidents, and caused them to be punished in expiation of their guilt. But eight or ten victims were too few, and a dreadful measure, characteristic of the spirit of that period, was resorted to. It was proclaimed that all those persons who had been employed in the arsenal whilst the English were in possession of the town, were to repair to the *Champ de Mars,* and give in their names; and they were led to believe that it was for the purpose of employing them again. Nearly two hundred persons, head workmen, inferior clerks, and other subalterns went accordingly, in full confidence. Their names were registered; it was proved by their own confession that they had retained their places under the English government, and the revolutionary tribunal, in the open field, immediately sentenced them to death. A battalion of Sans-Culottes and Marseillese, brought expressly for the purpose, shot them. This action requires no comment; but it was the only execution that took place at Toulon; it is false that any persons whatever were killed by grape-shot: neither I nor the cannoneers of the line would have lent themselves to such an action. It was the cannoneers of the revolutionary army who committed such atrocities at Lyons.

By a decree of the Convention, the name of *Port de la Montagne* was given to the Port of Toulon, and it was ordered that all the public edifices should be demolished, except those deemed necessary for the navy and the public service. This extravagant decree was put in execution, but very tardily; only five or six houses were demolished, and those were rebuilt shortly after. The English squadron remained a month or six weeks in Hyeres roads; this created some anxiety; there were no mortars in Toulon capable of throwing projectiles above 1,500 toises,* and the squadron was anchored 2,400 toises from the shore. Had we then had some Villantroys mortars, such as were afterwards used, the squadron would not have been able to anchor in the

* A toise equals 2·13 yards or 1·95 metres. S. de C.

TOULON

roads. At length, after blowing up the forts of Porquerolles and Porteros, the enemy proceeded to the roads of Porto-Ferrajo, where they landed a great number of the emigrants from Toulon.

The news of the taking of Toulon, at the moment when it was least expected, produced a wonderful effect in France, and throughout Europe. On the 25th of December the Convention ordered a national festival. The taking of Toulon was the signal of the successes which attended the campaign of 1794. Shortly afterwards the Army of the Rhine retook the lines of Weissemburg, and raised the blockade of Landau. Dugommier, with part of the army, marched for the Eastern Pyrenees, where Doppet was only making blunders. Another part of this army was sent into la Vendée, and many battalions returned to the Army of Italy. Dugommier ordered me to follow him, but other orders arrived from Paris, directing me first to replace the coasts of the Mediterranean in a state of defence, especially Toulon; and afterwards to proceed to the Army of Italy to command the artillery.

It was at Toulon that my reputation commenced. All the generals, representatives, and soldiers, who had heard my opinions given in the different councils, three months before the taking of the place, anticipated the military career I afterwards fulfilled. From that moment I had acquired the confidence of all the soldiers of the Army of Italy. Dugommier wrote to the Committee of Public Safety, soliciting the rank of brigadier-general for me, and using these words 'Reward this young man and promote him, for, should he be ungratefully treated, he would promote himself'. In the Army of the Pyrenees, Dugommier was continually talking of his commandant of the artillery a Toulon, and impressed a high opinion of him on the minds of all the generals and officers who afterwards went from the Army of Spain to the Army of Italy. Whenever he gained successes, he used to send couriers from Perpignan to me at Nice.

Chapter III

THE WAR OF ITALY

Fortifying the shores of the Mediterranean. Taking of Saorgio. Positions of the French Army. Accused. Action of Cairo. I direct the army in the Campaign of 1794. Taking of Saorgio, Oneglio, the Col di Tende and all the upper chain of the Alps (April 1794). I appease general insurrections in Toulon. I quit the army of Italy and arrive in Paris (June 1795). Kellermann, being defeated, rallies in the lines of Borghetto (July 1795). Battle of Loano (November 1796)

During the siege of Toulon, the Army of Italy had been attacked on the Var. The Piedmontese had attempted to invade Provence, and got nearly as far as Entrevaux; but being defeated at Gillette, they retreated, and retired within their lines.

The news of the taking of Toulon caused a sensation in Provence and throughout France, the more lively as such success was unexpected and almost unhoped-for. From this event my reputation commenced: I was made Brigadier-General of artillery in consequence, and appointed to the command of that department in the Army of Italy. General Dugommier was appointed Commander-in-Chief of the Army of the Eastern Pyrenees.

Before I joined the Army of Italy, I fortified the coasts of Provence, and the isle of Hyeres, immediately after they were evacuated by the English. There are no fixed rules in France with respect to the fortifying of coasts. This causes endless disputes between the artillery officers and the local authorities; the latter always requiring too much, the former being perhaps contented with too little.

MAP TO ILLUSTRATE THE ITALIAN CAMPAIGN

THE WAR OF ITALY

On being ordered to fortify the coasts of the Mediterranean, and finding that the artillery officers were everywhere denounced, because the French cannon did not carry so far as the English, I mounted some of the guns so as to fire at an angle of 43°; in order that, if the complaint came to be examined into, it might immediately be proved that the powder and the reach of the cannon were altogether equal to that of the English. But carriages constructed in this manner are much sooner unfit for service than those which are calculated to fire at 17°, and should only be employed in batteries defending anchorages at a distance of more than 1,500 toises.

I repaired to the mouths of the Rhône, where I commenced my survey for the fortification of the coasts of the Mediterranean. In every town I came to, I had to encounter the arguments of the public authorities and the popular societies, who were desirous to have batteries erected at every little village or hamlet that might be situated near the sea-side.

The interior extremity of the Gulf of Lyons used to be considered by the seamen of the Mediterranean as an innavigable sea, but the English have proved the contrary. They have been seen to anchor at the mouth of the Rhône, and ride there in safety, in the worst weather. This anchorage likewise enabled them to profit by the river, for the purpose of taking in water. The anchorage of the Buc is good; it is defended by a small castle; the entrance to it is very narrow, but ships of war may get in.

Buc is destined to be the chief port in the Mediterranean for building men-of-war, as Toulon and Spezia are for fitting them out, and dismantling them. From Buc to Marseilles there are only small batteries to defend the coasting-vessels, and there are no moorings for anything but sloops and little vessels.

At Marseilles, the best anchorage is at Istac. I had two strong batteries constructed there, each mounted with eight pieces of cannon. They were placed in such a manner as to afford a strong support to the two wings of a naval line of defence; they have never been made use of; but, inferior as we are in naval force, it was prudent to secure the safety of these moorings.

The defence of Toulon is of the highest importance; and in providing for it, nothing should be spared. The road is protected by the batteries of Cape Cepet and Cape Brun.

Saint Tropez ought to be reckoned a battery of the second class; Frejus and Juan afford anchorage to ships of war; it was therefore necessary to give them batteries of the first class.

The Gulf of Juan, which is close upon Antibes, has the best roads of any on the coast of Provence, after Toulon. Squadrons of twelve ships have been seen there, blockaded by English fleets, far superior in number, yet perfectly safe under the protection of the batteries which I constructed.

The anchorage of Antibes and Nice need only be defended by batteries of the second class. From Nice to Vado, a distance of about thirty leagues, there are only batteries of the third class. The roads of Vado, though not very superior, are regarded as the fourth best, in this part of the Mediterranean. Strong batteries were therefore constructed for their defence. From Vado to Genoa there are only batteries for the protection of the coasters. Genoa is only a middling port: nevertheless it occasionally affords shelter to vessels, and there was an intention of making new embankments, to render the anchorage more secure.

I joined the head-quarters of the Army of Italy at Nice, in March, 1794. It was at that time commanded by General Dumerbion, an old and brave officer, who had been ten years a captain of grenadiers in the troops of the line. His military knowledge was considerable, but he was confined to his bed by the gout half his time; he had carried on war between the Var and the Roya, and knew perfectly the positions of all the mountains that cover Nice.

As the new General of artillery I visited all the advanced posts and reconnoitred the line occupied by the army. It is the duty of a General of artillery to make himself acquainted with the whole operations of an army, as he is required to furnish the different divisions with arms and ammunition. His connection with the commandants of artillery in each division procures him information of everything that takes place, and the arrangement of his grand park is regulated by the communications he receives.

On returning from this inspection, I laid a memorial before General Dumerbion, relating to the unfortunate attack of General Brunet, and to the method of driving the enemy beyond the high Alps, by taking possession of the Col di Tende. If the French could thus fix themselves in the upper chain of the Alps, they would obtain impregnable positions, which, requiring but few men to maintain them, would leave a great number of troops disposable for other service.

These suggestions were laid before a council at which the representatives Ricors and young Robespierre were sitting: they were agreed to unanimously. Since the taking of Toulon my reputation as the General of artillery was quite enough of itself to inspire confidence in my designs.

The territory of Nice is comprised between the Var and the Roya; and the road from Nice to Turin, which passes by Saorgio, does not follow the course of any valley, but crosses hills and mountains, the valley of the Col di Tende and the Roya. This river rises, indeed, in the Col di Tende and goes down to the sea, near Vintimiglia. It affords some debouches. The Nervia, taking its rise near Menton, below Saorgio and the Col Ardente, does not come from the chain of the high Alps, any more than the Taggio, the source of which is between Triola and the Col Ardente.

On 8 April, in consequence of my plans, a part of the army, under the command of General Massena (General Dumerbion being confined to his bed by a fit of the gout), filing along the edge of the Roya by Menton, crossed the river. It then divided into four columns: the first marched up the bank of the Roya, the second up that of the Nervia, the third up that of the Taggio, and the fourth moved upon Oneglia.

The movements of the three columns along the valleys of the Roya, the Taggio, and the Nervia, and those of the troops which had debouched in Piedmont by the sources of the Tanaro, very naturally alarmed the Court of Sardinia. The Piedmontese army occupying the camps supported on Sargio might be cut off, or taken prisoners; and the loss of an army of that kind, of twenty thousand men, would involve the ruin of the monarchy itself. The Piedmontese army, therefore, hastily abandoned those famous positions which had been washed with so much blood, and in which the Piedmontese troops had acquired considerable renown.

By these manoeuvres the Army of Italy had gained more than sixty pieces of cannon. Saorgio was well provided with provisions and ammunition of every kind: it was the principal depot of all the Piedmontese army.

The commandant of Saorgio was tried and shot by order of the King of Sardinia; and justly, for he might have held out twelve days or a fortnight longer. It is true the event would have been the same, as the Piedmontese could not have come to his assistance; but in war the commandant of a place is not to judge of events; he ought to defend it until the very last hour, and he deserves death if he gives it up a single instant sooner than he is compelled to do so. The French Army remained in these positions until September; when they learned from Nice, that a considerable Austrian force was advancing on the Bormida. General Dumerbion, in consequence, marched the army to reconnoitre the Austrian force, and to seize its stores which he was informed had been advanced as far as Cairo. The representatives Albitte and Salicetti accompanied the French army; as General Commandant of the artillery I directed the operations, which saved me from being summoned to the bar of the Convention.

Whilst making my inspections at Marseilles, I was summoned by the representative ... who informed me that certain popular societies intended to plunder the powder-magazines. I, therefore, gave him a plan for constructing a little wall, with battlements, upon the ruins of Fort Saint-James, and Fort Saint-Nicolas which had been destroyed by the Marseillese at the beginning of the Revolution. The expense was trifling, but some months after, there was a decree for summoning 'the Commandant of artillery at Marseilles' to the bar of the Convention as having projected a plan for restoring the forts of Saint-James and Saint-Nicolas, in order to oppose the patriots.

The decree mentioned the Commandant of artillery at Marseilles; but I was at this time General of artillery in the Army of Italy. Colonel Seigny, who was the person specified by the text of the decree, went to Paris according to its literal tenor.

THE WAR OF ITALY

When he presented himself at the bar, he proved that the plan was not in his handwriting, and that he knew nothing about the matter. All was explained, and I was found to be the person in question; but the representatives of the Army of Italy, who wanted me to direct the affairs of the army, wrote to Paris, and gave such explanations to the Convention as it was satisfied with.

The French proceeded from Loano to Bardinetto, where they passed the straits of the Bormida, and on 26 September came to Balastreno, whence they proceeded to Cairo or Cair; where they fell in with from 12 to 13,000 Austrians, manoeuvring in the plain, who no sooner saw the French army, than they retreated upon Dego. The French quickly attacked them there; and after an action with the rearguard, in which the Austrians lost some prisoners, the latter retired upon Acqui. Having taken Dego, the French halted; their end was attained. They had now several magazines, and had ascertained that there was nothing to fear from the expedition of the Austrians. The march of the French spread consternation through all Italy; the army returned upon Savona, traversing upper and lower Montenotte.

The right of the army moved from Loano to the heights of Vado, in order to command the roads of that port which are the best and most important of any of these seas; and to prevent the English privateers from anchoring there. The line of the French army then passed by Septipani, Melagno and Saint-James, and extended to Bardinetto and the Col di Tende.

I spent part of March in visiting the positions occupied by the army, and collecting information respecting the various actions which had taken place in 1792. I remained several days at the camp of Brouis occupied by General Macquart, and convinced myself of the strength of the enemy's positions, and the imprudence of the attacks of the 8th and 12th of June, which had proved disastrous to the army. Amongst mountains there are many positions to be found of great natural strength, which we must take care not to attack. The genius of this kind of warfare consists in occupying camps, either on the flanks or in the rear of those of the enemy, which leave him only the alternative of evacuating his positions without fighting, or of coming out of them to attack you. In mountain-war, he who attacks is always under a disadvantage; even in offensive war, the art consists in engaging only in defensive actions, and in obliging the enemy to attack. The enemy's positions were well connected; the right was supported in a solid manner, but the left not so well; the country was much more practicable on that side. I, therefore, conceived a plan of operations, which, without engaging the army in difficult affairs, was adapted to put it in possession of the upper chain of the Alps, and to oblige the enemy to abandon of his own accord the formidable camps of Raus and Fourches. There was no reason to fear that the enemy would avail themselves of the detachment which would be made by the French army on its right, in

THE WAR OF ITALY

order to act on the offensive; such a movement in a hilly country would only be formidable in proportion to the time that might be lost in striking the decisive blow; for if the troops have gained a few marches on the enemy, they have arrived on his flanks, and then it is too late for him to take the offensive part. In mountain warfare, to oblige the enemy to leave his positions to attack yours, is, as we have already said, the spirit and true method of conducting this kind of war.

This plan was laid before a council, at which were present the two popular representatives, commissioners to the army, General Dumerbion, the general of the artillery (myself), General Massena, General Vial of the engineers, and Brigadier-General Rusca, a light-infantry officer, born in these mountains, and particularly acquainted with them. The reputation of the author saved him all long discussions. My predictions concerning Toulon were remembered, and my plan was adopted.

There was one political objection, it was necessary to *borrow* the territory of the Republic of Genoa; but the allies themselves had borrowed it six months before, when 2,000 Piedmontese crossed the Genoese territory and embarked at Oneglia for Toulon. They were only to have proceeded in small detachments disarmed, but they had marched in a body, under arms, with drums beating. The catastrophe of the *Modeste* was also remembered; this frigate had anchored in the port of Genoa, and was moored against the quay. On 15 October, 1793, three English ships and two frigates anchored in the port; an English seventy-four moored alongside the *Modeste*. The master civilly requested the officer on the quarter-deck of the frigate to remove a boat which was in the way of the manoeuvres of the English ship, which was readily done by the French. Half an hour after, the English captain requested the commander of the *Modeste* to hoist the white flag, saying, he did not know what the tri-coloured flag was (the Allies were then masters of Toulon). The French officer answered this insult as honour dictated: but the English had three platforms prepared, which they threw on the frigate and boarded her; at the same time commencing a brisk fire of musquetry from the tops and deck; the crew of the *Modeste* were unprepared for any attack; part of them threw themselves into the water; the English pursued the fugitives with their boats, killing and wounding them. The rage of the people of Genoa was unbounded; the English agent Drake was hooted and threatened, and incurred some danger, but Doria was doge; the senate made excuses, and the frigate was never restored. The representatives of the people at Marseilles laid an embargo on the Genoese shipping; they expected that the Convention would declare war; but France, and particularly the South, was desolated by famine; the Genoese flag was necessary to supply Provence with provisions; the Convention therefore dissembled, declaring that the whole affair was to be attributed to the weakness of the Genoese, and that the usual relations between the two countries should continue unaltered. It was nevertheless true that the independence and neutrality of this republic had been violated.

On 6 April a division of 14,000 men, forming five brigades, passed the Roya, and took possession of the castle of Vintimiglia; one brigade, commanded by Massena, marched on Mount Tanardo, and took up a position there; a second, after having passed the Taggia, took up a position at Monte-Grande; the three others, under my immediate command, advanced on Oneglia and overthrew an Austrian division posted on the heights of Sainte-Agatha. The French Brigadier-General Brulé was killed in this affair. The next day the army entered Oneglia, where twelve pieces of cannon were found. The whole population of the town and valley had fled.

The loss of the army was slight. The fall of Saorgia and of all those grand positions for which so many plans had been formed, and so much blood shed, increased my reputation in the army; and public opinion already called me to the chief command.

The Piedmontese Army, encamped in the plains and hills at the foot of the Alps, enjoyed the greatest abundance; it was recovering from its fatigues and repairing its losses; and was daily reinforced by the arrival of fresh Austrian battalions: whilst the French armies, encamped on the ridges of the upper chain of the Alps, on a semi-circumference of sixty leagues in extent, between Mont Blanc and the sources of the Tanaro, were perishing through want and sickness. All communication was attended with great difficulty, provisions were scarce and very expensive, the horses suffered, and all the material of the army was damaged. The hard waters of those elevated regions caused much sickness. The losses which the army suffered every three months in hospital might have supplied the casualties of a great battle; these defensive operations were more burthensome to our finances, and more perilous to the men, than an offensive campaign.

Defensive operations in the Alps, in addition to these disadvantages, are attended with others which arise from the topography of the country. The different corps encamped on these summits cannot assist each other; they are insulated; twenty days are necessary for proceeding from right to left, whilst the army defending Piedmont is in a fine plain, occupies the diameter, and can, in a few days, assemble in force at the point which it is intended to attack. The Committee of Public Safety was desirous that the army should assume the offensive. I had conferences on this subject at Colmar, with officers from the Army of the Alps: but a difference of opinion prevailed; it was necessary, in the first place, that these two armies should be under one commander-in-chief.

I spent the rest of the autumn in fortifying the promontories from Vado to the Var with good coast-batteries, in order to protect the passage from Genoa to Nice. In January I passed one night on the Col di Tende, whence, at sunrise, I surveyed those fine plains which were already the subject of my meditations. *Italiam! Italiam!*

The remainder of the year 1794 was spent in putting the positions occupied by the army into a state of defence, particularly Vado. The knowledge that I acquired, under these circumstances, of all the positions of Montenotte, was very useful to me when I became commander-in-chief of the same army, and enabled me to make the bold manoeuvre to which I owed the victory of Montenotte, at the opening of the campaign of Italy, in 1796.

From 9 Thermidor (27 July, 1794) the South had been much agitated. The revolutionary tribunal of Marseilles had brought to the scaffold all the principal merchants of that city. The Jacobins, composing the popular society, had still the upper hand; they deplored the ruin of the Mountain faction, and were enraged at the moderate laws which then prevailed; besides, the remains of the party of the Sections, although much weakened by emigration and losses of all kinds, excited disturbances from a violent thirst for vengeance. The population of Toulon, all the artificers belonging to the arsenal, and the crews of the squadron, were attached to the former party, and were inimical to the representatives Mariette and Cambon, whom they accused of being of the party of the *Refracteurs*. Under these circumstances, a French privateer brought into Toulon a Spanish prize, on board of which were about twenty emigrants, most of them of the Chabrillant family. A tumultuous mob assembled at the arsenal and in the streets, and proceeded to the prisons to slaughter these unfortunate persons. The representatives went to the arsenal, and after haranguing the officers of the department in a hall, they addressed the men in the workshops, promising to deliver up the emigrants to an extraordinary commission, and to have them tried within twenty-four hours; but they themselves were suspected, they had no influence over public opinion; their speeches were misinterpreted, a voice called out, 'To the *Lanterne* with the protectors of the emigrants!' It was late in the day, and they were just beginning to light the lamps. The uproar became horrible, the crowd outrageous, the guard came up and was repulsed. At this crisis I recognised amongst the principal rioters several gunners who had served under me at the siege of Toulon; I mounted a platform, the gunners enforced respect to their general, and obtained silence; I had the good fortune to produce an effect; the representatives got safe out of the arsenal, but the tumult was still greater in the streets. At the gates of the prisons the resistance of the guards began to slacken; I repaired thither, the populace was restrained from violence by my promise that the emigrants should be delivered up and sentenced the following morning. It would have been no easy matter to persuade them of what was perfectly evident, namely, that these emigrants had not infringed the law, as they had not returned voluntarily. During the night I had them put into some artillery waggons, and carried out of the town as a convoy of ammunition; a boat was waiting for them in Hyeres roads, where they embarked and were thus saved.

The committees of government presented the lists of general officers who were to serve in the campaign of 1795. A great number of officers, who had been unemployed from the end of 1792 to that of 1794, were now ordered on service, but there were many generals of artillery who could not be employed. I, then twenty-five years of age, was the youngest of all; I was entered on the list of generals of infantry, to be employed in the artillery when there should be inspections vacant. I was to quit the Army of Italy, of which Kellermann had just taken the command. I conferred with that general at Marseilles, gave him all the information he could want and set out for Paris. At Châtillon-sur-Seine, I visited the father of my aide-de-camp Marmont, where I heard the news of the events of the first of Prairial, which induced me to remain there a few days until tranquillity should be restored in the capital. On reaching Paris, I waited on Aubry, a member of the Committee of Public Safety, who had made the report on the military service; observed to him that I had commanded the artillery at the siege of Toulon, and that of the Army of Italy for two years; that I had fortified the coasts of the Mediterranean, and that it was painful to me to leave a corps in which I had served from childhood. The representative objected that there were many generals of artillery, and that I was the youngest, and that when there should be a vacancy I should be employed. But Aubry himself had been a captain of artillery six months before; he had not served in the field since the Revolution, and yet he had placed himself on the list as a general of division and inspector of artillery. A few days after, the Committee of Public Safety despatched orders to me to proceed to the army of La Vendée to command a brigade of infantry; in answer to which I gave in my resignation. In the meantime Aubry's report had excited many complaints; the officers displaced repaired in crowds to Paris; many were distinguished officers, but the greater part undeserving, and indebted to the clubs for their promotion; all of them, however, finding me a man of unblemished reputation, took care to mention me in their memorials and petitions as an instance of the partiality and injustice of the report.

Eight days after I had given in my resignation, and whilst I was waiting for the answer of the Committee of Public Safety, Kellermann was defeated, lost his positions at Saint-Jacques, and wrote that unless he received reinforcements speedily, he should even be obliged to quit Nice. This excited great alarm; the Committee of Public Safety assembled all the deputies who had been with the Army of Italy, in order to obtain information. The latter unanimously nominated me as the person best acquainted with the positions occupied by the army, and most capable of pointing out the measures proper to be adopted; I received a requisition to attend the Committee, and had several conferences with Sieyes, Doulcet, Pontecoulant, Letourneur, and Jean de Brie.

THE WAR OF ITALY

I drew up the instructions which the Committee adopted. I was attached to the topographical committee. I laid down the line of Borghetto for the Italian army—a line so strong that it only required an army of half the strength of ours to maintain it. It saved the French army, and preserved the coast of Genoa. The enemy attacked it several times in great force, but they were always repulsed with considerable loss. I was then by a special decree appointed Brigadier-General of artillery, to be specially attached, until farther order, to the direction of the military operations. In this situation I passed the two or three months previous to the thirteenth of Vendemiaire.

At the end of the year, the government, convinced of the incapacity of General Kellermann, superseded him in his command, and appointed General Scherer. On 22 November, this general, having received reinforcements from the army of the Pyrenees, attacked Devins, the enemy's general, at Loano, took his lines, made many prisoners, and took a considerable number of cannon: had he been sufficiently enterprising, he might at the time have made the conquest of Italy—he could not have had a more favourable opportunity; but Scherer was incapable of so important an operation; and, far from endeavouring to profit by his advantages, he returned to Nice, and went into winter quarters.

The Generals of the enemy, after having rallied their troops, also went into winter quarters.

Chapter IV

THE
THIRTEENTH OF VENDEMIAIRE

Constitution of the Year III. Additional Laws. The Sections of Paris take up arms in resistance. Dispositions for the attack and defence of the Tuileries. Action of 13 Vendemiaire. Commander in chief of the Army of the Interior.

The fall of the municipality of 31 May of Danton and Robespierre, led to the overthrow of the revolutionary government. The Convention was afterwards successively governed by factions which never succeeded in acquiring any preponderance; its principles varied every month; a dreadful system of reaction afflicted the interior of the Republic; domains ceased to be saleable, and the credit of the assignats grew daily worse; the armies were unpaid, requisitions and the maximum alone supplied them with the means of subsistence; the soldier was no longer certain even of bread; the recruiting of the troops, the laws on which subjects had been executed with the greatest rigour under the revolutionary government, ceased. The armies still continued to obtain brilliant successes, because they were more numerous than ever, but they suffered daily losses, which there were now no means of repairing.

The foreigners' party, supported by the pretext of the restoration of the Bourbons, increased daily in strength; foreign communications had become more easy; the destruction of the Republic was openly contriving. The Revolution had lost its novelty, it had alienated many persons by affecting their interest; an iron hand had oppressed individuals; many crimes had been committed; they were now eagerly recalled to memory, and popular animadversion was thereby daily excited with increasing violence against those who had governed, held administrative posts, or in any manner whatever participated in the success of the Revolution. Pichegru had sold himself, yet the proselytes

THE THIRTEENTH OF VENDEMIAIRE

of the enemies of the Republic were far from numerous in the army, which remained faithful to the principles for which it had shed so much of its blood and gained so many victories. All parties were tired of the Convention; it was even tired of its own existence, and at length saw that the safety of the nation, and its own, required that it should fulfil its commission without delay. On 21 June, 1795, it decreed the constitution known under the name of the Constitution of the year III, which confided the government to five persons called the Directory, and the legislature to two councils called those of the Five Hundred and of the Ancients. This constitution was submitted to the acceptance of the people convoked in primary assemblies.

It was the general opinion that the short duration of the Constitution of 1791 was to be attributed to the law of the Constituent Assembly, which had excluded its members from the legislature. The Convention did not fall into the same error, but annexed to the constitution two additional laws, by which it prescribed that two-thirds of the new legislature should be composed of members of the Convention, and that the electoral assemblies of the departments should on this occasion only have to nominate one-third of the two councils. These two additional laws were submitted to the acceptance of the people. They excited general dissatisfaction. The partisans of the foreigners saw all their schemes frustrated: they had flattered themselves that the majority of the two councils would be composed of men inimical to the Revolution, or even of those who had suffered by it, and had hoped to accomplish a counter-revolution by means of the legislature itself. This party was at no loss for excellent reasons to disguise the true motives of its discontent. It alleged that the rights of the people were disregarded by the Convention, which, having been empowered only to propose a constitution, was usurping the functions of an electoral body. As to the constitution itself, it was, undoubtedly, preferable to what then existed; and on this point all parties were unanimous. Some, indeed, would have preferred a president to the five directors, others would have desired a more popular council; but in general this new constitution was favourably received. The secret committees, which directed the foreign party, were by no means anxious about forms of government which they did not mean to maintain; they studied nothing in the constitution but the means of availing themselves of it to operate the counter-revolution; and whatever tended to wrest authority out of the hands of the Convention and conventionals was conducive to that end.

The forty-eight Sections of Paris assembled, forming forty-eight tribunes, which were immediately occupied by the most violent orators, La Harpe, Serizi, Lacretelle the younger, Vaublanc, and Regnault de Saint Jean d'Angely. It required little talent to excite people against the Convention, but several of these orators displayed much.

After 9 Thermidor, the city of Paris had organized its national guard; its

THE THIRTEENTH OF VENDEMIAIRE

object had been to get rid of the Jacobins, but it had fallen into the contrary extreme, and the counter-revolutionists formed a considerable number of its members. This national guard consisted of 40,000 men armed and clothed, and participated in all the exasperation of the Sections against the Convention. The Sections having rejected the additional laws, succeeded each other at the bar of the Convention, loudly declaring their opinions. The Convention, however, imagined that all this agitation would subside as soon as the provinces should have manifested their opinions by the acceptance of the constitution and the additional laws; it erroneously compared this agitation in the capital to the commotions so common in London, or which so often occurred in Rome at the time of the Comitia. On 23 September, the Convention proclaimed the acceptance of the constitution and additional laws, by the majority of the primary assemblies of the Republic; but on the following day the Sections of Paris, taking no notice of this acceptance, appointed deputies to form a central assembly of electors, which met at the Odeon.

The Sections of Paris had measured their strength; they despised the weakness of the Convention. This assembly at the Odeon was a committee of insurrection. The Convention awoke from its lethargy, annulled the meeting at the Odeon, declared it illegal, and ordered its committees to dissolve it by force. On the 10th of Vendemiaire the armed power proceeded to the Odeon, and executed this order. A few men collected on the square of the Odeon, indulged in some murmuring and abuse, but offered no resistance. But the decree for closing the Odeon excited the indignation of the Sections. That of Lepelletier, the district house of which was the Convent of the Filles Saint-Thomas, was the most exasperated. The Convention decreed that the place of its sittings should be closed, the meeting dissolved, and the Section disarmed. On 12 Vendemiaire (3 October), at seven or eight o'clock in the evening, General Menou, accompanied by the representatives of the people, Commissioners to the Army of the Interior, proceeded with a numerous body of troops to the place of meeting of the Section Lepelletier, to put the decree of the Convention in execution. The infantry, cavalry, and artillery were all crowded together in the Rue Vivienne, at the extremity of which is the Convent of the Filles Saint-Thomas. The Sectionaries occupied the windows of the houses in this street. Several of their battalions drew up in line in the courtyard of the convent, and the military force which General Menou commanded, found itself compromised. The Committee of the Section had declared themselves a representation of the sovereign people in the exercise of its functions; they refused to obey the orders of the Convention, and after spending an hour in useless conferences, General Menou and the Commissioners of the Convention withdrew by a sort of capitulation, without having dissolved or disarmed the meeting. The Section, thus victorious, declared itself in permanence; sent deputations to all the other Sections, boasted its

THE THIRTEENTH OF VENDEMIAIRE

success, and urged the measures calculated to ensure the triumph of its resistance. In this manner it prepared for the action of the thirteenth of Vendemiaire.

I had been some months attached to the Committee directing the movements of the armies of the Republic, and was at the Feydeau theatre, when I heard of the extraordinary scene that was passing so near me. I felt curious to observe all its circumstances. Seeing the conventional troops repulsed, I hastened to the tribunes of the Convention to witness the effect of this news, and observe the character and colouring which it would receive. The Convention was in the greatest agitation. The representatives deputed to the army, wishing to exculpate themselves, eagerly accused Menou, attributing to treachery what arose from unskilfulness alone. Menou was put under arrest. Different representatives then appeared at the tribune, stating the extent of the danger, the magnitude of which was but too clearly proved by the news which arrived every moment from the Sections. Every one proposed the general who possessed his confidence to succeed Menou; the Thermidorians proposed Barras, but he was by no means agreeable to the other parties. Those who had been at Toulon with the Army of Italy, and the members of the Committee of Public Safety, who were in daily communication with me, proposed me as the person most capable of extricating them from their present danger, on account of the promptitude of my coup-d'oeil, and the energy and moderation of my character. Mariette, who belonged to the party of the Moderates, and was one of the leading members of the Committee of Forty, approved this choice. I, who was in the crowd and heard all that passed, deliberated for about half an hour on the course I was to adopt. At length I made up my mind, and repaired to the Committee, where I represented in the most forcible manner the impossibility of directing so important an operation while clogged by three representatives, who in fact would exercise all power, and impede all the operations of the general: I added, that I had witnessed the occurrence in the Rue Vivienne; that the commissioners had been most to blame, and had nevertheless appeared in the Assembly as triumphant accusers. Struck with the truth of this reasoning, but unable to remove the commissioners without a long discussion in the Assembly, the Committee, to conciliate all parties (for it had no time to lose), determined to propose Barras as general-in-chief, appointing me second in command. Thus they got rid of the three commissioners without giving them any cause of complaint. Barras was of tall stature; he sometimes spoke in moments of violent contention, and his voice would then fill the hall. His moral faculties, however, did not allow him to go beyond a few phrases; the passionate manner in which he spoke might have made him pass for a man of resolution. He did not possess habits of application, yet he succeeded better than was expected. He was censured for his extravagance, his connexions with con-

THE THIRTEENTH OF VENDEMIAIRE

tractors, and the fortune he made during the four years he was in office, which he took no pains to conceal, and which greatly contributed to the corruption of the administration at that period. As soon as I found myself invested with the command of the forces which were to protect the Assembly, I went to one of the cabinets of the Tuileries, where Menou remained in order to obtain from him the necessary information respecting the strength and disposition of the troops and the artillery. The army consisted of only 5,000 soldiers of all arms; the park was composed of forty pieces of cannon, then parked at the Sablons, and guarded by twenty-five men. It was one o'clock in the morning. I immediately despatched a major of the 21st chasseurs (Murat), with 300 horse, to the Sablons, to bring off all the artillery to the garden of the Tuileries. Had another moment been lost, he would have been too late. He reached the Sablons at three in the morning, where he fell in with the head of a column from the Section Lepelletier, which was coming to seize the park; but his troops being cavalry, and the ground a plain, the Sectionaries judged that all resistance was useless; they accordingly retreated and at five in the morning the forty pieces of cannon entered the Tuileries.

Between six o'clock and nine, I placed my artillery at the head of the Pont Louis XVI, the Pont Royal and the Rue de Rohan, at the Cul de Sac Dauphin, in the Rue Saint-Honoré, at the Pont Tournant, etc., confiding the guarding of them to officers of known fidelity. The matches were lighted, and the little army was distributed at the different posts, or in reserve in the garden and at the Carrousel. The drums beat to arms in every quarter. During this time the battalions of the national guard were posting themselves at the outlets of the different streets, surrounding the palace and the garden of the Tuileries; their drums had the audacity to come and beat the *generale* on the Carrousel and the Place Louis XV. The danger was imminent; 40,000 national guards well armed, and long since organized, were in the field, and highly exasperated against the Convention. The troops of the line intrusted with its defence, were few in number, and might easily be led away by the sentiments of the population which surrounded them: in order to increase its forces, the Convention distributed arms to 1,500 individuals called the Patriots of 1789; these were men who, after 9 Thermidor, had lost their employments and quitted their departments, where they were persecuted by public opinion; they were formed into three battalions, and placed under the command of General Berruyer. These men fought with the most determined valour; their example influenced the troops of the line, and they were mainly instrumental to the success of the day.

A committee of forty members, consisting of the Committees of Public Safety and General Security, directed all the affairs, discussed much, but resolved on nothing; whilst the urgency of the danger increased every moment. Some proposed that the Convention should lay down arms, and receive the

THE THIRTEENTH OF VENDEMIAIRE

Sectionaries as the Roman senators received the Gauls. Others wished the members to withdraw to Caesar's camp on the heights of Saint Cloud, there to be joined by the Army of the Coasts of the ocean; and others proposed that deputations should be sent to the forty-eight Sections, to make them various proposals.

During these vain discussions, a man named Lafond debouched on the Pont Neuf, about two o'clock in the afternoon, at the head of three columns, which came from the Section Lepelletier, whilst another column of the same force advanced from the Odeon to meet them. They joined in the place Dauphine. General Carteaux, who was stationed on the Pont Neuf with 400 men and four pieces of cannon, with orders to defend the two sides of the bridge, quitted his post and fell back under the wickets of the Louvre. At the same time a battalion of national guards occupied the Infant's Garden. They called themselves faithful to the Convention, but nevertheless seized this post without orders; on another side, Saint Roche, the Theatre Français, and the Hotel de Noailles, were occupied in force by the national guard. The Conventional posts were not above twelve or fifteen paces from them. The Sectionaries sent women to corrupt the soldiers; even the leaders presented themselves several times, unarmed, and waving their hats, to fraternize, they said!

The danger rapidly increased. Danican, the general of the Sections, sent a flag of truce to summon the Convention to remove the troops which threatened the people, and to disarm the Terrorists. The bearer traversed the posts, with his eyes bandaged and all the formalities of war, about three o'clock. He was thus introduced into the midst of the Committee of the Forty, amongst whom his threats caused much alarm, but he obtained nothing. Night was coming on; the Sectionaries would have availed themselves of the darkness to climb from house to house to the Tuileries itself, which was closely blockaded. I had eight hundred musquets, belts and cartridge-boxes, brought into the hall of the Convention, to arm the members themselves and the clerks, as a corps of reserve. This measure alarmed several of them, who then began to comprehend the extent of the danger. At length, at four o'clock, some musquets were discharged from the Hotel de Noailles, and some balls fell on the steps of the Tuileries, and wounded a woman who was going into the garden. At the same moment Lafond's column debouched by the quay Voltaire, marching on the Pont Royal and beating the charge. The batteries then fired; an eight-pounder at the Cul de Sac Dauphin opened the fire and served as a signal. After several discharges Saint-Roche was carried. Lafond's column, taken in front and flank by the artillery placed on the quay even with the wicket of the Louvre, and at the head of the Pont Royal, was routed; the Rue Saint-Honoré, the Rue Saint-Florentin, and the places adjacent, were swept by the guns. About a hundred men attempted to make a stand at the Theatre de la République, but were dislodged by a few shells. At six o'clock in the

THE THIRTEENTH OF VENDEMIAIRE

evening all was over. A few cannon shot were heard during the night at a distance; but they were only fired to prevent the barricades, which some of the inhabitants attempted to form with casks. There were near two hundred of the Sectionaries killed or wounded, and almost as many on the side of the Convention; the greater part of the latter fell at the gates of Saint-Roche. Three representatives, Freron, Louvet and Sieyes, evinced resolution. The Section of the Quinze-Vingts, in the Faubourg Saint-Antoine, was the only one that assisted the Convention, to whose aid it sent 250 men: so completely had the late political oscillations of that body alienated the good will of the people. The Faubourgs, however, although they did not rise in favour of the Convention, did not act against it. The strength of the army of the Convention was 8,500 men, including the representatives themselves.

Assemblages still continued to form in the Section Lepelletier. On the morning of the 14th some columns debouched against them by the Boulevards, the Rue de Richelieu, and the Palais Royal; cannon had been placed at the principal avenues; the Sectionaries were speedily dislodged; and the rest of the day was occupied in traversing the city, visiting the rendezvous of the Sections, collecting arms, and reading proclamations; in the evening order was universally restored, and Paris was completely quiet. After this grand event, when the officers of the Army of the Interior were presented to the Convention in a body, I was appointed by acclamation, Commander-in-Chief of the Army of the Interior, Barras being no longer allowed to combine the title of Representative with military functions. General Menou was delivered up to a council of war; the Committees were desirous of his death. I saved him, by telling the members that if Menou merited death, the three Representatives, who had directed the operations and parleyed with the Sectionaries, were equally deserving of that punishment; that the Convention had, therefore, only to pass sentence on the three Deputies, and then Menou also might be condemned. The *esprit de corps* prevailed over the voices of the General's enemies. He was acquitted. The Commission condemned several persons to death in contumacy; Vaublanc amongst others. Lafond was the only person executed. This young man had displayed great courage in the action; the head of his column, on the Pont Royal, reformed thrice, under the fire of grape, before it entirely dispersed. He was an emigrant; it was impossible to save him, although the officers were very desirous to do so; the imprudence of his answers constantly frustrated their good intentions. It is not true that the troops were ordered to fire with powder only at the commencement of the action; that would only have served to embolden the Sectionaries and endanger the troops; but it is true that during the latter part of the action, when success was no longer doubtful, they fired with blank cartridges.

After 13 Vendemiaire, I had to reform the national guard, which was an

THE THIRTEENTH OF VENDEMIAIRE

object of the greatest importance, as it amounted to no less than 104 battalions. At the same time I organized the guards of the Directory, and reformed those of the Legislative Body. These very circumstances were afterwards amongst the principal causes of my success on the famous 18 Brumaire. I left such impressions on those corps, that on my return from Egypt, although the Directory had recommended its guards not to render me any military honours, their request was ineffectual, and the soldiers could not be prevented from beating *To the field,* the moment I appeared. The interval of a few months during which I commanded the Army of the Interior, was replete with difficulties and trouble, arising from the installation of a new government, the members of which were divided amongst themselves, and often opposed to the councils; the silent ferment which existed amongst the old Sectionaries, who were still powerful in Paris; the active turbulence of the Jacobins, who used to meet in a patriotic assembly, under the name of the Society of the Pantheon; the agents of the foreigners who fomented discord in all quarters; and above all, from the horrible famine which at that time desolated the capital. Ten or twelve times, the scanty distributions of bread which the government usually made every day, failed entirely. An uncommon degree of activity and dexterity was requisite to surmount so many obstacles, and maintain tranquillity in the capital under such unfavourable and afflicting circumstances. The Society of the Pantheon daily caused the Government increased solicitude; the police was afraid to attack this society openly. I caused the doors of their assembly-rooms to be sealed up. The members stirred no more, as long as I was present; but after my departure, they appeared once more, under the influence of Baboeuf, Antonelle, and others, and occasioned the affair of the camp of Grenelle. I frequently had occasion to harangue the people in the markets, and streets, at the sections, and in the faubourgs; and it is worthy of remark, that of all parts of the capital, the faubourg Saint-Antoine was that which I always found the readiest to listen to reason, and the most susceptible of a generous impulse.

It was whilst I commanded at Paris, that I became acquainted with Madame de Beauharnais. After the disarming of the Sections, a youth ten or twelve years of age presented himself to the staff, soliciting the return of a sword which had belonged to his father, formerly a general in the service of the Republic. This youth was Eugene de Beauharnais, afterwards Viceroy of Italy. Affected by the nature of his petition, and by his juvenile grace, I granted his request. Eugene burst into tears when he beheld his father's sword. Touched at his sensibility, I behaved so kindly to him that Madame de Beauharnais thought herself obliged to wait on me the next day, to thank me for my attention. Every one knows the extreme grace of the Empress Josephine, and her sweet and attractive manners. The acquaintance soon became intimate and tender; and it was not long before we married.

THE THIRTEENTH OF VENDEMIAIRE

Scherer, who commanded the Army of Italy, was reproached with not having profited by his victory at Loano; his conduct had not given satisfaction. There were many more agents than officers at his head-quarters. He was constantly applying for money to pay his troops, and refit different branches of the service, and for horses to replace those which had died for want of forage. The government being unable to supply him with either, gave him dilatory answers, and misled him with vain promises. Scherer perceived this, and gave notice that if any further delay took place, he should be obliged to evacuate the Riviera de Genoa, to return on the Roya, and perhaps to repass the Var. The Directory consulted the General of the Army of the Interior, who presented a memorial on this subject.

A young man of twenty-five could no longer remain at the head of the army of Paris. The reputation of his talents and the confidence reposed in him by the Army of Italy, pointed him out as the only person capable of extricating it from the embarrassing situation in which it was placed. These considerations determined the government to appoint me General-in-Chief of the Army of Italy; I left Paris on 4 March, 1796. General Hatry, a veteran of sixty, succeeded me in the command of the army of Paris, which had become less important, now that the crisis of the scarcity was over, and the government was established.

Chapter V

DESCRIPTION OF ITALY

Italy. The Alps. The Apennines. The great plain of Italy. The Valley of the Po, and the Valleys, the waters of which fall into the Adriatic, north and south of the Po. Frontiers of Italy on the land side. Lines which cover the Valley of the Po. Capitals of Italy. Her maritime resources.

Italy is surrounded by the Alps and the sea. Her natural limits are determined with the same precision as those of an island. This country is comprised between the thirty-sixth and forty-sixth degree of latitude, and the fourth and sixth of longitude from Paris. It naturally divides into three parts, the continental portion, the Peninsula, and the islands. The first of these is separated from the second by the isthmus of Parma.

The third part, or the islands, that is to say, Sicily, Sardinia and Corsica (which last belongs, in a geographical point of view, to Italy rather than to France) forms a surface of 4,000 square leagues; making the total surface of Italy fifteen thousand square leagues.

The frontiers of Italy, towards the continent of Europe, are only 150 leagues in extent; which line is fortified by the strongest barrier that can be opposed to mankind, the highest mountains of Europe, defended by eternal snows and steep rocks. The population of the Continental part is 7,000,000 of souls; that of the Peninsula 8,000,000; and that of the Islands 2,300,000. The total population of Italy amounts to between seventeen and eighteen millions.

The ancients divided Italy into three parts; Cisalpine Gaul, which comprised the whole of the Continental part, and was bounded by the Rubicon on the East; and the Magra on the West; Italy, properly so called, containing Tuscany, the Roman States, and part of the kingdom of Naples; and Magna Graecia, or the Southern part of the Peninsula. The first part was inhabited by the Gauls; those of Autun having founded Milan 600 years before the

DESCRIPTION OF ITALY

Christian era: those of the Loire, Cremona and Mantua. The second part was inhabited by the Italians, properly so called; and the third by Grecian colonies. In the time of Augustus, the Roman citizens inhabiting Italy were reckoned at 4,600,000.

The Alps, the greatest mountains in Europe, divide Italy from the Continent. There are many passes through them, but a few only are frequented by armies, travellers, and traders. At an elevation of 1,400 toises, the last traces of vegetation disappear; at a greater elevation it is with difficulty that man breathes and lives; at a height exceeding 1,600 toises are glaciers and mountains of eternal snow, whence rivers issue in all directions, which run into the Po, the Rhône, the Rhine, the Danube, and the Adriatic. The part of the Alps which pours its waters into the Po and the Adriatic belongs to Italy; that part, the streams from which flow into the Rhône, belongs to France; that from which the waters fall into the Rhine and the Danube, to Germany.

The Apennines are mountains of the second order, far inferior to the Alps; they cross Italy, and divide the waters which empty themselves into the Adriatic, from those which flow into the Mediterranean. They commence where the Alps terminate, at the hills of Saint-Jacques, near Mount Ariol, the last of the Alps.

The Ligurian Apennines commence at the mountains of Saint-Jacques, at the source of the Bormida, near Savona; and terminate at Mount Saint-Pellegrino on the confines of Tuscany. They extend fifty leagues, and separate the states of Genoa from Montferrat and the Duchy of Parma. The upper ridge is from three to twelve leagues from the sea, and from twelve to twenty from the Po. At the time of the campaign of 1796, there was no road along the sea-side practicable for artillery; in order to proceed from Nice to Genoa, it became necessary to transport the pieces on mountain carriages, and, on the opening of the campaign, the different trains had to reach Savona by sea, whence they penetrated into Italy by the Col di Cadibona, which was easily rendered practicable for carriages. There was at that time but one road by which it was possible to proceed from the sea into the interior of Italy, which was that of Genoa, called the Bocchetta road. But in 1812 the road from Nice to Genoa, called the Corniche road, was open for thirty leagues, and afforded an easy communication for carriages between those two cities.

At the time of the campaign in Italy, in 1796, there were two roads which crossed the Apennines and formed communications between the Mediterranean and Adriatic; that of Modena, called the Grafignana, came out on Lucca, and crossed Mount Cimone.

The great plain of Northern Italy is comprised between the Alps, the Apennines, and the Adriatic. It is composed of the valley of the Po, and the valleys which open into the Adriatic, North and South of the Po. This plain includes Piedmont, Lombardy, the Duchies of Parma and Modena, the Legations of

DESCRIPTION OF ITALY

Bologna, Ferrara and Romagna, and all the States of the Republic of Venice. It is one of the richest in the world, being covered with great and populous cities, and maintaining a population of five or six millions of inhabitants.

The Po, which the Greeks called Eridanus, may be considered as a sea, from the great number of rivers which run into it.

The rivers North of the Po, which fall into the Adriatic, are the Adige, which rises at the foot of the Brenner; the Brenta, the source of which is in the last hills of the Alps, on the Trent side; the Piave, the Livenza, and the Tagliamento, which rise in the Cadorian Alps; and, lastly, the Isonzo, the source of which is at the foot of the Col de Tarvis. All these rivers fall into the Adriatic, or into the Lagunes of Venice. The Adige alone remains a river throughout its course, whilst the others are only torrents.

France borders on Italy from the mouth of the Var, in the Mediterranean, to the Little Saint Bernard. From the foot of the Saint Bernard, on the French side, at the village of Scez, to the valley of Barcelonetta, it is thirty leagues: on the Italian side it is only eighteen, measuring from the valley of Aosta to the valley of the Stura opposite the Col d'Argentieres. But from the Stura it is necessary to clear the upper chain of the Alps in order to descend into the county of Nice and proceed along the left bank of the Var. An army from Italy, which has passed the Var, has entered France; but an army from France, which has passed that river, has not entered Italy; it is only on the acclivities of the Maritime Alps. Until it has cleared the upper ridge of the Alps to descend into Italy, that obstacle remains in full force.

The frontiers of states are either chains of mountains, great rivers, or vast and arid deserts. Thus France is defended by the Rhine, Italy by the chain of the Alps, and Egypt by the deserts of Libya, Nubia and Arabia. Of all these obstacles deserts are undoubtedly the most difficult to pass; mountains are the second class of impediments, and large rivers are only the third.

In 1796 the Alps were passable for the purpose of entering Italy: first, by the road of the Col di Tende, at the debouché of which was the fortress of Coni; secondly, by the Col d'Argentieres, but there was no road in that direction practicable for artillery, and the position of the Pas de Suze and Fort Demonte defended the valley of the Stura; thirdly, from Grenoble and Briançon by Mount Genèvre; but this road was impracticable for artillery; and at its opening into Piedmont were Fenestrelles and Exilles; fourthly, by Savoy, Chambery and Mount Cenis, but from Lanslebourg to la Novalese the roads were impracticable for waggons, and the valley was closed by the fortresses of Suza and la Brunette; fifthly, the Tarentaise led to the foot of the Little Saint Bernard; sixthly, the Valais led to the Great Saint Bernard; but the passage of these two mountains was not practicable for waggons; and Fort Bard, which closed the valley, intercepted the passage into the plain; seventhly, by the Valais there was a road reaching to Brig, where it ceased to be practicable for waggons. The passage of the Simplon was impossible, as were those of the Saint Gothard and of the Splugen.

Italy, insulated within its natural limits, separated by the sea and by very lofty mountains from the rest of Europe, seems destined to form a great and powerful nation; but she has a capital defect in her geographical form, which may be regarded as one of the causes of the calamities she has suffered, and of the parcelling out of this fine country into several independent monarchies or republics: her length is disproportionate to her breadth. If this country had been bounded by Mount Velino; that is to say, if it had extended about as far as Rome and all that part of its territory which is comprised between Mount Velino and the Ionian sea, including Sicily, had been thrown between Sardinia, Corsica, Genoa and Tuscany, Italy would have had a centre near every part of her circumference, with a unity of rivers, climate and local interests. But the three great islands, which form a third of her surface, have insulated interests and positions, and are each under peculiar circumstances; and that part of the Peninsula which is south of Mount Velino and which forms the kingdom of Naples, is unacquainted with the interests, climate and wants of the whole of the valley of the Po.

Thus, whilst the Gauls were passing the Cottian Alps, six hundred years before the Christian era, and settling in the valley of the Po, the Greeks were landing on the southern coasts from the Ionian sea, and founding the colonies of the Tarentines and Salentines, of Croto and Sabargte, states which were known under the generic name of Magna Graecia. Rome subjugated both Gaul and Greece, and reduced all Italy under her command. Several ages after Christ, when the seat of empire was transferred to Constantinople, the barbarians passed the Isonzo and the Adige, and founded several states; the throne of the powerful monarchy of the Lombards was fixed at Pavia. The fleets of Constantinople maintained the imperial sway on the coasts of the southern part. At a later period the Kings of France often penetrated into Italy by the Cottian Alps; and the Emperor of Germany by the Cottian and Rhetian Alps; the Popes opposed these princes to each other, and by that policy maintained themselves in a kind of independence, promoted by the divisions and anarchy that prevailed in the different cities. But although the South of Italy is, by its situation, separated from the North, Italy is one single country; the unity of manners, language and literature, must, at some future period, more or less remote, at length unite its inhabitants in one single government. The first and essential condition of the existence of this monarchy must be to become a maritime power, in order to maintain its supremacy over its islands, and to defend its coasts.

There are various opinions respecting the place best adapted to become the capital of Italy. Some point out Venice, because it is of the first importance to Italy to become a maritime power. Venice, protected by its situation from

DESCRIPTION OF ITALY

every attack, is the natural depot of the commerce of the Levant and of Germany: it is, commercially speaking, the nearest point to Turin and Milan, even more so than Genoa; the sea places it near every part of the coasts. Others are led by history and the memorials of antiquity to fix on Rome; these say, that Rome is more central; that it is convenient to the three great islands of Sicily, Sardinia, and Corsica, as well as to Naples, the seat of the greatest population in Italy; that it is at a proper distance from every point of the assailable frontier; whether the enemy advance by the French, Swiss or Austrian frontier, Rome is still at a distance of 120 leagues; that, should the frontier of the Alps be forced, Rome is covered by the frontier of the Po, and after that by the frontier of the Apennines; that France and Spain are great maritime powers, whose capitals, nevertheless, are not established in seaports; that Rome, near the coasts of the Mediterranean and Adriatic, is in a situation to provide for the victualling and defence of the frontiers of the Isonzo and Adige from Ancona and Venice, with economy and despatch by way of the Adriatic; that, by means of the Tiber, Genoa, and Villa Franca, she can take care of the frontier of the Var and the Cottian Alps; that, by means of the Adriatic and Mediterranean, she is favourably situated for harassing the flanks of any army which should pass the Po, and penetrate into the Cottian Alps, without commanding the sea; that the depots which a great capital contains might be transferred from Rome to Naples and Tarento, to save them from a victorious enemy, and finally that Rome exists; that she affords more resources for the occasions of a great capital than any city in the world; that she has, moreover, on her side, the magic influence and dignity of her name. It is accordingly my opinion that Rome is unquestionably the capital which the Italians will one day choose.

The population and wealth of Italy would enable her to maintain a military force of 400,000 soldiers, independently of her navy.

No part of Europe is so advantageously situated as this peninsula for becoming a great maritime power.

Chapter VI

BATTLE OF MONTENOTTE

Plan of the Campaign. State of the Armies. I arrive at Nice towards the end of March, 1796. Battle of Montenotte (12 April). Battle of Millesimo (14 April). Action of Dego (15 April). Action of Saint-Michel (20 April). Action of Mondovi (22 April). Armistice of Cherasco (28 April). Examination of the expediency of passing the Po, and proceeding farther from France.

In 1796 the King of Sardinia, whose military and geographical position had procured him the title of Porter of the Alps, had fortresses at the outlets of all the passes leading into Piedmont. For the purpose of penetrating into Italy by forcing the Alps, it was necessary to gain possession of one or more of these fortresses; the roads did not allow of bringing up a battering train; the mountains are covered with snow during three-quarters of the year, which leaves but little time for besieging fortresses. I conceived the idea of turning the whole of the Alps, and entering Italy precisely at the point where those lofty mountains terminate and where the Apennines begin, as has already been stated in Chapter III. Mont Blanc is the most elevated point of the Alps, whence the chain of these mountains decreases in height towards the Adriatic, as well as towards the Mediterranean as far as Mount Saint Jacques, where they end, and where the Apennines begin, which rise gradually as far as Mount Velino near Rome. Mount Saint Jacques is therefore the lowest point, both of the Alps and Apennines, the spot where the former end and the latter begin. Savona, a seaport and fortified town, was well situated for a depot and point of *appui*; from this town to la Madonna it is three miles; a firm road leads to that town, whence it is six miles to Carcari by a road which might in a few days be rendered practicable for artillery.

BATTLE OF MONTENOTTE

From Carcari there are carriage roads leading into the interior of Piedmont and Montferrat. This was the only point by which Italy could be entered without passing mountains; the elevations of the ground there are so trifling, that at a later period, under the Empire, a canal was planned for joining the Adriatic to the Mediterranean by the Po, the Tanaro, the Bormida, and locks from that river to Savona. The scheme of penetrating into Italy by Savona, Cadibona, Carcari, and the Bormida, afforded hopes of separating the Sardinian and Austrian armies; because Lombardy and Piedmont would be equally menaced from those points; Milan and Turin might be marched upon with equal facility. The Piedmontese were interested in covering Turin and the Austrians in covering Milan.

The army of the enemy was commanded by General Beaulieu, a distinguished officer, who had acquired reputation in the campaigns of the North. It was provided with all that could render it formidable, and was composed of Austrians, Sardinians and Neapolitans. Its numbers were double those of the French army, and were to be successively increased by the contingents of Naples, of the Pope, of Modena, and of Parma. These forces were divided into two grand corps; the active Austrian army, composed of four divisions of infantry of forty-two battalions, forty-four squadrons of cavalry, and one hundred and forty pieces of cannon: in all, 45,000 strong; under Lieutenants-General d'Argenteau, Melas, Wukassowich, Liptay, and Sebottendorf. The active army of Sardinia, composed of three divisions of infantry and one division of cavalry, in the whole 25,000 men, and sixty pieces of cannon, was commanded by the Austrian General Colli, and by generals Provera and Latour; the rest of the Sardinian forces garrisoned the fortresses, or defended the frontier, opposite to the French army of the Alps, under the command of the Duke of Aoste.

The French army was composed of four effective divisions of infantry, and two of cavalry, under Generals Massena, Augereau, Laharpe, Serrurier, Stengel and Kilmaine; it amounted to 25,000 infantry, 2,500 cavalry, 2,500 artillery, sappers, civil list, etc. Total 30,000 men present under arms. The effective strength of the army amounted, according to the returns of the ministry, to 106,000 men; but 36,000 were prisoners, dead or deserted. A regular review had long been expected for the purpose of striking them out of the states of situation. 20,000 were in the 8th military division, at Toulon, Marseilles, and Avignon, between the mouths of the Rhône and those of the Var; they could only be employed in the defence of Provence, depending on the ministry. There remained an effective force of 50,000 men on the left bank of the Var; of whom 5,000 were in the hospitals, 7,000 formed the depots of the corps of infantry, cavalry, (the latter being 2,500 men, not mounted) and artillery; there remained 30,000 men actually under arms, ready to take the field; 8,000 men, infantry and artillery, were employed in the garrisons of

BATTLE OF MONTENOTTE

Nice, Villa Franca, Monaco, the coasts of Genoa, and Saorgio, and in guarding the upper ridge of the Alps from the Col d'Argentieres to the Tanaro. The cavalry was in the worst condition possible, although it had long been on the Rhône to recruit itself; but it had suffered for want of provisions. The arsenals of Nice and Antibes were well provided with artillery, but destitute of means of carriage, all the draught horses having perished for want. The poverty of the finances was such that the government, with all its efforts, could only furnish the chest of the army with 2,000 louis in specie to open the campaign with, and a million in drafts, part of which were protested. The army was totally destitute, and had nothing to expect from France; all its dependence was on victory; it was only in the plains of Italy that it could organize means of conveyance, procure horses for the artillery, clothe the soldiers, and mount the cavalry. It consisted, however, of only 30,000 men actually under arms, and thirty pieces of cannon; and it stood opposed to 80,000 men and two hundred pieces of cannon. If it had been under the necessity of engaging in a general battle, its inferiority in numbers and in artillery and cavalry would undoubtedly have prevented it from making an effectual resistance; it had, therefore, to compensate for its inferiority in number by rapid marches; for the want of artillery by the nature of its manoeuvres; and for its inferiority in cavalry by the choice of positions. The character of the French soldiers was excellent; they had distinguished themselves and grown inured to war on the summits of the Alps and Pyrenees. Privations, poverty and want, are the school that forms good soldiers.

I reached Nice on 27 March; the picture of the army which General Scherer laid before me, was even worse than anything I had been able to conceive. The supply of bread was precarious, and no distribution of meat had been made for a long time. There were no means of conveyance but 500 mules; it was useless to think of carrying above thirty pieces of cannon. The state of affairs daily grew worse; there was not a moment to be lost; the army could no longer subsist where it was; it was indispensably requisite either to advance or to fall back. I gave orders to advance and thus surprise the enemy in the very opening of the campaign and dazzle him by striking and decisive successes. The head-quarters had never been removed from Nice since the commencement of the war; I instantly put them on their march for Albenga. All the civil lists had long considered themselves as permanently stationed, and were much more intent on procuring the comforts of life for themselves than on supplying the wants of the army. I reviewed the troops and addressed them thus: 'Soldiers, you are naked and ill-fed; the government owes you much, and can give you nothing. The patience and courage you have shown in the midst of these rocks are admirable, but they gain you no renown, no glory results to you from your endurance. It is my intention to lead you into the most fertile plains in the world. Rich provinces and great cities will be in your power; there you will find honour, glory and wealth. Soldiers of Italy, will you be wanting in courage or perseverance?' This speech from a young general of twenty-six already renowned for the operations of Toulon, Saorgio and Cairo, was received with eager acclamations.

For the purpose of turning the Alps and entering Italy by the Col di Cadibona, it was necessary to collect the whole army on its extreme right; a dangerous operation, had not the snow then covered all the debouchés of the Alps. The transition from the defensive to the offensive order is one of the most delicate of military operations. Serrurier posted himself at Garessio with his division to observe Colli's camps near Ceva; Massena and Augereau took positions at Loano, Finale, and Savona. Laharpe was placed so as to menace Genoa; his vanguard, commanded by Brigadier-General Cervoni, occupied Voltri. The French minister demanded of the senate of Genoa a passage by the Bocchetta, and the keys of Gavi, declaring that the French wished to penetrate into Lombardy, and support their operations on Genoa. This caused a great bustle in the city; the councils placed themselves in permanence. The effects of these measures were also felt in Milan.

Beaulieu, greatly alarmed, hastened precipitately to the aid of Genoa. He advanced his head-quarters to Novi, and divided his army into three corps: the right, composed of Piedmontese, and commanded by Colli, whose head-quarters were at Ceva, was ordered to defend the Stura and Tanaro. The centre, under the command of d'Argenteau fixed their head-quarters at Sasello, and marched on Montenotte to intercept the French army, during its march on Genoa, by falling on its left flank, and cutting it off from the road of la Corniche. Beaulieu in person marched with his left, by the Bocchetta, on Voltri to cover Genoa.

At first sight these dispositions appeared to be skilfully made; but on a more attentive examination of local circumstances, it was discovered that Beaulieu was dividing his forces, as no communication was practicable between his centre and his left, except round the back of the mountains; whilst the French army, on the contrary, was stationed in such a manner as to be able to unite in a few hours, and fall, in a mass, on either of the enemy's corps; on the defeat of one of which the other would be absolutely compelled to retreat. General d'Argenteau, commanding the centre of the enemy's army, encamped at Lower Montenotte, on 10 April; on the 11th he marched on Montelegino, to debouch by la Madonna on Savona. Colonel Rampon, who was ordered to guard the three redoubts of Montelegino, having received intelligence of the enemy's march, pushed forward a strong reconnoitring party to meet him, which was driven back from noon to two o'clock, when it regained the redoubts, which d'Argenteau attempted to carry by assault. He was repulsed by Rampon in three consecutive attacks; and as his troops were fatigued, he took up a position, intending to turn the redoubts in the morning in order to

BATTLE OF MONTENOTTE

reduce them. Beaulieu debouched on Genoa on the 10th; he attacked General Cervoni, before Voltri, the same day; the latter defended his position throughout the day, took up another on Mount la Fourche on the 11th, fell back in the course of the evening and night, and rejoined his division, that of Laharpe, which on the 12th before daylight was in position in the rear of Rampon, on Montelegino. During the night I marched with Augereau's and Massena's divisions; the latter by the Col di Cadibona and by Castellazzo debouched behind Montenotte. At day-break on the 12th, d'Argenteau, surrounded on all sides, was attacked in front by Rampon and Laharpe, and in rear and flank by Massena's division; the rout of the enemy was complete; they were all killed, taken, or dispersed: four stand of colours, five pieces of cannon, and 2,000 prisoners were the trophies of this day. During these occurrences Beaulieu presented himself at Voltri, but found nobody there; he conferred, without impediment, with the English admiral Nelson; it was not until the 13th that he heard of the loss of the battle of Montenotte and the entrance of the French into Piedmont. He was then obliged to make his troops fall back precipitately, and repass the bad roads into which the dispositions he had made had led him. Such was the circuit he was obliged to take, that two days elapsed before part of his troops could reach Millesimo, and he was twelve days in evacuating his magazines at Voltri and la Bocchetta, which compelled him to leave troops there to protect them.

On the 12th the head-quarters of the army reached Carcari; the Piedmontese had retreated on Millesimo, and the Austrians on Dego. These two positions were connected by a Piedmontese brigade, which occupied the heights of Biestro: at Millesimo the Piedmontese occupied both sides of the road which covers Piedmont; they were joined by Colli, with all the force he could muster from the right. At Dego the Austrians occupied the position which defends the Acqui road, the direct road to the Milanese: they were joined by Beaulieu with all the force he could bring from Voltri. In this position General Beaulieu was conveniently situated for receiving all the reinforcements which Lombardy could afford him: thus the two great openings into Piedmont and the Milanese were covered. The enemy was in hopes to fix and intrench himself there; for, advantageous as the battle of Montenotte had been to the French, the superiority of the enemy in number had enabled him to repair his losses.

But on the next day but one, the 14th, the battle of Millesimo opened the two roads of Turin and Milan. Augereau, forming the left, marched on Millesimo; Massena with the centre advanced on Biestro and Dego; and Laharpe with the right proceeded by the heights of Cairo. The French army thus occupied four leagues of ground from right to left; the enemy had supported his right by causing the hill of Cossaria, which commands both branches of the Bormida, to be occupied. But on the 13th General Augereau,

BATTLE OF MONTENOTTE

whose troops had not engaged at the battle of Montenotte, attacked the right of the enemy with such impetuosity that he carried the defiles of Millesimo, and surrounded the hill of Cossaria. The Austrian general, Provera, with his rear guard 2,000 strong, was cut off: in this desperate condition, he resorted to a desperate expedient; he took refuge in an old ruined castle, where he barricaded himself. From its top he saw the Sardinian army making dispositions for the battle of the following day, and conceived hopes of being extricated. I was sensible of the urgent importance of gaining possession of the castle of Cossaria in the course of the 13th, but this post was too strong; several attacks failed: the next day the two armies engaged. Massena and Laharpe carried Dego, after an obstinate conflict; Menard and Joubert took the heights of Biestro. All Colli's attacks, for the purpose of delivering Provera, were fruitless; he was constantly beaten and closely pursued: Provera, in despair, laid down his arms. The enemy was briskly pursued into the gorges of Spigno, on the Acqui road, by 400 men of the 22nd Chasseurs, 7th Hussars, and 15th Dragoons, and left behind him thirty pieces of horse-artillery, sixty ammunition waggons, fifteen stand of colours, and 6,000 prisoners, amongst whom were two generals and twenty-four superior officers. I was everywhere present at the most decisive moments.

The separation of the Austrian and Sardinian armies was thenceforth very evident. Beaulieu removed his head-quarters to Acqui on the Milanese road; and Colli proceeded to Ceva, to oppose the junction of Serrurier, and to cover Turin.

In the meantime, Wukassowich's division of Austrian grenadiers which had been directed from Voltri by Sassello, reached Dego at three in the morning of 15 April. The position was then occupied only by a few French battalions; these grenadiers easily carried the village, and occasioned great alarm at the French head-quarters, where it was found difficult to conceive how the enemy could be at Dego, when the advanced posts stationed on the Acqui road were undisturbed. I marched to Dego, which place was retaken after a very hot action of two hours, and nearly the whole of the enemy's division were taken or killed. Adjutant-General Lanusse, who was afterwards a general of division, and fell at the battle of Alexandria in Egypt (in 1801), decided the victory, which for a moment appeared doubtful. At the head of two battalions of light troops, he climbed the left side of the hill of Dego; some battalions of Hungarian grenadiers hastened up to prevent their reaching the summit: the two columns thrice advanced and fell back again; but the third time, Lanusse, placing his hat on the point of his sword, boldly advanced and decided the victory. This action, which took place in my sight, obtained Lanusse the rank of brigadier-general. Generals Causse and Bonnel were killed; they came from the Eastern Pyrenees; the officers who had served in that army always displayed remarkable courage and impetuosity. It was at

BATTLE OF MONTENOTTE

the village of Dego that, for the first time, I took notice of a lieutenant-colonel whom I made a colonel: this was Lannes, who afterwards became a marshal of the empire, and duke of Montebello, and evinced the greatest talents: in the sequel he will be constantly seen taking a most conspicuous part in all events.

After the action at Dego, operations were directed against the Piedmontese, and it was thought sufficient to keep the Austrians in check. Laharpe was placed in observation at the camp of San-Benedetto on the Belbo; Beaulieu was so much weakened that he attempted nothing more than to rally and organize the wreck of his army. Laharpe's division, being obliged to remain several days in this position, suffered through the scarcity of provisions, the want of means of conveyance, and the exhausted state of this country through the presence of so many troops; and this division abandoned itself to some disorders.

Serrurier, having heard at Garessio of the battles of Montenotte and Millesimo, occupied the heights of San Giovanni di Murialto, and entered Ceva on the same day that Augereau arrived on the heights of Montezemoto. On the 17th, after a fruitless resistance, Colli evacuated the intrenched camp of Ceva, repassed the Tanaro, and retreated behind the Corsaglia, occupying la Madonna di Vico by his right. On the same day the head-quarters were advanced to Ceva; the enemy having left there the artillery of his camp, which he had not had time to carry off, and contented himself with placing a garrison in the fort.

The arrival of the army on the heights of Montezemoto was a sublime spectacle: from that position the troops beheld the immense and fertile plains of Piedmont; the Po, the Tanaro, and a multitude of other rivers meandered in the distance: in the horizon a white girdle of snow and ice bounded this rich valley of the promised land. Those gigantic barriers, which appeared the limits of another world, which nature had delighted to render formidable, and on which art had lavished all its resources, had fallen as by enchantment. 'Hannibal forced the Alps', said I, contemplating those mountains, 'and we have turned them.' A happy expression, which in two words conveyed the idea and principle of the campaign. The army passed the Tanaro, and for the first time found itself in the plains: the cavalry became necessary; General Stengel, who commanded it, passed the Corsaglia at Lezegno on the right bank of that river, near its junction with the Tanaro.

On the 20th General Serrurier passed the bridge of Saint-Michel to attack the right of Colli's army, whilst Massena was passing the Tanaro to turn his left: but Colli, sensible of the danger of his position, had abandoned it during the night, and was himself marching on his right, to take position at Mondovi. By this fortuitous circumstance, he arrived with his forces before Saint-Michel, precisely at the moment when Serrurier was debouching from the

BATTLE OF MONTENOTTE

bridge. He halted, opposed Serrurier with superior numbers, and compelled him to fall back. The French general would nevertheless have maintained his ground in Saint-Michel, had not one of his light infantry regiments taken to pillage. He debouched on the 22nd by the bridge of Torre, Massena by that of Saint-Michel, and I by Lezegno. These three columns advanced on Mondovi: Colli had already raised some redoubts and taken up a position there, with his right on la Madonna di Vico, and his left on la Bicoque. Serrurier carried the redoubt of la Bicoque, and decided the battle of Mondovi. This town and all its magazines fell into the power of the victor. General Stengel, who had advanced too far into the plain with a thousand horse, in pursuit of the enemy, was attacked by the Piedmontese cavalry, which was brave and in excellent condition. He made every disposition that might be expected from a consummate general, and was operating his retreat on his reinforcements, when, in a charge, he received a mortal thrust and fell dead. Colonel Murat, at the head of three regiments of cavalry, repulsed the Piedmontese, and in his turn pursued them for several hours. General Stengel, a native of Alsace, was an excellent hussar officer; he had served under Dumouriez, and in the other campaigns of the North; he was adroit, intelligent, and active, combining the qualities of youth with those of maturity; he was the true general for advanced posts. Two or three days before his death, he having been the first to enter Lezegno, I arrived some hours later, and found everything I could want ready. The defiles and fords had been reconnoitred; guides had been secured; the curate and postmaster had been interrogated; an understanding had been entered into with the inhabitants; spies had been sent in several directions; the letters at the post-office seized, and those which contained any military information translated and analyzed; and all proper measures taken for forming magazines of provisions for the refreshment of the troops. Stengel, unfortunately, was near-sighted, an essential defect in his situation, and which proved fatal to him.

The loss of the Piedmontese in this battle amounted to 3,000 men, eight pieces of cannon, ten stand of colours, and 1,500 prisoners, amongst whom there were three generals. After the battle of Mondovi, I marched on Cherasco, Serrurier advanced on Fossano, and Augereau on Alba. Beaulieu had marched from Acqui on Nizza-della-Paglia with half his army, to make a diversion in favour of the Piedmontese, but too late; he fell back on the Po as soon as he heard of the treaty of Cherasco.

These three columns entered Cherasco, Fossano, and Alba, all at the same time. Colli's head-quarters were at Fossano; Serrurier dislodged him thence. Cherasco, at the junction of the Stura and Tanaro, was a fortified place, but ill armed, and unfurnished with stores, because it was not a frontier place. This acquisition was important; not a moment was lost in putting it in a state of defence; its artillery magazines contained everything necessary for the

BATTLE OF MONTENOTTE

completion of its armament. The French army passed the Stura, and arrived before the little town of Bra. Serrurier's junction had afforded the means of communication with Nice by Ponte-di-Nave; and reinforcements of artillery, with all the stores that could be got ready, arrived from thence. In all these actions the army had enriched itself with a great quantity of cannon and horses; many more of the latter were levied in the plain of Mondovi: a few days after entering Cherasco, the artillery could furnish sixty guns well supplied and horsed. The soldiers, who had been without distributions during the ten days of this campaign, now received them regularly: pillage and disorder, the usual attendants of rapid movements, ceased; discipline was restored; the appearance of the army was speedily improved amidst the abundance and resources which this fine country afforded; besides, the losses had not been so great as might have been supposed.

The rapidity of the movement, the impetuosity of the troops, and, above all, the art of always opposing them to the enemy in at least equal numbers, and often superior, added to the constant success obtained, had saved numbers of men. These losses, moreover, were repaired, soldiers arrived by every road from all the depots and hospitals of the Riviera di Genoa, on the mere report of the victories gained, and of the abundance which the army enjoyed. The condition of the French army had previously been so wretched that it would almost be rash to describe it; for several years the pay received by the officers had only been eight francs per month; and the staff had been entirely on foot. Marshal Berthier preserved amongst his papers an order of the day, dated from Albenga, granting a gratification of three louis to each general of division. Cherasco is ten leagues from Turin, fifteen from Alessandria, eighteen from Tortona, twenty-five from Genoa, and twenty from Savona.

The Court of Sardinia no longer knew what course to adopt; its army was discouraged and partly destroyed; the Austrian army no longer thought of anything but covering Milan. Throughout Piedmont great agitation prevailed; the Court was far from enjoying the confidence of the public. It placed itself at my discretion, and solicited an armistice. Many persons would have preferred marching on Turin; but Turin was a fortified place; heavy cannon would have been requisite for forcing its gates. The King still had a great number of fortresses; and notwithstanding the victories which had just been gained, the slightest check, the least caprice of fortune, might overturn everything. The two armies of the enemy were still, taken together, superior to the French army, notwithstanding the reverses they had sustained; they had a considerable train of artillery, and their cavalry, in particular, had suffered no loss. The French troops, in spite of their victories, were alarmed; they were struck with the magnitude of the enterprise; success appeared problematical when the feeble means that were to produce it were considered; they were disposed to exaggerate the least reverse. There were officers, and

BATTLE OF MONTENOTTE

even generals, who could not conceive how anyone could dare to think of the conquest of Italy with so little artillery, so bad a cavalry, and so feeble an army, which sickness and the distance from France would daily weaken still more. Traces of these sentiments in the army may be seen in the proclamation which I addressed to my soldiers at Cherasco:

'Soldiers, you have, in fifteen days, gained six victories, taken twenty-one stand of colours, fifty-five pieces of cannon, and several fortresses, and conquered the richest part of Piedmont; you have taken 15,000 prisoners, and killed or wounded upwards of 10,000 men. Hitherto you have fought for barren rocks, now celebrated through your valour, but useless to the country; but your services now equal those of the Armies of Holland and the Rhine. You were utterly destitute; and you have supplied all deficiencies. You have gained battles without cannon, passed rivers without bridges, performed forced marches without shoes, and bivouacked without brandy, and often without bread. None, but republican phalanxes, the soldiers of liberty, could have endured what you have; thanks be to you, soldiers, for your exertions. Your grateful country owes its prosperity to you; and if the conquest of Toulon was an omen of the immortal campaign of 1793, your present victories foreshow one still more glorious. The two armies which lately attacked you with confidence now fly before you in consternation; the perverse men who laughed at your distress, and inwardly rejoiced at the triumphs of your enemies, are confounded and trembling. But, soldiers, you have yet done nothing, for there still remains much to do. Neither Turin nor Milan are yours; the ashes of the conquerors of Tarquin are still trodden under foot by the assassins of Basseville. It is said that there are some amongst you whose courage is enervated; who would prefer returning to the summits of the Apennines and Alps! No, I cannot believe it. The victors of Montenotte, Millesimo, Dego and Mondovi, are eager to extend the glory of the French people!'

Conferences on the subject of a suspension of hostilities were held at headquarters in the house of Salmatoris, then maître d'hôtel to the King of Sardinia, and afterwards prefect of the palace to me. The Piedmontese General Latour, and Colonel Lacoste were charged with the King's powers. Count Latour was an old soldier, a Lieutenant-General in the Sardinian service, decidedly hostile to all new ideas, of little information, and but moderate capacity. Colonel Lacoste, a native of Savoy, was in the prime of life; he expressed himself with facility, was a man of talent, and made a favourable impression. The conditions were: That the King should secede from the coalition, and send a plenipotentiary to Paris to treat for a definite peace; that in the meantime there should be an armistice; that Ceva, Coni and either Tortona or Alessandria, should immediately be surrendered to the French army, with all their artillery and stores; that the army should continue to occupy all that part of the country which was then actually in its possession; that a free communication should be allowed by the military roads in all directions from the army to France, and from France to the army; that Valenza should immediately be evacuated by the Neapolitans, and placed in my possession until I should have effected the passage of the Po; and lastly, that the militia of the country should be disbanded, and the regular troops dispersed in the garrisons so as to give no umbrage to the French army.

From that moment the Austrians, left to themselves, might be pursued into the interior of Lombardy. Part of the troops of the Army of the Alps, which had now become disposable, were about to descend into Italy. The line of communication with Paris was shortened by one half; and lastly, we had points of *appui* and grand depots of artillery to form our battering trains, and to besiege Turin itself, if the Directory should not accede to the peace.

The armistice being concluded, and the fortresses of Coni, Tortona and Ceva occupied, it became a subject of deliberation whether to advance, and how far? It was allowed that the Armistice by which all the fortresses had fallen, and the Piedmontese army had been separated from that of Austria, was useful. 'But would it not be still more advantageous (it was asked) to avail ourselves of the means already acquired, and to revolutionize Piedmont and Genoa completely, previously to any farther advance? The French government possessed the right of refusing the negotiations proposed, and declaring its will by an ultimatum. Would it not be impolitic to remove farther from France, and pass the Ticino, without securing the rear? The kings of Sardinia, who have been so useful to France as long as they remained faithful, have likewise been the most effectual contributors to her reverses when they changed their policy. At this time the disposition of that Court does not allow of the slightest misapprehension. The nobles and priests rule it; they are the irreconcilable enemies of the republic. If we advance and suffer a defeat, what shall we not have to dread from their hatred and revenge? Even Genoa may well excite much anxiety. The oligarchical system still predominates there; and however numerous the partisans of France may be, they are without influence in political decisions. The Genoese citizens may declaim as much as they please, but that is the extent of their power. The Oligarchs govern; they command the troops, and have at their disposal from eight to ten thousand peasants of Fontana-Bona and other valleys, whom they summon to their aid when they want them. Lastly, are we to stop after passing the Ticino, or to pass the Adda, the Oglio, the Mincio, the Adige, the Brenta, the Piave, the Tagliamento, and the Isonzo? Is it prudent to leave in our rear such a numerous and hostile population? In order to proceed rapidly, is it not best to proceed deliberately, and to form points of support in every country we occupy, by changing the government, and intrusting the administration to persons of the same principles and interests as ourselves? If we advanced into the Venetian countries, should we not oblige the Republic of Venice, which has 50,000 men at its disposal, to side with the enemy?'

To all this it was answered: 'The French army ought to profit by its victory; it ought not to halt except on the best line of defence against the Austrian armies which will speedily debouch from the Tyrol and the Frioul. This line is the Adige; it covers all the valleys of the Po; it cuts off lower and middle Italy; it insulates the fortified city of Mantua, which may probably be taken before the enemy's army can recover itself, and be in a position to succour it. It was through overlooking this principle that Marshal Villars missed the whole object of the war in 1733. He was at the head of 50,000 men assembled at the camp of Vigevano in October; there was no army before him, and he might have gone wherever he would. He confined himself to remaining in observation of the Oglio, occupying positions on both sides of the Po; having thus lost the opportunity, he never found another. Three months after, Mercy arrived in the Seraglio with an army. Marshal de Coigny, although at the head of a very superior army during the whole campaign of 1734, and victorious in two pitched battles, those of Parma and Guastalla, did not know how to take advantage of such great successes; he manoeuvred alternately on the two banks of the Po. Had these generals been well acquainted with the topography of Italy, Villars would have taken up a position on the Adige in the month of November, thus intercepting all Italy; and Coigny would have availed himself of his victories to hasten thither with all possible despatch.

'On the Adige it is easy to provide for all the expenses of the army, because the burthen will be divided amongst a great population—that of Piedmont, Lombardy, the Legations of Bologna and Ferrara, and the Duchies of Parma and Modena. Is it feared that Venice will declare war against France? The best way of preventing her is to carry the war, in a few days, into the midst of her states; she is not prepared for such an event; she has not had time to levy troops and form resolutions; the Senate must be prevented from deliberating. If the army remain on the right bank of the Ticino the Austrians will force that republic to make common cause with them, or she will throw herself into their arms, under the influence of party spirit. The King of Sardinia is no longer formidable; his militia is disbanded; the English will stop their subsidies; the domestic affairs of that country are in the worst state possible. Whatever course the Court adopts, the number of malcontents will increase; after fever comes debility. All his remaining forces do not amount to more than from fifteen to eighteen thousand men; and these, dispersed through a great number of towns, will scarcely suffice to maintain internal tranquillity. Besides, the dissatisfaction of the Court of Vienna with the Cabinet of Turin will be constantly increasing: the latter will be reproached by Austria with having despaired of the common cause on the loss of a single battle. It was not

BATTLE OF MONTENOTTE

thus that Victor Amadeus acted in 1705, after the victory gained by Vendome at Cassano, when Prince Eugene was driven back to the banks of lake Iseo, and when three French armies invaded all his dominions, even the county of Nice: he had nothing left but Turin; yet he remained firm, and persisted in his alliance with Austria. He was rewarded the following year by the battle of Turin, in which he reconquered all his territories, in consequence of that most daring march by Prince Eugene, which it pleased fortune to crown with the most signal success.

'There is nothing to fear from the oligarchs of Genoa; the best guarantee against them is to be found in the immense profits they make by their neutrality. It is wished to protect the principles of liberty in Piedmont and Genoa; but for that purpose a civil war must be kindled, the people must be excited to revolt against the nobles and priests; and this course will incur the responsibility of all the excesses which such contests never fail to occasion. On the other hand, the army, on reaching the Adige, will command all the States of the house of Austria in Italy, and all those of the Pope on this side of the Apennines; it will be in a situation to proclaim the principles of liberty, and to excite Italian patriotism against the sway of foreigners. It will not be necessary to sow dissension between the various classes of citizens. Nobles, citizens, and peasants, will all be called on to exert themselves unanimously for the restoration of the Italian nation. The word *Italiam! Italiam!* proclaimed at Milan, Bologna, and Verona, will produce a magical effect. But were it pronounced on the right bank of the Ticino, the Italians would say, *Why do you not advance?*'

Colonel Murat, principal aide-de-camp, was despatched to Paris with twenty-one stand of colours and the treaty for the armistice of Cherasco. His arrival at Paris, by way of Mount Cenis, with so many trophies and the King of Sardinia's act of submission, caused great joy in the capital, and excited the most lively enthusiasm. The aide-de-camp Junot, who had been despatched after the battle of Millesimo by the Nice road, arrived after Murat.

The province of Alba, the whole of which the French occupied, was more hostile to the royal authorities than any other part of Piedmont, and that which contained the greatest quantity of revolutionary germs. Some disturbances had already broken out, and others occurred at a later period. If the French had wished to continue the war against the King of Sardinia, they would have found the most aid and the greatest disposition to insurrection in that province. Thus, in fifteen days, the principal point of the plan of the campaign was secured. Great results were obtained; the Piedmontese fortresses of the Alps had fallen; the coalition was deprived of the aid of a power which furnished from sixty to seventy thousand men, and was still more important on account of its situation. In the course of a month from the commencement of this campaign, the legislature five times decreed that the

BATTLE OF MONTENOTTE

Army of Italy had deserved well of its country; in the sittings of the 21st, 22nd, 24th, 25th, and 26th of April; and each time for new victories.

According to the conditions of the armistice of Cherasco, the King of Sardinia sent Count Revel to Paris to treat for a definite peace; which treaty he concluded and signed on 15 May, 1796. By this treaty the fortresses of Alessandria and Coni were surtendered to the Army of Italy; Suza, la Brunette, and Exilles, were demolished, and the Alps opened: thus the King of Sardinia was placed at the mercy of the Republic, having no other fortified points than Turin and Fort Bard.

Chapter VII

BATTLE OF LODI

Passage of the Po (7 May). Action of Fombio (8 May). Armistice granted to the Duke of Parma (9 May). Battle of Lodi (10 May). Entrance into Milan (14 May). Armistice granted to the Duke of Modena (20 May). Berthier. Massena. Augereau. Serrurier.

The gates of the fortresses of Coni, Tortona, and Ceva, were opened to the French in the beginning of May. Massena marched with his division to Alessandria, where he captured numerous stores belonging to the Austrian army. The headquarters reached Tortona, by way of Alba, Nizza-della-Paglia, and the convent of Bosco. Tortona was a very fine fortress: it was abundantly provided with artillery and military stores of all kinds. Beaulieu had retreated in consternation beyond the Po to cover Milan; he intended to defend the passage of the Po, opposite Valenza, and after that passage should be forced, to dispute those of the Sesia and Ticino. He stationed his troops on the left bank of the Cogna, at the camp of Valeggio; he was there reinforced by a reserve of ten battalions, which made his army equal to the French force. In all the military and political arrangements, Valenza had been designated as the place where the French would attempt the passage of the Po. In the conferences at Cherasco this supposition had been suffered to appear, though in a mysterious manner. An article in the concluding part of the armistice prescribed the surrender of that town to the French, to enable them to effect the passage of the river. Scarce had Massena reached Alessandria when he pushed forward parties in the direction of Valenza. Augereau set out from Alba, and encamped at the mouth of the Scrivia. Serrurier repaired to Tortona, where Laharpe had arrived by the Acqui road. The grenadiers of the army had been assembled there to the number of 3,500; they formed ten battalions. With

BATTLE OF LODI

these choice troops, the cavalry and twenty-four pieces of cannon I advanced by forced marches on Piacenza, to surprise the passage of the Po. The moment the intended passage was unmasked, all the French divisions abandoned their positions, and marched with all possible speed on Piacenza. On 7 May, at nine o'clock in the morning I arrived before that town, having marched sixteen leagues in thirty-six hours. I proceeded to the bank of the river, where I remained until the passage was effected, and the van was on the opposite bank. The ferry-boat of Piacenza carried 500 men or fifty horses, and crossed in half an hour. Colonel Andreossy of the artillery, director of the bridges, and Adjutant-General Frontin had taken, on the Po, between Castel-Sainte-Joane and Piacenza, ten boats carrying 500 wounded men, and the pharmacy of the Austrian army. Colonel Lannes passed first, with 900 grenadiers. Two squadrons of the enemy's hussars in vain attempted to oppose their landing. A few hours after, the whole of the van was on the opposite side. In the night of the 7th the whole army arrived; on the 9th the bridge was completed. In the evening of the 7th, General Laharpe, commanding the grenadiers, fixed his head-quarters at Emetri, between Fombio and the Po. This river is very rapid at Piacenza; it is two hundred and fifty toises in breadth. The passage of rivers of such importance is amongst the most critical of military operations.

Liptay's division of the Austrian army consisting of eight battalions and eight squadrons, having marched from Pavia, arrived during the night at Fombio, one league from the bridge of Piacenza. On the 8th, in the afternoon, it was discovered that the steeples and houses of the village were embattled and filled with troops; and that cannon were planted on the roads, which crossed some rice-fields. It became of the utmost importance to dislodge the enemy from Fombio. He might receive great reinforcements; it would have been much too dangerous to be compelled to give battle with so large a river in the rear. I gave orders for such dispositions as the nature of the ground required. Lannes attacked on the left; Lanusse in the centre; Dallemagne on the right: in one hour the village was carried, and the Austrian division which defended it routed, with the loss of their cannon, 2,500 prisoners, and three standards. The wreck of this corps threw themselves into Pizzighettone, and there passed the Adda. A few days before, the fortress of Pizzighettone had not been put in a state of defence, and was considered so far from the theatre of war and from all danger, that the enemy had not thought of it; but Liptay had time enough to raise the drawbridges and place some field-artillery on the ramparts. The French vanguard halted at night at the landing place of Malleo, at half cannon-shot distance from Pizzighettone. Laharpe executed a retrograde movement, in order to place himself in advance of Codogno, and to cover the roads to Pavia and Lodi. It had been ascertained from the prisoners taken at Fombio, that Beaulieu was on his march to encamp with his army behind Fombio. It was therefore possible that some of

BATTLE OF LODI

his corps, not knowing what had taken place in the afternoon might advance to Codogno to take up their quarters there; and the troops were instructed accordingly. After giving orders for the most vigilant look-out I returned to my head-quarters at Piacenza. During the night Massena passed the Po, and placed himself in reserve at the head of the bridge, to support Laharpe in case of need. What had been foreseen took place: the march of the troops from Tortona to Piacenza, rapidly as it was executed, had not been so secret but that Beaulieu had received information of it. He put all his troops in march to occupy the country between the Ticino and the Adda, in hopes of arriving opposite Piacenza in time to prevent the passage of the river; he knew that the French were unprovided with pontoons. One of the regiments of cavalry which preceded the column in which he was, presented itself at General Laharpe's advanced posts, coming by way of Pavia, and gave the alarm there. The bivouacs were speedily under arms; after a few discharges they heard no more of the enemy; nevertheless Laharpe, followed by a piquet and several officers, went forward to ascertain what was the meaning of this attack, and to interrogate in person the inhabitants of the first farmhouses on the road, who told him that this alarm had been caused by a regiment of cavalry which was ignorant that the French had passed the Po, and that it had turned to the left to make for Lodi. Laharpe returned to his camp. But, instead of returning by the road by which the troops had seen him set out, he unfortunately took a by-path. The soldiers were on the watch; they received their general with a very brisk fire of musquetry. Laharpe fell dead, pierced by the bullets of his own soldiers. He was a Swiss of the canton of Vaud. His hatred of the government of Berne had exposed him to persecutions, from which he had sought an asylum in France. He was an officer of distinguished bravery; a grenadier both in stature and in courage; he commanded his troops skilfully, and was much beloved by them, though of an unquiet temper. It was remarked that during the action of Fombio, throughout the evening preceding his death, he had seemed very absent and dejected; giving no orders, appearing as it were deprived of his usual faculties, and entirely overwhelmed by a fatal presentiment. The news of this melancholy event reached head-quarters at four in the morning. Berthier was instantly sent to this division of the vanguard, and found the troops in the greatest affliction.

On entering the states of Parma, I received, at the passage of the Trebbia, envoys from the prince, requesting peace and my protection. The Duke of Parma was of no political importance; the seizure of his states could be of no advantage. I left him in possession of the government, imposing on him, as the conditions of the armistice, all the sacrifices of which his states were capable. Thus every benefit was obtained from them, without the trouble of undertaking the administration; this was the wisest and simplest course. On the morning of the 9th, the armistice was signed at Piacenza. The duke paid

BATTLE OF LODI

two millions in money, furnished the magazines of the army with a great quantity of hay, wheat, etc., supplied sixteen hundred horses for the artillery and cavalry, and engaged to defray the expenses of all the military routes, and the hospitals which should be established in his states. It was on this occasion that I imposed a contribution of works of art for the Museum at Paris; being the first instance of the kind that occurs in modern history. Parma furnished twenty pictures, chosen by the French Commissioners, amongst which was the famous Saint-Jerome. The duke offered two millions to be allowed to keep this picture; the opinion of the army-agents was decidedly in favour of the acceptance of the money. I said that there would very soon be nothing left out of the two millions proposed; whilst the possession of such a masterpiece by the city of Paris would be ornamental to that capital, and would produce other chefs-d'oeuvre of art.

The city of Parma is situate thirty leagues from the gulf of Rapallo in the Mediterranean, at the same distance from the mouths of the Po in the Adriatic; sixty leagues from the mouth of the Var, the western frontier of Italy on the French side; twenty-five leagues from the Isonzo, the eastern frontier of Italy, and boundary of that country towards Germany; sixty leagues south from the pass of the Saint-Gothard, the boundary of Switzerland; two hundred and ten leagues from the Ionian sea; twenty leagues from Spezia, and four leagues from the Po. Its population was 40,000 souls. Its citadel was in a bad condition. The duchies of Parma, Piacenza, and Guastalla, were possessed by the house of Farnese. Elizabeth, wife of Philip V, heiress of that house, brought these duchies into the house of Spain. Don Carlos, his son, possessed them in 1714, who being afterwards called to the throne of Naples, these duchies passed to the house of Austria, in 1748, by the treaty of Aix la Chapelle; the infant Don Philip was invested with them, whose son Ferdinand succeeded him in 1762. He was Condillac's famous pupil, and died in 1802. He inhabited the castle of Colorno, surrounded with monks, and occupied with the most minute and rigid observance of religious practices.

The army levied four hundred artillery horses in the city of Piacenza. On the 10th it marched from Casal-Pusterlengo on Lodi, where Beaulieu had effected the junction of Sebottendorf's and Roselmini's divisions, and had directed Colli and Wukassowich on Milan and Cassano. The fate of these last troops depended therefore on rapidity of marching. They might be cut off from the Oglio, and made prisoners; but within a league of Casal the French army met with a strong rearguard of Austrian grenadiers, posted in an advantageous position, defending the Lodi road. It became necessary to manoeuvre, which was performed with the utmost ardour, the enemy resisting with all the obstinacy which circumstances required; at length his ranks fell into disorder, and he was hotly pursued even into the town of Lodi. This place was walled; the enemy attempted to close the gates, but the French

BATTLE OF LODI

soldiers entered pell-mell with the fugitives, who rallied behind the line of battle, which Beaulieu had taken up on the left bank of the Adda. This general unmasked from five and twenty to thirty pieces of cannon to defend the bridge; the French immediately opposed a like number to him. The strength of the Austrian line was 12,000 infantry and 4,000 cavalry, which, with the 10,000 who were retreating on Cassano, the 8,000 who had been beaten at Fombio, and the remains of whom had retreated to Pizzighettone, and the 2,000 of the garrison of the castle of Milan, made up about 35 or 36,000 men, being all that remained of the Austrian army.

In the hopes of cutting off the division which was marching by Cassano, I resolved to pass the bridge of the Adda the same day, under the enemy's fire, and to astonish them by so daring an operation. Accordingly, after a few hours' rest at Lodi, about five o'clock in the evening, I ordered General Beaumont, commanding the cavalry, to pass the Adda half a league above the town, where there was a ford which was then practicable; and as soon as he should reach the opposite side, to open a cannonade on the right flank of the enemy with a battalion of light artillery. At the same time I placed at the debouché of the bridge and on the right bank all the disposable artillery of the army, directing it against the enemy's guns which enfiladed the bridge; I formed the grenadiers in close column behind the rampart of the town on the edge of the Adda, where it was nearer the enemy's batteries than the line of the Austrian infantry itself (which had withdrawn to a distance from the river to take advantage of a rise in the ground which sheltered it from the balls of the French batteries), and when I perceived the fire of the enemy's artillery slacken, I ordered the charge to be beaten. The head of the column, by a mere wheel to the left, reached the bridge, which it crossed at a running step, in a few seconds, and instantly took the enemy's cannon; the column was only exposed to the enemy's fire at the moment of wheeling to the left to pass the bridge. It accordingly reached the opposite side in a twinkling, without any sensible loss, fell on the enemy's line, broke it, and forced him to retreat on Crema in the greatest disorder, with the loss of his artillery, several stand of colours, and 2,500 prisoners. This vigorous operation, conducted, under such a murderous fire, with all suitable prudence, has been regarded by military men as one of the most brilliant actions of the war. The French did not lose above 200 men; the enemy was destroyed. But Colli and Wukassowich had passed the Adda at Cassano, and were retreating by the Brescia road, which determined the French to march on Pizzighettone; they considered it important to drive the enemy instantly from that fortress, before he should have time to put it in a state of defence and victual it; it was scarcely invested when it surrendered; it contained 300 men, whom the enemy sacrificed to facilitate his retreat. In my nightly rounds, I fell in with a bivouac of prisoners, in which was an old garrulous Hungarian officer, whom I asked how matters went with them; the old captain could not deny but that they went on badly enough; 'but', added he, 'there is no understanding it at all; we have to do with a young general, who is this moment before us, the next behind us, then again on our flanks; one does not know where to place oneself. This manner of making war is insufferable, and against all usage and custom.' The French cavalry entered Cremona after a brilliant charge, and pursued the Austrian rear-guard as far as the Oglio.

No French troops had yet entered Milan, although that capital was several days' march in the rear of the army, which had posts at Cremona. But the Austrian authorities had abandoned it, and taken refuge in Mantua. The town was guarded by the national guards. The municipality and the states of Lombardy sent a deputation to Milan, with Melzi at its head, to make a protest of their submission, and implore the clemency of the victor. It was in memory of this mission that as King of Italy I afterwards created the duchy of Lodi, in favour of Melzi. On 15 May, as victor, I made my entrance into Milan under a triumphal arch, amidst an immense population, and the numerous national guard of the city, clothed in the three colours, green, red, and white. At the head of this corps was the duke of Serbelloni, whom the members had chosen for their commander. Augereau retrograded to occupy Pavia; Serrurier occupied Lodi and Cremona; and Laharpe's division Como, Cassano, Lucca, and Pizzighettone, which place was armed and victualled.

I addressed the following order of the day to my men: 'Soldiers, you have rushed like a torrent from the top of the Apennines, you have overthrown and dispersed all that opposed your march. Piedmont, delivered from Austrian tyranny, indulges her natural sentiments of peace and friendship towards France. Milan is yours; and the republican flag waves throughout Lombardy. The dukes of Parma and Modena are indebted for their political existence only to your generosity. The Army which so proudly threatened you, can now find no barrier to protect it against your courage; neither the Po, the Ticino, nor the Adda could stop you a single day: these vaunted bulwarks of Italy opposed you in vain; you passed them as rapidly as the Apennines. These great successes have filled the heart of your country with joy; your representatives have ordered a festival to commemorate your victories, which has been held in every commune of the Republic. There your fathers, your mothers, your wives, sisters and mistresses, rejoiced in your victories, and proudly boasted of belonging to you. Yes, soldiers, you have done much.— But remains there nothing more to perform?—Shall it be said of us that we knew how to conquer, but not how to make use of victory? Shall posterity reproach us with having found Capua in Lombardy?—But I see you already hasten to arms. An effeminate repose is tedious to you; the days which are lost to glory, are lost to your happiness. Well then! let us set forth, we have

BATTLE OF LODI

still forced marches to make, enemies to subdue, laurels to gather, injuries to avenge. Let those who have sharpened the daggers of civil war in France, who have basely murdered our ministers, and burnt our ships at Toulon, tremble! The hour of vengeance has struck; but let the people of all countries be free from apprehension; we are the friends of the people everywhere, and more particularly of the descendants of Brutus and Scipio, and the great men whom we have taken for our models. To restore the Capitol, to replace there the statues of the heroes who rendered it illustrious, with suitable honours, to awaken the Roman people, stupefied by several ages of slavery—such will be the fruit of our victories; they will form an historical era for posterity: you will have the immortal glory of changing the face of the finest part of Europe. The French people, free, and respected by the whole world, will give to Europe a glorious peace, which will indemnify her for the sacrifices of every kind which for the last six years she has been making. You will then return to your homes, and your countrymen will say, as they point you out, "*He belonged to the Army of Italy*".'

The army spent six days of the rest in improving its *matériel*; nothing was spared to complete the trains of artillery. Piedmont and the Parmesan had afforded great resources, but those found in Lombardy were much more considerable, and furnished the means of discharging the arrears of pay, supplying all the wants of the troops, and establishing regularity in the different branches of the service.

Milan is situate in the midst of one of the richest plains in the world, between the Alps, the Po, and the Adda.

The cathedral is the finest and most vaunted in Italy, next to Saint Peter's at Rome; it is faced with white marble, was begun by Galeasso in 1300, and finished in 1810 by me.

Milan was the capital of Austrian Lombardy, which was divided into seven provinces.

At Milan, as in all the great towns of Italy, and perhaps throughout Europe, the French Revolution at first excited the most lively enthusiasm, and found partisans everywhere; but at a later period, the hideous scenes acted during the Reign of Terror, dissipated these favourable sentiments. Yet revolutionary ideas still had warm partisans at Milan; the mass of the people was allured by the attraction of equality. The Austrians, notwithstanding their protracted rule, had not inspired the people of Lombardy with any feelings of attachment, with the exception of a few noble families; they were generally disliked on account of their pride and the rudeness of their manners. The governor-general, the archduke Ferdinand, was neither beloved nor esteemed; he was accused of being fond of money, of influencing the government in favour of depredations, of speculating in wheat, and other offences of this kind, which are always very unpopular. He was married to

BATTLE OF LODI

the princess Beatrice d'Este, daughter and heiress of the last duke of Modena, then reigning.

The citadel of Milan was in a good state of defence, and well supplied with provisions. Beaulieu had left in it a garrison of 2,500 men. The French general Despinois was intrusted with the command of Milan and the blockade of the citadel. The artillery department formed the besieging train by drawing the guns and military stores from the Piedmontese fortresses occupied by French garrisons, namely, Tortona, Alessandria, Coni, Ceva and Cherasco.

The three duchies of Modena, Reggio and Mirandola, on the right bank of the lower Po, were governed by the last prince of the house of Este, a covetous old man, whose only pleasure was to amass gold. He was despised by his subjects. On the approach of the French, he sent the commander d'Este, his natural brother, to solicit an armistice and my protection. The city of Modena was surrounded by a wall with bastions, and had a well-furnished arsenal, its military establishment was 4,000 men. This prince was of no political importance; he was treated in the same manner as the duke of Parma, and without regard to his consanguinity to the house of Austria. The armistice was concluded and signed at Milan on 20 May. He paid ten millions, gave horses and provisions of all kinds, and a certain number of works of art. He sent plenipotentiaries to Paris to treat for peace, but it was not concluded; the negotiations went on slowly, and were at last broken off. Wishing to place his treasures in security, he sought asylum at Venice, where he died in 1798. On his death the house of Este, so famous in the middle ages, and celebrated with so much taste and genius by Ariosto and Tasso, became extinct. His daughter, the Princess Beatrice, wife of the archduke Ferdinand, was the mother of the Empress of Austria, who died in 1816.

The successive arrivals of the news of the passage of the Po, the battle of Lodi, the occupation of Lombardy, and the armistices concluded with the dukes of Parma and Modena, so intoxicated the Directory, that it adopted the fatal plan of dividing the Army of Italy into two armies. I, with 20,000 men, was to pass the Po, and march on Rome and Naples; and Kellermann, with the other 20,000 was to command on the left bank of the Po, and to cover the siege of Mantua. Indignant at this piece of ingratitude, I sent in my resignation, refusing to be instrumental to the destruction of the Army of Italy and of my brethren in arms. I declared that all the men who should penetrate deep into the Peninsula would be lost; that the principal army, entrusted to Kellerman, would be inadequate to maintain its ground, and would be compelled to repass the Alps in a few weeks. One bad general, said I, is better than two good ones. The government became sensible of its error, and recalled its liberticidal decrees; and from that time interfered no farther with the Army of Italy than merely to approve whatever I did or projected.

BATTLE OF LODI

Berthier was then about forty-two years of age. His father, a geographical engineer, had had the honour of seeing Louis XV and Louis XVI occasionally, being employed to draw plans of the chases, and these princes being fond of pointing out the errors they discovered in the plans, on their return from hunting. Berthier, in his youth, served in the American war as lieutenant-adjoint to Rochambeau's staff; he was a colonel at the period of the Revolution, and commanded the National Guard of Versailles, where he strongly opposed Lecointre's party. Being employed in la Vendée as quarter-master-general of the revolutionary armies, he was wounded there. After the 9 Thermidor he was quarter-master-general to General Kellerman, in the Army of the Alps, and followed him to the Army of Italy. He it was who caused the army to take the line of Borghetto, which stopped the enemy. When Kellerman returned to the Army of the Alps, he took Berthier with him; but when I took the command of the Army of Italy, Berthier solicited and obtained the place of quarter-master-general, in which capacity he constantly followed me in the campaigns of Italy and Egypt. He was afterwards minister at war, major-general of the grand army, and prince of Neufchatel and Wagram. He married a Bavarian princess, and was loaded with favours by me. His activity was extraordinary; he followed his general in all his reconnoitring parties and all his excursions, without in the least neglecting his official duties. He was of an irresolute character, unfit for a principal command, but possessed of all the qualifications of a good quarter-master-general. He was well acquainted with the map, understood the reconnoitring duty perfectly, attended personally to the despatch of orders; and was thoroughly trained to presenting the most complicated movements of an army with perspicuity. There was an attempt made, at first, to disgrace him with his general, by describing him as my Mentor, and asserting that it was he who directed operations; but this did not succeed. Berthier did all in his power to silence these reports, which rendered him ridiculous in the army. After the campaign of Italy, he had the command of the army ordered to take possession of Rome, where he proclaimed the Roman Republic.

Massena was born at Nice, and entered the French service in the Royal Italian regiment; he was an officer at the commencement of the Revolution. He advanced rapidly, and became a general of division. In the Army of Italy, he served under the generals-in-chief Dugommier, Dumorbion, Kellerman, and Scherer. He was of a hardy constitution, and an indefatigable character; night and day on horseback amongst rocks and mountains, the warfare peculiar to which he was particularly acquainted with. He was resolute, brave, intrepid, full of ambition and pride; his distinguishing characteristic was obstinacy; he was never discouraged. He neglected discipline, and took little care of the affairs of the army, for which reason he was not much beloved by the soldiers. He used to make very indifferent dispositions for an attack. His conversation was uninteresting; but on the report of the first cannon, amongst balls and dangers, his ideas gained strength and clearness. If defeated, he began again as if he had been victorious. After the campaign of Italy, he was commissioned to carry the preliminaries of Leoben to the Directory. During the campaign of Egypt, he was commander-in-chief of the army of Helvetia, and saved the Republic by winning the battle of Zurich. He was afterwards a Marshal, duke of Rivoli, and prince of Essling.

Augereau, who was born in the faubourg Saint-Marceau, was a serjeant when the Revolution broke out. He must have been a distinguished sub-officer, for he was selected to go to Naples to instruct the Neapolitan troops. He at first served in La Vendée. He was made a general in the Army of the Eastern Pyrenees, where he commanded one of the principal divisions. On the peace with Spain he led his division to the Army of Italy, and served in all the campaigns of that army, under me, who sent him to Paris on the occasion of 18 Fructidor. The Directory afterwards gave him the chief command of the Army of the Rhine. He was incapable of conducting himself in this capacity, being uninformed, of a narrow intellect, and little education; but he maintained order and discipline amongst his soldiers, and was beloved by them. His attacks were regular, and made in an orderly manner; he divided his columns judiciously, placed his reserves with skill, and fought with intrepidity: but all this lasted but a day; victor or vanquished, he was generally disheartened in the evening; whether it arose from the peculiarity of his temper, or from the deficiency of his mind in foresight and penetration. In politics he was attached to Baboeuf's party, that of the most decided anarchists, and he was surrounded by a great number of them. He was nominated a deputy to the Legislative Body in 1798, engaged in the intrigues of the Manège, and frequently made himself ridiculous. The members of that society were not devoid of information; nobody could be less adapted than Augereau for political discussions and civil affairs, with which, however, he was fond of meddling. Under the empire, he became duke of Castiglione and Marshal of France.

Serrurier was a native of the department of the Aisne; and at the commencement of the Revolution was a major of infantry; he retained all the formality and strictness of a major: was very severe in point of discipline, and passed for an aristocrat, in consequence of which opinion he ran great risks in the midst of the camps, especially during the first few years. He gained the battle of Mondovi, and took Mantua, and had the honour of seeing Marshal Wurmser file off before him. He was a brave man, of great personal intrepidity, but not fortunate. He had less energy than the other two, but excelled them by the morality of his character, the soundness of his political opinions, and the strict integrity he observed in all his intercourse. He had the honourable commission to carry the colours taken from Prince Charles to the Directory. He was afterwards made a Marshal of France, governor of the *Invalides,* and a senator.

Chapter VIII

REVOLT OF PAVIA

The army quits its cantonments to take up the line of the Adige. Revolt of Pavia (24 May). Taking and Sack of Pavia (26 May). Causes of this revolt. The army enters the territories of the Republic of Venice (28 May). Battle of Borghetto; passage of the Mincio (30 May). The army arrives on the Adige (3 June). Description of Mantua. Blockade of Mantua (4 June). Armistice with Naples (5 June).

On the opening of the campaign, the city of Mantua was disarmed. The Court of Vienna was in hopes that its army would assume and preserve the offensive; it calculated on victories, not on defeats: and it was not until after the treaty of Cherasco, that it ordered Mantua and the fortresses of Lombardy to be armed and victualled. Some military men have been of opinion that if the French army, instead of taking up cantonments in the Milanese, had continued its march to drive Beaulieu beyond the Adige, Mantua would have been surprised: but it would have been against all principle to leave so many large towns and a population of more than a million of inhabitants behind, without taking possession of the former, and ascertaining the dispositions of the latter. The French remained only seven or eight days in Lombardy. On 27 May all the cantonments were raised. These few days had been well employed; the French dominion was secured by the national guards formed in all the towns of Lombardy, the change of all the public authorities, and the new organization of the country. General Despinois took the command of Milan; a brigade invested the citadel; the divisions of infantry and cavalry formed small depots of convalescents and wearied men, who kept garrison in the most important points; the depot of Augereau's division, 300 strong, was collected in the citadel of Pavia, and seemed a sufficient force to guard that city and the bridge over the Ticino.

On the 24th the headquarters were fixed at Lodi. Two hours after my arrival at that place, I was informed of the insurrection of Pavia, and of all the villages of that province, which Augereau's division had quitted on the 20th. A slight commotion had even taken place at Milan. I instantly set out again for that capital with 300 horse, six pieces of artillery, and a battalion of grenadiers. I arrived there the same evening, and found tranquillity restored. The garrison of the citadel, which had made a sortie to favour this revolt, had returned within its ramparts; the mobs had entirely dispersed. I proceeded to Pavia, sending on the archbishop of Milan before me, and despatching agents in all directions with proclamations for the information of the peasants. This archbishop was an old man of eighty, of the house of Visconti, respectable for his age and character, but without talent or reputation; his mission was wholly fruitless; he persuaded nobody. The insurgents of Pavia, who were to have joined the garrison of the castle of Milan, had pushed a vanguard of 800 men as far as Binasco. Lannes attacked it: Binasco was taken, pillaged, and burnt: it was hoped that the conflagration, which was visible from the walls of Pavia, would overawe that city. This was by no means the case; 8 or 10,000 peasants had entered the town, and made themselves masters of it; they were led by some turbulent individuals and agents of Austria, who cared little for the misfortunes of the country, and, in case of failure, had secured means of reaching Switzerland. In the evening the following proclamation was published in Milan, and was posted, during the night, on the gates of Pavia: 'A misled multitude, destitute of all effectual means of resistance, is committing the greatest excesses in several communes, disregarding the republic, and defying the army which has triumphed over kings; this unaccountable delirium deserves pity; these poor people are led astray and allured to their destruction. The General-in-chief, faithful to the principle adopted by his Nation of not making war upon the people, is willing to leave a door open to repentance; but after twenty-four hours, those who shall not have laid down their arms shall be treated as rebels; their villages shall be burnt. Let the terrible example of Binasco induce them to open their eyes! Its fate will be that of every commune that persists in the revolt.'

On the 26th the French column left Binasco, and reached Pavia at four in the afternoon; the gates were closed. The French garrison had capitulated; the insurgents had for several hours been masters of the citadel; this success had emboldened them. It seemed a difficult thing, with only 1,500 men and six field-pieces, to gain possession of a city containing 30,000 souls in a state of insurrection, enclosed within a wall, and even an ancient rampart with bastions, in very bad condition, it is true, but not to be taken by a *coup de main.* The tocsin was sounding throughout the adjacent country; the least retrograde step would have increased the evil and rendered it necessary to recall the army which had reached the Oglio. Under these circumstances temerity was the dictate of prudence; I risked the attack. The six pieces of artillery continued firing a long time, for the purpose of battering down the gates, but without success; the grape and shells, however, dislodged the peasants posted on the walls, and enabled the grenadiers to break down the gates with axes. They entered at the charge, debouched on the square, and lodged themselves in the houses at the tops of the streets. A troop of cavalry proceeded to the bridge of the Ticino, and made a successful charge; the peasants were fearful of being cut off, fled from the city, and gained the fields; the cavalry pursued them, and sabred a great number of them. The magistrates and principal inhabitants, with the archbishop of Milan and the bishop of Pavia at their head, then came to implore pardon. The 300 French who had been taken prisoners in the citadel, liberated themselves during this tumult, and came to the square unarmed, and in bad plight. My first impulse was to have this garrison decimated. 'Cowards,' said I, 'I intrusted you with a post essential to the safety of the army, and you have abandoned it to a mob of wretched peasants, without offering the least resistance.' The captain commanding this detachment was arrested. He was a weak man, and attempted to justify himself by an order given by General Haquin. The latter was coming from Paris; he had been stopped by the insurgents whilst changing horses at the post-house; they had clapped a pistol to his breast, threatening him with death unless he caused the citadel to surrender. He persuaded the garrison of the fort to deliver it up. But the guilt of General Haquin, however great, could not justify the commandant of the fort, who was, in no respect, under his command; and even if he had been so, ought to have ceased to obey, the moment the general was made prisoner; this captain was accordingly delivered over to a council of war, and shot. The confusion in the city was extreme. Fires were already lighted to set several quarters in flames; but compassion prevailed. The pillage, nevertheless, lasted several hours; but occasioned more fear than damage: it was confined to some goldsmiths' shops; but report exaggerated the losses suffered by the city, which was a salutary lesson for all Italy. Light columns were sent into the country, and effected a general disarming. Hostages were taken throughout Lombardy, and the selection fell on the principal families, even when no suspicion attached to them. It was conceived to be advantageous that some of the persons of most influence should visit France. In fact they returned a few months after, several of them having travelled in all our provinces, where they had adopted French manners.

The city of Pavia is situate seven leagues from Milan, on the Ticino, two leagues from its junction with the Po. It is eight hundred and fifty toises in breadth, and two thousand five hundred in circuit; it has a stone bridge over the Ticino, the only one which crosses that river: it is surrounded by a rampart of bastions, in ruins, and was the capital of the monarchy of the Lombards. In the eleventh and twelfth centuries this city was very powerful, and the rival of Milan, being the seat of the Ghibelline party, that of the emperors and nobles; whilst Milan was for the Guelphs, that is to say, on the side of the Popes and the people. In 1525, Francis I by his own fault, lost the famous battle of Pavia, where he was taken prisoner. The University of Pavia is celebrated; Volta, Spallanzani, Marcotti, Fontana, etc., were professors there.

This insurrection was attributed to the extraordinary contribution of twenty millions which had just been imposed, to the requisitions necessarily made by the army, and perhaps to some particular instances of oppression. The troops were destitute of clothing, which occasioned the titles of banditti and brigands, bestowed upon them by the enemy. The Lombards and other Italians did not consider themselves conquered; it was the Austrian army that had been defeated, there was no Italian corps in the Austrian service; the country even paid a tax to be exempt from recruiting: it was a settled principle with the Court of Vienna that it was impossible to make good soldiers of the Italians. This circumstance, the necessity under which the French army lay, of subsisting upon the local resources, materially retarded the progress of public spirit in Italy. If, on the contrary, the troops could have been maintained at the expense of France, numerous levies of Italians might have been raised at the very commencement. But to attempt to call a nation to liberty and independence, to require public spirit to arise amongst her inhabitants, to expect her to raise troops, and at the same time to take away her principal resources, are two contradictory ideas, and their reconciliation is a proof of talent. Nevertheless, discontent, murmurs, and conspiracies existed at first. The conduct of a general in a conquered country, is surrounded with difficulties: if he is harsh he irritates his enemies, and increases their numbers; if he is gentle, he excites hopes which afterwards make the abuses and oppressions necessarily attached to a state of war the more severely felt. Nevertheless, if under such circumstances an insurrection be suppressed in time, and if the conqueror exert a mixture of severity, justice, and mildness, the affair will have a good effect, will be rather advantageous than otherwise, and will be a security for the future.

In the meantime the army had continued its march on the Oglio, under the command of Berthier; I rejoined it at Soncino, and on the 28th marched with it into Brescia, one of the largest towns of the Venetian Terra Firma; the inhabitants of which were discontented with the government of the Venetian nobles. Brescia is eleven leagues from Cremona, fifteen from Mantua, twenty-eight from Venice, twenty-four from Trent, and fourteen from Milan. It submitted to the Republic of Venice in 1426. Its inhabitants amount to 50,000; those of the whole province to 500,000, some living in the mountains, others inhabiting rich plains. The following proclamation was posted: 'It is to deliver the finest country in Europe from the iron yoke of the proud house of Austria, that the French army has braved the most formidable obstacles. Victory, uniting with justice, has crowned its efforts with success; the wreck of the enemy's army has retreated beyond the Mincio. In order to pursue them, the French army enters the territory of the Republic of Venice, but it will not forget that the two republics are united by ancient friendship. Religion, government, and customs shall be respected. Let the people be free from apprehension, the severest discipline will be kept up; whatever the army is supplied with shall be punctually paid for in money. The General-in-chief invites the officers of the Republic of Venice, the magistrates and priests, to communicate his sentiments to the people, in order that the friendship which has so long united the two nations may be cemented by confidence. Faithful in the path of honour as in that of victory, the French soldier is terrible only to the enemies of his liberty and his government.'

The Senate sent Proveditores to meet the army, to make protestations of its neutrality. It was agreed that the senate should supply all necessary provisions, to be afterwards paid for. Beaulieu had received great reinforcements on the Mincio; on the first news of the movements of his army, he had removed his head-quarters behind the Mincio, being desirous to defend that river in order to prevent the investing of Mantua, the fortifications and supplies of which were daily increased. Disregarding the protestations of the Venetians, he forced the gates of the fortress of Peschiera, and made that place the *appui* of his right, which was commanded by General Liptay; he supported his centre on Valeggio and Borghetto, where he placed Pittony's division, while Sebottendorf's took up a position at Pozzuolo, and Colli's at Goito; the garrison of Mantua stationed posts on the Seraglio. The reserve, under Melas, 15,000 strong, encamped at Villa Franca, to advance on any point that should be menaced.

On 29 May, the French army had its left at Dezenzano, its centre at Montechiaro, and its right at Castiglione, wholly neglecting Mantua, which place it left on its right. On the 30th at daybreak, it debouched on Borghetto, after having deceived the enemy by various movements, which led him to think it would pass the Mincio at Peschiera, and drew his reserve from Villa Franca to that place. On approaching Borghetto, the French vanguard fell in with 3,000 Austrian and Neapolitan cavalry in the plain, and 4,000 infantry intrenched in the village of Borghetto, and on the heights of Valeggio. General Murat charged the enemy's cavalry; he obtained an important success in this action: it was the first time that the French cavalry, on account of its bad condition, had measured its strength to advantage with the Austrian cavalry: it took nine pieces of cannon, two standards, and 2,000 men, amongst whom

REVOLT OF PAVIA

was the Prince de Cuto, who commanded the Neapolitan cavalry. From that time forth the French cavalry emulated the infantry. Colonel Gardanne, who was marching at the head of the grenadiers, charged into Borghetto; the enemy burnt the bridge, which it was impossible to restore under the fire from the height of Valeggio. Gardanne threw himself into the water; the Austrians imagined they saw the terrible column of Lodi, and beat a retreat; Valeggio was carried. It was then ten in the morning, by noon the bridge was restored, and the French divisions passed the Mincio. Augereau went up the left bank, advancing on Peschiera, and occupied the heights of Castel Nuovo; Serrurier followed the troops which were evacuating Valeggio and retiring on Villa Franca. I marched with this division as long as the enemy was in sight, but, as they avoided an engagement, I returned to Valeggio, which place had been fixed on for head-quarters. Massena's division, appointed to cover Valeggio, was preparing dinner on the right bank of the Mincio, and had not yet passed the bridge. Sebottendorf's division, having heard the cannonade at Valeggio, had begun its march up the left bank of the river; their scouts approached Valeggio without meeting with any troops; they entered the town, and penetrated as far as the lodgings where I was; my piquet guard had barely time enough to shut the carriage gateway, and cry to arms, which afforded me an opportunity of mounting my horse and escaping through the gardens behind the house. Massena's soldiers overturned the kettles and passed the bridge. The sound of the drums put the Austrian hussars to flight. Sebottendorf was closely and vigorously pursued during the whole evening, and lost a great number of men.

The danger which I had incurred, convinced me of the necessity of having a guard of picked men trained to this service, and especially charged to watch over my personal safety. I formed a corps to which I gave the name of Guides. Major Bessieres was directed to organize it. This corps thenceforth wore the uniform which was afterwards worn by the Chasseurs of the Guard, of which it was the nucleus: it was composed of picked men who had served ten years at least, and rendered great services in the field. Thirty or forty of these brave fellows, opportunely set on, always produced the most important results. The Guides had the same effect in a battle, as the squadrons on duty afterwards had under their Emperor; which is easily explained, because both were under my immediate direction, and I ordered them forward at critical moments.

Bessieres, who was born in Languedoc, served originally in the 22nd Chasseurs, in the army of the Eastern Pyrenees. He possessed a cool species of bravery, was calm amidst the enemy's fire; his sight was excellent, he was much habituated to cavalry manoeuvres, and peculiarly adapted to command a reserve. In all the great battles he will be seen to render the greatest services. He and Murat were the first cavalry officers in the army, but of very opposite

REVOLT OF PAVIA

qualities. Murat was a good vanguard officer, adventurous and impetuous; Bessieres was better adapted for a reserve, being full of vigour, but prudent and circumspect. From the period of the creation of the Guides, he was exclusively intrusted with the duty of guarding me and the head-quarters. He was afterwards Duke of Istria, Marshal of the Empire, and one of the marshals of the Guard.

In order to cover the siege of Mantua and Italy, it was necessary for the French army to occupy the line of the Adige, and the bridges of Verona and Legnago. All the insinuations of the Proveditore Foscarelli against marching on Verona were fruitless. On 3 June, Massena took possession of that city, situate thirty-two leagues from Milan, twenty-five from Venice, and sixteen from Trent, with three stone bridges over the Adige. Ponte-Vecchio is sixty toises in length and has three arches; this town contains 60,000 inhabitants, and is handsome, large, rich, and very healthy. It became subject to the Venetians in 1405; its walls occupy both sides of the river, and are six thousand toises in extent: its forts are situate on the heights, commanding the left bank. Porto-Legnago was armed, and the army of observation occupied Montebaldo with its left, Verona with its centre, and the lower Adige with its right, thus covering the siege of Mantua. The object was attained; the tricoloured flag waved on the passes of the Tyrol. It was now time to force Mantua, and take that bulwark from Austria: hopes were entertained of accomplishing this undertaking before the arrival of the new Austrian army; but what battles, what events, what dangers were first to be encountered!

Mantua is situate amidst three lakes formed by the waters of the Mincio, which springs from the Lake of Garda at Peschiera and runs into the Po near Governolo. The city then communicated with the town by means of five dykes; the first, that of la Favorite, which separated the upper from the middle lake, is a hundred toises in length; it is of stone, the mills of the town are built against it; it has two floodgates for discharging the water; at its outlet is the citadel of la Favorite, a regular pentagon, tolerably strong, and protected, on several of its fronts, by inundations. It is by this causeway that people leave Mantua to go to Roverbella, and thence to Verona or Peschiera. The causeway of Saint-George is sixty toises long; it leads into the faubourg Saint-George; it is the road to Porto-Legnago. This causeway was closed by a stone gate, and in the middle of the lake by drawbridges. The third dyke is the causeway of Pietoli; the lower lake is there only eighty toises wide; but the ground between the lake and the place is occupied by an intrenched camp under the place, with ditches full of water. The fourth dyke is that of the gate of Ceresa, which leads to Modena; it was closed by a stone gate; the lake at that part, was of considerable breadth. Lastly, the fifth dyke or causeway was that of Pradella; it is two hundred toises long, and is the road to Cremona, defended by a hornwork placed in the midst of the lake. Thus, of the five

REVOLT OF PAVIA

causeways, that of la Favorite or Roverbella was the only one defended by a citadel; the four others were without defence; so that the besiegers, placing a handful of men at the extremities of these causeways, could blockade the garrison. In the time of the kingdom of Italy, there being an intention of completing this grand fortress, it was thought important to occupy all the debouches of the dykes by fortifications; the engineer Chasseloup had a permanent fort constructed before the causeway of Pradella; so that it would now be necessary, in order to blockade Mantua, to blockade the four forts placed at the four outlets.

The Seraglio is the space comprised between the Mincio, Mantua, the Po, and la Fossa Maestra, a canal which runs from the Lake of Mantua into the Po at Borgo-forte: it is a triangle of five or six square leagues, an island. Mantua requires a garrison of at least 12,000 men; this garrison ought to maintain itself as long as possible in the Seraglio to make use of the resources which are to be found there, the land being very fruitful, and in order to continue masters of the course of the Po, and draw supplies from the right bank of that river. Governolo was formerly fortified. The abbey of Saint-Benedetto, the central seat of the Benedictines, is on the right bank of the Po, opposite the mouth of the Mincio: the garrisons of Mantua make use of this abbey in time of peace, by fixing an hospital for convalescents there, the air being better than at Mantua.

The besieged, who were fully sensible of the importance of maintaining themselves at the head of the five causeways, proceeded with great activity in the construction of retrenchments there; but the French did not allow them sufficient time. On 4 June I proceeded myself to the faubourg Saint-George; carried it, after a brisk action, and drove the enemy into the place: they had scarcely time to raise the draw-bridges of the dyke; had they delayed a few minutes longer, the place itself would have been in danger. Augereau gained possession of the Ceresa gate after a firm resistance; the enemy evacuated Pietoli, and retired into the hornwork. The besiegers being thus masters of the heads of the four dykes, the besieged could now make no sortie except by the citadel of la Favorite, so that the garrison was kept in check by a besieging army of inferior force. Serrurier was intrusted with the direction of the blockade; he fixed his head-quarters at Roverbella, as the point nearest to the citadel of la Favorite, on which he placed 3,600 men in observation; 600 men were posted at Saint-George, 600 at Pietoli, 600 at Ceresa, and 1,000 at Pradella; and 2,000 men, including artillery, cavalry, and infantry, formed flying columns round the lakes, while a dozen gun-boats, manned by French seamen, cruised in them. Thus, with an army of only 8,000 soldiers of all descriptions actually in the field, Serrurier blockaded a garrison amounting to 14,000 effective men, of whom more than 10,000 were under arms. It was not conceived necessary to form lines of circumvallation, which was an error; but the engineers held out hopes that the place would be surrendered before the Austrian army would be able to come to its relief. Undoubtedly such lines would have been of no use against Wurmser, when he revictualled the place on the eve of the battle of Castiglione. I, who then raised the blockade and abandoned my besieging train, would have also abandoned my lines of circumvallation; but when Wurmser was driven into Mantua after the battle of Bassano, it is probable that if there had been lines of circumvallation, I would not have been able to force them, and would have been obliged to lay down my arms; this was the third blockade. When lines of circumvallation were constructed round Saint-George, they produced the surrender of the general's corps, and the success of the battle of la Favorite, in January, 1797.

The King of Naples, seeing Upper Italy in the power of the French, sent Prince Belmonte to head-quarters to request an armistice, which was signed on 5 of January. The Neapolitan division of cavalry, of 2,400 horse, quitted the Austrian army. A Neapolitan plenipotentiary repaired to France to conclude a definite peace with the Republic. As the King of Naples could bring 60,000 men into the field, this armistice was an important event; and the more so as this prince, remote from the theatre of the war, is, on account of his geographical situation, out of the influence of an army commanding Upper Italy; it being 200 leagues from the Po to the extremity of the peninsula.

I found it difficult to induce the French Government to adopt my policy; they wished to revolutionize Rome, Naples, and Tuscany, without calculating the distances, chances, or strength they would have to contend with. They had formed erroneous ideas respecting the localities, the spirit of the people, and the power of the revolutionists. The principles of war which regulated the determinations of the Cabinet, were erroneous, and contrary to rule.

Colonel Chasseloup commanded the engineers in the Army of Italy; he was made a general. He was one of the best officers of his corps; of an unsteady character, but well acquainted with all the resources of his art.

Lespinasse, who commanded the artillery, was an old officer of great personal bravery and zeal.

Dammartin, Sugny, and Songis, were officers of merit. The artillery general Dujard, who was sent to fortify the coasts of Nice and Provence, was assassinated in the Col di Tende by the Barbets.

Beaulieu, after all these disasters, fell into disgrace with his master; he was recalled and Melas took the command of the Austrian army *ad interim,* and fixed his head-quarters at Trent. Marshal Wurmser was removed from the command of the Army of the Upper Rhine to that of Italy.

Chapter IX

MARCH ON THE RIGHT BANK OF THE PO

Motives of the march of the French army on the Apennines. Insurrection of the Imperial Fiefs. Entrance into Bologna and Ferrara (19 June). Armistice granted to the Pope (23 June). Entrance into Leghorn (29 June). At Florence. Revolt of Lugo. Opening of the trenches before Mantua (18 July). Favourable posture of affairs in Piedmont and Lombardy.

The army fulfilled its destination. It occupied the line of the Adige, covered the siege of Mantua, middle and lower Italy; and was in readiness to oppose the Austrian armies, whether they should debouch by the Tyrol, or the Frioul. The French could advance no farther until Mantua should be taken, and the princes of the right bank of the Po disarmed. But in order to besiege Mantua, a battering train was requisite: that of the army had been left at Antibes; that which had been formed of the heavy cannon taken from the fortresses of Tortona, Coni, and Ceva, was engaged in the siege of the citadel of Milan: it was, therefore, of primary importance to accelerate the siege of that fortress.

Gerola, the Austrian minister at Genoa, had excited the Imperial Fiefs to insurrection, organized free companies, composed of the Austrian prisoners who had escaped and were daily escaping, of Piedmontese deserters, or natives of Piedmont, who had turned smugglers since the disbanding of the Piedmontese army. The oligarchy of Genoa contemplated with pleasure all the schemes put in execution by this minister to annoy the French army. The evil had become intolerable; the routes of the army by Genoa, Savona, and Nice, were almost intercepted, so that a battalion of 600 men had been compelled

MARCH ON THE RIGHT BANK OF THE PO

to fight several times in order to join the army. A prompt and efficacious remedy was necessary.

The Court of Rome was arming; and if its body of troops had been reinforced by the 6,000 English in Corsica, a formidable diversion would have been effected on the right bank of the Po, the moment the Austrian army was ready to resume offensive operations. It was therefore necessary to repass the Po, force the Pope's army beyond the Apennines, compel the Court of Rome to conclude an armistice, pass the Apennines, occupy Leghorn, drive out the English factory, unite the five or six hundred Corsican refugees in that city, and send them to Corsica to raise an insurrection, which would detain the English division there to defend itself. Marshal Wurmser, who had quitted the Rhine with 30,000 chosen troops, was marching on Italy. He could not arrive before 15 July; there were then, thirty or forty days left, during which the necessary detachments might conveniently be spared, so as to return to the Adige by the middle of July.

I repaired to Milan, had the trenches opened before the citadel, proceeded thence to Tortona, and directed a column of 1,200 men, commanded by Colonel Lannes, to march into the Imperial Fiefs. Colonel Lannes entered Arquata after an obstinate resistance, shot the brigands who had slaughtered a detachment of 150 French, and demolished the chateau of the Marquis de Spinola, the principal instigator of these commotions. At the same time the aide-de-camp Murat proceeded to Genoa, and being introduced into the Senate by Faypoult, the minister of the republic, demanded and obtained the dismission of the governor of Novi, the expulsion of the Austrian agents, and the ambassador Gerola from Genoa, and the establishment of columns of Genoese troops at the different halting-places, with instructions to clear the roads, to escort the French convoys, and to restore the safety of the communications.

General Augereau, with his division, passed the Po on 14 June, at Borgoforte, reached Bologna and Ferrara in four marches, and took possession of these two legations, which belonged to the Pope. General Vaubois collected a brigade of 4,000 men and 700 horses at Modena. I left Tortona, passed through Piacenza, Parma, and Reggio, and on the 19th arrived at Modena. My presence electrified the people of those two cities, who loudly called for liberty; but the armistice was scrupulously observed by the Regency. I exerted all my influence to retain these people in the obedience they owed to their sovereign, and to still the ferment which existed amongst them. At Modena I accepted the fetes which the Regency offered me, studied to inspire it with confidence, and to give it that respectability in the eyes of the people of which it stood in need. The old duke had long before fled to Venice with his treasures. The road from Modena to Bologna passes under the glacis of Fort Urbino, belonging to the Pope; this fort had old bastions and advanced works; it was armed, victualled, and defended by a garrison of 800 men. The troops of Augereau's division, which had entered Bologna the same day, had not had time to take possession of it, or to blockade it. Colonel Vignoles, deputy quarter-master-general, advanced against it with 200 Guides, and made the garrison capitulate; they surrendered as prisoners of war. The fort was lined with sixty pieces of cannon, half of which were forwarded to Borgo-forte, where was the park of the besieging train.

Augereau's division found at Bologna a cardinal and 400 men, and took them prisoners. The cardinal obtained leave to go to Rome on his parole; a few months afterwards, as he conducted himself very ill, General Berthier sent him orders to return to head-quarters; he answered in a very specious style, that he was released from his parole by a brief from his Holiness, which caused much laughter in the army. In the citadel of Ferrara were found 114 pieces of cannon, with abundance of ammunition. Forty of these guns were sent to Borgo-forte.

Bologna is surnamed the Learned. It is situate at the foot of the Apennines, on the Reno, and contains from fifty to sixty thousand inhabitants. The Academy at Bologna, called the Institute of the Sciences, is the most renowned in Italy; its noble streets are adorned with porticoes in arcades for the convenience of foot-passengers; it has a canal communicating with Venice. This city exercises a great influence over all the three legations, which were dissatisfied with the government of the Popes, a bastard, disgraceful government for all secular people. What can be worse, said they, than to be governed by priests? We have no country; we are ruled by men devoted to celibacy, who belong to the Christian religion, and consider affairs in a false point of view; they are accustomed from infancy to theological studies, which do not tend in the least to qualify them to judge of the affairs of the world. Bologna, in particular, was ardently desirous of liberty; that town and Brescia contained the warmest partisans, and those best disposed to work the triumph of the Italian cause. There was no place that testified a more sincere affection for the French than these. Bologna persisted in these sentiments; the entrance of the army was a triumph. Caprara, Marescalchi, and Aldini, deputies of the senate, did the honours; the two former were of the best families in the country. Caprara, then a senator, was afterwards master of the horse to the King of Italy, and Marescalchi minister of exterior relations; Aldini was the best advocate in Bologna; he was the confidential man of the senate; and he afterwards became minister secretary of state to the King of Italy. There were three or four hundred Spanish Jesuits at Bologna at that period; they were alarmed; the richest and youngest had sought an asylum at Rome; the staff of the army dispelled their fears, and ordered that all proper respect should be paid to them. There were men of distinguished merit amongst them. In the course of the few days that I remained at Bologna the appearance of this city

MARCH ON THE RIGHT BANK OF THE PO

was entirely changed. Never was a general revolution in the manners and habits of a people more promptly effected. All who were not priests assumed the military dress and the sword; and even a great number of ecclesiastics were drawn in by the spirit that animated the people. The city as well as individuals gave a great number of entertainments, bearing a character of popularity and grandeur which had not previously been seen in Italy. I shewed myself constantly in the midst of the people, without guards; and made a point of going to the theatre every evening with no other escort than the Bolognese.

In the meantime the Vatican was struck with alarm. Azara, the Spanish minister, provided with powers from the Pope, came with all possible despatch to conclude an armistice, which was signed on 23 June, and removed the apprehensions of his Holiness, who engaged to send a minister to Paris to treat for a definite peace with the Republic; and agreed that the armistice should last until the conclusion of peace; that Bologna and Ferrara should remain in the possession of the French army; that the French should garrison Ancona; that he, the Pope, should pay twenty-one millions in money, horses, and articles necessary for the army; and that he should give up one hundred works of art, to be chosen by the French commissioners, for the museum at Paris. Military circumstances were such that it could never have been my intention to march to Rome. Nevertheless the philosophers and the enemies of the Holy See, regarded this suspension of hostilities with dissatisfaction: the people of Bologna in particular were apprehensive of returning under the Pope's authority; but they were easily convinced that the French being now masters of the conditions of peace, it would not be made without securing their liberty. They exacted a promise to this effect, and immediately armed a body of national guards.

This important affair, which secured the flanks of the army from molestation, and contributed to conciliate the people to the French, being ended, I passed the Apennines, and on 26 June joined Vaubois' division at Pistoia. I lodged at the bishop's, the same who afterwards contended so warmly for religious opinions conformable to those of the constitutional priests. Manfredini, the prime minister of the Grand Duke of Tuscany, alarmed at the report that the French troops were to pass through Florence, came to headquarters; he was satisfied, and convinced that the French were extremely desirous to cultivate the friendship of the Grand Duke, and that they only passed over his territories on their way to Siena. On 29 June, Murat, who commanded the van, on leaving Firenzuola, turned suddenly on Leghorn, and arrived there in eight hours, hoping to surprise the English merchants, who had a hundred ships laden in the port; but they received timely notice, and took refuge in the ports of Corsica.

The walls of Leghorn must have been intended to inclose 8 or 10,000 inhab-

MARCH ON THE RIGHT BANK OF THE PO

itants: but commerce has made such progress there, that the population has increased to above 60,000 souls; whence it has become necessary to build immense faubourgs, which obstruct the glacis. It is difficult to enter the port. The roads are distant from the land, and far from safe; some accident happens every year. They have succeeded the port of Pisa, which was situate at the mouth of the Arno, the principal river of Tuscany. This is the port of Florence; it is much frequented by the English, who have established a factory there as an entrepot for their manufactures, and for their Indian and colonial merchandize. The occupation of Leghorn and the destruction of the factory, was sensibly felt by the trade of London. The Corsican refugees in France assembled to the number of 600 at Leghorn. The communication with Corsica by the shores of Fiumorbo and la Rocca, could not be intercepted. A multitude of agents penetrated into the interior of the isle with proclamations, The viceroy, Elliot, soon perceived the effects. Several insurrections took place. The refugees were persons of importance: their vicinity and correspondence excited the war-like population of the mountains. A series of sanguinary actions took place; the English daily lost numbers of men; they were not sufficiently numerous to maintain their footing in the country; there was no longer any fear of their disturbing the coasts of Italy. At length, in the month of October, Gentili and the Corsican refugees landed in a body in the isle, raised a general insurrection, and drove out the English. Spanocchi, the Tuscan commandant of Leghorn, was distinguished for his extreme partiality to the English; some instances of misconduct of which he was guilty, filled up the measure of his offences; he was arrested and taken to Florence, where he was placed at the disposal of the Grand Duke. The French Consul Belleville had the management of the contentious business relating to the English merchandize. Notwithstanding the efforts of a multitude of robbers who flocked from Genoa and Marseilles, the chest of the army received twelve millions from this property. Vaubois was left in command of the city with a garrison of 2,000 men; the rest of the troops repassed the Apennines and the Po, to rejoin the army on the Adige.

I went from Leghorn to Florence, in consequence of the invitation of the Grand Duke. I arrived there without any escort, and alighted at the residence of the French minister, where a battalion of the prince's guards awaited me as a guard of honour. I was highly satisfied with the Archduke, and visited with curiosity every object calculated to excite my attention in this ancient and important capital. The French troops twice crossed the grand duchy, but they passed at a great distance from Florence, observed the strictest discipline, and gave rise to no complaints. The Tuscan minister confessed that the English had more authority than himself in Leghorn, and complained of the arrogance of the English general.

Whilst at dinner with the Grand Duke, I received the news of the taking of

MARCH ON THE RIGHT BANK OF THE PO

the Castle of Milan, which had capitulated on 29 June. This castle had several large towers, the remains of the Visconti palace, which commanded the country; some pieces mounted thereon swept the trenches, and had retarded the approaches for several days. The garrison, 2,500 strong, were made prisoners of war; a hundred pieces of cannon were found in this castle. The besieging train was immediately embarked on the Po for Mantua, and with the pieces taken from the castle of Urbino and Ferrara made up two-hundred guns well supplied, which were thought sufficient for the siege of Mantua. After dinner, the Grand Duke conducted me (his guest) into the celebrated gallery of Florence, to view the masterpieces of art which it contained; I admired the Venus de Medicis. The Anatomist Fontana shewed me some very fine models in wax, and I ordered similar ones for Paris. Manfredini, the Grand Duke's major-domo and principal minister, had been preceptor to this prince as well as to the Archduke Charles; he was a native of Padua in the Venetian States, and proprietor of the Austrian regiment of Manfredini. He was an enlightened man, as much attached to all the philosophical ideas of the Revolution as shocked at their excesses, he had constantly opposed the pretensions of the Court of Rome, which after the death of Leopold had endeavoured to overturn the acts of that prince. He was a man of a clear understanding, generally esteemed, and had, moreover, a secret inclination for the independence of Italy. There was not a generous heart or noble mind in the country that did not feel involuntarily impelled, whatever might be their rank or situation in the world, to sacrifice their dearest affections to the independence and restoration of the fine country of Italy.

After a short stay at Florence, I proceeded to Bologna, where I spent several days in regulating the public impulse towards liberty. Lugo had revolted, excesses had been committed there against small French detachments. General Beyrand marched thither with his brigade, he met with some resistance; 4 or 5,000 peasants had thrown themselves into the town; he attacked and defeated them, and took the town by assault; it was pillaged. The Bishop of Imola, afterwards Pius VII, in whose diocese this insurrection had broken out, published a mandate to open the eyes of the deluded populace. *Render unto Cæsar that which is Cæsar's,* said he: *Christ commands us to obey him who has power*. He even sent the Bishop of Edessa, then his grand-vicar, and afterwards his almoner, to Lugo, who failed in his mission. The rebels received him with respect, but did not obey his orders. They submitted only to force. The army passed the Po; there were only a few piquets of gensd'armes and some depots left on the right bank. The country was so well disposed, that the national guards were sufficient; although the regency of Modena was entirely devoted to the enemy, it was powerless; in Reggio and Modena the patriots were by far the most powerful party.

Mantua was commanded by General Canto d'Irles, who had under him

MARCH ON THE RIGHT BANK OF THE PO

Generals Roccavina, Roselmini, and Wukassowich, with 12,000 infantry, 500 cavalry, 600 artillery, 150 miners, and 100 seamen, total 14,000 men. The head-quarters of the army were removed from Bologna, to Roverbella, where was Serrurier, who commanded the blockade; there were several French sloops on the lower lake. Colonel Andreossy had collected a considerable number of boats, in hopes of surprising the place. One hundred grenadiers had embarked, they were to land at two in the morning under the battery and bastion of the palace, to seize the postern gate, and let down the drawbridges of the causeway of Saint George, by which the army was to enter the city. This scheme appeared infallible. Colonel Lahoz, a native of Mantua, was to head the column, accompanied by several patriots of the country. But the Po having fallen considerably, and the waters of the lower lake having run off with great rapidity, there was not sufficient water for the boats, which were obliged to get amongst the reeds, to avoid being perceived from the place; they grounded there during the night, and it was impossible to get them off. The next night the waters abated still more, and this expedition was, therefore, abandoned. It was debated whether the trenches should be opened or not. The storm from the Tyrol seemed ready to burst. But Chasseloup promised to take the place in fifteen days, open trenches, it being ill armed and the garrison much weakened. I resolved to make the attempt. Generals Murat and Dallemagne passed the lower arm of the lake at Pietoli, where it was very narrow, and after a warm action got possession of the ground which was not overflowed from Pietoli to the palace del T, and of the intrenched camp of Migliazetto; on 18 July, all the natural obstacles were surmounted, there was nothing before the besiegers but a simple bastion and a large ditch full of water. General Chasseloup of the engineers opened the trenches; the siege became merely an ordinary one. On the 22nd, the trench was fifty toises from the covered way; the enemy attempted several sorties to retard the approaches; the skirmishes became sanguinary, but he was always repulsed with loss. Colonel Dupont, at the head of a battalion of grenadiers, behaved gallantly; he was the same officer who afterwards distinguished himself at the time of the surrender of Cairo in Egypt.

But the moment of the resumption of offensive operations by the Austrians was approaching. Being freed from anxiety respecting the works of the siege of Mantua, I wished to accelerate the progress of the internal organization of Lombardy, in order to secure my rear during the contest which was about to begin; I proceeded to Milan, in order to return by the time of the recommencement of hostilities. The King of Sardinia had placed himself absolutely at the disposal of the Republic; he had given up all his fortresses. Suza, Exilles, and Demonte, were demolished. Alessandria was in the possession of the Army of Italy. The chevalier Borgues resided at Milan, as charged with the temporary affairs of Sardinia, but the King frequently sent the Count de

MARCH ON THE RIGHT BANK OF THE PO

Saint-Marsan to head-quarters, either to give particular explanations, or to request the assistance necessary for maintaining tranquillity in the country; his affairs could not have been in better hands; the Count was, both personally and in point of character, agreeable to me as commander-in-chief. He was of one of the best families in Piedmont; was from twenty-five to thirty years of age, of a cool, mild, enlightened character; he suffered no prejudices to sway his mind, and consequently saw things as they really were. He was personally hostile to the Austrian policy, a sentiment inherited from his ancestors and confirmed by his own experience.

Chapter X

BATTLE OF CASTIGLIONE

Marshal Wurmser arrives in Italy at the head of a new army. Situation of the French army. Plan of the campaign. Wurmser debouches in three columns (29 July), the right by the road of the Chiesa, the centre on Montebaldo, between the Adige and the lake of Garda, and the left by the valley of the Adige. Prompt resolution taken by me. Action of Salo. Action of Lonato (31 July). Battle of Lonato (3 August). Surrender of the three divisions of the enemy's right, and of part of his centre. Battle of Castiglione (5 August). Second blockade of Mantua (end of August). Conduct of the different nations of Italy, on the news of the success of the Austrians.

The court of Vienna being informed of the arrival of the French on the borders of the Tyrol, and of the blockade of Mantua, relinquished its intended offensive operations in Alsace, and detached Marshal Wurmser at the head of 30,000 men from the Army of the Upper Rhine, into Italy, which detachment, added to Beaulieu's army, which had been recruiting for two months, and to the garrison of Mantua, raised that army to 80,000 men, exclusive of the sick in Mantua. The French army had fulfilled its task in destroying that of Beaulieu: had the armies of the Rhine been equally successful, this grand contest would have been finished. But reports of the preparations making by the house of Austria were spread throughout the Venetian territory; they were greatly exaggerated in commercial letters, in which it was stated that before the end

BATTLE OF CASTIGLIONE

of August Austria would be mistress of Milan, and the French expelled from the peninsula, without being able to reach the Alps; the proverb would again be verified this year, that *Italy was their tomb*.

I contemplated all these preparations with attention, and was seriously alarmed at them. I convinced the Directory that it was impossible for 40,000 men to withstand, alone, the efforts of the whole Austrian power; I required either that reinforcements should be sent to me, or that the armies of the Rhine should take the field without delay. I reminded them of the promise which had been made to me on my quitting Paris, that they should commence operations on 15 April; and that nevertheless, although two months had elapsed, they had not left their winter-quarters. They opened the campaign at last, in the month of June, but the diversion was then useless to the Army of Italy. Wurmser's 30,000 men were on their march, and expected to arrive. In this situation, reduced to my own force alone, I assembled all my army on the Adige and Chiesa, left only one battalion in the citadel of Ferrara, and two at Leghorn, and depots only at Coni, Tortona, Alessandria, Milan, and Pizzighettone. The siege of Mantua began to produce sickness; although the troops which I kept before that unhealthy place were only equal in number to two-thirds of the garrison, the losses were nevertheless considerable. I could not muster, with the army of observation on the Adige, above 30,000 men actually under arms; yet with this small number of brave soldiers, I was to contend with the principal army of the house of Austria. A very active correspondence was kept up between Italy and the Tyrol, where the enemy were assembling; and the fatal influence of these grand preparations on the minds of the people became every day more evident. The partisans of the French trembled; those of Austria behaved in a haughty and threatening manner; but all were astonished that such a power as France should leave an army which deserved so well of its country without assistance or support; these remarks even reached the soldiers themselves, by means of their daily communications with the inhabitants.

Soret's division, posted at Salo, covered the country between the lakes of Idro and Garda, intercepting the road from Trent to Brescia, by the valley of the Chiesa; Massena, placed at Bussolengo, occupied la Corona and Montebaldo with Joubert's brigade; the rest of his division encamped on the level of Rivoli. Dallemagne's brigade of Despinois' division guarded the bridges of Verona; the other brigade of this division, the Adige as far as Porto Legnago; Augereau's division, Porto Legnago and the lower Adige. General Guillaume commanded at Peschiera, where six galleys, under the command of Captain Lallemand, kept possession of the lake of Garda; Serrurier was besieging Mantua; Kilmaine commanded the cavalry of the army, Dammartin the artillery. Head-quarters were fixed at Castel-Nuovo, which place was within a convenient distance of the Adige, the Chiesa, and Mantua.

BATTLE OF CASTIGLIONE

Wurmser fixed his head-quarters at Trent, and assembled his whole army in the Italian Tyrol: he divided it into three corps; that of the left commanded by Generals Davidowich, Mezaros, and Metroski, 20,000 strong, was intended to debouch by the valley of the Adige; Mezaros was to proceed along the road on the left bank, and to penetrate into Verona by the heights; Davidowich and Metroski, the cavalry and artillery, were to pass the Adige on a bridge built opposite la Dolce, and to advance on Cassario; the centre, 30,000 strong, under Wurmser, forming four divisions, under Generals Melas, Sebottendorf, Bayalitsch and Liptay, were to penetrate by Montebaldo and the country between the Adige and the lake of Garda; the right, consisting of 20,000 men, under Quasdanowich, the Prince de Reuss and Ocskay, was to pass by the Chiesa, advance on Brescia, and turn the whole of the French army, which, being separated from Milan, would thus have its retreat cut off: its entire destruction was to be the result of this skilful plan. Proud of his great superiority, Wurmser meditated not how to conquer, but how he should make use of his victory, and render it decisive and fatal to the enemy.

I had been at Milan but a few days when I heard of the movements in the Tyrol. I repaired with all possible speed to Castel-Nuovo, where I fixed my head-quarters; in this little town I was within reach of the mountains, Monte-Baldo and Verona. On the 29th in the morning, I was informed that la Corona was attacked by an army; that the light troops of Mezaros's division were debouching upon the heights of Verona on the left bank of the Adige; and that numerous columns were descending by the Rocca d'Anfo. In the course of the night, farther intelligence arrived every hour; it appeared that Joubert, being attacked at la Corona, had resisted throughout the day, but that in the evening he had fallen back on the level of Rivoli, which Massena occupied in force; that the numerous lines of the fires of the Austrian bivouacs covered the country between the lake of Garda and the Adige; that on the heights of Verona, the whole division of Mezaros had joined his light troops; that on the Brescia side, Quasdanowich, who had debouched by the valley of the Chiesa, had divided his force into three columns, one of which covered the heights of Saint-Ozetto, appearing to direct its march on Brescia; that another had taken up a position at Gavardo, and threatened to advance on Ponte di San Marco and Lonato; and that the third had marched on Salo, where it had been fighting ever since three o'clock in the afternoon. On the 30th, at daybreak, advices arrived that the column of Saint-Ozetto had penetrated to Brescia, where it had met with no resistance, and had made prisoners of four companies left there to guard the hospitals. One of the communications of the army with Milan was thus intercepted; that of Cremona was the only one which now remained. Scouts already appeared on all the roads from Brescia to Milan, Cremona, and Mantua, announcing that an army of

BATTLE OF CASTIGLIONE

80,000 men had debouched by Brescia, and that another, of 100,000 was at the same time debouching by Verona; that Soret, fearful of finding himself cut off from Brescia and the army, had retreated on the heights of Dezenzano, leaving General Guyeux at Salo, with 1,500 men, in an ancient castle, a kind of fortress, secure from a *coup de main*; that the enemy's column at Gavarda had sent a few light horse towards Ponte di San Marco, but that they had been kept in check there by a company of chasseurs, ordered to guard that bridge.

Wurmser's plan was now unmasked; he had taken the lead in moving, and expected to keep it. But he considered the army as fixed about Mantua, and imagined that by surrounding this fixed point, he should surround the French army. In order to disconcert his schemes, it was necessary for me myself to take the lead, to render the army moveable by raising the siege of Mantua, sacrificing the trenches and besieging train, for the purpose of advancing rapidly, with the whole army in junction, upon one of the enemy's corps, and afterwards against the two others successively. The Austrians were superior in number in the proportion of five to two; but if the three corps were attacked separately by the whole French army, the latter would be superior in number on the field of battle. The right under Quasdanowich, which had debouched on Brescia, was the farthest advanced, and I, therefore, marched against this corps first. Serrurier's division burned the carriages of their besieging train, and their platforms, threw their powder into the water, buried their shot, spiked the guns, and raised the siege of Mantua in the night of 31 July. Augereau's division proceeded from Legnago to Borghetto on the Mincio; Massena's troops defended the heights between the Adige and the lake of Garda during the whole of the 30th. Dallemagne's brigade directed its march on Lonato. I proceeded to the heights behind Dezenzano; made Soret march back on Salo, to disengage General Guyeux, who was compromised in the disadvantageous post in which General Soret had left him; nevertheless he had engaged a whole division of the enemy's troops there for forty-eight hours, who had five times attacked him by assault, and been five times repulsed. Soret came up at the very moment when the enemy was making a final attempt, fell on his flanks, totally defeated him, and took a number of colours, cannon, and prisoners. At the same time General Ocskay's Austrian division had advanced from Gavardo on Lonato, to take up a position on the heights, and effect a junction with Wurmser on the Mincio. I myself led Dallemagne's brigade against it. It performed prodigies of valour; the 32nd was part of it. Ocskay was routed, and suffered great loss; the remains of these two divisions, beaten by Soret and Dallemagne, rallied at Gavardo. Soret was fearful of compromising himself; he came back, and took up an intermediate position between Salo and Dezenzano. In the meantime Wurmser's cavalry and artillery had passed the Adige. Being now master of

BATTLE OF CASTIGLIONE

all the country between the Adige and the lake of Garda, he placed one of his divisions on the heights of Peschiera, to mask that place and guard his communications; he directed two others with part of his cavalry on Borghetto, to seize the bridge over the Mincio and debouch on the Chiesa, in order to place himself in communication with his right. Lastly, with his two last divisions of infantry, and the rest of his cavalry, he marched on Mantua, to force the French to raise the siege of that place; but it had already been raised twenty-four hours before; he found the trenches and batteries entire, the guns overturned and spiked; the whole place covered with the wreck of carriages, platforms, and ammunition of all kinds. The precipitation with which these measures seemed to have been effected, probably gave him great satisfaction; for everything he saw around him seemed much more like the effect of terror than the result of a calculated plan.

Massena, after having kept the enemy in check throughout the 30th, passed the Mincio in the night at Peschiera, and continued his march on Brescia. The Austrian division, which appeared before Peschiera, found the right bank of the Mincio lined with skirmishers detached by the garrison and by Massena's rearguard, commanded by Pigeon, who had orders to dispute the passage of this river, and, when he should be forced, to retire and rally on Lonato. When Augereau marched for Brescia, he had passed by Borghetto, broken down the bridge, and left a rearguard to line the right bank, with orders to fall back on Castiglione when it should be forced. I marched the whole night of 31 July, with Augereau's and Massena's divisions, on Brescia, which place I reached at ten o'clock in the morning. The Austrian division, hearing that the French army was debouching upon it by all the roads, retreated precipitately. On entering Brescia they had found 500 sick, but their stay was so short and their departure so hasty that they had no time to reconnoitre or dispose of their prisoners. General Despinois and Adjutant-General Herbin, each with several battalions, went in pursuit of the enemy on Saint-Ozetto and the debouches of the Chiesa; and I, with two divisions of Augereau and Massena, then returned, by a rapid counter-march on the side of the Mincio, to the Chiesa, whence those two divisions had marched to support their rearguards, which by this counter-march became their vanguards.

On 2 August, Augereau, on the right, occupied Montechiaro; Massena, in the centre, encamped at Ponte di San Marco, connecting his line with that of Soret, who, on the left, occupied an eminence between Salo and Dezenzano, facing about to keep Quasdanowich's right in check, which was already thrown into disorder. In the meantime the rearguards which Augereau and Massena had left on the Mincio, had retreated before the enemy's divisions, which had forced the passage of that river. That of Augereau, which had orders to join at Castiglione, quitted its post too soon, and returned in a dis-

BATTLE OF CASTIGLIONE

orderly manner to rejoin its corps. General Valette, who commanded this rearguard, was cashiered before the troops, for not having shewn more resolution on this occasion. As for General Pigeon, with Massena's rearguard, he reached Lonato in good order, and established himself there. The enemy, taking advantage of General Valette's error, entered Castiglione on the 2nd, and intrenched themselves there. On the 3rd the battle of Lonato took place; it was fought by Wurmser's two divisions that passed the Mincio over the bridge of Borghetto (that of Liptay being one), and by Bayalitsch's division, which he had left before Peschiera; which, with the cavalry, composed a body of 30,000 men: the French had from 20 to 23,000. The victory was not doubtful. Neither Wurmser, with his two divisions of infantry and the cavalry which he had taken to Mantua, nor Quasdanowich, who was already retreating, could be present at this battle.

At daybreak the enemy advanced on Lonato, and commenced a vigorous attack, intending by this point to effect his junction with his right, respecting which he now began to be anxious. Massena's vanguard was overthrown, and Lonato was taken. I, who was at Ponte di San Marco, placed myself at the head of the troops. The Austrian general having extended his line too far, still with the intention of gaining on his right, in order to open his communications with Salo, his centre was broken; Lonato was retaken at the charge, and the enemy's line intersected. One part fell back on the Mincio and the other threw themselves into Salo; but the latter being taken in front by General Soret, whom they met, and in the rear by General Saint-Hilaire, and turned on every side, were obliged to lay down their arms.

The French had been attacked in the centre, but on the right they were the assailants. Augereau encountered Liptay's division, which covered Castiglione, and broke it after an obstinate action, in which the valour of the troops supplied the want of numbers. The enemy suffered greatly, lost Castiglione, and retreated on Mantua, whence his first reinforcements reached him but not until after the engagement. Augereau's division lost many brave men in this hard-fought action; the army particularly regretted General Beyrand and Colonel Pourailles, highly distinguished officers.

During the night Quasdanowich was informed of the result of the battle of Lonato; he had heard the cannon all day: his position was rendered very precarious; his junction with the main body of the army was becoming impossible. Besides, he believed that the French divisions which had manoeuvred against him on the 2nd were still following him, which made the French Army appear to him immense: he saw it in all directions. Wurmser had directed part of his troops from Mantua towards Marcaria in pursuit of Serrurier: he could not avoid losing time in recalling them on Castiglione. On the 4th he was not ready for action: he spent the whole day in collecting his troops, rallying those who had fought at Lonato, and renewing the sup-

BATTLE OF CASTIGLIONE

plies of his artillery. About two or three o'clock in the afternoon, I reconnoitred the line of battle taken up by the Austrian army, which I found to be formidable; it still presented from 25 to 30,000 combatants. I ordered Castiglione to be intrenched, rectified the position taken by Augereau, which was defective, and set out for Lonato, in order to superintend, personally, the movements of all my troops, which it became of the utmost importance to assemble in the course of the night round Castiglione. Throughout the day, Soret and Herbin on the one side, and Dallemagne and Saint-Hilaire on the other, had followed the march of the three divisions of the enemy's right, and of those cut off from the centre at the battle of Lonato, and had pursued them closely, making prisoners at every step: whole battalions had laid down their arms at Saint-Ozetto, others at Gavardo, and others were still wandering in the neighbouring valleys. Four or five thousand men having been informed by the peasants that there were only 1,200 French in Lonato, marched thither in hopes of opening a road towards Mantua. It was five o'clock in the evening. I was also entering Lonato, coming from Castiglione; a flag of truce was brought to me; and I heard at the same time that some columns of the enemy's troops were debouching by Ponte di San Marco, that they wished to re-enter Lonato, and summoned the town to surrender. But as I was still master of Salo and Gavardo, it was evident that these could only be straggling columns that wanted to clear themselves a passage. I ordered my numerous staff to mount, had the officer who came with the flag of truce brought in, and ordered the bandage to be taken off his eyes in the midst of all the bustle of the head-quarters of a commander-in-chief. 'Go and tell your general', said I, 'that I give him eight minutes to lay down his arms; he is in the midst of the French army: after that time there are no hopes for him.' These four or five thousand men who had been harassed for three days, wandering about and uncertain of their fate, were convinced that they had been deceived by the peasants, and laid down their arms. This one fact may convey an idea of the confusion and disorder of those Austrian divisions which, having been defeated at Salo, Lonato, and Gavardo, and pursued in all directions, were almost destroyed. All the rest of the 4th, and the whole night, were spent in rallying all the columns and concentrating them on Castiglione.

Before daybreak on the 5th, the French army, 20,000 strong, occupied the heights of Castiglione, an excellent position. Serrurier's division, consisting of 5,000 men, had received orders to set out from Marcaria, to march all night, and to attack Wurmser's left in the rear, at daylight; the firing of this division was to be the signal for the battle. A great moral success was looked for from this unexpected attack, and in order to render it more sensible, the French army made a feint of falling back; but on the report of the first cannon fired by the division of Serrurier (who being ill, his place was supplied by General

BATTLE OF CASTIGLIONE

Fiorella), the troops marched briskly forward and attacked the enemy, whose confidence was already shaken, and whose first ardour had evaporated. The hill of Medole, in the midst of the plain, was the *appui* of the enemy's left; Adjutant-General Verdier was ordered to attack it; the Aide-de-camp Marmont directed several batteries of artillery against it: the post was carried. Massena attacked the right, Augereau the centre, and Fiorella took the left in rear. The light cavalry surprised the head-quarters of the enemy, and were very near taking Wurmser. The enemy retreated from all points. Nothing but the excessive fatigue of the French troops could have saved Wurmser's Army, which reached the left bank of the Mincio in great disorder, hoping to rally and make a stand there. That position afforded the advantage of a communication with Mantua; but Augereau's division marched on Borghetto and Massena's on Peschiera. General Guillaume, commandant of that fortress, having only 400 men, had walled up the gates, and some hours were lost in clearing them again. The Austrian troops which blockaded Peschiera were fresh; they long maintained the conflict with the 18th of the Line, commanded by Colonel Suchet, but at length they were broken, and lost eighteen pieces of cannon and many prisoners. I marched with Serrurier's division on Verona, where I arrived on the 7th, during the night. Wurmser had had the gates shut, wishing to gain the night for his baggage to file off, but they were battered down by the cannon, and the French took the town. The Austrians lost a great number of men. Augereau's division, finding it difficult to effect its passage at Borghetto, passed the Mincio at the bridge at Peschiera. Wurmser, having lost the line of the Mincio, tried to preserve the important positions of Montebaldo and Rocca d'Anfo. General Saint-Hilaire attacked Quasdanowich, by the valley of the Idro, on the 12th, took possession of Rocca d'Anfo, Lodrone, and Riva, and made many prisoners, which obliged the Austrians to burn the flotilla on the lake. Massena marched on Montebaldo, and retook la Corona on the 11th. Augereau reascended the left bank of the Adige, traversing the ridges of the mountains, until he reached the heights of Alla. The fighting and manoeuvres of these two divisions produced 200 prisoners and several pieces of cannon. After the loss of two such battles as those of Lonato and Castiglione, Wurmser perceived that he could no longer dispute the power of the French to occupy whatever position they might choose; he therefore retreated to Roveredo and Trent. The French army itself stood in need of repose. The Austrians, notwithstanding their defeat, were still 40,000 strong; but there was this difference, namely, that one battalion of the Army of Italy was now sufficient to put to flight four battalions of the enemy and that the French troops were picking up cannon, prisoners, and military effects in all directions.

Wurmser had, indeed, revictualled the garrison of Mantua; and withdrawn from it the brigades of Rocca Vina and Wukassowich; but he had

BATTLE OF CASTIGLIONE

only brought back half his fine army. Nothing could equal the discouragement and dejection of his troops since their reverses, except the extreme confidence with which they had opened the campaign. The Austrian general's plan, which might have succeeded under other circumstances and against another antagonist, was calculated to produce the fatal result with which it was attended; and although at the first glance the defeat of this numerous and excellent army in so few days, seems attributable only to my talents, who incessantly invented new manoeuvres as occasion required, whilst the enemy was confined to a general plan laid down beforehand, it must be allowed that this plan rested on an erroneous foundation; it was an error to make corps which had no communication with each other act separately in the face of a centralized army, whose communications were easy; the right could only communicate with the centre by Roveredo and Ledro. It was a second error to subdivide the corps of the right, and to allot different tasks to its several divisions. That which went to Brescia found nobody opposed to it, and that which reached Lonato had to contend with the troops which were at Verona the preceding day, opposed to the left which was now entering the Veronese with no enemy before it. The Austrian army contained some very good troops, but it had also some of very indifferent quality: all those who came from the Rhine with Wurmser were excellent; but the skeleton of Beaulieu's old army, which had been so often defeated, were disheartened. In the different engagements and battles which occurred between 29 July and 12 August, the French army took 15,000 prisoners, 70 pieces of cannon, and nine stand of colours, and killed or wounded 25,000 men; the loss of the French army was 7,000 men; 1,400 being taken, 600 killed, and 5,000 wounded, half of whom were only slightly hurt.

The garrison of Mantua employed the first few days after the raising of the siege in destroying the works of the besiegers, and in getting in the guns and stores which they had abandoned; but the reverses sustained by Wurmser speedily brought the French once more before the place. But the loss of their artillery had left them destitute of the means of resuming the siege. This train of artillery, formed, by great exertions, of pieces collected in the different fortresses of Italy, was a very severe loss. Besides, the opening of the trenches and the duty therein would have been too dangerous for the troops, at the moment when the malignity of the climate was about to commence its usual ravages during the dog-days. I did not attempt to form a second besieging train, as it could not have been ready before new enemies would have exposed me to the chance of losing it as I had lost the former, by forcing me to raise the siege a second time. I, therefore, contented myself, with a mere blockade. General Sahuguet was appointed to the command of it; he attacked Governolo, and caused General Dallemagne to attack Borgo-Forte; on 24 August he was master of the whole of the Seraglio, had driven the enemy into the place, and increased the strictness of the blockade. He then proceeded to multiply the redoubts and works on the line of countervallation. The troops were daily diminished in number by the ravages of the fever, and it was foreseen with consternation that this destruction would increase during the autumn. The garrison, was, indeed, subject to the same calamity, but was better sheltered in the houses, and enjoyed more accommodation than the besiegers.

On the first rumours of the reverses sustained by the French army, the Italians of the different states discovered their secret inclinations. The enemy's party appeared the stronger at Cremona, Casal Maggiore, and Pavia; but, in general, Lombardy continued to manifest a good spirit; at Milan, in particular, the people showed great firmness, which subsequently gained them my confidence. I supplied them with arms, which they had constantly and earnestly solicited, and of which they afterwards made a good use. I wrote, shortly after, to the Milanese, in these terms: 'When the French army beat a retreat, and the partisans of Austria and enemies of the liberty of Italy, regarded it as irretrievably lost; when you yourselves could not possibly suspect that this retreat was only a stratagem, you proved your attachment to France and to liberty; you displayed a zeal and resolution by which you have merited the esteem of the army, and well deserve the protection of the Republic. Your people render themselves daily more worthy of liberty; they are constantly acquiring fresh energy, and they will, no doubt, one day appear with glory on the stage of the world. Accept the testimony of my satisfaction, and of the sincere prayers of the French nation to see you free and happy.'

The people of Bologna, Ferrara, Reggio, and Modena, evinced a lively interest in the cause of the French; the news of their defeats was ill received, but the accounts of their victories were hailed with enthusiasm. Parma remained faithful; the Regency of Modena assumed a hostile attitude. At Rome the French were insulted in the streets; and the execution of the conditions of the armistice was suspended. Cardinal Mattei, archbishop of Ferrara, testified his joy at the raising of the siege of Mantua, and called on the people to revolt. He took possession of the citadel of Ferrara, and hoisted the colours of the Church; the Pope immediately sent a legate thither; they thought the French army already beyond the Alps. After the battle of Castiglione, Cardinal Mattei was ordered to Brescia; when brought before me, he answered only by the word *peccavi*, which disarmed me as victor; I merely confined him three months in a seminary. This cardinal was afterwards the Pope's plenipotentiary at Tolentino. He was of a princely family in Rome; a man of little talent or information, but who passed for sincerely devout; he was a scrupulous observer of the practices of religion. After the death of Pope Pius VI, the Court of Austria made great efforts in the conclave at Venice to get

BATTLE OF CASTIGLIONE

him elected Pope, but did not succeed; Chiaramonti, bishop of Imola, gained the election, and took the name of Pius VII.

It was to reward Augereau's good conduct at the battle of Lonato, when he commanded the right, and was ordered to attack Castiglione, that he was afterwards made a duke with that title. That day was the most brilliant of General Augereau's life, nor did I ever forget it.

Chapter XI

MANOEUVRES AND ACTIONS BETWEEN THE MINCIO AND THE BRENTA (SEPTEMBER)

Position of the Austrian army in the Tyrol, on 1 Sept. Battle of Roveredo (4 Sept.). Wurmser descends into the plains of the Bassanese. Actions of Primolano, Covolo, and Cismone (7 Sept.). The French army forces the defiles of the Brenta. Action of Verona (7 Sept.). Battle of Bassano (8 Sept.). Wurmser passes the Adige by the bridge of Porto Legnago (11 Sept.). Battle of Saint-Georges (19 Sept.). Wurmser is shut up in Mantua (18 Sept.). Third blockade of Mantua.

The Armies of the Sambre and Meuse, and of the Rhine and Moselle, had at length passed the Rhine; they advanced rapidly into the heart of Germany; the former had reached the Rednitz, and the latter the Lech. Wurmser, recruited with 20,000 men, was in the Tyrol; he was commencing his movement to advance from Trent, with 30,000 men, to the relief of Mantua, marching by the defiles of the Brenta, Bassano, and the Lower Adige, and leaving Davidowich, with 25,000 men, in charge of the Tyrol. I was sensible to the importance of occupying the Austrian army, in order to prevent its detaching any troops against the army of the Rhine, which was approaching the plains of Bavaria. As soon, therefore, as I discovered Wurmser's intentions, I resolved to assume the offensive, defeat him in detail, by surprising him in *flagrante delicto*, and complete the destruction of this army, which had caused me so

THE MINCIO AND THE BRENTA

much anxiety, and had not sufficiently expiated its offences by the disasters of Lonato, and Castiglione.

General Kilmaine, with a corps of 2,500 or 3,000 soldiers of all weapons, was charged with the guarding of the Adige, in order to cover the blockade of Mantua, which was commanded by General Sahuguet; Kilmaine occupied the plains of Verona and Porto Legnago. That part of the walls of Verona which is on the left bank of the Adige, had been restored, and the forts put in a state of defence capable of sustaining a siege. In the instructions which Kilmaine received, all the events which took place were foreseen.*

On the first of September, Wurmser and his head-quarters were still at Trent; Davidowich's headquarters were at Roveredo, covering the Tyrol by Wukassowich's division, which was encamped at Saint-Marc, having its vanguard at Serravalle, and its advanced posts at Alla, and by Reuss's division, encamped at Mori, on the right bank of the Adige, with its vanguard at the bridge of Serea, and its advanced posts on Lodrone, its reserve in the excellent position of Calliano, behind Roveredo; the three divisions and the reserves of cavalry with which Wurmser wished to operate on the Adige, were on their march between Trent and Bassano; Mezaros's division near that town; Sebottendorf's at Rovigo and Magano; and Quasdanowich's at Lavis.

Vaubois' division, forming the left of the French army, marched on the same day, the first of September, from Ladrone up to the Chiesa, along the road leading to Trent. Massena's division, the reserve of cavalry, and the head-quarters, passed the Adige by the bridge of Pola, directing their march by the road of the left bank. Augereau's division left Verona, and marched as a second line by the same road; its light infantry occupying the upper ridge of the mountains which command the valley on the left bank of the Adige.

The Tyrol is one of the most ancient possessions of the house of Austria, to which the people are strongly attached. The Trentine country, which is the southern part, also called the Italian Tyrol, was governed by a bishop, who was sovereign of Trent. There are three roads leading from Trent into Italy; one to Bassano, along the Brenta; one to Verona, by Roveredo, along the left bank of the Adige; and one to Brescia, crossing the Sarca, doubling the lake of Garda, running along the Chiesa, and passing Rocca d'Anfo. There is a communication between the Verona road, and that of Bassano, by a cross road, without going back to Trent, from which place both roads branch out.

The prince of Reuss wished to defend the bridge of the Sarca; but General Saint-Hilaire, who commanded the vanguard of Vaubois' division, attacked him furiously, carried the bridge at the point of the bayonet, made a great number of prisoners, and pursued the enemy closely as far as their camp at Mori. At the same time General Pigeon, commanding Massena's vanguard,

* These instructions, which must be in the hands of Kilmaine's heirs, are an important document.

overthrew that of Wukassowich at Serravalle, pursuing them to the camp of Saint-Marc and taking several hundred prisoners.

The two armies met on 4 September at daybreak, on both sides of the Adige. The attack was impetuous, the resistance obstinate. As soon as I perceived some hesitation in the Austrian line, I made General Dubois charge with 500 horse; the charge was successful, but Dubois received three bullets, and fell dead on the spot. He was a brave officer, and had distinguished himself in the preceding campaigns on the Rhine. The troops entered Roveredo intermixed with the enemy, who were unable to rally until they reached the defile before Calliano, a very strong position, where the Adige is inclosed between very steep mountains. The defile is not four hundred toises wide, and the entrance is defended by fortifications and a wall supported by several batteries. General Davidowich was posted there with a reserve; General Dammartin planted a battery of light artillery so as to take the gorge obliquely. The skirmishers engaged, and obtained some success on the mountains. Nine battalions in close column rushed into the defile, attacked and overthrew the enemy; his artillery, cavalry, and infantry, were all thrown into confusion and intermixed. Fifteen pieces of cannon, seven stand of colours, and 700 men were taken. At the same time General Vaubois forced the camp of Mori, and pursued the enemy briskly up the right bank of the river, in the direction of Trent. Lemarrois, my aide-de-camp, was grievously wounded in a daring and brilliant charge at Roveredo. This young man had distinguished himself in Vendemiaire at Paris; he was of a very ardent character, and came from the department of La Manche.

The army continued its march during part of the night. On the 5th, at daybreak, it entered Trent. In the evening Vaubois' division, continuing its march, took up a position on the Avisio, three leagues from Trent; the wrecks of Davidowich's army were in a position behind that river. I ordered the general commanding the cavalry to ford the river with three squadrons, to cut the enemy's line, and to take the troops which defended the bridge in the rear, whilst he caused them to be charged in front. The enemy was thrown into the greatest disorder, and abandoned his position; and General Vaubois established himself on the banks of the Avisio.

The loss of the battle of Roveredo, instead of stopping Wurmser's movement on Bassano, only accelerated it: indeed, being cut off from Trent and the Tyrol, it was necessary for him to get out of the defiles as speedily as possible, and to collect his army at Bassano, in order to take up his line of operations by the Frioul. But another motive determined him to take this step: he suffered himself to be persuaded that I wished to march to Innsbruck to join the Army of the Rhine, then arrived in Bavaria; and on this false supposition he ordered Mezaro's division to march on Mantua. On 7 September it arrived before Verona; and at the same time Wurmser's head-quarters, with Sebotten-

THE MINCIO AND THE BRENTA

dorf's and Quasdanowich's divisions and his reserves, reached Bassano; and his rearguard took position at Primolano, to defend the passes of the Brenta. In the night of 5 September, intelligence reached Trent from General Kilmaine at Verona, that Mezaros's division had passed the Brenta and was marching on the Adige, and that it would probably attack Verona on 7 September. I instantly conceived the idea of hemming in Wurmser between the Brenta and the Adige, or, if on the approach of the French, he should fall back on the Piave, of surrounding and taking Mezaros's division, which was already compromised, and too far advanced to retreat. I intrusted the defence of the Italian Tyrol to General Vaubois, who from his position at the Avisio, could easily advance to the Brenner to meet Mezaros's general, should his right reach Innsbruck. At night I organized the administration of the country, and caused the following proclamation to be posted.

'Tyrolese! you solicit the protection of the French Army: you must render yourselves worthy of that protection; and, since the majority of you are well disposed, compel the few obstinate men amongst you to submit. Their senseless proceedings tend to draw the horrors of war upon their country; the superiority of my arms is now sufficiently proved. The Emperor's ministers, purchased by English gold, are betraying their master, and that unfortunate prince does not take a single step without committing an error. You wish for peace, and the French are fighting for the same object. We only enter your territories to force the Court of Vienna to yield to the wishes of distracted Europe, and to listen to the cries of its own people! We do not come to aggrandize France; Nature has marked our limits by the Rhine and the Alps, whilst she has placed the limits of the house of Austria in the Tyrol. Tyrolese, whatever may have been your conduct heretofore, return to your homes, quit the colours so often defeated and so powerless in your defence: the conquerors of the Alps can have nothing to fear from a few additional enemies, but the generosity of my nation commands me to endeavour to save unnecessary victims. We have rendered ourselves formidable in battle, but we are the friends of all who receive us with hospitality. The religion, customs, and property of all the communes which submit shall be respected;' etc.

On the 6th, at daybreak, I commenced my march, with Augereau's divisions in front, Massena and the reserve, by the defiles of the Brenta, to proceed on Bassano with all possible expedition. It was necessary to perform this march of twenty leagues, over a difficult road, in two days at the utmost. In the evening the head-quarters and the army were at Borgo-Val-Sugagna.

On the 7th, at daybreak, I recommenced my march; my van soon fell in with that of Wurmser, in position behind Primolano: it seemed impossible to dislodge them from this post; but nothing could withstand the French army; the Fifth Light Infantry, dispersed as skirmishers, and supported by the three battalions of the Fourth of the Line in three close columns, broke the double line of the Austrians. The Fifth Dragoons, commanded by Colonel Milhaud, cut off the road. Almost the whole of the enemy's vanguard laid down their arms; all the artillery, colours, and baggage, were taken. The little fort of Covolo, a kind of Chiusa, in vain attempted to resist; it was turned and taken. At night the French army bivouacked in the village of Cismone, where I took up my head-quarters, without attendants or baggage, and passed the night half dead with hunger and fatigue. A soldier (who reminded me of the circumstance at the camp of Boulogne, in 1805, when I was emperor) shared his ration of bread with me. Several parks of ammunition waggons, twelve pieces of cannon, five stand of colours, and 4,200 men were taken.

The same evening Mezaros's division attacked Verona, which place it was in hopes to occupy without resistance. But all the ground before Verona had been put in a defensive state; a strong half-moon had been constructed before the Vicenza gate. General Kilmaine expected Mezaros. He defended the approaches of the town by means of some squadrons of cavalry, which, falling back behind the fortifications, allowed thirty guns from the ramparts to shower grape on the Austrian column. After a few vain attempts, Mezaros, considering it impossible to take the town by main force, encamped at Saint-Michel, and demanded reinforcements and pontoons to enable him to pass the Adige and surround the town; but Wurmser being just then surprised and menaced in Bassano, ordered him to fall back and join him with all possible expedition. He hoped to collect his army together in time to stop the French before Bassano. It was too late. Mezaros's division did not reach Montebello until the 8th, the day on which the battle of Bassano was fought.

On 8 September, before daylight, I was at the advanced posts; at six o'clock the vanguard attacked, and overthrew six battalions which were in position in the passes on the two banks of the Brenta; their remains fell back on the line of battle, which was about 20,000 strong, but which made only a weak resistance. Augereau's division attacked the left; Massena's the right; the enemy was broken in all directions, and driven back on Bassano. The Fourth of the Line, in a close column, passed the bridge as at Lodi. At three o'clock, the army entered Bassano, and took 6,000 prisoners, eight stand of colours, two pontoon trains, two hundred baggage waggons, thirty-two pieces of cannon, and one hundred ammunition waggons of all kinds, all of which waggons had teams of four horses. Wurmser retreated in disorder on Vicenza, being now unable to retreat on the Piave; at Vicenza he rallied Mezaros's division. He thus found himself cut off from the hereditary states, and from his communications with Austria. General Quasdanowich, with 3,000 men, being cut off from Bassano, fell back on the Frioul. On the 9th, Massena's division marched on Vicenza, and Augereau's on Padua, intercepting those two great roads, in case Wurmser should attempt to return to the Brenta, in order to reach the Piave. But that general, after his defeats at

THE MINCIO AND THE BRENTA

Roveredo, in the passes of the Brenta, at Bassano and before Verona, had now no troops under his command but such as were much disheartened; he had lost the flower of his army; out of a force of 60,000 men, he had now but 16,000 in junction under his command. Never was there a more critical situation. He himself despaired, and the French were every hour in hopes of seeing him lay down his arms.

Of these 16,000 men, 600 were cavalry, of good quality, and not discouraged, not having suffered loss or been defeated. These horsemen spread themselves over the country in search of a passage across the Adige; two squadrons of them passed to the right bank of the Adige at the ferry of Albaredo, to reconnoitre the position of the French, and obtain some intelligence from Mantua. It was impossible for Wurmser to pass the Adige at this ferry, closely followed as he was by the French army, and after having lost his pontoons at Bassano. His position was become desperate, when the French evacuated Legnago without destroying the bridge. This error, committed by a lieutenant-colonel, saved Wurmser. Kilmaine when attacked at Verona by Mezaros's division, had ordered the 400 men who guarded Legnago to join him, and directed Sahuguet to replace them by a detachment from forces blockading Mantua. The lieutenant-colonel who commanded this detachment, having had a few men sabred on the road from Legnago to Mantua, suffered himself to be persuaded that the whole of the Austrian army had passed at Albaredo, and was about to cut off his retreat. He gave credit to the report spread by the enemy of the disasters experienced by the French army, which was said to have perished in the Tyrol. Believing himself intercepted, he was perfectly bewildered, evacuated the place, and retreated on Mantua. Wurmser, informed of this fortunate occurrence, instantly marched on Legnago, entered the place without firing a shot, and availed himself of the bridge to pass the Adige. At the same time I reached Arcole. On receiving this vexatious intelligence, I took possession of the ferry of Ronco, sent Massena over to the right bank, and ordered Augereau to march from Padua on Legnago: still entertaining hopes of surrounding the Marshal once more by reaching the Molinella before him. Kilmaine, with all the disposable force he could muster, had stationed himself on that river, intercepting the road to Mantua: but his force being inconsiderable, it was necessary to join him before the enemy should reach him. Wurmser lost valuable time at Legnago; whether excessive fatigue compelled him to give his troops a little rest, or whether, supposing the French to be on the road from Vicenza to Ronco, he hesitated for a time, in hopes to open once more his natural communications by way of Padua. As he had a great number of cavalry, he was enabled to obtain intelligence and watch the French at a great distance. His scouts informed him that the French were at Montagnana, a place in his front, where they had arrived by way of Padua; and that they were approaching Legnago by the two roads. He then commenced his march on Mantua.

There are two roads leading from Ronco to Sanguinetto, where it was intended to intercept the enemy: one of them runs on the left, along the Adige, and intersects the road from Legnago to Mantua at Cerea; the other leads direct from Ronco to Sanguinetto. General Pigeon, with Massena's vanguard, marched directly on Sanguinetto; but Murat, who was sent forward to reconnoitre with the light horse, had taken the Cerea road, as that which would bring him nearest to the enemy. He soon began a cannonade with them. Pigeon, hearing the cannon, rested his left on Cerea, advanced to that place, and drew up the 4th light demi-brigade in line behind the rivulet to stop the way. Wurmser was cut off; he would have been lost, had he not succeeded in forcing a passage. He attacked Cerea, deploying his whole army, and surrounded the small vanguard of the French, which was soon broken; 3 or 400 men remained in his power. Being left master of the field of battle, he continued his march on Sanguinetto without delay. It was during the conflict at Cerea that I, having galloped up to the village just as my vanguard was routed, had only just time enough to turn round, clap spurs to my horse, and get clear off.

Wurmser came up, a few minutes after, to the very spot where I had been, and learning the circumstance from an old woman, sent in pursuit of me in every direction, particularly recommending that I should be brought in alive. After reaching Sanguinetto, Wurmser marched all night. Having discovered that Sahuguet's and Kilmaine's reserves were waiting for him at the Molinella, he quitted the high road, turned to the left, and reached Villa-Impenta on the 12th, where there was a little bridge guarded by a small detachment; his cavalry surprised it. General Charton, who hastened with 500 men of the 12th light demi-brigade from the army before Mantua, to defend this bridge, could not reach it in time; he then formed the square, on the road, and made a vigorous resistance; but he was sabred by the Austrian cuirassiers, and left dead on the field. This detachment was lost. On the 14th the reverses of the old Marshal were again alleviated by another slight advantage at Due-Castelli similar to those of Cerea and Villa-Impenta; a battalion of light infantry was there cut off and broken by two regiments of cuirassiers, and lost 300 men. The troops were excessively fatigued, and their duty began to be negligently performed.

The trifling successes obtained by the Austrian army, in the actions of Cerea, Villa-Impenta, and Due-Castelli, encouraged it to keep the field. The garrison of Mantua came out, and Wurmser encamped his army between Saint-George and the citadel. He had then 33,000 men under his command; 5,000 were in the hospitals; he left 5,000 to guard the place; and encamped with 25,000, of whom 5,000 were cavalry; he was in hopes, by thus occupy-

THE MINCIO AND THE BRENTA

ing the country, to find an opportunity of reaching Legnago, and repassing the Adige: but General Bon, who commanded Augereau's division, entered Legnago on 13 September, made 1,700 prisoners, took twenty-four pieces of horse artillery, and liberated 500 French soldiers, who had been taken at Cerea and in other petty engagements. On the 16th he reached Governolo, forming the left of the army; Massena, who was at Due-Castelli, formed the centre; Sahuguet, with the troops engaged in the blockade, was at la Favorite, forming the right; Kilmaine had collected all the cavalry. The forced marches performed during this last fortnight, had greatly weakened the regiments. On the 16th, in the evening, the army amounted to 24,000 men under arms, of whom 3,000 were cavalry. The two armies were equal in strength, but their quality was very different; of the enemy's troops the cavalry alone retained their confidence.

On 19 September, General Bon began his march from Governolo, supported his left on the Mincio, and approached Saint-George. The action became very brisk; the Austrians sent their reserve to take part in it. Bon was not only stopped, but even lost a little ground. Sahuguet engaged on the right; the enemy thought the whole line was in action, when Massena debouched in column on the centre, and carried disorder into the enemy's army, which retreated precipitately into the town, after having lost 3,000 prisoners, amongst whom was a regiment of cuirassiers, completely mounted, with three standards and eleven pieces of cannon. After the battle of Saint-George, Wurmser spread his troops throughout the Seraglio, threw a bridge over the Po, and got provisions into the place. On 21 September he attacked Governolo, and was repulsed with the loss of 1,000 men, and six pieces of cannon; had he gained possession of this point, he meant to have endeavoured to reach the Adige. At length, on 1 October, Kilmaine, who commanded the blockade, entered the Seraglio, seized Pradella and Ceresa, and completely blockaded the place. This operation, which occasioned several very hot actions, maintained with a few men, did the General great credit. From 1 June to 18 September, the enemy had lost 27,000 men, of whom 18,000 were taken prisoners, 3,000 killed, and 6,000 wounded, seventy-five pieces of cannon, twenty-two ensigns and standards, thirty generals, eighty of the civil list from headquarters, and 6,000 horse. The Marshal and 16,000 men had been obliged to throw themselves into Mantua: 10,000 men out of this army had escaped into the Tyrol under Davidowich, and into the Frioul under Quasdanowich. The French army had lost 7,500 men; of whom 1,400 were taken, 1,800 killed, and 4,300 wounded.

Marmont, whom I despatched to Paris, with the colours taken in the battles of Roveredo, Bassano, and Saint-George, and the actions of Primolano and Cismone, was one of my aides-de-camp: I had found him an ensign of artillery at Toulon and had taken him into my service. He was afterwards Duke of

MANOEUVRES AND ACTIONS

Ragusa and a marshal of France. He came from the department of the Côte d'Or.

The troops, having, for the present, no enemy before them, took a little rest. Vaubois occupied Trent, and intrenched himself on the banks of the Avisio; Massena's division occupied Bassano, observing the passage of the Piave. Augereau's division occupied Verona; Kilmaine commanded the blockade of Mantua. The battles of Roveredo, Bassano, and Saint-George, the intermediate actions, and the sickness incident to the blockade, had weakened the troops. The garrison of Mantua at first made numerous sorties in great force; but reverses and sickness soon cooled its ardour. At the end of October it amounted to 17,000 men under arms, and about 10,000 in the hospitals; that is to say, nearly 30,000 mouths to feed; whence it was hoped that the place would speedily be surrendered; but the old Marshal had the greater part of his cavalry horses salted, which, added to the provisions of all kinds which he had collected in the vicinity, and particularly those he had obtained from the Regency of Modena, which on both occasions, when the siege was raised, had sent in convoys prepared long beforehand, put the place in a condition to make a longer defence than had been expected. Contrary to all probability, and to the opinion of all Italy, the French army was yet to gain more sanguinary and glorious victories, and Austria was yet to levy and to lose two armies, before this bulwark of Italy was to yield to its fate.

Kilmaine was of Irish origin, and an excellent cavalry officer: he possessed coolness and a quick eye; he was well adapted for the command of detached corps of observation, and all delicate commissions which require discernment, talent, and sound judgment. He had been employed in Prairial against the faubourg Saint-Antoine. At the period of the campaign of Italy he was about fifty years of age. He rendered the army important services, and would have been one of its principal generals, but for the delicacy of his health. He was well acquainted with the Austrian troops; and, understanding their tactics thoroughly, never suffered himself to be imposed upon by false reports which they are accustomed to spread in the rear of an army, nor by those heads of columns which they place on the communications, in all directions, to make the enemy believe there are great forces present, when in fact there are none. His political opinions were very moderate.

Chapter XII

BATTLE OF ARCOLE

Marshal Alvinzi arrives in Italy at the head of a third army. Good condition of the French army; all the nations of Italy confident of its success. Battle of the Brenta (5 Nov.); Vaubois evacuates the Tyrol in disorder. Battle of Caldiero (12 Nov.). Murmurs and various sentiments of the French soldiers. Nocturnal march of the army on Ronco, where the troops pass the Adige over a bridge of boats (14 Nov.). The army re-enters Verona in triumph, by the Venetian gate, on the right bank (18 Nov.).

All the couriers who reached Vienna with news of Prince Charles's successes, were followed by couriers from Wurmser, bringing accounts of his disasters. The court passed the whole month of September in these alternations of joy and sorrow. The satisfaction derived from its triumphs, did not compensate for the consternation excited by its defeats. Germany was saved, but Italy was lost: the army which guarded that frontier had disappeared. Its numerous staff, its old Marshal, and a remnant of troops, had only been able to find temporary safety by shutting themselves up in Mantua, which place, reduced to the last extremity, in want of everything, and ravaged by the autumnal fevers, would soon be compelled to open its gates to the conqueror. The Aulic Council felt the necessity of making extraordinary efforts; it assembled two armies; the first in the Frioul, the other in the Tyrol, appointed Marshal Alvinzi to command them, and ordered him to march to save Mantua and deliver Wurmser.

The influence of the proceedings of the Armies of the Sambre and Meuse and Rhine was calculated to be speedily felt in Italy. If those two armies

BATTLE OF ARCOLE

should not maintain themselves on the right bank of the Rhine, it was of the utmost importance that they should send strong detachments to reinforce the Army of Italy. The Directory promised much, but performed little; they sent, however, twelve battalions, drafted from the Army of la Vendée, who reached Milan in the course of September and October; care was taken to make them march in twelve columns. The notion was spread abroad that each of these columns was a regiment, and had its full complement of men, which would have been a very considerable reinforcement. It is true that the French soldiers did not need encouragement; they were full of confidence in their chief and in their own superiority; they were well paid, clothed, and fed; the artillery was fine and numerous; the cavalry well mounted. The Italians of every state had connected themselves with the interest of the army on which their liberty and independence depended; they were as much convinced of the superiority of the French over the German soldiers, as of that of the general who had vanquished Beaulieu and Wurmser, over Marshal Alvinzi. Public opinion had undergone a great change since the preceding month of July. At that time, when Wurmser's approach was announced, all Italy expected his triumph; at present no one doubted that of the French army. The public spirit of the Transpadan States, of Bologna, Modena, and Reggio, was such that they might be depended on for repulsing the Pope's army themselves, if it should enter their territories according to the threats held out.

In the beginning of October Marshal Alvinzi was still with his army before the Isonzo; but at the end of that month, he removed his head-quarters to Conegliano, behind the Piave. Massena, stationed at Bassano, was watching his movements. Davidowich had assembled a corps d'armée of 18,000 men in the Tyrol, inclosing the Tyrolese militia. The General of division Vaubois covered Trent, occupying the Avisio with a corps of 12,000 men. Augereau's division, the reserve of cavalry, and the head-quarters of the French army, were at Verona. Alvinzi's plan was to effect his junction with Davidowich in Verona, and to march thence on Mantua. On 1 November he threw two bridges across the Piave, and marched in three columns towards the Brenta. Massena, threatening to attack him, compelled him to deploy his whole army; and when he had ascertained that it amounted to upwards of 40,000 men, he raised his camp of Bassano, repassed the Brenta, and approached Vicenza, where I joined him with Augereau's division and my reserve; and on the 6th, at daybreak, advanced to give battle to Alvinzi, who had followed Massena's movement. He had fixed his head-quarters at Fonte Niva; his van, under General Liptay, on the right bank of the Brenta, at Carmignano, in advance of his left, which was commanded by General Provero. His right, under the command of Quasdanowich, was in position between Bassano and Vicenza. General Metrouski commanded a corps of observation in the gorges of the Brenta, and General Hohenzollern commanded his reserve. Massena

BATTLE OF ARCOLE

attacked at dawn of day, and after an action of several hours drove back the van, Quasdanowich, Liptay, and Provera's division, to the left bank of the river, killing a great number of men, and making many prisoners. I advanced against Quasdanowich at the head of Augereau's division, and drove him from Lenova upon Bassano. It was four o'clock in the afternoon; I considered the passage of the bridge and the taking of the town on this day as of the greatest importance; but Hohenzollern having come up, I ordered my brigade of reserve to advance for the purpose of seconding the attack of the bridge; a battalion of 900 Croats, which had been cut off, had thrown themselves into a village on the high road; as soon as the head of the reserve appeared to cross the village, it was received with a very brisk fire; it became necessary to bring up howitzers. The village was taken, and the Croats shot; but a delay of two hours had taken place, and the troops did not reach the bridge until night; they were obliged to postpone the forcing of this passage until the following day.

Vaubois had received orders to attack the enemy's positions on the right bank of the Avisio. On 1 November, he attacked those of Saint-Michael and Segonzano. The enemy were in considerable force, and defended themselves with the greatest intrepidity. Vaubois was not altogether successful, nor was the attempt he made the following day more fortunate. At length he was himself attacked in turn, his position of the Avisio was forced, and he was obliged to abandon Trent. Having rallied his troops, he took up a position at Calliano; but Landon, manoeuvring by the right bank of the Adige, with his Tyrolese, had outflanked him, and got possession of Nomi and Torbole. It appeared to be his intention to advance on Montebaldo and Rivoli. Vaubois had no longer any troops on the right bank, or any means of opposing this manoeuvre, which, had it been executed by the enemy, would have endangered not only his corps but the whole of the French army. This news reached the French head-quarters at two in the morning. There was now no room for hesitation; it was indispensably necessary to hasten to Verona, now so imminently threatened, and to abandon the former plan, with every idea of making a diversion. My original scheme was, after driving Alvinzi beyond the Piave, to proceed up the defiles of the Brenta, and to cut off Davidowich. Colonel Vignolles, of the staff, a confidential officer, was sent to collect all the troops he could muster at Verona, and to march with them on la Corona and Rivoli. He found there a battalion of the 40th, just arrived from la Vendée, and overawed the first skirmishers of the enemy, who came up to la Corona. On the following day, Joubert reached that important position, with the 4th light demi-brigade, brought from the blockade of Mantua: after this there was nothing to apprehend. At the same time Vaubois threw bridges over the Adige, crossed back to the right bank, and proceeded to occupy the position of la Corona and Rivoli in force.

BATTLE OF ARCOLE

From the Brenta, the French army filed through the city of Vicenza, during the whole of the 7th. The inhabitants who had witnessed the victory it had gained, could not account for this movement in retreat. Alvinzi had also commenced his retreat, at three in the morning, to pass the Piave; but he was soon informed by his light cavalry of the retrograde movement of the French army. He returned on the Brenta, and the next day passed that river to follow his antagonist's movement.

I had Vaubois' division assembled on the plain of Rivoli, and addressed them thus: 'Soldiers, I am not satisfied with you: you have shown neither discipline, perseverance, nor bravery; no position could rally you; you abandoned yourselves to a panic terror. You suffered yourselves to be driven from positions in which a handful of brave men might have stopped an army. Soldiers of the 39th and 85th, you are not French soldiers. Quarter-master-general, let it be inscribed on their colours, *They no longer form part of the Army of Italy*!' This harangue, pronounced in a severe tone, drew tears from these old soldiers; the rules of discipline could not suppress the accents of their grief. Several grenadiers, who had received honorary arms, cried out, 'General, we have been calumniated; place us in the van, and you shall see whether the 39th and 85th belong to the Army of Italy.' Having thus produced the effect I wished, I addressed a few words of consolation to them. These two regiments a few days after covered themselves with glory.

Notwithstanding the reverses which Alvinzi had sustained on the Brenta, his operations were crowned with the most brilliant success. He was master of the whole of the Tyrol, and of all the country between the Brenta and the Adige. But the most difficult task still remained, namely, to force the passage of the Adige in the face of the French army, and to effect his junction with Davidowich by marching over the bodies of the brave soldiers posted before Verona. The road from Verona to Vicenza runs along the Adige for three leagues, as far as Villa-Nuova, where it turns at right angles to the left, and runs straight to Vicenza. At Villa-Nuova the little river Alpon cuts it, and after running through Arcole falls into the Adige, near Albaredo. To the left of Villa-Nuova are some heights known by the name of the position of Caldiero, by occupying which Verona is covered, and it becomes easy to fall on the rear of an enemy manoeuvring on the lower Adige. As soon as the defence of Montebaldo was provided for, and Vaubois' troops had regained their confidence, I determined to occupy Caldiero, as affording more chances in favour of defensive operations, and more energy to my attitude. On the 11th, at two o'clock in the afternoon, the army passed the bridges of Verona. Verdier's brigade, which was at the head overthrew the enemy's vanguard, made several hundred prisoners, and took up a position, at night, at the foot of Caldiero. The fires of the bivouacs and the reports of spies and prisoners left no doubt respecting Alvinzi's intentions: he meant to receive battle, and had

BATTLE OF ARCOLE

fixed himself firmly in these fine positions, resting his left on the marsh of Arcole, and his right on Mount Olivetto and the village of Colognola. This position is good in both directions. He had covered himself by some redoubts and formidable batteries. At daybreak the enemy's line was perceived: his left was impregnable; his right seemed ill supported. Massena received orders to march with his division to take advantage of this defect by occupying a hill which outflanked the enemy's right, and which he had neglected to occupy. Brigadier-General Launay intrepidly climbed the acclivity at the head of a corps of skirmishers; but, having advanced too far, the division which was to support him could not come up with him in time, being stopped by a ravine, and he was repulsed and taken prisoner. The enemy, now apprised of their error, immediately rectified their position; and it was no longer possible to attack them with any hope of success. In the meantime the whole line engaged, and the fire was maintained throughout the day. The rain fell in torrents; the ground was so completely soaked that the French artillery could make no movement, whilst that of the Austrians, being in position and advantageously placed, produced its full effect. The enemy made several attempts to attack in his turn, but was repulsed with loss. The two armies bivouacked in their respective positions. It continued to rain all night so heavily that I judged it expedient to return into my camp before Verona. The loss in this affair was equal on both sides; the enemy, with reason, claimed the victory; his advanced posts approached Saint-Michael's, and the situation of the French was become truly hazardous.

Vaubois had suffered considerable loss; he had not now above 8,000 men left. The other two divisions, after having fought valiantly on the Brenta, and failed in their operation on Caldiero, did not now amount to more than 13,000 men under arms. The idea of the superior strength of the enemy pervaded every mind. Vaubois' soldiers, in excuse for their retreat, declared that the enemy were three to one against them. The enemy had also suffered loss, no doubt, but he had gained great advantages. He had counted the small number of the French at his ease; and accordingly he had no longer any doubt of the deliverance of Mantua, or of the conquest of Italy. In his delirium of confidence, he had a great number of scaling-ladders made, and loudly threatened to take Verona by storm. The garrison of Mantua had awakened from its lethargy, and made frequent sorties, incessantly harassing the besiegers, who amounted only to 8 or 9,000 men, and had to restrain a garrison of 25,000, out of which number, however, there were 10 or 12,000 sick. The French were no longer in a situation to carry on offensive operations in any directions; they were checked on one side by the position of Caldiero, and on the other by the defiles of the Tyrol. But even if the enemy's position had allowed of any enterprise against him, his numerical superiority was too well known: it was therefore necessary to let him make the first move, and to wait patiently

BATTLE OF ARCOLE

until he should make some attempt. The weather was extremely bad; every movement was made in the mud. The affairs of Caldiero and the Tyrol had evidently damped the confidence of the French soldier; he was, indeed, still persuaded of his superiority on equal terms, but did not now feel capable of resisting such superior numbers. A great number of the bravest men had been wounded two or three times in different battles since the army entered Italy. Discontent began to show itself. 'We cannot,' said the men, 'do everybody's duty. Alvinzi's army, now present, is the same that the Armies of the Rhine, and Sambre and Meuse, retreated before, and they are now idle; why are we to perform their work? If we are beaten, we must make for the Alps as fugitives and without honour; if, on the contrary, we conquer, what will be the result of our new victory? We shall be opposed by another army like that of Alvinzi, as Alvinzi himself succeeded Wurmser, and as Wurmser succeeded Beaulieu; and in this unequal contest we must be annihilated at last.'

To these remarks, I caused the following answer to be made. 'We have but one more effort to make, and Italy is our own. The enemy is, no doubt, more numerous than we are, but half his troops are recruits; when he is beaten, Mantua must fall, and we shall remain masters of all; our labours will be at an end; for not only Italy, but a general peace is in Mantua. You talk of returning to the Alps, but you are no longer capable of doing so: from the dry and frozen bivouacs of those sterile rocks, you could very well conquer the delicious plains of Lombardy; but from the smiling flowery bivouacs of Italy, you cannot return to the Alpine snows. Succours have reached us; there are more on the road; let not those who are unwilling to fight seek vain pretences; for only beat Alvinzi and I will answer for your future welfare.' These words, repeated by everyone in the army that possessed a generous heart, raised the spirits of the troops, and brought the mover by degrees to an opposite way of thinking. Thus, one while, the army, in its dejection, was desirous of retreating; at another moment it was filled with enthusiasm and talked of advancing. 'Shall the soldiers of Italy patiently endure the insults and provocations of these slaves?'

When it became known at Brescia, Bergamo, Milan, Cremona, Lodi, Pavia, and Bologna, that the army had sustained a check, the wounded and sick left the hospitals, before they were well cured, to resume their stations in the ranks; the wounds of many of these brave men were still bleeding. This affecting sight filled the mind with the most lively emotion.

At length, on 14 November, at nightfall, the camp of Verona got under arms: three columns began their march in the deepest silence, crossed the city, passed the Adige by three bridges, and formed on the right bank. The hour of departure, the direction taken, which was that of a retreat, the silence observed in the order of the day, contrary to the invariable custom of announcing that an engagement is to take place, the state of affairs, everything, in short, indi-

BATTLE OF ARCOLE

cated that the army was retreating. The first step in retreat would necessarily be followed by the raising of the siege of Mantua, and foreboded the loss of Italy. Those amongst the inhabitants who placed the hopes of their future lot in the victories of the French, followed with anxious and aching hearts the movements of this army, which was depriving them of every hope. But the army, instead of keeping the Peschiera road, suddenly turned to the left, marched along the Adige, and arrived before daylight at Ronco, where Andreossy was completing a bridge. By the first rays of the sun, the troops were astonished to find themselves, by merely facing to the left, on the opposite shore. The officers and soldiers who had traversed this country before, when in pursuit of Wurmser, now began to guess their General's intention; I intended to turn Caldiero, which I had not been able to carry by an attack in front: not being able with 13,000 men to withstand 40,000 in the plain, I was removing my field of battle to roads surrounded by vast marshes, where numbers would be unavailing, but where the courage of the heads of the columns would decide everything. The hopes of victory now animated every heart, and every man vowed to surpass himself in order to second so fine and daring a plan. Kilmaine had remained in Verona with 1,500 men of all arms, with the gates closed, and all communications strictly prohibited; the enemy was therefore completely ignorant of this movement. The bridge of Ronco was constructed on the right of the Alpon, about a quarter of a league from its mouth; which situation has been censured by ill-informed military men. In fact, if the bridge had been carried to the left bank opposite Alberedo; first, the army would have had to debouch on a vast plain, the very thing which I wished to avoid; secondly, Alvinzi, who occupied the heights of Caldiero, might have covered the march of a column which he would have directed on Verona, by stationing troops on the right bank of the Alpon: he would have forced Verona, feebly guarded as it was, and would have effected his junction with the Army of the Tyrol; the division of Rivoli, taken between two fires, would have been obliged to retreat on Peschiera, and the whole army would have been strangely compromised: Whereas, by constructing the bridge to the right of the Alpon, the invaluable advantages were secured first, of drawing the enemy into three roads crossing an immense marsh; secondly, of being in communication with Verona, by the dyke which runs up the Adige and passes by the villages of Porcil and Gambione, where Alvinzi's head-quarters were, without leaving any position for the enemy to take, or any natural obstacle to cover the movement of any troops he might detach to attack Verona. Such an attack was, indeed, now impossible, for the whole French army would have taken such troops in the rear, whilst the walls of the city would have stopped them in front. Three roads branch out from the bridge of Ronco; the first, on the left, goes up the Adige towards Verona, passes the villages of Bionde and Porcil, where it debouches in a plain; the second and

BATTLE OF ARCOLE

centre one, leads to Villa-Nuova, and runs through the village of Arcole, crossing the Alpon by a little stone bridge; the third, on the right, runs down the Adige and leads to Albaredo. It is 3,600 toises from Ronco to Porcil, 2,000 from Porcil to Caldiero, and three leagues from Caldiero to Verona. It is 2,200 toises from Ronco to Arcole, 3,000 from the bridge of Arcole to Villa-Nuova; 100 from Ronco to the mouth of the Alpon, and 500 thence to Albaredo.

Three columns entered upon these three roads; the left one marched up the Adige as far as the extremity of the marshes, at the village of Porcil, whence the soldiers perceived the steeples of Verona; it was thenceforth impossible for the enemy to march upon that city. The centre column marched on Arcole, where the French skirmishers got as far as the bridge unperceived. Two battalions of Croats, with two pieces of cannon, had bivouacs there for the purpose of guarding the rear of the army, and watching any parties which the garrison of Legnago might send into the country; that place being only three leagues off, on the right. The ground between Arcole and the Adige was not guarded; Alvinzi had contented himself with ordering patrols of hussars, who thrice every day visited the dykes of the marshes on the side of the Adige. The road from Ronco to Arcole meets the Alpon 1,200 toises from Ronco; it then runs along the right bank of that little rivulet for 10,000 toises, as far as the stone bridge which turns to the right, at right angles, and leads into the village of Arcole. The Croats were bivouacked with their right supported on the village and their left towards the mouth of the rivulet, with the dyke in their front, separated from them by the stream; by firing in front, they took the column, the head of which was near Arcole, in flank; the soldiers fell back precipitately as far as the point where the road ceases to expose the flank to the left bank. Augereau, indignant of this retrograde movement of his van, rushed upon the bridge at the head of two battalions of grenadiers; but, being received by a brisk flank-fire, he was driven back on his division. Alvinzi, being informed of this attack, could not at first comprehend, but at daybreak he was enabled to observe the movement of the French from the neighbouring steeples. His reconnoitring parties of hussars were received with discharges of musquetry on all the dykes, and pursued by the cavalry; he then plainly saw that the French had passed the Adige and were in his rear. It seemed to him absurd to suppose that a whole army could thus have been thrown into impassable marshes; he thought it must be some light troops which had moved in this direction to alarm him, and to mask a real attack by troops which would debouch by the Verona road. But his reconnoitring parties having brought him intelligence that all was quiet towards Verona, he thought it important to drive these light troops from the marshes. He therefore directed a division, commanded by Metrouski, on the dyke of Arcole, and another on the left dyke, commanded by Provera. Towards nine o'clock

BATTLE OF ARCOLE

in the morning they attacked with impetuosity. Massena, who was intrusted with the left dyke, having allowed the enemy to get fairly upon the dyke made a desperate charge, broke his column, repulsed him with great loss, and took a number of prisoners. The same thing happened on the dyke of Arcole. As soon as the enemy had passed the elbow of the road, he was charged and routed by Augereau, leaving prisoners and cannon in the victor's hands: the marsh was covered with dead. It became of the utmost importance to gain possession of Arcole, for, by debouching thence on the enemy's rear, we should have seized the bridge of Villa-Nuova over the Alpon, which was his only retreat, and established ourselves there before it could be occupied against us; but Arcole withstood several attacks. I determined to try a last effort in person; I seized a flag, rushed on the bridge, and there planted it; the column I commanded had reached the middle of the bridge, when the flanking fire and the arrival of a division of the enemy frustrated the attack; the grenadiers at the head of the column, finding themselves abandoned by the rear, hesitated, but being hurried away in the flight, they persisted in keeping possession of their General; they seized me by my arms and by my clothes, and dragged me along with them amidst the dead, the dying, and the smoke; I was precipitated into a morass, in which I sunk up to the middle, surrounded by the enemy. The grenadiers perceived that their General was in danger; a cry was heard of '*Forward, soldiers, to save the General!*' These brave men immediately turned back, ran upon the enemy, drove him beyond the bridge, and I was saved. This was the day of military devotedness. Lannes, who had been wounded at Governolo, had hastened from Milan; he was still suffering; he threw himself between the enemy and myself, covering me with his body, and received three wounds, determined never to abandon me. Muiron, my aide-de-camp, was killed in covering his General with his own body. Heroic and affecting death! Belliard and Vignolles were wounded in rallying the troops forward. The brave General Robert was killed; he was a soldier who never shrunk from the enemy's fire.

General Guieux passed the Adige at the ferry of Albaredo with a brigade. Arcole was taken in the rear; but in the meantime Alvinzi, having ascertained the real state of affairs, had become fully sensible of the danger of his position; he had abandoned Caldiero precipitately, destroyed his batteries, and made all his parks and reserves repass the bridge. From the top of the steeples of Ronco the French had the mortification to see this booty escape them; and it was only by witnessing the precipitate movements of the enemy that the whole extent and consequences of my plan could be comprehended. Everyone then saw what might be the results of so profound and daring a combination. The enemy's army was escaping from destruction by a hasty retreat; General Guieux was not able to march on Arcole by the left bank of the Alpon until near four o'clock; the village was carried without striking a blow;

BATTLE OF ARCOLE

but it was now unimportant, being six hours too late; the enemy had resumed his natural position. Arcole was now only an intermediate post between the fronts of the two armies, whereas in the morning it had been in the rear of the enemy. The day was, however, crowned with important results. Caldiero was evacuated; Verona was no longer in danger; two divisions of Alvinzi's army had been defeated with considerable loss; numerous columns of prisoners, and a great number of trophies, filed off through the camp, and filled the officers and soldiers with enthusiasm; the troops regained their spirits, and the confidence of victory.

In the meantime Davidowich with the corps of the Tyrol had attacked and taken la Corona; he occupied Rivoli. Vaubois occupied the heights of Bussolengo; Kilmaine, relieved from all apprehensions for the left bank by the evacuation of Caldiero, had directed his attention to the walls of Verona and the right bank; but if Davidowich should march on Vaubois, and force him to throw himself on Mantua, he would oblige the French to raise the blockade of that city, and cut off the retreat of the head-quarters and the army which were at Ronco. It is thirteen leagues from Rivoli to Mantua, and ten from Ronco to that city; by very bad roads; it was therefore necessary to be ready, by daylight, to support Vaubois, protect the blockade of Mantua and the communications of the army, and beat Davidowich, who had advanced in the course of the day. In order to succeed in this plan, it was necessary to calculate the hours. Uncertain what might have passed during the day, I thought it best to suppose that everything had been unfortunate on Vaubois' side; that he had been forced, and had taken up a position between Roverbella and Castel-Nuovo. I caused Arcole, which had cost so much blood, to be evacuated; made the army fall back on the right bank of the Adige, leaving on the left bank only one brigade and a few pieces of cannon, and ordered the soldiers to prepare their mess in this position. If the enemy had marched on Rivoli, the bridge over the Adige must have been raised, and the army must have disappeared before Alvinzi, and reached Vaubois in time to assist him. I left bivouacs at Arcole with lighted fires kept up by piquets of the grand guard, in order that Alvinzi should perceive nothing. At four in the morning the army got under arms; but at the same time one of Vaubois' officers brought word that he was at six o'clock the preceding evening still at Bussolengo, and that Davidowich had not moved. That general had commanded one of Wurmser's corps; he remembered the lesson he had received, and was not forward to compromise himself. Alvinzi, however, being informed of the retrograde march of the French about three in the morning, had Arcole and Porcil occupied, and at daylight directed two columns on the two dykes. The firing began about 200 toises from the bridge of Ronco, which the French crossed again in charging-time, fell on the enemy, broke them, and pursued them as far as the outlets of the morasses, which they filled with Austrian dead.

BATTLE OF ARCOLE

Several standards and cannon, and a number of prisoners, were the trophies of this day, on which two more Austrian divisions were defeated. In the evening I, from the same motives and calculations as the preceding day, made the same movements as before, concentrating all my troops on the right bank of the Adige, and leaving only a vanguard on the left bank.

Alvinzi, deceived by a spy who assured him that the French were marching on Mantua and had only left a vanguard at Ronco, debouched from his camp before dawn. At five in the morning, it was known at the French headquarters that Davidowich had made no movement, and that Vaubois was still in the same positions; the army again crossed the bridge; the heads of the columns of the two armies met half way up the dykes; the action was obstinate, and for a moment doubtful, the 75th being broken; the balls reached the bridge. I placed the 32nd in ambush, lying on their faces, in a little wood of willows, along the dyke, near the head of the bridge; they rose at the proper moment, fired a volley, charged bayonets, and overthrew into the morass a close column of 3,000 Croats, who all perished there. Massena, on the left, experienced some vicissitudes; but he marched at the head of his troops, with his hat at the end of his sword by way of a standard, and made a horrible carnage of the division opposed to him. In the afternoon I conceived the decisive moment had at length arrived; for if Vaubois had been defeated this day by Davidowich, I would have been obliged to proceed the next night to his aid and to that of Mantua. Alvinzi would then advance on Verona, and would carry off the honour and benefit of victory; and all the advantages gained during these last three days would be lost; whereas by repulsing Alvinzi beyond Villa-Nuova, I would be enabled to march to the assistance of Vaubois, by Verona. I had the prisoners carefully counted, and recapitulated the losses of the enemy, by which means I convinced myself that the Austrian force had been diminished by upwards of 25,000 men, in the course of these three days; so that henceforth, his number in the field would not exceed those of the French by much more than a third. I ordered the army to march out of the morasses, and to attack the enemy in the plain. The events of these three days had so materially altered the characters of the two armies, that victory was certain. The army passed the bridge constructed at the mouth of the Alpon; Elliot, aide-de-camp to me, had been charged to construct a second; he was killed there. At two o'clock in the afternoon the French army was formed in line, with its left on Arcole, and its right in the direction of Porto Legnago. The enemy was in front, with his right resting on the Alpon and his left on some marshes; he occupied both sides of the Vicenza road. Adjutant-General Lorset had marched from Legnago with 6 or 700 men, four pieces of cannon, and 200 horse, to turn the marshes on which the enemy supported his left. Towards three o'clock, when this detachment was advancing, the cannonade being brisk throughout the line, and the skirmishers engaged,

BATTLE OF ARCOLE

Major Hercule was ordered to proceed with twenty-five Guides and four trumpets across the reeds, and to charge the extreme left of the enemy when the garrison of Legnago should begin to cannonade them in the rear. That officer executed the movement in an able manner, and contributed greatly to the success of the day; the line was broken, the enemy commenced his retreat. The Austrian general had placed 6 or 7,000 men in echelon in his rear, to secure his parks and his retreat; he had not more troops than the French on the field of battle; he was closely pursued all the evening, and had a great number of men taken prisoners. The army passed the night in its position.

Notwithstanding the victories of these three days, it was matter of speculation amongst the generals and superior officers, what orders I would give for the next day; they thought that I would be content with having dispersed the enemy, and would not enter the plains of the Vicentine, but return to Verona by the left bank of the Adige, to march thence against Davidowich and occupy Caldiero, which had been the first object of my manoeuvre. But the enemy's loss had been so severe, during these three days, both in men and confidence, that he was no longer formidable in the plain; at daylight it was perceived that he had retreated on Vicenza; the army pursued him, but, after reaching Villa-Nuova the cavalry alone continued the pursuit, the infantry waiting for reports of the stand which should be made by his rearguard.

I entered the convent of Saint Boniface, the church of which had served as an hospital; between 4 and 500 wounded had been crowded into it, the greater part of them were dead; a cadaverous smell issued from the place. I was retiring, struck with horror, when I heard myself called by my name. Two unfortunate soldiers had been three days amongst the dead, without having had their wounds dressed; they despaired of relief, but were recalled to life at the sight of their General. Every assistance was afforded them.

Having ascertained by the reports that the enemy was in the utmost confusion, was making no stand in any direction, and that his rearguard had already got beyond Montebello, I faced to the left, and proceeded to Verona to attack the Army of the Tyrol. The scouts captured a staff-officer, sent by Davidowich to Alvinzi; he came from the mountains, and supposed himself in the midst of his friends. It was found by his despatches that the enemy had had no communications for three days, and that Davidowich was ignorant of all that had taken place. In the three days' engagements at Arcole, Alvinzi had lost 18,000 men, of whom 6,000 were taken prisoners, four standards, and eighteen pieces of cannon.

The French army re-entered Verona in triumph by the Venice gate, three days after having quitted that city almost clandestinely by the Milan gate. It would be difficult to conceive the astonishment and enthusiasm of the inhabitants; the most declared enemies of the French could not suppress their admiration, and added their homage to that of the patriots. The army, however,

BATTLE OF ARCOLE

made no stay there, but passed the Adige and advanced on Davidowich, who had attacked Bussolengo on the 17th, and driven Vaubois on Castel-Nuovo. Massena marched thither, joined Vaubois, and attacked Rivoli. Augereau marched on Dolce, on the left bank of the Adige, took 1,500 men, two pontoon trains, nine pieces of cannon, and a great quantity of baggage.

But these grand results were not obtained without loss. The army stood more than ever in need of repose; it was not expedient for it to enter the Tyrol and spread itself so far as Trent. It was to be expected that Mantua would open its gates before the Austrian general could form a new army: the garrison of that place had been reduced to half rations; desertion from it had become frequent; the hospitals were crowded to excess; everything announced a speedy surrender: the mortality was dreadful, and diseases daily swept off more men than would have sufficed to win a great battle.

Chapter XIII

NEGOTIATIONS IN 1796

1: With the Republic of Genoa. 2: With the King of Sardinia. 3: With the Duke of Parma. 4: With the Duke of Modena. 5: With the Court of Rome. 6: With the Grand Duke of Tuscany. 7: With the King of Naples. 8: With the Emperor of Germany. 9: Congress of Lombardy. Cispadan Republic.

I

The minority of the aristocracy which governed the Republic of Genoa, the majority of the third-estate, and the whole population of the Riviere di Ponente, were friendly to the French ideas. The city of Genoa was the only city of that state of any strength; it was defended by double walls with bastions, a great quantity of artillery, 6,000 soldiers of the line, and 6,000 national guards. At the first signal of the Senate 30,000 men of the inferior corporations, such as those of the colliers and porters, and the peasants of the valleys of Polcevera, Beragno, and Fontana-Bona, were ready to take up arms in defence of the prince. It would have required an army of 40,000 men, a besieging-train, and two months' works, to have gained possession of this capital. In 1794, 1795, and at the beginning of 1796, the Austro-Sardinian army covered Genoa on the North, and communicated with that city by the Bocchetta; the French army covered it on the West, and communicated with it by the Corniche di Savona. Genoa, thus placed between the two belligerent armies, could with equal facility, receive aid from either, and held the balance between them; had she declared for either, that one would have acquired a great advantage; under these circumstances Genoa possessed great weight in the scale of Italian affairs. The Senate was sensible of all the delicacy of this position, and of all the strength it acquired thereby; it availed itself of this strength to preserve its neutrality, and constantly disregarded the offers as well as the threats of the coalition. The commerce of the city increased, and brought immense wealth into the Republic. But the Port of Genoa had been violated by the English squadron; the catastrophe of the frigate *la Modeste* had made a powerful impression on the minds of the French; the Convention had dissembled, but only waited for a favourable opportunity to exact a memorable reparation. Several of the noble families most attached to France had been banished, which was another insult that the French government had to avenge. After the battle of Loano, in the winter of 1796, the Directory was the more inclined to think the moment favourable, because the extreme poverty of its Army of Italy made it attach great importance to an extraordinary aid of five or six millions. Negotiations on the subject had commenced, when I arrived to take the command of the army; I disapproved of this mean policy, which could never have succeeded, and must necessarily have had the effect of exasperating and disgusting the important population of this capital. 'We must,' said I, 'either scale the ramparts, fix ourselves there by a vigorous *coup de main*, and destroy the aristocracy; or respect its independence, and above all, leave it in possession of its money.' A few days after, the enemy's armies having been driven beyond the Po, and the King of Sardinia having laid down his arms, the Republic of Genoa was at the mercy of France. The Directory would have established democracy there, but the French armies were already too far advanced. The presence of a corps of 15,000 French under the walls of Genoa, and perhaps their stay there for several weeks, would have been necessary to ensure the success of such a revolution.

Nothing was now talked of but the march of Wurmser, who was then crossing Germany and entering the Tyrol. From that time it became necessary to concentrate the Army on the Adige, first for the purpose of defeating Wurmser, and afterwards on account of the manoeuvres in the Tyrol, and Alvinzi's movements to extricate Wurmser when blockaded in Mantua. The army had, moreover, nothing to fear from the Genoese; their rulers were divided amongst themselves, and the people were favourable to us.

Gerola, the Emperor's minister, taking advantage of the removal of the army, and being secretly favoured by the feudatory families, had kindled an insurrection in the Imperial Fiefs, and formed bands of Piedmontese deserters, of vagabonds thrown out of employment by the disbanding of the Piedmontese light troops, and of Austrian prisoners, who, having been ill guarded by the French, had escaped on their route. These bands infested the whole of the Apennines, and the rear of the army. In the course of June it became of urgent importance to put an end to this state of affairs; a detachment of 1,200 men, and my presence at Tortona, proved sufficient to restore order and tranquillity. I then gave instructions to the French minister at Genoa to set negotiations on foot for the purpose of increasing our influence in the government,

NEGOTIATIONS IN 1796

as far as that could be done without rendering the presence of an army necessary.

I required, first, the expulsion of the Austrian minister Gerola; secondly, that of the feudatory families, conformably to one of the statutes of the Republic; and, thirdly, the recall of the banished families.

These negotiations were much protracted. In the meantime five French merchantmen were captured under the Genoese batteries, which did not attempt to protect them. The Senate, alarmed at the menaces of the French agents, sent the senator Vincente Spinola, who was much in favour with the French, to Paris, where, after some negotiation, he signed on 6 October, 1796, a convention with Charles Lacroix, the Minister of exterior relations. All the causes of complaints which France had against Genoa were consigned to oblivion; the Senate paid a contribution of four millions, and recalled the persons banished. This event would have afforded an opportunity, which ought to have been seized, of forming an offensive and defensive alliance with this Republic, adding to the Genoese territory the Imperial Fiefs and Massa di Carara, and requiring a contingent of 4,200 infantry, 400 cavalry, and 200 artillery. But notwithstanding its utility, this system of alliance with oligarchs was repugnant to the feelings of the democrats of Paris. This convention, however, restored tranquillity, which continued up to the time of the convention of Montebello in 1797; and as long as the French army remained in Germany there was no reason to complain of the conduct of the people of Genoa.

2

The armistice of Cherasco had insulated the Austrian army, and enabled the French army to drive it out of Italy, to invest Mantua, and to occupy the line of the Adige. The peace concluded at Paris in the succeeding month of May placed all the fortresses of Piedmont, except Turin, in the power of France. The King of Sardinia thus found himself at the disposal of the Republic. His army was reduced to an effective force of 20,000 men; his paper money threatened both individuals and the state with ruin; his subjects were discontented and divided; even the French ideas had a few partisans. Some politicians wished to revolutionise Piedmont, in order to get rid of all anxiety with respect to the rear of the army, and to increase our means of annoying Austria, but it was impossible to overturn the throne of Sardinia, without direct interference by means of an imposing force; and the scenes which were passing before Mantua were sufficient to occupy all the troops of the Republic in Italy; besides the revolution in Piedmont might draw on a civil war; in which case it would become necessary to leave in Piedmont, in order to overawe the people, more French troops than we could obtain of Piedmontese. In case of retreat, the populace, which would have been thrown into a ferment, would inevitably be guilty of excesses. Besides, might not the Kings of Spain and Prussia become alarmed, at seeing the Republic, from its hatred to monarchs, overthrow with its own hands a prince with whom it had concluded peace only a few days before? These considerations led me to the same result by an opposite road; that of an offensive and defensive treaty of alliance with the King of Sardinia. This plan combined all advantages, and was liable to no objection. In the first place, this treaty was, in itself, a proclamation which would keep the discontented in awe, who would no longer confide in the protestations of the democrats of the army, and their promises of the assistance of France; the country would, therefore, remain in tranquillity. Secondly, a division of fine well-disciplined veteran Piedmontese troops, consisting of 10,000 men, would reinforce the French army and afford new chances of success. Thirdly, the example of the Court of Turin would have a beneficial influence on the Venetians, and contribute to determine them to seek, in an alliance with France, a guarantee for the integrity of their territory and the maintenance of their constitution; and yet the Piedmontese troops, being joined to the French army, would imbibe its spirit, and attach themselves to the general who had led them to victory; at all events they would be hostages placed in the midst of the army as a security for the disposition of the people of Piedmont towards it; and if the King could not maintain himself, placed as he was between the democratic republics of Liguria, Lombardy, and France, his fall would be the result of the nature of things, and not of a political act calculated to excite the resentment of other kings in alliance with France. 'The alliance of France with Sardinia,' said I, 'is like that of a giant embracing a pigmy; if he stifles him, it is against his will, and merely owing to the extreme difference of their organs.'

The Directory was not willing to comprehend the wisdom and profundity of this policy; it authorized the opening of negotiations but threw obstacles in the way of their conclusion. M. Poussielgues, secretary of legation at Genoa, had conferences at Turin during several months; he found the Court disposed to form an alliance with the Republic, but evinced little diplomatic skill in suffering himself to be drawn into concessions which were evidently extravagant. He promised Lombardy to the King of Sardinia. Now it was totally out of the question to think of increasing the territories of that prince, nor should hopes have been held out to him that were not to be realized: he was a sufficient gainer by a treaty which guaranteed the integrity of his kingdom.

When Mantua opened its gates, and I marched on Tolentino to dictate the terms of peace to the Holy See, and place myself in a situation to march on Vienna, I perceived the importance of bringing the affairs of Piedmont to a conclusion and authorized General Clarke to negotiate, with M. de Saint-Marsan, a treaty of offensive and defensive alliance, which was signed at Bologna on 1 March, 1797. The King received from the Republic the guarantee of his estates; he furnished to the French army a contingent of 8,000 infantry, 2,000 cavalry, and twenty pieces of cannon. Having no doubt of the ratification of a treaty ordered by me, the Court of Turin hastened to assemble its contingent, which would have joined the army in Carinthia, but the Directory hesitated to ratify this treaty, and the contingent remained in Piedmont, in cantonments near Novarre, during the whole campaign in 1797.

3

The policy proper to be observed towards the Infant Duke of Parma was prescribed by our relations with Spain; in the first instance an armistice was granted him on 9 May, 1796, and a few months after he signed, at Paris, his peace with the Republic; but the French ministry did not know how to accomplish the object which I had in view. The successes of the Army of Italy had induced the King of Spain to conclude a treaty of offensive and defensive alliance with the Republic, in August, 1792; in consequence of which it would have been easy to prevail on the court of Madrid to send a division of 10,000 men to the Po, to guard the Infant Duke of Parma, and by means of the lure of an increase of territory for that prince, to allow that division to march under the French colours. Its presence would have overawed Rome and Naples, and would have contributed in no small degree towards the success of the military operations. The alliance with Spain having determined the English to evacuate the Mediterranean, the French and Spanish squadrons were masters of that sea, which facilitated the movements of the Spanish troops into Italy. The sight of a Spanish division in the ranks of the French army, would have had a beneficial influence on the decision of the Senate, with respect to an alliance with France, and reinforced the army with 10,000 Sclavonians.

4

The armistice of Milan of 20 May had terminated hostilities with the Duke of Modena; the French army was not numerous, the country it occupied was immense, and to detach two or three battalions for any secondary object would have been blameable. The armistice with Modena placed all the resources of that duchy at the disposal of the army, and did not require the employment of any troops to maintain public tranquillity. The commander d'Est, invested with the duke's powers, commenced negotiations at Paris for a definitive peace: the French ministry prudently took care not to expedite its conclusion. The Duke, who was entirely devoted to the Austrians, had retired to Venice, and the Regency, which governed his states, had passed several convoys of provisions into Mantua, during the raising of the blockade, in the beginning of August and latter part of September. As soon as I was informed of this direct infringement of the armistice, I complained to the Regency, who in vain attempted to justify themselves under colour of certain ancient treaties. Under these circumstances, however, a detachment from the garrison of Mantua, which had passed the Po at Borgo-forte, was cut off; they marched to Reggio on 20 October, intending to proceed into Tuscany; the inhabitants of Reggio shut the gates of the town. The detachment took refuge in the fort of Monte Cherigio, where the patriots surrounded it, and forced it to lay down arms. Two of the inhabitants of Reggio were killed in this petty encounter, and were the first Italians who sealed the liberty of their country with their blood! The prisoners being conducted to Milan by a detachment of the national guard of Reggio, were there received in triumph by the congress of Lombardy, the national guard of Milan and myself. Several civic feasts were given on this occasion, which contributed to heighten the enthusiasm of the Italians. Reggio proclaiming its liberty; the people of Modena wished to follow the example, but were restrained by the garrison: in this state of affairs there was no choice. I declared that the armistice of Milan had been violated by the conduct of the Regency in revictualling Mantua; I caused the three duchies of Reggio, Modena and Mirandola to be occupied by my troops and on 8 October, by virtue of my right of conquest proclaimed their independence. This resolution improved the situation of the army, by substituting, for a malevolent regency, a provisional government wholly devoted to the French cause. National guards, consisting of warm patriots, were raised and armed in all the towns of the three duchies.

5

Hostilities having ceased with Rome, by the armistice of Bologna of 23 June, 1796, that Court sent Monsignor Petrarchi to Paris. After spending several weeks in conferences, that minister sent to his Court the terms of peace proposed by the Directory. The assembly of Cardinals was of opinion that they contained matters contrary to the faith, and were inadmissible. Monsignor Petrarchi was recalled. In September the negotiations were renewed at Florence; the commissioners from government to the army were furnished with the powers of the Directory. At one of the first conferences, they presented to Monsignor Galeppi, the Pope's plenipotentiary, a treaty in sixty articles, as a *sine qua non*, declaring that they could alter nothing in it. This was also judged at Rome, to contain matters contrary to the faith; Monsignor Galeppi was recalled, and the negotiations were broken off on 25 September. The Court of Rome, no longer doubting but that the French government had resolved on its destruction, abandoned itself to despair, and determined to ally itself exclusively with the Court of Vienna. It began by suspending the armistice of Bologna; it had still sixteen millions to pay, which were on their way to Bologna, where they were to be delivered over to the treasury of the army. These convoys of money returned to Rome, where their re-entrance was a triumph. Monsignor Albani set out for Vienna on 6 October, to solicit the support of that court; the Roman Princes offered patriotic gifts, and raised regiments. The Pope dispersed proclamations to kindle a holy war in case the territory of the sacred see should be attacked. All these efforts of the Court of Rome were considered capable of producing an army of about 10,000 men, the worst troops possible; but this court relied on the King of Naples, who secretly engaged to support it with an army of 30,000 men; and although the enmity and bad faith of the Cabinet of the Two Sicilies were known to the Vatican, its aid was invoked: 'All means seem good to them, in their delirium,' wrote the minister Cacault; 'they would cling to red hot iron.' This state of affairs had a pernicious effect on all Italy.

I had no need of this increase of difficulties; I was already menaced by Alvinzi, whose troops assembled in the Tyrol and on the Piave. I reproached the French ministry with having left me ignorant of negotiations which I alone was able to direct. Had I been appointed to conduct them, as ought to have been the case, I would have delayed the opening of them for two or three weeks, in order to have received 16,000,000 due from the Holy See, by virtue of the armistice of Bologna. I would not have suffered spiritual and temporal affairs to be mingled in the treaty, because when once the latter, which were the most essential, were settled, the delay of a few months in coming to an arrangement with respect to the former was of no consequence; but the mischief was done. The government acknowledged this, and invested me with the authority necessary to remedy it, if possible. The object was to gain time to calm the agitation of the passions, to restore confidence and to prevent the effects of the alarm excited in the Vatican. I directed M. Cacault, the French agent at Rome, to disavow confidentially all the spiritual part of the negotiations of Paris and Florence; to intimate that I was instructed with the negotiation; and that neither the Directory nor the commissioners had anything more to do with it, but myself alone. These overtures produced a good effect. To make a greater impression, I went to Ferrara, on 21 October, alighted at the house of Cardinal Mattei, archbishop of that city, and had several conferences with him; I convinced him of my pacific intentions and got him to set off for Rome to carry words of peace directly to the Pope. A few days after, the battle of Arcole put an end to all the hopes which had been raised in Italy by Alvinzi's Army. I judged this a favourable moment for concluding the affairs of Rome; I proceeded to Bologna with 1,500 French and 4,000 Cispadans and Lombards, threatening to march on Rome; but the Court of Rome this time despised my threats; it was in correspondence with its minister at Vienna for the purpose of treating, and knew that two new and

NEGOTIATIONS IN 1796

powerful armies were advancing into Italy. The cardinal and the Austrian Minister at Rome said openly, 'The Pope will evacuate Rome, if necessary; for the farther the French general removes from the Adige, the nearer we shall approach our deliverance.' In fact, a few days after, I, being informed of Alvinzi's movements, repassed the Po, and proceeded with all possible speed to Verona. But the battle of Rivoli, in the month of January, 1797, destroyed the hopes of the enemies of France for ever. Mantua shortly after opened its gates; the moment for punishing Rome had now arrived; a small Gallo-Italian army marched on the Apennines. All disputes between France and the Court of Rome were at length ended by the treaty of Tolentino, as will be seen in Chapter XV.

6

The Grand Duke of Tuscany was the first prince in Europe who acknowledged the Republic. When the army invaded Italy, he was at peace with France; his states, situated beyond the Apennines, had no influence on the theatre of the war. Although a French brigade advanced on Leghorn, after Mantua was invested, it was only to drive out the English traders, and facilitate the deliverance of Corsica; in other respects the independence of the states of Tuscany was not infringed. The garrison of Leghorn never amounted to more than 1,800 men. It was, no doubt, a sacrifice, to employ three battalions on a secondary object, but the 57th demi-brigade, which had suffered severely and needed repose, was at first put on this duty. Manfredini, the Grand Duke's first minister, exerted much talent and activity in removing the obstacles which might have been prejudicial to his master, who was, on that occasion, indebted to him for the preservation of his states. Three or four conventions of little importance were signed between the French general, and the Marquis of Manfredini; by the last, signed at Bologna, Leghorn was evacuated by the French garrison; on this occasion the Grand Duke poured two millions into the chest of the army to liquidate old accounts. At the treaty of Campo Formio, this prince preserved the integrity of his states. He had suffered some alarm, but no damage, during the war of Italy; care was taken to do him no injury, as well from respect for existing treaties, as from a desire to mitigate the animosity entertained by the house of Lorraine against the Republic, and to detach it from the English.

7

When the French army had arrived on the Adige, and Middle and Lower Italy were thereby cut off from Germany, Prince Pignatelli came to headquarters, to demand an armistice for the King of Naples, which he obtained.

NEGOTIATIONS IN 1796

It was signed on 5 June, 1796. The Neapolitan division of 2,400 horse, which formed part of Beaulieu's army, went into cantonments round Brescia, in the midst of the French army. A Neapolitan plenipotentiary went to Paris to negotiate and sign a definite treaty with the Republic. The conclusion of this treaty was impeded by the ill-timed chicanery practised at Paris, and also through the system of bad faith constantly pursued at the Court of the Two Sicilies. The Directory ought to have thought themselves extremely fortunate in disarming the King of Naples, a prince who had 60,000 men under arms, and could have spared from 25 to 30,000 to march on the Po. I incessantly urged the conclusion of this treaty. The Ministry of exterior relations at Paris wanted a contribution of some millions, which the Court of Naples very reasonably refused to pay; but in the course of September, when it became known that the alliance between Spain and France and the deliverance of Corsica from the English yoke had determined the Cabinet of Saint James's to recall its squadrons from the Mediterranean, which left the command of the Mediterranean and the Adriatic to the Toulon fleets, the Court of Naples was alarmed, and subscribed to all that the Directory required; peace was signed on 8 October. But the hatred and insincerity of this cabinet, and its disregard of its signature and treaties were such, that, long after the peace, it took a pleasure in alarming Italy by movements of troops on her frontiers, and offensive demonstrations, as if war had actually existed. It would be difficult to describe the indignation excited by this want of all decency and contempt of all human engagements, which eventually brought on the ruin of that cabinet.

8

The French government charged me in the beginning of September, when the Armies of the Rhine and Sambre and Meuse were still in Germany, to write to the Emperor, that unless he would consent to peace, I would destroy his naval establishments at Fiume and Trieste. There was no advantage to be expected from so unbecoming a step. At a later period, when the Armies of the Sambre and Meuse and Rhine had been forced to retreat into France, and the *têtes-de-pont* of Kehl and Huningen were besieged, Moreau proposed an armistice, which the Archduke refused, declaring that he claimed the possession of the two *têtes-de-pont*; but as Marshal Wurmser, with nearly 30,000 Austrians, was blockaded in Mantua, and Alvinzi's efforts to relieve him had failed at Arcole, the Directory conceived hopes of getting the principle of a general armistice acknowledged, by which France should preserve Huningen and Kehl, and Austria Mantua. General Clarke consequently received the necessary powers for proceeding to Vienna to propose this general armistice, which was to last till June, 1797. The sieges of Kehl and Huningen were to be raised, and Mantua placed *in statu quo*. Austrian and French commissioners were daily to send the provisions necessary for the troops and inhabitants into the place. General Clarke arrived at Milan on 1 December, to make arrangements with me; I was instructed to adopt all necessary means for procuring this plenipotentiary the passports for which he had occasion. I said to him, 'It is easy to force the enemy to raise the sieges of Kehl and Huningen; the Archduke has only 40,000 men before Kehl; Moreau must march out of his intrenched camp at break of day with 60,000 men, beat the Archduke, take his parks, and destroy all his works; that moreover Kehl and the *tête-de-pont* of Huningen were not equivalent to Mantua; that it would be impossible to prove the number of inhabitants, men, women, and children, or even that of the garrison; that Marshal Wurmser, by reducing everybody to half allowance, would save in six months wherewithal to subsist six months longer; that if the armistice was intended to pave the way for negotiations for peace, that was a new reason for not proposing it whilst Mantua was in the power of Austria; that it was, therefore, necessary to gain a victory under the walls of Kehl, and to wait for the surrender of Mantua; after which an armistice and peace might be offered.' But the orders of government were positive. General Clarke wrote to the Emperor and sent him a letter from the Directory, in consequence of which, Baron Vincent, aide-de-camp to the Emperor, and General Clarke, met on 3 January at Vicenza, where they had two conferences. Baron Vincent declared that the Emperor could not receive at Vienna a plenipotentiary from the Republic, which he did not acknowledge; that he could not, moreover, separate from his allies; and lastly, that if the French minister had any communication to make, he might apply to M. Giraldi, the Austrian minister at Turin. Thus, fortunately, this disastrous idea of an armistice was eluded by the enemy. The French minister had scarcely reached the Adige on his return, when Alvinzi began to manoeuvre to raise the blockade of Mantua, which occasioned the battles of Rivoli and la Favorite, as may be seen in Chapter XIV.

Nevertheless, the Cabinet of the Luxembourg chose to see in this answer of Baron Vincent's, although it does not appear wherefore, a door opened to negotiation; and in the course of January, 1797, the Directory sent instructions to General Clarke for the peace he was authorized to sign, on condition, first, that the Emperor should renounce Belgium and the Luxembourg country; secondly, that he should ratify the cession of Liége to the Republic, and some other little acquisitions that had been made; thirdly, that he should promise his influence to give the Stadtholder an indemnity in Germany; fourthly, that the Republic should restore to Austria all her Italian dominions. These conditions were not approved of by me; I thought that the Republic had a right to require the limits of the Rhine and a state in Italy to support the French influence, and keep the Republic of Genoa, the King of Sardinia, and

NEGOTIATIONS IN 1796

the Pope dependent on France; for Italy could never be looked upon as in the situation it stood in before the war. If the French should ever again pass the Alps without having kept a powerful auxiliary there, the aristocracies of Genoa and Venice, and the King of Sardinia, would unite still more closely with Austria by indissoluble ties, influenced by the necessity of securing their internal existence against democratical and popular ideas. Venice, who for a century had possessed no influence in the balance of Europe, now enlightened by experience and the danger she had recently incurred, would collect energy, treasures, and armies to reinforce the Emperor and to repress ideas of liberty and independence in the Terra-firma. Pontiffs, king, and nobles, would combine to defend their privileges, and prevent modern ideas from passing the Alps.

Three months later, I signed preliminaries of peace, on the conditions of the limits of the Rhine; that is to say, with the fortress of Mentz, and an additional population of 1,500,000 souls to the Republic, beyond what the Directory demanded, and the existence of one or two democratical republics in Italy, communicating with Switzerland, barring all Italy, from North to South, from the Alps to the Po, surrounding the King of Sardinia, and covering Middle and Lower Italy along the line of the Po. In case of necessity the French armies, debouching by Genoa, Parma, Modena and Bologna, would at once reach the Piave, after turning the Mincio, Mantua, and the Adige. This Republic, with 3,000,000 of inhabitants, would secure the influence of the French over the 3,000,000 of inhabitants of the kingdom of Sardinia, and the 3,000,000 belonging to the States of the Church and to Tuscany, and even over the kingdom of Naples.

9

The line of conduct to be observed towards the people of Lombardy was a matter of delicacy; France had determined to conclude peace the moment the Emperor would renounce Belgium and the Luxembourg; and restore Lombardy to him at that price. No engagement, therefore, could be contracted, no guarantee given contrary to these secret arrangements of the cabinet. On the other hand, the country had to support all the expenses of the army, which not only absorbed its revenues, but occasioned additional burthens of greater or less amount, according to the longer or shorter stay of the troops in particular places. In France the indirect taxes had been suppressed; the system of contributions was very insufficient; the treasury was independent; everything was conducted in a disorderly, corrupt and unskilful manner; every branch of the public service was left unprovided for; it became necessary to send contributions from Italy; very important sums to assist the Army of the Rhine, the Toulon and Brest fleets, and even the establishments at Paris. In

NEGOTIATIONS IN 1796

Italy, however, it became essential to counterbalance the influence of the Austrian party, composed of the nobility, and of a part of the clergy, on which the influence of Rome was exerted with more or less success. I supported the party that aimed at the independence of Italy, but without committing myself; and, notwithstanding the critical state of the times, I captivated the opinion of the majority of these people. I not only paid great respect to religion, but I omitted nothing that was calculated to conciliate the minds of the clergy. I knew when and how to use the talisman, the magic word of liberty, and, above all, of national independence, which from the days of Rome had never ceased to be dear to the Italians. I intrusted the administration of the provinces, towns and communes, to the inhabitants, choosing the most eligible men and those who enjoyed the greatest popularity and I confided the police to the national guards, who throughout Italy, were raised in imitation of those of France, under the Italian colours, red, white and green. Milan had been of the Guelph party, and this was still the general disposition of the minds of the people. The patriots daily increased in number, the French ideas made rapid progress, and the public spirit was such that after Wurmser's destruction, I authorized the Congress of Lombardy to levy a legion of 3,000 men. In the course of November, the Polish generals Zayoncheck and Dombrowski, arrived from Poland, with a great number of their officers, to offer their services to Italy; upon which the congress was authorized to raise a Polish legion of 3,000 men. These troops were never brought into the field to oppose the Austrians in line; but they served to maintain public tranquillity, and to keep the Pope's army in check. When difficulties afterwards arose, which induced me to proclaim the Cispadan republic, the Congress of Lombardy was much alarmed; but it was satisfactorily explained that the difference was occasioned by a difference of circumstances. The army's line of operations did not pass through the Cispadan territory; and, in short, it was not difficult to convince the most enlightened persons, that even had it been true that this was connected with the wish of the French government not to form engagements which the fortune of war might possibly prevent it from fulfilling, that ought not to alarm them; for after all, it was very evident that the fate of the French party in Italy depended on the chances of battles; that, moreover, this guarantee which France thenceforth gave to the Cispadan republic was equally favourable to them; because, should it one day happen that the course of events should oblige France to consent to the return of the Austrians into Lombardy the Cispadan republic would then be a refuge for the Lombards, and an altar on which the sacred fire of Italian liberty would be preserved from extinction.

Reggio, Modena, Bologna, and Ferrara, situate on the right bank of the Po, composed the whole extent of the country from the Adriatic to the states of Parma, by which they were joined to the Republic of Genoa, and by the latter to France. If there was an apprehension of the necessity of restoring Lombardy to Austria, in order to facilitate peace, the importance of maintaining a democratical republic on the right bank of the Po, against which the house of Austria could bring forward no right or claim, was the more clearly perceived.

These four states existed several months in independence, under the government of their municipal authorities; a junta of general safety, composed of the Capraras, etc., was organized to concert defensive measures, and keep the disaffected in awe. A congress composed of a hundred deputies assembled at Modena in the course of November; the colours of Lombardy were displayed as the Italian colours; some fundamental principles of government were resolved on; that is to say, the suppression of the feudal system, equality, and the rights of man. These small republics formed a confederacy for common defence, and taxed themselves to raise an Italian legion 3,000 strong. The congress was composed of persons of all conditions; cardinals, nobles, merchants, lawyers, and men of letters. Their ideas expanded insensibly; the press was free, and at length, at the commencement of January, 1797, after some resistance, local prejudices were overcome, and these people united in a single state, entitled the Cispadan republic, of which Bologna was declared the capital; and a representative constitution was adopted. The effect of this step was felt in Rome. The organization and spirit of these new republicans were an effectual barrier against the principles propagated by the Holy See, and against the troops it was assembling in Romagna. The Congress of Lombardy formed an alliance with the Cispadan republic, which at this period fixed the attention of all the people of Italy. Of all the Italian cities, Bologna is that which has constantly shown the greatest energy, and the most considerable share of real information. In February, 1797, after the peace of Tolentino, Romagna, having been ceded by the Pope, was naturally reunited to the Cispadan republic, which augmented its population to near two million of souls.

Such was the state of Italy at the end of the year 1796 and in the spring of 1797, when the French army resolved to pass the Julian Alps, and to march on Vienna.

Chapter XIV

BATTLE OF RIVOLI

Affair of Rome. Situation of the Austrian army. Situation of the French army. Plan of operations adopted by the Court of Vienna. Action of Saint-Michel (12 Jan.). Battle of Rivoli (14 Jan.). Passage of the Adige by General Provera; and his march on Mantua (14 Jan.). Battle of la Favorite (16 Jan.). Capitulation of Mantua (2 Feb.).

The animosity of the Senate of Venice against the French cause increased daily; but a two-fold dread fettered its enmity; the presence of the victorious army, and the mental agitation that pervaded most of its towns in the Terra-firma. However, it raised levies of Sclavonians; new battalions successively arrived in the Lagunes. The two parties were now face to face, in all the towns of the Terra-firma. The castles of Verona and Brescia were occupied by French troops. Some commotions which had happened at Bergamo showed the necessity of occupying the citadel. General Baraguey d'Hilliers took possession of it. This precaution, according to my hopes of the speedy surrender of Mantua, seemed sufficient. I did not wish to engage the Senate in discussions which would have led to new difficulties, previously to the fall of that place. Thus both parties were still dissembling.

The negotiations with Rome were broken off; experience had proved that nothing could be obtained of that court but by the presence of force. It was requisite to put an end to this state of uncertainty, which kept up a ferment in Italy. Before the arrival of the new Austrian armies, 3,000 French and 4,000 Italians passed the Po and entered Bologna on 6 January; I had arrived there from Milan. Manfredini, first minister to the Grand Duke of Tuscany, hastened thither to attend to the interest of that prince, and returned to Florence convinced that the French were marching on Rome. The Vatican did not become the dupe of these menaces, being acquainted with the plans adopted at Vienna, and in hopes of their success. The Austrian minister encouraged the Court of Rome. Nothing, he said, could be more favourable to their views than to draw the French into the heart of Italy; the Pope must even quit Rome, if necessary; the defeat of the French on the Adige would thereby be rendered the more inevitable; it was on the banks of the Tiber that the fate of Italy was to be decided!

In fact, Alvinzi was daily receiving considerable reinforcements; the Paduan, Trevisan, and Bassanese countries were covered with his troops. Austria had employed the two months which had elapsed since the battle of Arcole, in bringing into the Frioul divisions drafted from the banks of the Rhine, where the French armies were in winter-quarters. A national impulse had been given to the whole monarchy. Several battalions of excellent sharp-shooters were raised in the Tyrol. They were easily persuaded that it was incumbent on them to defend their territory and reconquer Italy, which country was so essential to the prosperity of their mountains. The successes of Austria in Germany, in the last campaign, and her defeats in Italy, had both, in different ways, animated the public spirit of her subjects. The great towns offered battalions of volunteers: Vienna raised four battalions, who received from the Empress colours embroidered with her own hands: they lost them, but not before they had defended them with honour. At the beginning of January, 1797, the Austrian army of Italy consisted of eight divisions of infantry, of equal strength, to which were attached several brigades of light cavalry, and a division of cavalry of reserve; making in all from 65 to 70,000 fighting men (sixty-four battalions and thirty squadrons), and 6,000 Tyrolese, besides 24,000 men of the garrison of Mantua; making a total of from 96 to 100,000 men.

The French army had been reinforced since the battle of Arcole by two demi-brigades of infantry from the coast of Provence, of which the 57th formed part, and by a regiment of cavalry; in all 7,000 men; which compensated for the loss sustained at Arcole and in the blockade of Mantua. It was formed in five divisions: Joubert commanded one of them, and occupied Montebaldo, Rivoli, and Bussolengo; Rey, with a less numerous division, was in reserve at Dezenzano; Massena was at Verona, with a vanguard at Saint-Michel; Augereau at Legnago, with a vanguard at Bevilacqua; Serrurier was blockading Mantua. These five divisions amounted to 45,000 men, under arms, of whom only 30,000 belonged to the Army of Observation. Joubert had covered la Corona with intrenchments; Verona, Legnago, Peschiera, and Pizzighettone, were in a good state of defence; the citadels of Brescia and Bergamo, the fort of Fuentes, the citadel of Ferrara, and fort Urbino, were likewise occupied by the French, whose gun-boats also rendered them masters of the four lakes of Garda, Como, Lugano, and Maggiore.

BATTLE OF RIVOLI

Wurmser had attacked by three debouchés, that is to say, by the road of the Chiesa, by Montebaldo, and the valley of the Adige. His columns were to join at Mantua. A few months after, Alvinzi had entered Italy with two armies, one advancing by the Tyrol, the other by the Piave, the Brenta, and the Adige; they were to join at Verona. The Court of Vienna adopted this time a new plan, connected with the operations of Rome, and ordered two grand attacks to be made, the principal one by Montebaldo, the second on the Lower Adige by the plains of the Paduan country; they were to be independent of each other. The two corps-d'armée were to unite before Mantua. The principal one was to debouch by the Tyrol; if it defeated the French army it would arrive under the walls of Mantua, and would there find the corps which would have reached that place by crossing the Adige. If the principal attack should fail, and the second should succeed, the siege of Mantua would still be raised and the place victualled; this corps-d'armée would then throw itself into the Seraglio, and establish its communications with Rome; Wurmser would take the command of the army which was forming in Romagna, with his 5,000 cavalry, his staff, and his numerous train of field-pieces. The great number of generals, officers, and dismounted cavalry, who were in Mantua, would serve to discipline the Pope's army, and form a diversion, which would compel the French to have two armies also, one on the right and the other on the left bank of the Po. A very intelligent secret agent sent from Vienna to Mantua, was arrested by a sentinel as he was passing the last post of the blockading army. He was forced to give up his despatches, although he had swallowed them; they were inclosed in a ball of sealing-wax, and consisted of a small letter written in very minute characters, and signed by the Emperor Francis. He informed Wurmser that he would be relieved without delay; at all events, he ordered him not to capitulate, but rather to evacuate the place, pass the Po, proceed into the Pope's territories, and there take the command of the army of the Holy See.

Pursuant to the plan adopted by the Court of Vienna, Alvinzi commanded the principal attack, at the head of 5,000 men, and advanced his head-quarters from Bassano to Roveredo; General Provera took the command of the corps-d'armée destined to act on the Lower Adige, which was formed of three divisions, and 20,000 strong. He fixed his head-quarters at Padua. On 12 January his left division, commanded by Bayalitsch, took up a position at Caldiero; and Hohenzollern, with the vanguard, at Montagnana. On the 12th, Hohenzollern marched on Bevilacqua, where he found the French vanguard commanded by the brave General Duphot, who, after a slight resistance, retreated behind the Adige, passing the bridges of Porto Legnago. Bayalitsch's division attacked Saint-Michel: it consisted of eight battalions and six squadrons. Massena marched to the aid of his vanguard; the Austrians were broken, and hotly pursued as far as Caldiero, leaving 900 prisoners.

BATTLE OF RIVOLI

Having been informed, at Bologna, by the agents from Venice, of the movement of the Austrian army on Padua, I had ordered the Italian troops to encamp on the frontiers of the Transpadan country, to keep the Pope's army in check; and had directed the 3,000 French from Bologna on Ferrara, where they had passed the Po at Ponte di Lagoscuro. I had crossed that river at Borgo-Forte, and proceeded to head-quarters at Roverbella. I arrived at Verona during the action of Saint-Michel. In the evening I ordered Massena to withdraw his whole division behind Verona in the course of the night. The enemy was in operation; it was therefore necessary to keep all the troops beyond the defile, that they might be able to march without delay to whatever point the true attack should be made on. During the night I received from Legnago a report that the Austrian army was in movement on the Lower Adige, that its general staff was there, and that two pontoon trains had been seen. General Duphot's report left no doubt as to the numerous forces deployed before him; he had seen above 12,000 men, and supposed that they were only the first line. Joubert sent word from la Corona, that he had been attacked during the whole of the 12th, but that he had kept the enemy in check and repulsed him: and this seemed to confirm the opinion that the true attack was on the Lower Adige.

The enemy had not yet unmasked his plans, and the moment for adopting a decisive course had not yet arrived. The troops held themselves in readiness for a nocturnal march. The division encamped at Dezenzano proceeded on the 13th to Castel-Nuovo, to wait for fresh orders. The news from the Chiesa was satisfactory as to that point. It rained very heavily; at ten o'clock the troops were under arms, but I had not yet determined in what direction I should move them; whether they were to march up or down the banks of the Adige. At ten in the evening the reports from Montebaldo and the Lower Adige arrived. Joubert intimated that on the 13th, at nine o'clock in the morning, the enemy had deployed numerous forces; that he had fought all day; that his position was very much confined; that he had been fortunate enough to maintain his ground; but that, at two in the afternoon, perceiving that he was outflanked on his left, by the march of an Austrian division along the lake of Garda, which threatened to place itself between him and Peschiera, and on the right by another division, which had marched along the left bank of the Adige, constructed a bridge near Dolce, a league from Rivoli, passed the river, and was filing along the left bank, past the foot of Monte Magnone, to carry the level of Rivoli, he had considered it indispensably necessary to send a brigade to secure this important level, the key of the whole position; and that at four o'clock he had likewise judged it necessary to follow this movement in retreat, in order to reach the level of Rivoli, by daylight; that he should be obliged to evacuate his position in the night and retreat on the Lower Adige, unless he received orders to the contrary. Provera had lined the

BATTLE OF RIVOLI

left bank with troops, and a fire of musquetry was kept up on each side. The enemy's plan was now unmasked. It was evident that he was operating with two corps; the principal one on Montebaldo, and a minor one on the Lower Adige. Augereau's division appeared sufficient to dispute the passage of the river with Provera, and defend it against him; but on the Montebaldo side the danger was imminent; there was not a moment to lose, for the enemy was about to effect a junction with his artillery and cavalry, by taking possession of the level of Rivoli, and if he could be attacked before he could get possession of that important point, he would be obliged to fight without artillery or cavalry. All the troops were therefore put in march to reach Rivoli by daybreak; I proceeded to the same point, and arrived there at two in the morning.

The weather had cleared up; the moon shone brilliantly; I ascended several heights, and observed the lines of the enemy's fires, which filled the whole country between the Adige and the lake of Garda, and reddened the atmosphere. I clearly distinguished five camps, each composed of a column, which had commenced their movements the preceding day. From the fires of the bivouacs I calculated that there must be from 40 to 45,000 men. The French could not bring more than 22,000 men into action on this field; this was a great disproportion; but then the French had the advantage of sixty pieces of cannon and several regiments of cavalry. It seemed evident from the positions of the five bivouacs of the enemy, that Alvinzi would not attack before ten in the morning. The first column, that of Luzignan, on the right, was at a great distance; its intention seemed to be to get behind the level of Rivoli in order to surround it; it could not reach its destination before ten o'clock. The second column, that of Liptay, seemed to intend to attack the position on the left of the level. The third, that of Koblos, was spread along the foot of Monte Magnone, in the direction of Saint-Mark's chapel. The fourth column was composed of fourteen battalions, and of the artillery, cavalry, and baggage of the army; it had passed the Adige at Dolce, having marched down the right bank to the foot of Monte Magnone: it was now opposite Osteria della Dugana, in echelons near the hamlet of Incanole, at the foot of the level of Rivoli: it was to debouch by this road, and thus Alvinzi would have united his infantry, artillery and cavalry. The fifth column, under Wukassowich, was on the left bank of the Adige, opposite the Venetian Chiesa.

Upon this general view I formed my plan. I ordered Joubert, who had evacuated Saint-Mark's chapel on Monte Magnone, and who now occupied the level of Rivoli only with a rear guard, to resume the offensive forthwith, to regain possession of the chapel without waiting for daylight, and to repulse the fourth column, under Ocskay, as far as possible. Ten Croats, having been informed of the evacuation of Saint-Mark's by a prisoner, had just entered the chapel, when Joubert sent General Vial up to it, about four o'clock

BATTLE OF RIVOLI

in the morning, and retook it. The firing began with a regiment of Croats, and successively with the whole of Ocskay's column, which by daylight was repulsed as far as the middle of the ridge of Monte Magnone. The third Austrian column, that of Koblos, then hastened its march, and reached the heights on the left of the level of Rivoli a little before nine o'clock, but without artillery. The 14th and 85th French demi-brigades, which were in line in this position, had each a battery. The 14th, which occupied the right, repulsed the enemy's attacks; the 85th was outflanked and broken. I hastened to Massena's division, which, having marched all night, was taking a little rest in the village of Rivoli, led it against the enemy, and in less than half an hour this column was beaten and put to flight at half past ten. Liptay's column hastened to the aid of that of Koblos. Quasdanowich, who was at the bottom of the valley, perceived that Joubert had left no troops at Saint-Mark's chapel, that he had advanced in pursuit of Ocskay, and that the firing approached the level of Rivoli; he therefore considered the opportunity favourable for debouching. He detached three battalions to climb the heights up to the chapel, and two to protect the passage of his cavalry and artillery. The victory depended on the success of this enterprise, but its execution was very difficult, it was an absolute escalade. Joubert ordered three battalions to run back, who reached the chapel before those of the enemy, and repulsed them to the bottom of the valley. The French battery of fifteen pieces of cannon, placed at the level of Rivoli, overwhelmed all who offered to debouch, with grapeshot. Colonel Leclerc charged with 300 horse in platoons, and Major Lasalle, farther on, with 200 hussars; the intrepidity of these charges decided the success of the day; the enemy was overthrown into the ravine; all who had debouched, infantry, cavalry, and artillery, were taken. Half the army, consisting of the columns of Quasdanowich and Wukassowich, not having been able to debouch, became useless and afforded no assistance. In the meantime, the first column, that of Luzignan, was coming up to its appointed position; it had fallen in with the French reserve of Dezenzano, composed of the 57th and 58th, in position at Orza, and left one of its brigades to keep them in check. The other brigade, 5,000 strong, deployed on the heights of Pipolo, on both sides of the Verona road, behind the level of Rivoli, supporting its right on the Adige. These troops had no artillery; they thought they had turned the French army; but it was too late; scarcely had they arrived on the height when they witnessed the rout of Ocskay, Koblos, and Liptay; they then foresaw the fate which awaited them, and which they had no means of avoiding. They were first cannonaded by fifteen twelve-pounders of the reserve, for a quarter of an hour, and immediately afterwards attacked and entirely taken. The second brigade of this column, which had been left in the rear to oppose the reserve of Dezenzano, then began to retreat; it was pursued and dispersed, and the greater part killed or taken. It was two o'clock in the afternoon, the

BATTLE OF RIVOLI

enemy was everywhere defeated, and dreadfully cut up. Joubert advanced with such rapidity that at one moment it was supposed that the whole of Alvinzi's army was taken. La Scaliera was the only retreat open to the enemy; but their general, aware of the danger he stood in, faced about with a reserve, checked Joubert, and even made him give ground a little. The battle was won; the French had taken the twelve pieces of cannon which debouched by Incanole, several colours and 7,000 prisoners. Two detachments of the 18th and 32nd which were joining the army, had fallen in with Luzignan's division whilst it was cutting off the Verona road. They spread a report in the rear that the French army was surrounded and lost. This day I was several times surrounded by the enemy; I had several horses killed. General Chabot occupied Verona with a few men.

On the same day, Provera constructed a bridge at Anghiari, near Legnago, passed the river and marched on Mantua; leaving a reserve to guard his bridges. Augereau could not attack them until the 15th; he then had an engagement, which lasted several hours, killed or took all the guard, and burned the pontoons. It is difficult to prevent an enemy who is provided with pontoons from passing a river, when the object of the army defending the passage is to cover a siege; the latter should have taken measures for reaching an intermediate position between the river which it defends and the place it covers, before the enemy. As soon as Provera had passed the Adige, Augereau should have directed his march on the Molinella, where he would have arrived before Provera. Being informed, on the 14th, at two o'clock in the afternoon, in the midst of the battle of Rivoli, that Provera was constructing a bridge at Anghiari, I immediately foresaw what was about to take place. I left the task of pursuing Alvinzi on the following day to Massena, Murat, and Joubert, and instantly marched with four regiments to station myself before Mantua. I had thirteen leagues to march. I entered Roverbella as Provera arrived before Saint-George. Hohenzollern with the vanguard had presented himself on the 16th, at break of day, at the gate of Saint-George, at the head of a regiment wearing white cloaks; he knew that this suburb was merely covered by a simple line of countervallation, and was in hopes to surprise it. Miollis, who commanded there, had no guard except towards the city; he knew that a French division was on the Adige, and thought the enemy far distant. Hohenzollern's hussars resembled those of the first French hussar regiment. But an old serjeant of the garrison of Saint-George, who was gathering wood about two hundred yards from the walls, observed this cavalry; he conceived doubts which he communicated to a drummer who accompanied him; it seemed to them that the white cloaks were too new for Berchini's regiment. In this uncertainty these brave fellows threw themselves into Saint-George, crying, 'To arms, and shut the barrier': Hohenzollern galloped up, but he was too late; he was recognized, and fired upon with grape. The troops

BATTLE OF RIVOLI

speedily manned the parapets. At noon Provera surrounded the place. The brave Miollis, with 1,500 men, defended himself all day, and thus gave time for the succours from Rivoli to arrive.

Provera communicated with Mantua by means of a bark which crossed the lake, and concerted operations for the ensuing day. On the 16th, as soon as it was day, Wurmser made a sortie with the garrison, and took up a position at la Favorite. At one o'clock in the morning, I stationed General Victor, with the four regiments he had brought with him, between la Favorite and Saint-George, to prevent the garrison of Mantua from joining the succouring army. Serrurier, at the head of the troops of the blockade, attacked the garrison; Victor's division attacked the army of succour; it was in this battle that the 57th earned the title of *Terrible*. They attacked the Austrian line, and overthrew all who attempted to resist; by two o'clock in the afternoon the garrison was driven back into the place, and Provera capitulated and laid down his arms. A number of standards, much baggage, several parks, 6,000 prisoners, amongst whom were several generals, fell into the victor's power. In the meantime a rearguard, which Provera had left at the Molinella, was attacked by General Point of Augereau's division, defeated and taken. Of all Provera's troops, only 2,000 men who remained beyond the Adige, escaped; all the rest were taken or killed. This action was called the Battle of la Favorite, from the name of a palace belonging to the dukes of Mantua, situate near the field of battle.

On the Pazzone side, Joubert chased Alvinzi throughout the 15th, and reached the Scaliera (ladder-path) di Brentino so rapidly, that 5,000 men were intercepted and taken. Murat, with two battalions of light troops, embarked on the lake of Garda, and turned la Corona; it was with difficulty that Alvinzi escaped. Joubert marched on Trent, occupied the old positions of the Avisio, and made 1,000 prisoners in different reconnaissances. General Augereau marched to Castel Franco, and thence to Treviso; he was also obliged to engage in several slight affairs. Massena occupied Bassano, and placed his advanced posts on the Piave; he made 1,200 prisoners in two actions fought with his vanguard.

The Austrian troops retreated across the Piave. All the passes of the Tyrol were blocked up by the snow, which was the greatest difficulty Joubert had to surmount. The French infantry triumphed over all obstacles. Joubert entered Trent, and occupied the Italian Tyrol. All the Austrian sick were taken as well as considerable stores. The army occupied the same positions as before the battle of Arcole. The trophies acquired in the course of January in the several actions were 25,000 prisoners, twenty-four colours and standards, and sixty pieces of cannon. And lastly, the enemy's loss was at least 35,000 men.

Bessieres carried the colours to Paris. The prisoners were so numerous that they created some difficulty; many escaped in passing through Switzerland;

there was a system organized for this purpose; nevertheless General Rey escorted them with 4,000 men.

It was in acknowledgment of the services rendered in so many battles by General Massena, that I afterwards made him Duke of Rivoli.

The garrison of Mantua had long subsisted on half rations; the horses had been eaten. Wurmser was informed of the results of the battle of Rivoli. He had no longer anything to hope for. He was summoned to surrender, but proudly answered that he had provisions for a twelvemonth. A few days after however, Klenau, his first aide-de-camp, came to Serrurier's head-quarters. He protested that the garrison had still sufficient provisions for three months, but that the marshal not believing that Austria would be able to succour the place in sufficient time, his conduct would be regulated by the conditions which should be prescribed to him. Serrurier replied that he would take the orders of his General-in-Chief on the subject. I went to Roverbella; I remained incognito, wrapped in my cloak, whilst the conversation between the two generals was proceeding. Klenau, employing all the customary expedients, expatiated at length on the great resources which Wurmser still possessed, and the quantities of provisions he still had in his magazines of reserve. I approached the table, took a pen and spent nearly half an hour in writing my decisions in the margin of Wurmser's proposals, whilst the discussion was proceeding with Serrurier. 'If Wurmser,' said I to Klenau, when I had finished, 'had but provisions for eighteen or twenty days, and talked of surrendering, he would not deserve an honourable capitulation; but I respect the Marshal's age, his bravery, and misfortunes. Here are the conditions I grant him if he opens his gates to-morrow. If he delays a fortnight, a month, or two, he shall still have the same conditions; he may therefore hold out to his last morsel of bread. I am about to set out instantly to pass the Po, and I shall march on Rome. You know my intentions; go and communicate them to your general.' Klenau, who had been quite at a loss to understand the first words, soon comprehended who it was that addressed him. He examined the decisions, the perusal of which filled him with gratitude for such generous and unexpected treatment. Dissimulation was now useless; he acknowledged that they had not provisions for more than three days. Wurmser sent to request me, as I was to cross the Po, to pass it at Mantua, which would save much circuitous travelling over bad roads, but all arrangements were already made. Wurmser wrote to me to express his gratitude, and a few days after despatched an aide-de-camp to me at Bologna, to apprise me of a conspiracy to poison me, which was to be carried into effect in Romagna, and to give me the necessary information to preserve myself from the attempt. This notice proved useful. General Serrurier presided at the ceremony of the surrender of Mantua, and saw the old marshal and all the staff of his army file off before him: I was by that time in Romagna. The indifference with which I withdrew

BATTLE OF RIVOLI

myself from the very flattering spectacle of a Marshal of great reputation, Generalissimo of the Austrian forces in Italy, delivering up his sword at the head of his staff, was remarked throughout Europe. The garrison of Mantua still amounted to 20,000 men, of whom 12,000 were fit for service; there were thirty generals, eighty commissaries and agents of all descriptions, and Wurmser's grand staff. In the three blockades since the month of June, 27,000 soldiers had died in the hospitals or been killed in the different sorties.

Joubert, who was born in the department of the Aisne (formerly Bresse), had studied for the bar; the Revolution induced him to adopt the profession of arms. He served in the Army of Italy, and was successively made a brigadier-general, and general of division. He was tall and thin, and seemed naturally of a weak constitution; but he had strengthened his frame amidst fatigues, camps, and mountain warfare. He was intrepid, vigilant and active. In November, 1796, he was made a general of division, to succeed Vaubois. He had the command of the corps of the Tyrol. It will be seen that he acquired honour in the campaigns of Germany. He was much attached to me, and I sent him to the Directory, in November, 1797, with the colours taken by the Army of Italy. In 1799 he engaged in the intrigues of Paris, and was appointed General-in-Chief of the Army of Italy, after the defeat of Moreau. He then married the daughter of the senator Semonville. He fell gloriously at the battle of Novi. He was still young, and had not acquired all the experience necessary. His talents were such that he might have attained great military renown.

Chapter XV

TOLENTINO

Rupture of the armistice with the Court of Rome. Army of the Holy See. Action of the Senio; submission of Romagna. The prisoners taken at the action of the Senio sent home. Action of Ancona; taking of that place. Our Lady of Loretto. Mission of the General of the Camaldolites to Pope Pius VI. Treaty of Tolentino. Mantua. Arrival of two divisions of the armies of the Sambre and Meuse, and Rhine, in Italy.

Six months had now elapsed since Cardinal Busca had succeeded Cardinal Zelada in the post of secretary of state at Rome. The new minister had come to a rupture with France, formed a declared alliance with Austria, and was exerting himself with more zeal than success to form a respectable army. He wished to renew the times when the pontifical armies decided the fate of the Peninsula. So urgently had he stimulated the Roman nobility, that with more ostentation than sincerity they offered regiments equipped for service, horses and arms. This cardinal had great confidence in the attachment of the Italians to their religion, and in the warlike disposition of the people of the Apennines. I had hitherto abstained from taking notice of all these injuries and insults; but the fall of Mantua at length gave me an opportunity of inflicting signal vengeance.

A courier from Cardinal Busca to Monsignor Albani, *chargé d'affaires* of Rome at Vienna, was intercepted near la Mezzola on 10 January, 1797; the whole policy of the Vatican was unveiled in his despatches. The Roman minister stated in his letter: 'That the French were desirous of peace, and even earnestly solicited it; but that he was delaying its conclusion because the Pope was resolved to trust wholly to the fortune of the House of Austria; that the conditions of the armistice of Bologna neither were nor would be performed, notwithstanding the strongest protests on the part of the French minister, Cacault; that fresh levies of troops were actively making in the States of the Holy See; that His Holiness accepted General Colli, whom the Emperor offered to command his army; that it was necessary that this general should bring with him a considerable number of Austrian officers, particularly of engineers and artillery; that orders should be given for their reception at Ancona; that he was sorry to find that Colli would be obliged to confer with Alvinzi, of whose manoeuvres he did not approve; that it was desirable he should go and review the Pope's troops in Romagna, previously to his coming to Rome', etc.

A courier was immediately despatched to Cacault, the French minister, with orders to quit Rome. 'You have now,' I wrote, 'been for several months treated with continual humiliations; and every expedient has been tried to force you to leave Rome. Resist, now, all entreaties to stay there: depart immediately on the receipt of this letter.' The Minister wrote to the Secretary of State, Busca: 'I am recalled by order of my government, which requires me to set out this evening for Florence; I have the honour to inform your Eminence of this circumstance, and to renew the expressions of my respect.' Busca persisted in his enterprise to the last: he replied—'Cardinal Busca was far from expecting the news which the highly respectable M. de Cacault has communicated to him. His sudden departure for Florence only allows the Cardinal to assure him of his profound esteem.' At the same moment General Victor passed the Po at Borgo-forte, at the head of 4,000 infantry and 600 horse; he joined the Italian division, commanded by General Lahoz, amounting to 4,000 men, at Bologna. These 9,000 men were sufficient to conquer the States of the Church. A few days later, I arrived at Bologna, where I published a manifesto conceived in these terms:

'ART. I. The Holy See has formally refused to perform articles VIII and IX of the armistice concluded at Bologna on 23 June, under the mediation of Spain, and solemnly ratified at Rome on 27 June.

'II. It has also incessantly continued to arm its subjects, and to excite them to war by its manifestoes; it has violated the territory of Bologna; its troops have approached within ten miles of that city, and threatened to occupy it.

'III. It has opened negotiations hostile to France with the Court of Vienna, as is proved by Cardinal Busca's letters, and the mission of the Prelate Albani to Vienna.

'IV. It has entrusted the command of its troops to Austrian generals and officers sent by the Court of Vienna.

'V. It has refused to meet the official advances made by Citizen Cacault, the Minister of the French Republic, for the opening of pacific negotiations.

'VI. The treaty of armistice has therefore been violated and infringed by

TOLENTINO

the Holy See: in consequence whereof I declare that the armistice concluded on 23 June between the French Republic and the Court of Rome, is broken.'

The intercepted letters of Cardinal Busca were published in support of this manifesto. Many other documents might have been added, but these letters explained everything. Cardinal Mattei, after having been three months in a seminary at Brescia, had obtained permission to return to Rome. Availing himself of the advantage of being known to me, he had written to me several times; which gave me an opportunity of forwarding to him the intercepted letters of Cardinal Busca. The perusal of these papers filled the Sacred College with confusion, and stopped the mouths of this minister's partisans.

On 2 February head-quarters were fixed at Imola, in the palace of bishop Chiaramonte, afterwards Pius VII. On the 3rd, the little army of the French reached Castel-Bolognese, and found the Pope's army on the opposite or right bank of the Senio, defending the passage of the bridge. This army consisted of 6 or 7,000 men, including regular soldiers and peasants collected by the tocsin, commanded by monks, and wrought up to fanatical enthusiasm by preachers and missionaries. They had eight pieces of cannon. The French took up a position; the day's march had been fatiguing. As they were stationing their grand guards, a flag of truce came up, and declared, in a ridiculous manner, on the part of his Eminence the Lord Cardinal, commander-in-chief, *that if the French army continued to advance, he would fire upon it*. This terrible threat excited much laughter amongst the French, who replied, *that they did not wish to expose themselves to the Cardinal's thunders, and that they were going to take up a position for the night*. Cardinal Busca's hopes had, however, been fulfilled. All Romagna was in a flame; a holy war had been proclaimed there; the tocsin had been incessantly sounding for three days; the lowest class of the people was in a delirium and frenzy. Prayers of forty hours, missions in public places, indulgences, and even miracles—every engine, in short, had been set to work. Martyrs were bleeding in one place; Madonnas weeping in another; and everything foreboded a conflagration about to consume this fine province. Cardinal Busca had told the French minister Cacault, 'We will make a Vendée of Romagna, of the mountains of Liguria; nay, of all Italy.'

The following proclamation was posted at Imola:

'The French army is about to enter the territories of the Pope. It will be faithful to the maxims it professes, and will protect religion and the people. The French soldier bears in one hand the bayonet, the sure pledge of victory; in the other, the olive branch, the symbol of peace and the gage of his protection. Woe to those who may be seduced by men of consummate hypocrisy, to draw upon their houses the vengeance of an army which has, in six months, made 100,000 of the Emperor's best troops prisoners, taken 400 pieces of cannon, and 110 standards, and then destroyed five armies!'

TOLENTINO

At four o'clock in the morning General Lannes, commanding the van of the little French army, marched a league and a half up the bank of the Senio, passed it at a ford, at daybreak, and drew up in line in the rear of the Pope's army, cutting it off from Faenza. General Lahoz, supported by a battery and covered by a cloud of skirmishers, passed the bridge in close column. The armed mob of the enemy was routed in an instant; artillery, baggage, and everything was taken; four or five hundred men were sabred; a few monks perished, crucifix in hand; these were mostly mendicants. Nearly all the troops of the line were taken. The Cardinal-general escaped. The action did not last above an hour. The loss of the French was trifling; they arrived before Faenza the same day. The gates were shut; the tocsin sounded; the ramparts were lined with a few pieces of cannon; and the delirious populace insulted their conqueror by all sorts of insults. When summoned to open the gates, they gave an insolent answer; and it became necessary to pull down the gates, and enter the town by main force. '*This is the same thing as happened at Pavia,*' cried the soldiers, by way of demanding the pillage of the place. '*No,*' answered I: '*at Pavia they had revolted after taking an oath, and they wanted to massacre our soldiers who were their guests. These are only senseless people, who must be conquered by clemency.*' In fact a few convents only were attacked. This interesting town being thus saved from its own delirium, the salvation of the province was the next object of attention. Agents were despatched into every district to make the people acquainted with the state of affairs, and to calm their excessive agitation and frenzy. But the most efficacious step was that of sending home the prisoners of war.

The prisoners taken at the action of the Senio were collected at Faenza in a garden belonging to a convent. Their first terror had not yet subsided; they trembled for their lives. At my approach they threw themselves on their knees, crying out for mercy. I addressed them in Italian in these words: 'I am the friend of all the nations of Italy, and particularly of the people of Rome. I come for your good; you are free; return to your families, and tell them that the French are the friends of religion, of order, and of the poor.' The consternation of the prisoners now gave way to joy. These poor people abandoned themselves to their sentiments of gratitude with all the vivacity that belongs to the Italian character.

From the garden I proceeded to the refectory, where I had caused the officers to be assembled: they amounted to several hundreds, and some of them belonged to the best families of Rome. I conversed with them a long time; talked of the liberty of Italy, of the abuses of the pontifical government, of all that was contrary to the spirit of the gospel in it, and of its folly in attempting to resist a victorious army, composed of the best disciplined and most experienced troops in the world. I permitted them to return to their homes; and required them, in return for my clemency, to make known my sentiments

TOLENTINO

towards Italy in general, and the people of Rome in particular. These prisoners became so many missionaries, who dispersed themselves in the States of the Pope, and loudly proclaimed the favourable treatment they had met with. They carried proclamations with them, which thus reached the most remote castles of the Apennines. This measure succeeded; the sentiments of the people underwent a change; the army on reaching Forli, Cesena, Rimini, Pezaro, and Sinigaglia, found the people favourably disposed. They had passed to the opposite extreme, and now received with demonstrations of joy those Frenchmen whom, a few days before, they had thought the most terrible enemies of their religion, property and laws. The monks themselves, with the exception of the mendicants, began to consider how much they had to lose, and to use sincere endeavours to enlighten the people. There were many individuals of merit amongst them, who deplored the folly of their cabinet.

Colli, who commanded the Pope's army, had commanded that of Piedmont at Mondovi and Cherasco. He well knew with whom he had to deal. He chose a good position on the heights before Ancona, where he had encamped the 3,000 men he still had left. But he and the Austrian officers, under different pretexts, retired to Loretto as soon as the French army appeared. The position occupied by the Romans was a very fine one. General Victor sent a flag of truce to persuade them to surrender. During the parley the French and Italian troops outflanked them both on the right and left, surrounded them, took them prisoners without firing a shot, and entered the citadel without resistance. The prisoners made on this occasion were treated in the same manner as those taken at the action of the Senio. They were sent home with proclamations; and thus became additional missionaries to precede the army in its march. Ancona is the only port between Venice and Brindisi, which is the extremity of the eastern point of Italy; but it was neglected and in bad condition; even frigates could not enter it. It was at this period that I perceived what it was necessary to do in order to fortify the place and repair the port. Great works were executed there during the kingdom of Italy. At this time the port receives ships of all kinds, not excepting three-deckers. The Jews, who were numerous at Ancona, as well as the Mahometans of Albania and Greece, were subject to ancient customs, which were humiliating and contrary to the laws of hospitality. It was one of my first cares to free them from this oppression. In the meantime, notwithstanding the presence of the army, the people were running in crowds to prostrate themselves at the feet of a Madonna, which was said to shed tears in abundance. Some of the more rational citizens gave information of the circumstance; Monge was sent to the spot. He reported that the Madonna actually wept. The chapter received orders to bring her to head-quarters. It was an optical illusion, ingeniously managed by means of a glass. The following day the Madonna was restored to her place in the church, but without a glass; she wept no more. A chaplain, the inventor of this artifice, was arrested. It was an offence against the army, and an insult to the sanctity of our religion.

On the 10th the army encamped at Loretto. This is a bishopric, and contains a magnificent convent. The church and buildings are sumptuous; there are vast and well-furnished apartments for the treasures of the Madonna, and the accommodation of the abbots, the chapter, and the pilgrims. In the church is the *Casa Santa*, once the residence of the Virgin at Nazareth, and the very place in which she received the visit of the angel Gabriel. It is a little cabin five or six toises square, in which is a Madonna placed on a tabernacle. The legend states that the angels carried it from Nazareth into Dalmatia, when the infidels conquered Syria; and thence across the Adriatic to the heights of Loretto. From all parts of Christendom pilgrims flocked to see the Madonna. Presents, diamonds, and jewels sent from all parts formed her treasures, which amounted to several millions. The court of Rome, on hearing of the approach of the French army, had the treasures of Loretto packed up and placed in safety: there was, nevertheless, property left in gold and silver to the value of upwards of a million. The Madonna was forwarded to Paris. It is a wooden statue clumsily carved; a proof of its antiquity. It was to be seen for some years at the national library; when First Consul, I restored it to the Pope at the time of the Concordat, and it has been replaced in the *Casa Santa*.

Several thousands of French priests, expelled from their country, had taken refuge in Italy. As the French army had advanced in the Peninsula, they had fled to Rome. But now that the army had entered the States of the Pope, they found themselves without an asylum. Some of the most timid had crossed the Adige in time, and retired into Germany: Naples had refused them shelter. The heads of the different convents in the States of the Pope, who were anxious to get rid of the burthen of feeding and maintaining them, made a pretext of the arrival of the army, and affecting to be apprehensive that the presence of these priests would draw the animosity of the victor upon their convents, turned their unfortunate guests out of doors. I made an order, and published a proclamation, by which I encouraged the priests, ordering the convents, bishops, and different chapters to receive them, and furnish them with everything necessary for their subsistence and comfort. I commanded the army to look upon these priests as friends and fellow-countrymen, and as such to behave to them and protect them. The army adopted these sentiments, which gave rise to many affecting scenes. Some of the soldiers found their former pastors again; and these unfortunate old men, banished many hundred leagues from their country, now received, for the first time, tokens of respect and affection from their countrymen, who until then had treated them as enemies and criminals. This measure was much talked of throughout the Christian world, especially in France: there were some attempts to find fault;

but these murmurs were drowned in the general approbation, and above all in that of the Directory.

In the meantime consternation reigned in the Vatican. Bad news arrived every hour. The first intelligence was that the papal army, of which such hopes had been entertained, was entirely destroyed, without having made the slightest resistance. Next came the couriers who announced the arrival of the French army in the different towns successively, and described the changes which had taken place in public opinion. Hatred and fanaticism had given place to friendly sentiments and the desire of liberty. Busca had now an opportunity of finding out that *Vendées* were not to be excited at pleasure; and that if extraordinary circumstances give rise to them, nothing but great errors can establish and prolong them. Soon afterwards it was found that the French army had taken possession of Ancona, Loretto, and Macerata; and thus its vanguard was already on the summit of the Apennines. '*The French*', said the prelates, '*do not march, but run.*'

The officers and soldiers who had been taken prisoners and sent home from Faenza and Ancona propagated the confidence they felt in every quarter of Rome. The friends of liberty raised their heads, and openly shewed themselves even within the city. The members of the Sacred College, seeing no hope left, began to think of providing for their own safety. Every preparation was made for proceeding to Naples. The horses were already put to the court carriages, when the general of the Camaldolites arrived at the Vatican, and prostrated himself at the feet of the holy father. In passing through Cesena, I had particularly noticed this ecclesiastic; and knowing that Pius the VI reposed great confidence in him, I had charged him to assure his Holiness that his destruction was not aimed at; that the French general revered his position and character; that he might remain at Rome; and that he had only to change his ministers, and send plenipotentiaries to Tolentino to conclude and sign a definitive treaty of peace with the Republic. The general of the Camaldolites successfully accomplished this mission: the Pope took courage; dismissed the ridiculous Busca; entrusted the direction of his cabinet to Cardinal Doria, a man who had long been celebrated for the moderation of his opinions; countermanded his departure from Rome, and appointed plenipotentiaries to conclude and sign a definitive treaty of peace.

The instructions of the Directory were against any negotiations with Rome: the Directors thought that an end must be put to the temporal reign of the Pope, in order that it might give no farther trouble; that no case would arise in which the court of Rome would be more evidently in the wrong than on this occasion; that it would be a mere folly to think of a sincere peace with theologians, so violently hostile to the principles which governed the new republics. The temporal existence of the Pope was undoubtedly incompatible with the happiness of Italy. Experience proved that neither moderation nor good faith were to be expected from that court: but I thought that I could neither revolutionize Rome, nor unite her territories with the Cispadan Republic, without marching on Naples and overturning the throne. The partisans of liberty in that kingdom were sufficiently numerous to give some uneasiness to the court, but too feeble to afford support and effectual aid to the French army. The Court of Naples felt that the revolution of Rome would produce its fall. But an army of 20 or 25,000 men was requisite for marching on Naples; and this measure was therefore inconsistent with my grand project of dictating peace under the walls of Vienna.

The van of the French army had passed the Apennines, and was within three days' march of Rome; head-quarters were at Tolentino on 13 February. Cardinal Mattei, Monsignor Galeppi, the Duke of Braschi, and the Marquis Massimi, the Pope's ministers plenipotentiary, arrived there the same day. Conferences began on the 14th. Monsignor Galeppi opened the negotiation. This prelate was endowed with a most copious eloquence; he delivered a great number of homilies. But the Court of Rome was guilty, and was to be punished; which could only be effected by the cession of the conquered provinces, or by equivalent contributions. The three legations, the duchy of Urbino, the marquisate of Ancona, the provinces of Macerata and Perugino, were conquered. These terms being at length agreed on, the conclusion of the treaty occupied only five days in discussion. Galeppi, who had at first talked of the absolute ruin of the papal finances, found resources as soon as they were wanted for the purpose of redeeming provinces, or diminishing the number of those which the Pope was to cede. The treaty was signed in the form and on the conditions following:

The General-in-Chief Bonaparte, commanding the Army of Italy, and Citizen Cacault, agent for the French Republic in Italy, plenipotentiaries charged with the full powers of the Executive Directory; and his Eminence Cardinal Mattei, Monsignor Galeppi, the Duke of Braschi, and the Marquis Massimi, plenipotentiaries of his Holiness—have agreed on the following articles:

ARTICLE I. There shall be peace, friendship, and good understanding between the French Republic and Pope Pius VI.

II. The Pope revokes all adherence, consent, and accession, patent or secret, given or entered into by him, to or with the armed coalition against the French Republic; and renounces all treaties of offensive and defensive alliance with all powers and states whatsoever. He engages not to afford to any of the powers in arms against the French Republic in the present or any future war, any succours of men, ships, military stores, provisions, or money, under any pretence or denomination whatsoever.

III. His Holiness shall, within five days from the ratification of the present

TOLENTINO

treaty, disband his newly levied troops, retaining only the regiments which existed before the armistice signed at Bologna.

IV. No ships of war or privateers belonging to the powers armed against the Republic shall enter or remain in any of the ports or roads of the Ecclesiastical States during the present war.

V. The French Republic shall continue to enjoy, as before the war, all the rights and prerogatives which France enjoyed at Rome; and shall in all respects be treated in the same manner as the most favoured powers, especially with respect to its ambassador or minister, consuls, and vice-consuls.

VI. The Pope wholly and simply renounces all rights which he might claim in the city and territory of Avignon and the county of Venasque, with its dependencies; and transfers, yields, and abandons the said rights to the French Republic.

VII. The Pope likewise renounces in perpetuity, yields, and transfers to the French Republic, all his rights in the territory known by the name of the Legations of Bologna, Ferrara, and Romagna. No offence shall be offered to the Catholic religion in the said legations.

VIII. The town, citadel, and villages forming the territory of the city of Ancona, shall remain in the possession of the French Republic until a continental peace.

IX. The Pope undertakes, for himself and those who shall succeed him, not to transfer to any persons whomsoever the titles of lordships attached to the territory by him ceded to the French Republic.

X. His Holiness engages to cause to be paid and delivered to the treasurer of the French army, at Foligno, before the 15th of the current month of Ventose (5 March, 1797, old style), the sum of fifteen millions of livres of France; ten millions of which are to be paid in specie, and the remaining five millions in diamonds and other valuable effects; out of the balance of about sixteen millions which remains due, according to Article IX of the armistice signed at Bologna on 5 Messidor, year 4, and ratified by his Holiness on 27 June.

XI. For the definitive discharge of what will remain to be paid to complete the performance of the armistice signed at Bologna, his Holiness shall furnish the army with 800 cavalry horses, harnessed, 800 draught horses, oxen, and buffaloes, and other articles the produce of the States of the Church.

XII. Independently of the sum specified in the preceding Articles, the Pope shall pay to the French Republic, in coin, diamonds, and other valuables, the sum of fifteen millions of livres Tournois of France; ten millions to be paid in the course of the month of March, and five millions in the course of the month of April next.

XIII. Article VIII of the treaty of armistice signed at Bologna, concerning manuscripts and works of art, shall be fully executed as speedily as possible.

XIV. The French Army shall evacuate Umbria, Perugia, and Camerino, as soon as the tenth article of the present treaty shall be executed and accomplished.

XV. The French army shall evacuate the province of Macerata, with the exception of Ancona, Fano, and their territories, as soon as the first five millions of the sum mentioned in article XII of the present treaty shall have been paid and delivered.

XVI. The French army shall evacuate the territory of the town of Fano and the duchy of Urbino, as soon as the second five millions of the sum mentioned in article XII of the present treaty shall have been paid and delivered, and articles III, X, XI, and XIII shall have been executed.

The last five millions, forming part of the sum stipulated by article XII shall be paid, at latest, in the course of April next.

XVII. The French Republic cedes to the Pope all its rights in the different religious foundations in the cities of Rome and Loretto; and the Pope cedes in full property to the French Republic all the allodial estates belonging to the Holy See in the three provinces of Bologna, Ferrara, and Romagna; and particularly the estate of La Mezzola and its dependencies. The Pope nevertheless reserves to himself, in case of sale, the third of the produce thereof, which is to be remitted to his agents.

XVIII. His Holiness shall cause his Minister at Paris to disavow the murder committed on the body of the secretary of legation Basseville.

His Holiness shall also pay, in the course of the year, the sum of 300,000 livres, to be divided amongst the sufferers on that occasion.

XIX. His Holiness shall cause all persons detained in prison on account of their political opinions to be set at liberty.

XX. On receipt of the ratification of the present treaty, the General-in-Chief shall give permission to all prisoners of war taken in his Holiness's service, to return to their homes.

XXI. Until a treaty of commerce shall be concluded between the French Republic and the Pope, the commerce of the Republic shall be re-established and maintained in his Holiness's states, upon the footing of the most favoured nation.

XXII. Conformably to article VI of the treaty concluded at the Hague, on 27 Floreal, year 3, the peace concluded by the present treaty, between the French Republic and his Holiness, is declared common to the French Republic.

XXIII. The French post shall be re-established at Rome, in the same manner as it formerly existed.

XXIV. The school of arts instituted at Rome for all Frenchmen shall be re-established, and continue its proceedings as before the war: the palace belonging to the Republic, in which this school was conducted, shall be restored without dilapidation.

XXV. All the articles, clauses, and conditions of the present treaty, without exception, are obligatory in perpetuity both on his Holiness Pope Pius VI and on his successors.

XXVI. The present treaty shall be ratified with the least possible delay.

Done and signed at head-quarters at Tolentino, by the above-named plenipotentiaries, on 1 Ventose, in the 5th year of the French Republic, one and indivisible (19 February, 1797).

(Signed), BONAPARTE; CACAULT; Cardinal MATTEI; L. GALEPPI; L. Duca BRASCHI-ONESTI; and CAMILLO, Marquis Massimi.

I long insisted that the Court of Rome should undertake to suppress the Inquisition. It was represented to me that the Inquisition was no longer what it had been; that it was now rather a tribunal of police than of religious belief; that *autos-da-fé* no longer existed. I appreciated these arguments at their just value; but I gave up this article to gratify the Pope, who attached great importance to it, and explained himself on the subject in his private correspondence. I contented myself with the legations of Bologna and Ferrara, with Romagna, and the occupation of Ancona by a French garrison. This was also in consequence of the principle which had induced me to respect the temporal existence of the Pope. Had I, according to the wishes of the patriots of the Transpadan republic, added to their new state the duchy of Urbino, Ancona, the province of Ferrara and Macerata, and extended its boundaries to the Tronto and the Apennines, it would have been placed in contact with Naples. A war with that power would infallibly have been the result; it must have taken place, even though France and the Court of Naples had not wished it.

The importance attached by this Court to these stipulations was such, that Prince Pignatelli, its minister, followed the French staff from Bologna; which is a sufficient proof of his apprehensions. This prince was not deficient either in intellect or activity, but he would do anything to gain information. He was several times caught listening at doors, particularly at Loretto, and during the negotiations of Tolentino; thus exposing himself to be turned out by the porters. The peace stopped the march of the French troops.

After the signature of the treaty, I entrusted General Victor with the superintendance of its execution, despatched my aide-de-camp, Colonel Junot, with a respectful letter to the Pope, and set out for Mantua. This letter and the answer of his Holiness, which were published, formed a contrast to the language then in general use, and were accordingly remarked.

Mantua had now been a month in the power of the Republic; its hospitals were all crowded with the Austrian sick. I alighted at the ducal palace, where I remained several days. A great number of very fine pictures had been found in this city; I had them sent to the Museum of Paris. The fine frescoes of the war of the Titans by Titian, in the palace del T, excited the admiration of

TOLENTINO

connoisseurs. The committee of artists presented several plans for removing and transporting them to Paris; but such an attempt must have exposed these extraordinary works to imminent hazard of loss and destruction. I had an arsenal of construction established, and directed General Chasseloup, who commanded the engineers, to improve the fortifications. The weak side, at that period, was that towards La Pradella and Pietoli. Works were immediately commenced, and carried on without remission, in order to place it on an equality with the other parts. I gave all proper orders for the armament of the place. I then proceeded to Milan, the centre of the administration and policy of Italy. Public spirit had there made great progress.

At the time of the battle of Arcole the French government imagined that Italy was lost, which led it to reflect seriously on the effect that circumstance was likely to produce on the state of France. People were indignant at the incomprehensible circumstance that the whole burthen, and consequently all the glory, was left to a single army. The Army of Italy also complained loudly, and at length the government began to think seriously of sending succours to its relief. The Directory ordered one division of six regiments of infantry and two of cavalry, from the Army of the Sambre and Meuse, and a similar force from the Army of the Rhine, to pass the Alps, in order to enable the Army of Italy to fight on an equality with the enemy in the expected new contest. This army was then menaced by the forces which were destroyed at Rivoli. The march of these reinforcements was delayed by several circumstances. Meantime the distress to which Mantua was reduced hastened Alvinzi's operations; so that these reinforcements had only just reached the foot of the Alps, when the victories of Rivoli and La Favorite, and the surrender of Mantua, placed Italy beyond the reach of danger. It was not until my return from Tolentino that I reviewed my new forces. They were fine troops, in good condition, and well disciplined. The division of the Sambre and Meuse, commanded by Bernadotte, had suffered little desertion on its march; that of the Rhine, commanded by Delmas, was weaker, and had lost more men by desertion. This detachment was estimated at 30,000 men; but its actual strength did not exceed 19,000. The Army of Italy was henceforth equal to any enterprise; and sufficiently powerful, alone, to undertake to force the cabinet of Vienna to renounce its alliance with England.

Chapter XVI

THE TAGLIAMENTO

Plan of the Campaign for 1797. Passage of the Piave (12 March). Battle of the Tagliamento (16 March). Retreat of Prince Charles. Action of Gradisca (19 March). Passage of the Julian Alps and the Drave (29 March). Actions in the Tyrol.

The reverses which the two armies of the Sambre and Meuse and Rhine had sustained in the late campaign, the timid conduct of those two armies during the siege of Kehl and the *tête-de-pont* of Huningen, had encouraged the Aulic Council, and rendered it perfectly confident of security on this side. Towards the end of February they detached six divisions of their best troops of the Rhine, amounting to 40,000 men, and ordered four of them into Friuli and two into the Tyrol. Prince Charles, who had lately acquired the most brilliant glory in Germany, took the command of the Austrian armies of Italy, and advanced his head-quarters to Inspruck on 6 February, whence he soon transferred them successively to Villach and Goritz. In the course of February his engineers visited the debouchés of the Julian and Noric Alps. They projected fortifications which they were to construct as soon as the snow should be melted. I was impatient to anticipate them, and ardently hoped to attack the Archduke and chase him out of Italy before the arrival of the powerful reinforcements which were marching through Germany.

My army was composed of eight divisions of infantry and a reserve of cavalry, consisting of the following troops under arms, viz. 53,000 infantry, 3,000 artillery serving 120 guns, and 5,000 cavalry. The King of Sardinia's contingent amounted to 8,000 infantry, 2,000 cavalry, and twenty pieces of cannon. I had long been negotiating for the purpose of engaging Venice to enter into alliance with France; and the Venetian contingent was to be similar

THE TAGLIAMENTO

to that of Piedmont. Thus I expected to enter Germany with 70,000 infantry, 9,000 cavalry, and 160 pieces of cannon. But the Directory, with the strangest infatuation, refused to ratify the armistice of Bologna, and thus deprived the French army of the Sardinian contingent. The Venetian Senate refused all proposals of alliance, and even betrayed so hostile a disposition that it became necessary for the French to be on their guard; and thus they were not only disappointed of the Venetian contingent, but obliged to leave 10,000 men in reserve on the Adige, to secure the rear, and watch the inimical proceedings of the oligarchy of Venice. I, therefore, had but 50,000 men to enter Germany with; and of these 5,000 were cavalry and 2,500 artillery. I had thought that the armies of the Sambre and Meuse and Rhine would have been united in one army of 120,000 men and would have marched from Strasburg into Bavaria, passed the Inn, arrived on the Ens, and joined the army of Italy, which, crossing the Tagliamento, the Julian Alps, Carinthia, the Drave, and the Muer, would have directed its march on the Simering; and that the French, thus united in the number of near 200,000 men, would have entered Vienna, whilst an army of observation of 60,000 men guarded Holland, blockaded Ehrenbreistein, Mentz, Manheim, and Philippsberg, and defended the *têtes-de-pont* of Dusseldorf, Kehl, and Huningen. But the Directory, persisting in their false principles of war, continued to keep the armies of the Sambre and Meuse and Rhine separate; the experience of the last campaign was lost upon them.

There are three high roads from Italy to Vienna: first, that of the Tyrol; secondly, that of Ponteba or of Carinthia; thirdly, that of Carniola.

The first runs from Verona along the left bank of the Adige as far as Trent, crosses the high chain of the Alps at the pass of the Brenner, sixty leagues from Verona, and thence proceeds, by Salzburg, towards the Danube, and descends that river as far as Vienna, crossing the Ens in its way. By this road it is 170 leagues from Verona to Vienna. The second road runs through the Vicentine and the Trevisan, passes the Piave, the Tagliamento, the Ponteba, and the Carnic Alps at the pass of Tarwis; whence it descends into Carinthia, crosses the Drave at Villach, runs through Klagenfurth, the capital of the province, meets the Muer, which it follows as far as Bruck, crosses the Simering, and descends into the valley of Vienna. It is 95 leagues by this road from San-Daniele to Vienna.

The Carniolan road crosses the Isonzo at Gradisca, runs towards Laybach, the capital of the province, passes the Drave at Marburg, enters Styria, passes through Gratz, the capital of that province, and joins the Carinthian road at Bruck. It is 105 leagues from Goritz to Vienna by this road.

The Tyrolese road communicates with that of Carinthia by five cross roads. The first, called the Pusterthal, commences at Brixen, turns to the right, meets one of the tributary streams of the Adige, runs through Lienz and Spittal, and

THE TAGLIAMENTO

joins the road of Carniola, near Villach; it is forty-five leagues in length. The second begins at Salzburg, runs through Rastadt, and goes to Spittal, being thirty-two leagues in extent. Four leagues below Rastadt there is a branch from this road which runs along the Muer as far as Scheifling, where it meets the Carinthian road: this branch runs sixteen leagues. The third road begins at Linz on the Danube, passes the Ens near Rotenmann, crosses some high mountains, and after running thirty-six leagues falls into the Carinthian road at Judenburg. The fourth begins at Ens, runs up the Ens twenty leagues, and ends at Leoben, being twenty-eight leagues in length. And the fifth, of twenty-four leagues, begins at Saint-Polten, and runs to Bruck.

The roads of Carinthia and Carniola communicate together by three crossroads. The first commences at Goritz, runs up the Isonzo, through Caporetto and Austrian Chiusa, and joins the Carinthian road at Tarwis, after a course of twenty-one leagues. The second begins at Laybach, crosses the Save and Drave, and runs to Klagenfurth, being seventeen leagues in length. The third leads from Marburg, along the Drave, to Klagenfurth, a distance of twenty-six leagues. Beyond Klagenfurth the Carinthian and Carniolan roads have no further communication; they proceed in a parallel direction at a distance of twenty-nine leagues from each other, as far as Bruck, where they join.

In the beginning of March the Archduke's army was 50,000 strong; it was behind the Piave, covering Friuli, except 15,000 men, who were in the Tyrol. This army was to be joined in the course of April by six divisions, which had commenced their march from the Rhine; which reinforcement would have made it upwards of 90,000 men. So great a superiority justified the flattering hopes of the cabinet of Vienna. The French army, at the same period, was stationed as follows: the three divisions of Delmas, Baraguay d'Hilliers, and Joubert, and General Dumas' brigade of cavalry, were united in the Italian Tyrol, under the command of Lieutenant-General Joubert, and formed a corps of 17,000 men. The divisions of Massena, Serrurier, Guieux (formerly Augereau), and Bernadotte, with General Dugua's division of cavalry of reserve, were in junction in the Bassanese and Trevisan countries, having advanced posts along the right bank of the Piave. Victor's division was still on the Apennines; it was expected to reach the Adige in the beginning of April, to form the nucleus of the corps of observation opposed to the Venetians; it was estimated that the successive arrivals of the French marching battalions, and of the Lombard, Cispadan, and Polish battalions would increase this corps-d'armée to 20,000 men.

When it was found that the Archduke had arrived at Inspruck on 6 February, it was concluded that he would collect all his forces in the Tyrol, and content himself with detaching a division of 6,000 men behind the Tagliamento. This would have enabled the six divisions detached from the Rhine to join his army twenty days earlier; he might then have attacked General

THE TAGLIAMENTO

Joubert, forced him in his positions of the Lavis, and driven him into Italy. In the beginning of February I had informed General Joubert of his danger, and on this hypothesis had ordered him to choose three positions between the Lavis and the line of Torbole and Mori, where, with his corps-d'armée, he might retard the Archduke's march, and gain eight or ten days, so as to give the divisions which were on the Brenta time to take the Archduke's army in flank, by the gorges of the Brenta.

But the Archduke, abiding by the plan which had been laid down for him by the Aulic Council, had assembled his principal forces in Friuli, which gave the French army an opportunity of attacking him before the arrival of the divisions of the Rhine, which were still twenty days' march behind. I consequently fixed my head-quarters at Bassano on 9 March. I addressed my army, by means of the order of the day, in these terms: 'Soldiers! The taking of Mantua has now put an end to the war of Italy, which has given you eternal claims to the gratitude of your country. You have been victorious in fourteen pitched battles and seventy actions; you have taken 100,000 prisoners, 500 field-pieces, 2,000 heavy cannon, and four pontoon-trains. The contributions laid on the countries you have conquered have fed, maintained, and paid the army; besides which you have sent thirty millions to the minister of finance for the use of the public treasury. You have enriched the Museum of Paris with 300 masterpieces of the arts of ancient and modern Italy, which it has required thirty centuries to produce. You have conquered for the Republic the finest countries in Europe. The Transpadan and Cispadan Republics are indebted to you for their liberty. The French flag waves, for the first time, on the shores of the Adriatic, opposite the native country of Alexander, and within twenty-four hours' sail of it. The kings of Sardinia and Naples, the Pope, and the Duke of Parma are separated from the coalition. You have expelled the English from Leghorn, Genoa, and Corsica—yet higher destinies await you!!! You will prove yourselves worthy of them!!! Of all the foes who combined to stifle the Republic in its birth, the Emperor alone remains before you. He has now no other policy or will than those of that perfidious cabinet, which, unacquainted with the horrors of war, smiles with satisfaction at the woes of the continent. The Executive Directory has spared no effort to give peace to Europe; and the moderation of its proposals was uninfluenced by the strength of its armies. It has not been listened to at Vienna; there is therefore no hope of obtaining peace, but by seeking it in the heart of the hereditary states. You will there find a brave people. You will respect their religion and manners, and protect their property. It is liberty that you carry to the brave Hungarian nation.'

It was necessary to pass the Piave and the Tagliamento in the presence of the Austrian army, and to turn its right, in order to anticipate it at the gorges of Ponteba. Massena marched from Bassano, passed the Piave in the moun-

THE TAGLIAMENTO

tains, beat Luzignan's division, pursued him closely, took six hundred prisoners, including General Luzignan, and several pieces of cannon, and drove the wreck of this division beyond the Tagliamento, taking Feltre, Cadore, and Belluno. Serrurier's division advanced, on 12 March, on Asolo, passed the Piave at daybreak, marched on Conegliano, where the Austrian head-quarters were, and thus turned all the divisions which defended the lower part of the Piave, which allowed Guieux's division to effect its passage at two in the afternoon, at Ospedaletto, before Treviso. The river is pretty deep at this spot, and a bridge would have been desirable; but the goodwill of the soldiers supplied that deficiency. A drummer was the only person in danger, and he was saved by a woman who swam after him. On the same day, Serrurier's division and that of Guieux encamped, with the head-quarters at Conegliano. Bernadotte's division, which was at Padua, joined on the following day. The enemy had chosen the plains of the Tagliamento for his field of battle; they were favourable to his excellent and numerous cavalry. His rearguard attempted to make a stand at Sacile, at night, but was overthrown, on the 13th, by General Guieux.

On 16 March, at nine o'clock in the morning, the two armies met. The French army with its staff, arrived before Valvasone on the right bank of the Tagliamento; Guieux's division forming the left, Serrurier's the centre, and Bernadotte's the right. The Austrian army, nearly equal in force, was drawn up in the same order on the opposite bank. By this position it did not cover the road of the Ponteba. Ocskay's column, and the remains of Luzignan's division were no longer able to stop Massena. Yet the Ponteba road was the shortest, and the natural direction to cover Vienna.

This conduct of the Archduke can only be explained by supposing that he feared only for Trieste, the centre of the naval establishments of Austria; or, that his positions were not definitively taken, and that being covered by the Tagliamento, he was in hopes to gain a few days, which would have allowed time for a division of grenadiers on its march from the Rhine, and which had reached Klagenfurth, to reinforce Ocskay's division, which was opposed to Massena.

The cannonade began from one bank of the Tagliamento to the other; the light cavalry made several charges on the beach of that torrent. The French troops, seeing the enemy too well prepared, ceased firing, formed the bivouacs, and prepared their mess. The Archduke was deceived by this appearance; he thought that as they had marched all night, they were taking up a position. He fell back, and returned into his camp. But two hours afterwards, when all was quiet, the French army suddenly got under arms. Duphot, at the head of the 27th light demi-brigade, being Guieux's van, and Murat with the 15th light demi-brigade, Bernadotte's van, each supported by its division, each regiment with its second battalion deployed, and its first and third in column

THE TAGLIAMENTO

by divisions, at platoon distance, rushed into the river. The enemy flew to arms; but the whole of this first line had already passed in the finest order, and was drawn up in line of battle on the left bank. The cannonade and musquetry began in all directions. The light cavalry attached to these two divisions was on the right and left of the line. General Dugua's division of cavalry of reserve, and Serrurier's division, formed the second line, which passed the river as soon as the first line had advanced a hundred toises from the shore. After several hours' fighting, and different charges of infantry and cavalry, the enemy having been repulsed in the attacks of the villages of Gradisca and Codroipo, and finding themselves turned by a successful charge made by Dugua's division, beat a retreat, abandoning eight pieces of cannon and some prisoners to the victors.

At the commencement of the cannonade, Massena had effected his passage at San-Daniele; he met with little resistance, occupied Osopo, the key to the Ponteba road, which the enemy had neglected, and Venetian Chiusa. He was thus master of the gorges of the Ponteba; and he forced the remains of Ocskay's division to retreat on Tarwis.

The Archduke being now unable to retreat by way of Carinthia, because Massena occupied Ponteba, resolved to gain that road by way of Udine, Cividale, Caporetto, Austrian Chiusa, and Tarwis. He sent forward three divisions and his parks, under the command of General Bayalitsch, in that direction, and marched with the rest of his army by way of Palma-Nuova and Gradisca, to defend the Isonzo and cover Carniola; but Massena was only two days' march from Tarwis. Bayalitsch was six days' march from that place, by the road he took; this manoeuvre therefore placed the corps-d'armée under his command in jeopardy, as the Archduke soon perceived. He hastened, in person, to Klagenfurth, placed himself at the head of the division of grenadiers which he found there, and took up a position before Tarwis, to oppose the progress of Massena. This general had been delayed two days, but having received orders to march with all possible expedition upon Tarwis, he hastened thither accordingly. He found the Archduke's forces formed in line, consisting of the remains of Ocskay's troops, and the fine division of grenadiers from the Rhine. The action was obstinate; the importance of victory was felt on both sides; for the Austrians knew that if Massena made himself master of the debouché of Tarwis, the three Austrian divisions, which were on their march through the valley of the Isonzo, were lost. The Prince exposed himself to the greatest dangers, and was repeatedly on the point of being taken by the French skirmishers. General Brune, afterwards a marshal of France, who commanded a brigade of Massena's division, behaved on this occasion with distinguished bravery. The Austrians were broken; they had engaged their very last battalion in the action; they could operate no retreat; the remains of their force made for Villach, beyond the Drave, in order to rally there.

THE TAGLIAMENTO

Massena, being master of Tarwis, occupied that place, facing towards Villach and Austrian Chiusa, in which directions the three divisions which had been ordered to take this route from the field of the battle of the Tagliamento, were expected to debouch.

The day after the battle of the Tagliamento, the Archduke's head-quarters had entered Palma-Nuova, a fortress belonging to the Venetians. He had established magazines there, but judging that it would be necessary to leave five or six thousand men to guard the place, his artillery not having arrived, he evacuated it. The French left a garrison in it, and secured it from a *coup-de-main*. Bernadotte's division appeared before Gradisca, in order to pass the Isonzo, but found the gates shut, and was greeted with a cannonade. The Governor refused to parley. I myself then proceeded, with Serrurier, to the left bank of the Isonzo, by the Montefalcone road. It would have occupied too much valuable time to construct a bridge. Colonel Andreossy, the director of bridges, was the first to throw himself into the Isonzo, in order to sound the depth: the columns followed his example; the soldiers passed the river up to the middle in water, under the fire of the musquetry of two battalions of Croats, who were routed. Having thus effected the passage, Serrurier's division proceeded to Gradisca, and arrived opposite that place at five o'clock in the evening. During this march, a brisk fire of musquetry was kept up on the right bank, where Bernadotte was engaged. This general had imprudently attempted to take the place by assault, and had lost upwards of four hundred men; but the excuse for this excessive ardour was the eagerness of the troops of the Sambre and Meuse to distinguish themselves, and to reach Gradisca before the old troops of the Army of Italy. When the Governor of Gradisca perceived Serrurier on the heights, he capitulated, and surrendered prisoner of war with 3,000 men, two standards, and twenty field-pieces, with their teams. Head-quarters were at Goritz the next day. Bernadotte's division marched on Laybach; General Dugua, with 1,000 horse, took possession of Trieste. Serrurier marched from Goritz up the Isonzo, through Caporetto and Austrian Chiusa, to support General Guieux, and regain the Carinthian road at Tarwis.

General Guieux had marched from the field of the Tagliamento on Udine and Cividale, and entered the road of the Isonzo at Caporetto: he had had brisk actions every day with Bayalitsch's rearguard, killed a great number of men, made many prisoners, and taken much baggage and artillery, which had forced the enemy to precipitate their march. On reaching Chiusa di Pletz, the Austrians thought themselves safe, for they did not know that Massena had been two days in possession of Tarwis. They were attacked in front by Massena, and in the rear by Guieux. The position of Chiusa, although strong, could not withstand the 4th of the Line (called *the impetuous*). This demi-brigade climbed the mountain that commands the left, and thus turning this important post, left Bayalitsch no resource but to lay down his arms. His baggage, guns, park, and colours, were all taken. The prisoners, however, did not amount to more than 5,000, because a great number of men had been killed, wounded, or taken, in different actions, since the battle of the Tagliamento; and many soldiers, natives of Carniola and Croatia, seeing that all was lost, had disbanded themselves in the passes, and endeavoured to reach their villages singly. The French took thirty-two pieces of cannon, four hundred ammunition and baggage waggons, with their teams, four generals, and many persons employed in the civil department.

Head-quarters were successively fixed at Caporetto, Tarwis, Villach, and Klagenfurth. The army passed the Drave over Villach bridge, which the enemy had not had time to burn. It was now in the valley of the Drave, having passed the Carnic and Julian Alps; it was in Germany. The language, manners, climate, soil, and state of cultivation, were all different from those of Italy. The soldiers were pleased with the hospitality and simplicity of the peasants: the abundance of vegetables, and the quantities of waggons and horses were very useful; in Italy there were only carts drawn by oxen, whose slow and clumsy labours did not suit the vivacity of the French. The army occupied the castles of Goritz, Trieste, and Laybach. The two Austrian divisions, under Kaim and Mercantin, which had marched from the Rhine, were in position at Klagenfurth, and attempted to defend that place; the former lost from 4 to 500 men, and was repulsed.

Klagenfurth was surrounded with a bastioned wall, which had for ages been neglected; the engineer officers filled the ditches with water, repaired the parapets, demolished the houses built on the ramparts, and established hospitals and magazines of every kind in the place. As a point of *appui,* at the debouché of the mountains, it seemed important. The following proclamation was published in all the provinces, in French, German, and Italian: 'Inhabitants of Carinthia, Carniola, and Istria, the French army does not enter your country to conquer it, or to introduce any alterations in your religion, manners, or customs; it is the friend of all nations, and particularly of the brave Germans. Inhabitants of Carinthia, you, I well know, detest as much as we do, both the English, the only gainers by the present war, and your ministry, which is sold to them. Although we have now been upwards of six years at war it has been against the wish of the brave Hungarians, of the enlightened citizens of Vienna, and of the honest, worthy inhabitants of Carinthia, Carniola, and Istria. Well, then, in spite of England and the ministers of the court of Vienna, let us be friends. The French Republic possesses the rights of conquest over you; let them be superseded by a contract mutually binding between us. You will not meddle with a war of which you do not approve! You will supply the wants of my army. On my side, I will protect your property, and require no contribution from you. Is not war of itself sufficiently horrible? Do you not already suffer too much, innocent victims of the passions of others? All the taxes you are accustomed to pay to the Emperor will serve to indemnify you for the damage necessarily attending the march of an army, and to pay you for what you may supply me with.'

This proclamation produced a good effect; it was faithfully observed on both sides. No extraordinary contribution was levied, and the inhabitants gave no occasion for complaint of any kind. Four governments, composed of the richest proprietors, were organized for the four provinces. The English merchandize at Trieste was confiscated. Quicksilver to the value of several millions was found in the imperial warehouses of the mine of Idria.

Ten days had elapsed since the campaign had been opened on the banks of the Piave and Tagliamento, and in Friuli, whilst in the Tyrol both armies had remained inactive. General Kerpen, who commanded the Austrian corps, was in hourly expectation of the arrival of the two divisions of the Rhine. General Joubert had received no orders to attack; his instructions only directed him to keep the enemy in check, and to maintain his position of the Avisio. But immediately after the battle of the Tagliamento, when the Austrian army was driven entirely out of Italy, when Massena had rendered himself master of the Carinthian road, and when I had resolved to march by that road with my whole army, I despatched orders to General Joubert to beat the enemy, to whom he was superior, to march up the banks of the Adige, drive General Kerpen beyond the Brenner, and march by facing to the right and by the Pusterthal, along the road that runs by the side of the Drave, to join the army at Spittal on the Carinthian road. I ordered him to leave a brigade to defend the Avisio, with directions, in case of being forced, to fall back on Montebaldo, there to wait for the orders of General Kilmaine, who commanded in Italy, and to correspond with General Balland at Verona. I knew that when the French army should arrive victorious on the Simering, menacing Vienna, all that might occur in the lower Tyrol would be of secondary importance.

On 20 March, as soon as General Joubert had received his instructions, he commenced his movement. The head-quarters of the army were then at Goritz on the Isonzo. General Kerpen encamped, with his principal forces, at Cambra, behind the Avisio, covering Saint-Michael, by which place he communicated with General Laudon, who occupied the right bank of the Adige. Joubert's division passed the Avisio at Segonzano, whilst the divisions of Delmas and Baraguay d'Hilliers passed it over Lavis bridge, and directed their march on Saint-Michael by the road of the right bank. Thus all the French forces were now in a situation to share in the attack of General Kerpen's camp, whilst Laudon's corps, separated from him by the Adige, remained idly looking on. The action was not doubtful. General Kerpen, driven from all his positions, lost half his men and several standards and pieces of cannon; he had 2,000 men killed, and 3,000 taken prisoners. This battle of Saint-Michael opened the Tyrol. Whilst Baraguay d'Hilliers and Delmas entered Saint-

THE TAGLIAMENTO

Michael and cut down the bridge, Joubert advanced through the mountains directly on Neumarck, took that place after a slight action, passed the bridge, and completely defeated and dispersed the troops under General Laudon, who, with all the force he had been able to collect, was in position between Neumarck and Tramin. In the evening Joubert returned into Neumarck, with 2,500 prisoners, and several pieces of cannon.

In the meantime the van entered Bolzano, a rich trading town of great importance, where it captured all the enemy's magazines. The first Austrian division of the Rhine, commanded by General Sporck, had reached Clausen. In the rear of this division General Kerpen rallied the remains of his corps; and, stationed in a position which seemed inexpugnable, he resolved to await his conqueror. On the 24th General Joubert marched against him with the greater part of his corps d'armée. The attack was brisk; the obstacles presented by the nature of the ground appeared at first insurmountable; but the intrepid French fusiliers, active as the Tyrolese themselves, climbed the mountains which supported the enemy's right, and thereby compelled him to retreat. General Kerpen, all whose hopes now depended on the junction of the second division which he expected from the Rhine, retreated on Mittenwald, thus leaving the Pusterthal road at General Joubert's command; but the latter conceived that it would be dangerous for him to commence his movement on the right, as he would have had to defile so near the enemy's camp. He attacked him on 28 March. A charge of cavalry, under General Dumas, contributed to the success of this action. General Kerpen, now defeated for the third time, evacuated Sterzing and retreated on the Brenner. The alarm spread as far as Inspruck; there was no longer any doubt but that it was General Joubert's intention to march on that place in order to connect his force with the Army of the Rhine. This plan would have been fatal, for the Army of the Rhine was still in cantonments in Alsace. But nothing now remained to prevent Joubert from marching, according to his instructions, by the Pusterthal, to join the grand army on the Carinthian road. On 2 April he began his movement, caused Pruneken and Tolbach to be occupied: and as soon as he had ascertained that nothing could now oppose his debouching in the valley, and his movement on Carinthia, he called in all his posts from the Tyrol. On 4 April his movement was decided. He left a column of 1,200 men, under the command of General Serviez, with orders to resume his positions on the Avisio, in order to cover Italy. General Joubert joined the army with 12,000 men; he was encumbered with 7,000 prisoners taken in these engagements.

Thus, in less than twenty days, the Archduke's army had been defeated in two pitched battles and several actions, and driven beyond the Brenner, the Julian Alps and the Isonzo; Trieste and Fiume, the only two ports of the monarchy, were taken. The provinces of Goritz, Istria, Carniola, and Carin-

THE TAGLIAMENTO

thia obeyed the French government; twenty thousand prisoners, twenty standards, and fifty pieces of horse artillery, taken on the field of battle were the trophies that attested the superiority of the French soldiers. Two of the six divisions, which the Archduke expected from the Rhine, had been defeated. The French head-quarters were in Germany, and not above sixty leagues from Vienna. Everything tended to indicate that in the course of May the victorious French armies would be in possession of that capital; for Austria had not, in the beginning of March, above 80,000 men left, whilst the French Army of the Sambre and Meuse and Rhine amounted to upwards of 130,000.

Chapter XVII

LEOBEN

The Imperial Court leaves Vienna. Overtures of Peace. Action of Neumarck (1 April). Action of Unzmark. Armistice of Judenburg (8 April). Junction of the divisions of the Tyrol, Carniola and Carinthia. Preliminaries of peace of Leoben (18 April). Motives which actuated the French. Of the Armies of the Rhine and Sambre and Meuse; they commence hostilities on 18 April, the very day of the signature of the preliminaries of peace.

The news of the battles of the Tagliamento and of Tarwis, of the action of Goritz, and the entrance of the French into Klagenfurth and Laybach, struck the inhabitants of Vienna with consternation. The capital was menaced, and was destitute of all effectual means of resistance. The most valuable effects and important papers were packed up. The Danube was covered with boats, which were transporting goods into Hungary, whither the young archdukes and archduchesses were sent. Amongst these was the Archduchess Maria Louisa, then five years and a half old, who was afterwards empress of the French. General discontent prevailed. 'In less than a fortnight,' said the people of Vienna, 'the French will probably be before our walls. The ministry does not think of making peace, and we have no means of resisting this terrible army of Italy.'

The armies of the Rhine and Moselle and the Sambre and Meuse were to have opened the campaign, and passed the Rhine on the same day as the army of Italy passed the Piave; and they were to advance as speedily as possible into Germany. When I sent home an account of the battle of the Tagliamento, I announced that I should pass the Julian Alps in a few days, and enter the heart of Germany; that between 1 and 10 April I should be at Klagenfurth, the

LEOBEN

capital of Carinthia, that is to say, within sixty leagues of Vienna; and before 20 April, on the top of the Simering, twenty-five leagues from Vienna; that it was therefore of importance that the armies of the Rhine should put themselves in motion, and that I should be informed of their march. The government, on 23 March, wrote to me in answer, complimenting me on the victory of the Tagliamento, stating reasons why the armies of the Rhine had not taken the field, and assuring me that they would march without delay; but three days afterwards, on 26 March, the ministers wrote that Moreau's army could not take the field, that it was in want of boats to effect the passage of the Rhine, and that the army of Italy was not to reckon upon the co-operation of the armies of Germany, but on itself alone. These despatches, which reached Klagenfurth on 31 March, gave rise to many conjectures. Was the Directory apprehensive that these three armies, comprising all the forces of the Republic, might, if united under the command of one general, render him too powerful? Was it the remembrance of the reverses which the armies of the Rhine and Sambre and Meuse had suffered the year before that intimidated them? Was this strange pusillanimity to be ascribed to a want of vigour and resolution in the generals?—That was impossible. Or was there an intention to sacrifice the Army of Italy, as had been attempted in June, 1796, by ordering half the army to be sent against Naples? As I could no longer calculate on the assistance of these two armies, I was obliged to relinquish all thoughts of entering Vienna; I had not sufficient cavalry to descend into the plain of the Danube; but I thought I might safely advance to the summit of the Simering, and that the most advantageous use I could make of my position was to conclude a peace, which was the general wish of all France.

Within twelve hours from the receipt of the despatches of the Directory, on 31 March, I wrote to Prince Charles in the following terms: 'Whilst brave soldiers carry on war they wish for peace. Has not this war already lasted six years? Have we not killed men enough, and inflicted sufficient misery on the human race? Humanity calls loudly upon us. Europe has laid down the arms she took up against the French Republic. Your nation alone remains; yet blood is to flow more copiously than ever. Fatal omens attend the opening of this sixth campaign. Whatever be its issue, we shall kill some thousands of men on both sides; and after all we must come to an understanding, since all things have an end, not excepting vindictive passions.

'The Executive Directory of the French Republic communicated to his Majesty the Emperor, its wish to put an end to the war which oppresses both nations. The intervention of the court of London opposed this measure. Is there then no hope of arrangement? And must we, on account of the interests and passions of a nation which is a stranger to the horrors of the war, continue to slaughter each other? You, General, whose birth places you so near the throne, and above those petty passions which often actuate ministers and governments, are you disposed to merit the title of a benefactor to the whole human race, and the saviour of Germany? Do not imagine, Sir, that I mean to deny that it may be possible to save Germany by force of arms: but even supposing the chances of war should become favourable to you, the country would nevertheless be ravaged. For my part, General, if the overture I have now the honour to make to you should only save the life of a single man, I should feel more proud of the civic crown I should think I had thereby merited, than of all the mournful glory that the most distinguished successes can afford.'

On 2 April Prince Charles replied as follows: 'Most certainly, General, whilst I carry on war in obedience to the call of honour and duty, I am desirous, as you are, of peace, for the sake of the people and of humanity. Nevertheless, as it does not belong to me, in the functions with which I am entrusted, to inquire into, or terminate the quarrel of the belligerent nations, and as I am not furnished with any powers to treat on the part of his Majesty the Emperor, you will not consider it extraordinary that I do not enter into any negotiation with you, and that I wait for superior orders on this important subject, which is not essentially within my province. But whatever may be the future chances of war, or whatever hopes of peace may exist, I beg you to rest convinced, General, of my esteem, and particular consideration.'

In order to support this overture for negotiation it was important to march forward, and to approach Vienna.

The van was at Saint-Veit, and the head-quarters at Klagenfurth. On 1 April at break of day, Massena advanced on Freisach. In front of the castle he met with the enemy's rearguard, which covered considerable magazines collected by the Archduke; he attacked them briskly, and entered Freisach pell-mell with them, took all the stores, and continued the pursuit almost as far as Neumarck, where he met the Archduke with four battalions from the Rhine, those of the Prince of Orange, General Kaim, and General Mercantin, the reserve of grenadiers, and the remains of the old army, in position to defend the gorges of Neumarck. I immediately ordered Massena to join with all his division on the left of the high road; I placed Guieux's division on the heights on the right, and Serrurier's in reserve. At three o'clock in the afternoon the 2nd light infantry of Massena's division charged the enemy's first line, and covered themselves with glory. These troops came from the Rhine, and the soldiers used to call them the *contingent,* alluding to the troops of the German princes, which were not considered the best in the world; and the soldiers of the 2nd light infantry, being piqued by this appellation, challenged the old soldiers of the army of Italy to go as fast and as far as themselves; they performed prodigies: Prince Charles exposed himself to the greatest personal danger, in vain; he was driven from all his positions, and lost 3,000 men. The French troops entered Neumarck at night, pell-mell with the Austrians, and took 1,200 prisoners, six pieces of cannon, and five standards. Scheifling,

LEOBEN

where the third cross-road joins the highway, was still twelve leagues off. The Austrian general, being unable to retard the victor's march, had recourse to a stratagem to gain twenty-four hours, and give General Kerpen time to debouch at Scheifling. He proposed a suspension of arms, in order, as he said, to take into consideration the letter which had been written to him on 31 March. Berthier answered, that they might negotiate and fight at the same time; but that there could be no armistice until the French reached Vienna, unless for the purpose of treating for a definite peace. At daybreak the French vanguard commenced its march on the Muer. Strong reconnoitring parties had been sent as far as Murau, to meet Kerpen's corps; I went thither in person; but that corps had fallen back; its rearguard, under General Sporck, was slightly harassed. On the 4th and 5th the French head-quarters remained at Scheifling, a castle situate on the banks of the Muer.

From Scheifling to Knittelfeld, the road runs along the Muer, through formidable defiles. Positions which might have stopped the French army were found at every step. It was of the utmost importance to the Archduke to gain a few days to give Vienna time to make preparations, and to enable the troops, which were hastening with all possible expedition from the Rhine, to arrive and cover that great capital. The same reasons dictated to the French the necessity of accelerating their march by all possible means. On the 3rd, the van had a furious engagement with the enemy in the defiles of Unzmarkt; they overthrew the enemy notwithstanding his superiority, drove him from all his positions at the point of the bayonet, and entered Knittelfeld. The loss of the Austrians was considerable; 1,500 prisoners and four pieces of cannon were taken. Colonel Carrère, a distinguished officer commanding the artillery of the vanguard was killed; he was much regretted, being a good officer in battle. One of the frigates found at Venice received his name; it was one of those with which I sailed from Egypt, when I returned to France and landed at Frejus. On 6 April the head-quarters of the army were fixed at Judenburg, the principal town of one of the circles of Carinthia.

After the action of Unzmarkt, the army met with no further resistance; its van reached Leoben on the 7th. Lieutenant-General Bellegarde, Prince Charles's adjutant-general, and Major-General Merfeld, presented themselves at that place under a flag of truce. After a conference with me, they delivered the following note: 'General, His Majesty the Emperor and King has nothing more at heart than to contribute to the repose of Europe, and to terminate a war which is ravaging both nations. In consequence of the overtures which you made to his Royal Highness by your letter from Klagenfurth, his Majesty the Emperor has sent us to meet you for the purpose of conferring on this important subject. After the conversation we have just had with you, and persuaded of the sincere wish and intention of both powers to put an end to this disastrous war as speedily as possible, his Imperial Highness desires a

LEOBEN

suspension of arms for ten days, that he may attain this desirable object with the greater celerity, and in order to remove all the delays and obstacles which the continuation of hostilities would occasion in the negotiations, so that everything may concur to restore peace between the two nations.'

I answered this note the same day in the following terms: 'In the military position of the two armies, a suspension of arms is wholly prejudicial to the French army; but if it is to prove a step towards the peace so much wished for, and so necessary to the people, I am happy to consent to your wishes. The French Republic has often testified to his Majesty its desire to put an end to this cruel contest; it persists in the same sentiments, and I doubt not, after the conference I have had the honour of holding with you, but that peace may be made between the French Republic and his Majesty.'

The armistice was signed on the 7th, in the evening. It was to last five days. The whole country, as far as the Simering, was occupied by the French army. Gratz, one of the largest towns of the Austrian monarchy, was surrendered with its citadel. General Berthier, at dinner, asked the Austrian commissioners, where they supposed Bernadotte's division to be?—'About Laybach,' they replied. 'And Joubert's?'—'Between Brixen and Mulback.'—'No;' answered he, 'they are all in echelons: the most distant is only a day's march behind.' This surprised them much. On the 9th head-quarters were at Leoben, and the vanguard reached Bruck, pushing parties forward as far as the Simering. Adjutant-General Leclerc was sent to Paris to acquaint the government with the signature of the armistice. He was a distinguished officer, intrepid in the field of battle, and skilful in official business.

I had sent my aide-de-camp Lavalette, at the head of a party of cavalry, from Klagenfurth, on 30 March, to meet General Joubert. He proceeded as far as Lienz, but General Joubert had not then debouched from the Tyrol. The townsmen, perceiving that the French were but sixty men, took up arms against them; and this detachment was saved only by the coolness and intrepidity of the aide-de-camp who commanded it. One dragoon only was assassinated. A few days afterwards, General Zajonczek, with several squadrons of dragoons, occupied Lienz, and communicated with the corps of the Tyrol. The town was disarmed and the inhabitants punished. On 8 April, Joubert arrived at Spittal, near Villach, and formed the left of the army. He had the prisoners immediately removed into the rear.

General Bernadotte, having completed the organization of Carniola, received orders to pass the Save and the Muer, and to join the army at Leoben. He left General Friant, with a column of 1,500 men, to cover the evacuation of Fiume, and keep Carniola in awe. It was easy to foresee that with so inconsiderable a force he might probably be repulsed; in that case he was to defend the Isonzo, and finally, to throw himself into Palma-Nuova, to complete the garrison of that place. The event proved as had been expected; a body of

LEOBEN

6,000 Croats attacked him on 15 April. Friant's troops, although only one to four, repulsed the enemy, who suffered great loss; but the general saw the necessity of evacuating Fiume; and the armistice of Judenburg found him on 19 April at Materia, covering Trieste. These events, exaggerated like those which had occurred in the Tyrol, were reported at Venice, and were the principal cause of the commotions and hostilities which produced the fall of that state.

During the five days of the armistice, from 7 to 12 April, Massena's division established itself at Bruck, at the foot of the Simering, having advanced posts half-way up the mountain. Head-quarters were removed to the Bishop's palace at Leoben. Serrurier's division occupied the important town of Gratz, and began the necessary works for putting the castle in a state of defence. These five days of rest were extremely necessary and useful. The armistice expired on the 13th; but at nine in the morning Count Merfeld arrived, furnished with full powers to negotiate and sign preliminaries of peace, conjointly with the Marquis di Gallo, ambassador from Naples to Vienna, who enjoyed the favour of the Empress, whose influence over the affairs of the empire was remarkable. A prolongation of the suspension of arms to 20 April was signed, and conferences for the negotiation of the preliminaries were opened. On 16 April, after long debates, three plans were agreed upon, which were despatched to Vienna, and to which the French plenipotentiary gave his consent. On the 17th the answer of the cabinet of Vienna having been brought by Baron Vincent, the Emperor's aide-de-camp, the patent and secret preliminary articles were drawn up; the secretaries of legation neutralized a country seat, a league from Leoben, where the preliminaries of peace were signed on the morning of the 18th. General Clarke was furnished, as has been stated, with the full powers of the government, but he was then at Turin. It required time for him to reach head-quarters; and as he had not arrived on the 18th I took the responsibility on myself, as on many other occasions, and signed the treaty. General Clarke reached head-quarters a few days afterwards. The Austrian plenipotentiaries thought they had done something very agreeable in setting down, as the first article, that the Emperor acknowledged the French Republic. 'Strike that out,' said I: 'the Republic is like the sun, which shines by its own light; none but the blind can fail to see it.' In fact, this acknowledgment would have done mischief, because, if the French people had afterwards wished to create a monarchy, the Emperor might have said that he had acknowledged the Republic.[1] It was stipulated by the preliminaries, that the

---

[1] There is evidently some confusion in Napoleon's mind as to whether he made this remark during the signature of the preliminaries at Leoben on 18 August or when signing the peace treaty at Campo-Formio on 17 October, as described on page 260 of these Memoirs. In either case it is virtually an admission that he already had the Crown in mind in 1797. S. de C.

definitive treaty should be negotiated in a congress to be assembled at Berne, and that the peace of the empire should be the business of another congress, which should be held in a German city. The limits of the Rhine were guaranteed to France. The Oglio was the limit of the states of the house of Austria in Italy, and of the Cisalpine Republic, composed of Lombardy, the Modenese, Bergomasque and Cremasque countries. The city of Venice was to receive the legations of Ferrara and Bologna, and Romagna, as a compensation for the loss of its states of the Terra-Firma. By this treaty the Emperor had Mantua, but the Republic gained Venice. The French armies were enabled to communicate from Milan to Venice by the right bank of the Po, to debouch on the Piave, and to disregard the lines of the Mincio, the Adige, and Mantua. Nothing now prevented the two Republics from uniting in one, if it suited their convenience. Venice had existed nine centuries, without possessing any territory in Italy, being only a maritime state; and this was the period of her greatest power. The truth is, however, that these arrangements were stipulated in enmity to the Venetians. It was just when General Kilmaine's despatches of 3 and 5 April arrived. The army was transported with indignation at the murders which were perpetrating in its rear. An insurrectionary cockade was displayed at Venice, and the English minister wore it in triumph; the Lion of Saint Mark was seen on his gondola; this minister had great influence.

On 27 April the Marquis di Gallo presented the preliminaries, ratified by the Emperor, to me as General-in-Chief at Gratz. The exchange did not take place immediately, because it was necessary to wait for the ratification of the Executive Directory; but as there could be no doubt respecting this ratification, the army evacuated Styria and part of Carniola and Carinthia. Several overtures having been made by the Emperor's plenipotentiaries, the aide-de-camp Lemarrois carried the answers to Vienna. He was received with distinction; this was the first time since the Revolution that the tri-coloured cockade had been seen in that capital. It was in one of these conferences at Gratz, that one of the plenipotentiaries, authorized by an autograph letter of the Emperor's, offered to procure me, on the conclusion of peace, a sovereignty of 250,000 souls in Germany, for myself and my family, in order to place me beyond the reach of republican ingratitude. I smiled; I desired the plenipotentiary to thank the Emperor for this proof of the interest he took in my welfare, and said, that I wished for no greatness or riches, unless conferred on me by the French people. It is affirmed that I added: 'and with that support, believe me, Sir, my ambition will be satisfied.'

Adjutant-General Dessolles was despatched to Paris with the news of the opening of the negotiations. General Massena carried the preliminary treaty to the Directory. He was received on 9 May in a solemn audience. All the distinguished generals of the Army of Italy had been successively sent to Paris to carry home trophies of victory. Massena alone, who ranked foremost of them on account of the share he had had in every victory, had not yet been sent.

The situation of the Army of Italy was prosperous; the musters of 16 April stated 38,500 infantry, 4,500 cavalry; total 43,000 men; and 120 pieces of cannon. These forces were assembled on one spot, and ready to post themselves on the Simering in a single march. The losses they had suffered since the opening of the campaign were but trifling. The fortresses of Palma-Nuova, Klagenfurth, and Gratz, were victualled and armed; numerous magazines of all kinds were collecting in them. The French soldiers were animated with the utmost courage and alacrity; at the action of Neumarck a third only of Massena's division were engaged, and proved sufficient to overthrow the *élite* of the Austrian troops, although advantageously posted. The Archduke's army, on the contrary, was discouraged; he had now scarce any of the troops of his old army of Italy. The six divisions from the Rhine had been successively attacked, and suffered severe loss; they were considerably diminished. I might have entered Vienna at once; but this would have produced no good effect; it would have been difficult for me to maintain my ground there, for the armies of the Rhine had not taken the field, and had moreover declared themselves unable to do so. The councils and the Directory were at variance; there was even a difference amongst the directors themselves; the government was devoid of strength; public spirit was a nullity in France; the finances were in a deplorable state. The Army of the Rhine was unpaid, and in the greatest penury. One of the principal obstacles of its passing the Rhine, was the total inability of the treasury to supply Moreau with the 30 or 40,000 crowns he wanted for the purpose of organizing his pontoon train. Regiments raised in La Vendée for the Army of Italy, and increased to 4,000 men by the incorporation of various corps, arrived at Milan only 900 or 1,000 strong; three-fourths of the men having deserted on the march. The government had no system for making the deserters rejoin, and recruiting the armies.

In the first conferences the Austrian plenipotentiaries consented to the cession of Belgium, and to the line of the Rhine; but they demanded indemnities, and when it was proposed to give them indemnities in Germany, for instance in Bavaria, they immediately added that, in that case, Venice must also be guaranteed in its existing constitution, and the aristocracy of the Golden Book confirmed, as Austria would never under any pretence, permit the Italian Republic to extend itself from the Alps and Apennines to the Isonzo and the Julian Alps. But this was strengthening the most active and constant enemy of the French Republic; an enemy, who, apprized of his danger by recent events, was thenceforth likely to have no other policy than that of combining more closely with Austria, and making common cause with that power, which, in fact, would have made an offensive and defensive league with the Venetian oligarchy against the democratic Italian Republic.

LEOBEN

This was increasing the power of Austria by the addition of Bavaria and of territory of Venice. In the instructions given by the Directory to General Clarke, as already stated in Chapter XIII, he had been authorized to sign much less advantageous conditions. Peace was the will of the people, the government, and the legislative body: I therefore signed the preliminaries.

Hoche had just been promoted to the command of the Army of the Sambre and Meuse; he was a young man full of talent, bravery, and ambition. He had a superb army under his command, which he acknowledged to amount to 80,000 men under arms: he felt himself able to conduct it, and his heart swelled with impatience at the news he was constantly receiving from the Army of Italy. By every courier he sent, he entreated the Directory to allow him to enter Germany. The troops shared his ardour; even the inhabitants, informed by their correspondents of my rapid march on Vienna, and the retrograde movement of the Austrian armies of the Rhine, enquired why the French of the Sambre and Meuse and Rhine remained inactive and lost so much valuable time.

On 18 April Hoche passed the Rhine at the bridge of Neuwied, whilst Championnet, who had marched from Dusseldorf, arrived at Uckerath and Altenkirchen. Kray commanded the Austrian army. Hoche attacked him at Hedersdorf, took several thousand prisoners, some cannon and colours, and forced him to fall back on the Maine. On 22 April, Hoche arrived before Frankfort, when General Kray's staff transmitted to him despatches from General Berthier, informing him of the signature of the treaty of Leoben. He immediately concluded an armistice, and advanced his head-quarters to Friedberg, occupying the Nidda and Wetzlar. Moreau was at Paris, soliciting pontoons to pass the Rhine at Strasburg; but as soon as Desaix, who commanded the Army of the Rhine, *ad interim*, found that Hoche was engaged with the enemy, he constructed a bridge on 20 April, at six o'clock in the morning, at the village of Kilstett, several leagues below Strasburg. On the 21st, at two o'clock in the morning, the army passed the Rhine. Moreau, who had posted with all possible speed from Paris, found himself at the head of the army just as Sztarray, who had collected 20,000 men and twenty pieces of cannon, was attacking it. The action was hot; the Austrians were completely beaten; they left a number of prisoners and twenty pieces of cannon in the power of the conquerors. All the equipages of the Austrian chancery were taken. Amongst these was Klinglin's waggon, which contained Pichegru's correspondence with the Prince of Condé, which Moreau kept secret for four months without communicating it to the government. After this victory the army marched up the Rhine and took Kehl. The van had arrived beyond Offenbach, in the valley of the Kintzig, on the 22nd, when a courier from the Army of Italy brought the news of the signature of the preliminaries of Leoben. Moreau put a stop to hostilities, and concluded an armistice with Sztarray.

LEOBEN

Hostilities did not commence on the Rhine until eight hours after the treaty of Leoben had been signed; and I received the intelligence seven days after the signature of that treaty. Why was not the campaign re-commenced five days sooner, or at least why had the Directory written that the co-operation of the armies of the Rhine was not to be reckoned upon? But the affairs of the war were conducted without energy or talent; the administration was corrupt, and never produced any satisfactory result. By one of the clauses of the constitution of year III, the treasury was made independent of the government; an idea equally false and disastrous, and the most absurd that could have been found out by the metaphysics of our modern legislators! This alone was sufficient to endanger the existence of the Republic.

Chapter XVIII

OBSERVATIONS

On Field-Marshal Beaulieu. On my manoeuvres against Field-Marshal Beaulieu. On Field-Marshal Wurmser. On my manoeuvres against Field-Marshal Wurmser. On Field-Marshal Alvinzi. On my manoeuvres against Field-Marshal Alvinzi. On the march against the army of the Holy See. On the Archduke Charles. On my manoeuvres against the Archduke Charles.

FIRST OBSERVATION: (1) An army in position on the upper ridge of the Maritime Alps, resting its left on the Col d'Argentieres, and its right on the Col di Tende, would cover the whole country of Nice. It would be from fifteen to eighteen leagues distant from the sea;—three or four days' march. In its rear there would be a great number of good positions, in which it might rally and arrest the march of a conqueror; it would have time to effect its retreat at pleasure upon Genoa or the Var. This theatre of operations possesses sufficient depth to admit of being defended to advantage.

An army occupying the upper ridges of the Apennines, from Tanarello to the Saint Bernard (of the Tanaro), would cover part of the *Riviere di Ponente*, it would occupy positions two days' march from the sea; in its rear it would have Monte Grande, San Bartolomeo, and Rocca Barbena: the little river of the Arosoia, which passes near Pieva and Albenza, is very defensible.

This army might, therefore, defend the ground, cover Oneglia, and advance on Genoa or Nice at pleasure; but an army occupying the upper ridge of the Apennines, from Bardinetto to the Bocchetta, that is to say, the heights of Saint-Jacques, Cadibona, Montelegino, Stella, and Montefaiale, would undoubtedly cover the other part of the *Riviere di Ponente* as far as Genoa; but as

OBSERVATIONS

this army would be only from two to five leagues from the sea, it might be cut off in one day, and would be in danger of not having time to rally and effect its retreat. This is a bad field of operations, essentially dangerous, not having sufficient depth.

(2) Had General Beaulieu reflected on these topographical circumstances, he would not have marched on Voltri to cover Genoa; he would have advanced by Acqui, and on Cairo, whence he would have debouched in three columns at once, each 15,000 strong; the left by Montenotte, Montelegino, and Savona; the centre on Cadibona and Vado; and the right on la Madonna della Neva, Saint-Jacques and Finale. He would have had a reserve in a proper situation to succour these three attacks. The French army would soon have fallen back from Voltri and Genoa, to defend these three important positions. The Austrian general would have drawn the war into a field entirely advantageous to him; for he might have cut off the French army, driven it back to the seashore, and ruined it in one day.

(3) After the battle of Montenotte, the Austrians rallied on the Montferrat road; they could act no otherwise, because the greater part of their forces were about Voltri and Sassello, and dispersed on their left. But the Piedmontese army, under the command of General Colli, should have supported itself on Dego, and formed Beaulieu's left, instead of marching on Millesimo. It was an error to imagine that, in order to cover Turin, it was necessary to be posted on both sides of the road to that city. The armies united at Dego would have covered Milan, because they would have been posted across the high road of Montferrat; they would have covered Turin, because they would have been on the flank of the road to that city. If Beaulieu had had five or six days to spare for the purpose of rallying his left, he should have marched on Ceva to join the Piedmontese army, because it was most advantageous to the allies to remain near the line of operations of the French army. There was no fear that the latter would enter Montferrat whilst the enemy had an army near Ceva. United, the two armies were still superior to the French army; but, if separated, they were lost.

(4) Dego and Millesimo were too near Montenotte to be safe rallying-points for the Austrian and Piedmontese armies. Beaulieu should have collected his army before Acqui, and Colli, since they would separate, on the heights of Montezemolo; they would thus have avoided the battle of Millesimo, and the action of Dego. The divisions of each army would have had time to reach these two points of assemblage, before the French army could have attacked them there. *When you are driven from a first position, you should rally your columns at a sufficient distance in the rear, to prevent the enemy from anticipating them; for the greatest misfortune you can meet with is to have your columns separately attacked before their junction.*

(5) In order to contest the passage of the Po, General Beaulieu took up a

position on the left bank of that river, near Valeggio; this operation could never fulfil its intention, in the face of an army accustomed to manoeuvres. He should have posted himself across the Po, by throwing two bridges over at Stradella, and covering them by strong *têtes-de-pont*. By this alone he would have prevented the French army from marching down the right bank, and obliged it to pass the Po above Stradella, which would have given the Austrian general the important advantage of protecting his defensive operations, by the two great barriers of the Po and the Ticino.

(6) General Beaulieu wished to defend the Mincio by a cordon. This is the very worst plan in the whole system of defence. It was only May; he should have occupied the Seraglio with his whole army; he might have remained there seventy days without danger of sickness. He left a garrison of 13,000 men in Mantua, and he had 26,000 on the Mincio. He might, therefore, have collected 40,000 men, that is to say, a force superior to the French army, in the formidable position of the Seraglio; he would thus have maintained his communications with Modena and Lower Italy, and got a great quantity of provisions into Mantua. Had the French general succeeded in forcing this intrenched camp, it would have been no easy matter for him to invest an army which occupied Saint-George, Cerea, Pietoli and Pradella in force. By this line of conduct, Beaulieu would have avoided violating the neutrality of Venice. The Emperor would have been able to insist effectually on the maintenance of neutrality by the Senate of Venice, which would have been highly advantageous to him.

(7) But not having taken these steps, Marshal Beaulieu might, after passing the Oglio, have proceeded to the heights of Gavardo, and taken the position of Saint-Ozetto, with his right to the Chiesa, and his left to the lake of Garda; the French army would then have been forced to take up an opposite position before Brescia, and could not have extended itself beyond the Mincio, so long as the Austrian army occupied that position, or any other between the lakes of Idro and Garda.

(Lastly) As the Austrian General, in the dispirited state of his army, could not give battle, he ought not to have deceived himself so far as to expect much protection from the Mincio. By dispersing his army along that river, he weakened himself; he could have been stronger had he occupied a good position on the hills between the lake of Garda and the Adige, before the level of Rivoli, covering himself there with retrenchments. He might then have required the Venetians to occupy the fortress of Peschiera in force, and to refuse entrance to the French army, as they would have been thought to have refused it to the Austrian army. Verona, which was a fortified place, with a garrison of 3,000 Sclavonians, would also have refused admission to the French, since it would likewise have been considered as having refused it to the Imperialists. These great advantages were sacrificed by the Austrian

OBSERVATIONS

general, for the sake of strengthening his cordon of the Mincio. He himself violated the neutrality of Venice by occupying Peschiera.

SECOND OBSERVATION: (1) When the French army directed its march on Ceva to attack the Piedmontese army, Laharpe's division was left in observation against the camp of Acqui, where Beaulieu was rallying all the Austrian army. It would appear that the natural position of this corps of observation would have been on the banks of the Bormida, before Dego, in order to cover the line of operations on Savona. It is to be remarked that I only preferred the position on the Belbo, before San Benedetto, two days' march on the left of Dego, leaving the Savona road uncovered, because I wished to keep my army in junction, that Beaulieu might not throw himself between my divisions and insulate them. The camp of San Benedetto covered the army which was manoeuvring on Ceva. If Beaulieu had marched on Dego, the corps placed at San Benedetto would have attacked him in flank and rear; besides, the communications of Garessio and Ormea were open; the choice of the camp of San Benedetto for the corps of observation against Beaulieu deserves consideration.

(2) The divisions of Serrurier and Massena marched on Mondovi; they were sufficient; and, in the meantime, Beaulieu having detached some troops from Acqui on Nizza della Paglia, Augereau's division was ordered to proceed to the support of the camp of San Benedetto, and, after the battle of Mondovi, marched on Alba, pushing forward a vanguard on Nizza della Paglia.

(3) It has been said that I should have passed the Po, not at Piacenza, but at Cremona; but this is erroneous. My operation was sufficiently daring as it was; for, in marching along the Po from Alessandria, I exposed my flank for twenty leagues to the Austrian army; had I prolonged this march seven leagues more, it is evident that I would have been still more exposed. Beaulieu, after reaching Fombio, would have passed the Po at Piacenza, would have fallen on the columns in march, and cut off the line of operations of the right bank, as he intercepted that of the left by observing the Adda. Besides, Piacenza is situate on the right bank, and afforded resources for the passage of the river; Cremona is situate on the left bank, and the few Austrians who were there would have been sufficient to delay the passage.

(4) It has been said, that if the French army, after the battle of Lodi, had marched on Mantua, it would have found that place without provisions or means of defence, and might have taken it; but this conjecture is rashly thrown out. The army had, in a few days, conquered all Lombardy; it was necessary to stay there long enough to establish the blockade of the fortresses, occupy the most important points, and organize the administration. What the French performed, under these circumstances, is the very maximum of what may be

required of rapidity and activity. To demand anything more would be asking impossibilities. During the six days that the French army remained in Lombardy, it doubled its means, by increasing its artillery and ammunition, remounting its cavalry, and rallying the stragglers, who had remained in the rear in consequence of forced marches.

(5) The revolt of Pavia might have had important consequences: the activity and vigour of the repressive measures adopted, the burning of Binasco, the sacking of a few houses in Pavia, the taking of four hundred hostages, selected throughout Lombardy and sent into France, the respectable character of conciliators, with which I invested the bishops and clergy—all these proceedings were worthy of applause and imitation. The tranquillity of this fine country was never after disturbed. By confiding the police of the country to the city and country guards and to national magistrates, I organized the country, spared my own army, and obtained auxiliaries.

(6) The battle of Borghetto was fought on 30 May; Wurmser's attack took place on 1 August; it was in this interval of sixty days that part of the army passed the Po, took the legations of Ferrara and Bologna, fort Urbino, the citadel of Ferrara and Leghorn, and disarmed these provinces. The troops had returned to the Adige before Wurmser was in a situation to commence his operations: surely their time had been well employed. The strength of an army, like the quantity of movements in mechanics, is estimated by the mass multiplied by quickness. This march, instead of weakening the army, increased its resources and its courage, and added to its means of conquest.

(7) Had I carried into execution the orders of my government, I would have marched on Rome and Naples with 20,000 men, leaving the rest of the army before Mantua, under the command of Kellermann. Italy and the army would have been lost. I would certainly have been only obeying the orders of my superiors, but this would not have been a sufficient excuse for me. A general-in-chief is not completely justified by the order of a minister or prince far from the field of operations, and ill-informed or uninformed of the latest posture of affairs. First: Every general-in-chief who undertakes to execute a plan which he considers bad and likely to prove disastrous, is criminal; he ought to make representations on the subject, to insist upon a change, and, in short, to give in his resignation rather than become the instrument of his men's destruction. Secondly: Every general-in-chief who, in consequence of orders from his superiors, fights a battle that he is certain to lose, is equally guilty. Thirdly: A general-in-chief is the first officer of the military hierarchy. The minister or the prince gives instructions to which, in spirit and conscience, he is to adhere; but these instructions are never military orders, and do not require passive obedience. Fourthly: Even military orders do not require passive obedience, unless they are given by a superior who, being present at the moment of giving them, is acquainted with the state of

OBSERVATIONS

affairs, and has an opportunity of listening to objections, and of giving explanations to the person who is to execute the order.

Tourville attacked eighty English ships with only forty French, and the French fleet was destroyed. The orders of Louis XIV do not justify this commander: they were not military orders requiring passive obedience, but instructions. The clause understood was, provided there be an equal chance of success. In that case the Admiral's responsibility was covered by the prince's letter; but when, from the state of affairs, the loss of the battle was certain, the literal execution of the order shewed little understanding of its spirit. Had the Admiral, when he waited on Louis XIV said to him, 'Sire, if I had attacked the English, your whole squadron would have been lost; I have brought it back into such a port,' the King would have thanked him, and the royal order would in fact have been executed.

The conduct of the Duke of Orleans before Turin in 1706 has been justified; historians acquit him of all blame. The Duke of Orleans was a prince; he was afterwards regent; he was a liberal man, and writers have been favourable to him; whilst Marsin, who was left dead on the field of battle, could not defend himself. It is well known, however, that he protested, with his dying breath, against the resolution that was adopted of remaining in the lines. But who was the general-in-chief of the French army of Italy? The Duke of Orleans. Marsin, Lafeuillade, and Albergotti, were under his command; it depended on him whether to take the opinion of a council of war; he presided at it: it was at his option whether to abide by the opinion of this council or not. The Prince was not disturbed in his command; no one refused obedience to him. First: Had he ordered the French army to march out of his lines; secondly, had he given orders for the left to pass the Doire in order to reinforce the right; thirdly, had he positively ordered Albergotti to repass the Po, and the generals had refused to comply, under the pretext that they were not bound to obey him, all would have been well; the Prince would have been exculpated. But, it is said, Albergotti did not obey the order he received to detach a body of troops to the right bank of the Po; he indulged in remarks; a thing that happens daily. This was not an act of disobedience: had the Prince sent him a positive order; had he galloped up to his camp, ordered the troops to fall in, and given the word—*Head of column to the left,* he would have been obeyed; fourthly, the battle being lost, the army retreated on Asti to cover Lombardy, and join Medavi's army, who had the same day gained a victory at Castiglione. The Commander-in-chief (the Duke) changed his mind, and retreated on Pignerol, because he thought himself cut off from the road to Lombardy. If the obscure anecdote which has been circulated, that the Duke of Orleans was only nominally general and that Marsin was furnished with a secret order from the King, authorizing him to command, were really true, the performance of such a part by the Duke of Orleans at the age of thirty-

OBSERVATIONS

two would have been a dishonourable, contemptible action, which would have disgraced the most inconsiderable private gentleman. Had the French been victorious, who would have reaped the glory? Count Marsin was provided with a recommendation from the King requiring the Prince to attend to his advice; this was all. The Duke of Orleans was the Commander-in-Chief acknowledged by the generals, officers, and soldiers; no one refused, or would have refused to obey him, and he was responsible for all that took place.

General Jourdan, in his Memoirs, says, that the government had intimated to him that they wished him to give battle at Stockach: thus endeavouring to exculpate himself from the unfortunate result of that affair; but this justification could not be admitted, even had he received positive and formal orders, as we have already proved. When he determined on giving battle, he thought he had a fair chance of gaining the victory, and he was deceived.

But might not a minister or a prince express his intentions so clearly that no condition could possibly be understood? Might he not say to a general-in-chief, 'Give battle. The enemy, from his number, the excellence of his troops, and the positions he occupies, will beat you; that is of no importance; it is my will.' Ought such orders to be passively executed? No. If the General comprehended the utility, and therefore the morality, of so strange an injunction, he ought to execute it; but if he did not understand it, he ought not to obey it.

Something of the kind, however, frequently occurs in war; a battalion is left in a difficult position in order to save the army; but the commanding officer of that battalion receives a positive order to that effect from his general, who is present when he gives it; and answers all objections, if any reasonable objections can be made: these are military orders given by a present chief, and are entitled to passive obedience. But if the minister or prince were with the army? In that case, if they take the command, they are the generals-in-chief, and the general is only a subordinate general of division.

It does not follow that a general-in-chief is not bound to obey a minister who orders him to give battle; on the contrary, he ought to do it whenever the chances are, in his opinion, equal, and there is as much probability of his success as of his defeat; for the foregoing observation applies only to cases where the chances appear to him wholly unfavourable.

THIRD OBSERVATION: (1) Marshal Wurmser's plan, in the beginning of August, was defective; his three corps, one of which was immediately under his own command, another under that of Quasdanowich, and the third under that of Davidowich, were separated from each other by two great rivers, the Adige and the Mincio, several chains of mountains, and the lake of Garda.

Wurmser should either have debouched with all his forces between the

OBSERVATIONS

lake of Garda and the Adige; possessed himself of the level of Rivoli, and made his artillery join him at Incanale (70 or 80,000 men, thus posted, with the right supported on the lake of Garda and the left on the Adige, with a front of three leagues, would have overawed the French army, which, containing scarce 30,000 fighting men, could not have made head against them);

Or he should have debouched, with his whole army in junction, by the Chiesa on Brescia, where artillery can pass.

(2) In the execution of his plan he committed an error which cost him dear; this was his losing two days in advancing on Mantua. He should, on the contrary, have thrown two bridges over the Mincio, a cannon-shot from Peschiera, and promptly crossed that river, joined his right at Lonato, Dezenzano, and Salo, and thus made up for the defects of his plan by the rapidity of its execution.

(3) To operate in directions remote from each other and without communications between them, is a fault which commonly produces a second error. The column detached has orders only for the first day; its operations for the second depend on what may have happened to the principal column; thus it either loses time in waiting for orders, or acts at random. On this occasion Wurmser ought to have avoided this disadvantage, and given orders to Quasdanowich, not only for debouching on Brescia, but even on Mantua, and advanced himself, with the principal corps, on that fortress with all possible expedition. Quasdanowich would have reached Mantua, if he had not been stopped at Brescia; he would have compelled the French to raise the siege; would have found protection behind the ramparts of the place, and subsisted on its magazines; the junction with the army would have been effected at a fixed point, which was not exposed to the vicissitudes of the campaign; and if Wurmser had been defeated before he reached Mantua, Quasdanowich would, nevertheless, have supplied the garrison with provisions; he might have occupied the Seraglio a long time; in short, he could have acted according to circumstances.

It is therefore a principle that an army should always keep its columns in junction, so that the enemy may not be able to introduce himself between them; and when, from particular circumstances, this principle is departed from, the detached corps must be independent in their operations; and, in order to join again, must direct their course towards a fixed point, upon which they must march without hesitation, and without fresh orders, that they may be the less exposed to separate attacks.

(4) In the beginning of September, Wurmser put himself in motion to advance with 30,000 men into the Bassanese, leaving Davidowich with 30,000 men in the Tyrol. He ought to have foreseen the possibility that the French General would debouch in the Tyrol, and to have ordered Davidowich not to accept battle at Roveredo, but to fall back on Bassano, that they might together give battle to the French army; the Tyrolese militia were sufficient

OBSERVATIONS

to observe the Avisio. Or else he should have contrived to be on the field of battle in the Tyrol, ordering Davidowich to retreat on Calliano and the Avisio. San Marco, Mori, and Roveredo are good positions; but against impetuous troops they will not compensate for inferiority of numbers. In all these affairs of defiles, the columns, when once broken, throw each other into confusion, and are sure to fall into the enemy's power.

(5) When Wurmser conceived the idea of directing General Mezaros's division on Verona, it was too late for that movement, which had been foreseen. Kilmaine was there with a small corps of observation. Wurmser would have done better in keeping this division at Bassano, to support the two others; but at all events, as he was determined to operate on Mantua with part of his troops, he should have given this division 2,000 cavalry, thirty pieces of cannon, and an equipage of pontoons; directing it, not on Verona, but on Albaredo, where it would have constructed its bridge, and whence it might have marched with the utmost expedition upon Mantua. The blockade of that place would have been raised, and the rear of the French much harassed; even Verona might have been taken in the rear; and the garrison of Mantua, thus reinforced, might long have maintained the command of the country. The Marshal might then have retreated from Bassano, with his two other divisions, his parks, and his staff, upon the Piave. The left of the French army would have been obliged to remain on the Avisio, before Trent; its centre, on the Piave, to oppose the principal corps of the enemy's army; and it must have extended its rear to Mantua, in order to renew the blockade: this would have been no inconsiderable share of employment for a small army, and might have given rise to vicissitudes of fortune.

(6) Wurmser's march on the Adige, with the remaining 16,000 men of his army, was compulsory; he ought to have been surrounded, driven to the river, and forced to lay down his arms, because he had no pontoons, his two trains and his parks of reserve having been taken at Bassano. He was entirely indebted, for his success in making his way to Mantua, to the error of a lieutenant-colonel, who evacuated Legnago.

(7) The Marshal left 1,800 men and several batteries in Legnago to no purpose; there was no possibility of his retreating in the direction of the Adige, where there was the whole of the French army. It was necessary for him to regain Mantua; and if that proved impossible, it was easier for him to enter Milan than to return to Legnago. He thus weakened his army unnecessarily, and made a useless sacrifice.

(8) Wurmser was also wrong in risking the battle of Saint George; it would have been more advantageous to him to have remained in the Seraglio, which is the proper field of battle for the garrisons of Mantua, when they are numerous.

(9) The Marshal, whilst master of the Seraglio, might also have passed the

OBSERVATIONS

Po with the whole of his cavalry, some battalions of grenadiers, and a few well-horsed batteries, marched down the right bank of that river, repassing the Po lower down, crossed the Adige, and regained Padua; the French general would not have been apprised of this operation until it would have been too late to oppose it. Wurmser might thus have saved all his cavalry, a great part of his artillery, the staff of his army, all that belonged to his head-quarters, and the honour of the Austrian army.

FOURTH OBSERVATION: (1) There were at Brescia a French magazine and hospital, with a garrison of only three companies; they were made prisoners of war. If the citadel had been secured from a *coup-de-main*, this would not have happened. It was done at a subsequent period, and ought to have been done before.

(2) Soret's division, which was at Salo, should have kept a vanguard on the lake of Idro, at la Rocca d'Anfo, to watch the Chiesa road as far as Lodrone, which would have prevented Brescia and Salo from being surprised; twelve hours' notice would have been secured, which would have allowed time to make preparations for defence.

(3) Since there is but one road practicable for artillery between the lakes of Garda and Idro, that is to say the road which runs through la Rocca d'Anfo, and it was necessary to pass through that defile in order to reach Salo, would it not have been more judicious to have placed Soret's division in position on the lake of Idro, behind the defile of Anfo, occupying the avenues and the lake of Idro with redoubts, entrenchments, and two gun-boats? It would have taken Quasdanowich twenty-four hours to carry this position, which would have allowed of sending intelligence to Brescia, Salo, Verona, and to head-quarters. The position occupied by Soret's division at Salo, neither defended nor covered anything; it must therefore be acknowledged that this division was ill posted, and did not occupy the positions it should have been placed in, in order to fulfil its object, that is to say, to cover the country from the Chiesa to the lake of Garda.

(4) It has been said that the march of Massena's division on the left bank of the Adige, and that of Vaubois' division on the Chiesa, in September, were liable to the same objections as those of Wurmser and Quasdanowich, in August; for in both cases the columns were separated by the Adige, the Mincio, the lake of Garda, and the mountains. This assertion is not correct. These marches, far from similar, are inverse to each other. Wurmser and Quasdanowich separate at Roveredo, where they were in junction, and march in two directions, which form an obtuse angle; so that the distance between them daily increases: on their third day's march, the one was at Brescia and the other at Rivoli, and it was then that they were separated by two rivers, a lake, and mountains; that is to say, at the moment when they were to meet

OBSERVATIONS

the enemy, and were commencing operations and debouching in the plain. But of the two French columns, on the contrary, previously to their beginning to move, one was on the Adige and the other at Brescia, and they marched also on lines meeting in an angle, but towards its vertex, so that on the third day one of them reached Mori, and the other San-Marco; they were then close to each other, or at least separated only by the Adige, over which river they had thrown two bridges, at Seravalle and Roveredo. These columns were constantly in communication and their communications became shorter and easier, in proportion as they approached the enemy, so that at the last moment they could speak together. Wurmser's two columns were leaving the mountains to debouch in the plain, whilst the French columns were quitting the plain to enter defiles, where number was less important; and it being the object of both to reach Trent, they evidently aided each other on their march, as they were approaching a narrow area.

(5) If it has been proved that these two operations cannot be compared, does it follow that my march was conformable to rule and free from danger? It cannot be said, in the abstract, that this march was absolutely without danger, but it was attended with very little. If Vaubois had not left Brescia and Lodrone, it was to be concluded that he had returned to Polo to pass the Adige, which would have occasioned a delay of five days. The divisions of Massena and Augereau were already in columns on a single road, in narrow passes; Vaubois' division would only have brought an increase of difficulties. I contented myself with giving particular instructions with respect to all that could happen, not only to General Vaubois, but to General Saint-Hilaire, a confidential officer, commanding the vanguard. I recommended them to keep a good look-out, and not to engage, if the enemy should by a sudden and unexpected movement advance to attack them; with this view they were to keep the parks and baggage far behind, that they might be able to fall back one march without inconvenience. But in fact Vaubois' division was constantly in communication with the army, at first by Riva, and afterwards by the bridge of Sarca; it sent and received intelligence three times a day.

(6) It has been thought that if I had had Legnago occupied as a fortified place, if I had stationed a commandant, adjutants, officers of artillery and engineers, and a commissary, with magazines, and a garrison of 4 or 500 men besides depots, the commandant would never have conceived the idea of evacuating the place: and as Wurmser could not have forced it, being cut off from Mantua, his ruin would have been certain. I was sensible of this, for I afterwards had Legnago fortified.

(7) Had I, in the first instance, constructed lines of circumvallation at Saint-George, they would have materially annoyed Wurmser. I had some constructed afterwards, which contributed to the success of the battle of la Favorite.

OBSERVATIONS

A French army besieging Mantua should have, independently of the corps of observation on the Adige and Montebaldo, advanced posts on the banks of the Molinello and Tartaro, and should cover its bridges by works, with ditches full of water, and inundations. With a little labour, the roads from Legnago to Mantua, and the whole country from the Po to Roverbella, may be rendered impassable by means of the waters.

(8) It has been said that this march of the French army across the Tyrol, and its movement to the right by the defiles of the Brenta, and on Bassano, placed it in jeopardy; that if Wurmser had marched on Verona, he would have cut off its retreat and surrounded it in the defiles of the Tyrol; and that this operation was not merely daring, but rash, and contrary to the rules of War.

The battle of Roveredo took place on 3 September, and the battle of Bassano on the 8th. In the evening of 3 September, the French had made 9,000 prisoners, and put half the Austrian army *hors de combat*. On the 5th Wurmser's head-quarters were still at Borgo di Valsugana, with two divisions on their march to Bassano, and one division lay that night at Bassano. It was not possible, then, for the Marshal to attempt anything on the Adige; in fact the French army reached Bassano at daybreak on the 8th, and Wurmser's head-quarters had only arrived there very late on the preceding evening. An operation of this nature may be meditated beforehand, and conceived at once; but its execution is progressive, and is sanctioned by the events which take place each day. But after all, suppose Wurmser had reached Verona and passed the Adige, the French army would always have been certain of a retreat on the Chiesa and Brescia, three days' march in the rear. This operation was therefore strictly conformable to the rules of war; daring, indeed, but well considered.

FIFTH OBSERVATION: (1) The Court of Vienna was not disheartened by the failure of the second plan it had prescribed to Wurmser. Alvinzi debouched, in November, with two corps d'armée; the one by the Tyrol, commanded by Davidowich, and the other by the Vicentine, under his own command. Nothing could be more faulty than this plan; and, in order to remedy its defects, he should, as soon as he was master of Bassano, and Davidowich in possession of Trent, have ordered the latter to come to Bassano, through the passes of the Brenta, leaving the Tyrolese militia at Trent; and thus he should have presented himself on the Adige, with his whole army in junction.

(2) In occupying the position of Caldiero, he should have established posts in the morasses of Arcole, and opposite Ronco; he unluckily took it for granted that these marshes were impracticable, which enabled the French army to construct a bridge, pass it, and debouch in his rear on the left bank, before he knew what was passing.

(3) The communications between the corps of Alvinzi and Davidowich

OBSERVATIONS

were so difficult, that, although they were only ten or twelve leagues apart (the distance from Caldiero to Rivoli) they had no correspondence for eight days. The aspect of the country, north of Verona, is extremely rugged—there are no outlets.

(4) At the battle of Rivoli, Alvinzi had in the field forty-four battalions, twenty-four squadrons, and a hundred and thirty pieces of cannon;—in all 50,000 men under arms: but he made twenty battalions and all his artillery (25,000 men), with his waggons and baggage, debouch by the valley of the Adige; that is to say, one column by the left bank, commanded by Wukassowich, six battalions strong, marching on la Chiusa, where it was stopped by thirty men in garrison in that fort: this column was useless. The column which debouched by the right bank of the Adige, reached that side by passing the bridge of Dolce, and marched along the foot of Monte Magnone for the space of a league, hemmed in between that mountain and the river. In several places there is but the width of the road; the side of Monte Magnone is almost perpendicular to the Adige; there is no outlet as far as the chapel of San Marco; on one side is the level of Rivoli, on the other the road from Trent to Peschiera, which, after reaching the end of the level of Rivoli, crosses Osteria della Dogana and the little hamlet of Incanale; but this road is commanded by the height on which the chapel of San Marco stands on the north side, and by the side of the level of Rivoli on the south side.

Alvinzi, with his remaining twenty-four battalions, without cavalry or artillery, that is to say, with less than 25,000 men, passed the heights of Montebaldo and occupied the whole space comprized between Monte Magnone and the lake of Garda. These dispositions were contrary to the grand principle, which requires an army *to be every day and at all hours in readiness to fight.* Now, Alvinzi was not in readiness to fight when he arrived on these mountains, nor during the time that was requisite for reaching the level of Rivoli. For an army must be in junction to be ready for battle; but the twenty battalions which were marching in the valley of the Adige were separated from the rest, and could not join them until after having taken the level of Rivoli. To be in readiness for battle, an army wants its cavalry and artillery; now the cavalry and artillery, which were under the command of Quasdanowich, could only join the army by the level of Rivoli. Alvinzi supposed, then, that he should not have to fight between la Corona and Rivoli; yet that did not depend upon him. He had exposed twenty-four battalions, without cavalry or artillery, to the attack of the whole French army of 20,000 infantry, 2,000 cavalry, and 60 pieces of cannon; the contest was unequal. But Marshal Alvinzi thought he had to deal only with Joubert's brigade of 9,000 men, which, being ordered to guard the whole country from la Corona to Rivoli, and from the lake of Garda to the Adige, would be obliged, he thought, to place at least 3,000 men at Rivoli, to defend the level, and prevent Quasdanowich from debouching by the valley of the Adige. Alvinzi had at his disposal 25,000 men against, as he imagined, 5 or 6,000; he consequently detached Luzignan's division, which he caused to pass between Montebaldo and the lake of Garda, in order to march on Montepopoli and turn the level of Rivoli. He had then only 18,000 to oppose Joubert, who could not, he thought, have more than 6,000 on Montebaldo and Monte Magnone. This calculation would have been very clever, if men, like mountains, were immoveable; but he had forgotten the popular proverb, *that, although mountains are motionless, men walk and meet together.* The Austrian tacticians have always been apt to fall into this error. The Aulic Council, which drew up Wurmser's plan, supposed the French army motionless, and fixed to the fortress of Mantua; and this gratuitous assumption produced the destruction of the finest army of the house of Austria. Lauer, who directed Alvinzi's operations took it for granted that Massena's division would be kept in check by the division which debouched from Caldiero, and would remain nailed, as it were, to the ramparts of Verona; in short, that I would not understand the importance of anticipating the Austrian army on the level of Rivoli.

(5) What should Alvinzi have done? He should have marched in such a manner as to be ready for battle every day and hour. For this purpose he should, first, have kept his forty-four battalions so placed on the mountains between Monte Magnone and the lake of Garda, as to be united, in communication, and forming only a single mass; secondly, he should also have united with them his thirty squadrons of cavalry; for it is a prejudice to suppose that the cavalry cannot pass wherever the infantry can pass; and each column should have been provided with guns on sledge carriages; thirdly, he should not have made his dispositions for the attack of Joubert's corps until the very morning of the attack, after having ascertained and satisfied himself of the state of things, by the return of reconnoitring parties, and the reports of deserters, prisoners, and spies. For it is a principle *that no detachment should be made on the eve of the day of attack, because the state of affairs may alter during the night, either by means of the enemy's movements in retreat, or the arrival of great reinforcements, which may place him in a situation to assume an offensive attitude, and to turn the premature dispositions you may have made to your own destruction.*

Generals are often deceived respecting the strength of the enemy they have to engage. Prisoners are only acquainted with their own corps; officers make very uncertain reports; hence an axiom adapted to all cases has been generally adopted: *that an army ought always to be ready by day, by night, and at all hours, to make all the resistance it is capable of making.* This requires the soldiers to be constantly provided with their arms and ammunition; the infantry to have its artillery, cavalry, and generals always with it; the different divisions of the army to be always ready to support and cover each other; and points out, that in all camps, halts, and marches, the troops should always be in advantageous

OBSERVATIONS

positions possessing the qualities requisite for every field of battle, that is to say:—first, that the flanks be supported, and secondly, that all the artillery may be brought into action in the most advantageous positions possible. To fulfil these conditions, when troops are in marching columns, it is necessary to have vanguards and flankers, to watch the motions of the enemy in front and on the right and left, at a sufficient distance to allow the principal corps to deploy and take position. The Austrian tacticians have always deviated from these principles, by drawing up plans founded on uncertain reports, and which, even if they had been true at the moment of preparing the plans, had ceased to be so the following day, or the next day but one, that is to say, when they were to be executed.

A great captain ought every day to ask himself several times this question: If the enemy's army should now appear in my front or on my right or left, what should I do? and if he should find himself embarrassed, he must be ill-posted, or irregular in his arrangements, and should endeavour to remedy the evil. If Alvinzi had said to himself, *Should the French army meet me before I reach Rivoli, and whilst I have only half my infantry and no cavalry or artillery to oppose it;* he must have added: *I shall be beaten by forces inferior to my own.* How happened it that what had taken place at Lodi, Castiglione, the Brenta, and Arcole, did not make him more circumspect?

(6) Alvinzi debouched in January; Mantua was at the last extremity. He operated with two corps: the first marched on Montebaldo, commanded by himself in person; the other down the Adige, commanded by Provera. Provera's success could be of no advantage if Alvinzi should be defeated. These defects in the plan of the campaign were aggravated by combining these two attacks with a central attack on Verona, which had no object, and only weakened the two principal attacks without connecting them, which local circumstances rendered it impossible to do. It is true that the orders from Vienna were, that if Alvinzi should be beaten, and Provera should succeed in raising the blockade of Mantua, Wurmser should pass the Po with the garrison of Mantua, and retreat on Rome; but without being certain of the co-operation of the King of Naples, which was not secured, these measures would have been fruitless.

(7) Provera, after having surprised the passage of the Adige at Anghiari, should have crossed to the right bank with his whole corps, including Bayalitsch's division, raised his bridge, and made for Mantua, which was his only asylum. He might have reached that place with 20,000 men. Instead of this he conducted but 8,000 men to Mantua, for he left Bayalitsch's division on the right, 2,000 men to guard his bridge (who were taken prisoners), and having wasted time, his vanguard suffered loss. Arriving in the morning before Saint-George, he ought to have entered into the place before noon, either by the citadel, where there were no lines of circumvallation, or by Pietoli, crossing

the lake, which is very narrow at that spot; there were upwards of a hundred boats in the port of Mantua. He lost the day and night. By five in the afternoon, I, having reached la Favorite with part of the army of Rivoli, the whole posture of affairs was altered. Provera was obliged to capitulate the next morning. *The Austrians, in general, do not know the value of time.*

(8) General Provera had been taken at Cossaria, the day after the battle of Millesimo; he had evinced little talent, and this was my true reason for extolling him, as I wished to keep up his credit. This plan succeeded; Provera was again employed, and suffered himself to be taken a second time at la Favorite. We ought therefore to look with suspicion on the praises of an enemy, unless they are given after the cessation of hostilities.

SIXTH OBSERVATION: (1) It has been said that the bridge over the Adige should have been placed at Albaredo and not at Ronco; but this is erroneous. Kilmaine had but 1,500 men in Verona. After having passed the bridge at Ronco, and previously to marching on Arcole, a reconnoitring party was sent forward on the dyke of Porcil; that village was taken, and Massena proceeded thither, who thus found himself two leagues in the rear of Marshal Alvinzi. If this marshal had marched on Verona the same day, as it was probable he would, the French army would have followed at his heels; there was no obstacle to separate them, and Alvinzi would have been hemmed in between the French army and Verona. If the bridge had been placed opposite Albaredo, on the left of the Alpon, that river, or the morass of Arcole, would have covered Alvinzi's march, and allowed him time to force Verona. The circumstances were so delicate! The operation of passing into the rear of Alvinzi's army at Ronco was bold, but secure from all disadvantage; that of passing the Adige at Albaredo would have been rash and hazardous; it would have compromised both Verona and the army.

(2) Why was Arcole abandoned on the first and second day? In order to have an opportunity of raising the bridge of Ronco at midnight, if the news from Rivoli should require it, and then marching on Roverbella and reaching that place before Davidowich. If the latter arrived before Mantua before the French army, all was lost; if the French army got there first, all was won. After effecting a junction with Vaubois, I would have beaten Davidowich, driven him into the Tyrol, and returned to the Adige before Alvinzi could have passed that river.

(3) It has also been said that on the first day, a bridge should have been thrown over the Alpon, and the army should have debouched in the plain; or at least that this should have been done on the second day! No. It was not until the third day of this battle that the enemy's army was sufficiently weakened and discouraged to allow of a hope of beating it in deployed line. It was even contrary to the opinion of the generals, who thought this man-

OBSERVATIONS

oeuvre too daring, and after an hour's hesitation, that I gave the order on the third day. It is necessary to bear in mind that the French army had been weakened by the battles of the Brenta and of Caldiero; it now amounted only to 13,000 men, and the first and second days of the battle of Arcole had still further reduced it. The manoeuvres of this battle are not to be understood without a thorough knowledge of the topographical situation of Rivoli, Verona, Castel-Nuovo, Mantua, Ronco, Caldiero, Villa-Nuova, and Vicenza.

(4) The capitulation granted to Wurmser is unexampled. I was induced to grant it by a generous feeling towards the Marshal, who was old enough to have been my grandfather; by a wish to acquire a reputation for clemency towards the vanquished; and in order to testify my extreme indignation at the order the Directory had sent me to treat this respectable marshal as an emigrant taken in arms, being a native of Alsace.

(5) I should have had the level of Rivoli, la Corona, the chapel of San Marco, and la Rocca d'Anfo occupied with good works of timber, and even of masonry. The Adige is covered with loads of timber, which are brought down by traders from the Tyrol to be carried to Ferrara and Venice; lime and stone are in great abundance there; Verona and Brescia afford resources of all kinds. In the course of six weeks four forts might have been completed, on the level of Rivoli, at the chapel of San Marco, and at la Rocca d'Anfo, which, when each lined with fifteen pieces of cannon, and manned with garrisons four or five hundred strong, would have secured all these debouchés from any surprise or *coup-de-main*; and this would have been more serviceable to the army than a reinforcement of 15,000 men. It is said that after Wurmser's operation in August, when the full extent of the danger that the army was in from the debouché of the Chiesa was perceived, I gave orders to occupy la Rocca d'Anfo, but the engineers made out plans which were far too extensive, and would have required a twelvemonth's labour to carry into execution. But this opinion of the engineers was evidently erroneous; in war the general-in-chief alone understands the importance of certain things; and he alone, by his superior information and authority, can overcome all difficulties.

(6) Mantua at length fell, after having been eight months invested. Some Italian engineers had proposed to divert the waters of the Mincio, and thus to dry up the lakes of Mantua, which would have deprived that place of its principal means of defence. This operation was attempted by the Visconti in their wars against the Dukes of Mantua; but they were not masters of Peschiera; and, besides, the Milanese engineers conducted their works upon false principles: they endeavoured to bar the Mincio with dykes, which the river always carried away. It is well known that the course of water must never be directly opposed: it was by humouring it and submitting to all its caprices, that the Dutch subdued the ocean. This plan might, however, have been accomplished by drawing off the waters into the Tartaro and Molinella.

OBSERVATIONS

(7) In order to shorten the line of the Adige, it has several times been proposed, as an effectual experiment, to cut the dyke of the right bank of that river, near Legnago. The waters drawn off would mingle with those of the Tartaro and Molinella, and would make a morass of all the country comprised within the Adige from Legnago to the Po. But the consequences of such an operation would be ruinous to that province. At the time of the second attack of Alvinzi and Provera, in January, the plan was submitted to me, who did not think that the critical state of affairs could justify such a devastation. The English did not act with so much moderation in Egypt: in order to obtain a very slight advantage they cut the dyke of Lake Maadieh, and let the Mediterranean into Lake Mareotis, which had very nearly ruined Alexandria.

SEVENTH OBSERVATION: There were but 4,000 French in the army that marched against Rome, although it consisted of 9,000 men, including the newly-levied Milanese and Bolognese battalions, which were not yet fit to face regular troops in line. The court of Rome made great efforts, but with little success. A nation that has no skeleton regiments, no principle of military organization, will always find it very difficult to organize an army. France raised good armies with great celerity in 1790; but this was because she had a good foundation, which the emigration rather improved than injured. Romagna and the mountains of the Apennines were worked up to a high pitch of fanaticism; the all-powerful influence of the priests and monks, missions, sermons and miracles, were effectually employed. The people of the Apennines are naturally brave; some sparks of the character of the ancient Romans are still to be found amongst them; yet they could make no resistance against a handful of well-disciplined and well-conducted troops. Cardinal Busca alluded to la Vendée. The situation of la Vendée was very peculiar; the population was warlike, and included a great number of officers and non-commissioned officers who had served in the army, whilst the troops sent against them had been levied in the streets of Paris, were commanded by men who knew nothing of military affairs, and committed the greatest blunders, which insensibly inured the Vendeans to war. At last the desperate measures adopted by the Committee of Public Safety and the Jacobins, left these people no middle course; death being inevitable, it was still best to make a defence. It may easily be conceived that in this war against the Holy See, if, instead of endeavouring to calm the people, and gaining victories, the French had suffered defeats at first, and had then resorted to measures of violence and extermination, a Vendean war might have been established in the Apennines: severity, bloodshed, and death create enthusiasts and martyrs, and excite courageous and desperate determinations.

OBSERVATIONS

EIGHTH OBSERVATION: (1) In the campaign of 1797, Prince Charles, wishing to cover Vienna and Trieste, ought to have collected all his forces in the Tyrol, where he would have been supported by local circumstances and the disposition of the inhabitants. He could readily have received his reinforcements from the army of the Rhine; and as long as he maintained himself in the Tyrol, he had no reason to fear the march of the French army to the Isonzo. On the first move of that army on the Piave, he would have recalled it by passing the Avisio and possessing himself of the Trentine, which would have obliged the French general to have carried the war into the Tyrol with his whole army, a very difficult and hazardous operation. If Prince Charles's head-quarters had been at Bolzano instead of Conegliano; if the 40,000 men he had on the Piave and the Tagliamento had been on the Avisio, Vienna and Trieste would have been perfectly covered. There would, however, have been nothing to prevent his arming and occupying the fortress of Palma-Nuova, and making it the point of *appui* for a division of five or six thousand men of all weapons, employed in observing the Piave and Tagliamento.

(2) My plans at the battle of the Tagliamento admit of no doubt; I wished to possess myself of the Col de Tarwis. It was not, therefore, at Codroipo that the Archduke should have fixed his head-quarters, but on the heights of San Daniele so as to be able, in case of need, to operate his retreat on la Ponteba and the heights of Tarwis.

(3) After the battle of the Tagliamento, he should not have retreated in the direction of the passes of Cividale and the Isonzo, upon Tarwis, because Massena was already master of them, which circumstance produced the destruction of all the troops he sent in this false direction, and ruined his army.

(4) The fortress of Gradisca was not tenable after the passing of the Isonzo; the battalions he had placed there were sacrificed to no purpose; they did not delay the march of the French army a single moment.

(5) As it was of the utmost importance to the Archduke in April, to gain three or four days in order to give Kerpen and Sporck time to join him; and as he had reached Murau, one day's march from Scheifling, he should have availed himself of the opportunity of gaining that time which I, as French General, afforded him by the proposal of peace. He should have answered this offer by sincerely embracing it, by promising to use his influence, and requesting an armistice to enable him to go to Vienna to speak to the Emperor on the subject. The armistice would have been signed. But the Archduke gave a cold vague answer, and twenty-four hours after, upon second thoughts, applied for a suspension of hostilities; but it was then too late; his object was too evident.

NINTH OBSERVATION: (1) Was not the march into Germany by two lines of operation, those of the Tyrol and la Ponteba, contrary to the principle

OBSERVATIONS

that an army should never have more than one line of operations? Was not the junction of these two corps d'armée in Carinthia, so far from the point from which they departed, contrary to the principle of *never joining your columns before the enemy and near him?* Would it not have been preferable to leave seven or eight thousand men before Trent, on the defensive, and to make ten or twelve thousand more men join on the Piave? By this plan the French would have avoided carrying the war into the Tyrol, a difficult theatre of operations; nor would they have exposed themselves to the chances unfavourable to a junction; yet the whole of the forces would have been concentrated in the very outset of operations.

Neither of the above-mentioned principles were violated. If only 8,000 men had been left with Joubert on the Avisio, he would have been attacked, and Davidowich's corps d'armée would have reached Verona before the French army had arrived at Villach. Joubert would have wanted at least 14,000 men to enable him to maintain himself on the Avisio. It appeared preferable to avoid depriving him of any part of his forces, and to allow him by means of the superiority he thus retained over Davidowich's army, to beat that general, weaken his army, and drive it beyond the Brenner. The Tyrol is a difficult theatre of war, but a fatal one to the vanquished. The French troops had acquired a great superiority over those of Germany.

The army did not enter Germany by two lines of operations; for the Pusterthal is on the Italian side of the upper ridge of the Alps, and, as soon as Joubert had passed Lienz, the line of operations was that of Villach and the Ponteba. The junction of the two corps d'armée was not effected in presence of the enemy; for when Joubert left Brixen, to march to Spittal, wheeling to the right, through the Pusterthal or the valley of the Drave, the principal corps of the army had reached Klagenfurth, and had patrols advanced as far as Lienz. It was therefore impossible for the Archduke to invent any manoeuvre to oppose this junction. Joubert remained on the defensive until the battle of the Tagliamento. After that battle he attacked, beat, and destroyed the greater part of Davidowich's corps, and repulsed it beyond the Brenner; which was attended with no disadvantage, because, had he been beaten, he would merely have retreated from position to position, into Italy. When he was informed that the army had passed the Julian Alps and the Drave, he effected his movement of junction by the Pusterthal, which was also unattended with any disadvantage. This operation, thus executed in three movements, was strictly conformable to rule: it was calculated to succeed, and did in fact succeed, in every respect.

(2) It has been asked why Serrurier's division, and the head-quarters, did not support Guieux's division by directing their march from the field of battle of the Tagliamento, on Cividale and Caporetto, under the pretence that Berna-

OBSERVATIONS

dotte's division was alone sufficient to follow the enemy's left on Palma-Nuova and Goritz.

From Cividale to Tarwis, by way of Caporetto, the road presents but one defile. Guieux's troops, which contained 8,000 fighting men, all excellent troops, were more than sufficient to drive Bayalitsch's corps as far as Caporetto; but as the Archduke had ordered this corps to take an erroneous direction, which was certain to produce its destruction if Bayalitsch, on reaching Caporetto, should persist in marching in the direction of Tarwis, it was supposed that the Archduke would reconsider the matter, and send him orders at Caporetto, to go down to Gradisca and return on Carniola, which induced me to march on Palma-Nuova and Gradisca, with Serrurier's and Bernadotte's divisions; from Goritz I sent Bernadotte's division into Carniola, to follow Prince Charles's left, and proceeded with Serrurier's division on Caporetto. If Bayalitsch's corps, instead of going up the Isonzo, marched down it to seek safety by way of Goritz, it would be attacked in front, whilst Guieux would push its rearguard; this corps would be taken. If, on the contrary, he advanced to Tarwis, disregarding Massena's position, who occupied that place, as in fact he did, Serrurier's division formed a second line in the rear of Guieux. I had provided for all contingencies.

(3) Bernadotte's division marched on Laybach, because it was necessary to subdue Carniola, to take possession of Trieste and the mines of Idria, and to drive Prince Charles's left out of Carniola and beyond the Drave; but immediately after attaining these objects, this division proceeded, by a wheel to the left, to join the army; and the French general took care not to direct it, as many generals would have done, by way of Cilli and Goritz, on the Simering, because in that case this division would not have been in a situation to support the army in all the actions which took place, or might have taken place, at Judenburg, Bruck, etc. The march of Bernadotte's division on Groetz, which, if it had been performed without any bad consequences, might have been attended with some advantage, would have been contrary to rule; whilst the march it actually performed was agreeable to the principles of concentration, which are the true principles of war.

(4) I determined to conclude the treaty of Leoben, and to stop on the Simering, because, as we have already seen, I had been informed by a letter from the Directory, that I was not to calculate upon the co-operation of the armies of the Rhine. Had the government informed me, on the contrary, that such co-operation would be afforded, had it been even as late as the month of June, I would have waited, and not have concluded the peace; for my position was good: I had above 60,000 men with me in Carinthia, and reserves on the Adige, which were more than sufficient to suppress the insurrections of the Venetians and check the Tyrolese levies; and I was desirous of entering Vienna.

OBSERVATIONS

(5) The order given to Joubert after the battle of the Tagliamento, to enter the Tyrol and advance to Villach in Carinthia, by the Pusterthal, was communicated to Lallemant, the French minister to the Republic of Venice, that he might take measures to prevent the commotion that was expected to break out; it was apprehended that, as soon as the oligarchs should learn that the Tyrol was evacuated, they would imagine that the French were beaten, and would take rash and premature measures. Lallemant had several conferences on this subject with the persons who were deputed to him; he shewed them a copy of the instructions given to Joubert. This produced some effect, but the communication came too late: the Senate had secretly taken its measures thirty-six hours before, in the persuasion of the destruction of Joubert's corps. This delay of thirty-six hours was the principal cause of the ruin of the Republic of Venice. On what trifles does the fate of nations depend!

(6) Certain foreign officers, imperfectly acquainted with the circumstances of the case have blamed me for having left the divisions of Victor and Kilmaine in the Marches and in Romagna, to observe the Pope's army and Naples, which, said they, was useless, because peace was restored with those powers.

General Kilmaine commanded on the Adige: his head-quarters were at Verona when the insurrection of that city, and the arrival of General Fioravanti, placed him under the necessity of ordering the commandants of the forts to shut themselves in. He quitted the Adige, and retired to the Mincio, with 6 or 700 men, infantry, cavalry, and artillery, wishing to avoid being surrounded, and to keep up his communications with Mantua and Peschiera. General Victor's division consisted of 8,000 men, including 3,000 Milanese under the command of General Lahoz. This division had orders to march to the Adige, to form a corps of observation, and keep down the Venetians. Victor made General Lahoz precede him, and delayed his own march with the French brigade for a fortnight; whether he was not fully sensible of the importance of expediting his movement, or whether that time was requisite for his executing the Articles of Tolentino, or from any other cause is unworthy of the attention of history. The fact is, however, that this fortnight's delay was the sole cause of the massacres of Verona. Perhaps Pesaro and his party would have been more circumspect, had they seen this general's division quartered on the Adige, as it ought to have been; and this would have been very fortunate for the Senate, and prevented its ruin. The Pope had disbanded his army: it was on the peace establishment, and excited no apprehension. The Bologna troops were more than sufficient to occupy Romagna, and overawe all the malevolent on the right bank of the Po. There was never, therefore, any intention of leaving a single man in observation on the Rubicon. But dates are not to be disputed: the peace of Tolentino was signed on 19 February; the battle of the Tagliamento was fought on 16 March; and the preliminaries of Leoben were signed on 14 April.

Chapter XIX

VENICE

Description of Venice. The Senate. Conduct of the Provedi׳ tores Mocenigo and Foscarelli. Factions; Brescia; Bergamo. Difficulties attending the affairs of Venice. Conferences of Goritz, on 20 March. Verona. Mission of the Aide-de-camp Junot to the Senate; Declaration of war of Palma-Nuova. Entrance of Venice by the French; Revolution of that capital. Revolution of the Terra-Firma States; the colours taken from the Venetians and in the last days of the campaign forwarded to Paris.

Venice, founded in the fifth century by the inhabitants of Friuli and the Paduano, who sought refuge in the lagoons from the incursions of the barbarians, at first occupied the sites of Heraclea and Chiozza. The patriarch of Aquilea afterwards established himself at Grado with his clergy, on occasion of the Arian schism. Grado became the capital. In the earliest times Padua gave laws and consuls to the Venetians.

Venice is the best situated commercial port in all Italy. Merchandize from Constantinople and the Levant arrives there by the shortest road, crossing the Adriatic; whence it is dispersed through Upper Italy, as far as Turin, by the Po; and throughout Germany, by going up the Adige as far as Bolzano, and thence by the high roads to Ulm, Augsburg, Munich, and Nuremberg. Venice is the sea-port of the Upper Danube, the Po, and the Adige. Nature has destined this spot to be the entrepôt of the Levant, of Italy, and of Southern Germany. Before the discovery of the Cape of Good Hope, Venice carried on the trade with India by Alexandria and the Red Sea; and she therefore

VENICE

struggled to intercept the navigation of the Portuguese. She equipped a considerable fleet in the Red Sea, and established an arsenal, watering places, and magazines near Suez; the remains of them are still seen at the fountains of Moses. But the Portuguese beat these fleets, which had been constructed at vast expense: and the anarchy which prevailed in Egypt completed the work of closing this road against the commerce of India.

The lagoons are formed by the waters of the Piave, the Brenta, and the Livenza; they communicate with the sea by three great channels, the Chioggia, the Malamoco, and the Lido.

After the abolition of the democracy in 1200, the sovereignty resided in the aristocracy of several hundred families inscribed in the Golden Book, which contained the names of 1,200 persons entitled to vote in the grand council. The population of the states of the Republic consisted of three millions of individuals dispersed around Venice in rich countries and fertile plains.

In 1796 this republic was much reduced; it was but the shadow of its former self. Three generations had succeeded each other without engaging in war. These unworthy descendants of the Dandolos, Zenos and Morosinis, trembled at the sight of a gun. During the war of the succession, and those of 1733 and 1740, they had submitted with base resignation to the insults and outrages of the Austrian, French, and Spanish armies.

The Venetian navy consisted of a dozen ships of 64 guns, as many frigates, and a great number of small vessels, sufficient to overawe the Barbarians, rule the Adriatic, and defend the lagoons. The army, 14,000 strong, was composed of Italian regiments, recruited in the Terra Firma, and of Sclavonians raised in Dalmatia—brave men and wholly devoted to the republic. The latter had the advantage of being strangers to the language and manners of the Terra Firma.

The families of the Golden Book alone had any share in the administration; they composed exclusively the senate, the councils, the forties, and other magistracies. This rendered the nobles of the Terra Firma discontented: amongst these were many rich, illustrious, and great families, which, thus subdued and deprived of all power, lived unnoticed, and entertained a strong jealousy of the supreme nobility. They were descended partly from the ancient Condottieri, the ancient *Podestas,* and other personages who had acted distinguished parts in the republics of their cities, and whose ancestors, after having long opposed the enterprises of the Venetians, had at length fallen victims to their policy. The jealousy and hatred with which the nature of the government inspired them, were thus strengthened by historical resentments carefully perpetuated. The people of the Terra Firma were in general discontented, the greater part of them making common cause with the nobility. The noble Venetians, however, who had property and establishments in almost all the provinces, had their partisans also. The clergy possessed no credit or influence in this republic, which had freed itself as far as possible from the temporal influence of the Pope at a very early period.

In 1792 the combined powers invited Venice to take part in the war. It does not appear that any serious discussions took place in the senate on this occasion: there was an unanimous vote for neutrality. This republic was so distant from the theatre of war, that it thought itself unconcerned in the affairs of France. When the Count de Lille took refuge at Verona, the senate did not grant him permission to remain there, until it had obtained the consent of the committee of public safety, which preferred Verona to any other place for the residence of this prince.

When the French troops marched towards Oneglia, in 1794, it was thought that Italy was threatened with an invasion, and several powers held a congress at Milan. Venice refused to appear there, not because she approved of the principles of the French, but as fearing to place herself at the mercy of Austria, and unwilling to deviate from that base and enervated policy which she had for several generations followed. But when I arrived at Milan, and Beaulieu fled, struck with consternation, beyond the Mincio, occupying Peschiera, where he stationed his right, in hopes of defending that line, great anxiety and alarm prevailed in the senate. The immense space which had previously separated Venice from the struggle between democracy and aristocracy had now been traversed; the wars of principles and cannon were now raging in the bosom of the state. Stormy discussions accordingly took place in the councils, in which three different opinions were maintained by their respective adherents.

The young oligarchs wished for an armed neutrality: they advised that strong garrisons should be thrown into Peschiera, Brescia, Porto Legnago, and Verona; that these places should be declared in a state of siege; that the army should be increased to 60,000 men; that the lagoons should be put in a state of defence and covered with gun-boats; that a squadron should be fitted out to guard the Adriatic; and that in this formidable attitude the republic should declare war against the first power that should violate her territory.

The partisans of this opinion went still further. 'If our last hour is come,' said they, 'it is less disgraceful to die in arms. By defending the territory, we shall prevent the French ideas from gaining ground in the great cities of the Terra Firma: the more respect we are in a condition to insist on from both the hostile parties, the more we shall obtain. If, on the contrary, our gates are peaceably opened, the war of the two powers will be established on the territories of the republic, and from that moment the sovereignty is lost to the prince. His first duty is to protect his subjects: if their fields and property become a prey to the war, the wretched people will lose all esteem and respect for the authority which abandoned them. The germs of discontent and jealousy which already exist will be thrown into a violent ferment, and the republic will expire unregretted.'

The partisans of the old policy maintained that it would be best to take no decisive measures; but to temporize, gain time, and watch the course of events. They confessed that all the dangers pointed out really existed; that the ambition of Austria and the principles of France were both to be dreaded: but they insisted that these evils were temporary; that the troubles apprehended might be avoided by means of circumspection and patience; that the French were of a conciliable disposition, easily won over by caresses; that an influence might be gained over the minds of their leaders, and their goodwill might be acquired by liberal behaviour towards them; that in the present state of men's minds an armed neutrality must lead to war, which was above all things to be avoided; that Providence had placed the capital in a position which secured it from all insult; and that patience, moderation, and time, were weapons to be relied on.

Battaglia said: 'The republic is certainly in danger. On one side, the French principles are subversive of our constitution; on the other, Austria aims at the destruction of our independence. Between these two evils, one of which is inevitable, let us take care to choose the least. In my opinion Austrian despotism is the worst. Let us augment the Golden Book; let us inscribe in it the names of such of the nobles of the Terra Firma as merit that honour: we shall thus conciliate our own subjects, and there will be no opposition amongst ourselves. Let us garrison our fortresses, fit out our fleets, raise our army, and hasten to meet the French general and offer him an offensive and defensive alliance. This may, perhaps, lead to a few slight alterations in our constitution, but we shall preserve our independence and liberty. An armed neutrality is talked of. Two years ago this plan would have been the best; it would have been just, because equal towards both the belligerent parties; and it was possible, because there was then time to make preparations accordingly. But you cannot now refuse the French what you have permitted or tolerated on the part of the Austrians; this would be declaring war against the French army, when it is victorious and will be at Verona in eight days, and without even being assured of Austria; but for the next two months that power can do nothing for you. What will become of the republic, during those two months, attacked by an enemy equally enterprising and active? This is of all possible schemes the worst; it is rushing into the midst of the danger instead of avoiding it.

'The second plan which has been proposed to you, that of patience and time, is little better than the former. Political circumstances are no longer the same; times are much altered; the present crisis resembles none of those over which the prudence of our ancestors triumphed. The French principles are in every head; they are propagated in various forms; they are an overwhelming torrent which has burst its banks, and which it would be vain to attempt to stop by patience, moderation, and pliancy. The measure I propose to you is the only one that can save us: it is simple, noble, and generous. We are able to offer the French a contingent of 10,000 men, reserving sufficient forces for the defence of our fortresses. They will soon take Mantua and carry the war into Germany. The first step being taken, all the rest will be easy; because all the parties by which the state is divided will go on unanimously together: our independence will be secured; we shall save the grand foundations of our constitution. Austria has no influence over our subjects; and she has no fleets, whilst we know not from one hour to another, but that signals may be made from the Lido of the appearance of the Toulon fleet.'

This opinion excited the passions of all parties and struck all judicious minds, but it gained but few votes. Aristocratical prejudices prevailed over the interests of the country. This resolution would have been too noble for degenerate men incapable of elevated notions.

The proveditore Mocenigo received me at Brescia in a magnificent style: he made protestations of the goodwill of the senate towards France. Splendid fêtes were given, which formed connexions between the officers of the army and the principal families. Every noble endeavoured to become the particular friend of a French general. At Verona, the proveditore Foscarelli imitated this example; but the haughtiness of his character was incompatible with dissimulation: he could ill disguise his secret sentiments. He was one of the senators who were most hostile to modern ideas: he had not dared to protest against the entrance of the French into Peschiera, because they succeeded Beaulieu's troops there; but when he was asked by the French for the keys of the arsenal, in order to line the ramparts with artillery, and when steps were taken to arm the galleys, he complained of this violation of the neutrality of the republic. On my arrival at Peschiera, this proveditore endeavoured to dissuade me from marching on Verona; he even went so far as to threaten to close the gates and fire the cannon. 'It is too late,' said I; 'my troops have entered the place; I am obliged to take up my line of defence on the Adige, during the siege of Mantua. You would not be able to oppose the passage of the Austrian army with your 1,500 Sclavonians. Neutrality consists in having the same weight and measure for all parties. If you are not my enemies, you must grant or allow me what you have granted, or at least tolerated, in my enemies.'

These various discussions being reported to the senate, determined it to recall Foscarelli, and to appoint Battaglia in his stead, conferring on him the dignity of proveditore-general of all the provinces beyond the Adige, including Verona. He was a pliant, well-informed man, of agreeable manners, and sincerely attached to his country, quite an enthusiastic admirer of the French of times past, and preferring even republican France to Austria. The theatre of war gradually extended over the whole of the Venetian possessions; but it was always the Austrians who first entered new territories. Beaulieu occupied Peschiera and Verona; Wurmser threw himself into Bassano, and marched through Vicenza and Padua; Alvinzi and the Archduke Charles occupied Friuli, Palma-Nuova, and the most easterly parts of the republic.

A strong agitation was manifested in the Terra Firma; discontent spread with rapidity. The inveterate animosity that was entertained against the oligarchy was strengthened by the charm of the new opinions. Italy was generally regarded as lost to the Austrians, and the fall of the aristocracy appeared the necessary consequence. I constantly endeavoured to moderate this feeling, which was supported by the general disposition of the army. When I returned from Tolentino, wholly occupied with my scheme of marching on Vienna, I found it necessary to pay immediate attention to this state of affairs, which in some measure embarrassed me. The irritation had continued to increase: Brescia and Bergamo were in a state of insurrection. The Fenaroli, Martinengo, Lecchi, and Alessandri families, some of the principal and wealthiest in the Venetian states, were at the head of the insurgents. The municipal authorities of these two cities possessed great power; they were entrusted with the public money, disposed of the revenues, and appointed officers. Although the lion of Saint Mark was still to be seen there, it was more out of deference to the French general, than in token of submission to the sovereignty of Venice. Continual and violent attacks on the Venetian nobility were heard in all companies, and kept the press employed. The injustice of their supremacy was passionately urged by all possible means. 'What right has Venice,' said the disaffected, 'to govern our cities? Are we less brave, enlightened, opulent, or noble than the Venetians?' The pride of the senators was severely wounded at seeing subjects who had for so many ages submitted to their yoke, forgetting their immense superiority, and comparing themselves to their masters. Everything announced the approach of a violent concussion. Battaglia, in his dispatches to the senate, concealed the outrages of the Brescians as much as possible, and softened the rage and violence of the senate in the eyes of the latter. Constantly anxious to conciliate, in all his numerous communications with me, he endeavoured to interest me in the welfare of the republic.

It would have been dangerous to leave in the rear of the army three millions of individuals abandoned to disorder and anarchy. I was well aware that I had no more influence over the friends of France than over the senate itself:—I could restrain them from action, but not from speaking, writing, and directly provoking the government in a multitude of details of administration to which I was a stranger. To disarm the patriots of Brescia and Bergamo, to declare for the senate, proscribe the partisans of innovation, and throw them into the dungeons of Venice, would have ensured me the hatred of the popular party without gaining the affection of the aristocracy; and could so base a policy have entered into my calculations, it would infallibly have ended, as in the time of Louis XII, in raising the whole population against us. To induce the senate to enter into an alliance with France, and to modify its constitution to the satisfaction of its Terra Firma subjects was the best, and indeed the only eligible plan. This was accordingly the constant object of my endeavours. Whenever I gained a new victory, I repeated this proposal, but always in vain.

A third course presented itself, namely, to march on Venice, to occupy that capital, to effect by force the political alterations which circumstances made indispensable, and to confide the government to the partisans of France. But it was impracticable to march on Venice whilst Prince Charles remained on the Piave; the first thing to be done was, therefore, to beat the Austrian army and expel it from Italy: and supposing this to be effected, it was a question whether it would be advisable to lose the fruits of victory, and defer the passage of the mountains, for the purpose of bringing back the war to the neighbourhood of Venice; which would give the Archduke time to reconnoitre, obtain reinforcements and create new obstacles. It was under the walls of Vienna that peace was to crown the victories of the French. Venice was, moreover, a place of great strength, defended by her lagoons, her armed vessels, and 10,000 Sclavonians; and being mistress of the Adriatic, she could easily receive fresh troops: besides, her walls contained the moral strength of all those sovereign families which would be called upon to fight for their political existence. Who could say how much inestimable time the French army might lose by this enterprize? And if the contest should happen to be prolonged, who could foresee the effects of a stout resistance on the rest of Italy?

This new war was sure to meet with many impediments at Paris. The senate had a very active minister there; the legislative body opposed the directory, and the directors were divided amongst themselves. If consulted upon the war with Venice, they would give no answer, or evade the question. If I acted, as I had hitherto done, without authority, I was sure to be reproached, unless in case of immediate success, with the violation of all principles. As a general-in-chief I had no further right than to repel force by force. To undertake a new war against an armed power, without the orders of my government, was to incur the charge of usurping the rights of sovereignty; and I was already but too much exposed to republican jealousy.

It was possible that the episode of Venice might become the principal affair. I, therefore, resolved to adopt only common military precautions with respect to the Venetians. I was sure of Brescia, Bergamo, and all the right bank of the Adige. I garrisoned the castles of Verona, Saint-Felix, and Saint-Peter, as well as the old palace, which rendered me master of the stone bridges. The troops employed in the expedition against the Pope were on their march back to the Adige; they formed a sufficient reserve to overawe the senate. Arrangements were made for all the convalescents and wounded, who

VENICE

should leave the hospitals, to be organized into marching battalions, and added to the reserve; but this was taking so many men from the active army.

I resolved, however, to make one more effort. I desired an interview with Pesaro, who at that period managed all the affairs of the republic. Pesaro represented the critical situation of his country, the disaffection of the people, and the legitimate complaints of the senate; he stated that these trying circumstances required strong measures and extraordinary levies of troops, which ought to give no umbrage to the French; that the senate was obliged to arrest persons at Venice and in the Terra Firma; and that it would be unjust to treat the merited punishment of rebellious subjects, who wished to subvert the laws of their country, as a rigorous persecution of the partisans of France.

I acknowledged the critical situation of Venice; but without losing time in discussing its causes, I came at once to the question. 'You want,' said I, 'to arrest persons whom you call your enemies, but whom I call my friends. You entrust power to men well-known for their hatred of France; you raise new troops: what more is requisite for a declared war? Yet this would be your complete and immediate ruin. In vain would you reckon on the support of the Archduke; I shall have driven his armies from Italy in less than eight days. There is, however, one way of extricating your republic from the unfortunate situation in which it is placed. I offer it the alliance of France; I guarantee its possessions in the Terra Firma, and even its authority in Brescia and Bergamo; but I require it to declare war against Austria, and to furnish me a contingent of 10,000 infantry, 2,000 cavalry, and twenty-four pieces of cannon. I think it would be right to inscribe the principal families of the Terra Firma in the Golden Book; but I do not make this a condition *sine qua non*. Return to Venice, get the senate to deliberate, and come back to sign a treaty, which is the only means of saving your country.' Pesaro acknowledged the wisdom of this plan. He departed for Venice, promising to return in less than a fortnight.

On 11 March the French army put itself in motion to pass the Piave. As soon as this intelligence reached Venice, orders were despatched to arrest fourteen of the principal inhabitants of Bergamo, and bring them before the Council of Ten. The leaders of the patriotic party, having timely warning from a Venetian commissary devoted to their interest, intercepted the courier, arrested the proveditore himself, raised the standard of revolt and proclaimed the liberty of Bergamo. The deputies whom they sent to the French head-quarters, reached them on the field of the Tagliamento. This event embarrassed me, but was irremediable. The people of Bergamo had already entered into a confederation with Milan, the capital of the Lombard republic, and Bologna, the capital of the Transpadan republic. A similar revolution took place a few days afterwards at Brescia: and 2,000 Sclavonians who were there were disarmed; the proveditore Battaglia was respected, but

VENICE

sent to Verona. The Venetian general Fioravanti advanced against the insurgents, occupied Salo, and menaced Brescia; the Milanese general Lahoz marched to meet him, defeated him, and drove him from Salo.

Pesaro returned to head-quarters, according to his promise; he found them at Goritz. The Archduke had been defeated on the Tagliamento; Palma-Nuova had opened its gates; the French flag waved at Tarwis beyond the Isonzo, and on the summit of the Julian Alps. 'Have I kept my word?' said I. 'The Venetian territory is covered with my troops; the Austrians are flying before me. In a few days I shall be in Germany. What does your Republic mean to do? I have offered the alliance of France; is it accepted?'

'Venice,' replied Pesaro, 'rejoices in your triumphs; she knows that she cannot exist but by means of France; but, faithful to her ancient and wise policy, she wishes to remain neutral. In the days of Louis XII, and Francis I, her armies were of some importance in the field of battle. But now that whole nations are in arms, of what value can our aid be to you?'

I made a last effort, but failed. As Pesaro took his leave, I said to him: 'Well, as your republic is resolved to remain neutral, I consent to it; but let her cease her armaments. I leave sufficient forces in Italy to render me master there. I am marching on Vienna. Things that I might have forgiven at Venice, when I was in Italy, would be unpardonable crimes when I am in Germany. Should my soldiers be assassinated, my convoys harassed, and my communications interrupted in the Venetian territories, your republic would cease to exist. She would have pronounced her own sentence.'

General Kerpen had imitated the movement of Joubert, who had commenced operations on 20 March; he had abandoned the Tyrol, and advanced by Salzburg and Rottenmann, into the valley of the Muer, where he was in hopes of joining the Archduke; but being anticipated at Scheifling by the rapid march of the French, he repassed the mountains, and did not operate his junction until he arrived in the plain of Vienna. General Laudon, left by him to guard the Tyrol with only 2,000 men, troops of the line, contrived to collect 10,000 Tyrolese militia, who, discouraged by so many defeats, had dispersed themselves. This reinforcement gave him a great numerical superiority over the little corps of observation which Joubert had ordered to cover the Trent road. General Serviez had about 1,200 men; he evacuated the two banks of the Avisio on the approach of the enemy, and retreated on Montebaldo. Laudon occupied Trent. Being master of the whole Tyrol, he inundated Italy with proclamations. He circulated reports in Venice, Rome, Turin, and Naples, that the French had been defeated several times. 'The Tyrol had been the tomb of Joubert's troops; Napoleon had been beaten on the Tagliamento; the imperial armies had gained brilliant victories on the Rhine; he was debouching from Trent into Italy with 60,000 men, to cut off the retreat of the wreck of the army which the Archduke was pursuing;

finally, he called on Venice and all Italy to take up arms and rise against the French.'

On this intelligence the Venetian oligarchy no longer kept any terms. The French minister endeavoured in vain to convince the senate that it was digging a pit into which it must necessarily fall; he denied the alleged reverses of Joubert in the Tyrol; and those which it was pretended, with equal falsehood, that the armies of the Sambre and Meuse and Rhine had sustained. He proved that they had not yet begun hostilities; he went so far as to communicate the plan of campaign, from which it appeared that Joubert's leaving the Tyrol was a concerted movement; that he was marching by Carinthia on the Pusterthal; and that, instead of being lost, he had accomplished his object. Pesaro gave no credit to these communications; he was too eagerly desirous of the defeat of the French. At the same time the Court of Vienna used every endeavour to excite the passions of the enemies of France. It was of essential importance to Austria to raise insurrections in the rear of the French army.

The corps of reserve left at Palma-Nuova, the garrison of Osopo, and the prudence of the proveditore Mocenigo,* maintained order in Friuli: perhaps too the inhabitants, being less remote from the theatre of operations, were better informed of the state of affairs.

The levy *en masse* of the Veronese had long been prepared: more than 30,000 peasants had received arms, and awaited only the signal for slaughter; 3,000 Venetian and Sclavonian troops had been sent to Verona to garrison the town. The proveditore Emili, who was devoted to the senate, had a conference with Laudon: he informed him of the weakness of the French garrison; and the moment he thought himself certain of the assistance of the Austrian troops, he gave the signal of revolt. On 17 April, Tuesday in Easter week, after vespers, the tocsin sounded; the insurrection broke out at the same time in the city and in the country; the French were massacred on all sides; and the fury of the people carried them so far as to murder four hundred sick in the hospitals. General Balland shut himself up in the castle with the garrison. The artillery of the forts, the fire of which he directed against the city, induced the Veronese authorities to demand a parley, but the rage of the multitude opposed this measure. A reinforcement of 2,000 Sclavonians, sent from Vicenza by the proveditore Foscarini, and the approach of the troops commanded by the Austrian General Nieperg, increased the madness of the people, who revenged the mischief done to the city by the bombardment, by slaughtering the garrison of Chiusa, which had been obliged to capitulate to the levy *en masse* of the mountaineers.

General Kilmaine, the chief commandant of Lombardy, made dispositions for the relief of General Balland, on the first intelligence he received of the insurrection of the Veronese. On the 21st his first columns appeared before

* Not the Mocenigo who had been proveditore at Brescia.

VENICE

Verona. Generals Chabran, Lahoz and Chevalier, after several engagements, succeeded in investing Verona in the course of the 22nd. On the 23rd the signature of preliminaries of peace with Austria became known to the insurgents, who, at the same time, heard that Victor's division had marched from Treviso, and was rapidly approaching. They were now seized with consternation; their dejection was equal to their former fury; they requested to be allowed to capitulate, and accepted on their knees the conditions which General Balland imposed upon them. They gave hostages and order was universally restored.

The French were entitled to terrible reprisals; the blood of their brethren in arms, basely murdered, was still running in the streets; yet no revenge was taken; three inhabitants only were delivered up to the tribunals; a general disarming was effected, and the peasants were sent home to their villages.

The oligarchs, no less blind at Venice, suffered the crew of a French privateer, which, being pursued by an Austrian frigate, had taken refuge under the batteries of the Lido, to be murdered before their eyes. The French minister protested against this violation of the law of nations, and demanded justice on the assassins. The senate laughed both at his representations and his threats, and passed a decree granting reward to such of its satellites as had participated in the murder of Captain Laugier and his sailors.

When I heard of the outrages and murders which were taking place in the rear of the army, I sent my aide-de-camp Junot to Venice, charging him to present to the senate the following letter, dated at Judenburg, 9 April: 'Throughout the Terra Firma the subjects of the most Serene Republic are in arms; their rallying cry is *Death to the French!* Several hundred of the soldiers of the army of Italy have already fallen their victims. In vain you affect to disclaim assemblages of mobs which you yourselves collected. Do you then imagine that because I am at a distance, in the heart of Germany, I shall not be able to enforce respect to the soldiers of the first nation in the world? Do you think that the legions of Italy can leave unpunished the assassins who are covered with the blood of their brethren in arms? There is not a Frenchman living who would not feel his courage and strength increased threefold by the commission to fulfil this vengeance. Did you think this was the age of Charles VIII? But minds are greatly changed in Italy since that period.'

Junot had orders to read this letter to the senate himself, and to express the extreme indignation of his Commander-in-chief: but terror already prevailed in Venice, all illusion had vanished. It was known that the armies of the Rhine had not commenced hostilities; that Joubert was at Villach with his forces; that Victor was approaching Verona; that the French were already on their march for the lagoons; and finally, that I, victorious in every battle, had spread terror as far as Vienna; that I had just granted an armistice to the Archduke; and that the Emperor had sent to me to solicit peace.

VENICE

The French minister Lallemant presented Junot to the senate; and that officer fulfilled his mission with all the plain bluntness of a soldier. The senate humbled itself, and endeavoured to find excuses. The friends of liberty now raised their heads, foreseeing their approaching triumph. A deputation of senators was sent to Gratz, to me to offer all the reparation I might require, and, above all, to bribe every one who might seem to have any credit with me: but all was unavailing.

At the same time the senate despatched couriers to Paris, and placed considerable sums at the disposal of its minister there, in hopes of gaining the leaders of the Directory, and getting such orders sent to the General of Italy as might save the republic. This intrigue succeeded at Paris: by the distribution of ten millions in bills of exchange, the minister of Venice obtained the despatch of the orders he solicited; but it was found that these orders were not authenticated with all the legal forms. Some despatches, intercepted at Milan, enabled me to baffle the whole plot: I had in my hands the account of the sums distributed at Paris, and I annulled, of my own authority, all that had been done.

On 3 May, I published, from Palma-Nuova, my declaration of war against the republic of Venice, grounding it on the principle of repelling force by force. My manifesto was conceived in the following terms:

'Whilst the French army is in the defiles of Styria, having left Italy and its principal establishments far behind, where only a few battalions remained, this is the line of conduct pursued by the government of Venice.

'It takes the opportunity of Passion Week to arm 40,000 peasants, adds ten regiments of Sclavonians to that force, forms them into several corps-d'armée, and posts them at different points to intercept the communications of the army. Extraordinary commissions, musquets, ammunition of all kinds, and artillery, are sent from the city of Venice, to complete the organization of the different corps. All who received the French in a friendly manner in the Terra Firma are arrested; whilst those who are distinguished by an outrageous hatred of the French name, obtain the favours and entire confidence of the government; and especially the fourteen conspirators of Verona, whom the proveditore Priuli had caused to be arrested three months ago, as convicted of having plotted the slaughter of the French.

'In the squares, coffee-houses, and other public places of Venice, the French are insulted; they are called Jacobins, regicides and atheists; and at length they are expelled from the city, and forbidden ever to return.

'The people of Padua, Vicenza, and Verona are ordered to take up arms, to second the different corps-d'armée; and, in short, to begin these new Sicilian Vespers. It is ours, say the Venetian officers, to verify the proverb that *Italy is the tomb of the French*. The priests in their pulpits preach a crusade; and in the states of Venice, priests never say anything but what is dictated by the government. Pamphlets, perfidious proclamations, and anonymous letters are printed in various towns, and begin to work upon the minds of the people; and in a state in which the liberty of the press is not allowed—in a government as much dreaded as secretly abhorred—authors and printers write and print only what is wished by the senate.

'At first everything seems to favour the treacherous scheme of the government; French blood flows in all directions. On every road the convoys, couriers, and all belonging to the army, are intercepted.

'At Padua a chief of battalion and two other Frenchmen are murdered; at Castiglione di Mori, several soldiers are disarmed and murdered; on the high roads from Mantua to Legnago, and from Cassano to Verona, upwards of 200 French are murdered.

'Two battalions, on their way to join the army, are met at Chiari by a Venetian division, which opposes their progress. An obstinate action commences, and our brave soldiers force a passage over the bodies of the enemies. At Valeggio there is another engagement; and at Dezenzano they are again obliged to fight. The French are in all these cases few in number, but they are accustomed to disregard the numbers of their enemies.

'On the second holiday of Easter, at the ringing of the bell, all the French in Verona are murdered: the assassins spare neither the sick in the hospitals, nor those who are convalescent and walking in the streets: they are thrown into the Adige, after receiving a thousand stabs of stilettoes. Upwards of four hundred soldiers are thus massacred. During eight days the Venetian army besieges the three castles of Verona; the cannon it plants against them are taken by the French at the point of the bayonet; the city is set on fire; and the corps of observation, which comes up during these transactions, completely routs these cowards, taking 3,000 prisoners, amongst whom are several generals.

'The house of the French consul at Zante is burnt down. In Dalmatia, a Venetian man-of-war takes an Austrian convoy under her protection, and fires several shots at the sloop *La Brune*. The Republic ship *Le Libérateur d'Italie*, carrying only three or four small guns, is sunk in the port of Venice by order of the government. The young and lamented Lieutenant Laugier, her commander, finding himself attacked both by the fire of the fort and that of the admiral's galley, being within pistol-shot of both, orders his crew under hatches. He alone mounts on deck, amidst a shower of grape-shot, and endeavours to disarm the fury of these assassins, by addressing them; but he falls dead on the spot. His crew betake themselves to swimming, and are pursued by six boats manned by troops in the pay of the republic of Venice, who kill several of the French with axes, as they are endeavouring to save their lives by swimming towards the sea. A boatswain, wounded in several places, weakened, and bleeding profusely, is fortunate enough to make the shore, and clings to a piece of timber projecting from the harbour castle; but the commandant himself chops off his hand with an axe.

'Considering the above mentioned grievances, and authorized by title XII article 328 of the Constitution of the Republic, and seeing the urgency of the occasion, the General-in-chief requires the Minister of France to the republic of Venice to depart from the said city;

'Orders the different agents of the Venetian republic in Lombardy and the Venetian Terra Firma, to depart within twenty-four hours;

'Orders the different generals of division to treat the troops of the republic of Venice as enemies; and to pull down the lion of Saint Mark in every town of the Terra Firma. To-morrow, in the order of the day, each of them will receive particular instructions respecting further military operations.'

On reading this manifesto, the weapons fell from the hands of the oligarchs, who no longer thought of defending themselves. The Grand Council of the aristocracy dissolved itself, and restored the sovereignty to the people. A municipal body was now entrusted with the supreme power. Thus these haughty families, who had so long been treated with the utmost consideration, and to whom an alliance had been offered with so much sincerity, fell without offering the least resistance. In their last agonies they in vain supplicated the court of Vienna; they made fruitless applications to it to include them in the suspension of arms, and in the negotiations for peace. That court was deaf to all their entreaties; it had its views.

On 16 May, Baraguay d'Hilliers entered Venice at the call of the inhabitants, who were threatened by the Sclavonians. He occupied the forts and batteries, and hoisted the tri-coloured flag in Saint-Mark's Place. The partisans of liberty immediately met in popular assembly. The aristocracy was destroyed for ever; the democratic constitution of twelve hundred was proclaimed. Dandalo, a man of hot, impetuous temper, an enthusiast in the cause of liberty, a very worthy man, and one of the most distinguished advocates, was placed at the head of all the affairs of the city.

The lion of Saint Mark and the Corinthian horses were carried to Paris. The Venetian navy consisted of twelve sixty-four-gun ships, and as many frigates and sloops. These were manned and sent to Toulon.

Corfu was one of the most important points of the republic. General Gentili, the same who had reconquered Corsica, proceeded to Corfu with four battalions and a few companies of artillery, on board of a squadron composed of Venetian ships. He took possession of this place, the key of the Adriatic; as well as of the five other Ionian islands, Zante, Cerigo, Cephalonia, Saint Maura (anciently Ithaca), etc.

Pesaro was overwhelmed with general reprobation; he had ruined his country; he escaped to Vienna. Battaglia sincerely regretted the fall of Venice. He had long blamed the proceedings of the senate, and foreseen this

VENICE

catastrophe but too clearly. He died some time afterwards, regretted by all honest men. Had his advice been listened to, Venice would have been saved. The doge Manini suddenly fell down dead, whilst taking the oath to Austria, administered by Morosini, who had become the Emperor's commissioner.

On receipt of the order of the day declaring war against Venice, the whole Terra Firma revolted against the capital. Every town proclaimed its independence and constituted a government for itself. Bergamo, Brescia, Padua, Vicenza, Bassano, and Udine, formed so many separate republics. It was on this system that the Cispadan and Transpadan republics had begun. They adopted the principles of the Fench Revolution; they abolished convents, but respected religion and the property of the secular priests; constituted national domains, and suppressed feudal privileges. The *élite* of the nobility and great proprietors formed themselves into squadrons of hussars and light horse, under the title of the Guard of Honour; the inferior classes formed battalions of national guards. The colours of these new republics were those of Italy.

Notwithstanding my extreme vigilance to prevent abuses and peculation, there were more disorders of this kind committed on this occasion than at any other period of the war. The country was divided between two very hostile factions: the passions of the people were here peculiarly ardent and daring. At the time of the surrender of Verona, the *Mont-de-Piété* of that city, containing property to the value of seven or eight millions, was plundered. Bouquet, a commissary of the war department, and Andrieux, a colonel of hussars, were accused of being the authors of this robbery, the atrocity of which was increased by other crimes committed both before and after it, in order to keep it concealed. All that was found in the houses of the accused was restored to the city, which, nevertheless, suffered a very considerable loss.

General Bernadotte carried the colours taken from the Venetian troops, and the remainder of those which had been taken at Rivoli and in Germany from Prince Charles's army, to Paris. He presented these trophies to the Directory, a few days before 18 Fructidor.

These frequent presentations of colours were at this period very useful to the government, for the disaffected were silenced and overawed by this display of the spirit of the armies.

Chapter XX

NEGOTIATIONS IN 1797

1: Head-quarters at Montebello. 2: Negotiations with the Republic of Genoa. 3: With the King of Sardinia. 4: With the Pope. 5: With Naples. 6: The Cispadan and Transpadan Republics; they form the Cisalpine Republic. 7: Negotiations with the Grisons and the Valteline.

I

Montebello is a castle situate a few leagues from Milan on a hill which commands the whole plain of Lombardy. The French head-quarters remained there during the months of May and June. The daily assemblage of the principal ladies of Milan to pay their court to Josephine; the presence of the Ministers of Austria, the Pope, the Kings of Naples and Sardinia, the Republics of Genoa and Venice, the Duke of Parma, the Swiss Cantons, and of several of the German princes; the attendance of all the generals, of the authorities of the Cisalpine Republic, and the deputies of the towns; the great number of couriers going and returning every hour to and from Paris, Rome, Naples, Vienna, Florence, Venice, Turin and Genoa; and the style of living at this great castle—induced the Italians to call it *the Court of Montebello*. It was, in fact, a brilliant court. The negotiations for peace with the Emperor, the political affairs of Germany, and the fate of the King of Sardinia, of Switzerland, Venice, and Genoa, were here settled. The Court of Montebello made several excursions to lake Maggiore, the Borromean islands, and the lake of Como; taking up its temporary residence in the different country-houses which surround these lakes. Every town and village was eager to distinguish itself, and to testify its homage and respect to the *liberator of Italy*. These circumstances made a strong impression on the diplomatic body.

NEGOTIATIONS IN 1797

General Serrurier carried the last colours taken from the Archduke to Paris, and presented them to the Directory. 'This officer,' said I in my letter, 'has displayed in the last two campaigns equal talent and *civism*. It was his division that gained the victory of Mondovi, contributed so materially to that of Castiglione, and took Mantua. It also distinguished itself at the passage of the Tagliamento, at the passage of the Isonzo, and especially at the taking of Gradisca. General Serrurier is severe to himself, and sometimes towards others: he is a rigid supporter of discipline, regularity, and the virtues most necessary to the maintenance of social order. He disdains intrigue, and has consequently found enemies amongst men who are always ready to prefer the charge of *incivism* against those who wish to maintain the dominion of the laws. I think he would be very fit to command the troops of the Cisalpine Republic. I entreat you to send him back to his post as soon as possible.' Serrurier was well received at Paris; the frankness of his character met with general approbation there. He made a journey in his native department of the Aisne. He had always been very moderate in his revolutionary principles. But on his return from France he appeared a very warm and decided supporter of the republic, being highly incensed at the prevalent spirit of disaffection which he had observed.

At the moment of the entrance of the French army into Venice, the Count d'Entraigues escaped from that city. He was arrested on the Brenta by the troops of Bernadotte's division, and sent to the head-quarters at Milan. Count d'Entraigues was a native of the Vivarais. As a deputy of the *noblesse* to the Constituent, he was an ardent patriot in 1788 and 1789; but at the commencement of the Assembly (he was nephew to M. Saint-Priest) he changed sides— emigrated, became one of the principal agents of the foreigners, and a complete go-between in political intrigues. He had been two years at Venice, apparently attached to the English legation, but in fact as the minister of the counter-revolution, and heading all the plots of *espionage* and insurrection against the French army. He was suspected of having had an important share in the massacres at Verona. Generals Berthier and Clarke examined his portfolio, drew up a *procès-verbal* of all the papers found, marked them, and sent them to Paris. The French Government, in answer, ordered that d'Entraigues should be brought before a military commission, and tried according to the laws of the Republic; but in the interval he had made interest with me who had seen him several times. Fully aware of the danger of his situation, he did all in his power to please the man who was master of his fate, made unreserved communications, discovered all the intrigues of the time, and compromised his party more than it was necessary to do. He succeeded, and obtained permission to reside in the city on his parole, and without guard. Some time afterwards he was allowed to escape into Switzerland. So little was he attended to, that it was not discovered that he had broken his parole,

NEGOTIATIONS IN 1797

until six or seven days after his departure from Milan. Soon afterwards he published and circulated throughout Germany and Italy a kind of pamphlet against his benefactor, describing the horrible dungeon in which he had been confined, and the tortures he had suffered, the boldness he had displayed, and the dangers he had braved in making his escape. This excited great indignation at Milan, where he had been seen in all companies, in the public walks and theatres, enjoying the greatest liberty. Several members of the diplomatic body participated in the feelings of the public, and published declarations to this effect.

2

The Republic of Genoa, during the three wars of the successions of Spain, Parma, and Austria, had formed part of the belligerent forces; its little armies had then marched with the troops of the French and Spanish kingdoms. In 1747 the people had driven the Austrian garrison, commanded by the Marquis de Botta, out of Genoa; and had afterwards sustained a long and obstinate siege against the armies of Maria Theresa. In the eighteenth century Genoa maintained a sanguinary war against Corsica. National animosities occasioned continual skirmishes between the people of Piedmont and the Genoese. This continuance and concurrence of military events had kept up a spirit and energy in the citizens of this republic, inconsiderable as it was in population and territory, which rendered its composition wholly different from that of the Republic of Venice. The Genoese aristocracy had accordingly withstood the storm, preserved their freedom and independence, and suffered neither the Allied Powers nor France, nor the popular party, to intimidate them. The Republic had maintained the constitution which Andrea Doria had given it in the sixteenth century, in all its original purity.

But the proclamation of the independence of the Cispadan and Transpadan Republics, the abdication of the aristocracy of Venice, the establishment of a popular government throughout the Venetian territories, and the enthusiasm which the victories of the French excited, had given such a preponderance to the popular party, that a change in the constitution became indispensable. France thought she could place no confidence in the aristocracy; but it was desirable that the revolution should take place without her open interference, and merely through the progress and force of public opinion. Faypoult, the French minister at Genoa, was an enlightened man, moderate in his principles, and of an irresolute character; which was an advantageous circumstance, as matters stood, since he was more inclined to repress than to excite the enthusiasm of the revolutionary party.

Men who watched the progress of events expected a crisis about the end of August, conceiving that the aristocracy would be unable to prolong its

NEGOTIATIONS IN 1797

resistance beyond that period. The revolutionists of the Morandi club, impatient at the slow progress of the revolution, and probably excited by secret agents from Paris, drew up a petition requiring the abdication of the aristocracy and the proclamation of liberty. A deputation waited on the Doge with this petition. He did not seem averse to comply with the wishes of the public; he even named a junta of nine persons, four of whom were of the plebeian class, to propose alterations in the constitution to him.

The three state inquisitors, or supreme censors, who were the leaders of the oligarchy and the enemies of France, beheld this state of affairs with dissatisfaction. Being themselves convinced that the aristocracy had but a few months to exist, if they permitted events to take their course and did not find means to direct them, they called in the aid of fanaticism, by which they hoped to obtain that of the inferior corporations. They knew that if they could but excite the enthusiasm of the colliers and porters, they should acquire sufficient strength to overawe the other citizens of every class. They made use of the confessional and the pulpit, of preachers in the squares and public places, or miracles, of the exposing of the Host, and even of prayers of forty hours, to entreat God to avert from the Republic the storm which threatened it: but by this imprudent conduct they drew upon themselves the very calamities they sought to avoid. The Morandists, on their side, were not inactive; they declaimed, printed, excited the people against the nobles and priests by a thousand expedients, and continually made proselytes. It was not long before they found a favourable opportunity, and took up arms. On 22 May, at ten o'clock in the morning, they took possession of the principal gates, especially those of the arsenal, Saint Thomas, and the port. The terrified inquisitors gave the signal to the colliers and porters, who, led by their syndics, advanced with shouts of *Viva Maria!* to the armoury, and declared for the aristocracy. In a few hours 10,000 men were thus armed and organized for the defence of the Prince. The French minister, alarmed at their vociferations against the Jacobins and the French, went to the palace, and used his endeavours to reconcile these hostile parties. Perceiving the preparations of the oligarchy and the numbers of their defenders, the patriots became sensible of their weakness. They had reckoned on the aid of the citizens, who might have turned the scale by declaring in their favour; but the citizens were intimidated by the fury of the colliers, and shut themselves up in their houses. The patriots, thus deceived in their expectations, perceived no means of safety but in mounting the French cockade; which, they hoped, would overawe the oligarchs: but this had nearly proved fatal to the French families settled at Genoa. The conflict now began, and the patriots were beaten and driven from their posts. During the night of the 23rd they kept possession of the gate of Saint Thomas, but lost it on the 24th at daybreak. The triumphant oligarchy issued orders that everyone should wear the Genoese cockade, and suffered the houses of

NEGOTIATIONS IN 1797

the French to be pillaged; several of them were thrown into dungeons. The minister Faypoult only escaped insult through a guard of honour of 200 men which the Doge sent him. The naval commissioner Menard, a prudent man, who had particularly abstained from all interference in the troubles of the times, was dragged by the hair as far as the lighthouse fort; the consul La Chaise had his house plundered; all that was French was exposed to outrage and assassination. The citizens were indignant, but so much afraid of the victors that they durst not stir. Between the 23rd and 29th, the minister Faypoult presented several notes on this subject, but obtained no satisfaction. At this juncture Admiral Brueys, returning from Corsica with two men-of-war and two frigates, came in sight of the port. The Doge objected to the entrance of this squadron, under the pretext that its presence would irritate the populace, and provoke them to all sorts of excesses against the French families. Faypoult had the weakness to yield to these arguments, and sent orders to Brueys to make for Toulon.

When it was observed in the senate by moderate men that this conduct was extremely imprudent, the oligarchs replied, that the French, who were engaged in negotiations with Austria, would not dare to march a body of troops against Genoa; that the prevailing opinion at Paris was unfavourable to democratical ideas; that they knew that I myself disapproved of the principles of the Morandi club, and that I would consider twice before I exposed myself to the censure of my government and of the Clichy party, which ruled the legislature.

All these fallacious hopes were defeated. No sooner was I informed of the events which had taken place, and the shedding of French blood, than I despatched my aide-de-camp Lavalette to Genoa, and required of the Doge that all the French who had been arrested should be immediately placed at the disposal of the French minister; and that the colliers and porters should be disarmed, and the inquisitors arrested; declaring, at the same time, that the heads of the patricians should be responsible to me for the lives of the French, and that all the magazines and property of the Republic should answer for their property. I ordered the minister Faypoult to quit Genoa and repair to Tortona, with all the French who might think proper to follow him, unless these arrangements were carried into execution within twenty-four hours. The aide-de-camp Lavalette arrived at Genoa on 28 May, at half after four o'clock; and at six he was introduced to the senate, which, after hearing his speech, and being acquainted with my letter to the Doge, promised to give an answer the same evening. In fact, the French were immediately set at liberty and taken to the house of the Embassy, amidst an immense concourse of people, who seemed gratified at their release. The citizens and the real people, encouraged by what I had done, and by my assurances of protection, roused themselves, and loudly demanded the disarming of the assassins of the oligrachy. That

NEGOTIATIONS IN 1797

very evening 4,000 musquets were brought back to the arsenal. Strong debates took place in the petty council; the aristocracy was in the minority. A division of French troops was entering Tortona. Genoa, besieged by land and sea, would soon have been reduced to obedience; it is even probable that the sight of the French troops would have sufficed to give the citizens and the mass of the third estate strength enough to shake off the yoke of the aristocracy.

The answer of the senate was not, however, satisfactory; it was a middle course. Faypoult resolved to depart. Lavalette was to remain at Genoa, to protect the French. When the French minister demanded his passports, the Doge assembled the senate, which alone was authorized to deliver them. The senate now took into deep consideration the situation in which it appeared that the Republic would shortly be placed. After some discussion, they adopted a resolution to coincide sincerely in my views. It was resolved, first, that a deputation, composed of Cambiaso the Doge, Serra, and Carbonari, should immediately proceed to Montebello; secondly, that the three inquisitors should be put in a state of arrest; and thirdly, that the colliers and porters should be disarmed.

In consequence of this resolution, the French minister remained at his post, which tranquillized the populace. The colliers and porters, who had only acted under the orders of the government, and who had, in reality, no interest in the affair, became very tractable as soon as submission was sincerely resolved on.

On 6 June, the deputies from the senate signed a convention at Montebello, which put an end to Doria's constitution, and established the democratical government at Genoa.

The people triumphed with that extravagance which distinguishes the spirit of party and the southern nations; they committed excesses, burned the Golden Book, and broke the statue of Doria to pieces. This outrage on the memory of that great man displeased me; I required the Provisional Government to restore this statue. The exclusionists, however, got the upper hand, and the constitution was influenced by their predominance; the priests were rendered discontented, and the nobles were exasperated, being excluded from all functions. This constitution was to be submitted to the approbation of the people on 14 September; it was printed and posted in all the communes. Several of the country cantons declared they would not accept it; the priests and nobles were actively endeavouring, on all sides, to induce the peasants to revolt: insurrections broke out in the valleys of Polcevera and the Bisagno. The insurgents possessed themselves of the *Eperon,* the *Tenaille,* and the bastion of the lighthouse which commands the port. General Duphot, who had been sent to Genoa to organize the troops of the Republic, whose effective force amounted to 6,000 men, was required by the Provisional Government to fight in its defence. He expelled the insurgents, and retook the walls

NEGOTIATIONS IN 1797

and forts. On the 7th tranquillity was restored in both valleys, and the peasants were disarmed.

This news was a disappointment to me. I was then wholly occupied in the negotiations with Austria; I had not been able to pay particular attention to the affairs of Genoa; but I had recommended that the nobles should be conciliated and the priests satisfied. I suspended the publication of the constitution; I made all the alterations required by the clergy and the nobles; and, thus purged from the anarchical spirit that pervaded it, it was carried into execution by general assent. I was partial to Genoa, and would have proceeded thither in order to reconcile and unite all parties; but important events followed each other so rapidly, that they prevented my fulfilling this intention. After the treaty of Campo Formio, just as I was leaving Italy, I wrote the following letter from Milan to the Genoese government, on 11 November, 1797:—

'I am going to justify the confidence which you, citizens, have placed in me —You feel it necessary to diminish the expenses of the administration in order to avoid the necessity of over-burthening your people—It is not enough to do nothing against religion; it is necessary to avoid giving the slightest grounds of disquiet to the most timorous minds, or the least pretence to the ill-disposed. *To exclude all the nobles from public functions would be a shocking piece of injustice: you would be doing what they have done*—The freedom of the port is an apple of discord which has been thrown amongst you—The city of Genoa ought to owe the freedom of its port to the will of the Legislative Body.

'*Why is the Ligurian nation already so much altered? Fear and terror have succeeded its first transports of fraternity and enthusiasm. The priests were the first to rally round the tree of liberty; they were the first who told you that the morality of the Gospel is purely democratical; but men in the pay of your enemies, men who in all revolutions are the immediate auxiliaries of tyranny, have taken advantage of the errors—the crimes, if you will—of a few priests, in order to write against religion; and the priests have withdrawn. Proscriptions have been declared against whole bodies of men, and this has but increased the number of your enemies—Whenever the people of any state, but particularly of a small state, accustom themselves to condemn without hearing, and to applaud speeches merely because they are passionate: when they call exaggeration and fury, virtue; and equity and moderation, crimes; the ruin of that state is at hand.* Rest assured, that, wherever my duty and the service of my country may lead me, I shall look upon any opportunity of being useful to your Republic as one of the most fortunate moments of my life. It will give me great satisfaction to hear that the people of Genoa are united and prosperous.'

The Council of Five Hundred at Paris was then debating on a motion made by Sieyes, tending to expel all the nobles from France, on giving them the value of their property in manufactured goods. This advice, given by me to the Republic of Genoa, appeared to be addressed in fact to the French Republic, which at all events profited by it; for this violent and terrific plan, which caused universal alarm and disorder, was abandoned, and was no more heard of.

Not a single French battalion had passed beyond Tortona. The Genoese revolution was effected entirely by the influence of the third estate; and but for the plots of the inquisitors and the Morandi club, it would have been effected without any disturbance or commotion, and without even the indirect intervention of France.

3

The King of Sardinia was in a false position. The following treaty, negotiated by me at Bologna, and signed at Turin by Clarke, might be said to exist and not to exist:

'The Executive Directory of the French Republic and his Majesty the King of Sardinia, wishing by all means in their power, and particularly by a closer union of their respective interests, to contribute to effect, as speedily as possible, a peace which is the object of their wishes, and which may secure the repose and tranquillity of Italy, have resolved to enter into a treaty of alliance, offensive and defensive; and for this purpose have given full powers in manner following; that is to say: The Executive Directory of the French Republic, to citizen Henri Jacques Guillaume Clarke, general of division in the armies of the French Republic; and his Majesty the King of Sardinia, to the chevalier D. Clement Damian de Priocca, knight grand cross of the orders of Saint Maurice and Saint Lazarus, principal secretary of state to his Majesty for the department of foreign affairs, and regent of that of internal affairs; who, after exchanging their respective powers, have agreed on the following articles:

'ARTICLE I. There shall be an offensive alliance between the French Republic and his Majesty the King of Sardinia, until a continental peace. At that period this alliance shall become merely defensive, and shall be established on terms suitable to the reciprocal interests of the two powers.

'II. It being the principal object of the present alliance to hasten the conclusion of peace and secure the future tranquillity of Italy, it shall be carried into execution, during the present war, solely against the Emperor of Austria, who is the only continental power that impedes the attainment of this truly desirable object. His Majesty the King of Sardinia will remain neutral with respect to England and the other powers still at war with the French Republic.

'III. The French Republic and his Sardinian Majesty mutually guarantee, by all means in their power, their present possessions in Europe during the continuance of the present alliance. The two powers shall unite their forces against their common foreign enemies, and shall give no direct or indirect assistance to the domestic enemies of each other.

'IV. The contingent of the troops which his Sardinian Majesty is to furnish, in the first instance and in consequence of the present alliance, shall be 8,000 infantry, 2,000 cavalry, and 40 pieces of cannon. In case the two powers should think it necessary to increase this contingent, the augmentation shall be settled and regulated by commissioners, furnished with the full powers of the Directory and of his Sardinian Majesty for that purpose.

'V. The contingent of troops and artillery shall be taken and join at Novara, in manner following: 500 cavalry, 4,000 infantry, and 12 pieces of heavy artillery by the 30th of the present month of Germinal, 19 April (old style), and the remainder within fifteen days next following.

'This contingent shall be maintained at the expense of his Sardinian Majesty, and shall be under the command of the General-in-Chief of the French army in Italy.

'The mode of service for this contingent shall be settled by a particular convention drawn up with the approbation of the said general.

'VI. The troops which shall form the said contingent shall participate, in proportion to their numbers present under arms, in the contributions to be imposed on the conquered countries, reckoning from the day on which this contingent shall join the army of the Republic.

'VII. The French Republic promises to procure for his Sardinian Majesty, at the general or continental peace, all the advantages which circumstances may enable it to obtain.

'VIII. Neither of the two contracting powers shall conclude any separate treaty of peace with the common enemy; nor shall any armistice be entered into by the French Republic with the armies covering Italy, without including his Sardinian Majesty therein.

'IX. All contributions laid on the states of his Sardinian Majesty, not yet acquitted or discharged, shall cease immediately after the exchange of the ratifications of the present treaty.

'X. The supplies which from the same period shall be furnished in the states of his Majesty the King of Sardinia to the French troops and the prisoners of war taken to France, as well as those which have been furnished pursuant to particular agreements for that purpose, and which have not yet been paid or compensated for by the French Republic in consequence of the said agreements, shall be rendered in kind to the troops forming the contingent of his Sardinian Majesty; and in case the supplies to be so rendered should exceed the occasions of the contingent, the balance shall be discharged in money.

'XI. The two contracting powers shall forthwith appoint commissioners empowered to negotiate in their names a treaty of commerce, conformably to the terms agreed upon in the seventh article of the treaty of peace,

NEGOTIATIONS IN 1797

concluded at Paris between the French Republic and his Majesty the King of Sardinia: in the meantime the posts and commercial relations shall be re-established without delay, as they existed previously to the war.

'XII. The ratifications of the present treaty of alliance shall be exchanged at Paris with the least delay possible.

'Done and signed at Turin, 16 Germinal, year V of the French Republic, one and indivisible.

(Signed) H. CLARKE.
CLEMENT DAMIAN.'

The Directory did not openly declare its intentions, but it was evident that it would not ratify this treaty. I, on the other hand, persisted in regarding this ratification as indispensably necessary. I justly thought it highly important to add to my army a division of good veteran Piedmontese troops, whose valour I esteemed. Considering myself as personally engaged to the Court of Sardinia, I used all means in my power to guarantee the interior tranquillity of the King's dominions. The Piedmontese malcontents nevertheless increased in numbers daily; they took up arms, and the revolutionists were defeated. This situation was extremely delicate; it excited the resentment of the French and Italian Jacobins in the highest degree; and when the royalists had triumphed at Turin, the arrests and oppressive proceedings in which they indulged gave rise to innumerable complaints addressed to head-quarters.

At the end of September, when the Directory signed the ultimatum for the negotiations of Campo-Formio, they intimated to me their perseverance in the determination not to sign the treaty of alliance with Sardinia. The minister of exterior relations, in communicating the intentions of the Directory, suggested to me the expediency of having the Sardinian soldiers enticed to desert by the Italian recruiting agents; which would enable me, said the minister, to obtain the 10,000 men of the Piedmontese contingent without incurring any obligation to the Court of Turin. But the establishments, which constitute strength of troops, could not be enticed to desert: besides, an operation of this kind could not be accomplished without a great loss of time, and it was necessary to take the field immediately. This conduct of the Directory was one of the causes which determined me to sign the peace of Campo-Formio, without attending to the ultimatum of the French government of 29 September, which could not, in my opinion, be inserted in the protocol without producing a rupture. But the Directory at last perceived the importance of reinforcing the army of Italy with the 10,000 men of the Piedmontese contingent; they determined on ratifying the treaty of Turin, and sent it on 21 October to the Legislative Body; but it was now too late, for peace with Austria had been signed on the 17th at Campo-Formio.

Thus, after my campaigns in Italy, the King of Sardinia retained this throne, weakened indeed by the loss of Savoy and the county of Nice, and by that of his fortresses, part of which had been demolished, and the remainder were in the power of the French, who placed garrisons in them; but he had gained the immense advantage of being in alliance with the Republic which guaranteed the integrity of his estates. This prince, however, did not deceive himself with respect to the situation in which he stood: he knew that he owed the preservation of his throne solely to me, and that the apparent alliance of the Directory was far from sincere. He had a presentiment of his approaching fall. Surrounded on every side by the French, Ligurian, and Cisalpine democracies, he had also to contend with the power of public opinion amongst his own subjects: for the Piedmontese loudly called for a revolution, and the Court already looked to Sardinia as a place of refuge.

4

The Court of Rome, at first, faithfully abided by the treaty of Tolentino; but soon afterwards yielded to the influence of Cardinal Busca and Albani, recommenced its levies of troops, and had the imprudence to bid open defiance to France, by sending for General Provera to command its troops. It also refused to acknowledge the Cisalpine republic. The victorious attitude of France, and the threats of her ambassador, soon put an end to this empty affectation of independence. Provera remained but a few days at Rome, and departed once more for Austria. The Cisalpine Republic, rejoicing in this opportunity to get possession of some of the provinces of the Holy See, declared war against the Vatican. Perceiving the approaching storm which threatened them, these feeble, rash old men fell on their knees, and gave the Cisalpine Directory every satisfaction it could require.

If this conduct presents no traces of the ancient policy which for so many centuries distinguished the Vatican, it is because that government was worn out. The temporal power of the Pope was no longer predominant; it was drawing towards its end, as the sovereignty of the ecclesiastical electors of the empire had terminated.

5

The Court of Naples was governed by the Queen, a woman of remarkable strength of mind, but all whose ideas were as disorderly as the passions which agitated her bosom. The treaty of Paris of 10 October, 1796, had made no alteration in the disposition of this Cabinet, which continued to raise troops and excite anxiety during the whole of the year 1797.

When I was in the Marches, menacing Rome, Prince Belmonte Pignatelli, the Neapolitan minister, who was at head-quarters, shewed me, in confidence,

NEGOTIATIONS IN 1797

a letter from the Queen, informing him that she was about to order 30,000 men to march to cover Rome. 'I thank you for this confidential communication,' said I, 'and in return I will make you a similar one.' I rang for my secretary, ordered him to bring the papers relating to Naples, took out a despatch which I had written to the Directory in the month of November, 1796, before the taking of Mantua, and read as follows: 'The difficulties arising from Alvinzi's approach would not prevent me from sending 6,000 Lombards and Poles to punish the Court of Rome; but as it is probable that the king of Naples might send 30,000 men to defend the Holy See, I shall not march on Rome until Mantua shall have fallen, and the reinforcements you announce shall have arrived, in order that, in case the Court of Naples should violate the treaty of Paris, I might have 25,000 men disposable to occupy its capital and compel it to take refuge in Sicily.' In the course of the night Prince Pignatelli despatched an extraordinary courier, doubtless for the purpose of informing the Queen of the manner in which her insinuation had been received.

Ever since the treaty of Paris the Neapolitan legations had generally behaved with more hostility and arrogance towards the French than during the war; and the ambassadors of Naples often had the temerity to say openly that the peace would not be of long duration. This rash and foolish conduct did not prevent the Court of Naples from indulging in dreams of ambition. During the conferences of Montebello, Udine, and Passeriano, the Queen's envoy tried to obtain the islands of Corfu, Zante, Cephalonia, and Santa Maura, the Marches of Macerata, Ferrara, and Ancona, and the duchy of Urbino. He even went so far as to express her wish to enrich herself with the spoils of the Pope and the Republic of Venice; and the Queen expected to gain these acquisitions through the patronage of France, and particularly by my intervention. The Court of Naples survived the peace of Campo-Formio, and might have remained tranquil and prosperous amidst the storms which agitated Europe and Italy, had it been directed by sound policy.

6

It was found necessary to yield to the wishes of the people of Lombardy, and form them into a democratical and independent state under the title of the Transpadan Republic, comprising all the left bank of the Po, from the Mincio to the Ticino. The Cispadan Republic was on the right bank of the Po, from the states of Parma (which it did not include) to the Adriatic. The constitution of the Cispadan state had been decreed in a congress of the representatives of the nation, and submitted to the people for acceptance, who had voted its establishment by an immense majority, and it had been carried into execution at the latter end of April. The nobles and priests had succeeded in getting themselves elected to all public situations; the citizens accused them of not

NEGOTIATIONS IN 1797

being well affected towards the new order of things; the discontent was general. I felt the necessity of giving these two republics a definitive organization.

Immediately after the refusal of the Court of Vienna to ratify the convention signed at Montebello, with the Marquis di Gallo, which contained the terms of the definitive peace, I created the Cisalpine Republic. This was composed of the Cispadan and Transpadan Republics; whereby four millions of inhabitants were united under the same government, composing a mass of force calculated to have a powerful influence on subsequent operations. But the authorities of the Cispadan state obstinately objected to a union which was repugnant to all their prejudices. The Governments of Reggio, Modena, Bologna, and Ferrara, considered the necessity of uniting under one government as a great hardship. The spirit of locality everywhere opposed the junction of the people on the two banks of the Po; and the attempt to effect this fusion by the consent of the people would probably have failed, but for the hopes they were led to form that it was but a prelude to the union of all the nations of the peninsula under a single government. The secret inclination of all the Italians to form a single great nation prevailed over all the petty passions of the local administrations. Two peculiar circumstances strengthened this motive. Romagna, which the Pope had ceded by the Treaty of Tolentino, had proclaimed itself independent under the title of the Emilian Republic, having declined a union with the Cispadan on account of its antipathy to Bologna; but this republic ardently embraced the idea of forming part of the Cisalpine Republic, the formation of which it solicited by several petitions. In the meantime Venice and the Terra Firma states, uneasy at the secrecy of the preliminaries, voted in the popular assemblies the formation of the Italian Republic. These two circumstances removed all difficulties. The spirit of locality gave way to public spirit; private interests yielded to the good of the community; the amalgamation was decreed by general consent.

The new republic took the name of Cisalpine. Milan was its capital. This excited some disapprobation at Paris, where there were some persons who would have had it called the Transalpine Republic. But as the Italians fixed their hopes upon Rome, and the union of the whole peninsula in a single state, the denomination of Cisalpine was that which flattered their passions, and which they insisted on adopting, not daring to call this state the Italian Republic.

By the treaty of Campo-Formio the Cisalpine Republic obtained the addition of that part of the states of Venice which was situated on the right bank of the Adige; which, added to the acquisition of the Valteline, gave it a population of 3,600,000 souls. These provinces, the richest and finest in Europe, composed ten departments. They extended from the mountains of Switzerland to the Tuscan and Roman Apennines, and from the Ticino to the Adriatic.

I would willingly have given the Cisalpine state a different constitution

NEGOTIATIONS IN 1797

from that of France. With this view I had desired to have some celebrated publicist, such as Sieyes, sent to me at Milan; but this idea did not please the Directory: they required the Cisalpine Republic to adopt the French constitution of 1795. The first Cisalpine Directory was composed of Serbelloni, Alessandri, Paradisi, Moscati, and Containi, leaders of the French party in Italy. Serbelloni was one of the greatest lords in Lombardy. On 30 June they were installed in the palace of Milan. The independence of the Cisalpine Republic had been proclaimed on the 29th in the following terms:—

'The Cisalpine Republic had for many years been subject to the sway of the house of Austria. The French Republic had succeeded to the latter by right of conquest, which it henceforth renounces, and leaves the Cisalpine Republic free and independent. Acknowledged by France and by the Emperor, it will speedily be recognized by all Europe. The Executive Directory of the French Republic, not content with having employed its influence and the victories of the Republican armies in securing the existence of the Cisalpine Republic, extends its solicitude still farther; and convinced, that, if liberty is the first of blessings, a protracted revolution is the most terrible of calamities, gives the Cisalpine people its own constitution, which is the result of the knowledge of the most enlightened nation in the world. The Cisalpine people is therefore on the point of exchanging a military for a constitutional government. In order to effect this transition without any shock, without anarchy, the Executive Directory has deemed it expedient to appoint, for this time only, the members of the Government and Legislative Body; so that the people will not appoint to vacant places, conformably to the constitution, until after the expiration of a year. No republic has existed in Italy for many years. The sacred fire of liberty has been extinguished, and the finest part of Europe has been subjugated by foreigners. It belongs to the Cisalpine Republic to convince the world, by its prudence, its energy, and the organization of its armies, that modern Italy has not degenerated, but is still worthy of liberty.

'The General-in-chief Bonaparte, in the name of the French Republic, and in consequence of the above proclamation, nominates as members of the Directory of the Cisalpine Republic, Citizens Serbelloni, Alessandri, Moscati, and Paradisi: the fifth member shall be appointed without delay. These four members will be installed to-morrow at Milan.'

A general federation of the national guards and the authorities of the new Republic took place at the Lazaretto of Milan. On 14 July 30,000 national guards or deputies from the departments took an oath of fraternity, and swore to employ their utmost efforts to revive the liberty of Italy, and make her once more a nation. The Cisalpine Directory appointed its ministers and executive authorities, constituted its military establishment, and governed the Republic as an independent state. The keys of Milan and of all the fortresses were delivered by the French to the Cisalpine officers. The army left the states of the

Republic, and went into cantonments in the territory of Venice. From this period may be dated the first formation of the Italian army, which afterwards became numerous, and acquired a great share of glory.

The manners of the Italians underwent an immediate change; a few years afterwards they were no longer the same people. The cassock, which was the fashionable dress of youth, gave place to regimentals; instead of passing their time at the feet of women, the young Italians now frequented the riding and fencing-schools, and fields of exercise; the children no longer played at *chapel*; they had regiments armed with tin guns, and imitated the occurrences of war in their games. In the comedies, and the street farces, there had always been an Italian, represented as a very cowardly though witty fellow, and a kind of bullying captain—sometimes a Frenchman, but more frequently a German—a very powerful, brave and brutal character, who never failed to conclude with caning the Italian, to the great satisfaction of applauding spectators. But such allusions were now no longer endured by the populace; authors now brought brave Italians on the stage, putting foreigners to flight, and defending their honour and their rights, with the approbation of the public. A national spirit had arisen: Italy had songs at once patriotic and warlike; and the women contemptuously repulsed those men who affected effeminate manners in order to please them.

7

The Valteline is composed of three valleys; the Valteline properly so called, the Bormio, and the Chiavenna; its population is 160,000 souls; its inhabitants profess the Roman Catholic religion, and speak Italian. It belongs geographically to Italy; it borders the Adda down to its discharge into the lake of Como, and it is separated from Germany by the Higher Alps. It is eighteen leagues in length, and six in breadth. Chiavenna, its capital, is situate two leagues from the lake of Como, and fourteen leagues from Coire, which is seventeen leagues from Bormio. The Valteline was anciently part of the Milanese. Barnabas Visconti, Archbishop and Duke of Milan, in 1404, gave these three valleys to the church of Coire. In 1512, the Grison Leagues were invested with the sovereignty of the Valteline by Sforza, upon certain conditional statutes which the Dukes of Milan were to guarantee. The people of the Valteline thus found themselves subject to the three Leagues, most of the inhabitants of which speak German and are protestants, and are separated from the Valteline by the high chain of the Alps.

There is no condition more dreadful than that of a nation which is subject to another nation. It was thus that the Lower Valais was subject to the Upper Valais, and the *Pays de Vaud* to the canton of Berne. The unfortunate people of the Valteline had long complained of the oppressions they suffered, and the humiliating yoke to which they were subjected. The Grisons, poor and ignorant, used to come to enrich themselves in the Valteline, the inhabitants of which were richer and more civilized. The lowest peasant of the Leagues considered himself as much superior to the richest inhabitant of the Valteline, as a sovereign to his subjects. Unquestionably, if there be any situation which justifies insurrection and demands a change, it is that in which the Valteline groaned.

In the course of May, 1797, the people of the three valleys revolted, took up arms, drove out their pretended sovereigns, unfurled the Italian tri-coloured flag, appointed a provisional government, and addressed a manifesto to all powers, setting forth their grievances, and the resolution they had adopted to regain by force of arms the rights of which no people can be deprived. They sent the deputies Juidiconni, Planta, and Paribelli, men of merit, to Montebello, to claim the execution of their statutes, which had been violated by the Grisons in every point.

I was reluctant to interfere in questions which might affect Switzerland, and which, in that point of view, were of general importance. But having, nevertheless, had the documents relating to this business examined in the archives of Milan, I found that the Milanese Government was in fact invested with the right of guaranteeing the statutes; and as the Leagues also solicited my assistance to compel the people of the Valteline, their subjects, to return to subordination and obedience, I accepted the office of mediator, and appointed both parties to appear before my tribunal in the course of the following July, to defend their respective rights. In this interval the Leagues implored the intervention of the Helvetic body. Barthelemy, the French minister at Berne, solicited strongly in their favour. At length, after many intrigues on both sides, I, previously to giving a final decision, invited both parties, by way of suggestion, to come to an amicable arrangement; and proposed to them, as a mode of reconciliation, that the Valteline should form a fourth League equal in every respect to the three former. This suggestion deeply wounded the pride of the Grison peasants. *How could it be imagined that a peasant who drinks the water of the Adda could be the equal of one who drinks the water of the Rhine?* They were highly offended at so unreasonable a proposal as that of equalizing *catholic peasants who spoke Italian and were rich and enlightened to protestant peasants who spoke German and were poor and ignorant.* The leading characters amongst them did not share these prejudices, but were misled by avarice. They found the Valetline an important source of revenues and riches, which they could not make up their minds to abandon. They intrigued at Paris, Vienna, and Berne. Promises were held out to them; they were advised to gain time; and they were blamed for having provoked and agreed to the mediation. They declined conciliatory measures, and sent no deputies at the period fixed for discussing the execution of the statutes before the mediator, in opposition to the deputies of the Valteline.

NEGOTIATIONS IN 1797

I gave judgment by default against the Leagues; and as the arbitrator chosen by both parties, and as representing the sovereign of Milan, who was pledged to the performance of the statutes of the Valteline, pronounced my decision in these terms, on 19 Vendemiaire, year VI (10 October, 1797):—

'The people of the Valteline, Chiavenna, and Bormio revolted against the laws of the Grisons, and declared themselves independent in Prairial last. The government of the Republic of the Grisons, after having used all means in its power to reduce its subjects to obedience, resorted to the mediation of the French Republic, in the person of General Bonaparte, to whom they sent Gaudenzio Planta as their deputy.

'The people of the Valteline, on their side, having also required the same mediation, the General-in-Chief assembled the respective deputations at Montebello, on 4 Messidor (22 June); and, after a conference of considerable length, accepted in the name of the French Republic the proposed mediation. He wrote to the Grisons and the Valtelines, requiring them to send their deputies to him as soon as possible.

'The people of the Valteline, Chiavenna, and Bormio, punctually sent the deputies demanded.

'Several months elapsed, and the Grison government sent no deputies, notwithstanding the reiterated requests of Citizen Comeyras, resident of the Republic at Coire.

'On 6 Fructidor (23 August), the General-in-Chief, considering the anarchy that prevailed in the Valteline, had a letter written to the Grison government, giving it notice to send its deputation before 24 Fructidor (10 September).

'19 Vendemiaire (10 October) is arrived, and no deputies from the Grisons have appeared.

'They have not only failed to appear, but there is no room to doubt that, in contempt of the mediation accepted by the French Republic, the Leagues have prejudged the question, and the refusal to send deputies arises from deep intrigues.

'In consequence whereof, the General-in-Chief, in the name of the French Republic:

'Considering: First. That the good faith, honourable conduct, and confidence of the people of the Valteline, Chiavenna and Bormio, towards the French Republic, claim a similar return from the latter, as well as its assistance;

'Secondly. That the French Republic, in consequence of the demand made by the Grisons, is become the mediatrix, and as it were, the arbitress, of the fate of the people;

'Thirdly. That it is beyond doubt that the Grisons have infringed the statutes they were bound to observe towards the people of the Valteline, Chiavenna, and Bormio; and that, consequently, the latter have regained the rights which Nature gives to all mankind;

NEGOTIATIONS IN 1797

'Fourthly. That a people cannot be subject to another people, without an infraction of public and natural rights;

'Fifthly. That the wishes of the inhabitants of the Valteline, Chiavenna, and Bormio are decidedly in favour of their union with the Cisalpine Republic;

'Sixthly. That a conformity of religion and language, the local peculiarities, the nature of the communications, and the course of commerce, also justify this incorporation of the Valteline, Chiavenna, and Bormio with the Cisalpine Republic, from which, moreover, these three countries were in former times severed;

'Seventhly. That, since the decree of the communes which compose the three Grison Leagues, the course which the mediator might have adopted, of organizing the Valteline as a fourth Grison League, stands rejected; and that, consequently, the Valteline has no refuge from tyranny, except in a union with the Cisalpine Republic;

'Determines, by virtue of the power with which the French Republic is invested, by the demand made of its mediation by the Grisons and Valtelines, that the people of the Valteline, Chiavenna, and Bormio are at liberty to unite themselves with the Cisalpine Republic.'

The question was now decided. The unfortunate inhabitants of the Valteline were now transported with joy and enthusiasm; the Grisons were frantic with rage and mortification. Immediately after this award, the Valteline and Cisalpine people negotiated and effected their incorporation. The Grisons then perceived their error. They wrote to me that their deputies were setting out to appear before me and defend their rights, thus pretending to be ignorant of what had occurred. I informed them, in reply, that it was too late; that my judgment had been pronounced on 10 October; that the Valteline was already united with the Cisalpine Republic; and that the question was now settled for ever.

The justice thus done to this petty nation made a strong impression on all generous minds. The principles on which my sentence was founded echoed throughout all Europe, and aimed a mortal blow at the usurpation of the Swiss cantons, which held more than one people in subjection. It might have been expected that the aristocracy of Berne would have been sufficiently warned by this example, to feel that the moment for making some concessions to the enlightened state of the age, to the influence of France, and to justice, had arrived. But prejudices and pride never listen to the voice of reason, nature, or religion. An oligarchy yields to nothing but force. It was not until several years afterwards that the inhabitants of the Upper Valais consented to look upon the inhabitants of the Lower Valais as their equals; and that the peasants of the *Pays de Vaud* and Argovie forced the oligarchs of Berne to acknowledge their rights and independence.

Chapter XXI

THE EIGHTEENTH OF FRUCTIDOR

Of the Executive Directory. Public spirit. Religious affairs. New system of weights and measures. The Factions which divide the Republic. Conspiracy against the Republic, headed by Pichegru. I defeat this conspiracy. 18 Fructidor. Law of 19 Fructidor.

The apparent advantages attendant on the form of government prescribed by the constitution of 1795, placed it at first very high in public opinion. A council of five magistrates, having responsible ministers for the execution of its orders, was likely to have sufficient leisure to give all business mature deliberation; the same spirit, the same principles were to be transmitted uninterruptedly from age to age; there were no more regencies or minorities to fear. But these visionary ideas were soon dispelled; disadvantages of every description, the inevitable results of the amalgamation of five separate interests, the jarring of the passions and opposite character of five individuals, were soon perceived. Men now perceived all the difference that exists between an individual created by nature, and an artificial being which has neither heart nor soul, and inspires neither confidence, love, nor veneration.

The five directors divided the palace of the Luxembourg amongst themselves, and settled there with their families, which they brought into notice. Hence arose five little city courts, placed side by side, and disturbed by the passions of the women, the children, and the servants. The supreme magistracy was degraded; the men of 1793 and the elevated classes of society were equally shocked. The spirit of the constitution was violated. A director was neither a minister, a prefect, nor a general; he was but a fifth part of a whole. He ought never to have attracted public attention but when in council. His wife, children, and servants ought not to have seemed to know that he was a

THE EIGHTEENTH OF FRUCTIDOR

member of the government; the director should have remained a private citizen. But the Directory should have been surrounded with all the pomp, etiquette, and splendour which become the supreme magistracy of a great nation. This splendour should have been that of power, and not that of a court. The director going out of office would then have perceived no alteration in his domestic condition, and would have suffered no privation. It was from this feeling that the consitution had allowed him only the moderate sum of 100,000 francs for his appointments, and that the expenses of ceremony, for the Directory, were stated in the budget at five millions, under the title of *House Expenses*. A salary of 100,000 francs was therefore sufficient; but it should have been secured to the director for life, which would have rendered it fair to require a director going out of office never more to fill any public situation, and would have secured his independence.

The Republic was disunited. One party had confidence in the constitution of 1795; another would have had a president at the head of the government; a third regretted the constitution of 1793. Lastly, the emigrants, the remains of the privileged classes, ardently wished for a counter-revolution: but this last party was composed only of a few individuals. The emigrants were dying of want in foreign countries; and the three first-mentioned parties comprised the whole population of France. Many people would have wished to have the Directory composed of persons who had taken no part in public affairs since 10 August.

The five directors had voted for the death of the King: it had been expected that they would employ all those of their colleagues in the convention who had not been re-elected to the councils; but this was not the case. The title of a *Conventional* soon became a cause of dislike, and shortly afterwards a ground of proscription. The state police took measures to expel them from Paris, and compel them to withdraw to their place of domicile. The men of 1793 had at first appeared disposed to attach themselves to the car of a government composed of men who had all been violent Jacobins; but the proceedings of the Directory displeased them; they did not find that simplicity of manners which flattered their passions; they were enraged at the appearance of a court; and being accustomed to respect no consideration whatever, to observe no bounds, they indulged freely in all kinds of sarcasms. This exasperated the Directory, which took severe measures against them. Being thus driven to extremities, they conspired together to deliver themselves from the yoke of the *five gentlemen* of the Luxembourg. They now remembered that Rewbell had shut up the Jacobins' meeting; that Barras had marched against them on 9 Thermidor; and that La Reveillere Lepeaux was one of the seventy-three: Carnot, alone, was irreproachable in their opinion.

The party which wished for the government of a president would have sincerely attached themselves to the Directory, had the latter appeared to place

THE EIGHTEENTH OF FRUCTIDOR

confidence in them: but, on the contrary, they were designated as enemies on the very first opportunity. This party was therefore disaffected, and became inimical, if not to the Republic, at least to the administration.

The Directory endeavoured to gain partisans in the privileged classes, but without success. These shewed no respect whatever for persons destitute of the advantages of birth, and of all personal claims to distinction.

The armies, however, rallied round a government founded on the principles for which they had been fighting for five years, and which secured them more stability and consideration.

Thus the two extreme parties came forward again: the men of 1793, because they were persecuted; and the privileged classes, because they were courted.

Soon afterwards the Directory adopted the fatal system of policy known by the name of *bascule* (see-saw): this was founded on the principle of equally keeping down both parties; so that when either of them compromised itself and incurred the severity of government, the other was always visited by the same act and at the same moment, even when it had on that occasion seconded the intentions of the ruling party. A general sense of the injustice, absurdity, and immorality of this system excited universal exasperation and disgust. The factions increased daily in strength and violence; and there was even a kind of union between them. The splendour which the victories obtained in Italy diffused over the Directory could not efface the ungenerousness of its administration. Its sceptre was a leaden one!

The laws had proclaimed liberty of conscience; they afforded equal protection to the exercise of every kind of worship; but under the revolutionary government, priests of all religions had been imprisoned, driven from the territory of the Republic, and at length transported. After 9 Thermidor this state of affairs had improved; afterwards the director La Reveillere Lepeaux put himself at the head of the theophilanthropists, and gave them temples. The persecution of the catholic priests was renewed, and they were impeded in the exercise of their religion under various pretexts. A great number of good citizens were thus once more alarmed and disturbed in all that mankind esteems most sacred.

The republic calendar had divided the year into twelve equal months of thirty days, and each month into three decades: there was no longer a Sunday; the *decadi* was appointed as the day of rest. The Directory went farther still, and prohibited the people, under correctional penalties, from working on the *decadi,* and from resting on the Sunday; employing the peace-officers, gendarmes, and commissaries of police to enforce the execution of these absurd regulations. The people were thus tormented and exposed to penalties and vexations for matters which have nothing to do with order and social interest. The public voice appealed in vain to the rights of man, the dispositions of constitutions, the laws which guaranteed liberty of conscience, and the right

THE EIGHTEENTH OF FRUCTIDOR

of everyone to do whatever injures neither the state nor any other individual. It is difficult to conceive the hatred which this conduct excited against a government which thus tyrannized over the citizens in all the affairs of life, in the name of liberty and the rights of man.

The want of uniformity in the French weights and measures is an inconvenience which has always been felt; it has several times been noticed by the states-general. The Revolution was expected to remedy this evil. The law on this subject is so simple that it might have been drawn up in the course of twenty-four hours, and adopted in practice throughout France in less than a year. The system of weights and measures used in the city of Paris ought to have been rendered common to all the provinces. The government and artists for centuries used this system; and by sending standards into all the communes, and obliging the administrations and tribunals to admit no other weights or measures, the benefit would have been produced without effort, without difficulty, and without coercive laws. But geometricians and algebraists were consulted upon a question which was wholly within the province of administration. They thought that the unity of weights and measures ought to be deduced from natural principles, in order to secure its adoption by all nations. They conceived that it was not sufficient to confer a benefit on 40,000,000 of people: they wished the whole world to participate in it. They found that the metre was an aliquot part of the meridian; this they demonstrated and proclaimed in an assembly composed of French, Italian, Spanish, and Dutch geometricians. A new system of unity of weights and measures was thenceforth enacted, which neither agreed with the regulations of public administration, with the tables of dimensions used in all arts, nor with those of any of the existing machines. There was no real advantage to be expected from the extension of this system to the world in general. Besides, this scheme was impracticable; it would have been opposed by the national spirit of the English and Germans. Gregory VII, indeed, reformed the calendar, and rendered it common to all Europe; but this was because that reformation was connected with religious ideas, and was not effected by a nation, but by the power of the church. But in the new system, the good of the present generation was sacrificed to abstractions and vain hopes; for in order to make an ancient nation adopt a new system of weights and measures, all the regulations of government, and all the calculations of the arts, must be altered; an undertaking the immensity of which startles the understanding. The new system of weights and measures, whatever it be, has an ascending and descending scale which does not agree in simple numbers with the scale of the system of weights and measures which has for ages been used by the government, by men of science, and by artists. The translation from one nomenclature to the other cannot be made; because what is expressed by the simplest figure in the one, would become a compound cypher in the other. It is there-

THE EIGHTEENTH OF FRUCTIDOR

fore necessary to increase or diminish by some fractions, so that the matter or weight expressed in the new nomenclature may be expressed in simple cyphers. Thus, for instance, a soldier's ration is expressed by twenty-four ounces in the old nomenclature: this is a very simple number; but when translated into the new one, it becomes seven hundred and thirty-four grammes, and two hundred and fifty-nine thousandths. It is therefore evident that it must be increased or diminished, to make it seven hundred and thirty-four, or seven hundred and thirty-five grammes. All the dimensions and lines that compose architectural works, all the tools and measures used in clock-making, jewellery, paper-making, and all the arts, all instruments and machines, had been invented and calculated according to the ancient nomenclature, and were expressed by simple numbers, which could only be translated by five or six figures. All was therefore to begin again.

The *savants* conceived another idea, wholly unconnected with the benefit of the unity of weights and measures; they adopted the decimal numeration, taking the metre for unity, and suppressed all complex numbers. Nothing can be more contrary to the organization of the mind, the memory, and the imagination. A fathom, a foot, an inch, a line, or a point, are fixed portions of extension, which the imagination conceives independently of their reciprocal relations: if, therefore, the third of an inch be demanded, the mind immediately acts, and divides the extent called an inch into three parts. But by the new system, the operation which the mind had to perform was not to divide an inch into three parts, but to divide a metre into one hundred and eleven parts. The experience of all ages had so completely established the difficulty of dividing a space or a weight into a greater number of parts than twelve, that a new complex name had been given to each of these divisions. If the twelfth of an inch were required, the operation was already performed; it was the complex number called a line. Decimal numeration applied to all the complex numbers as well as to unity; and if a hundredth part of a point or of a line was the quantity required, a hundredth was written: by the new system, if it is wished to express a hundredth part of a line, it is necessary to refer to its relation with the metre, which leads to an infinite calculation. The divisor 12 had been preferred to the divisor 10, because 10 has but two factors, 2 and 5; whilst 12 has four, viz. 2, 3, 4, and 6. It is true that decimal numeration, generalized and exclusively adapted to the metre as unity, facilitates the labours of astronomers and calculators; but these advantages are far from compensating the disadvantage of rendering thought more difficult. The first object of every method ought to be to assist the conception and imagination, to facilitate recollection, and to increase the power of thought. Complex numbers are as old as man, because they are as inherent in the nature of his organization, as it is in the nature of decimal numeration to adapt itself to every unity, to every complex number, and not to one unity exclusively.

THE EIGHTEENTH OF FRUCTIDOR

Finally, they made use of Greek roots, which farther multiplied difficulties; for these denominations, although they might be useful to the learned, did not suit the people. The weights and measures were one of the principal affairs of the Directory. Instead of leaving time to work the change, and merely encouraging the new system by all the power of example and fashion, they made compulsory laws, and had them rigorously executed. Merchants and citizens found themselves harassed about matters which were in themselves indifferent; and this increased the unpopularity of a government which placed itself above the wants and the reach of the people, infringing their usages, habits, and customs with all the violence that might have been expected from a Greek or Tartar conqueror, who, with the staff in his hand, insists upon obedience to all his commands, which are dictated only by his own prejudices and interests, to the total exclusion of those of the vanquished. The new system of weights and measures will be a subject of embarrassment and difficulties for several generations; and it is probable that the first learned commission employed to verify the measure of the meridian will find it necessary to make some corrections. Thus are nations tormented about trifles!

The elections to the Legislative Body brought men into public business who were of a contrary opinion to the Directory; the natural consequence of its false policy and bad administration. General Pichegru, deputy from the Jura to the Five Hundred, was named by acclamation president of that council; (his connexions with foreigners were then unknown;) Barthelemy was appointed to the Directory in the place of Letourneur. These two nominations were highly approved by the public. Pichegru was then the most renowned general of the Republic; he had conquered Holland. Barthelemy was the minister who had negotiated the peace with the King of Prussia and the King of Spain.

The Directory divided into two parties: Rewbell, Barras, and La Reveillere, formed the majority; Carnot and Barthelemy the minority.

The ministry was changed. Benezech, minister of the interior, and Cochon l'Apparant, minister of police, were implicated in the discoveries of Duverne de Presle. Petiet and Truguet adhered to the moderate party in the councils; they had contributed to restore to their country a great number of emigrants, whose presence gave umbrage. Not all the eminent services which the minister Petiet had performed in the war department—nor even the merit of having been the first, since the Revolution, who had rendered a clear and exact account of the expenses of his administration—could save him from the displeasure of the factious; although he was then, as throughout his long career of administration, remarkable for extraordinary integrity. He left no fortune at his death, and his children inherited nothing but the esteem which he had so honourably acquired. Ramel and Merlin were the only ministers retained. Three parties were formed in the councils; the determined republicans, who sided with the majority of the Directory, excepting as far as their particular affections were concerned;—the partisans of the princes and of foreigners; of which party Pichegru, Willot, Imbert Colomès, Rovere, and two or three more, were the only persons in the secret;—and the Clichy clubbists; amongst whom were several highly respectable and well-meaning men, but ignorant of affairs, discontented, and enemies to the directors, the conventionals and the revolutionary government.

The *Clichy* party represented themselves as wise, moderate, good Frenchmen. Were they republicans? No. Were they royalists? No. They were for the constitution of 1791, then? No. For that of 1793? Still less. That of 1795, perhaps? Yes and no. What were they, then? They themselves did not know. They would have consented to such a thing, *but*—; to another, *if*—. What gave them life and activity was the applauses they obtained in the saloons, and the praises resulting from the successes in the tribunes. They voted with the royalist committee without knowing it; they were astonished, when convinced, after their fall, that Pichegru, Imbert Colomès, Willot, De La Haye, etc. were conspirators; and that all those fine harangues and grand speeches which they had pronounced were acts of conspiracy, in furtherance of the policy of Pitt and the princes. Nothing could have been farther from their thoughts; they had not courage enough to conspire. Carnot and many of the Clichy club have since proved by their conduct that they were far from intending to contrive any plot against the Republic. Carnot was misled by his hatred of the Thermidorians; his feelings had been deeply wounded, ever since 9 Thermidor, by the general opinion, which attributed all the blood shed on the scaffold to the Committee of Public Safety; he stood in need of the respect of the world. He was influenced by those who ruled the tribunes, and the public prints.

The great majority of the writers of those journals were against the Directory, the Convention, and the Revolution. Some of them endeavoured by these sentiments to purchase oblivion of the crimes they had committed during the reign of the revolutionary government, whose agents they had been; and several were in the pay of the treasury of London. The Directory did not oppose journal to journal, press to press, and pen to pen; whether they were not sensible of the importance of such measures, or whether they were unable or unwilling to make the necessary pecuniary sacrifices. They did not profit by the example of the English government, which not only kept in pay and profusely distributed morning, evening, weekly, monthly, and yearly papers, but even furnished them with extracts of such despatches as public curiosity was interested in. The Cabinet of Saint James's deceives foreigners when it disclaims these wretched scribblers with such disdain, and loads them with so much contemptuous language: this contempt is all

THE EIGHTEENTH OF FRUCTIDOR

affected; the fact is, that it pays and directs them, and that its archives are open to them.

The tribune of the Council of Five Hundred and that of the Ancients, and almost all the public prints, were full of vociferations against the government and the revolution; against the laws respecting emigration, the sale of national property, and public worship; against the embezzlements of government, and the enormous taxation. National property ceased to sell; those who had purchased it were alarmed; the emigrants returned; the priests raised their heads. General Pichegru was the soul of this plan of counter-revolution. The Directory went on in a precarious manner, amidst this tempest.

Pichegru, born in Franche-Comté, was admitted at the age of eighteen into the military school at Brienne, in the capacity of *maître-de-quartier*. His plan was to enter into the convent of Vitri, to pass his noviciate there; but he was dissuaded from this scheme, and entered the Metz regiment of artillery, in 1789. He was a serjeant in that regiment when the Jacobin society of Besançon appointed him to the command of a battalion of volunteers. In 1793 the representative Saint-Just promoted him to the rank of a general-in-chief. He conducted the campaign of 1795 successfully, and conquered Holland. In 1795 he commanded the Army of the Rhine, during which period his treasonable practices began. He had a criminal understanding with the enemy's generals, and concerted his operations with them. The Armies of the Sambre and Meuse, and Rhine, had orders to operate a combined movement, in order to unite at Mentz; he frustrated this manoeuvre by leaving the majority of his forces on the Upper Rhine. Some time afterwards the line of contravallation which he occupied on the left bank of the river, before Mentz, was forced by Clairfait, who possessed himself of all his field artillery. He retired with the remains of his troops into the lines of Weissemberg. These events, with other circumstances, excited suspicions of his fidelity. The government was alarmed: in the beginning of 1796 it deprived him of the command of the army, and offered him an embassy to Sweden. Pichegru refused this, and retired into Franche-Comté, where he continued his correspondence with the enemy. When appointed to the Council of the Five Hundred by the electoral assembly of the Jura, he thought the moment had arrived for effecting the triumph of the foreigners' party. He was called, in private company, the French General Monck.

In the course of April, Duverne and the Abbé Brottier were apprehended, brought before the tribunals, and condemned. Duverne de Presle made important discoveries: a corner of the veil which covered France was now lifted up. In the meantime, d'Entraigues' portfolio reached Paris. All the papers in it had been indorsed and numbered by General Clarke and General Berthier. They contained circumstantial particulars respecting Pichegru's conduct. Fauche Borel, a bookseller at Neuschâtel, was the principal actor in this plot. In several long conversations which I had with the Count d'Entraigues, I penetrated the mystery of the intrigues which excited and kept up agitation in France, encouraged the hopes of foreign powers, and had an unfavourable effect on the negotiations with Austria.

The signal had been given to the party: all the journals were full of censures, calumnies, and harangues against the General of the Army of Italy; they depreciated my successes, vilified my character, calumniated my administration, threw out suspicions respecting my fidelity to the Republic, and accused me of ambitious designs. From the journals these slanders ascended to the tribune, in which I was denounced for the war I had undertaken against Venice, for my political conduct towards Genoa, and for the award I had given in favour of the Valteline against the Grison leagues. They went so far as to deny the massacre of the French in the Venetian States, and even that of Verona, as well as the infringement of neutrality towards the sloop *Libérateur d'Italie*, which had been fired upon in the port of Venice by the Admiral's galley and the batteries of the Lido fort.

The Parisian journals soon became the subject of conversation in the camps. 'What!' said the soldiers, 'are the men who call themselves our representatives become the panegyrists of our enemies? The Venetians have shed French blood; and instead of avenging it, they accuse us, not of having shed it ourselves, but of having excited acts of revenge! Are they ignorant that we are here a hundred thousand bayonets, all unexceptionable witnesses? These enemies of the Republic having neither been able to conquer nor to purchase our general, are endeavouring to assassinate him juridically; but they will not succeed; they shall never reach him without first marching over our bodies.'

The Italian artists published engravings in which they represented the Clichy deputies as making common cause with the Sclavonians. The soldiers grew so enthusiastic that they were quite enraged when they read the Parisian journals.

On the festival of 14 July, previously to reviewing the army, I had addressed it in the order of the day as follows:—'Soldiers! this is the anniversary of 14 July. You see before you the names of our companions in arms who have fallen in the field of honour in defence of the liberty of their country. They have set you a noble example; you owe your entire devotion to the Republic, and to the welfare of thirty millions of Frenchmen; you owe it to the glory of the French name, to which you have added new lustre by your victories.

'I well know, soldiers, that you are deeply affected at the calamities which threaten our country. But our country cannot be in real danger. The same men through whose means she has triumphed over all Europe combined against her, are still there. We are separated from France by mountains; but you would pass them with the rapidity of the eagle, were it necessary, in order

THE EIGHTEENTH OF FRUCTIDOR

to maintain the constitution, defend liberty, and protect the government and the republicans. The government, soldiers, watches over the deposit of the laws which is entrusted to its care. Whenever the royalists shew themselves, that moment is their last. Dismiss all anxiety; and let us swear by the *manes* of the heroes who have fallen by our side for liberty—let us swear on our colours, war against the enemies of the Republic and of the constitution of the year III!'

This was the spark that kindled the conflagration. Each division of cavalry and infantry drew up its address; the officers, non-commissioned officers, and privates voted and signed them. These addresses evinced the violent agitation that prevailed. General Berthier sent them to the Directory and the Councils. The people recovered themselves; the Armies of the Sambre and Meuse, and the Rhine, shared the same sentiments. A total alteration in the disposition of the public immediately took place. The majority of the Directory appeared lost; the Republic was in danger.

Hoche marched a division of the Army of the Sambre and Meuse upon Paris, under pretext of the expedition to Ireland. The Council of the Five Hundred was highly displeased at the conduct of the military in infringing the constitutional circle. Hoche left the capital; his only refuge was his own head-quarters.

Under these critical circumstances a powerful party invited me to overthrow the Directory, and seize the reins of government myself. The enthusiasm which the conquest of Italy had excited in France, and the devotion of the army which had acquired so many laurels under my command, seemed to smooth all obstructions. Had ambition been the guide of my life, I would not have hesitated: what I afterwards did on 18 Brumaire, I might have done on 18 Fructidor; but the independence, power, and prosperity of France were then, as throughout my life, the principal objects of my thoughts. When victorious at Arcole and Rivoli, I was as far from thinking it was in my power to secure these grand objects at that time, as I afterwards was at Paris, after my disasters, from the moment when the Legislative Chamber abandoned me. In 1797, as in 1815, the ferment of revolutionary ideas misled the leaders of faction and deluded the multitude; the same men who had overturned the throne of Louis XVI directed public opinion, and fancied themselves destined to save the Revolution. I resolved to support the Directory, and for that purpose sent General Augereau to Paris: but had the conspirators gained the day, contrary to my expectations, everything was arranged for my making my entrance into Lyons at the head of 15,000 men within five days after receiving intelligence of their triumph; whence, marching on Paris, and rallying all the republicans and those interested in the Revolution, I would have passed the Rubicon, like Cæsar, at the head of the popular party.

THE EIGHTEENTH OF FRUCTIDOR

On General Augereau's arrival, he was appointed by the Directory to the command of the seventeenth military division. On 18 Fructidor (4 Sept.) at daybreak, the peace-officers went to the houses of the directors Barthelemy and Carnot. They seized the former; but the latter, who had been warned of his danger, fled to Geneva. At the same moment the Directory had Pichegru, Willot, fifty deputies to the Council of the Ancients and Council of Five Hundred, and one hundred and fifty other individuals, most of whom were journalists, arrested. The same day the Directory addressed a message to the legislature, communicating the conspiracy which had been formed against the Republic, and laying before it the papers found in d'Entraigues' portfolio, and the declarations made by Duverne de Presle. The law of 19 Fructidor condemned to deportation two directors, fifty deputies, and one hundred and forty-eight individuals; the elections of several departments were annulled; several laws were repealed; new measures of public safety were decreed; the nomination of Carnot and Barthelemy to the Directory was revoked, and they were replaced by Merlin and François de Neufchâteau. Thus the schemes of the enemies of the Republic were defeated.

The public was equally astonished and incredulous. It was supposed that d'Entraigues' papers and Duverne's discoveries were forged; but all doubt ceased when the following proclamation appeared from Moreau to his army, dated from his head-quarters at Strasburg, 23 Fructidor (9 Sept., 1797):—

'Soldiers! I have this instant received the proclamation of the Executive Directory, dated the 18th of this month (4 Sept.), informing France that Pichegru has rendered himself unworthy of the confidence with which he has so long inspired the whole Republic, and the armies in particular. I have also been informed that several military men, too confident in the patriotism of that representative, and considering the services he had rendered to the state, doubted this assertion. I owe it to my brethren in arms and fellow-citizens to inform them of the truth. It is but too true that Pichegru has betrayed the confidence of all France. I informed one of the members of the Directory, on the 17th of this month (3 Sept.), that a correspondence with Condé and other agents of the Pretender had fallen into my hands, which left no doubt of these treasonable acts. The Directory has summoned me to Paris, requiring, no doubt, more complete information respecting this correspondence. Soldiers! be calm and dismiss all anxiety respecting the state of affairs at home: depend upon it, that the government will keep down the royalists, and vigilantly maintain the republican constitution which you have sworn to defend.'

On 24 Fructidor (10 September) Moreau wrote as follows to the Directory: —'I did not receive your order to come to Paris until a very late hour on the 22nd, when I was ten leagues from Strasburg. Some hours were necessary for me to make arrangements for my departure, to secure the tranquillity of the army, and to apprehend several persons compromised in an interesting correspondence which I shall myself deliver to you. I send you subjoined a proclamation which I have issued, which has had the effect of convincing many incredulous persons; and I confess I found it difficult to believe that a man who had done his country such important services, and had no interest in betraying it, could have been guilty of such infamous conduct. I was thought to be a friend of Pichegru's; but I have long ceased to esteem him. You will see that no one was in greater danger than myself, for the whole scheme was founded on the expected reverses of the army which I commanded: its courage has saved the Republic.'

On 19 Fructidor (5 September) Moreau had written to Barthelemy as follows:

'Citizen Director, you will recollect, no doubt, that on my last visit to Bâle, I informed you that at the passage of the Rhine we took a waggon from General Klinglin, containing two or three hundred letters of his correspondence; those of Wittersbach formed part of them, but were the least important. Many of these letters are in cypher, but we have found out the key to them: the whole are now decyphering, which occupies much time. No person is called by his real name in these letters, so that many Frenchmen who are in correspondence with Klinglin, Condé, Wickham, D'Enghien, and others, are not easily discovered. We have, nevertheless, such indications, that several are already known. I had determined not to give publicity to this correspondence, since, as peace might be presumed to be at hand, there seemed to be no danger to the Republic: besides, these papers could have afforded proofs against but few persons, as no one is named in them. But seeing at the head of the parties which are now doing so much mischief to our country, and in possession of an eminent situation of the highest confidence, a man deeply implicated in this correspondence, and intended to act an important part in the recall of the Pretender (the object to which it relates), I have thought it my duty to apprise you of the circumstance, that you may not be duped by his pretended republicism; that you may watch over his proceedings, and oppose his fatal projects against our country; since nothing but a civil war can be the object of his schemes.

'I confess, Citizen Director, that it is with deep regret that I inform you of this treason; and the more so, because the man I denounce to you was once my friend, and would certainly have remained so still, had I not detected him. I speak of the representative of the people, Pichegru. He has been too prudent to commit any thing to writing; he only communicated verbally with those who were intrusted with this correspondence, who carried his proposals and received his answers. He is designated under several names, that of Baptiste amongst others. A brigadier-general named Badouville was attached to him, and is mentioned by the name of *Coco*. He was one of the couriers whom Pichegru and the other correspondents employed; you must frequently have seen him at Bâle. Their grand movement was to have taken place at the beginning of the campaign of the year IV; they reckoned on the probable occurrence of some disasters on my taking the command of the army; which, as they expected, discontented at its defeat, would call for its old commander, who, in that case, was to have acted according to circumstances and the instructions he would have received. He was to have 900 louis for the journey which he took to Paris at the time of his discharge; which circumstance accounts, in a natural way, for his refusal of the Swedish embassy.

'I suspect the Lajolais family of being concerned in this plot. The confidence which I have in your patriotism and prudence alone determined me to give you this intelligence. The proofs are as clear as day, but I doubt whether they are judicial. I entreat you, Citizen Director, to have the goodness to assist me with your advice on this perplexing occasion. You know me well enough to conceive how dear this disclosure costs me; nothing less than the danger which threatened my country would have induced me to make it. The secret is confined to five persons; General Desaix, General Regnier, one of my aides-de-camp, and an officer employed in the secret service of the army, who is constantly employed in pursuing the clue of information afforded by the decyphered letters.'

The letters found in Klinglin's waggon were soon afterwards published, in April, 1797; Moreau, Desaix, and Regnier alone had been acquainted with their contents. Proofs of Pichegru's treachery soon poured in from all quarters; he became the object of public execration. The persons condemned were embarked at Rochefort and transported to Guiana.

When I was informed of the law of 19 Fructidor, I was deeply afflicted, and loudly declared my dissatisfaction. I reproached the three directors with not having known how to act with moderation in the hour of victory. I thought it right that Carnot, Barthelemy, and the fifty deputies should be deprived of their functions, as a measure of public safety, and placed under inspection in one of the towns of the interior of the Republic. I would have had Pichegru, Willot, Imbert Colomès, and two or three more only, brought to trial, and condemned to expiate on the scaffold the treasonable crime which they had committed, and of which government possessed the proofs; but there I would have stopped. I was shocked to see men of great talent, such as Portalis, Tronçon-Ducoudray, and Fontanes, patriots like Boissy. d'Anglas, Dumoulard, and Muraire, and supreme magistrates, as Carnot and Barthelemy, condemned, without information or trial, to perish in the marshes of Sinamari. What! inflict the punishment of transportation on a multitude of journalists, who merited only contempt and the disgrace of a correctional punishment! This was renewing the proscriptions of the Roman triumvirate; it was acting in a more cruel and arbitrary manner than Fouquier-Tinville's tribunal; for he at least heard the accused, and he condemned them only to death! The armies,

THE EIGHTEENTH OF FRUCTIDOR

and the whole mass of the people, were for the Republic. Nothing but the danger of the state could have justified such a flagrant piece of injustice, such a violation of equity and of the laws.

The conspirators wished to effect the destruction of the Republic by means of the Legislative Body; to render the Directory unpopular, by the powerful agency of the national tribune; to impede its proceedings by the authority of the legislative; to compose a Directory of men of weak characters, or devoted to the party; and, lastly, to proclaim the counter-revolution as the only remedy for the calamities which afflicted the country.

The three directors, intoxicated with their victory, saw only their own triumph in that of the Republic. The Councils appointed Merlin and François de Neufchâteau to succeed Carnot and Barthelemy; they did not convoke the electoral assemblies in order to fill up the vacancies, but remained in an imperfect state, without respectability or independence. It was difficult to conceive what advantage they proposed to themselves from such an attack on the constitution—such a disregard of public opinion. Did these three men, unsupported by the prepossessions attendant on ancient greatness, or even by the honours of victory, pretend to set themselves up as kings of France, and to govern of their own authority, without the aid of the law, or the concurrence of the Legislative Body? The acts of 22 Floreal in the following year, and those which took place two years afterwards on 30 Prairial, were the consequences of this illegal and impolitic conduct. In Fructidor, the government attacked the legislature; on 22 Floreal the legislature and the government violated the sovereignty of the people, by refusing to receive the deputies nominated by electoral assemblies which had been declared legal, as members of the Councils. Lastly, on 30 Prairial the Councils, infringed the rights, the prerogatives, and the liberty of the government. The events of these three days were subversive of the republican system, and annihilated the constitution of 1795.

In the month of October, 1796, the Cabinet of Saint James's, alarmed at the pecuniary sacrifices which it would be necessary to require from the English in order to maintain the war against France, had determined on peace. Lord Malmesbury had exchanged his powers as plenipotentiary with Charles Lacroix, minister of exterior relations, at Paris; but, after several conferences, this plenipotentiary having communicated his ultimatum, which required the retrocession of Belgium to the Emperor, the negotiations were broken off. The preliminaries signed at Leoben induced the English to renew them. Austria herself had renounced Belgium; and the possession of this province could no longer occasion any difficulty. Lord Malmesbury came to Lisle. Pitt was now desirous of peace, in consequence of the failure of his financial plans. The Directory appointed Letourneur, Pleville-le-Peley, and Maret, afterwards Duke of Bassano, as plenipotentiaries. The choice of the latter gave satisfaction at London; Pitt was acquainted with his pacific inclinations, and esteemed his character, having treated with him in 1792 for the preservation of Louis XVI and the maintenance of peace. Lord Malmesbury on his side, wished to efface the impression of his failure at Paris the preceding year, and to crown his long political career with new success. The plenipotentiaries on both sides being actuated by good faith, a favourable issue was anticipated. These important negotiations, which were proceeding at the same time in the north of France and in Italy, could not be unconnected with each other. Clarke was instructed to correspond with Maret. A peace concluded with England would have removed many difficulties at Campo-Formio, and it was on the point of signature, at Lisle, on terms more advantageous to France and her allies than those of the treaty of Amiens, when the events of 18 Fructidor took place. Maret was recalled. Treilhard and Bonnier, the new plenipotentiaries, demanded the restoration of all that England had conquered from France, Spain, and Holland. Lord Malmesbury, astonished at this singular demand, replied that he had orders to negotiate on terms of mutual compensation. The French ministers gave him twenty-four hours to accede to their demand, and desired him, in case he persisted in declining to explain himself, to return to London for fresh instructions and more extensive powers. On 17 September he quitted Lisle. The French plenipotentiaries carried their irony so far as to pretend to expect his return to Lisle, and to wait for him there. On 5 October, Lord Malmesbury notified to them, from London, that England would send no more plenipotentiaries to France, unless her negotiator were first furnished with some guarantee that would secure his independence, and the respect due to his character. The Directory was as clearly in the wrong, in the second negotiation, as right in the first, both in substance and form. It was just, when France was preserving part of her conquests on the Continent, that England should likewise retain part of hers. In forgetting the respect due to the character of an ambassador, the Directory forgot its own dignity.

Some time after 18 Fructidor, a law was enacted relating to the public debt, by which it was ordained that the third of the capital should be inscribed in a new book, and the interest paid at five per cent; that the other two-thirds should be reimbursed in *bons de deux tiers,* and that domains should be pledged for their liquidation: but every year the laws of the budget withdrew the pledge, and thus prolonged the immorality and misery of this bankruptcy. At length the *bons de deux tiers* were reduced to two per cent. It would have been less odious to leave the capital untouched, and merely to reduce the interest.

I was of opinion that the preservation of public faith was of the utmost importance, and to be preferred to every other consideration; that it was desirable to extinguish the debt by charging it upon all national domains whatsoever, including those under sequestration, and to pursue this measure with such energy as to effect the operation in three years. I thought the principle ought to be established, at the same time, as a constitutional law sanctioned by the people, that one generation cannot be pledged by another generation, and that the interest of a loan can only be demanded during the first fifteen years. This would have been a preservative against the abuse of this resource, and would have protected future generations against the cupidity of the present.

At the period of 18 Fructidor, the aide-de-camp Lavalette had been several months at Paris, as a mediator between me, the majority of the Directory, the minority, and the different parties into which the Councils and the capital were divided. A fortnight after the 18th he was molested by the government: he was a man of a mild character and moderate opinions; he set off precipitately for Milan, and sought my protection.

One of my first cares, on obtaining the consulate, was to annul the law of 19 Fructidor; to recall to their country a great number of individuals respectable for their talents and the services they had performed, and who were, in consequence of a few imprudent acts, persecuted and comprised in the proscription of Fructidor. Pichegru, Willot, Imbert Colomès, and a few others of that stamp, were alone excepted. Carnot, Portalis, Barbé Marbois, and Benezech, were afterwards my ministers, and entrusted with portfolios. Barthelemy, Lapparent, Pastoret, Boissy d'Anglas, and Fontanes, became senators: the latter was even president of the Legislative Body, and grand master of the University. Simeon, Muraire, Gau, Villaret Joyeuse, Dumas, and Laumont, were appointed to the Council of State; Vaublanc, Duplantier, etc. were prefects.

The government was daily losing in public opinion. The Council of Five Hundred, alarmed at the general discontent, aggravated the evil instead of providing a remedy for it. They thought that revolutionary measures alone could save them: they had the rashness to order all the nobles to quit France. There were great numbers of this class, not only in the constituted authorities, but even in the armies. It was partly for the purpose of giving advice to France that I wrote on 11 November to the provisional government of Genoa that remarkable letter which produced so great an effect in Paris, and in which I said: 'To exclude the nobles from all public functions would be a most flagrant piece of injustice; in committing which you would be acting as they have done.'

Chapter XXII

PEACE OF CAMPO-FORMIO

Exchange of the ratifications of the preliminaries of Leoben (24 May). Conferences of Montebello; conferences of Udine previous to 18 Fructidor. Conferences of Passeriano. After 18 Fructidor, the French government is no longer desirous of peace. Motives which determine me as French plenipotentiary to sign the treaty of peace. My interest and policy. Extravagant pretensions of the Imperial plenipotentiaries; threats; movements of the armies. Signature of the treaty of peace of Campo-Formio (17 Oct.). Of General Desaix and General Hoche. I leave Italy, and proceed to Paris, passing through Rastadt.

The exchange of the ratifications of the preliminaries of Leoben took place on 24 May at Montebello, between me and the Marquis di Gallo. A question of etiquette arose for the first time: the Emperors of Germany did not give the Kings of France the alternative; the Cabinet of Vienna was apprehensive that the Republic would not acknowledge this custom, and that the other powers of Europe, following the example of the French, would force the holy Roman empire to descend from the sort of supremacy it had enjoyed ever since the time of Charlemagne. It was in the first ecstasies of the Austrian minister, at the acquiescence of France in the customary etiquette, that he renounced the idea of the congress of Berne, consented to a separate negotiation, and agreed not to open the congress of Rastadt for preserving the peace of the empire until July then next. In a few days the plenipotentiaries had agreed on the following terms as the basis of a definitive treaty: first, the boundary of the

PEACE OF CAMPO-FORMIO

Rhine for France; secondly, Venice and the boundary of the Adige for the Emperor; and thirdly, Mantua and the boundary of the Adige for the Cisalpine Republic. The Marquis di Gallo declared that his next courier would bring him powers *ad hoc* to sign the treaty of peace on these terms; I and General Clarke had been invested with the necessary powers ever since 6 May. The conditions were more favourable to France than the Directory had expected: the peace might therefore have been considered as concluded.

Clarke was a captain in the Orleans dragoons when the Revolution took place. From 1789 he attached himself to the Orleans party. In 1795 he was placed by the Committee of Public Safety at the head of the topographical department. Being patronized by Carnot, he was chosen by the Directory, in 1796, to make overtures of peace to the Emperor, for which purpose he went to Milan. The real object of his mission was, not to open a negotiation, but to act as the secret agent of the Directory at head-quarters, and to watch me, whose victories began to give umbrage. Clarke sent reports to Paris respecting the first persons in the army, which excited murmurs, and drew unpleasant reflections on him. Convinced that it is necessary that governments should obtain information, I was glad they had confided this mission to a man who was known, rather than to one of those subaltern agents who pick up the most absurd information in antechambers and taverns. I therefore encouraged Clarke, and even employed him in several negotiations with Sardinia and the princes of Italy. After 18 Fructidor I defended him warmly, not only because he had gained my esteem in the very delicate mission he had been employed in, but also because it became me to grant protection to a man who had been in daily communication with me, and of whom I had had no ostensible cause to complain. Clarke's genius was not military; he was an official man, exact and upright in business, and a great enemy to knaves. He is descended from one of the Irish families, which accompanied the Stuarts in their misfortunes. His foible was that of priding himself on his birth; and he rendered himself ridiculous in the imperial reign by genealogical researches which were strangely at variance with the opinions he had professed, the course of his life, and the circumstances of the times: this was a blunder. I, nevertheless, entrusted him with the portfolio of the war department, as an able minister who was likely to be attached to me who had loaded him with favours. In the time of the empire Clarke rendered important services by the integrity of his administration; and it is to be regretted, for the sake of his memory, that towards the end of his career he was a member of the ministry which France will eternally reproach with having forced her whole people to pass under the Caudine Forks, by ordering the disbanding of an army that had for twenty-five years been its country's glory, and by giving up to our astonished enemies our still invincible fortresses. If the royal confidence, in 1814 and 1815, had

PEACE OF CAMPO-FORMIO

not been placed in men whose minds were unequal to the circumstances of that crisis, or who, like renegades to their country, could see no safety or glory for their master's throne but in the yoke of the Holy Alliance; if the Duke de Richelieu, whose ambition it was to deliver his country from the presence of foreign bayonets; if Chateaubriand, who had just rendered distinguished services at Ghent, had had the direction of affairs, France would have remained powerful and formidable after those two grand and critical trials. Chateaubriand has received from nature the sacred fire; his works prove it. His style is not that of Racine—it is that of prophecy. He is the only man in the world who could, with impunity, have said in the Chamber of Peers, 'Napoleon's grey great coat and hat hoisted on a stick, on the coast of Brest, would set all Europe in arms.' Should he ever take the helm of affairs, it is possible that Chateaubriand may lose himself: so many have found it their destruction! But it is certain that greatness and national spirit must always acknowledge his genius, and that he would have rejected with indignation the idea of those infamous actions by which the administration of that period disgraced itself.

Count Merfeld, a new Austrian plenipotentiary, arrived at Montebello on 19 June. The Cabinet of Vienna disavowed the Marquis di Gallo, and persisted in its resolution to treat for peace only in the congress of Berne and in the presence of its allies: it had evidently changed its plan. Was it engaged in a new coalition? Did it place its confidence in the Russian armies? Was this change one of the effects of Pichegru's conspiracy? Did the enemy flatter themselves that the civil war, which ravaged the departments of the West, would spread itself over all France; and that the supreme power would fall into the hands of the conspirators?

The Austrian plenipotentiaries confessed that they had nothing to say in reply, when I observed to them that England and Russia would never consent to allow the Emperor to take his indemnities at the expense of ancient Venice; that to decline to negotiate, except in concert with these powers, was to declare a determination to try the chances of war once more. The minister Thugut sent new instructions; he gave up the congress of Berne, and agreed to the principle of a separate negotiation. The conferences began at Udine on 1 July. General Clarke alone attended on the part of France. I intimated that I should not attend until I should see reason to conclude, from the protocol, that the Austrian plenipotentiaries were sincerely desirous of peace, and had power to make it. A few days afterwards I left Montebello and went to Milan; where I remained all July and August. Austria was waiting to see the result of the troubles in France: these two months were accordingly spent in idle parleys. The affair of 18 Fructidor baffled all her hopes. Count Cobentzel hastened to Udine, invested with the full powers of the Emperor, whose entire confidence he possessed. The Marquis di Gallo, Count Merfeld, and

PEACE OF CAMPO-FORMIO

Baron Engelmann took part in the conferences; but they were in reality only introduced for form's sake.

I went to Passeriano: Clarke having been recalled, I was now the only plenipotentiary on the part of France. On 26 September the negotiation with Count Cobentzel began. The conferences were alternately held at Udine and at Passeriano. The four Austrian plenipotentiaries sat on one side of a rectangular table; at the ends were the secretaries of legation; and on the other side was I, as French plenipotentiary. When the conferences were held at Passeriano the dinner was given by me; when they were held at Udine, it was given by Count Cobentzel. Passeriano is a handsome country house situate on the left bank of the Tagliamento, four leagues from Udine and three leagues from the ruins of Aquilea.

In the first conference Count Cobentzel disclaimed all that his colleagues had been saying for four months; he urged extravagant pretensions, and it became necessary to recommence the circle of nonsense which had been going on ever since May. With a negotiator of this kind, there was but one method of proceeding; namely, to go as far beyond the true medium as he himself did, in the opposite direction.

Count Cobentzel was a native of Brussels; a very agreeable man in company, and distinguished by studied politeness, but positive and untractable in business. There was a want of propriety and precision in his mode of expressing himself, of which he was sensible; and he endeavoured to compensate for this by talking loud and using imperious gestures.

The Marquis di Gallo, Neapolitan minister to Vienna, enjoyed the favour both of the Queen of Naples and the Empress. He was of an insinuating, supple character, but a man of honour.

Count Merfeld, colonel of a regiment of Hulans, had distinguished himself and gained the confidence of the minister Thugut. Baron Englemann belonged to the Chancery, and was a well-meaning, sensible man.

The progress of the negotiations after the arrival of Count Cobentzel, left no farther doubt respecting the real intentions of the Court of Vienna, which wished for peace, and had contracted no new engagement with Russia or England. Accordingly, the moment the Austrian negotiators were convinced that they could only obtain peace by adhering to the terms proposed at Montebello, it might have been signed, had not the Directory changed their policy. The affair of 18 Fructidor had led them to trust too much to their own strength, and they now thought they might with impunity require the nation to make new sacrifices. They conveyed insinuations to me calculated to induce me to break off the negotiations and recommence hostilities, whilst the official correspondence was still dictated in the spirit of the instructions of 6 May. It was evident that the Directory wished for war, but was anxious that the responsibility of the rupture should rest entirely with the negotiator. When

PEACE OF CAMPO-FORMIO

they perceived that this plan did not succeed—and, what they thought more important, when they believed their own power firmly established—they sent their ultimatum, by a despatch dated 29 September, which I received at Passeriano on 6 October. France now refused to yield to the Emperor either Venice or the line of the Adige; and this refusal was equivalent to a declaration of war.

I had fixed ideas respecting the degree of obedience which I owed to my government. With respect to military operations, I thought it my duty to execute my orders only so long as they seemed to me reasonable and likely to succeed; I would have considered it a crime to undertake the execution of a defective plan, and in that case would have thought myself obliged to offer my resignation. I had acted thus in 1796, when the Directory had wished to detach part of my army into the kingdom of Naples.

My ideas respecting the degree of obedience due from me as a plenipotentiary, were not so well settled. Could I renounce my mission in the midst of a negotiation, or thus hazard its result, by executing instructions of which I did not approve, and which were equivalent to a declaration of war? But my principal character at Passeriano was that of general-in-chief. It appeared to me absurd to suppose that I was to declare war as a plenipotentiary, and at the same time give up my command as a general, so as not to have to recommence hostilities, by executing a plan of campaign contrary to my opinion.

The minister of foreign relations extricated me from this anxiety. In one of his despatches he informed me that the Directory, in drawing up its ultimatum, had been persuaded that it was in the power of the general-in-chief to compel its acceptance by force of arms. I meditated profoundly on this communication; it was now evident that I held in my hands the destiny of France: war or peace depended on my decision. I resolved to abide by my instructions of 6 May, and to sign the peace on the terms settled at Montebello; which, before 18 Fructidor, had been approved by the government.

The motives which influenced my decision were: First, that the general plan of my campaign was defective; secondly, that having only received the ultimatum on 16 October, hostilities could not recommence before 15 November, when it would be difficult for the French armies to enter Germany, whilst the season would be favourable to the Austrians for collecting considerable forces in the plains of Italy; thirdly, that the command of the army of Germany was entrusted to Augereau, whose political opinions had become very violent since the events of Fructidor; his staff was principally composed of satellites of the propagandists, intoxicated with the principles of 1793, which was an insurmountable impediment to the harmony so necessary in the operations of the two armies; I had desired that the command of the army might be given to Desaix, Moreau being removed; fourthly, that I had required a reinforcement of 12,000 infantry and 4,000 cavalry, which had

PEACE OF CAMPO-FORMIO

been refused; yet that with only 50,000 men under arms I was twenty days' march nearer to Vienna than the armies of the Rhine, having to fight three-fourths of the forces of the House of Austria, which covered Vienna on the Italian side, whilst the armies of the Sambre and Meuse and Rhine were opposed only by a mere corps of observation; fifthly, that the Directory, in its delirium, had, by its despatches of 29 September, declared its refusal to ratify the treaty of offensive and defensive alliance of the preceding 5 April with the King of Sardinia. By that treaty the King of Sardinia had engaged to join the army of Italy with a contingent of 8,000 infantry, 2,000 cavalry, and forty pieces of cannon. The refusal of the Directory drove the Court of Turin to despair; it could no longer avoid perceiving the ultimate intentions of the French government; it had therefore no terms to keep; and the army of Italy would therefore have been under the necessity of detaching 10,000 men to reinforce the garrisons of Piedmont and Lombardy.

On 21 October, the Directory notified, that in consequence of my observations they had determined to reinforce my army with a body of 6,000 men, to be sent from the army of Germany, to modify the general plan of the campaign agreeably to my wishes; and to ratify the treaty of offensive and defensive alliance with the King of Sardinia; and that this resolution had been communicated to the legislative body the same day, 21 October.

But the Treaty of Campo-Formio had been signed three days before the writing of these despatches, which did not reach Passeriano until twelve days after the signature of the peace. Perhaps, if the Directory had taken this resolution on 29 September, when it sent its last ultimatum, I would have determined on war, in the hope of liberating all Italy as far as the Isonzo, of which I was more desirous than anyone.

It was my interest to conclude peace. The republicans openly manifested their jealousy of me. 'So much glory,' said they, 'is incompatible with liberty.' If I had recommended hostilities, and the French army had occupied Vienna, the Directory, constant to the principles by which they had been actuated ever since 18 Fructidor, would have wanted to revolutionize the empire, which would undoubtedly have involved France in a new war with Prussia, Russia, and the Germanic body; but the Republic was ill-governed; and the administration corrupt; the government inspired neither confidence nor respect. Had I broken off the negotiations, the responsibility of the consequences would have lain with me; but in giving peace to my country, I added to the glory of conquest and pacification that of being the founder of two great republics; for Belgium, the departments of the Rhine, Savoy, and the county of Nice, could not be legitimately annexed to France until the treaty of peace with the Emperor, nor could the existence of the Cisalpine Republic be regularly procured without that event. Thus crowned with laurels and with the olive branch in my hand, I thought I should safely return into private

PEACE OF CAMPO-FORMIO

life, with equal glory to the great men of antiquity; the first act of my public life would be concluded; circumstances and the interest of my country would regulate the remainder of my career; glory, and the love and esteem of the French nation, were sufficient means for the attainment of any object.

France was anxious for peace. The struggle of the allied Kings with the Republic, was a conflict of principles: it was a repetition of the contest between the Ghibellines and the Guelphs; a war between the oligarchs who reigned at London, Vienna, and Saint-Petersburg, and the republicans of Paris. As French plenipotentiary I conceived the idea of altering this state of affairs, which left France opposed singly to them all, and of throwing an apple of discord amongst the allies, and thus changing the state of the question by creating other passions and other interests. The Republic of Venice was wholly aristocratical; the cabinets of Saint-James's and Saint-Petersburg were most particularly interested in its fate. In seizing on the territories of this republic, the house of Austria would excite the highest degree of resentment and jealousy in those powers. The senate of Venice had conducted itself very ill towards France, but extremely well towards Austria. What opinion would nations form of the morality of the cabinet of Vienna, when they saw it appropriate to itself the dominions of its ally, the most ancient state in modern Europe, and that which entertained the most opposite principles to democracy and the French system; and all this without any pretext, and merely for its own convenience? What a lesson would this be for Bavaria and the powers of the second order! The Emperor would be obliged to give up to France the fortress of Mentz, which he only held as a pledge; and would appropriate to himself the spoils of the princes of Germany, whose protector he was, and whose armies were fighting under his standard. This was presenting to all Europe a complete satire on absolute governments and the European oligarchy. What could afford a more convincing proof of their being worn out, decayed, and illegitimate?

Austria would be content; for although she gave up Belgium and Lombardy, she received an equivalent, if not in revenue and population, at least in geographical convenience and commercial facilities. Venice was contiguous to Styria, Carinthia, and Hungary. The league of the European oligarchy would be divided, and France would avail herself of this circumstance to grapple with England singly, in Ireland, Canada, and the Indies.

The different factions which divided Venice would be extinguished; aristocrats and democrats would unite in opposition to the sway of a foreign nation. There was no reason to fear that a nation of such soft manners would ever conceive an affection for a German government; or that a great commercial city, which had for ages been a maritime power, would become sincerely attached to an inland monarchy without colonies; and if ever the opportunity of creating the Italian nation should arise, this cession would be no impediment. The years which the Venetians would have passed under the yoke of the house of Austria, would make them hail any national government with enthusiasm, whether a little more or less aristocratical, whether Venice should be its capital or not. The people of Venice, Lombardy, Piedmont, Genoa, Parma, Bologna, Romagna, Ferrara, Tuscany, Rome, and Naples, could not be converted into Italians without being decomposed and reduced to elements; they wanted recasting, as it were. In fact, fifteen years afterwards, that is to say, in 1812, the Austrian power in Italy, the throne of Sardinia, those of the dukes of Parma, Modena and Tuscany, and even that of Naples, with the oligarchies of Genoa and Venice, had disappeared. The temporal power of the pope, which had always been the cause of the parcelling out of Italy into so many portions, was on the point of ceasing to be an obstacle; the grand-duchy of Berg had remained vacant, and awaited the court of King Joachim. '*It will take me twenty years,*' said I, in 1805, at the council of Lyons, 'to create the Italian nation.' Fifteen had sufficed; all was ready; I waited only for the birth of a second son, in order to take him to Rome, crown him king of the Italians, give the regency to Prince Eugene, and proclaim the independence of the peninsula, from the Alps to the Ionian Sea, and from the Mediterranean to the Adriatic.

The court of Vienna, tired of the sanguinary struggle which it had for several years maintained, was not solicitous to retain Belgium, which it could never have defended; and thought itself fortunate, after so many disasters, in obtaining indemnities for losses already sustained, and in contracting engagements with the French Republic, which secured it certain advantages in the arrangement of the affairs of Germany; but although the principles of the treaty were agreed upon, the mode of execution was by no means settled. Count Cobentzel required, he said, 'the Adda as a boundary, or nothing'. He supported his demands by statistical calculations.

'You wish,' said he, 'to restore the system of 1756; you must therefore give us an advantageous treaty, framed without reference to the events of the war. Both powers have had their glorious days; our two armies ought to esteem each other; a peace disadvantageous to either power would never be anything but a truce. When you agree to this principle, why do you refuse to give us a complete and absolute indemnity? What are the foundations of power?—Population and revenue. What does the Emperor, my master, lose?—Belgium and Lombardy, the two most populous and richest provinces in the world. Belgium is doubly valuable to you, because it renders Holland subject to your power, and enables you to blockade England from the Baltic to the Straits of Gibraltar. We further consent to your adding Mentz, the four departments of the Rhine, Savoy, and the county of Nice, to the Republic. For all these extensive concessions, what do we ask of you in return?—Four millions of Italians—bad soldiers; but inhabiting, it is true, a tolerably fertile

PEACE OF CAMPO-FORMIO

country. We have, therefore, a right to require the *Thalweg* of the Adda as our boundary.'

As French plenipotentiary I replied: 'It is an advantage to the Austrian monarchy to be relieved of the possession of Belgium, which has always been burthensome to it. England alone had any interest in its remaining in your possession. If you calculate what this province cost you, you will be satisfied that it has always been a source of expense to your treasury: but at all events it can no longer be of any value to you, now that the new principles which have changed the state of France are established in it. To think of obtaining, on your Styrian, Carinthian, and Hungarian frontiers, an indemnity equivalent to the revenue and population of a detached possession is an extravagant expectation. Besides, were you to pass the Adige, you would weaken yourselves, and neither you nor the Cisalpine Republic would have any frontiers.'

These arguments, however, were far from convincing the Austrian plenipotentiaries; but they reduced their claims to the line of the Mincio. 'But this,' said Count Cobentzel, 'is our *ultimatum*; for if the Emperor, my master, were to consent to give you the keys of Mentz, the strongest fortress in the world, without exchanging them for the keys of Mantua, it would be a degrading act.' All the official measures of protocols, notes, and counternotes, having been adopted without producing any satisfactory result, confidential conferences were now tried; but neither side would give way any further. The armies put themselves in motion. The French troops, which were cantoned in the Veronese, Paduano, and Trevisano, passed the Piave, and stationed themselves on the right of the Isonzo. The Austrian army encamped on the Drave and in Carniola. When the Austrian plenipotentiaries came from Udine to Passeriano, they were obliged to pass through the French camp, in which all military honours were lavished upon them. The conferences were held within hearing of the drums; but Count Cobentzel remained immoveable; his carriages were got ready, and he announced his departure.

On 16 October, the conferences were held at Udine, at Count Cobentzel's. I recapitulated, in the form of a manifesto to be inserted in the protocol, the conduct of my government since the signature of the preliminaries of Leoben, and at the same time repeated my ultimatum. The Austrian plenipotentiary replied at great length, endeavouring to prove that the indemnities which France had offered the Emperor were not equivalent to a fourth part of what he was losing; that the Austrian power would be considerably weakened, whilst the French power would be so materially increased, that it would be dangerous to the independence of Europe; that by means of the possession of Mantua, and the line of the Adige, France would, in fact, add all Italy to the territories of the Gauls; that the Emperor was irrevocably determined to risk all the chances of war, and even to fly from his capital if necessary, rather than

PEACE OF CAMPO-FORMIO

consent to so disadvantageous a peace; that Russia offered him armies, that they were ready to come to his assistance, and that it would soon be seen what the Russian troops were; that it was very evident that I preferred my interest as a general to my character as a plenipotentiary, and that I did not wish for peace. He added, that he should depart that night, and that the French negotiator would be responsible for all the blood that would be shed in this new contest. Upon this I, with great coolness, although I was much irritated at this attack, arose, and took from a mantelpiece a little porcelain vase, which Count Cobentzel prized, as a present from the Empress Catherine, 'Well,' said I, 'the truce, then, is at an end, and war is declared; but remember that before the end of autumn I will shatter your monarchy as I shatter this porcelain.' Saying this, I dashed it furiously down, and the carpet was instantly covered with fragments. I then saluted the Congress, and retired. The Austrian plenipotentiaries were struck dumb. A few moments afterwards they found that as I got into my carriage I had despatched an officer to the Archduke Charles, to inform him that the negotiations were broken off, and that hostilities would recommence in twenty-four hours. Count Cobentzel, seriously alarmed, sent the Marquis di Gallo to Passeriano, with a signed declaration that he consented to the ultimatum of France. The treaty of peace was signed the following day, 17 October, at five o'clock in the evening. It was on this occasion that the person who drew the treaty having inserted, as the first article, 'The Emperor of Austria acknowledges the French Republic,' I said, 'Strike out that article; the French Republic is like the sun; they who cannot see it must be blind. The French people are the masters in their own country; they formed a republic; perhaps they may form an aristocracy tomorrow; and a monarchy the day after. It is their imprescriptible right; the form of their government is merely an affair of domestic law.' The treaty was dated at Campo-Formio, a small village between Passeriano and Udine, which had been neutralized for this purpose by the secretaries of legation; but it was thought unnecessary to remove thither, and there was no suitable house in the place for the accommodation of the plenipotentiaries.

By this treaty the Emperor acknowledged the natural limits of the Republic, the Rhine, the Alps, the Mediterranean, the Pyrenees, and the Atlantic Ocean: he consented to the formation of the Cisalpine Republic, composed of Lombardy, the Duchies of Reggio, Modena, and Mirandola; the three legations, Bologna, Ferrara, and Romagna; the Valteline and that part of the Venetian states which lay on the right bank of the Adige (the Bergomasco, Cremoese, Bresciano, and Polesino); and he ceded Brisgaw, which placed a greater distance between the Hereditary States and the French frontiers. It was agreed that the important bulwark of Mentz should be surrendered to the troops of the Republic, pursuant to a military convention which was to be agreed upon at Rastadt, where I as French plenipotentiary

PEACE OF CAMPO-FORMIO

and Count Cobentzel made an appointment to meet. All the princes dispossessed on the left bank of the Rhine were to be indemnified on the right bank, by the secularization of the ecclesiastical princes. The peace of Europe was to be negotiated at Rastadt; the cabinets of the Luxembourg and Vienna were to act in concert. The Prussian territory on the left bank was reserved; and it was agreed that it should be ceded to the Republic by the treaty of Rastadt, but with an equivalent for Austria in Germany. Corfu, Zante, Cephalonia, Santa Maura, and Cerigo, were ceded to France, who on her side consented to the Emperor's taking possession of the Venetian states on the left bank of the Adige, which added upwards of two millions of souls to his empire. By one of the articles of the treaty the property which the Archduke Charles possessed in Belgium, as the heir of the Archduchess Christina, was secured to him: it was in consequence of this article that I, when Emperor, purchased for a million of francs the mansion of Lacken, situate near Brussels, which, previously to the Revolution, was part of the property of the Archduchess; the rest of the Archduke's domains in the Low Countries were purchased by the Duke of Saxe-Teschen. This stipulation was a mark of esteem which I afforded to the general I had been fighting with, and with whom I had had communications honourable to us both.

During the conferences of Passeriano, General Desaix came from the army of the Rhine to visit the fields of battle which the army of Italy had rendered famous; I received him at head-quarters, and thought to astonish him by imparting to him the light which d'Entraigues's portfolio threw on Pichegru's conduct. 'We have long known,' said Desaix smiling, 'that Pichegru was a traitor; Moreau found proofs of the fact in Klinglin's papers, with all the particulars of the bribes he had received, and the concerted motives of his military manoeuvres. Moreau, Regnier, and I are the only persons in the secret. I wished Moreau to inform the government of it immediately, but he would not. Pichegru,' added he, 'is perhaps the only general who ever got himself beaten purposely.' He alluded to the manoeuvre by which Pichegru had intentionally moved his principal forces up the Rhine, in order to prevent the success of the operations before Mentz. Desaix visited the camps, and was received with the greatest respect in all of them. This was the commencement of the friendship between him and me. He loved glory for glory's sake, and France above everything. He was of an unsophisticated, active, pleasing character, and possessed extensive information. No one had more thoroughly studied the theatre of war up the Rhine, and in Swabia and Bavaria, than Desaix. The victor of Marengo shed tears for his death.

General Hoche, who commanded the army of the Sambre and Meuse, died suddenly, about this time, at Mentz. Many people thought he had been poisoned, but there was no foundation for such a rumour. This young general had distinguished himself at the lines of Weissemburg, in 1794. He had given

PEACE OF CAMPO-FORMIO

proofs of talent at La Vendée, in 1795 and 1796, and had the glory of establishing peace in that country, although it was but of short duration. Enthusiastic in patriotism, distinguished for bravery, active, ambitious, and restless, he knew not how to wait for opportunities, but exposed himself to failure by premature enterprises. By marching his troops on Paris, at the crisis of 18 Fructidor, he infringed the constitutional circle, and had nearly fallen its victim; the councils informed against him. He attempted an expedition to Ireland; no one was better qualified to conduct it with success. He expressed a great regard for me on all occasions. His death, and Moreau's disgrace, left the command of the armies of the Rhine and Sambre and Meuse vacant. The government united them in one, and gave the command to Augereau.

I had successively sent my principal generals home to Paris with colours taken, which afforded the government an opportunity of becoming acquainted with them, and securing their attachment by rewards. I commissioned General Berthier to carry home the treaty of Campo-Formio; and wishing to manifest my esteem and respect for the sciences, I sent Monge with him, who was a member of the Commission of the Sciences and Arts in Italy: Monge had belonged to the old Academy of the Sciences. I delighted in the very interesting conversation of this great geometrician, who was a natural philosopher of the first order, and a very warm patriot, but pure, sincere, and true. He loved France and the French people as his own family, and democracy and equality as the results of a geometrical demonstration. He was of an ardent character; but, whatever his enemies may have said, a truly worthy man. At the time of the invasion of the Prussians in 1792, he offered to give his two daughters in marriage to the first volunteers who should lose a limb in the defence of the territory; and this offer was sincere in him. He followed me into Egypt; he was afterwards a senator, and was always faithful to me. The sciences are indebted to him for the excellent work of descriptive geometry.

The treaty of Campo-Formio surprised the Directory, who were far from expecting it: they could not wholly conceal their vexation; it is even said that they thought, at first, of refusing to ratify it; but the opinion of the public was too positive, and the advantages which the peace secured to France were too evident, to allow of this rejection.

Immediately after the signature of the treaty, I returned to Milan, to complete the organization of the Cisalpine Republic, and the arrangements for the supply of my army. I was now to proceed to Rastadt, to terminate the grand work of the continental peace. I took leave of the Italians in these terms:

'Citizens!

'From the first of Frimaire next, your constitution will be in full operation. Your Directory, your Legislative Body, your Tribunal of Cassation, and the other subaltern branches of administration, will be completed.

PEACE OF CAMPO-FORMIO

'You afford the first instance which appears in history of a people liberated without factions, revolutions, or convulsions.

'We have given you liberty; do you take care to preserve it. Next to France, you are the most populous and richest of republics; and your situation must one day require you to act a great part in the affairs of Europe.

'Prove yourselves worthy of your destiny by making none but wise and moderate laws.

'Have them executed with vigour and energy.

'Promote the diffusion of knowledge, and respect religion.

'Compose your battalions, not of the refuse of society, but of citizens imbued with the principles of the Republic, or deeply concerned in its prosperity.

'Generally speaking, you require to be impressed with a sense of your own strength, and of the dignity which belongs to the free.

'Divided as you had been, and compelled to crouch under a tyrannical sway, you would not have acquired your liberty without assistance; but in a few years, should you be left to yourselves, no power on earth will be strong enough to deprive you of it.

'Until that period the *Great Nation* will protect you against the attacks of your neighbours. Its political system will be united with yours.

'Had the Roman people made the same use of its strength as the French people, the Roman eagles would still have been seen on the Capitol; and eighteen centuries of slavery and tyranny would not have disgraced mankind.

'I have performed a task, for the purpose of establishing liberty, and solely with a view to your happiness, which has hitherto never been undertaken but through ambition and the love of power.

'I have filled up a great number of places, and have incurred the risk of having passed over the honest man and given the preference to the intriguer: but there were still greater objections to leaving these first nominations to you; you were not sufficiently organized.

'I shall leave you in a few days. Nothing but the orders of my government, or any imminent danger that may threaten the Cisalpine Republic, will be likely to recall me into these parts.

'But wherever my country's service may place me, I shall always feel a lively interest in the welfare and glory of your Republic.

BONAPARTE.

'Head-quarters, Milan, 22 Brumaire, year VI. (12 Nov., 1797.)'

I set out for Turin. I alighted at Guinguené's, the French minister's, on 17 November. The King of Sardinia desired to see me, and express his gratitude to me in a public manner; but circumstances were already such that I did not

PEACE OF CAMPO-FORMIO

think it expedient to indulge myself in court entertainments. I continued my journey towards Rastadt. I crossed Mount Cenis: at Geneva I was received as I might have expected to be in a French town, and with the enthusiasm which characterizes the Genevese. On my entry into the Pays de Vaud, three parties of handsome young girls came to compliment me at the head of the inhabitants; one party was clothed in white, another in red, and the third in blue. These maidens presented me with a crown, on which was inscribed the famous sentence which had proclaimed the liberty of the Valteline, and that maxim so dear to the Vaudois, *that one nation cannot be subject to another*. I passed through several Swiss towns, Berne amongst others, and crossed the Rhine at Bâle, proceeding towards Rastadt.

The order of the day, on my leaving Milan, contained these expressions: 'Soldiers, I set out to-morrow for Rastadt. Separated from the army, I shall sigh for the moment of my rejoining it, and braving fresh dangers. Whatever post the Government may assign to the soldiers of the Army of Italy, they will always be the worthy supporters of liberty and of the glory of the French name. Soldiers, when you talk of the princes you have conquered, and of the nations you have set free, and the battles you have fought in two campaigns, say: "*In the next two campaigns we shall do still more!*" '

On reaching Rastadt I found the grand apartments of the palace prepared for my reception. Treilhard and Bonnier, whom the Directory had appointed to negotiate jointly with me with the Germanic body, had arrived a few days before me. Old Count Metternich represented the Emperor at this congress as head of the German confederation; whilst Count Cobentzel represented him as head of the house of Austria; thus forming two legations with opposite interests and instructions. Count Lherbach represented the circle of Austria to the Diet. Count Metternich's part was merely one of parade; Cobentzel transacted the business. After exchanging the ratifications of the treaty of Campo-Formio, the plenipotentiaries signed the convention respecting the surrender of Mentz, in execution of the treaty. In the first place, the Austrian troops were to quit Mentz, and to leave only the Elector's troops; at the same hour the French troops were to invest the place and take possession of it; secondly, the French were to quit Venice and Palma Nuova, leaving only the Venetian troops in those places of which the Austrians were to take possession, as well as the whole of the country. Albini, the minister of Mentz, made the strongest protestations; all the German princes loudly complained. They said that Mentz did not belong to Austria; and they accused the Emperor of having betrayed Germany for the sake of his interests in Italy. Count Lherbach, as deputy for the circle of Austria, was employed to answer all these protestations, which task he discharged with all the energy, arrogance and irony which distinguished his character.

Sweden appeared at Rastadt as a mediatrix, and as one of the powers

PEACE OF CAMPO-FORMIO

which had guaranteed the treaty of Westphalia. Russia had arrogated similar pretensions to herself ever since the treaty of Teschen; but she was at this moment at war with France. The state of Europe had undergone great changes since the treaty of Westphalia: Sweden then possessed great influence in Germany, being at the head of the protestant party, and dignified by the victories of the great Gustavus; Russia was not then an European power, and Prussia scarcely existed. The progress of these two powers had forced Sweden to fall back, and fixed her in the rank of a power of the third order. Her claims were therefore unseasonable. This court had, moreover, been foolish enough to send Baron Fersen as its representative to Rastadt. The favour which this nobleman had enjoyed at the court of Versailles, his intrigues in the time of the Constituent Assembly, and the hatred he had on all occasions expressed against France, rendered him so unfit for this mission, that his appointment might be regarded as an insult to the Republic. When he was introduced, on the visit of etiquette, to the French ambassador's residence, he was announced as ambassador from Sweden and mediator to the Congress. I told him that I could not acknowledge any mediator; and, moreover, that his former opinions did not allow of his acting in that capacity between the Republic and the Emperor of Germany; that I could therefore receive him no more. Baron Fersen was so completely disconcerted, and this reception made so much noise, that he left Rastadt the following day.

Immediately after the surrender of Mentz to the French troops, I held a conference with Treilhard and Bonnier, and after having demonstrated to them that the instructions of the Directory were insufficient, I declared that I would stay no longer at the Congress, but return home. Affairs were more complicated at Rastadt than at Campo-Formio; it was necessary to cut matters short, in order to come to a conclusion.

The Directory knew not what course to determine on; they named, however, new plenipotentiaries in addition to Treilhard and Bonnier. Already dissatisfied with the course of the foreign policy of the French government, I determined to meddle no further in a negotiation which was sure to take an unfavourable turn. At the same time, the internal situation of France foreboded, in my opinion, the approaching triumph of the demagogues; and that being the case, the same motives as had induced me to shun the civilities of the court of Sardinia, led me to withdraw myself from the testimonials of approbation which the German princes lavished upon me. I thought the treaty of Campo-Formio an appropriate termination to the first act of my political life; and resolved to live at Paris as a private individual, as long as circumstances might permit. During my short stay at Rastadt, I procured the French plenipotentiaries, who had previously been very much neglected, all the respect and consideration to which they were entitled, as the representatives of a great nation, from the foreign plenipotentiaries, as well as from the multitude of petty German princes who swarmed at this congress. I also induced the Government to place large sums at the disposal of the negotiators, to enable them to support their rank with proper dignity. The allowance which they had previously received was insufficient, which circumstance was detrimental to the respectability of the Republic.

Chapter XXIII

PARIS

My arrival at Paris. Affairs of Switzerland. Affairs of Rome. Bernadotte, the ambassador of the Republic at Vienna, is insulted by the populace. Plan of an expedition into the East. 21 January.

I left Rastadt, travelled through France incognito, reached Paris without stopping on the road, and alighted at my small house in the *Chaussée d'Antin, rue Chantereine*. The municipal body, the administration of the department, and the councils, vied with each other in expressing the gratitude of the nation towards me. A committee of the Council of the Ancients drew up an act for settling the estate of Chambord and a mansion in the capital upon me; but the Directory, from some unknown motive, was alarmed at this proposal, which its emissaries contrived to put off. At the same time, by a resolution of the municipality of Paris, which was then more independent than the councils, the name of *rue de la Victoire* was given to the *rue Chantereine*.

During the two years of my command in Italy, I had filled the whole world with the renown of my victories; and the coalition had been broken up by them. The Emperor and the princes of the empire had now acknowledged the Republic. Italy was entirely subjected to its laws. Two new Republics had been created there on the French system. England alone remained in arms, but she had testified a wish to make peace; and it was only owing to the folly of the Directory after 18 Fructidor that the treaty had not been signed. Besides the grand results thus obtained by the Republic in her foreign relations, she had gained many advantages in her internal administration and her military power. At no period of history had the French soldier been more thoroughly impressed with the sense of his superiority over all other soldiers in Europe. It was owing to the influence of the victories in

Italy, that the armies of the Rhine and Sambre and Meuse had been able to carry the French colours to the banks of the Lech, where Turenne had first unfurled them. In the beginning of 1796, the Emperor had 180,000 men on the Rhine, and meant to carry the war into France. The armies of the Sambre and Meuse and Rhine were not in sufficient force to resist him; their numerical inferiority was notorious; they were in want of everything, and although the valour of so many brave men assured the Republic of an honourable defence, the hope of conquest was entertained by no one. The battles of Montenotte, Lodi, etc., struck Vienna with alarm, and obliged the Aulic Council to recall, successively, from its armies in Germany, Marshal Wurmser, the Archduke Charles, and upwards of 60,000 men; by which equality was restored on the German side, and Moreau and Jourdan were enabled to undertake offensive operations.

Extraordinary contributions to the amount of upwards of 120 millions had been levied in Italy; 60 millions had sufficed to pay, feed and provide for the army of Italy, in every branch of the service; and 60 millions, which had been sent to the Treasury at Paris, had enabled it to supply the wants of the interior, and the army of the Rhine; but the system of the ministry of the finances of that period was so defective, the administration so corrupt, and the treasury so ill managed, that these armies experienced but little relief from this source. Independently of this important supply of sixty millions, the treasury owed to my victories an annual saving of seventy millions, the amount of the expense of the armies of the Alps and Italy in 1796. The naval department at Toulon had received considerable supplies in hemp and timber, and the shipping taken at Genoa, Leghorn and Venice. The national museum had been enriched with the *chefs-d'oeuvre* of the arts which had embellished Parma, Florence, and Rome, and which were valued at upwards of 200 millions.

The commerce of Lyons, Provence and Dauphiny, began to revive the moment the grand debouché of the Alps was opened to it. The Toulon squadron ruled the Mediterranean, the Adriatic and the Levant. Happy times for France seemed to be at hand, and she acknowledged with pleasure that she owed them to the conquerors of Italy.

On my arrival, the leaders of all parties immediately called upon me; but I refused to listen to them. The public was extremely eager to see me; the streets and squares through which I was expected to pass were constantly crowded with people, but I never showed myself. The Institute having appointed me a member of the class of mechanics, I adopted its costume. I received no constant visits, except from a few men of science, such as Monge, Berthollet, Borda, Laplace, Prony, and Lagrange; several generals, as Berthier, Desaix, Lefebvre, Caffarelli Dufalga, and Kleber, and a very few deputies.

I was received in public audience by the Directory who had had scaffoldings erected in the Place du Luxembourg for this ceremony, the pretext for

PARIS

which was the delivery of the treaty of Campo-Formio. I avoided all mention of Fructidor, of the affairs of the time, and the expedition to England; my address was simple, but nevertheless afforded room for much meditation. The following expressions were noticed in it. 'In order to attain freedom, the French people had to fight the allied kings; and to obtain a constitution founded on reason, they had to combat the prejudices of eighteen centuries. Religion, the feudal system, and despotism, have successively governed Europe for twenty ages; but the era of representative governments may be dated from the peace which you have just concluded. You have accomplished the organization of the grand nation, whose vast territories are bounded only by the limits which nature herself has set to them. I present you the treaty of Campo-Formio, ratified by the Emperor. This peace secures the liberty, prosperity and glory of the Republic. When the happiness of the French people shall be established upon the best organic laws, the whole of Europe will become free.'

General Joubert, and Brigadier-General Andreossy, carried, on occasion of this ceremony, the standard which the legislative body had presented to the Army of Italy, containing the following inscriptions in letters of gold. 'The Army of Italy took 150,000 prisoners, 170 standards, 550 pieces of garrison artillery, 600 field pieces, five pontoon trains, nine sixty-four gun ships, twelve frigates of thirty-two guns, twelve corvettes, and eighteen galleys.—Armistices with the kings of Sardinia, and Naples, the Pope, and the Dukes of Parma and Modena.—Preliminaries of Leoben.—Convention of Montebello with the republic of Genoa.—Treaties of peace of Tolentino and Campo-Formio.—Liberty given to the people of Bologna, Ferrara, Modena, Massa Carrara, Romagna, Lombardy, Brescia, Bergamo, Mantua, Cremona, part of the Veronese, Chiavenna, Bormio, and the Valteline; to the people of Genoa, the imperial Fiefs, and the people of the departments of Corcyra, the Egean sea, and Ithaca.—The *chefs-d'oeuvre* of Michael Angelo, Guercino, Titian, Paul Veronese, Corregio, Albano, the Carracci, Raphael, Leonardo da Vinci, etc., sent to Paris.—This army has triumphed in eighteen important affairs or pitched battles, and in sixty-seven actions: I. Montenotte; II. Millesimo; III. Mondovi; IV. Lodi; V. Borghetto; VI. Lonato; VII. Castiglione; VIII. Roveredo; IX. Bassano; X. Saint George; XI. Fontana Viva; XII. Caldiero; XIII. Arcole; XIV. Rivoli; XV. La Favorite; XVI. The Tagliamento; XVII. Tarwis; XVIII. Neumarckt.' Here followed the names of the sixty-seven actions in which the army had fought during the two campaigns of 1796 and 1797.

The Directory, the Legislative Body, and the minister of exterior relations, gave entertainments to me. I appeared at them all; but remained only a short time. That of the minister Talleyrand bore the stamp of good taste. A celebrated woman, determined to engage with the conqueror of Italy, addressed me in the midst of a numerous circle, demanding who was, in my opinion, the first woman in the world, dead or alive: '*She who has borne the greatest number of children,*' replied I, smiling. People thronged to the sittings of the Institute for the sake of seeing me, I always took my place there between Laplace and Lagrange; the latter of whom was sincerely attached to me. I never attended the theatre except in a private box, and positively refused the proposal of the managers of the opera, who wished to give a grand representation in my honour, although Marshal Saxe, Lowendahl, and Dumouriez had attended such representations on returning, respectively, from Fontenoy, Bergen-op-Zoom, and Champagne. When I afterwards appeared at the Tuileries, at the time of the revolution of Brumaire, after my return from Egypt, I was still unknown to the inhabitants of Paris, who were excessively eager to satisfy their curiosity.

The Directory showed me the greatest respect; when they thought proper to consult me, they used to send one of the ministers to request me to assist at the council, where I took my seat between two of the directors, and gave my opinion on the matters in question.

The troops, as they returned to France, extolled me to the skies in their songs; they proclaimed that it was time to turn the lawyers out, and make me king. The Directors carried the affectation of candour so far, as to show me the secret reports which were made by the police on the subject; but they could ill conceal the jealousy which all this popularity excited in their minds. I was sensible of all the delicacy and difficulty of this situation. The proceedings of the administration were unpopular, and many people fixed their hopes on the conqueror of Italy. The Directory wished me to return to Rastadt, but I refused to do so, under the pretext that my mission into Italy had terminated at Campo-Formio, and that it no longer became me to wield both the pen and the sword. I soon afterwards consented to accept the command of the army of England, in order to deceive Europe and cover the design and preparations of the expedition to Egypt.

The troops composing the Army of England were quartered in Normandy, Picardy, and Belgium. As their new General I inspected every point, but chose to travel through the departments *incognito*. These mysterious journeys increased the anxiety that was felt in London, and contributed to mask the preparations making in the South. It was at this period that I visited Antwerp, and conceived the grand plans of naval establishments, which I carried into execution when Emperor. It was also in one of these journeys that I perceived all the advantages which Saint-Quentin would derive from the canal which was opened under the Consulate, and settled my ideas respecting the superiority of Boulogne to Calais, on account of the tide, for the purpose of attempting an enterprise against England with mere pinnaces.

The principles which ought thenceforth to have governed the policy of the

Republic had been laid down by me at Campo-Formio, without regard to the instructions of the directors. In fact, the directors were strangers to this policy, and were, besides, incapable of overruling their passions. Switzerland became the first proof of this fact. France had always had to complain of the canton of Berne and the Swiss aristocracy; all the foreign agents who had raised disturbances in France had constantly made Berne their centre of action. The time had now arrived for destroying the preponderance of this aristocracy, by means of the great influence which the Republic had lately acquired in Europe. I highly approved of the resentment of the Directory; I also thought that the opportunity of establishing the political influence of France over Switzerland now presented itself; but I did not think it necessary for that purpose to overturn everything in that country. The proper course was to conform to the policy which dictated the treaty of Campo-Formio, and to attain the proposed object with as few alterations as possible. I wished the French ambassador to have presented a note to the Helvetic Diet, supported by two camps, one in Savoy, the other in Franche-Comté; and to have declared, by this note, that France and Italy considered it necessary to their policy, their safety, and the dignity of the three nations respectively, that the Pays de Vaud, Argau, and the Italian bailiwicks should become free and independent cantons, equal to the other cantons; that they had reason to complain of the aristocracy of certain families of Berne, Soleure, and Friburg, but that they would consign all their dissatisfaction to oblivion, provided the peasants of those cantons and of the Italian bailiwicks were restored to their political rights.

All these changes might have been effected without difficulty, and without resorting to arms: but Rewbell, listening to some Swiss demagogues, got a different system adopted in preference; and the Directory, without regard to the manners, religion, or local circumstances of the cantons, resolved to subject all Switzerland to an uniform constitution similar to that of France. The small cantons were enraged at the loss of their liberty; Switzerland took up arms on the approach of a convulsion fatal to so many interests, and exciting so many passions. The French troops were obliged to interfere and conquer. Blood was shed, and Europe was alarmed.

At the same time the court of Rome, still actuated by the vertigo that it seemed subject to, and rather incensed than corrected by the treaty of Tolentino, persisted in its system of aversion towards France. This cabinet of weak and imprudent old men set public opinion in a ferment around them; quarrelled with the Cisalpine republic, had the folly to place the Austrian general Provera at the head of their troops, and excited the fury of the people of all classes who adhered to their party. The tumult broke out. Young Duphot, a general of the most promising talents, who happened to be at Rome while travelling, was murdered at the gate of the French palace, whilst endeavouring to prevent disorder. The ambassador withdrew to Florence. Being consulted, I replied by my usual adage, '*That incidents ought not to govern policy, but policy incidents*; that however wrong the court of Rome might be, the measures to be adopted towards it were a most important question; that it ought to be corrected, but not destroyed; that by overthrowing the Holy See and revolutionizing Rome, a war with Naples would infallibly be produced, which ought to be avoided; that it would be best to order the French ambassador to return to Rome, and require that an example should be made of the guilty; to receive an extraordinary nuncio with excuses from the Pope; to expel Provera, place the most moderate prelates at the head of affairs, and force the Holy See to conclude a concordat with the Cisalpine republic; that by all these measures combined, Rome would be tranquillized and prevented from giving any further trouble; and that the concordat with the Cisalpine state would have the further advantage of preparing men's minds in France for a similar measure long beforehand.'

But La Reveillere, surrounded by his theophilanthropists, prevailed on the Directory to decide on marching against the Pope. 'It is now time,' said he, 'to abolish that idol. The word Roman Republic would be enough to throw all the ardent minds of the revolutionists into transports. The General of Italy had been too circumspect when he had the opportunity; and it was entirely his fault that there were now any quarrels with the Pope. But possibly he had his private views: in fact the civility of his behaviour, his considerate conduct towards the Pope, and his generous compassion for the exiled priests, had gained him many partisans in France who were no friends to the revolution.' As to the apprehension that the entrance of the army into Rome might bring on a war with Naples, he treated it as chimerical. According to him, France had a numerous party at Naples, and had nothing to fear from a power of the third class. Berthier received orders to march on Rome with an army, and to re-establish the Roman Republic, which was done. The Capitol once more beheld consuls, a senate, and a tribunate. Fourteen cardinals went to Saint Peter's church to sing the Te Deum in commemoration of the restoration of the Roman Republic, and the destruction of the throne of Saint Peter. The people, intoxicated with the idea of independence, drew the greater part of the clergy into their sentiments.

The hand which had hitherto restrained the officers and agents of the army of Italy, was no longer with them; the greatest robberies were committed in Rome; the Vatican was plundered of its furniture; pictures and curiosities were everywhere seized. The inhabitants were enraged; and even the soldiers cried out against some of their generals, whom they accused of misconduct. This commotion was extremely dangerous, and it was not without great difficulty that order was restored. There is reason to think that the clamour was excited by the intrigues of Neapolitan, English, and Austrian agents.

Bernadotte had been appointed ambassador to Vienna; this choice was a bad one; the character of this general was too enthusiastic; his head was not sufficiently cool, not to mention that a general can never be an agreeable envoy to a nation which has constantly been beaten: a magistrate would have been the proper person; but the Directory had few men of this class at its disposal, having disgusted most of those who were not too obscure for the purpose. However this may be, Bernadotte suffered his temper to master his judgment, and committed serious errors. One day, from what motive has never been divined, he hoisted the tri-coloured flag on the top of his hotel, at the instigation of certain agents who wished to embroil Austria with France. An instantaneous rising of the populace was the consequence; they tore down the tri-coloured flag, and insulted Bernadotte.

The Directors, in the first moments of rage, sent for me, in order to obtain the support of my influence over public opinion. They communicated to me a message to the councils, declaring war against Austria, and a decree investing me with the command of the army of Germany; but I was not of the opinion of government. 'If you intended war,' said I, 'you should have prepared for it independently of what has happened to Bernadotte; you should not have sent your troops to Switzerland, Southern Italy, and the coasts of the Atlantic: you should not have proclaimed the intention of reducing your army to one hundred thousand men; for although that scheme has not yet been executed, it is known, and discourages the army. These measures shew that you calculated on peace. Bernadotte is materially in the wrong. In declaring war you are only playing the game of England. It would indicate very little knowledge of the policy of the cabinet of Vienna to imagine, that, if it had wished for war, it would have insulted you: on the contrary, it would have flattered you and lulled your suspicions, whilst it was putting its troops in motion, and you would have learnt its real intentions only by the first cannon-shot. Depend upon it, Austria will give you every satisfaction. To be thus hurried away by every event is to have no political system at all.' The force of truth calmed the government; the Emperor gave satisfaction; the conferences of Seltz took place; but this incident delayed the sailing of the expedition to Egypt for a fortnight.

In the meantime I began to be apprehensive that, amidst the daily storms which the irresolute conduct of the government and the nature of events produced, an Oriental enterprise might not be conducive to the true interest of the nation. 'Europe,' said I to the Directory, 'is anything but tranquil: the congress of Rastadt does not close its negotiations: you are obliged to keep your troops in the interior to secure the elections: you require a force to keep the western departments in awe. Would it not be best to countermand the expedition, and wait for a more favourable opportunity?'

The Directory, alarmed, and fearing that it was my real intention to place myself at the head of affairs, urged the expedition more warmly than ever. They were not sensible of all the consequences of the changes they had introduced into the political system within the last six months. According to them, the events in Switzerland, far from weakening France, had given her excellent military positions, and the Helvetic troops as auxiliaries: the affair at Rome was at an end, for the Pontiff was already at Florence, and the Roman Republic had been proclaimed: Bernadotte's affair could lead to no unpleasant consequences, since the Emperor had offered amends. The present moment was therefore the most favourable that had ever occurred for attacking England, as had been determined, in Ireland and in Egypt. I then offered to leave Desaix and Kleber, whose talents might, I thought, prove serviceable to France. The Directory knew not their value, and refused them. 'The Republic,' said they, 'is not reduced to these two generals; multitudes would be found to effect the triumph of their country, if it were in danger; we are more likely to want soldiers than generals.'

The government was on the brink of an abyss which it did not perceive. Its affairs were going on ill; it had abused its victory in Fructidor, and committed an error in not rallying round the Republic all those who did not belong to the foreigners' party, but had only been drawn in to follow it. The Directory had thus deprived themselves of the assistance and talents of a great number of individuals, who, out of resentment, rushed into the party opposed to the Republic, although their interests and opinions naturally inclined them to that form of government. The Directory found themselves under the necessity of employing men devoid of morality; thence arose the public dissatisfaction, and the necessity of keeping up a great number of troops in the interior, to secure the elections and overawe La Vendée. It was easy to foresee that the new elections would produce violent differences. The Directory had no more system in administration than in foreign policy: they went on from day to day, actuated by the individual characters of the directors, or by the vicious nature of a government of five persons, foreseeing nothing, and only sensible of obstacles when actually stopped by them. When it was asked 'How will you manage at the approaching elections?' 'We shall provide for that by a law,' answered La Reveillere. The event shewed what kind of law he had in view. When it was asked, 'Why do you not bring forward all those friends of the Republic who were only misled in Fructidor? Why not recall Carnot, Portalis, Dumolard, Muraire, etc., in order to form a combination of knowledge and liberal ideas against the foreigners and emigrants?' They made no answer; they could not comprehend these anxieties; they thought themselves popular, and established on solid ground.

A party composed of the influential deputies in the two councils, the Fructidorians who sought a protector, and the most distinguished and enlightened generals, long urged me to step forward and place myself at the head of the Republic. I refused; the time was not yet come; I did not think myself popular enough to go alone; I had ideas on the art of governing and on what was requisite for a great nation, different from those of the men of the revolution and assemblies: I was fearful of compromising my character. I determined to sail for Egypt, resolved, nevertheless to appear again as soon as circumstances should render my presence necessary, as I already partly foresaw they would. To render me master of France, it was necessary that the Directory should experience disasters in my absence, and that my return should recall victory to the colours of the nation.

The government celebrated the anniversary of the death of Louis XVI, and it was a grand subject of discussion amongst the Directors and ministers, whether I should assist at this ceremony. On one side it was feared that, if I did not go, it would tend to render the festival unpopular; and, on the other, that, if I went, the Directory would be neglected, and I alone would occupy the attention of the public. It was nevertheless considered that my presence was necessary for political reasons; and one of the ministers was instructed to negotiate, as it were, this matter with me. I, who would have preferred being unconnected with acts of this description, observed 'that I had no public functions; that I had personally nothing to do with this pretended fête, which, from its very nature, was agreeable to but few people; that it was a very impolitic one, the event it commemorated being a tragedy, and a national calamity; that I very well understood why the fourteenth of July was observed, being the period when the people had recovered their rights; but that it might have recovered them, and established a republic, without polluting itself by the slaughter of a prince who had been declared inviolable and irresponsible by the constitution itself; that I did not undertake to determine whether that measure had been useful or injurious, but maintained that it was an unfortunate event; that national fêtes were held in celebration of victories, but that the victims left on the fields of battle were lamented; that to keep the anniversary of a man's death could never be the act of a government, although it might suit a faction, or a sanguinary club; that I could not conceive how the Directory, which had shut up the meetings of the jacobins and the anarchial clubs, could fail to perceive that this ceremony created the Republic many more enemies than friends; that it estranged, instead of conciliating; irritated, instead of calming; and shook the foundations of government, instead of adding to their strength.' The emissary brought all his rhetoric into play; he endeavoured to prove 'that this fête was just, because it was politic; that it was politic, for all countries and republics had celebrated the fall of absolute power and the murder of tyrants as a triumph; thus Athens had always solemnized the anniversary of the death of Peisistratus, and Rome the fall of the Decemvirs; that it was, moreover, a law of the country, and that everyone consequently owed submission and obedience to it; and lastly, that the influence of the General of Italy over public opinion was such, that it was incumbent on him to appear at this ceremony, as, otherwise, his absence might be prejudicial to the interest of the commonwealth.' After several conferences, a middle course was agreed upon: the Institute attended this ceremony; and it was settled that I should walk amongst the members, in the class to which I belonged, thus performing, as a duty attached to a public body, an act which I did not consider voluntary. This arrangement of the matter was very agreeable to the Directory. But when the Institute entered the church of Saint Sulpice, someone who recognized me having pointed me out, I instantly became the sole object of general interest. The fears of the Directory were realized; they were totally eclipsed. At the conclusion of the ceremony the multitude suffered the Directory to walk out by themselves, and remained to attend me who would have preferred being left unnoticed in the crowd, rending the air with shouts of *Long live the General of the Army of Italy!* This event, accordingly, only served to increase the displeasure of the rulers of the state.

Another circumstance placed me under the necessity of loudly condemning the proceedings of the Directory. At the Garchi coffee-house, two young men, under pretence of political raillery, excited by the manner in which they wore their hair in tresses, were insulted, attacked, and assassinated. This murder had been conducted under the orders of the Minister of Police, Sotin, and executed by his agents. Circumstances were already such that I, although living in the most profound retirement in my power, was obliged, with a view to my own safety, to keep a vigilant eye upon events of this nature. I gave vent to my indignation. The Directory were alarmed, and sent one of their ministers to explain to me the motives of their conduct, stating 'that such events were common in critical times; that revolutionary moments were exceptions from ordinary laws; that in this case it had become necessary to overawe the upper ranks of society, and check the audacity of the saloons; that there were faults which the tribunals could not reach; that the *Lanterne* of the Constituent Assembly could not, certainly, be approved of, but yet the revolution would never have proceeded without it; and that there are evils which must be tolerated, because they save us from greater calamities.' I replied, 'that such language could scarcely have been listened to before Fructidor, when the opposite parties were in the field and ready for action, and when the Directory had to defend itself, rather than to govern; that such an act, might, perhaps, at that time have been palliated by necessity, but that the Directory being now invested with undisputed power, the law meeting with no opposition, and all the citizens being, if not attached, at least subjected to the government; this action could only be considered as an atrocious crime, an absolute insult to civilized society; that wherever the words law and liberty were uttered, all the citizens were guards to each other; and that in this

PARIS

cut-throat affair, everyone would be struck with terror, and anxiously ask where such proceedings would stop.' These arguments were too plausible to need much illustration to a man of talent, and of this minister's character; but he had a commission, and endeavoured to justify a Government whose favour and confidence he was ambitious to preserve.

Chapter XXIV

NAVAL BATTLE OF ABOUKIR

Reports at London respecting the expedition preparing in the ports of France. Movement of the English squadrons in the Mediterranean, in May, June and July. Chances for and against the French and English naval armaments, if they had met on the way. The French squadron receives orders to enter the old port of Alexandria. It moors in Aboukir roads. I learn that it remains at Aboukir. My astonishment. The French squadron is reconnoitred at its moorings by an English frigate. Battle of Aboukir.

Intelligence was received in England, from various quarters at the same time, that considerable armaments were preparing at Brest, Toulon, Genoa, and Civita-Vecchia; that the Spanish squadron of Cadiz was fitting out with great activity; and that numerous camps were forming on the Scheldt, on the coasts of the Pas-de-Calais, of Normandy, and of Bretagne. Having been appointed general-in-chief of the Army of England, I was inspecting all the coasts of the ocean, and visiting every port. I had assembled about me at Paris, all that were left of the old naval officers who had acquired reputation during the American war, such as Buhor, Marigny, etc.; but they did not justify their celebrity. The intelligence which France maintained with the United Irishmen, could not be kept so secret but that the English Government should hear something of it. The first opinion of the Cabinet of Saint James's was, that all these preparations were directed against England and Ireland; and that France wished to take advantage of the peace, which had just been re-established on the Continent, in order to terminate this long struggle by a war hand to hand. That cabinet conceived that the armaments which were making in Italy, were merely intended to mislead;

NAVAL BATTLE OF ABOUKIR

that the Toulon fleet would pass the Straits, and effect its junction with the Spanish fleet at Cadiz; and that the two fleets would arrive before Brest, and carry one army to England, and another to Ireland. In this uncertainty the English admiralty contented itself with hastily fitting out a new squadron; and as soon as it heard that I had sailed from Toulon, it despatched Admiral Rogers with ten ships of war, to reinforce the English squadron before Cadiz, where Admiral Lord Saint-Vincent commanded, who, by this reinforcement, found a fleet of twenty-eight or thirty ships under his orders. There was another squadron of equal force before Brest.

Admiral Saint-Vincent had in the Mediterranean, a light squadron of three ships, cruising between the coasts of Spain, Provence, and Sardinia, in order to collect information and to watch that sea. On 24 May he detached ten ships from before Cadiz, and sent them into the Mediterranean, with orders to join those commanded by Nelson, and thus to form for that Admiral a fleet of thirteen ships, to blockade Toulon, or to follow the French squadron if it should have sailed from that port. Lord Saint-Vincent remained before Cadiz with eighteen ships to watch the Spanish fleet, being chiefly apprehensive that the Toulon squadron would escape Nelson and pass the Straits.

In the instructions sent by this Admiral to Nelson, which have been printed, it appears that everything had been foreseen, except an expedition against Egypt. The cases of the French expedition's proceeding to Brazil, the Black Sea, or Constantinople, were provided for. More than 150,000 men were encamped on the coast of the ocean, which produced agitation and continual alarm throughout England.

Nelson was cruising between Corsica, Provence, and Spain, with the three sail detached by Lord Saint-Vincent, when, in the night of 19 May, he suffered from a gale, which damaged his ships, and dismasted that in which he sailed. He was obliged to be towed. It was his design to anchor in the Gulf of Oristagni, in Sardinia; he could not succeed in this, but made the roads of Saint Peter's Isles, where he repaired his damage.

On the same night, the 18th, the French squadron sailed from Toulon; it arrived before Malta on 10 June, after doubling Cape Corso and Cape Bonara. Malta could not withstand a bombardment of twenty-four hours; the place certainly possessed immense physical means of resistance, but no moral strength whatever. The knights did nothing shameful; nobody is obliged to perform impossibilities.

Nelson having been joined by Lord Saint-Vincent's ten ships, and appointed to the command of this squadron, was cruising off Toulon on 1 June. He did not then know that the French squadron had left that port. On the 15th he reconnoitred the roads of Tagliamone, on the coast of Tuscany, which he supposed to be the rendezvous of the French expedition. On the 20th he appeared before Naples, where he was informed by the government, that the

NAVAL BATTLE OF ABOUKIR

French squadron had landed its troops at Malta, and that Garat, the ambassador of the Republic, had stated, that the expedition was intended for Egypt. On the 22nd Nelson arrived off Messina. The intelligence of the capture of Malta by the French expedition was confirmed to him; and he also learned that it was making for Candia. Upon this he passed the Faro of Messina, and proceeded to Alexandria, where he arrived on 29 July.

The French squadron received the first intelligence of the presence of an English fleet in the Mediterranean, off Cape Bonara, from a ship that fell in with it; and on the 25th, whilst the squadron was reconnoitring the coast of Candia, it was joined by the frigate *La Justice,* which had been cruising off Naples, and which brought positive news of the presence of an English squadron in these latitudes. I then gave orders that, instead of steering directly for Alexandria, the squadron should manoeuvre so as to make Cape Aza, in Africa, twenty-five leagues from Alexandria; and should not appear before Alexandria until farther intelligence should be obtained.

On the 29th, the coast of Africa, and Cape Aza were descried. Nelson was just then arrived before Alexandria; having gained no intelligence of the French squadron, he steered for Alexandretta, and from thence made for Rhodes. He then scoured the Isles of the Archipelago, reconnoitred the entrance of the Adriatic, and, on the 18th, was obliged to anchor at Syracuse to take in water. Up to this time he had obtained no information respecting the course of the French squadron. He sailed from Syracuse, and on 28 July anchored off Cape Coron, at the extremity of the Morea. It was there that he was first informed that the French army had landed in Egypt a month before. He supposed that the French squadron must have already effected its return to Toulon; but he proceeded to Alexandria in order to be able to furnish his government with positive intelligence, and to leave the necessary forces before that place for the purpose of blockading it.

When the French squadron left Toulon it was composed of thirteen sail of the line, six frigates, and a dozen brigs, sloops, and cutters. The English squadron consisted of thirteen sail, one of which carried 50 guns, and all the others 74. They had been fitted out very hastily, and were in bad condition. Nelson had no frigates. In the French squadron there were one ship of 120 guns, and three of 80. There was a fleet of several hundred sail under the convoy of this squadron, and particularly under the protection of two 64-gun ships, four Venetian-built frigates of 18 guns, and about twenty brigs and sloops. The French squadron, availing itself of its great number of light vessels, obtained intelligence from a great distance; so that the convoy had nothing to fear, and in case of falling in with the enemy, could easily take up the most advantageous position for remaining at a distance from the engagement. Every French ship had 500 old soldiers on board, with a company of land artillery amongst them. Twice a day, during the month they had been on board, the troops had been exercised in the manoeuvres of the guns. In every ship of war there were generals of experience, accustomed to stand fire, and to the chances of war.

The supposition of an engagement with the English was the general subject of conversation. The captains of ships had orders, in that case, to consider it as a permanent and constant signal, to take part in the action, and to assist the ships near them.

Nelson's squadron was one of the worst that England had ever fitted out of late years.

The French squadron received orders to enter Alexandria; this was necessary for the army, and for the success of my ulterior plans as the commander-in-chief. When the Turkish pilots declared they could not carry 74-gun ships, much less those of 80 guns, into the old port, much astonishment was excited. Captain Barré, a very distinguished naval officer, being ordered to examine the soundings, positively asserted the contrary. The 64-gun ships and frigates went in without difficulty; but the Admiral and several naval officers persisted in considering it necessary to take new soundings previously to risking the whole squadron. As the ships of war had the artillery and ammunition of the army on board, and the breeze was pretty strong, the Admiral proposed to land the whole at Aboukir, declaring that thirty-six hours would suffice for that purpose, whereas he should need five or six days for effecting this operation, whilst remaining under sail.

When I left Alexandria to advance to meet the Mamelukes, I repeated to the Admiral the order to enter the port of Alexandria; and in case he should consider that impossible, to proceed to Corfu, where he would receive from Constantinople the orders of the French minister Talleyrand; or in case there should be much delay in the arrival of those orders, to proceed from Corfu to Toulon.

The squadron might have entered the old port of Alexandria. It was allowed that a ship drawing twenty-one feet of water, might enter without danger. Seventy-fours, which draw twenty-three feet, would, therefore, only have to be lightened to the extent of two feet; 80-gun ships, drawing twenty-three feet and a half, would have been lightened by two feet and a half; and three deckers, drawing twenty-seven feet water, must have been lightened six feet. The ships might have been lightened in this manner without any inconvenience, either by throwing the water into the sea, or by taking out some of the guns. A 74 may be reduced so as to draw only .... feet water merely by taking out her water and provisions, and to draw only .... feet by taking out her artillery. This method was proposed by the naval officers to the Admiral. He replied that if all the thirteen ships had been seventy-fours, he would have adopted this expedient; but, as one of them carried 120 guns, and three others 80, he should run the risk, when once in the port, of not being able to get out

NAVAL BATTLE OF ABOUKIR

again, and of being blockaded by a squadron of eight or nine English ships; because it would be impossible for him to put the *Orient* and the three 80-gun ships in a condition to fight, if reduced to the draught of water requisite for passing the channel. This objection was of little weight; the winds which prevail in those latitudes render a rigorous blockade impracticable, and the squadron needed only twenty-four hours, after clearing the passage, to complete its armament. There was also a natural expedient; namely, to construct, at Alexandria, four floating half-butts, adapted to raise 80-gun ships two feet, and ships of 120 guns four feet; the construction of these floating butts for so trifling a rise, would not have required much labour. The *Rivoli,* built at Venice, came out of the Malamoko completely armed, on a floating butt, which raised her seven feet, so that she only drew sixteen feet of water. A few days after her launch, she fought extremely well against an English frigate and sloop. There were ships, frigates, and 400 transports in Alexandria, which would have furnished all the materials that could have been wanted. There was also a great number of naval engineers; amongst others M. Leroy, who had passed his whole life in the dock yards.

When the officers commissioned to examine Captain Barré's report had completed that operation, the Admiral sent their report to me; but it could not reach me in time to obtain an answer, because the communications were cut off for a month previous to the taking of Cairo. Had I received this report, I should have repeated the order to enter the port by lightening the ships, and ordered the works necessary at Alexandria to facilitate the squadrons getting out to sea again. But after all, as the admiral had orders, in case he should be unable to enter the port, to proceed to Corfu, he was a competent judge and umpire of his own conduct. Corfu had a good French garrison, and magazines of biscuit and meat for six months; the admiral might have touched on the coast of Albania, whence he might have drawn provisions, and finally, his instructions authorized him to proceed thence to Toulon, where there were five or six thousand men belonging to the regiments in Egypt. They were soldiers returned by permission, or from hospitals, and different detachments which had joined at that place after the sailing of the expedition. Admiral Brueys did nothing of the kind; he moored his squadron in line in Aboukir roads, and sent to Rosetta for rice and other provisions. There are many opinions with respect to the motives which induced the Admiral to remain in those bad roads. Some people have thought that, after having judged it impossible to effect the entrance of his squadron into Alexandria, he wished, previously to quitting the Grand Army, to be assured of the taking of Cairo, and to be free from all anxiety respecting the situation of the army. Brueys was much attached to me; the communications had been intercepted, and, as is usual in such cases, the most alarming rumours prevailed in the rear of the army. The admiral had, however, heard of the

NAVAL BATTLE OF ABOUKIR

success of the battle of the Pyramids, and the triumphal entrance of the French into Cairo, on 29 July. It seems that having waited a month, he still wished to wait a few days, in order to receive direct news from me. But the orders which the admiral had were positive, and such motives were insufficient to justify his conduct. In no case ought he to have remained in a situation in which his squadron was unsafe. He might have satisfied himself with respect to the anxiety he felt from the false reports which were spread relative to the army, and at the same time fulfilled his duty to his squadron, by cruising between the coasts of Egypt and Caramania, and by sending to obtain intelligence from the Damietta shore, or any other point from which news from the army and Alexandria might be obtained.

As soon as the Admiral had landed the artillery, and what he had on board belonging to the land forces, which was an affair of about forty-eight hours, he should have weighed anchor, and got under sail, whether he waited for fresh information to enter the port of Alexandria, or whether he waited for news from the army, previously to quitting these seas. But he entirely mistook his situation. He spent several days in rectifying his line of moorings; he supported his left behind the little Isle of Aboukir, where, thinking it unassailable, he placed his worst ships, the *Guerrier* and the *Conquerant*. This last, the oldest ship in the whole squadron, carried only eighteen-pounders in her lower tier. He had the little Isle occupied, and a battery of two twelve-pounders constructed. He placed his best ships, the *Orient,* the *Franklin,* and the *Tonnant,* in the centre, and at the extremity of his left the *Genereux,* one of the best and best-commanded ships in the squadron. Being fearful for his left, he had it sustained by the *Guillaume Tell,* his third 80-gun ship.

In this position, Admiral Brueys entertained no apprehension of any attack on his left, which was supported by the Isle; he was more solicitous respecting his right. But had the enemy advanced against it, he must have lost the wind; in that case it seems to have been the intention of Brueys to make sail with his centre and left. He considered this left so completely sheltered from attack, that he did not think it necessary to protect it by the fire of the Isle. The feeble battery he established there was merely intended to prevent the enemy from landing. Had the admiral understood his position better, he would have placed on this Isle twenty thirty-six pounders and eight or ten mortars; he would have moored his left near it; he would have recalled the two 64-gun ships from Alexandria, which would have made two excellent floating batteries, and which, drawing less water than the other ships, could have approached nearer the Isle; and he would have brought 3,000 seamen of the convoy from Alexandria, whom he would have distributed amongst his ships to reinforce their crews. He had recourse, it is true, to this expedient, but not until the last moment, after the commencement of the action, so that it only

NAVAL BATTLE OF ABOUKIR

increased the confusion. He completely deceived himself with respect to the strength of his line of moorings.

After the action of Rhamanieh, the Arabs of Bahire intercepted all the communications between Alexandria and the army; nor did they submit until the news of the battle of the Pyramids, and the taking of Cairo, alarmed them with respect to the resentment of the French. On 27 July, the second day after my entrance into Cairo, I received, for the first time, despatches from Alexandria, and the admiral's correspondence. I was extremely surprised to find that the squadron was not in safety, that it was neither in the port of Alexandria, in that of Corfu, nor on its voyage to Toulon; but in the Aboukir roads, exposed to the attacks of an enemy of superior strength. I despatched my aide-de-camp Julien from the army to the admiral, to inform him of my great dissatisfaction, and order him to set sail immediately, and get into Alexandria, or make for Corfu. I reminded him that all naval ordinances forbid the receiving battle in an open road. The chief of squadron Julien set out on the 27th at seven in the evening; he could not have arrived before 3 or 4 August; the battle took place on the 1st and 2nd. This officer had reached Teramea, when a party of Arabs surprised the jerm in which he was, and the brave young man was massacred whilst courageously defending the despatches of which he was the bearer, and the importance of which he well knew.

Admiral Brueys remained inactive in the bad position he had placed himself in; an English frigate, which had been detached twenty days before, by Nelson, of whom she was now in search, presented herself before Alexandria, and went to Aboukir to examine the whole line of moorings, which she effected with impunity; not a ship, frigate, or brig, was under sail. Yet the admiral had above thirty light ships with which he might have covered the sea; they were all at anchor. The principles of war required him to remain under sail with his whole squadron, whatever might be his ulterior plans. But he ought, at least, to have kept under sail a light squadron of two or three men of war, and eight or ten frigates and sloops, to prevent any light English ship from watching his motions, and to obtain the earliest intelligence of the enemy's approach. But destiny impelled him.

On 31 July, Nelson detached two of his ships, which reconnoitred the French line of moorings without molestation. On 1 August, the English squadron appeared towards three o'clock in the afternoon with all sails set. A fresh gale of the wind usual at that season was blowing. Admiral Brueys was at dinner; part of the crews were on shore; the decks were not cleared in a single ship. The admiral immediately made the signal to prepare for action. He despatched an officer to Alexandria to demand the seamen of the convoy; shortly afterwards he made a signal to prepare to get under sail; but the enemy's squadron came up so rapidly, that there was scarcely time to clear

NAVAL BATTLE OF ABOUKIR

the decks, which was done with extreme negligence. Even on board the *Orient*, the admiral's ship, some cabins, which had been constructed on the poop for the accommodation of the army officers during the passage, were not destroyed; they were left full of mattresses and buckets of paint and tar. The *Guerrier* and the *Conquerant* each cleared only one tier of guns for action; the side towards the land was encumbered with all that had been cleared out from the opposite side, so that when the ships were turned those tiers could not fire. The English were so much astonished at this that they sent to reconnoitre the reason of this inconsistency; they saw the French flag wave without a gun being fired.

The men who had been detached from the different crews had scarcely time enough to return on board. The admiral, judging that the enemy would not be within gun-shot before six o'clock, supposed that he would not attack until the following day, more particularly as he only observed eleven 74-gun ships; the two others had been detached on Alexandria, and did not rejoin Nelson until eight in the evening. Brueys did not think the Admiral would attack him the same day, and with only eleven ships. It is imagined that he thought at first of getting under way, but that he deferred giving the order, until the sailors, whom he expected from Aboukir, should be embarked. The cannonade then commenced, and an English vessel struck on the Isle, which gave Brueys fresh confidence. The sailors demanded at Alexandria did not arrive till towards eight o'clock, when the cannonade was already brisk between several ships. During the tumult and darkness, a great number of them remained on shore, and did not embark. The English admiral's plan was to attack ship after ship; every English ship anchoring astern, and placing herself athwart the head of a French ship; accident altered this disposition. The *Culloden*, intending to attack the *Guerrier*, and endeavouring to pass between the left of that ship and the Isle, struck. Had the Isle been supplied with a few pieces of cannon, this ship would have been taken. The *Goliath*, which followed her, manoeuvring to anchor athwart the head of the *Guerrier*, was carried away by the wind and current, and did not anchor until she had passed and turned that ship. Perceiving then that the larboard tiers of the *Conquerant* did not fire, for the reasons explained above, she placed herself alongside of that vessel, and soon disabled her. The *Zealous*, the second English ship, followed the movement of the *Goliath*, and anchoring alongside the *Guerrier*, which could not return her fire, speedily dismasted her. The *Orion*, the third English ship, executed the same manoeuvre, but was retarded in her movement by the attack of a French frigate, and anchored between the *Franklin* and the *Peuple Souverain*. The *Vanguard*, the English admiral's ship, cast anchor athwart the *Spartiate*, the third French ship. The *Defence*, the *Bellerophon*, the *Majestic*, and the *Minotaur*, followed the same movement, and engaged the centre of the French line as far as the *Tonnant*, the eighth ship.

NAVAL BATTLE OF ABOUKIR

The French admiral and his two seconds formed a line of three ships, very superior to those of the English. The fire was terrible; the *Bellerophon* was disabled, dismasted, and compelled to strike. Several other English ships were obliged to sheer off; and if, at that moment Admiral Villeneuve, who commanded the right wing of the French, had cut his cables and fallen on the English line, with the five ships under his command, the *Heureux, Timoleon, Mercure, Guillaume Tell, Genereux,* and the *Diane* and *Justice* frigates, it would have been destroyed. The *Culloden* had struck on the Bequieres bank, and the *Leander* was engaged in endeavouring to bring her off. The *Alexander* and *Swiftsure,* two other English ships, seeing that our right did not stir, and that the centre of the English line was hard pressed, made towards it. The *Alexander* took the place of the *Bellerophon,* and the *Swiftsure* attacked the *Franklin*. The *Leander,* which until then had been engaged in righting the *Culloden,* perceiving the danger in which the centre stood, hastened to reinforce it. The victory was still far from being decided. The *Guerrier* and *Conquerant* no longer fired, but they were the worst ships in the squadron; and, on the side of the English, the *Culloden* and *Bellerophon* were disabled. The centre of the French line had, by the great superiority of its fire, occasioned the ships opposed to it much more damage than it had sustained. The English had only seventy-fours, and those of a small rate. It was to be presumed that the fire being thus kept up all night, Admiral Villeneuve would at last get under way in the morning, and the greatest success might yet be expected from the attack of five good ships which, as yet, had neither fired nor sustained a single cannon shot. But, at eleven o'clock, the *Orient* took fire, and blew up. This unforeseen accident decided the victory. The dreadful explosion of this ship suspended the action for a quarter of an hour. Our line, undismayed by this shocking spectacle, recommenced firing. The *Franklin, Tonnant, Peuple Souverain, Spartiate,* and *Aquilon,* maintained the action till three o'clock in the morning. From three to five o'clock the firing slackened on both sides. Between five and six it redoubled, and became terrible. What would it have been if the *Orient* had not been blown up? In short, the battle was raging at noon, and was not over before two o'clock. It was not until then that Villeneuve seemed to awaken, and to perceive that the fleet had been fighting for twenty hours. He cut his cables, and stood out with the *Guillaume Tell,* his flag-ship, the *Genereux,* and the *Diane* and *Justice* frigates. The three other ships of his wing ran ashore without fighting. Thus, notwithstanding the terrible accident of the *Orient,* and the singular inactivity of Villeneuve which prevented five ships from firing a single gun, the loss and confusion of the English were such, that twenty-four hours after the battle the French flag was still flying on board the *Tonnant*; and Nelson had no ship in a condition to attack her. Not only the *Guillaume Tell* and *Genereux* were not pursued by any English ship, but the enemy, in the disabled state they were in, were glad

FACSIMILE OF A PORTION OF THE MANUSCRIPT REWRITTEN BY NAPOLEON HIMSELF

It reads: 'L'amiral Villeneuve étant brave et bon marin on se demande la rasion de cette singulière conduite—il attendait des ordres. On assure que l'amiral lui donna celui d'appareiller mais que la fumée l'empêcha de l'appercevoir. Mais fallait-il donc un ordre pour prendre part au combat et secourir ses camarades? L'Orient a sauté a 11 heures. Depuis ce temps jusqu'à 2 heures aprèsmidi c.à.d. pendant 13 heures on s'est battu. C'est alors Villeneuve qui commandait, pourquoi donc n'a-t-il rien fait? Villeneuve était d'un caractère irrésolu et sans vigueur.' (Translation on page 287).

to see them make off. Admiral Brueys obstinately defended the honour of the French flag; although he had received several wounds he would not go down to the cock-pit. He died on his quarter-deck giving his orders. Casabianca, Thermard, and Du Petit-Thouard, acquired glory on this unfortunate day. Rear-Admiral Villeneuve, according to Nelson and the English, might have decided the victory even after the explosion of the *Orient*. Even at midnight had he got under way, and engaged in the action with the ships of his wing, he might have annihilated the English squadron. He remained a peaceful spectator of the battle. As Rear-Admiral Villeneuve was a brave and good seaman, one has to ask what was the cause of this singular conduct? He waited for orders! It is positively asserted that the admiral made the signal for him to weigh anchor, but that the smoke prevented him from seeing it. But was there any need of an order to take part in the battle and assist his comrades?

The *Orient* blew up at eleven o'clock; from that time till two in the afternoon, that is to say, for fifteen hours, the fight was continued. It was then Villeneuve who commanded; why did he do nothing? Villeneuve was of an irresolute character, destitute of energy.

The crews of the three ships which grounded, and those of the two frigates, landed on the beach at Aboukir. A hundred men escaped from the *Orient*, and a great number of sailors from the other ships took refuge on land, at the moment of the decision of the battle, availing themselves of the disorder of the enemy. The army thus obtained 3,500 recruits; a nautical legion, three battalions strong, was formed of part of these men, to the number of 1,800. The rest recruited the artillery, infantry, and cavalry. The salvage was actively performed; many pieces of artillery, much ammunition, several masts and other pieces of timber were preserved, which became useful in the arsenal of Alexandria. We still had in the port the two ships the *Causse* and the *Dubois*, four Venetian built frigates, three French built frigates, all the light vessels and transports. A few days after the battle, Nelson set sail, and quitted the shores of Alexandria, leaving two ships of war to blockade the port. Forty Neapolitan transports solicited and obtained, from the commandant of Alexandria, leave to return home; the commander of the English cruisers collected them round him, took out the crews, and burnt the vessels. This violation of the rights of nations proved prejudicial to the English; the crews of the Italian and French transports saw that they had no resource but in the success of the French army, and took their measures accordingly with resolution. Nelson was received with triumph in the port of Naples.

The loss of the battle of Aboukir had great influence on the affairs of Egypt, and even on those of the world. Had the French fleet been saved, the expedition to Syria would have met with no obstacle; the battering-train could have been safely and easily conveyed beyond the Desert, and Saint-Jean d'Acre

NAVAL BATTLE OF ABOUKIR

would not have stopped the French army. But the French fleet being destroyed, the Divan took courage and ventured to declare war against France. The army lost a grand support; its position in Egypt was totally changed, and I was obliged to renounce the hope of establishing the French power permanently in the East, by the results of the expedition to Egypt.

Since the least ships of the line have been seventy-fours, the naval armaments of France, England and Spain, have never been composed of more than thirty ships. There have nevertheless, been armaments which have, for the time, been more considerable. A squadron of thirty ships of the line is equal to a land army of 120,000 men. An army of 120,000 men is a grand army, although there have sometimes been forces of still greater strength. A squadron of thirty ships contains at most a fifth part of the number of men in an army 120,000 strong. It carries five times more artillery, and of a very superior calibre. The expense of the *matériel* is very nearly the same. If the *matériel* of the whole artillery of 120,000 men, of their waggons, provisions, and hospitals, be compared with that of thirty ships, the expenses of both are equal, or nearly so. If we calculate 20,000 cavalry, and 20,000 artillery and waggon-train for the land force, the support of the army is incomparably more expensive than that of the navy.

France might have three fleets of thirty sail as well as three armies of 120,000 men.

War by land generally destroys more men than maritime war, being more perilous. The sailor, in a squadron, fights only once in a campaign; the soldier fights daily. The sailor, whatever may be the fatigues and dangers attached to his element, suffers much less than the soldier; he never endures hunger or thirst, he has always with him his lodging, his kitchen, his hospital, and medical stores. The naval armies, in the service of France and England, where cleanliness is preserved by discipline, and experience has taught all the measures proper to be adopted for the preservation of health, are less subject to sickness than land armies. Besides the dangers of battle, the sailor has to encounter those of storms; but art has so materially diminished the latter, that they cannot be compared to those which occur by land, such as popular insurrections, assassinations, and surprises by the enemy's light troops.

A general who is commander-in-chief of a naval army, and a general who is commander-in-chief of a land army, are men who stand in need of different qualities. The qualities adapted to the command of a land army are born with us, whilst those which are necessary for commanding a naval army can only be acquired by experience.

Alexander and Condé were able to command at a very early age; the art of war by land is an art of genius and inspiration; but neither Alexander nor Condé, at the age of twenty-two years, could have commanded a naval army.

NAVAL BATTLE OF ABOUKIR

In the latter, nothing is genius or inspiration, but all is positive and matter of experience. The marine general needs but one science, that of navigation. The commander by land requires many, or a talent equivalent to all, that of profiting by experience and knowledge of every kind. A marine general has nothing to guess; he knows where his enemy is, and knows his strength. A land general never knows anything with certainty, never sees his enemy plainly, nor knows positively where he is. When the armies are facing each other, the slightest accident of the ground, the least wood, may hide a party of the hostile army. The most experienced eye cannot be certain whether it sees the whole of the enemy's army, or only three-fourths of it. It is by the eyes of the mind, by the combination of all reasoning, by a sort of inspiration, that the land general sees, commands, and judges. The marine general requires nothing but an experienced eye; nothing relating to the enemy's strength is concealed from him. What creates great difficulty in the profession of the land commander, is the necessity of feeding so many men and animals; if he allows himself to be guided by the commissaries, he will never stir, and his expeditions will fail. The naval commander is never confined; he carries everything with him. A naval commander has no reconnoitring to perform, no ground to examine, no field of battle to study; Indian Ocean, Atlantic, or Channel, still it is a liquid plain. The most skilful can have no other advantage over the least experienced, than what arises from his knowledge of the winds which prevail in particular seas, from his foresight of those which will prevail there, or from his acquaintance with the signs of the atmosphere; qualities which are acquired by experience, and experience only.

The general commanding by land never knows the field of battle on which he is to operate. His *coup d'oeil* is one of inspiration, he has no positive data. The data from which a knowledge of the localities must be gained, are so contingent, that scarcely anything can be learnt from experience. It is a facility of instantly seizing all the relations of different grounds, according to the nature of the country; in short, it is a gift called *coup d'oeil militaire,* which great generals have received from nature. Nevertheless, the observations which may be made on topographical maps, and the facilities arising from education and the habit of reading such maps, may afford some assistance.

A naval commander-in-chief depends more on the captains of his ships, than a military commander-in-chief on his generals. The latter has the power of taking on himself the direct command of the troops, of moving to every point, and of remedying the false movements by others. The personal influence of the naval commander is confined to the men on board his own ship; the smoke prevents the signals from being seen. The winds change, or may not be the same throughout the space occupied by his line. Of all arts, then, this is the one in which the subalterns have the most to take upon themselves.

NAVAL BATTLE OF ABOUKIR

Our naval defeats are to be attributed to three causes: first, to irresolution and want of energy in the commanders-in-chief; secondly, to errors in tactics; thirdly, to want of experience and nautical knowledge in the captains of ships, and to the opinion these officers maintain that they ought only to act according to signals. The action off Ushant, those during the Revolution in the Ocean, and those in the Mediterranean in 1793 and 1794, were all lost through these different causes. Admiral Villaret, though personally brave, was wanting in strength of mind, and was not even attached to the cause for which he fought. Martin was a good seaman, but a man of little resolution. They were, moreover, both influenced by the Representatives of the People, who, possessing no experience, sanctioned erroneous operations.

The principle of making no movement, except according to signal from the admiral, is the more erroneous, because it is always in the power of the captain of a ship to find reasons in justification of his failure to execute the signals made to him. In all the sciences necessary to war, theory is useful for giving general ideas which form the mind; but their strict execution is always dangerous; they are only axes by which curves are to be traced. Besides rules themselves compel one to reason in order to discover whether they ought to be departed from.

Although often superior in force to the English, we never knew how to attack them, and we allowed their squadrons to escape whilst we were wasting time in useless manoeuvres. The first law of maritime tactics ought to be, that as soon as the admiral has made the signal that he means to attack, every captain should make the necessary movements for attacking one of the enemy's ships taking part in the action, and supporting his neighbours.

This was latterly the principle of English tactics. Had it been adopted in France, Admiral Villeneuve would not have thought himself blameless at Aboukir, for remaining inactive with five or six ships, that is to say, with half the squadron, for twenty-four hours, whilst the enemy was overpowering the other wing.

The French navy is called on to acquire a superiority over the English. The French understand building better than their rivals, and French ships, the English themselves admit, are better than theirs. The guns are superior in calibre to those of the English by one-fourth. These are two great advantages.

The English are superior in discipline. The Toulon and Scheldt squadrons had adopted the same practice and customs as the English, and were attempting as severe a discipline, with the difference belonging to the character of the two nations. The English discipline is perfectly slavish; it is patron and serf. It is only kept up by the influence of the most dreadful terror. Such a state of things would degrade and debase the French character, which requires a paternal kind of discipline, more founded on honour and sentiment.

NAVAL BATTLE OF ABOUKIR

In most of the battles with the English which we have lost, we have either been inferior in strength, or combined with Spanish ships, which, being ill organized, and in these latter times degenerate, have weakened our line instead of strengthening it; or, finally, the commanders-in-chief, who wished to fight while advancing to meet the enemy, have wavered when they fell in with him, retreated under various pretexts, and thus compromised the bravest men.

Chapter XXV

EGYPT

Alexandria. The Nile and its inundations. Ancient and modern population. Division and productions of Egypt. Commerce. Alexander. Of the different races by which Egypt is inhabited. The Desert and its inhabitants. Government and importance of Egypt. Army policy.

Alexandria was built by Alexander. It had become, under the Ptolemies, so considerable a city as to excite the jealousy of Rome. It was, unquestionably, the second city in the world. Its population amounted to several millions. In the seventh century it was taken by Amru in the first year of the hegira, after a siege of fourteen months. The Arabs lost 28,000 men in this siege. The walls of Alexandria were twelve miles round; the city contained 4,000 palaces, 4,000 baths, 400 theatres, 12,000 shops and above 50,000 Jews. The walls were raised in the wars of the Arabs and the Roman empire. This city remained, ever after, in a state of decline.

The Arabs erected a new wall, that which still exists; it is not more than 3,000 toises round; but even that extent denotes a large city. The whole city is now on the isthmus. The Pharos is no longer an island; the present town is on the isthmus which joins it to the continent. It is enclosed by a wall which bars the isthmus, and is only 600 toises long. It has two good ports, the new and old. The old port can shelter squadrons of men-of-war, however numerous, from the weather or a superior force. The Nile now only reaches Alexandria at the period of the inundations. Its waters are preserved in vast cisterns, by the appearance of which we were much struck. The old Arabian wall is covered by Lake Mareotis, which extends nearly to the tower of the Arabs; so that Alexandria is now only assailable on the Aboukir side. Lake Mareotis also leaves a part of the city walls uncovered, beyond that of the Arabs.

EGYPT

Pompey's column, situate without the Arabs' wall, and 300 toises from it, was formerly in the centre of the city.

I passed several days in laying down the principles of the fortifications of the city. All my orders were executed with the greatest intelligence by Colonel Cretin, the most skilful engineer officer in France. I ordered all the Arabs' wall to be restored; the labour was not very great. This wall was supported by the occupation of the triangular fort which formed its right, and which still exists. The centre and Aboukir side were each supported by a fort. They were erected on little mounts of rubbish which commanded all the country from an elevation of twenty toises behind the Arabs' wall. The wall of the present town was restored as a reduit; but it was commanded in front by a great mount of rubbish. This was occupied by a fort, to which the name of Caffarelli was given. This fort and the wall of the present town formed a complete system, susceptible of a long defence, even after the rest should have been taken. It required artillery to occupy these heights with promptitude and solidity. The conception and direction of these works were confided to Cretin.

In a few months he formed three inexpugnable forts, without much labour; he established ramparts of masonry, presenting scarps of eighteen or twenty feet, which place the batteries quite out of the reach of an escalade, and he covered these works of masonry with profiles which he contrived in the height; so that they were not seen from any part. It would have required millions of money and years of labour to have strengthened these forts so effectually, under a less skilful engineer. Towards the sea, the tower of Marabou, and the Pharos, were occupied. Strong side batteries were constructed, which produced a wonderful effect as often as the English presented themselves to bombard the town. Pompey's column strikes the imagination like everything that is sublime. Cleopatra's needles are still on the same spot. In searching the tomb in which Alexander was interred, a little statue in *terracotta* was found, ten or twelve inches high, dressed in the Greek fashion; the hair was curled with great art, and the locks meet on the nape of the neck; it is quite a masterpiece. There are, at Alexandria, large and handsome mosques, convents of Copts, and some houses in the European style belonging to the consuls.

It is four leagues from Alexandria to Aboukir; the ground is sandy and covered with palm-trees. At the extremity of the promontory of Aboukir is a fort built of stone; there is a little isle at the distance of 600 toises. A tower and thirty guns in this island would secure the anchorage for several ships of war, nearly as at the isle of Aix.

The way to Rosetta passes Lake Maadieh at its junction with the sea, which is 100 toises wide; ships of war, drawing eight or ten feet water, can enter it. One of the seven branches of the Nile formerly fell into this lake. To go to

EGYPT

Rosetta without passing the lake, it must be turned, which increases the distance by three or four leagues.

The Nile rises in the mountains of Abyssinia, flows from South to North, and falls into the Mediterranean, after passing through Abyssinia, the deserts of Nubia, and Egypt. It runs eight hundred leagues; of which extent its course through the Egyptian territory forms two hundred. It enters Egypt at the isle of Elfilah or Elephantina, and fertilizes the arid deserts through which it runs. Its inundations are regular and productive; regular, because they are caused by the tropical rains; productive, because these rains, falling in torrents on the mountains of Abyssinia, covered with wood, carry with them a fertilizing slime, which the Nile deposits on the lands. The North winds prevail during the rise of the river, and promote its productive effects by keeping back the waters.

It never rains in Egypt. The earth, in that country, is only rendered fertile by the regular inundation of the Nile. When it is high, the year is abundant; when it is low, the harvest is ordinary.

It is a hundred and fifty leagues from the Isle of Elephantina to Cairo, and this valley, watered by the Nile, is on an average five leagues in width. Beyond Cairo the stream separates into two branches, and forms a sort of triangle which it covers by overflowing. The base of this triangle is sixty leagues, from the Arabs' tower to Pelusium; and the sides are fifty leagues in length, from the sea to Cairo; one of these arms falls into the Mediterranean near Rosetta; the other near Damietta. In ancient times this river had seven mouths.

The Nile begins to rise at the summer solstice; the inundation increases till the equinox, after which it gradually decreases. It is, therefore, between Spetember and March that all agricultural labours must be performed. The landscape is then delightful; it is the season of flowers and of harvest. The dyke of the Nile is cut at Cairo in the course of September, and sometimes in the beginning of October. After the month of March the earth gets so completely soaked, that it is dangerous to cross the plains on horseback, and excessively fatiguing to do so on foot. A burning sun, which is never tempered by clouds or rain, burns up all the herbs and plants, except those which can be watered. Hence the salubrity of the stagnant waters, which are preserved in this country in the low grounds. In Europe, such marshes would cause death by their exhalations; in Egypt they do not even occasion fevers.

The surface of the valley of the Nile, such as it has just been described, is equal to a sixth part of ancient France; which would not imply, in a state of prosperity, above four or five millions of population. Yet the Arabian historians assure us that at the time of the conquest by Amru, Egypt contained twenty millions of inhabitants and upwards of twenty thousand cities. In this

EGYPT

calculation, however, they included not only the valley of the Nile, but the Oases,* and the deserts belonging to Egypt.

This assertion of the Arabian historians cannot be classed amongst those ancient traditions which judicious criticism disallows. A good administration, and a numerous population, might greatly extend the benefits of the inundation of the Nile. Undoubtedly, if the valley presented a surface of the same nature as our lands in France, it would be incapable of feeding more than four or five millions of people. But in France there are mountains, sands, heaths, and uncultivated lands, whilst in Egypt everything is productive. To this consideration it must be added that the valley of the Nile, fecundated by the waters, the mud, and the warmth of the climate, is more fertile than our best lands, and that two-thirds, or perhaps three-fourths of France produce but little. There is, moreover, reason to believe that the Nile fertilized several Oases.

Supposing all the canals which draw water from the Nile and carry it over the lands, to be ill kept up, or stopped, the course of the river would be much more rapid, the inundation would be less extensive, a greater mass of water would reach the sea, and the culture of the lands would be much diminished. But supposing, on the contrary, all the canals made for the purpose of irrigation to be kept in the best state, and as numerous, long, and deep as possible, and directed by art so as to water the greatest possible extent of desert in all directions, it may be conceived that a very small quantity of the waters of the Nile would be lost in the sea, and that the inundations fertilizing a greater extent of territory, cultivation would increase in the same proportion. Now there is no country in which government has more influence on agriculture, and consequently on population, than Egypt. The plains of Beauce and Brie are fecundated by a regular watering from the rains; government has, in this respect, no influence there. But in Egypt, where the irrigations can only be artificial, government is everything. If good, it adopts the best police regulations relative to the direction of the waters, the maintenance and construction of the irrigatory canals. If bad, partial, or weak, it favours localities or particular properties, to the detriment of the public interest, is unable to repress the civil dissensions of the provinces, when new canals are to be opened, or finally, allows them all to go to ruin; the consequence is, that the inundation is diminished, which lessens the extent of the lands capable of cultivation. Under a good administration the Nile gains on the Desert; under a bad one the Desert gains on the Nile. In Egypt, the Nile, or the genius of good, and the Desert, or the genius of evil, stand constantly opposed to each other; and it may be said that property there does not so much consist in the possession of a field, as in the right established by general rules of government, of having

* The Oases are parts of the desert where a little vegetation is found; they are isles, as it were, amidst a sea of sand.

the benefit of the inundation, at a certain period of the year, and by a certain canal.

Egypt has been continually declining for two hundred years. At the time of the French expedition, this country still contained from 2,500,000 to 2,800,000 inhabitants. If it continues to be governed in the same way, it will not contain above 1,500,000, fifty years hence.

By constructing a canal to draw the waters of the Nile into the great Oasis, a vast kingdom was acquired. It is reasonable to admit that in the times of Sesostris and the Ptolemies, Egypt was able to feed from twelve to fifteen millions of inhabitants, by agriculture alone, without the aid of commerce.

This country is divided into Upper, Middle and Lower Egypt. The Upper, which is called Saide, forms two provinces, namely, Thebes and Girgeh; Middle Egypt, named Vostanieh, forms four, namely, Benisouf, Siout, Fayoum, and Daifih; Lower Egypt, called Bahhire, has nine, Bahhire, Rosetta, Garbieh, Menouf, Damietta, Mansoura, Sharkieh, Kelioubieh, and Ghizeh.

Egypt likewise includes the Great Oasis, the valley of the Sea Without Water, and the Oasis of Jupiter Ammon.

The Great Oasis is situate parallel to the Nile, on the left bank; it is a hundred and fifty leagues in length. Its remotest points from this river are at a distance of sixty leagues; its nearest only twenty leagues from the Nile.

The valley of the Sea Without Water, near which are the Natron lakes, the source of a considerable branch of commerce, is fifteen leagues from the Rosetta branch. This valley was formerly fertilized by the Nile. The Oasis of Jupiter Ammon is eighty leagues distant, on the right bank of the river.

The Egyptian territory extends towards the frontiers of Asia, as far as the hills which are found between El-Arisch, El-Kanones, and Refah, about forty leagues from Pelusium, whence the line of demarcation crosses the Wilderness, passes by Suez, and along the shore of the Red Sea, as far as Berenice. The Nile runs parallel to this sea; its remotest points are fifty leagues from it, its nearest thirty. One of its elbows, indeed, is but twenty-two leagues distant from the Red Sea, but then it is separated from it by impassable mountains. The square superficies of Egypt is two hundred leagues in length, by a breadth varying from one hundred and ten to one hundred and twenty leagues.

Egypt produces abundance of wheat, rice, and pulse. This country was the granary of Rome, and is at present that of Constantinople. It also produces sugar, indigo, senna, cassia, nitre, flax, and hemp; but has neither wood, coal, nor oil. It is also destitute of tobacco, which it obtains from Syria; and of coffee, with which Arabia supplies it. It feeds numerous flocks, independently of those of the Desert, and a multitude of poultry. The chickens are hatched in ovens, and an enormous quantity is procured by this method.

EGYPT

This country serves as an intermediate district between Africa and Asia. The caravans arrive at Cairo like ships on a coast, at the moment when they are least expected, and from the most remote countries. Signals of their arrival are made at Ghizeh, and they approach by the Pyramids. At that spot they are informed of the place at which they are to cross the Nile, and where they are to encamp near Cairo. The caravans thus announced are those of pilgrims or traders of Morocco, Fez, Tunis, Algiers, or Tripoli, going to Mecca, and bringing goods to barter at Cairo. They are usually composed of several hundred camels, sometimes even of several thousands, and escorted by armed men. Caravans also come from Abyssinia, from the interior of Africa, from Tagoast, and the places in direct communication with the Cape of Good Hope and Senegal. They bring slaves, gum, gold dust, elephants' tusks, and in general all the produce of those countries, which they exchange for the merchandize of Europe and of the Levant. In short, caravans come from all parts of Arabia and Syria, bringing coals, wood, fruits, oil, coffee, tobacco, and in general, all that is supplied by the interior of India.

Egypt has at all times served as the mart for the commerce of India. It was anciently carried on by way of the Red Sea. The goods were landed at Berenice, and transported on the backs of camels for eighty leagues, as far as Thebes, or were sent up by water from Berenice to Cosseir; which lengthened the navigation by eighty leagues, but reduced the carriage to thirty. On arriving at Thebes they were embarked on the Nile, to be afterwards spread throughout Europe. Such was the cause of the great prosperity of Thebes with her hundred gates. Goods were also conveyed beyond Cosseir, as far as Suez, whence they were transported on the backs of camels as far as Memphis and Pelusium, that is to say, for the space of thirty leagues. In the time of Ptolemy, the canal from Suez to the Nile was open. From thence, therefore, there was no land carriage of merchandize; it reached Baboust and Pelusium, on the banks of the Nile and Mediterranean, by water.

Independently of the commerce of India, Egypt has a domestic trade of her own. Fifty years of a French administration would increase her population in a great proportion. She would afford such a market for our manufactures as would produce a great benefit in every branch of our industry; and we should soon be called upon to supply all the wants of the inhabitants of the deserts of Africa, Abyssinia, Arabia, and a great part of Syria. These people are destitute of everything; and what are Saint-Domingo and all our colonies compared to such vast regions?

France, in return, would obtain from Egypt wheat, rice, sugar, nitre, and all the productions of Africa and Asia.

If the French were established in Egypt, it would be impossible for the English to maintain themselves long in India. Squadrons built on the coasts of the Red Sea, victualled with the productions of the country, manned and filled with our troops stationed in Egypt, would infallibly render us masters of India, at the moment when England least expected it.

Even supposing the commerce of that country is free, as it has hitherto been, between the English and French, the former will be in no condition to stand the competition. The possibility of the reconstruction of the canal of Suez being a problem resolved, and the labour it would require being of little importance, the goods would arrive so rapidly by this canal, and with such a saving of capital, that the French might appear in the markets with immense advantages: the trade of India, by way of the ocean, would be annihilated.

Alexander distinguished himself more by founding Alexandria, and by the plan of transporting thither the seat of his empire, than by his most striking victories. That city was calculated to be the capital of the world. It is situated between Asia and Africa, with access to Europe and the Indies. Its port is the only anchorage on a coast of five hundred leagues, reaching from Tunis, the site of ancient Carthage, to Alexandretta; it is on one of the ancient mouths of the Nile. All the fleets in the world might lie there; and in the old port they are safe from the winds and from every attack. Ships drawing twenty-one feet of water have entered that port without difficulty. Those drawing twenty-three feet might do so; and by means of works which would not be very considerable, the entrance might be rendered easy, even for three-deckers. As First Consul I had twelve seventy-fours, drawing only twenty-one feet of water, built at Toulon, upon the English plan; and there was no reason to complain of their sailing when they were placed in our squadrons. They are, however, less fit for service in India, because they carry less water and provisions.

The dilapidation of the canals of the Nile prevents its waters from reaching Alexandria. They no longer arrive there except in the time of the inundation, and it is found necessary to have cisterns to preserve them. By the side of the port of this town is Aboukir road, which might be rendered safe for a few ships; if a port were constructed on Aboukir island, they would be as safe there as at the Isle of Aix.

Rosetta, Bourlos, and Damietta, can only receive small vessels, there being only six or seven feet water over the bars. Pelusium, El-Arisch, and Gaza, can never have had ports; and the lakes of Bourlos and Menzaleh, which communicate with the sea, can only be entered by ships which do not draw above six or seven feet of water.

At the period of the expedition to Egypt, that country was inhabited by three races of men; the Mamelukes or Circassians, the Ottomans or Janissaries, and Spahis, and the Arabs or natives of the country.

These three races differ in principles, manners, and language. They have nothing in common but their religion. The usual language of the Mamelukes and Ottomans is Turkish; the natives speak the Arabic language. At the time

EGYPT

of the arrival of the French, the Mamelukes governed the country, and possessed all wealth and power in it. They had for their chiefs twenty-three Beys, equal and independent of each other; that is to say, subject only to that one, who, by his talents and bravery could obtain all their suffrages.

The household of a Bey is composed of from four to eight hundred slaves, all horsemen, each of whom has two or three fellahs to attend him. They have several officers for the honorary duty of their houses. The Kiaschefs are the lieutenants of the Beys, under whom they command this militia, and are lords of the villages. The Beys have estates in the provinces, and a house at Cairo. One large building serves for their lodging and their harem; around the courts are those of the slaves, guards, and domestics.

The Beys can only recruit their numbers in Circassia. Young Circassians are sold by their mothers, or stolen by people who make it a trade, and sold at Cairo by the merchants of Constantinople. Blacks and Ottomans are sometimes admitted, but these exceptions are rare.

The slaves forming part of a Bey's household are adopted by him, and compose his family. They are intelligent and brave, and rise successively from rank to rank until they attain that of Kiaschef, or even of Bey.

The Mamelukes have few children, and those they have do not live so long as the natives of the country. They very seldom continue their race beyond the third generation. The sterility of their marriages has been attributed to an anti-physical inclination. The Arabian women are fat and clumsy; they affect inactivity, can scarcely walk, and remain whole days motionless on a divan. A young Mameluke of fourteen or fifteen, supple and active, displaying admirable grace and address in exercising a beautiful courser, excites the senses in a different manner. It is certain that all the Beys and Kiaschefs had been subjected in youth to the vices of their masters, and afterwards pursued the same course with their handsome slaves; they do not deny it themselves.

The Greeks and Romans were accused of the same vice. Of all nations, that which has been least addicted to this monstrous inclination, is undoubtedly France. This is ascribed to the fact that there is no country in which the women are more captivating, by the lightness and elegance of their figures, their vivacity, and grace.

There were in Egypt about 60 or 70,000 individuals of the Circassian race.

The Ottomans established themselves in Egypt at the time of the conquest by Selim, in the sixteenth century. They form the corps of Janissaries and Spahis, and have been increased by the addition of all the Ottomans enrolled in these companies, according to the customs of the empire. They amount to about 200,000, constantly debased and humbled by the Mamelukes.

The Arabs compose the mass of the population; their chiefs are the grand scheiks, the descendants of those of the Arabs, who in the time of the prophet, at the beginning of the Hegira, made the conquest of Egypt. They are at once the chief nobility and the doctors of the law; they possess villages and a great number of slaves, and never travel but on mules. The mosques are under their inspection; that of Jemil-Azar alone has sixty grand scheiks. It is a kind of Sorbonne, which decides all religious questions, and even serves as an university. The philosophy of Aristotle, and the history and morals of the Koran are taught there; it is the most renowned school in the East. Its scheiks are the principal ones of the country; the Mamelukes feared them; and even the Porte was cautious in its conduct towards them. It was only through them that the country could be influenced and excited. Some of them descend from the prophet, as the scheik El Bekry; others from the second wife of the prophet, as the scheik El Sadda. If the sultan of Constantinople were at Cairo, at the period of either of the two great festivals of the empire, he would celebrate it at the house of one of these scheiks. This sufficiently shews the high respect in which they are held. It is such that there is not a single instance of the infliction of an infamous punishment on one of them. When the government considers the condemnation of one of them indispensable, it causes him to be poisoned, and his funeral is performed with the honours due to his rank, and as if his death had been a natural one.

All the Arabs of the Desert are of the same race as the scheiks, and revere them. The fellahs are Arabs,—not that all their progenitors came at the commencement of the Hegira, with the army that conquered Egypt; it is supposed that not above 100,000 settled in Egypt through the conquest; but as all the natives of the country, at that period, embraced the Mahometan faith, they became mingled in the same manner as the Franks and Gauls. The scheiks are the men of law and religion; the Mamelukes and Janissaries the men of power and government. The difference between them is greater than that which exists in France between the military and the priesthood, for they are entirely distinct races and families.

The Copts are Catholics; but do not acknowledge the Pope; there are nearly 150,000 of them in Egypt. They enjoy the free exercise of their religion. They descend from families which remained Christian after the conquests of the caliphs. The Syrian Catholics are few in number. Some insist that they are the descendants of the crusaders; others that they spring from natives of the country, who, like the Copts, professed Christianity at the time of the Conquest, and who have preserved some differences in their religion. This is another Catholic sect. There are few Jews or Greeks. The Patriarch of Alexandria, who is the chief of the latter, considers himself equal to the Patriarch of Constantinople, and superior to the Pope. He lives in a convent at Old Cairo, in the manner in which the head of a religious order in Europe would live, with 30,000 livres per annum. The Franks are not numerous; they consist of English, French, Spanish, or Italian families, settled in the country for purposes of trade, or of persons sent thither in the service of European houses.

EGYPT

The Deserts are inhabited by tribes of wandering Arabs, who live under tents. Of these tribes there are about sixty, all dependent on Egypt, and forming a population of about 120,000 souls, capable of furnishing from 18 to 20,000 cavalry. They command the different parts of the Deserts, which they look upon as their property, and where they possess a great quantity of cattle, camels, horses, and sheep. These Arabs often make war amongst themselves, on account of differences respecting the limits of their tribes, the pasturage of their cattle, or other matters. The Desert alone cannot feed them, for it produces nothing. They possess some Oases, like isles, in the midst of the Desert, which furnish fresh water, grass and trees. These they cultivate, and retire to at certain seasons of the year. Nevertheless, the Arabs in general are in a state of wretchedness, and constantly stand in need of Egypt. They come every year to cultivate the borders of the country, sell the produce of their flocks, let their camels to carry burthens in the Desert, and employ the profit which they derive from this traffic in the purchase of the articles for which they have occasion. The Deserts are plains of sand, without water or vegetation, the monotonous aspect of which is varied only by hillocks, mounts, or banks of sand. It is, however, uncommon to travel twenty or four and twenty leagues in the Desert without finding a spring of water; but they afford only a scanty supply, are more or less brackish, and almost all of them exhale an alkaline odour. Great quantities of bones of men and animals are found in the Desert, which are used for making fires. Gazelles are also seen there, as well as flocks of ostriches, which look, at a distance, like Arabs on horseback.

There exists no trace of roads; the Arabs are accustomed, from infancy, to guide their course by the sinuosities of the sand hills or banks, by the accidents of the ground, or by the stars. The winds sometimes displace the mounts of moving sand, which renders marching in the Deserts very laborious, and often dangerous. Sometimes the ground is firm; at others it sinks beneath the feet. It is uncommon to meet with trees, except around the wells, where a few palm-trees are found. There are marshes in the Deserts, where the waters settle and remain for a longer or shorter period. Near these fens some thorns grow, to the height of a foot, or eighteen inches, which serve to feed the camels; this is the rich part of the Deserts. Disagreeable as it is to travel in these sands, people are often obliged to cross them, in order to communicate between the south and north of Egypt, as the distance would be tripled by following all the windings of the course of the Nile.

There are tribes of 1,500 or 2,000 souls, which have 300 horsemen, and 1,400 camels, and occupy a hundred square leagues of ground. They had formerly an excessive dread of the Mamelukes. One of the latter would put ten Arabs to flight, because the Mamelukes had not only a great military superiority over them, but a moral superiority also. Besides, the Arabs had reason to be cautious in their conduct towards them, as they wanted them to purchase

EGYPT

or hire their camels, to supply them with grain, and to allow them to cultivate the border of Egypt.

If the extraordinary situation of Egypt, whose prosperity depends upon the extent of the inundations, requires a good administration, the necessity of keeping in awe 20 or 30,000 thieves, who are independent of justice, because they take refuge in the immensity of the Desert, no less urgently requires an energetic administration. In modern times they have carried their audacity to such a pitch, as to come and plunder villages, and kill the fellahs; and yet this did not occasion any regular pursuit. One day, being surrounded by the divan of the grand-scheiks, I was informed that the Arabs of the tribe of Osnadis had killed a fellah, and carried off some flocks; I appeared highly indignant, and, in an animated tone, ordered a staff officer to march immediately into the Bahireh, with 200 dromedaries and 300 horsemen, to obtain reparation, and punish the guilty parties. The scheik Elmodi, who witnessed this order, and my emotion, said to me with a laugh, 'Was this fellah thy cousin, that his death excites so much anger in thee?'—'Yes', replied I, 'all whom I command are my children.' 'Taib'* said the scheik, 'that is spoken like the prophet himself.'

Egypt has, in all ages, excited the jealousy of the nations who have governed the world. Octavius, after the death of Antony, united this country to the empire. He would not send a proconsul to it, but divided it into twelve praetorships. Antony had drawn upon himself the hatred of the Romans, by giving rise to suspicions of an intention to make Alexandria the capital of the republic. It seems probable that Egypt, in the time of Octavius, contained from 12 to 15,000,000 of inhabitants. Her wealth was immense; her territories were the true canal of the commerce of India; and Alexandria, from its situation, seemed destined to become the seat of the empire of the world. But several obstacles prevented this city from attaining all the greatness of which it seemed capable. The Romans were apprehensive that the national spirit of the Arabs, a brave people, inured to fatigues, who were free from the effeminacy of the inhabitants of Antioch or Asia Minor, and whose immense cavalry had enabled Hannibal to triumph over Rome, might make their country a centre of revolt against the Roman empire.

Selim had still greater reason to dread Egypt. It was the holy land; the natural mother country of Arabia, and the granary of Constantinople. An ambitious Pacha, favoured by circumstances, and by a bold enterprising character, might have restored the Arabian nation, and struck terror into the Ottomans, already threatened by that immense Greek population, which forms the majority of the inhabitants of Constantinople and its environs. Accordingly, Selim was unwilling to intrust the government of Egypt to one Pacha only. He was even fearful that the division of the country into several

* A word used by the Arabs to express great satisfaction.

pachaships would not be a sufficient guarantee; and endeavoured to ensure the submission of this province, by confiding its government to twenty-three Beys, each having a household of from 400 to 800 slaves. These slaves were to be their sons, or natives of Circassia, but never of Arabia or of the country. By these means he created a militia completely foreign to Arabia. He established in Egypt the general system of the empire, Janissaries and Spahis, and placed at their head a Pacha, representing the Grand Signor, with the authority of a viceroy, over the whole province, but who, being restrained by the Mamelukes, could not carry into effect any plan for rendering himself independent.

The Mamelukes, thus called to the government of Egypt, sought for auxiliaries. They were too ignorant and too few to perform the functions of collectors of the revenues; but they were unwilling to intrust those duties to the natives of the country, whom they feared, through the same spirit of jealousy which made the Sultan fear the Arabs. They chose the Copts and Jews. The Copts are, it is true, natives of the country, but of a proscribed religion. As Christians, they are out of the protection of the Koran, and can only be protected by the sabre; they could therefore give no umbrage to the Mamelukes. Thus did this soldiery of 10 or 12,000 horse engage, as their agents and men of business, the 200,000 Copts who inhabit Egypt. Every village had a Coptic receiver: all the business of finances and administration was in the hands of the Copts.

The tolerance which prevails throughout the Ottoman empire, and the species of protection afforded to the Christians, are the result of ancient views. The sultan and the policy of Constantinople like to defend a class of men from which they have nothing to fear, because these men form a feeble minority in Armenia, Syria, and all Asia Minor; because, moreover, they are in a state of natural opposition to the people of the country, and could not, in any case, league with them to re-establish the Syrian or Arabian nation. This, however, will not apply to Greece, where the Christians are superior in number. The sultans have committed a great error in leaving so considerable a number of Christians collected together. Sooner or later this circumstance will produce the ruin of the Ottomans.

The moral situation resulting from the different interests and different races that inhabit Egypt did not escape my observation; and it was upon this that I built my system of government. The French had little inclination to undertake the administration of justice in this country, nor could they have effected it if they had been willing. I intrusted it to the Arabs, that is to say, the Scheiks, and gave them the whole preponderance. Thenceforth I addressed the people through the medium of these men, at once the nobility and doctors of the law, and thus interested the national Arabian spirit, and the religion of the Koran, in the support of his government. I made war against the Mamelukes alone, and them I pursued with the utmost rigour; after the battle of the Pyramids there was but a wreck of them left. By the same policy I endeavoured to conciliate the Copts. These latter were connected with me by similarity of religion, and were exclusively versed in the administration of the country. But even had they not possessed that advantage, it would have been my policy to give it them, that I might not depend exclusively on the native Arabs, or have to struggle, with 25 or 30,000 men, against the force of the national and religious spirit. The Copts, seeing the Mamelukes destroyed, had no choice but to attach themselves to the French; and thus our army had, in every part of Egypt, spies, observers, comptrollers and financiers, independent of the natives, and hostile to them. As to the Janissaries and Ottomans, policy required that the Grand Signor should be respected in their persons; the standard of the Sultan waved in Egypt, and I was persuaded that the minister Talleyrand had proceeded to Constantinople, and that negotiations respecting Egypt had been opened with the Porte. Moreover the Mamelukes had made a point of humbling, reducing, and disorganizing the Janissary soldiery, who were their rivals; from the humiliation of the Ottoman militia had arisen a total disregard of the Pacha and of the authority of the Porte, which had arrived at such a pitch, that the Mamelukes often refused the *miry*; and these warriors would even have declared themselves entirely independent, but for the opposition of the Scheiks, or doctors of the law, which attached them to Constantinople by a religious sentiment as well as by inclination. The Scheiks and the people preferred the influence of Constantinople to that of the Mamelukes; they even frequently sent complaints thither, and sometimes succeeded in mitigating the arbitrary sway of the Beys.

Since the commencement of the decline of the Ottoman empire, the Porte has often sent expeditions against the Mamelukes, but they have always had the advantage in the end; and these wars have always concluded by an arrangement which has left the Mamelukes their power. An attentive perusal of the history of the events which have taken place in Egypt during the last two hundred years, will shew, that if power, instead of being intrusted to 12,000 Mamelukes, had been confided to a Pacha, who, like the Pacha of Albania, had recruited his forces in the country, the Arabian empire composed of a nation entirely distinct, with its peculiar spirit, prejudices, history, and language, and comprising Egypt, Arabia, and part of Africa, would have become independent like that of Morocco.

Chapter XXVI

EGYPT:
BATTLE OF THE PYRAMIDS

March of the army on Cairo. Despondency and complaints of the soldiers. Position and forces of the enemy. Manoeuvres of the French army. Impetuous charge of Murad-Bey repulsed. Taking of the intrenched camp. French head-quarters at Gizeh. Taking of the Isle of Rodah. Surrender of Cairo. Description of the city.

The evening after the action of Shebreis, (13 July, 1798) the French army lay at Shabur. This day had been arduous; the troops marched in order of battle and in quick time, in the hope of cutting off some vessels of the enemy's flotilla. In fact the Mamelukes were obliged to burn several. The army bivouacked at Shabur, under some fine sycamores, and found the fields full of battechs, a species of water-melons, furnishing a wholesome and refreshing nourishment. We met with them continually, as far as Cairo; and the soldier expressed how agreeable this fruit was to him, by naming it, like the ancient Egyptians, the holy *battech*.

On the following day the army began its march very late; some meat had been procured, which it was necessary to distribute. We waited for our flotilla, which could not ascend the current before the North wind had risen, and we slept at Kounscheric. The following day we arrived at Alkam. At that place General Zayoucheck received orders to land on the right bank, with all the dismounted cavalry, and to advance on Menouf and the point of the Delta. As there were no Arabs there, he was at liberty to make what movements he pleased, and was of great assistance in procuring us provisions. He took position at the head of the Delta, called the *cow's belly*.

EGYPT: BATTLE OF THE PYRAMIDS

On the 17th the army encamped at Abou-Neshabe, on the 18th at Wardan. Wardan is a large place; the troops bivouacked there in a great forest of palm trees. The soldiers began to understand the customs of the country, and to dig up the lentils and other pulse which the fellahs are accustomed to bury in the earth. We made short marches, on account of the necessity of procuring provisions, and in order to be always in a condition to receive the enemy. We often took up a position by ten o'clock in the morning, and the first care of the soldier was to bathe in the Nile. From Wardan we went to lie at Omedinar, when we perceived the Pyramids. All the glasses in the army were instantly levelled at these most ancient monuments in the world. They might be taken for enormous masses of rock, but the regularity and right lines of the angles betray the hand of man. The Pyramids border the horizon of the valley on the left bank of the Nile.

We were approaching Cairo, and were informed, by the people of the country, that the Mamelukes, combined with the troops of that city, and with a considerable number of Arabs, Janissaries, and Spahis, were waiting for us between the Nile and the Pyramids, covering Gizeh. They boasted that our success would end there.

We halted a day at Omedinar. This repose served to get our arms in readiness, and to prepare us for battle. Melancholy and sadness prevailed in the army. As the Hebrews, wandering in the wilderness, complained, and angrily asked Moses for the onions and fleshpots of Egypt, the French soldiers constantly regretted the luxuries of Italy. In vain were they assured that the country was the most fertile in the world, that it was even superior to Lombardy; how were they to be persuaded of this when they could get neither bread nor wine? We encamped on immense quantities of wheat, but there was neither mill nor oven in the country. The biscuit brought from Alexandria had long been exhausted; the soldiers were even reduced to bruise the wheat between two stones, and to make cakes, which they baked under the ashes. Many parched the wheat in a pan, after which they boiled it. This was the best way to use the grain, but after all it was not bread. The apprehensions of the soldiers increased daily; and rose to such a pitch, that a great number of them said there was no great city of Cairo; and that the place bearing that name was, like Damanhour, a vast assemblage of mere huts, destitute of everything that could render life comfortable or agreeable. To such a melancholy state of mind had they brought themselves, that two dragoons threw themselves, completely clothed, into the Nile, where they were drowned. It is, nevertheless, true that though there was neither bread nor wine, the resources which were procured with wheat, lentils, meat, and sometimes pigeons, furnished the army with food of some kind. But the evil was in the ferment of the mind. The officers complained more loudly than the soldiers, because the comparison was proportionately more disadvantageous

EGYPT: BATTLE OF THE PYRAMIDS

to them. In Egypt they found neither the quarters, the good tables, nor the luxury of Italy. Wishing to set an example, I used to bivouac in the midst of the army, and in the least commodious spots. No one had either tent or provisions; the dinner of myself and my staff consisted of a dish of lentils. The soldiers passed the evenings in political conversations, arguments, and complaints. *For what purpose are we come here?* said some of them; *the Directory has transported us. Caffarelli,* said others, *is the agent that has been made use of to deceive the General-in-chief.* Many of them, having observed that wherever there were vestiges of antiquity, they were carefully searched, vented their spite in invectives against the *savans,* or scientific men, who, they said, *had started the idea of the expedition in order to make these searches.* Jests were showered upon them, even in their presence. The men called an ass a *savant*; and said of Caffarelli Dufalga, alluding to his wooden leg, *He laughs at all these troubles; he has one foot in France.* But Dufalga and the *savans* soon regained the esteem of the army.

On the 21st we marched from Omedinar at one in the morning. This was to be a decisive day. At dawn, for the first time since the action of Shebreis, a Mameluke vanguard of 1,000 horse shewed itself; but it retreated in order without attempting anything; a few balls from our vanguard kept it in check. At ten o'clock we perceived Embabeh, and the enemy in line. Their right was supported on the Nile, where they had constructed a large intrenched camp, lined with forty pieces of cannon, and defended by about 20,000 infantry, janissaries, spahis, and militia from Cairo. The Mamelukes' line of cavalry rested its right on the intrenched camp, and extended its left in the direction of the Pyramids, crossing the road to Gizeh. There were about nine or ten thousand horse, as nearly as could be estimated. Thus the whole army consisted of 60,000 men, or thereabouts, including the infantry troops and the foot soldiers who attended every horseman. Two or three thousand Arabs kept the extreme left, and occupied the space between the Mamelukes and the Pyramids. These dispositions were formidable. We knew not what sort of a stand the janissaries and spahis of Cairo would make, but we knew and were impressed with a full sense of the skill and impetuous bravery of the Mamelukes. The French army was drawn up in the same order as at Shebreis, the left resting on the Nile, the right on a large village. General Desaix commanded the right, and it took him three hours to form to his position, and rest a little. The intrenched camp of the enemy was reconnoitred, and it was soon ascertained that it was merely sketched out. It was a work which had only been begun three days previously, after the battle of Shebreis. It was composed of long *boyaux,* which might be of some service against an attack by infantry. We also perceived with good telescopes, that their cannon were not upon field carriages, but were only great iron pieces, taken from the vessels and served by the crews of the flotilla. As soon as I had satisfied myself

EGYPT: BATTLE OF THE PYRAMIDS

that the artillery was not moveable, it was evident to me that neither it nor the infantry would quit the intrenched camp; or that if the latter should come forth, it would be without artillery. The dispositions for the battle were to be made in consequence of these data; we resolved to prolong our right, and to follow the movement of that wing with our whole army, passing out of the range of the guns of the intrenched camp. Through this movement we had only the Mamelukes and the cavalry to deal with; and we placed ourselves on ground where the enemy's infantry and artillery could be of no service to him.

Murad-Bey, who was Commander-in-chief of the whole army, saw our columns put themselves in motion, and quickly guessed our purpose. Although this chief had no experience in war, nature had endowed him with a natural greatness of mind, with undaunted courage, and a quick and discerning eye. The three affairs which we had had with the Mamelukes already served him as experience. He comprehended, with a degree of skill that could hardly have been expected in the most consummate European general, that the fortune of the day depended on preventing us from executing our movement, and on his availing himself of his numerous cavalry to attack us on our march. He advanced with two-thirds of his cavalry (6 or 7,000), leaving the rest to support the intrenched camp and encourage the infantry; and came up at the head of this troop, to attack General Desaix, who was advancing by the extremity of our right. The latter was for a moment compromised; the charge was made with such rapidity that we thought the squares were falling into confusion; General Desaix, on his march at the head of his column, had entered a grove of palm-trees. However, the head of the corps of Mamelukes, which fell upon him, was not numerous. The mass did not arrive for some minutes; and this delay was sufficient. The squares were perfectly formed, and received the charge with coolness. General Regnier supported their left; I was in General Dugua's square and immediately marched on the main body of the Mamelukes, and placed myself between the Nile and Regnier. The Mamelukes were received with grape, and a brisk fire of musquetry: thirty of the bravest died near General Desaix; but the mass, by an instinct natural to the horse, turned round the squares, and this frustrated the charge. In the midst of the fire of grape and ball, of the dust, the cries, and the smoke, part of the Mamelukes regained their intrenched camp, according to the natural impulse of the soldier to retreat towards the place whence he set out. Murad-Bey, and the most expert, directed their course towards Gizeh. Thus this Commander-in-chief found himself separated from his army. The division of Bon and Menou, forming our left, then advanced on the intrenched camp; and General Rampon, with two battalions, was detached to occupy a kind of defile, between Gizeh and the camp.

The most horrible confusion prevailed at Embabeh; the cavalry had thrown

EGYPT: BATTLE OF THE PYRAMIDS

itself upon the infantry, which, not relying upon it, and seeing the Mamelukes beaten, rushed into the jerms, kaiks, and other boats, to repass the Nile. Many effected the passage by swimming; the Egyptians excel in this exercise, which the peculiar circumstances of their country render very necessary to them. The forty pieces of cannon which defended the intrenched camp did not fire two hundred shot. The Mamelukes, quickly perceiving that their retreat was in the wrong direction, wished to regain the Gizeh road, but were unable. The two battalions placed between the Nile and Gizeh, and supported by the other divisions, drove them back on their intrenched camp. Many of them fell there, and many more were drowned in attempting to pass the Nile. The intrenchments, artillery, pontoons, and baggage, all fell into our power. Of this army of above 60,000 men, not more than 2,500 horse escaped with Murad-Bey; the greater part of the infantry got off by swimming, or in boats. The number of Mamelukes drowned in this battle has been estimated as high as 5,000. Their numerous bodies carried the news of our victory, in a few days, to Damietta and Rosetta, and all along the banks.

It was at the beginning of this battle that I addressed to my soldiers those words which afterwards became so celebrated: '*From the tops of those Pyramids forty centuries look upon you!*'

It was night when the three divisions of Desaix, Regnier, and Dugua returned to Gizeh. I fixed my head-quarters there, in Murad-Bey's country-house.

The Mamelukes had sixty vessels on the Nile laden with all their riches. Seeing the unexpected result of the battle, and our cannon already placed on the river beyond the outlets of the Isle of Rodah, they lost all hopes of saving them, and set them on fire. During the whole night we perceived through the volumes of smoke and flame, the forms of the minarets and buildings of Cairo, and the City of the Dead. These columns of flame gave so much light that we could even discern the Pyramids.

The Arabs, according to their custom after a defeat, rallied far from the field of battle, in the Desert beyond the Pyramids.

For several days the whole army was engaged in fishing for the bodies of the Mamelukes; their valuable arms, and the quantity of gold they were accustomed to carry with them, rendered the soldiers very zealous in this search.

Our flotilla had not been able to follow the movement of the army, the wind having failed. If we had had it, the action would not have been more decisive, but we should probably have made a greater number of prisoners, and taken all the wealth which fell a prey to the flames. The flotilla had heard our cannon, notwithstanding the North wind, which blew with violence. As it grew calmer, the sound of the cannon continued to increase, so that at last it appeared to have come nearer them, and the seamen, in the evening,

EGYPT: BATTLE OF THE PYRAMIDS

thought the battle lost; but the multitude of bodies which passed near their ships, and which were all Mamelukes, soon restored their confidence.

Not long after his flight, Murad-Bey perceived that he was only followed by part of his people, and discovered the error his cavalry had committed by remaining in the intrenched camp. He tried several charges, in order to re-open a passage for it; but it was too late. The Mamelukes themselves were struck with consternation, and acted supinely. Fate had decreed the destruction of this brave and intrepid soldiery, unquestionably the flower of the Eastern cavalry. The loss of the enemy on this day may be reckoned at 10,000 men left on the field or drowned, including Mamelukes, Janissaries, militia of Cairo, and slaves to the Mamelukes. A thousand prisoners were made; and eight or nine hundred camels and as many horses were taken.

About nine in the evening, I entered the country-house of Murad-Bey at Gizeh. Such habitations bear no resemblance to our chateaux. We found it difficult to make it serve for our lodging, and to understand the distribution of the different apartments. But what chiefly struck the officers, was a great quantity of cushions and divans covered with the finest damasks and silks of Lyons, and ornamented with gold fringe. For the first time we found the luxury and arts of Europe in Egypt. Part of the night was passed in exploring this singular mansion in every direction. The gardens were full of magnificent trees, but without alleys, and not unlike the gardens belonging to some of the nunneries in Italy. What most delighted the soldiers (for everyone came to see the place), were great arbours of vines covered with the finest grapes in the world. The vintage was soon over.

The two divisions of Bon and Menou, which had remained in the intrenched camp, also enjoyed the greatest abundance. Amongst the baggage had been found a great number of canteens full of preserves, pots of confectionery, and sweetmeats. We every moment found carpets, porcelains, vases of perfumes, and a multitude of little elegancies used by the Mamelukes, which excited our curiosity.

The army then began to be reconciled to Egypt, and to believe, at last, that Cairo was not like Damanhour.

The next morning, at daybreak, I proceeded to the river, and seizing some barks, caused General Vial, with his division, to pass into the Isle of Rodah, which was taken after a few musquet-shot. The moment we had taken possession of the Isle of Rodah, and placed a battalion in the Mekias, and sentinels along the canal, the Nile might be considered as passed; there was nothing further to divide us from Boulac and Old Cairo but a large canal. The walls of Gizeh were inspected, and the closing up of the gates was immediately commenced. Gizeh was surrounded by a wall sufficiently extensive to inclose all our establishments, and strong enough to keep off the Mamelukes and Arabs. We impatiently awaited the arrival of the flotilla; the North wind was blow-

EGYPT: BATTLE OF THE PYRAMIDS

ing as usual, and yet it did not arrive! The Nile being low, there had not been sufficient water for it; the vessels were aground. Rear-Admiral Perré sent word that we must not reckon upon him, and that he could not name any day for his arrival. This was a great disappointment, for it was necessary to take Cairo in the first moment of stupor, instead of leaving the inhabitants time to recover from their alarm, by a delay of forty-eight hours. Fortunately it was not the Mamelukes alone who had been defeated in the battle; the Janissaries of Cairo, and all the brave men under arms in that city, had engaged in it, and were in the greatest consternation. All the reports of this affair represented the French in a light approaching the marvellous.

A dragoman was sent by me to the Pacha and Cadi-scheik, Iman of the grand mosque, and the proclamations which I had published on my entrance into Egypt were disseminated. The Pacha had already set off, but he had left his Kiaya. The latter thought it his duty to come to Gizeh, as I declared it was not against the Turks, but against the Mamelukes, that I made war. He had a conference with me, and I persuaded him it was, moreover, the best thing this Kiaya could do. By yielding to me, he preserved the hopes of acting a distinguished part, and making his fortune. By refusing, he would have been hastening to destruction. He, therefore, promised obedience to me, and engaged to persuade Ibrahim-Bey to retire, and the inhabitants of Cairo to submit. In the morning a deputation of the scheiks of Cairo came to Gizeh, and brought intelligence that Ibrahim-Bey had already left the city, and gone to encamp at Birketel-hadji; that the Janissaries had assembled and resolved to surrender, and that the scheik of the grand mosque of Jemilazar had been charged to send a deputation to treat for a surrender, and to implore the clemency of the victor. The deputies remained several hours at Gizeh, where all means that were thought most efficacious were employed to confirm them in their good intentions, and to inspire them with confidence. The following day General Dupuy was sent to Cairo as commandant, and possession was taken of the citadel. Our troops passed the canal, and occupied Old Cairo and Boulac. I made my entrance into Cairo on 26 July, at four o'clock in the afternoon. I went to lodge in the square of El-Bekir, in the house of Elphi-Bey, whither I removed my head-quarters. This house was situated at one of the extremities of the town, and the garden communicated with the country.

Cairo is situate half a league from the Nile; Old Cairo and Boulac are its ports. A canal which crosses the city, is usually dry, but fills during the inundation, at the moment when the dyke is cut, an operation which is never performed until the Nile is at a certain height, when it becomes the occasion of a public festival. The canal then distributes its waters amongst numerous channels; and the square of El-Bekir, as well as most of the squares and gardens of Cairo, is under water. All these places are traversed in boats, during the flood. Cairo is commanded by a citadel placed on a hill, which overlooks the whole

EGYPT: BATTLE OF THE PYRAMIDS

city. It is separated from the Mokattam by a valley. An aqueduct, which is a remarkable work, supplies the citadel with water. For this purpose there is at Old Cairo, an enormous and very high octagonal tower, inclosing a reservoir, to which the waters of the Nile are raised by an hydraulic machine, and from which they enter the aqueduct. The citadel also draws water from Joseph's Well, but it is not so good as that of the Nile. This fortress was not in a state of defence, but neglected and falling to ruin. Its repairs were immediately commenced, and regularly carried on from that time. Cairo is surrounded with high walls, built by the Arabs, and surmounted by enormous towers; these walls were in a bad state, and falling through age; the Mamelukes never repaired anything. The city is large; half its walls abuts on the Desert, so that dry sands are met with on going out by the Suez gate, or those which are towards Arabia.

The population of Cairo was considerable, being estimated at 210,000 inhabitants. The houses are built very high and the streets made narrow, in order to obtain shelter from the sun. From the same motive the bazaars, or public markets, are covered with cloth or matting. The beys have very fine palaces of an Oriental architecture, resembling that of India rather than ours. The scheiks also have very handsome houses. The okels are great square buildings with very large inner courts, containing whole corporations of merchants. Thus there is the okel of Seur rice, the okel of the merchants of Suez, and of Syria. On the outside and next the street, they have each a little shop of ten or twelve feet square, in which is the merchant with samples of his goods. Cairo contains a multitude of the finest mosques in the world; the minarets are rich and numerous. The mosques in general serve for the accommodation of pilgrims, who sleep in them; some of them occasionally contain as many as 3,000 pilgrims; amongst these is Jemilazar, which is said to be the largest mosque in the East. These mosques are usually courts, the circuit of which is surrounded by enormous columns supporting terraces; in the interior is found a number of basins and reservoirs of water, for drinking or washing. In one quarter, that of the Franks, are a few European families; a certain number of houses may be seen here, such as a merchant of 30 or 40,000 livres a year might have in Europe; they are furnished in the European style with chairs and beds. There are churches for the Copts, and some convents for the Syrian Catholics.

Close to the city of Cairo, towards the Desert, is the City of the Dead. This city is larger than Cairo itself; it is there that every family has its place of burial. A multitude of mosques, tombs, minarets, and domes, keep up the memory of the great who have been buried there and who have had them built. There are attendants to many of the tombs, who keep lamps burning in them, and shew the interior to the curious. The expenses of this custom are defrayed by the families of the dead, or by foundations. Even the popular

EGYPT: BATTLE OF THE PYRAMIDS

classes have their tombs, distinguished by families or quarters, which rise two feet above the ground.

There is a vast number of coffee-houses in Cairo, in which people take coffee, sherbet, or opium, and converse on public affairs.

Around this city, as well as near Alexandria, Rosetta, etc., there are mounts of considerable height, formed of ruins and rubbish, which are daily increasing, because all the rubbish from the city is brought thither; these produce a disagreeable effect. The French established police regulations to stop the progress of the evil; and the institute took into discussion the means of removing it entirely. But difficulties arose. Experience had convinced the people of the country that it was dangerous to throw this rubbish into the Nile, because it stopped up the canals, or was spread over the country by the flood. These ruins are the consequence of the declining state of the country, traces of which are perceived at every step.

Chapter XXVII

EGYPT: RELIGION

Of Christianity. Of Islamism. Of the difference in the spirit of these two religions. Hatred of the Caliphs against Libraries. Of the duration of Empires in Asia. Polygamy. Slavery. Religious Ceremonies. Feast of the Prophet.

The Christian religion is the religion of a civilized people, and is entirely spiritual; the reward which Jesus Christ promises to the elect is that they shall see God face to face. In this religion everything tends to mortify the senses, nothing to excite them. The Christian religion was three or four centuries in establishing itself, and its progress was slow. It requires much time to destroy, by the mere influence of argument, a religion consecrated by time; and still more when the new religion neither serves nor kindles any passion.

The progress of Christianity was the triumph of the Greeks over the Romans. The latter had subdued all the Greek republics by force of arms; and the Greeks conquered their victors by the arts and sciences. All the schools of philosophy and eloquence, and all the practice of the arts in Rome, were confined to the Greeks. The Roman youth did not consider their education complete unless they had been to Athens to finish it. There were yet other circumstances which proved favourable to the propagation of the Christian religion. The apotheosis of Julius Cæsar and that of Augustus were followed by those of the most abominable tyrants: this abuse of polytheism recalled men to the idea of one only God, the Creator and Ruler of the Universe. Socrates had already proclaimed this great truth: the triumph of Christianity, which borrowed it from him, was, as we have already mentioned above, a reaction of the philosophers of Greece upon their conquerors. The holy fathers were almost all Greeks. The morality they preached was that of Plato. All the subtlety which is found in the Christian theology is derived from the refinements of the sophists of his school.

EGYPT: RELIGION

The Christians, like the votaries of paganism, thought the rewards of a future life insufficient to repress the disorders, vices, and crimes which spring from the passions; they formed a hell entirely physical, and sufferings wholly corporeal. They went far beyond their models, and even gave so much preponderance to this dogma, that it may justly be said that the religion of Christ is a threat.

Islamism is the religion of a people in the infancy of civilization; it arose in a poor country, destitute of the necessaries of life. Mahomet appealed to the senses; he would not have been comprehended by his countrymen had he appealed to the mind. He promised his followers odoriferous baths, rivers of milk, fair black-eyed houris, and groves of perpetual shade. The Arab, thirsting for water, and parched by a burning sun, sighed for shade and coolness, and was ready to do anything for such a recompense. Thus it may be said that the religion of Mahomet, in opposition to that of Christ, is a promise.

Islamism especially attacks idolaters; there is no other God but God, and Mahomet is his prophet: this is the foundation of the Musulman religion; it consecrates the great truth announced by Moses and confirmed by Jesus Christ, in the most essential point. It is known that Mahomet had been instructed by Jews and Christians. The latter were a sort of idolaters in his sight. He did not well understand the mystery of the Trinity, which he expounded as an acknowledgment of three Gods. Nevertheless, he persecuted Christians with much less fury than Pagans. The former might be redeemed on paying a tribute. The doctrine of the Unity of God which Moses and Jesus Christ had spread, was carried by the Koran into Arabia, Africa, and to the extremity of India. Considered in this point of view the Mahometan religion is the successor of the two others; all three together have outrooted paganism.

Christianity arose amongst a corrupted, enslaved, oppressed people, and preached submission and obedience, in order to avoid opposition from sovereigns. It sought to establish itself by means of insinuation, persuasion, and patience. Jesus Christ, a simple preacher, exercised no power on earth: *My kingdom is not of this world,* said he. He preached this doctrine in the temple, and to his disciples in private. He bestowed on them the gift of tongues, wrought miracles, never revolted against established power, and died on a cross, between two thieves, in execution of the sentence of a mere praetor, who was an idolater.

The Mahometan religion, which originated in a free and warlike nation, preached intolerance, and the destruction of infidels. Unlike Jesus Christ, Mahomet became a king! He declared that the whole universe ought to be subjected to his sway, and ordered his followers to use the sabre to destroy the idolater and the infidel, to kill whom was a meritorious work. The idolaters of Arabia were soon converted or destroyed. The infidels in Asia, Syria, and Egypt, were attacked and conquered. As soon as Islamism had triumphed at

EGYPT: RELIGION

Mecca and Medina, it served as a rallying point to the different Arab tribes. They were all imbued with the fanatical spirit, and a whole nation precipitated itself upon its neighbours.

The successors of Mahomet reigned under the title of caliphs. They bore at once the sword and the censer. The first caliphs preached daily in the mosque of Medina, or in that of Mecca, and thence sent orders to their armies, which already covered part of Africa and Asia. An ambassador from Persia, who arrived at Medina, was much astonished to find the caliph Omar sleeping in the midst of a crowd of mendicants on the threshold of the mosque. When Omar afterwards went to Jerusalem, he travelled on a camel which carried his provisions, had only a tent of coarse canvass, and was distinguished from other Mussulmen only by his extreme simplicity. During the ten years of his reign he conquered forty thousand cities, destroyed fifty thousand churches, and built two thousand mosques. The caliph Abubekir, who took from the treasury only three pieces of gold daily for his household expenses, gave five hundred to every mossen who had fought under the Prophet at the battle of Bender.

The progress of the Arabs was rapid; their armies, impelled by fanaticism, at once attacked the Roman empire and that of Persia. The latter was speedily subjugated; and the Musulmans penetrated to the banks of the Oxus, got possession of innumerable treasures, destroyed the empire of Chosroes, and advanced as far as China. The victories they gained in Syria, at Aiquadiah and Dyrmonk, put them in possession of Damascus, Aleppo, Amasia, Cæsarea, and Jerusalem. The taking of Pelusium and Alexandria rendered them masters of Egypt. This whole country was Coptic, and decidedly separated from Constantinople through heretical discussions. Kaleb, Derar, and Amru, surnamed the Swords of the prophet, met with no resistance. All obstacles were unavailing before them. In the midst of assaults and battles those warriors saw the fair houris with black or blue eyes, covered with chaplets of diamonds, who called them with outstretched arms; their souls were fired at the sight, they rushed on blindly, and sought the death which was to place those beauties in their power. It was thus that they made themselves masters of the fine plains of Syria, of Egypt and of Persia; it was thus that they subdued the world.

It is a prejudice widely spread and yet contradicted by history, that Mahomet was an enemy to the sciences and arts, and to literature. The caliph Omar's expression, when he caused the library of Alexandria to be burnt, has often been quoted: If this library contains what is in the Koran, it is useless; if it contains anything else, it is dangerous. A fact like this, and many others of the same nature, ought not to make us forget what we owe to the Arabian caliphs. They were constantly extending the sphere of human knowledge; and embellishing society by the charms of their literature. It is nevertheless possible,

EGYPT: RELIGION

that the successors of Mahomet were, at first, apprehensive that the Arabs might suffer themselves to be enervated by the arts and sciences, which were carried to so high a pitch in Egypt, Syria, and the Lower Empire. They had before their eyes the decline of the empire of Constantine, partly owing to perpetual scholastic and theological discussions. Perhaps this spectacle had prejudiced them against most libraries, which, in fact, were principally filled with books of this kind. However this may be, the Arabs were, for five hundred years, the most enlightened nation in the world. It is to them we owe our system of numeration, organs, solar quadrants, pendulums, and watches. Nothing can be more elegant, ingenious, or moral than Persian literature, and in general everything that flowed from the pens of the writers of Bagdad and Bassora.

Empires have a shorter duration in Asia than in Europe, which may be attributed to geographical circumstances. Asia is surrounded by immense deserts, whence, every third or fourth century, rush warlike populations, which overthrow the most extensive empires. Thence came the Ottomans, and afterwards Tamerlane and Gengis Khan.

It appears that the sovereigns who have given laws to these nations, always made it a point to preserve their national manners and aboriginal character. Thus they prevented the Janissary of Egypt from ever becoming an Arab, and the Janissary of Adrianople from changing into a Greek. The principle which they adopted, of opposing all innovation in customs and manners, made them proscribe the sciences and arts. But this measure is neither to be attributed to the precepts of Mahomet, to the religion of the Koran, nor to the Arabian character.

Mahomet limited the number of wives that each Musulman was permitted to marry, to four. No Oriental legislator had ever allowed so few. It may be asked why he did not suppress polygamy; for it is very certain that the number of women, in the East, is nowhere superior to that of the men. It would, therefore, have been natural to allow only one, in order that all might be supplied.

This contrast between Asia and Europe is still a subject of meditation. Amongst us, legislators allow but one wife; Greeks, Romans, Gauls, Germans, Spaniards, Britons—all nations, in short, have adopted this custom.

In Asia, on the contrary, polygamy was always allowed. Jews and Assyrians, Tartars and Persians, Egyptians and Turcomans, were always permitted to have several wives.

Perhaps the reason of this difference is to be sought in the nature of the geographical circumstances of Africa and Asia. These countries were inhabited by men of several colours; polygamy is the only means of preventing them from persecuting each other. Legislators have imagined, that in order to prevent the whites from being enemies to the blacks, the blacks to the whites, and the

EGYPT: RELIGION

copper-coloured to both, it was necessary to make them all members of one identical family, and thus to oppose that inclination inherent in man, to hate whatever is not himself. Mahomet thought four wives sufficient for the accomplishment of this purpose, because every man could have a black one, a white one, a copper-coloured one, and one of some other colour. It was also, undoubtedly, agreeable to the nature of a sensual religion, to gratify the passions of its sectaries; in which respect policy and the prophet agreed.

It is perhaps difficult to comprehend the possibility of having four wives in a country where there are no more men than women. The fact is, that eleven-twelfths of the population have only one, because they can only support one. But this confusion of races, colours, and nations, produced by polygamy, existing in the upper ranks of a nation, is sufficient to establish union and perfect equality throughout it.

Whenever it is wished to emancipate the blacks in our colonies, and establish perfect equality there, the legislator must authorize polygamy, and allow every man to have one white, one black, and one Mulatto wife, at the same time. Thenceforth the different colours, each forming part of the same family, will obtain equal consideration from others; without this, no satisfactory result will ever be obtained. The blacks will be more numerous or better informed, and then they will hold the whites in subjection; and *vice versâ*.

In consequence of this general principle of the equality of colours, established by polygamy, there was no difference between the individuals composing the household of the Mamelukes. A black slave, bought by a Bey from an African caravan, might become a kiaschef, and be equal to the handsome white Mameluke, born in Circassia; nor was it even suspected that this could be otherwise.

Slavery neither is, nor ever was, in the East what it was in Europe. In this respect, manners have remained as they appear in scripture. The maid servant married the master.

The law of the Jews supposed so little distinction amongst them, that it prescribed regulations for the case of a servant who marries her master's son. Even at present, a Musulman buys a slave, brings him up, and if he thinks proper, unites him to his daughter and makes him the heir of his fortune, without acting in any respect contrary to the customs of the country.

Murad-Bey and Aly-Bey had been sold to some of the Beys at a tender age, by merchants who had purchased them in Circassia. They at first performed the meanest offices in their masters' households. But their personal beauty, their dexterity in bodily exercises, their bravery or intelligence, progressively raised them to the principal situations. It is the same with the pachas, viziers, and sultans. Their slaves are promoted in the same manner as their sons.

In Europe, on the contrary, whoever was impressed with the seal of slavery, remained for ever in the lowest rank of domestic society. Amongst the

EGYPT: RELIGION

Romans, the slave might be freed, but he retained a despised and base character; he was never considered equal to a free-born citizen. The slavery of the colonies, founded on the difference of colours, is still much more severe and degrading.

The consequences of polygamy, the manner in which the natives of the East consider slavery and treat their slaves, differ so widely from our manners and ideas on slavery, that we can scarcely conceive what is done amongst them.

It was, in the same manner, a long time before the Egyptians could understand that all the French were not my slaves; and after all, it was only the most enlightened amongst them who could comprehend it.

Every father of a family, in the East, possesses an absolute power over his wife, children, and slaves, which public authority cannot modify. Being himself a slave to the grand-signor, he exercises at home the despotism to which he is subject abroad; and there is no instance of a pacha or other officer having penetrated into a house to interrupt the master in the exercise of his authority over his family; such a thing would do violence to the national customs, manners, and character. The Orientals consider themselves masters in their own houses; and every agent of power who has to exercise his functions towards them, waits until they come abroad, or sends for them.

The Mahometans have many religious ceremonies, and a great number of mosques, in which the faithful go and pray, several times in a day. The feasts are celebrated by grand illuminations in the temples and streets, and sometimes by fireworks.

They have also feasts on their birthdays, their marriages, and the circumcision of their children; it is this last which they celebrate with the greatest joy. They are all conducted with more pomp than ours. Their funerals are majestic, and their tombs in a magnificent style of architecture.

At the appointed hours the Musulmans say their prayers, wherever they happen to be; the slaves spread carpets before them, and they kneel with their faces towards the East.

Charity and alms are recommended in every chapter of the Koran, as the means of being most agreeable to God and his prophet. To devote part of one's fortune to public establishments, particularly to dig a canal or a well, or to erect a fountain, are works of supereminent merit. The establishment of a fountain or a reservoir is frequently connected with that of a mosque; wherever there is a temple, there is abundance of water. The prophet seems to have placed this element under the protection of religion. It is the first of necessaries in the Desert, where it must be collected and preserved with care.

Ali has few followers in Arabia, the Turkish empire, Egypt, and Syria. We found there none but the Mutualis. But all Persia, as far as the Indus, is of this caliph's sect.

EGYPT: RELIGION

I went to celebrate the feast of the Prophet, at the house of the Scheik El-Bekir. The ceremony was begun by the recital of a kind of litany, containing the life of Mahomet from his birth to his death. About a hundred Scheiks, sitting in a circle, on carpets, with their legs crossed, recited all the verses, swinging their bodies violently backwards and forwards, and all together.

A grand dinner was afterwards served up, at which the guests sat on carpets, with their legs across. There were twenty tables, and five or six people at each table. That of myself and the Scheik El-Bekir was in the middle; a little slab of a precious kind of wood, ornamented with mosaic work, was placed eighteen inches above the floor, and covered with a great number of dishes in succession. They were pilaws of rice, a particular kind of roast, entrées, and pastry, all very highly spiced. The Scheiks picked everything with their fingers. Accordingly water was brought to wash the hands three times during dinner. Gooseberry water, lemonade, and other sorts of sherbets, were served to drink, and abundance of preserves and confectionary with the dessert. On the whole, the dinner was not disagreeable; it was only the manner of eating it that seemed strange to us.

In the evening the whole city was illuminated. After dinner the party went into the square of El-Bekir, the illumination of which, in coloured glass, was very beautiful. An immense concourse of people attended. They were all placed in order, in ranks of from twenty to a hundred persons, who, standing close together, recited the prayers and litanies of the prophet with movements which kept increasing, until, at length, they seemed to be convulsive, and some of the most zealous fainted away.

In the course of the year I often accepted invitations to dine with the Scheik Sadda, the Scheik Fayon, and others of the principal Scheiks. These days were festivals throughout the quarter. The same magnificence prevailed at all these entertainments, which were conducted nearly in a similar manner.

Chapter XXVIII

EGYPT:
CUSTOMS, SCIENCES AND ARTS

Women; Children. Marriages. Clothing of the men and women. Harness of Horses. Houses; Harems. Arts and Sciences. Navigation of the Nile and canals. Carriage, Camels, Dromedaries, Asses, and Horses. Institute of Egypt. Labours of the Scientific Commission. Hospitals; different diseases, etc. Plague. Works executed at Cairo. Anecdote.

Women, in the East, are always veiled; a piece of cloth covers their nose, and particularly their lips, and only allows their eyes to be seen. When any of the Egyptian women found themselves, by accident, surprised without their veils, and covered only with that long blue shift which forms the clothing of the fellah's wives, they used to take up the lower part of the shift to hide their faces, preferring the exposure of any other part.

I had several opportunities of seeing some of the most distinguished women of the country, to whom I granted audiences. They were either the widows of Beys or Kiaschefs, or their wives, who, in their absence, came to me to implore my protection. The richness of their dress, their noble deportment, their little soft hands and fine eyes, a noble and graceful carriage, and very elegant manners, distinguished them as women of education and rank superior to the vulgar. They always began by kissing the hands of Sultan Kabir (the Arabs gave this name to me; the word 'Kabir' signifies 'Great'), which they then placed on their foreheads, and afterwards on their stomachs. Many of them

EGYPT: CUSTOMS, SCIENCES AND ARTS

stated their requests with perfect grace, and an enchanting tone of voice, displaying all the intelligence and sweetness of the most accomplished women of Europe. The propriety of their demeanour, and the modesty of their dress, gave them additional fascinations; and the imagination delighted in guessing at charms of which they did not even allow a glimpse.

Wives are sacred amongst the Orientals; and in their intestine wars, they are always spared. Those of the Mamelukes stayed in their houses at Cairo, whilst their husbands were carrying on the war against the French. I sent Eugene, my son-in-law, to compliment the wife of Murad-Bey, who had under her command about fifty slaves belonging to this Mameluke chief and his Kiaschefs. It was a sort of convent of religious females, of which she was the abbess. She received Eugene on her grand divan, in the harem, to which he was admitted by special exception, and as the envoy of Sultan Kabir. All the women wished to see the young and handsome Frenchman, and the slaves found it very difficult to restrain their impatience. The wife of Murad-Bey was a woman of fifty, with the beauty and grace suitable to that age. She had coffee and sherbets served up, according to custom, in very rich plate, and in a sumptuous style. She took from her finger a ring worth a thousand louis, which she presented to the young officer. She then addressed various requests to me as General-in-Chief, who preserved her villages for her, and always protected her. She passed for a woman of distinguished merit. Women decay early in Egypt; and there are more of them brown than fair. In general their face is a little coloured, and they have a tinge of copper colour. The most beautiful are Greeks or Circassians, with whom the bazaars of the merchants who carry on this trade, are always abundantly provided. The caravans from Darfur and the interior of Africa, bring a great number of beautiful negresses.

Marriage takes place without either party's having ever seen the other; sometimes the wife may have seen the husband, but the latter has never beheld his betrothed, or at least the features of her face.

Those of the Egyptians who had rendered services to the French, sometimes the Scheiks themselves, would come and request me to grant them in marriage a person whom they pointed out. The first request of this kind was made by an Aga of Janissaries, a sort of police-agent, who had been very useful to the French, and who wished to marry a very rich widow; this proposal appeared singular to me. 'But does she love you?'—'No.'—'Will she?'—'Yes, if you command.' In fact, as soon as she was informed of the will of Sultan Kabir, she accepted the match, and the marriage was solemnized. Similar transactions often took place afterwards.

The wives have their privileges. There are things which their husbands cannot refuse without passing for barbarians and monsters, and enraging everybody against them; such, for instance, is the privilege of going to the bath.

EGYPT: CUSTOMS, SCIENCES AND ARTS

These are vapour-baths, where the women assemble, and where political and other intrigues are contrived, and marriages planned. General Menou having married a lady of Rosetta, treated her in the French fashion. He gave her his hand to enter the dining-room; the best place at the table, the best bits at dinner were always kept for her. If she dropped her handkerchief, he ran to pick it up. She related these circumstances in the bath at Rosetta, and the other women, in hopes of a change in the national manners, signed a request to Sultan Kabir, that their husbands might be obliged to treat them in the same manner.

The dress of the Orientals bears no resemblance to ours. Instead of a hat, they cover their heads with a turban, a much more elegant and convenient head-dress, and which being susceptible of great variety in form, colour, and arrangement, discovers the differences of nations and ranks at the first glance. Their necks and limbs are not confined by bandages or garters; a native of the East may remain a month in his clothes without feeling fatigued by them. The different nations and classes are, of course, differently dressed; but they all agree in wearing wide pantaloons, large sleeves, and every other part of their dress full and ample. To screen themselves from the sun, they wear shawls. A great quantity of silks, Indian stuffs, and Cachemires, is introduced in the dresses of both men and women. They wear no linen. The fellahs are covered only with a blue shirt, tied about the middle. The Arab chiefs who traverse the desert in the intense heat of the dog-days, are covered with shawls of all colours, which protect the different parts of their bodies from the sun, and which they fold over their heads. Instead of shoes, both men and women wear slippers, which they leave on the edge of the carpet when they enter an apartment.

The harness of the horses is extremely elegant. The dresses of the French staff, although covered with gold, and displaying all the magnificence of Europe, appeared to them mean, and were eclipsed by the Oriental clothing. Our hats, our tight breeches, our close coats, and the stock which strangles us, were objects of laughter and aversion to them. They have no occasion to change their dress for riding; they use no spurs, and place their feet in large stirrups which render boots unnecessary, and spare them the trouble of dressing on purpose for this exercise, as we are obliged to do. The Franks or Christians who inhabit Egypt, ride on mules or asses, unless they are persons of elevated rank.

The architecture of the Egyptians bears more resemblance to that of Asia than to ours. All the houses have terraces, on which people walk; on some of them they even bathe. They are several storeys high. In the ground-floor there is a sort of parlour, where the master of the house receives strangers, and gives refreshments. In the first-floor is usually the harem, to which there are only private staircases. The master has a little door in his **apartments**

EGYPT: CUSTOMS, SCIENCES AND ARTS

which leads to the harem. There are other little staircases of this kind for the servants. A grand staircase is a thing unknown in Egypt.

The harem consists of a large room in the form of a cross; opposite this runs a corridor, in which there are a great number of chambers. Round the saloon are divans more or less rich, and in the middle a little marble basin with a fountain playing in it. These fountains often throw out rose-water or essences, which perfume the apartment. All the windows are covered with a kind of lattice, in trellis-work. There are no beds in the houses; the natives of the East sleep on divans or carpets. When they have no strangers with them, they take their meals, sleep, and pass their leisure hours in the harem. As soon as the master arrives, all the women hasten to wait on him; one presents him his pipe, another his cushion, etc. Everything is there for the master's service.

The gardens have no walks, they are arbours of great trees, where one may take the air, and sit smoking. The Egyptian, like all the Orientals, spends a great part of the day in this amusement; it serves him for occupation and excuse.

The arts and sciences, in Egypt, are in their infancy. At Jemil-Azar they teach the philosophy of Aristotle, the rules of the Arabian language, writing, and a little arithmetic; the different chapters of the Koran are explained and discussed; and that part of the history of the caliphs which is necessary for understanding and judging of the different Mahometan sects is taught. But the Arabs are completely ignorant of the antiquities of their country, and their notions on geography and the spheres are very superficial and erroneous. There were a few astronomers at Cairo, whose knowledge went no further than to enable them to make out the almanack.

In consequence of this state of ignorance, they have little curiosity. This quality exists only amongst nations sufficiently informed to distinguish what is natural from what is extraordinary. Our balloons did not produce such an effect upon them as we had expected. The Pyramids interest them only because they have observed the interest they excite in foreigners. They know not who built them, and the people in general, except the best informed, look upon them as a production of nature; the most enlightened amongst them, seeing us attach so much importance to them, imagined they were raised by some ancient nation from which the Franks were descended. It is thus that they account for the curiosity of the Europeans. The science which would be most useful to them is hydraulic mechanics. They are almost destitute of machines: yet they have one of a very ingenious kind for pouring water from a ditch or well upon higher ground, the prop of which is also the arm. They have none but horse or hand mills; we did not find a single water mill or windmill in Egypt. The use of the latter kind to raise the waters would be a grand acquisition for them, and might be productive of important results in Egypt. Conté constructed one for them.

EGYPT: CUSTOMS, SCIENCES AND ARTS

All the artisans of Cairo are very intelligent; they executed everything they saw done very completely. During the revolt of that city they cast mortars and cannon, but in a clumsy manner, similar to that in which they were made in the thirteenth century.

They knew the use of frames for weaving cloth; they even had them for embroidering Mecca carpeting. These carpets are magnificent, and made with great art. One day when I dined with Scheik El-Fayoum, they were talking of the Koran: 'It contains all human knowledge', said the Scheiks. 'Does it tell us how to cast cannon and make gunpowder?' asked I. 'Yes,' replied they; 'but then you must know how to read it!' A scholastic distinction, of which all religions have made use, more or less.

The traffic on the Nile is very brisk; the navigation very easy; they go down the river with the current; and sail up it by the aid of the north wind, which at a certain season blows constantly. When the south wind prevails, it is sometimes necessary to wait a long time. The vessels that are used are called Jerms. Their masts and sails are higher than usual, nearly by one-third, which arises from the necessity of catching the wind over the mounts which enclose the valley.

The Nile was constantly covered with these jerms, some carrying goods, others passengers. They are of different sizes. Some float in the great canals of the Nile; others are constructed to enter the small. The river, near Cairo, is always covered with a great number of sails, going up and down. The staff-officers who used the jerms in carrying orders, often met with accidents. The Arab tribes at war with us used to wait for them at the turns of the river, where the wind failed them. Sometimes also, the boats would get aground in coming down the river, and the officers they carried were massacred. Kaiks are little sloops, or light narrow pinnaces, which serve to pass the Nile, and sail not only on the canals, but over the whole country as far as it is overflowed. The number of light vessels on the Nile is greater than on any river in the world, owing to the circumstances that during several months of the year, people are obliged to make use of these boats to pass from one village to another.

There is neither coach nor cart in Egypt. Water carriage is so abundant and so easy, that coaches are, perhaps, less necessary there than in any other part of the world. A carriage which Ibrahim-Bey had received from France was thought a very remarkable thing. (Cæsar, my coachman, astonished the Egyptians by his dexterity in driving my carriage with six fine horses, in the narrow streets of Cairo and Boulac. This carriage crossed the whole desert of Syria, as far as Saint-Jean d'Acre: it was one of the curiosities of the country.)

Horses are used for traversing the city by all but lawyers and women, who ride on mules or asses. Both are surrounded by a great number of officers and servants in liveries, and holding great staves in their hands.

EGYPT: CUSTOMS, SCIENCES AND ARTS

Camels are always used for burthen; and serve also for riding. The lightest sort, with only one hump, are called dromedaries. The animal is trained to kneel when his rider wishes to mount. The latter sits on a kind of pack-saddle, with his legs across, and guides the dromedary with a bridge attached to a ring passed through the nostrils of the animal. This part of the camel being very sensitive, the ring produces the same effect on him as the bridle on the horse. He takes a very long step; his ordinary pace is a long trot, which produces the same effect on the rider as the rolling of a ship. In this manner the camel will travel twenty leagues in a day with ease.

There are usually two panniers placed on each side of the camel, which receive two persons besides luggage. This is the way in which women usually travel. In every caravan of pilgrims there is a great number of camels equipped for them in this manner. These animals can carry half a ton; but their usual burthen is six hundredweight. Their milk and flesh are good nourishment.

The dromedary, like the camel, drinks little, and can even endure thirst for several days. He finds, even in the driest places, something eatable. He is made for the Desert.

There is an immense quantity of asses in Egypt; they are large, and of a fine breed; at Cairo they in some measure supply the place of hackney coaches: a soldier could hire one for a whole day, for a few paras. At the time of the expedition into Syria there were above eight thousand with the army: they were extremely serviceable.

The horses in the Deserts contiguous to Egypt are the finest in the world; the stallions of this race have improved every breed in Europe. The Arabs bestow great pains on the preservation of the purity of the race; they have the genealogy of their stallions and mares. The chief distinction of the Arabian horse is the swiftness, and particularly the ease and gentleness of his paces. He drinks only once a day, seldom trots, and almost always either walks or gallops. He can stop suddenly on his hind legs, which it would be impossible to get our horses to do.

The Institute of Egypt was composed of members of the French Institute, and of the men of science and artists of the commission who did not belong to that body. They assembled and added to their number several officers of the artillery and staff, and others who had cultivated the sciences or literature.

The Institute was placed in one of the palaces of the Beys. The grand hall of the harem, by means of some alterations, became the place of their sittings, and the rest of the palace served for the habitation of the members. Before this building there was a very extensive garden, which adjoined the country, and near which the fort called De l'Institut was erected on a mount.

A great number of machines, and physical, chemical and astronomical instruments, had been brought from France. They were distributed in the

EGYPT: CUSTOMS, SCIENCES AND ARTS

different rooms, which were also successively filled with all the curiosities of the country, whether of the animal, vegetable, or mineral kingdom.

The garden of the palace became a botanical garden. A chemical laboratory was formed at head-quarters: Berthollet performed experiments there several times every week, at which I and a great number of officers attended.

The establishment of the Institute excited great curiosity amongst the inhabitants of Cairo. Understanding that these meetings were not held for any purpose connected with religion, they persuaded themselves that they were assemblies of alchemists, for the purpose of endeavouring to discover the art of making gold.

The simple manners of the scientific men, their constant occupations, the respect which the army paid them, their usefulness in the works of art and manufactures, respecting which the artists of the country had to communicate with them, soon gained them the goodwill and respect of the whole population.

The members of the Institute were also employed in the civil administration. Monge and Berthollet were appointed commissioners to the grand divan, and the mathematician Fourrier to the divan of Cairo. Costaz was made the principal editor of a journal; the astronomers Nourris and Noel visited all the principal points of Egypt to fix their geographical positions, particularly that of the ancient monuments. It was wished by such means to reconcile the ancient and modern geography.

Lepeyre, the engineer of bridges and roads, was instructed to take the levels and draw the plans for the canal of Suez; and the engineer Gerard to study the system of navigation of the Nile.

One of the members of the Institute had the direction of the mint of Cairo. He had a great quantity of paras, a small coin of the country, made. This was a profitable operation; the treasury gained sixty per cent. by it. The paras circulated, not only in Egypt, but in Africa and the deserts of Arabia; and instead of impeding circulation and injuring the exchange, the disadvantages of copper money, these promoted them. Conté established several manufactures.

The ovens for hatching chickens, which Egypt had possessed from the remotest antiquity, strongly excited the attention of the Institute. In several other practices which were traditionally handed down in this country, traces were recognized which were preserved with the utmost solicitude as useful to the history of the arts, and capable of leading to the recovery of many lost arts of antiquity.

General Andreossy was charged with a scientific and military mission to reconnoitre Lakes Mensaleh, Bourlos, and Natron. Geoffroy employed himself on natural history. The draftsmen Dutertre and Rigolo made drawings of everything calculated to give an idea of costumes and monuments of anti-

EGYPT: CUSTOMS, SCIENCES AND ARTS

quity. They drew the portraits of all those natives who had devoted themselves to me, which distinction flattered them greatly.

At the Institute, General Cafarelli and Colonel Sukolski often read curious memoirs, which had been collected amongst the members of that society.

Upon the conquest of Upper Egypt, which was not effected until the second year, the whole scientific commission proceeded thither to prosecute their researches on antiquities.

These various labours gave rise to the magnificent work on Egypt, written and engraved during the first fifteen years of this century, at an expense of several millions.

The climate of Egypt is universally healthy; nevertheless one of the first subjects to which the government turned its attention was the formation of hospitals. For this purpose everything was to create. The house of Ibrahim-Bey, situate on the bank of the canal of Rodah, a quarter of a league from Cairo, was appropriated as the grand hospital. It was rendered capable of accommodating five hundred sick. Instead of bedsteads, large wicker panniers were used, on which mattresses of cotton or wool were placed, with palliasses made with wheaten and maize straw, which is very plentiful there. In a short time, this hospital was abundantly supplied in every respect. Similar establishments were formed at Alexandria, Rosetta, and Damietta, and the regimental hospitals were greatly extended.

The French army in Egypt was much incommoded by diseases of the eyes; more than half the soldiers were attacked by them. These disorders arise, it is said, from two causes; from the salts which exist in the sand and dust, and necessarily affect the sight, and from the irritation produced by the check of the perspiration in very cold nights succeeding burning days. Whether this explanation be correct or not, this ophthalmia evidently results from the climate. Saint Louis, on his return from his Oriental expedition, brought back a multitude of blind; and it was this circumstance that gave rise to the establishment of the hospital of the *Quinze-Vingts* at Paris.

The plague always comes from the coasts and never from Upper Egypt. Lazarettoes are placed at Alexandria, Rosetta, and Damietta; a very fine one was also constructed in the Isle of Rodah; and when the plague appeared, all the sanitary precautions of Marseilles were adopted. These precautions proved extremely beneficial. They were wholly unknown to the inhabitants, who at first submitted to them with repugnance, but eventually became sensible of their utility. The plague occurs during the winter, and disappears entirely in June. It has been much disputed whether this disorder be endemic to Egypt. Those who maintain the affirmative, think they have remarked that it manifests itself at Alexandria, or on the coast of Damietta, in those years distinguished by the uncommon occurrence of rain in these countries. There is, moreover, no instance of its ever having commenced in Cairo or Upper

EGYPT: CUSTOMS, SCIENCES AND ARTS

Egypt, where it never rains. Those who conceive that it comes from Constantinople, or other parts of Asia, also ground their opinion on the fact that the first symptoms always manifest themselves along the coasts.

At Elphi-Bey's House, in the square of El-Bekir, occupied by me; several works were executed for the purpose of adapting it to our use. The first was the construction of a grand staircase leading to the first storey, the ground-floor having been left for offices and the staff. The garden, also, underwent alterations. It had no walks, but a great number were made, as well as marble basins and *jets d'eau*. The natives of the East are not fond of walking; to walk when one might be sitting, appears to them an absurdity which they can only account for from the petulance of the French character.

Some projectors established a sort of Tivoli in the garden of Cairo, in which, like that of Paris, there were illuminations, fireworks, and promenades. In the evening it was the rendezvous of the army and people of the country.

A causeway was constructed, communicating between Cairo and Boulac, which was passable at all times, even during the flood. A theatre was built, and a great number of houses were arranged and adapted to our customs, like mine. Scavengers were appointed. (The Egyptians heat their ovens partly with reeds and partly with the dung of camels and horses, which, when dried in the sun, serves for fuel.)

At the extremity of the Isle of Rodah, several windmills were erected for making flour; and others had begun to be employed for raising the water and watering the lands. Several sluices had been made, and everything necessary for commencing the works of the canal of Suez had been prepared; but the fortifications and military buildings occupied all the strength and activity of the army during this first year.

I often invited the Scheiks to dinner. Although our customs were very different from theirs, they thought chairs, knives and forks, very convenient. After one of these dinners, I one day asked Scheik El-Mondi, 'What is the most useful thing I have taught you, in these six months that I have been amongst you?' 'The most useful thing you have taught me,' replied the Scheik, half in jest and half in earnest, 'is to drink at my dinner.' The Arabs never drink until their meal is ended.

Chapter XXIX

SYRIA

Motives of the Expedition into Syria. The Siege of Saint-Jean d'Acre.

Arabia is, in form, a trapezium. One of its sides, bounded by the Red Sea and the Isthmus of Suez, is five hundred leagues in length. That which extends from the straits of Babel-Mandeb to the cape of Razelgate, is four hundred and fifty. The third, which extends from Razelgate across the Persian Gulf and the Euphrates to the mountains near Aleppo, on the borders of Syria, is six hundred leagues in length, being the longest side. The fourth which is the least, is one hundred and fifty leagues from Raffa, the boundary of Egypt, to beyond Alexandretta and the mountains of Rosas; it separates Arabia from Syria. In this last country, throughout the extent above-mentioned, the cultivated lands run thirty leagues in width, and the Desert, which forms part of it, extends thirty leagues, as far as Palmyra. Syria is bounded on the North by Asia Minor, on the West by the Mediterranean, on the South by Egypt, and on the East by Arabia; thus it is the complement of the latter country, in conjunction with which it forms a large isle comprehended between the Mediterranean, the Red Sea, the Ocean, the Persian Gulf, and the Euphrates. Syria differs totally from Egypt, in population, climate and soil. The latter is a single plain, formed by the valley of one of the largest rivers in the world; the other is the assemblage of a great number of valleys. Five sixths of the land are hills or mountains, a chain of which crosses all Syria, and runs parallel with the coast of the Mediterranean for a distance of ten leagues. To the right, this chain pours its waters into two rivers, which run in the same direction as itself, the Jordan and the Orontes. These rivers rise in Mount Lebanon, which is the centre of Syria, and the most elevated point of this chain. The Orontes takes its course between the mountains and Arabia, from South to North, and after running sixty leagues, falls into the sea near the Gulf of Antioch. As this river

SYRIA

runs very near the foot of the mountains, it receives but a small number of tributary streams. The Jordan, which rises twenty leagues from the Orontes on the Ante-Lebanon, runs from North to South. It receives about ten smaller streams from the chain of mountains which crosses Syria. After a course of sixty leagues, it is lost in the Dead Sea.

Near the sources of the Orontes, on the Balbec side, two minor rivers arise. One, called the Baradee, waters the plain of Damascus, and spends itself in the lake of Bahar-El-Margi; the other, the course of which extends thirty leagues, likewise rises in the heights of Balbec, and falls into the Mediterranean near Sour, or Tyre. The country of Aleppo is washed by several rivulets, which rise in Asia Minor and run into the Orontes. The Koik, which passes Aleppo, is lost in a lake near that city.

It rains in Syria almost as much as in Europe. The country is very healthy, and affords the most agreeable spots. As it is composed of valleys and small mountains, very favourable to pasture, a great quantity of cattle is bred here. Trees of all kinds abound—particularly great numbers of olives. Syria would be very suitable to the cultivation of the vine; all the Christian villages make excellent wine.

This province is divided into twelve pachaships; that of Jerusalem, which comprises the ancient Holy Land; and those of Acre, Tripoli, Damascus, and Aleppo. Aleppo and Damascus are, beyond comparison, the two largest cities. On the hundred and fifty leagues of coast which Syria presents, there are the following towns:—Gaza, situate a league from the sea, without a trace of roads or a port, but with a fine level, two leagues in circumference, which points out the site of this city in the times of its prosperity; it is now of little importance: Jaffa or Joppa, the nearest port to Jerusalem, from which it is fifteen leagues distant; besides the port for shipping it has an open road: Cæsarea presents only ruins. Acre has an open road, but the town is inconsiderable; it contains ten or twelve thousand inhabitants. Sour, or Tyre, is now a mere village. Said, Bairout, and Tripoli, are small towns. The most important point of all this coast is the Gulf of Alexandretta, situate twenty leagues from Aleppo, thirty from the Euphrates, and three hundred from Alexandria. It affords anchorage for the largest squadrons. Tyre, which commerce formerly advanced to so high a pitch of splendour, and which was the mother-country of Carthage, seems to have been partly indebted for her prosperity to the trade of India, which was carried on by sailing up the Persian Gulf and the Euphrates, passing Palmyra and Amasia, and proceeding at one period to Tyre, at another to Antioch.

The most elevated point of all Syria is Mount Lebanon, which is but a mountain of the third order, and is covered with enormous pines; that of Palestine is Mount Tabor. The Orontes and Jordan, the largest streams of these countries, are both little rivers.

SYRIA

Syria was the cradle of the religions of Moses and Jesus; Islamism arose in Arabia. Thus the same corner of the earth produced the three religions which have destroyed polytheism, and carried to every part of the globe the knowledge of one only God, the Creator of the universe.

Almost all the wars of the Crusaders of the eleventh, twelfth and thirteenth centuries were carried on in Syria; and Saint-Jean d'Acre, Ptolemais, Joppa and Damascus, were the principal scenes of action. The influence of their arms, and their residence, which was protracted for several ages, have left traces, which may still be perceived.

There are many Jews in Syria, who come from all parts of the world to die in the Holy Land of Japhet. There are also many Christians, some of whom are descended from the Crusaders; others are indigenous families, who did not embrace Mahometanism at the time of the conquest by the Arabs. They are confounded together, and it is no longer possible to distinguish them. Chefamer, Nazareth, Bethlehem, and part of Jerusalem, are peopled by Christians only. In the pachaships of Acre and Jerusalem, the Christians and Jews together are superior in number to the Musulmans. Behind Mount Lebanon are the Druses, a nation whose religion approaches nearly to that of the Christians. At Damascus and Aleppo, the Mahometans form a great majority; there exists, however, a considerable number of Syriac Christians. The Mutualis, Mahometans of the sect of Ali, who inhabit the banks of the river which runs from Lebanon towards Tyre, were formerly numerous and powerful; but at the time of the expedition of the French into Syria they had greatly declined; the cruelty and oppression of Gezzar Pacha had destroyed a great number of them. All who remained, however, rendered us great services, and distinguished themselves by extraordinary intrepidity. All the traditions we possess relating to ancient Egypt, carry its population very high. But Syria cannot, in this respect, have exceeded the proportions known in Europe; for there are in that country, as in those which we inhabit, rocks and uncultivated lands.

Syria, however, like every part of the Turkish empire, presents, on almost all sides, little but heaps of ruins.

The principal object of the French expedition to the East was to check the power of the English. The army which was to change the destiny of India, was to march from the Nile. Egypt was to supply the place of Saint-Domingo and the Antilles, and to reconcile the freedom of the blacks with the interests of our manufactures. The conquest of this province would have produced the ruin of all the English establishments in America and the Peninsula of the Ganges. Had the French once become masters of the ports of Italy, Corfu, Malta, and Alexandria, the Mediterranean would have become a French lake.

The revolution of India was likely to be more or less near, according as the

SYRIA

chances of war should prove more or less fortunate, and the inhabitants of Arabia and Egypt should be more or less favourably disposed, in consequence of the policy the Porte should adopt under these new circumstances: the only object to be immediately attended to was to conquer Egypt and to form a solid establishment there; and the means of effecting this were all that had been provided. All the rest has been considered as a necessary consequence; the execution only had been anticipated. The French squadron refitted in the ports of Alexandria, victualled and manned by experienced crews, would have sufficed to keep Constantinople in awe. It could have landed a body of troops at Alexandria, if it had been thought necessary; and we should have been, in the same year, masters of Egypt and Syria, the Nile and the Euphrates. The happy issue of the battle of the Pyramids, the conquest of Egypt, achieved without any sensible loss, the goodwill of the inhabitants, the zeal of the chiefs of the law, seemed at first to ensure the speedy execution of these grand projects. But a short time only had elapsed, when the destruction of the French squadron at Aboukir, the countermanding of the expedition to Ireland by the Directory, and the influence of the enemies of France over the Porte, rendered success much more difficult.

In the meantime two Turkish armies assembled, one at Rhodes, and the other in Syria, to attack the French in Egypt. It appears that they were to act simultaneously in the month of May, the first by landing at Aboukir, and the second by crossing the Desert which divides Syria from Egypt. In the beginning of January news arrived that Gezzar Pacha had been appointed Seraskier of the army of Syria; that his vanguard, under the command of Abdalla, had already arrived at El-Arisch, had occupied that place, and was engaged in repairing the fort, which may be considered as the key of Egypt on the Syrian side. A train of artillery of forty guns, served by 1,200 cannoneers, the only troops of that kind in the empire that had been trained in the European manner, had landed at Jaffa; considerable magazines were forming in that town; and a great number of transports, part of which came from Constantinople, were employed for this purpose. At Gaza, stores of skins to hold water had been formed; report said there were enough of them to enable an army of 60,000 men to cross the Desert.

If the French had remained quiet in Egypt, they would certainly have been attacked by the two armies at once; it was also to be feared that the Turks would be joined by a body of European troops, and that the attack would be made at a moment of internal troubles. In this case, even if the French had been victorious, it would have been impossible for them to have profited by their conquest. By sea, they had no fleet; and by land, the Desert of seventy-five leagues, which separates Syria from Egypt, was not passable by an army in the height of the hot season.

The rules of war, therefore, required me to anticipate my enemies, to cross the great Desert during the winter, to possess myself of all the magazines which the enemy had formed on the coast of Syria, and to attack and destroy the troops in succession as fast as they collected.

According to this plan, the divisions of the army of Rhodes were obliged to hasten to the aid of Syria, and Egypt remained quiet, which allowed us to march the greater part of our forces into Syria. The Mamelukes of Murad-Bey and Ibrahim-Bey, the Arabs of the Desert of Egypt, the Druses of Mount Lebanon, the Mutualis, the Christians of Syria, and the whole party of the Scheik of Ayer, in Syria, might join the troops when masters of that country, and the commotion would communicate to every part of Arabia. The provinces of the Ottoman empire in which Arabic is spoken, heartily prayed for a change, and waited for a leader. We might, if fortunate, have been on the Euphrates by the middle of the summer, with 100,000 auxiliaries, who would have had a reserve of 25,000 French veterans, some of the best troops in the world, with a numerous train of artillery. Constantinople would then have been menaced; and if an amicable connexion could have been formed with the Porte, we might have crossed the Desert, and marched on the Indus by the end of autumn.

Jaffa, a town containing from seven to eight thousand inhabitants, which was the portion of the Sultana Valida, is situate sixteen leagues from Gaza, and one league from the little river of Maar, which, at its mouth, is not fordable. The wall, on the land side, is formed by a half hexagon; one of the sides looks towards Gaza, another towards the Jordan, a third towards Acre, and a fourth runs along the seaside in the form of a concave half-circle. There is a port for small ships, in a bad state, and tolerable open roads. On the Koich is the convent of the Fathers of the Holy Land (the Recollets Chaussés), stewards of Nazareth, and proprietors of several other communities in Palestine. The fortifications of Jaffa consist of great walls flanked with towers, without ditches or counterscarps. These towers were lined with artillery, but the range of the batteries had not been well understood, and the guns were unskilfully placed. The environs of Jaffa consist of a valley full of gardens and orchards; the ground affords many opportunities of approaching within a pistol-shot of the ramparts without being perceived. Above a cannon-shot from Jaffa is the rideau which commands the country; the line of countervallation was traced there. This was the proper place for the army to encamp in; but as it was far from the water, and exposed to the scorching heat of the sun, the rideau being open, the troops preferred stationing themselves in some groves of orange-trees, and having the military positions guarded by posts.

Mount Carmel is situate on a promontory of the same name, three leagues from Acre, forming the extreme left of the bay. It is steep on every side; at its summit there is a convent and fountains, and a rock on which there is the

SYRIA

print of a man's foot, which tradition states to have been left by Elijah when he ascended into heaven.

This mount commands the whole coast, and ships steer by it when they are making for Syria. At its foot runs the river Caisrum, the mouth of which is seven or eight hundred toises from Caiffa. This little town, situate on the sea-shore, contains three thousand inhabitants; it has a small port, a wall in the ancient style, with towers, and is commanded by the heights of Carmel at a very short distance. The way to Acre from the mouth of the Caisrum runs along the sands on the seashore for a league and a half, when it meets the mouth of the Belus, a little river which rises on the hills of Chefamer, and the waters of which scarcely flow. This river is marshy down to its mouth, and falls into the sea about fifteen hundred toises from Acre. It passes within a musquet-shot of the height of Richard Cœur de Lion, situate on its right bank, six hundred toises from Saint-Jean d'Acre.

The siege of Saint-Jean d'Acre may be divided into three periods.

First period. It began on 20 March, the day on which the trench was opened, and ended on 1 April. During this period our battering-train consisted of one thirty-two pounder carronade, which Major Lambert had taken at Caiffa, by seizing the long boat of the *Tiger* by main force; but it was not possible to make use of it with the carriage belonging to the boat, and we were destitute of balls. These difficulties speedily vanished. In twenty-four hours the park of artillery constructed a carriage. As for balls, Sir Sidney Smith took upon himself to provide them. A few horsemen or waggons made their appearance from time to time: upon which the commodore approached and poured in an alternate fire from all his tiers; and the soldiers, to whom the director of the park paid five *sous* per ball, immediately ran to pick them up. They were so much accustomed to this manoeuvre that they would go and fetch them in the midst of the cannonade, and the shouts of laughter it occasioned. Sometimes, also a sloop was brought forward, the construction of a battery was pretended to be begun. Thus we obtained twelve and thirty-two pounder balls. We had powder, for the park had brought some from Cairo, and more had been found at Jaffa and Gaza. On the whole, the total of our means, in the way of artillery, including our field-pieces, consisted of four twelve-pounders, provided with 200 rounds each, eight howitzers, a thirty-two-pounder carronade, and thirty four-pounders.

The engineer General Samson, being ordered to reconnoitre the town, declared positively on his return that it had neither counterscarp nor ditch. He said he had reached the foot of the rampart, in the night, and received a musquet-shot there by which he was severely wounded. His report was incorrect; he had in fact reached a wall, but not the rampart. Unfortunately measures were taken according to the information given. A hope was enter-

SYRIA

tained of taking the town in three days. It is not so strong as Jaffa, it was said: its garrison is only between 2 and 3,000 men, while Jaffa, with a much more limited space to defend, had 8,000 men when it was taken.

On 25 March, the carronade and the four twelve-pounders made a breach in the wall, in the course of four hours, which was deemed practicable. A young officer of engineers, with fifteen sappers and twenty-five grenadiers, was charged to mount to the assault, to clear the foot of the tower, and Adjutant-commander Laugier, who was stationed in the place of arms, a hundred toises from the spot, waited for the completion of this operation, to rush upon the breach. The sappers, on coming out from behind the aqueduct, had but thirty toises to go, but they were stopped short by a counterscarp of fifteen feet, and a ditch which they estimated at several toises in width. Five or six of them were wounded, and the rest, pursued by a dreadful fire of musquetry, regained the trench precipitately.

A miner was immediately sent to work to blow up the counterscarp. In three days, that is to say on the 28th, the mine was ready; the miners declared that the counterscarp might be blown up. This difficult operation was performed under the fire of all the ramparts and of a great quantity of mortars, directed by excellent gunners, furnished by the English ships, which scattered shells in all directions. All our eight-inch mortars and fine pieces which the English had taken, now strengthened the defence of the place. The mine was sprung on 28 March, but it did not succeed well; it had not been dug deep enough, and overthrew only half the counterscarp, above eight feet of which remained. The sappers, however, asserted that it was entirely destroyed. The Staff-officer Mailly was consequently sent with a detachment of twenty-five grenadiers to support an officer of engineers who advanced to the counterscarp with six sappers. They had taken the precaution to provide themselves with three ladders, with which they descended it. As they were annoyed by the musquetry, they fixed the ladders to the breach, and the sappers and grenadiers preferred mounting to the assault to clearing the foot of the breach. They gave notice to Laugier, who was ready to second them with two battalions, that they were in the fossé, that the breach was practicable, and that it was time to support them. Laugier hastened up to them at a running step; but on reaching the counterscarp he met the grenadiers returning, who said that the breach was too high by some feet, and that Mailly and several of their comrades had been killed.

When the Turks saw this young officer fastening the ladder, terror seized upon them; they fled to the port, and Gezzar himself had got on board ship. But the death of Mailly frustrated the whole operation; the two battalions dispersed themselves in order to return the enemy's fire of musquetry. Laugier was killed, and some loss was incurred without producing any result. This event was very unfortunate, for this was the day on which the town

SYRIA

ought to have been taken; reinforcements arrived by sea daily from that time.

Second period. From 1 April to the 27th.—A new well was now sunk for a mine, intended to blow up the whole counterscarp, in order that the fossé might no longer be any impediment. What had already been done was found useless; it was easier to make a new approach. Eight days were requisite for the miners. The counterscarp was blown up, the operation succeeded perfectly. On the 10th, the mine was continued under the fossé in order to blow up the whole tower. There was now no hope of getting in at the breach, the enemy having filled it up with all sorts of combustibles. The approaches were carried on for six days more. The besieged perceived what was doing, and made a sortie in three columns. That of the centre was headed by 200 English; they were repulsed, and a captain of marines was killed at the shaft of the mine.

It was during this period that the actions of Canaam, Nazareth, Saffet, and Mount Tabor, were fought. The first took place on the 9th, the second on the 11th, and the others on the 13th and 16th. It was on the latter day, 16 April, that the miners calculated that they were under the axis of the tower. At this period Rear-Admiral Perré had arrived at Jaffa, with three frigates, from Alexandria; he had landed two mortars and six eighteen-pounders at Tintura. Two were fixed to play upon the little isle that flanked the breach, and the four others were directed against the ramparts and curtains by the side of the tower. It was intended, by the overthrow of this tower, to widen the breach which it was supposed the mine would make, for it was apprehended that the enemy might have made an internal retrenchment, and isolated the tower, which was salient.

On the 25th the mine was sprung, but a chamber under the tower disappointed us, and only the part which was on our side was blown up. The effect produced was the burying of two or three hundred Turks and a few pieces of cannon, for they had embattled and occupied every storey of the tower. It was determined to take advantage of the first moment of surprise, and thirty men accordingly attempted to make a lodgement in the tower. Being unable to proceed, they maintained themselves in the lower storeys, whilst the enemy occupied the upper, until the 26th when General Devaux was wounded. It was then resolved to evacuate the place, in order to use the batteries against this tottering tower, and to destroy it altogether. On the 27th Cafarelli died.

Third period. From 27 April to 20 May.—During this period the enemy felt that if they remained on the defensive they were lost. The countermines they had formed did not make them feel secure. All the battlements of the walls were destroyed, and the guns dismounted by our batteries. A reinforcement of 3,000 men, which had entered the place, had, however, compensated for all these losses.

But the imagination of the Turks was struck with terror, and it was no longer possible to induce them to remain upon the walls. They supposed every spot to be undermined. Phelippeaux* formed lines of counter-attack; they began at Gezzar's palace, and the right of the front attack. He also dug two trenches, resembling two sides of a triangle, which took all our works in flank. The numerical superiority of the enemy, the great number of labourers in the city, and the quantity of bales of cotton with which they formed the epaulements, materially expedited the works. In a few days they flanked the whole tower on the right and left, after which they raised cavaliers, and lined them with twenty-four pounders; their counter-attack and batteries were several times carried and overthrown and their guns spiked; but we were never able to maintain these works, because they were so entirely commanded by the towers and the wall. The order was then given to proceed against them by sap, so that their workmen and ours were only separated by two or three fathoms of ground, and were marching directly against each other. Fougasses were also established, which afforded means of entering the enemy's boyau, and destroying all who were not on their guard.

It was thus that, on 1 May, two hours before daybreak, possession was obtained of the most salient part of the counter-attack without any loss. Twenty volunteers endeavoured, at the first peep of dawn, to effect a lodgement in the tower, the defences of which our battery had entirely razed. But at that moment the enemy made a sortie on their right, and their balls striking behind the detachment, which was endeavouring to lodge itself under the ruins, obliged it to fall back. The sortie was briskly repulsed; five or six hundred of the besieged were killed, and a great number driven into the sea. As the tower was totally destroyed, it was resolved to attack a portion of the rampart by mining, in order to avoid the retrenchment which the enemy had constructed. The counterscarp was blown up. The mine was already carried across under the ditch, and was beginning to extend under the scarp, when, on the 6th, the enemy debouched by a sap covered by the fossé, surprised the mask of the mine, and filled up the well.

On the 7th, the enemy received a reinforcement of fresh troops, amounting to 12,000 men. As soon as their arrival was announced by signals, it was calculated that according to the state of the wind they could not land for six hours. In consequence of this a twenty-four-pounder, which had been sent by Rear-Admiral Perré, was immediately brought into play; which battered down a piece of the wall to the right of the tower which was on our left. At night the troops attacked all the enemy's works, filled up the trenches, killed all they met with, spiked the guns, mounted the breach, made a lodgement in the tower, and entered the place; in short we were masters of the town, when the troops which had landed appeared in formidable numbers, to renew the battle. Rambaut was killed; 1,500 men fell with him, or were taken; Lannes

* A French emigrant, officer of engineers.

was wounded. The besieged sallied forth by every gate, and took the breach in rear; but there was an end of their success; our troops marched against them, and after driving them back into the town, and cutting off several columns, regained the breach. Seven or eight hundred prisoners were taken; they were armed with European bayonets, and came from Constantinople. The enemy's loss was enormous; all our batteries fired upon him with grape, and our success appeared so great, that on the 10th, at two in the morning, I ordered a new assault. General Debon was killed in this last action. There were 20,000 men in the place, and Gezzar's house and all the others were so thronged with defenders that we could not pass beyond the breach.

Under these circumstances what was I to do? On the one hand Rear-Admiral Perré, who had returned from a cruise, had for the third time landed artillery at Tintura. We were beginning to have sufficient artillery to entitle us to hope to reduce the town. But, on the other hand, the prisoners informed us that new succours were leaving Rhodes when they embarked. The reinforcements received and expected by the enemy might render the success of the siege problematical; remote as we were from France and Egypt, we could not afford fresh losses: we had at Jaffa and in the camp 1,200 wounded; the plague was in our hospital. On the 20th the siege was raised.

Chapter XXX

EGYPT: MARCH, APRIL AND MAY, 1799. BATTLE OF ABOUKIR

Insurrection against the French. Murad-Bey leaves the desert of Nubia, and advances into Lower Egypt. Mustapha-Pacha lands at Aboukir, and takes the fort. Movements of the French Army. I advance to Alexandria. Junction of the army at Birketh; I march against the Turkish army. Battle of Aboukir, 25 July, 1799.

During the expedition into Syria, the inhabitants of Egypt conducted themselves as if it had been a province of France. Desaix, in Upper Egypt, continued to repulse the attacks of the Arabs and to secure the country from the attempts of Murad-Bey, who made incursions from the desert of Nubia into different parts of the valley. Sir Sidney Smith, forgetting what he owed to the character of the French officers, had caused a great number of circulars and libels to be printed, which he sent to the generals and commandants remaining in Egypt, proposing to them to return to France, and guaranteeing their passage, if they chose to do so, *whilst the Commander-in-chief was in Syria*. These proposals appeared so extravagant, that it became the general opinion of the army that the commodore was mad. General Dugua, commanding the Lower Egypt, prohibited all communications with him, and indignantly rejected his insinuations.

The French forces in Lower Egypt were daily increased by the arrival of men from the hospitals, who reinforced the third battalions of the corps. The fortifications of Alexandria, Rosetta, Rhamanieh, Damietta, Salahieh, Belbeis, and the different parts of the Nile, which it had been thought proper to occupy with towers, went on constantly during these three months.

EGYPT: MARCH, APRIL AND MAY, 1799

General Dugua had only to repress the incursions of the Arabs, and some partial revolts; the mass of the inhabitants, influenced by the scheiks and ulemas,* remained submissive and faithful. The first event which attracted the General's attention was the revolt of the Emir-Hadji (Prince of the Caravan of Mecca). The privileges and emoluments attached to this place were very considerable. As General-in-chief I had authorized the Emir-Hadji to establish himself in Sharkieh, to complete the organization of his household. He had already 300 armed men; but he wanted 8 or 900 to form a sufficient escort for the caravan of the pilgrims of Mecca. He was faithful to 'Sultan Kabir' until the battle of Mount Tabor; but Gezzar having succeeded in communicating with him coastwise, and informing him that the armies of Damascus and the Naplousains were surrounding the French at the camp of Acre, and that the latter, weakened by the siege, were irremediably lost, he began to despair of the success of the French, and to listen to Gezzar, endeavouring to make his peace by rendering him some service. On 15 April, having received more false intelligence from an emissary of Gezzar, he declared his revolt by a proclamation published throughout Sharkieh. He asserted that 'Sultan Kabir' had been killed before Acre, and the whole of the French army taken. The mass of the population of the province remained deaf to these insinuations. Five or six villages only displayed the standard of revolt, and his forces were only increased by 400 horse, belonging to a tribe of Arabs.

General Lanusse, with his moveable column, left the Delta, passed the Nile, and marched against the Emir-Hadji; after several slight affairs, and various movements, he succeeded in surrounding him, attacked him briskly, put all who defended themselves to death, dispersed the Arabs, and burnt the most guilty village as an example. The Emir-Hadji escaped with four other persons, through the Desert, and reached Jerusalem.

During these occurrences in Sharkieh, others of greater importance were transacting in Bahireh. A man of the Desert of Derne, possessed of a great reputation for sanctity amongst the Arabs of his tribe, took it into his head, or attempted to persuade others, that he was the angel Elmody, whom the Prophet promises, in the Koran, to send to the aid of the elect, in the most critical circumstances. This opinion gained ground in the tribe; the man had all the qualities adapted to excite the fanaticism of the populace. He succeeded in persuading them that he lived without food, and by the special grace of the Prophet. Every day, at the hour of prayer, and before all the faithful, a bowl of milk was brought to him, in which he dipped his fingers and passed them over his lips; this being, as he said, the only nourishment he took. He formed himself a guard of 120 men of his tribe, well armed and completely infatuated with zeal. He repaired to the Great Oasis, where he met with a caravan of

* Priests. S. de C.

EGYPT: MARCH, APRIL AND MAY, 1799

pilgrims, consisting of 400 Maugrebins from Fez; he announced himself as the angel Elmody; they believed and followed him. These 400 men were well armed, and had a great number of camels; he thus found himself at the head of between 5 and 600 men, and marched to Damanhour, where he surprised 60 men of the nautical legion, killed them, and took their musquets and a four-pounder. This success increased the number of his partisans; he then visited all the mosques of Damanhour and the neighbouring villages, and from the pulpit, which is used by the readers of the Koran, announced his divine mission. He declared himself incombustible and ball-proof, and assured his hearers that all who would follow him would have nothing to fear from the musquets, bayonets, and cannon of the French. He was the angel Elmody! He convinced, and enlisted 3 or 4,000 men in Bahireh amongst whom there were 4 or 500 well armed. He armed the others with great pikes and shovels, and exercised them in throwing dust against the enemy, declaring that this blessed dust would frustrate all the efforts of the French against them.

Colonel Lefebvre, who commanded at Rhamanieh, left 50 men in the fort, and set out with 200 men to retake Damanhour. The angel Elmody marched to meet him; Colonel Lefebvre was surrounded by the superior forces of the angel. The action commenced, and when the fire was briskest between the French and the angel's armed followers, some columns of Fellahs outflanked the French, and passed to their rear, raising clouds of dust. Colonel Lefebvre could do nothing; he lost several men, killed a greater number, and took up a position at Rhamanieh. The wounded and the relations of those who were killed murmured, and loudly reproached the angel Elmody. He had told them that the balls of the French would not hit any of his followers, yet a great number had been killed and wounded! He silenced these murmurs by means of the Koran and of several predictions; he maintained that none of those who had rushed forward full of confidence in his promises had been either killed or wounded; but that those who had shrunk back had been punished by the Prophet, because they had not perfect faith in their hearts. This event, which ought to have opened their eyes to his imposture, confirmed his power; he reigned absolute at Damanhour. There was reason to fear that the whole of Bahireh, and by degrees the neighbouring provinces also, might revolt; but a proclamation from the Scheiks at Cairo arrived in time, and prevented a general revolt.

General Lanusse speedily crossed the Delta; and from the province of Sharkieh, proceeded to the Bahireh, where he arrived on 8 May. He marched on Damanhour, and defeated the troops of the angel Elmody. All those who were unarmed, dispersed and fled to their villages. He fell on the fanatics without mercy, and shot 1,500 of them, amongst whom was the angel Elmody himself. He took Damanhour, and the tranquillity of Bahireh was restored.

On the news that the French army had repassed the Desert, and was return-

EGYPT: MARCH, APRIL AND MAY, 1799

ing into Egypt, a general consternation prevailed in the East. The Druses, the Mutualis, the Christians of Syria, and the partisans of Ayer, could only effect their peace with Gezzar by making great pecuniary sacrifices. Gezzar was less cruel than formerly; almost all his military household had been killed at Saint-Jean d'Acre, and this old man survived all those whom he had brought up. The plague, which was making great ravages in that town, also increased his troubles, and gave the final blow to his power. He did not go out of his pachaship.

The pacha of Jerusalem resumed possession of Jaffa. Ibrahim-Bey, with 400 Mamelukes that he still had left, took up a position at Gaza; there was some parleying and some skirmishing with the garrison of El-Arisch.

Elphi-Bey and Osman-Bey, with 300 Mamelukes, a thousand Arabs, and a thousand camels, carrying their wives and their riches, went down through the Desert, between the right bank of the Nile and Red Sea, and reached the Oasis of Sebaiar in the beginning of July; they waited for Ibrahim-Bey, who was to join them at Gaza, and thus united they wished to induce all Sharkieh to revolt, to penetrate into the Delta, and advance on Aboukir.

Brigadier-General Lagrange left Cairo, with one brigade and a half the dromedary regiment; he arrived in presence of the enemy in the night of 9 July, and manoeuvred so skilfully that he surrounded the camp of Osman-Bey and Elphi-Bey, took their thousand camels and their families, and killed Osman-Bey, five or six kiaschefs, and a hundred Mamelukes. The rest dispersed in the Desert, and Elphi-Bey returned to Nubia. Ibrahim-Bey, being informed of this event, did not quit Gaza.

Murad-Bey, with the rest of the Mamelukes, amounting to between 4 and 500 men, arrived in the Fayoum, and thence proceeded by the Desert to Lake Natron, where he expected to be joined by between 2 and 3,000 Arabs of Bahireh and the Desert of Derne, and to march on Aboukir, the place appointed for the landing of the great Turkish army. He was to take camels and horses to this army, and to aid it by his influence.

General Murat left Cairo, reached Lake Natron, attacked Murad-Bey, and took a kiaschef and fifty Mamelukes. Murad-Bey briskly pursued, and having, moreover, no news of the army which was to have landed at Aboukir, but was delayed by the winds, turned back, and sought safety in the Desert. In the course of the 13th, he reached the Pyramids; it is said that he ascended the highest of them, and remained there part of the day, gazing with his telescope on the houses of Cairo, and his fine country-seat at Gizeh. Of all the power of the Mamelukes, he now retained only a few hundred men, disheartened, fugitive, and miserable!

As soon as I heard of his presence there, I instantly set out for the Pyramids; but Murad-Bey plunged into the Desert, making for the Great Oasis. A few camels and some men were taken from him.

EGYPT: MARCH, APRIL AND MAY, 1799

On 14 July, I heard that Sir Sidney Smith, with two English ships of the line, several frigates, and Turkish men-of-war, and from a hundred and twenty to a hundred and fifty sail of transports, had anchored in Aboukir roads on the 12th, in the evening. The fort of Aboukir was armed, victualled, and in good condition; the garrison amounted to 400 men, with a commander who might be depended on. Brigadier-General Marmont, who commanded Alexandria and the whole province, undertook to defend the fort during the time necessary for the army to come up. But this General had committed a great error; instead of razing the village of Aboukir, as I had ordered him to do, and increasing the fortifications of the fort, by constructing a glacis, a covered way, and a good demilune of masonry, General Marmont had taken on himself to preserve the village, which contained good houses, and which seemed to him necessary for the cantonment of the troops; and he had got a redoubt of fifty feet on each side, constructed by Colonel Cretin in advance of the village, near 400 toises from the fort. This redoubt seemed to him a sufficient protection for the fort and village; from the narrowness of the isthmus, which at that point is not above 400 toises over, he thought it impossible to pass and to enter the village without gaining possession of the redoubt. These dispositions were faulty, because they rendered the security of the important fort of Aboukir, which had a scarp and counterscarp of permanent fortifications, dependent on a field-work which was not flanked, or even palisaded.

Mustapha-Pacha sent his boats into Lake Maadieh; seized the ferry-boat, which was used in the communication between Alexandria and Rosetta, and effected his landing on the banks of that lake. On the 14th, the English and Turkish gun-boats entered Lake Maadieh, and cannonaded the redoubt. Several field-pieces, landed by the Turks, were placed so as to answer the four pieces which defended this work, and when it was thought to be sufficiently battered, the Turks surrounded it, kangiar in hand, mounted to the assault, carried the work, and took or killed the 300 French stationed there by the commandant of Aboukir, who was killed. They then took possession of the village; there remained in the fort but 100 men and a bad officer; these, intimidated by the immense forces which surrounded them, and by the taking of the redoubt, had the cowardice to surrender the fort; this unfortunate event baffled all calculation.

In the meantime as soon as I was informed of the landing of the Turks, I proceeded to Gizeh, and despatched orders to all parts of Egypt. On the 15th I slept at Wardan, on the 17th at Alkam, on the 18th at Shabur, and on the 19th at Rhamanieh, thus performing a journey of forty leagues in four days. The convoy, of which signals had been made at Aboukir, was considerable and there was every reason to suppose that there was not only a Turkish but an English army; in the uncertainty of the case I reasoned as if it had been so.

The divisions of Murat, Lannes, and Bon, marched from Cairo, leaving a

EGYPT: MARCH, APRIL AND MAY, 1799

good garrison in the citadel and the different forts; Kleber's division marched from Damietta. General Regnier, who was in Sharkieh, had orders to leave a column of 600 men, infantry, cavalry, and artillery, including the garrisons of Belbeis, Salahieh, Cathieh, and El-Arisch, and to march on Rhamanieh. The different generals who commanded the provinces advanced with their columns, and what disposable force they had, on that point. General Desaix had orders to evacuate Upper Egypt, to leave the guarding of the country to the inhabitants and to come to Cairo with all possible speed; so that, if it should be necessary, the whole army, amounting to 25,000 men, including above 3,000 excellent cavalry, and sixty well-horsed pieces of cannon, was in movement to join before Aboukir. The number of troops left in Cairo, including the sickly, and those of the depots, was not above 8 or 900 men.

I was in hopes to destroy the army which was landing at Aboukir, before that of Syria, if a new one had been raised during the two months which had elapsed since I had quitted that country, could arrive before Cairo. It was known, through our vanguard which was at El-Arisch, that none of the troops, of which such an army would have been composed, had yet arrived, at Gaza; it was, however, necessary to act as if the enemy, whilst he was landing at Alexandria, had an army marching on El-Arisch; and it was important that General Desaix should have evacuated Upper Egypt, and arrived at Cairo, before the army of Syria (if any such army existed, and would venture to pass the Desert) should reach that place.

Under these circumstances the Scheiks of Gemil-Azar issued proclamations to inform the people respecting the movements which were operating, and to prevent their imagining that the French were evacuating Egypt; on the contrary, they declared that this country was still the constant object of Sultan Kabir's solicitude. This had induced him to pass the Desert for the purpose of destroying the Turkish army, which was coming to ravage it; and now that another army had arrived at Aboukir, by sea, he was marching with his usual activity to oppose its landing, and to preserve Egypt from the calamities with which a country that is the theatre of war is usually afflicted.

On my arrival at Rhamanieh, I received, on 20 July, news from Alexandria, which gave the particulars of the enemy's landing, the attack and taking of the redoubt, and the capitulation of the fort. It was stated that the enemy had not yet advanced, and was labouring on intrenchments consisting of two lines; one joining the redoubt to the sea by intrenchments; the other three-quarters of a league in advance, having the right and left supported by two sand-mounts, one commanding Lake Maadieh, and the other extending to the Mediterranean: that the inactivity of the enemy, during the five days which had elapsed since his taking the redoubt, arose, according to some, from his waiting for the arrival of the English army, which he expected from Port Mahon; according to others, from the refusal of Mustapha to march on Alex-

EGYPT: MARCH, APRIL AND MAY, 1799

andria without artillery or cavalry, knowing that place to be fortified and defended by an immense quantity of artillery: that he expected Murad-Bey, who was to bring him several thousand cavalry and several thousand camels; that the Turkish army was estimated at from twenty to twenty-five thousand men: that about thirty cannon were seen on the strand, of French make, and like those taken at Jaffa: that he had no artillery horses and that his whole cavalry consisted only of two or three hundred horses belonging to the officers, which had been formed into companies to furnish guards for the advanced posts.

The events which had befallen Murad-Bey disconcerted all the enemy's schemes; the Arabs of Bahireh, amongst whom we had many partisans, feared to expose themselves to the vengeance of the French army; they did not seem to feel much confidence in the success of the Turks, whom they observed, moreover, to be destitute of artillery horses, and cavalry.

The fortifications which the Turkish army was making on the peninsula of Aboukir, gave reason to think that it wished to make this point its centre of operations: it could march thence either on Alexandria or Rosetta.

I thought proper to fix on Birketh for the centre of my movements. I sent General Murat thither, with his vanguard, to take up a position: the village of Birketh is at the head of Lake Maadieh. From thence we could fall on the right flank of the enemy's army, if he should make for Rosetta, and attack him between Lake Maadieh and the Nile, or fall on his left flank if he should march on Alexandria.

Whilst all the columns were effecting a junction on Rhamanieh, I proceeded to Alexandria: I was satisfied with the good condition in which I found that important place, which inclosed such quantities of ammunition, and such considerable magazines: and I rendered, in public, due testimony to the talents and activity of Colonel Cretin of the engineers.

The enemy's proceedings gave probability to the report spread by his partisans, that he was waiting for the English army; it was therefore important to attack and defeat him before its arrival. But my march had been so rapid, and the distances were so great, that there were still not more than 5 or 6,000 men in junction. From twelve to fifteen days more were, therefore, requisite for assembling the whole army, except Desaix's division, which required twenty days.

I resolved to advance with what troops I had, and to reconnoitre the enemy; the latter having neither cavalry nor moveable artillery, could not engage me in a serious action. My plan was, if the enemy should prove numerous and well posted, to take up a position parallel to theirs, supporting the right on Lake Maadieh, and the left on the sea, and to fortify myself there, by redoubts. By this method, I calculated that I should keep the enemy blockaded in the peninsula, prevent his having any communication with Egypt, and be in a

EGYPT: MARCH, APRIL AND MAY, 1799

situation to attack the Turkish army when the greater part of the French army should have arrived.

I set out from Alexandria on the 24th, and proceeded to Puits, half way across the isthmus, where I encamped and was joined by all the troops that were at Birketh.

The Turks, who had no cavalry, could not watch my movements; they were held in check by the grand guards of hussars and chasseurs, which the garrison of Alexandria had sent forth immediately after the debarkation. Some hopes of surprising the enemy's army were therefore entertained. But a company of sappers, escorting a convoy of tools, having left Alexandria very late on the 24th, passed the fires of the French army, and fell in with those of the Turkish army at ten o'clock in the evening. As soon as these sappers perceived their mistake, the greater part of them fled, but ten were taken, and from them the Turks ascertained that I and the army were opposite them. They passed the whole night in making their final dispositions, and we found them, on the 25th, prepared to receive us.

I then changed my first plan, and resolved to attack instantly, if not to gain possession of the whole peninsula, at least to oblige the first line of the enemy to fall back behind the second, whereby the French would be enabled to occupy the position of the first line and intrench themselves there. The Turkish army being thus hemmed in, it would be easy to overwhelm it with shells, howitzers, and balls; we had immense resources in artillery at Alexandria.

General Lannes, with 1,800 men, made his dispositions to attack the left of the enemy; Destaing, with a like number of troops, prepared to attack the right; Murat, with all the cavalry and a light battery, divided his force into three corps, the left, right and reserve. The skirmishers of Lannes and Destaing soon engaged with those of the enemy. The Turks maintained the battle with success, until General Murat, having penetrated through their centre, directed his left to the rear of their right, and his right to the rear of their left, thus cutting off the communication between the first and second lines. The Turkish troops then lost all confidence, and rushed tumultuously towards their second line. This corps consisted of between 9 and 10,000 men. The Turkish infantry are brave, but preserve no order, and their musquets have no bayonets; they are, moreover, deeply impressed with an opinion of their inferiority to cavalry in the plain. Encountered in the midst of the plain by our cavalry, this infantry could not join the second line; their right was driven into the sea, and their left into Lake Maadieh. The columns of Lannes and Destaing, which had advanced to the heights recently quitted by the enemy, descended them at the charge, and vigorously pursued him. An unprecedented spectacle was then seen. These 10,000 men, to escape from our cavalry and infantry, threw themselves into the water; and whilst our artillery poured grape-shot upon them, they were almost all drowned there. It is said that only twenty men succeeded in getting on board the sloops. This extraordinary success, obtained with so little loss, gave us hopes of forcing the second line. I went forward with Colonel Cretin to reconnoitre. The left was the weakest part.

General Lannes had orders to form his troops in columns, to cover the intrenchments of the enemy's left with skirmishers, and under the protection of his whole artillery to proceed along the lake, turn the intrenchments, and throw himself into the village. Murat, with all his cavalry, placed himself in close column in the rear of Lannes, for the purpose of repeating the same manoeuvre as that against the first line, and, as soon as Lannes should have forced the intrenchments, to get in the rear of the redoubt on the left of the Turks. Colonel Cretin, who was perfectly acquainted with the localities, was appointed to direct his march. General Destaing was instructed to make false attacks, to occupy the attention of the enemy's right.

All these dispositions were crowned with the most brilliant success. Lannes forced the intrenchments at the point of their junction with the lake, and made a lodgement in the first houses of the village; the redoubt and the whole right of the enemy were covered with skirmishers.

Mustapha-Pacha was in the redoubt; as soon as he perceived that General Lannes was on the point of reaching the intrenchment and turning his left, he made a sortie, debouched with four or five thousand men, and thereby separated our right from our left, which he took in flank at the same time as he placed himself in the rear of our right. This movement would have stopped Lannes short; but I, who was in the centre, marched with the 69th, checked Mustapha's attack, made him give ground, and thereby restored the confidence of General Lannes' troops, who continued their movement; the cavalry having then debouched, got in the rear of the redoubt. The enemy, finding themselves cut off, instantly fell into the most frightful disorder. General Destaing advanced at the charge on the intrenchments of the right. All the troops of the second line then tried to regain the fort, but they fell in with our cavalry, and not one Turk would have been saved, had it not been for the village, which a considerable number had time enough to reach. Three or four thousand Turks were driven into the sea. Mustapha, all his staff, and a body of from 1,200 to 1,500 men, were surrounded and made prisoners. The 69th were the first that entered the redoubt.

It was four in the afternoon: we were masters of half the village, and of the whole camp of the enemy, who had lost from fourteen to fifteen thousand men. He had three or four thousand left, who occupied the fort, and barricaded themselves in a part of the village. The fire of musquetry continued throughout the day. It was not thought possible to force the enemy in the houses he occupied, protected as he was by the fort, without risking an enormous loss. A position was taken, and the engineer and artillery officers reconnoitred the most advantageous points for placing cannon of heavy calibre, to raze the enemy's defences without hazard of greater loss.

Mustapha-Pacha had not surrendered until after making a valiant defence. He had been wounded in the hand. The cavalry had the greatest share in the success of this day. Murat was wounded by a tromblon shot in the head; the brave Duvivier was killed by the thrust of a kangiar. Cretin was shot dead by a musquet-ball, whilst he was conducting the cavalry. Guibert, my aide-de-camp, was struck by a ball in the breast and died shortly after the battle. Our loss amounted to near 300 men. Sir Sidney Smith, who did the duty of major-general to the Pacha, and who had chosen the positions occupied by the Turkish army, narrowly escaped being taken, and had great difficulty in reaching his sloop.

The 69th had behaved ill in an assault at Saint-Jean d'Acre, and, dissatisfied with them, I had commanded and inserted it in the order of the day, that they should cross the Desert with their arms reversed, and escorting the sick. By their noble conduct at the battle of Aboukir they regained their former reputation.

Chapter XXXI

EGYPT

Objects of the Expedition to Egypt. Project to convert the French Army to Islam. Arrival of English newspapers. My return to France. Events in Egypt after my departure. Résumé of the Egyptian Campaign. Comparison with St Louis' Campaign of 1250.

There were three objects in the expedition to Egypt: first, to establish a French colony on the Nile, which would prosper without slaves, and serve France instead of the republic of Saint-Domingo, and of all the sugar islands. Secondly, to open a market for our manufactures in Africa, Arabia, and Syria, and to supply our commerce with all the productions of those vast countries. Thirdly, setting out from Egypt, as from a place of arms, to lead an army of 60,000 men to the Indus; to excite the Mahrattas and oppressed people of those extensive regions to insurrection: 60,000 men, half Europeans and half recruits from the burning climates of the equator and tropics, carried by 10,000 horses and 50,000 camels, having with them provisions for fifty or sixty days, water for five or six days, and a train of artillery of a hundred and fifty field-pieces, with double supplies of ammunition, would have reached the Indus in four months. Since the invention of shipping, the ocean has ceased to be an obstacle; and the desert is no longer an impediment to an army possessed of camels and dromedaries in abundance.

The first two objects were fulfilled, and notwithstanding the loss of Admiral Brueys's squadron at Alexandria, the intrigue by which Kleber was induced to sign the Convention of El-Arisch, the landing of from 30 to 35,000 English commanded by Abercrombie at Aboukir and Cosseir, the third object would have been attained: a French army would have reached the Indus in the winter of 1801-2, had not the command of the army devolved, in consequence of the murder of Kleber, on a man who although abounding in courage, talents for business, and goodwill, was of a disposition wholly unfit for any military command.

The Koran ordains that idolaters shall be exterminated or subjected to tribute; it does not allow of obedience and submission to an infidel power, in which it is contrary to the spirit of our religion: '*Render unto Caesar the things that are Caesar's,*' saith Jesus Christ; '*my kingdom is not of this world; obey the powers that be.*' In the 10th, 11th and 12th centuries, the Christians reigned in Syria; but religion was the object of the war; it was a war of extermination, and cost Europe several millions of men.

If a similar spirit had animated the Egyptians in 1798, it would have been impossible to sustain such a struggle with 25 or 30,000 Frenchmen, who were not heated with fanaticism of any kind, and were already disgusted with the country. After taking Alexandria and Cairo, and defeating the Mamelukes at the Pyramids, the question of conquest was still undecided, unless the ulemas and all the ministers of the Musulman religion could be conciliated. Ever since the Revolution, the French army had exercised no worship: even in Italy it never attended church. Advantage was taken of this circumstance: the army was presented to the Musulmans as an army of converts, disposed to embrace Mahometanism. The Coptic, Greek, Latin, and Syrian Christians were numerous; they wished to avail themselves of the presence of the French army to elude the restrictions imposed on their worship. I opposed this proceeding, and took care to keep religious affairs on the footing on which I found them. Every morning at sunrise, the scheiks of the Grand Mosque of Gemil-Azar (a sort of Sorbonne) used to come to my levee: I caused all possible respectful attentions to be shown them; I discoursed with them at length on the various circumstances of the prophet's life, and on the chapters of the Koran. It was after my return from Salahieh that I proposed to them to publish a fetam, by which they should order the people to take an oath of obedience to me. This proposal startled them, and perplexed them much: after some hesitation, Scheik Cherkaoui, a respectable old man, replied: 'Why should not you and your whole army become Musulmans? In that case a hundred thousand men would flock to your standard, and when they were disciplined in your manner, you would re-establish the Arabian nation, and subdue the East.' I objected the necessity of circumcision, and the prohibition of wine, a beverage indispensable to the French soldier. After some discussions on this point, it was agreed that the grand scheiks of Gemil-Azar should endeavour to find out some way of removing these two obstacles. The disputes on the subject were animated; they lasted three weeks; but the report which was spread throughout Egypt, that the grand scheiks were engaged in making the French army Mahometans, filled all the faithful with joy. The French already perceived the amelioration of public spirit; they were no

EGYPT

longer looked upon as idolators. When the ulemas were agreed, the four muftis published a fetam, by which they declared that circumcision, being only a perfection, was not indispensable to being a Musulman: but that in that case Paradise must not be expected in the other world. Half the difficulty was thus removed; and it was easy to make the muftis comprehend that the second decision was not reasonable. This became the subject of six weeks' additional debates. At length they declared that it was possible to be a Musulman and drink wine, provided the fifth of one's income, instead of the tenth, were employed in acts of benevolence. I then had a plan drawn for a mosque larger than that of Gemil-Azar; I declared that I intended to have it built, by way of a monument, to commemorate the period of the conversion of my army; in fact, I only wished to gain time. The fetam of obedience was issued by the scheiks, and I was declared a close friend of the Prophet, and under his special protection. It was generally reported, that before the end of a year, the whole French army would wear a turban. This was the line of conduct which I constantly endeavoured to observe, reconciling my determination to remain in the religion in which I was born, with the occasions of my policy and ambition. During the whole stay of the army in Egypt, General Menou was the only person who became a Musulman, which was useful, and had a good effect. When the French left that country, only five or six hundred men remained behind, who enlisted with the Mamelukes, and embraced the Mahometan religion.

After the battle of Aboukir, on 3 August, 1799, the English commodore sent to Alexandria the English papers, and the French Gazette of Frankfort of the months of April, May and June, which communicated the news of the reverse sustained by the armies of the Rhine and of Italy. The commencement of the war of the second coalition had been heard of at the camp of Saint-Jean d'Acre.

I returned to France; first, because my instructions authorized me to do so; I had carte-blanche in all respects; secondly, because my presence was necessary to the Republic; thirdly, because the army of the East, which was victorious and numerous, could not, for a long time, have any enemy to contend with, and because the first object of the expedition was accomplished; the second could not be attained so long as the frontiers of the Republic should be menaced, and anarchy should prevail in its interior. The army of the East was victorious over two Turkish armies, which had been opposed against it during the campaign; that of Syria, defeated at El-Arisch, Gaza, Jaffa, Acre, and Mount Tabor, and which had lost its park of forty field-pieces, with all its magazines; and that of Rhodes, defeated at Saint-Jean d'Acre and Aboukir, where it had lost its train of thirty-four field-pieces, and its general-in-chief, the vizier with three tails, Mustapha-Pacha. The army of the East was numerous; it comprised 25,000 fighting men, of whom 3,500 were cavalry; it had

EGYPT

a hundred field-pieces of horse artillery, and 1,400 other pieces of artillery of all calibres, well supplied. It has been said that I left my army in distress, without artillery, clothing, or bread, and reduced to 8,000 effective men. These false reports deceived the English ministry; on 17 December, 1799, that Government determined to break the capitulation of El-Arisch, and ordered its admiral in the Mediterranean to suffer no capitulation to be carried into execution, which should allow the army of the East to return to France; but to stop the ships carrying the troops, and bring them to England. Kleber then comprehended his situation; he shook off the yoke of intrigue, and became himself again, turned on the Ottoman army, and defeated it at Heliopolis. After such a criminal violation of the law of nations, the Cabinet of Saint-James's perceived its error, and sent into Egypt 34,000 English, under the command of Abercrombie, who, joining 26,000 Turks under the grand-vizier and the capitain-pacha, succeeded in making themselves masters of that important colony in September, 1801, twenty-seven months after my departure; and not until after a very brisk campaign of 6 months, which would have ended in the overthrow of the English, if Kleber had not been assassinated, and if Menou, than whom a less military man never commanded, had not been at the head of the army. But after all, this campaign of 1801 cost the English Government several million sterling, 10,000 picked soldiers, and the commander-in-chief of its army. General Belliard obtained at Cairo, on 27 June, 1801, and General Menou at Alexandria, on 2 September in that year, the same capitulation which intriguing persons had made Kleber sign, at El-Arisch, twenty months before, on 24 January, 1800; that is to say, that the French army should be carried to France at the expense of the English, with its arms, cannon, baggage, and colours, and without being made prisoners of war. The reports of its state on arriving at the lazarettos of Marseilles and Toulon, prove that it consisted of 24,000 French; its losses in 1800 and 1801 had amounted to 4,000 men. When, therefore, I left the command to Kleber, it must have been 28,000 men, of whom 25,000 were in a condition to take the field. It is notorious, that when I left Egypt in the month of August, 1799, I thought that country forever secured to France, and hoped to be one day able to realize the second object of the expedition. As to the ideas I then entertained on the affairs of France, I communicated them to Menou, who has often repeated them; I projected the revolution of 18 Brumaire.

General Kleber had never commanded in chief; he had served in the army of the Sambre and Meuse as a general of division, under the orders of Jourdan. Having fallen into disgrace with the Directory, he was living in obscurity at Chaillot, when I arrived from Radstadt in November, 1797, after having conquered Italy, dictated peace at Vienna, and taken possession of the fortress of Mentz. Kleber followed my fortunes and went to Egypt with me. He there behaved with equal talent and bravery; he gained my esteem as his commander-in-chief, and I regarded him, next to Desaix, as the best officer in my army: he was also one of the most distinguished for subordination, which surprised the officers of his staff, who were accustomed to hear him censure and criticize the operations of the army of the Sambre and Meuse. He expressed the highest admiration of the fine manoeuvre of the battle of Mount Tabor, in which as commander-in-chief I saved Kleber's honour and his life. Some weeks afterwards he was marching at the head of his division to storm Acre; I sent him orders to join me, not choosing to risk so valuable a life on an occasion in which his brigadier-general could supply his place. When I determined to hasten back to Europe, to the aid of the Republic, I at first thought of leaving the command to Desaix; I afterwards intended to take Desaix and Kleber with me to France; but at length I resolved to take the former with me, and to invest the latter with the command. To raise a general of division to the rank of a general-in-chief, would be a singular way of showing a jealousy of him. It is vexatious to read such an assertion; for, after all, what should engender jealousy in a man who had been victorious in so many battles? and in what respect did I ever evince such a feeling?

The army of Egypt might have maintained, nay, might have perpetuated itself in that country, without receiving any assistance from France; provisions, clothing, all that is necessary for an army, abounded in Egypt. There were military stores and ammunition enough for several campaigns; besides, Champy and Conté had established powder-mills; the army had sufficient officers, etc., to organize a force of 80,000 men; it could obtain as many recruits as might be desired, especially amongst the young Copts, the Greeks, Syrians, and negroes of Darfur and Sennaar.

The 21st demi-brigade recruited 500 Copts, many of whom were made sub-officers, and received the decoration of the Legion of Honour; there are, no doubt, some of them now in France. But what power was there that could possibly attack Egypt?—The Ottoman Porte? It had lost its two armies of Syria and Rhodes; the battles of the Pyramids, of Mount Tabor, and of Aboukir, had completely exposed the weakness of the Ottoman armies. The Grand Vizier, with his mob of Asiatic rabble, was not even formidable to the inhabitants—Russia? a mere phantom. The Czar wished the French army to be established in Egypt; it was playing his game, and opening the gates of Constantinople to him.—What remained? England. But it required an army of at least 36,000 men to succeed in such an operation, and England had no such force disposable; and it was evident, since she had succeeded in forming a new coalition, that she would attempt the conquest of Egypt in Italy, Switzerland, or France.

Besides this, the army of Egypt might have received succours from France during the winter; nothing could have prevented it.

The destruction of the Aboukir squadron was a great misfortune; but the

EGYPT

loss of eleven vessels, three of which were very old, was not irreparable. From the month of August, 1797, Admiral Brueys commanded the Mediterranean, with forty ships of war: had he thought proper to land 15,000 men in Egypt, he could have done so; he did not, because the war which broke out on the Continent, required all the French troops in Italy, Switzerland, or on the Rhine. In the month of January, 1800, immediately after 18 Brumaire, any number of men might have been sent to Egypt by embarking them in the Brest squadron, or that of Rochefort: but men were wanted in France to dissolve the second coalition. It was not until after the battle of Marengo, when the state of the Republic was considerably altered, that it began to be thought expedient to send reinforcements to the army of Egypt.

Gantheaume sailed from Brest with seven ships of war, carrying 5,000 men. Forty ships were ready to put to sea, the moment a gun should be fired in the Baltic; which would have obliged England to send thither a reinforcement of thirty ships. These forty ships from Brest would have commanded the Mediterranean, during a part of the summer; they would have taken on board the troops necessary for Egypt at Tarentum.

In the month of October, 1800, advice-boats, frigates, merchant-ships, frequently arrived in Egypt; European wines and merchandize were very plentiful there, and the army received news from Europe every month. It was impossible to prevent frigates and corvettes from Toulon, Ancona, Tarentum, Brindisi, from arriving at Damietta or Alexandria, in the months of November, December, January, February, and March. *L'Egyptienne* and *La Justice* sailed from Toulon, and arrived in January, after a voyage of ten days: *La Régénérée* arrived in seventeen days from Rochefort. We must, therefore, conclude: First, that the army of the East needed no succours; secondly, that it might have remained several years without making new recruits; thirdly, that it might have made as many recruits as it pleased, by selecting Christians, and even Musulmans; and finally, by purchasing negroes from Darfur and Sennaar. Egypt is not a fortress, it is not a barren island, but an immense kingdom with a coast of 120 leagues. To apply the principles which relate to a citadel to so rich and extensive a country, is to mislead one's self and others in the most absurd manner. The crusaders were masters of Syria, for more than a hundred years; but theirs was a religious war.

The particular instructions which I, as commander-in-chief, transmitted to General Kleber and my letter dated from Aboukir, 5 Fructidor, which was written just as I was about to embark, and has been printed, are sufficient to explain my projects with respect to Egypt, and to prove my expectations of returning thither to complete the objects of the expedition, and the perfect confidence which I felt that Kleber would establish the colony. Whilst France should be at war, and the second coalition should remain undissolved, to remain stationary in Egypt, and merely preserve the country, were all that

EGYPT

could be done, and for these purposes Kleber, or Desaix, were more than sufficient. I obeyed the voice of France, which recalled me to Europe. On commencing this expedition, I had received a *carte blanche* from the Directory, for all my operations, whether for the affairs of Malta, or for those of Sicily, Egypt or Candia. I had regular powers to make treaties with Russia, the Porte, the India governments and princes; I was at liberty to retreat with my army, name my successor, or return myself, whenever I thought proper.

When I received the intelligence of the murder of Kleber, and found that General Menou, as the eldest officer, had assumed the command, I thought of recalling Menou and Reynier, and of giving the command to General Lanusse. General Menou had every qualification necessary for the command; he was very well informed, skilful in business, and a man of integrity. He had become a Mahometan, a circumstance certainly very ridiculous, but extremely agreeable to the prejudices of the country: some doubts were entertained respecting his military talents; it was, however, well known that he was extremely brave; he had behaved well in La Vendée, and at the storming of Alexandria. General Reynier was more habituated to war; but he was deficient in the most important quality of a chief: excellent as he was in the second rank, he seemed ill adapted for the first. He was taciturn, and partial to silence and solitude: he could not electrify, influence, or lead men at his will. General Lanusse possessed the sacred fire; he had distinguished himself by brilliant actions in the Pyrenees, and in Italy; he had the talent of communicating his sentiments to the two former; but what determined me as First Consul to leave matters as they stood, was the apprehension that the decree of nomination might be intercepted by the enemy's cruisers; and that they might use it for the purpose of sowing division and discord in the army, which had already evinced a tendency to disunion. It was impossible to foresee, at that time, the extent of Menou's incapacity for the direction of military affairs, as he had been a soldier all his life, had read much, had served in several campaigns, and was perfectly acquainted with the scene of action in which he was now placed.

I had no party in Egypt; I was the head of the army. Berthier, Desaix, Kleber, Menou, and Reynier, were all equally subordinate to me; and even supposing there had been parties, is it likely that petty narrow party views should influence a man who, throughout his administration always silenced the spirit of party—whose very first act of authority was to carry the law of 19 Fructidor, to fill the ministry, the council of State, and all the great offices of administration with *Fructidorisés,* such as Portalis, Benezech, Carnot, in the ministry; Dumas, Laumond, Fievé, in the council of state; Barthelemy, Fontanes, Pastoret, etc., in the senate?

Gantheaume sailed from Brest 25 January; he passed the straits 6 February; had he continued his route, he would have been at Alexandria on 20 February, where he would have found only the two ordinary cruisers; he might have

EGYPT

landed 5,000 men whom he carried with him, and 1,000 men forming the crews of three frigates or corvettes which he would have left at Alexandria; in seventy-two hours he might have landed all his charge, and then returned to Toulon: there was no squadron in the Mediterranean but that of Admiral Keith, of nine ships of war, which was in the bay of Maire, encumbered with the charge of a convoy of 180 sail. Rear-Admiral Warren was at Gibraltar, with some dismantled ships; he was not able to put to sea till a long time afterwards. Admiral Calder, with seven sail, had gone in pursuit of Gantheaume to America; so ably had the English spies been imposed upon. In fact the agents of administration for Guadaloupe and Saint-Domingo, with a great number of inhabitants, both men and women, embarked at Brest, intending to go to America. The frigate *La Régénérée* sailed from Rochefort, passed the straits 19 February, and arrived at Alexandria 1 March; which is a sufficient proof that Admiral Gantheaume, who passed the Straits on 6 February, would have arrived before that time: and it was not till 1 March that Admiral Keith anchored at Alexandria and landed Abercrombie's army. General Friant who commanded at Alexandria, would, therefore, have had 8,000 men to oppose the landing of the English, who must have failed, and thus Egypt would have been saved. The English army and fleets were divided by the war which France and Spain were carrying on against Portugal, and by the quadruple alliance, which required a fleet in the Baltic. After having succeeded in deceiving Admiral Calder, there was nothing more to fear in the Mediterranean.

The French admiral's resolution having thus failed him, he anchored, about the middle of February, in the port of Toulon; after having taken an English frigate and sloop of war: I, as First Consul, was extremely dissatisfied; I ordered him to sail again, but he could not put to sea until 19 March. On the coast of Sardinia he fell in with Admiral Warren's squadron, which had been equipped at Gibraltar: it was inferior to his own; but, as it was not his object to fight, he manoeuvred with great skill, and during the night altered his course, and escaped. Warren, finding at daybreak that the French admiral had disappeared, steered for Alexandria, to fall in under the flag of Admiral Keith. Gantheaume ought to have made for Alexandria likewise, reconnoitring Mount Carmel or Mount Cassins, and to have landed his little army at Damietta: instead of which he returned again to Toulon. I was still dissatisfied: I made him sail again, with orders to land his troops at Damietta, if he should keep the Syrian coast, or at El Baratoun, in case he should coast the African shore. El Baratoun is a good port, with plenty of water. From thence to Alexandria water and pastures are every day met with: and the admiral would have landed with the 5,000 men, two months' provisions, clothes, and money. In five or six days' march these 5,000 men would have arrived at Alexandria. This third time, Gantheaume reached the Egyptian shore on 8

EGYPT

June: these 5,000 men would therefore have arrived towards 15 or 20 June, at the most propitious moment: the reinforcements from England not having reached the English army. In June, General Cool had but 4,000 men at the Roman camp opposite Alexandria: Hutchinson, with 5,000 men, was near Gesch. General Menou, strengthened by this reinforcement, could have attacked General Cool with 10,000 men, would have defeated him, and disengaged Belliard from Cairo; the victory was certain. Thus the French admiral had three opportunities of saving Egypt; but he suffered himself to be imposed on by false reports: had he possessed the decision of Nelson, his squadron being light, very fast sailers, and well manned, he might have despised Keith's squadron: he could not have defeated, but he might have escaped it. Gantheaume was perfectly acquainted with the coasts of Syria and Egypt: and the circumstances were unprecedented. All the English fleets were required in the Baltic. A little squadron of light, fast-sailing, well-manned vessels might have undertaken anything. Three frigates, commanded by Rear-Admiral Perée, traversed all the seas between Rhodes and Acre, during the siege of Saint-Jean d'Acre, frequently communicated within two leagues of Sir Sidney Smith, behind Mount Carmel, and intercepted several ships of the army of Rhodes, on their way to Acre, laden with provisions, guns, and ammunition for the besieged army; nevertheless *L'Alceste, La Courageuse,* and *La Junon,* were very ordinary sailers; if the rear-admiral had had three such frigates as *La Justice* and *La Diane,* he would have manoeuvred much more boldly; he would have done as he pleased, in spite of the *Tiger* and the *Theseus,* Sir Sidney Smith's two eighty-gun ships.

To resume: the expedition to Egypt was completely successful. I landed at Alexandria on 1 July, 1798; on 1 August I was master of Cairo, and of all lower Egypt; on 1 January, 1799, I had conquered the whole of Egypt; on 1 July, 1799, I had destroyed the Turkish army of Syria, and taken its train of 42 field-pieces and 150 ammunition waggons. At length, in the month of August, I destroyed the select troops of the army of the Porte, and at Aboukir took its train of 32 field-pieces. Kleber allowed himself to be intimidated by the Grand Vizier; he surrendered all the fortresses to him, and consented to a most extraordinary convention, that of El-Arisch. But Colonel Latour-Maubourg, arriving on 1 March, 1800, before Cairo had been surrendered, defeated the Grand Vizier, drove him into the Desert, and reconquered Egypt. In March, 1801, the English landed an army of 18,000 men, without horses for the artillery, or cavalry: this army must have been destroyed; but Kleber had been assassinated, and by an overwhelming fatality this brave army was consigned to the command of a man, who, although competent enough for many other purposes, was detestable as a military commander. The vanquished army, after six months feigned manoeuvres, landed on the coast of Provence, to the number of 24,000 men. The army of Egypt, on its

EGYPT

arrival at Malta, in 1798, was 32,000 strong: it received there a reinforcement of 2,000 men, but left a garrison of 4,000; and arrived at Alexandria 30,000 strong. It received 3,000 men from the wreck of the squadron at Aboukir, which increased it to 33,000 men. 24,000 returned to France: 1,000 had previously gone home as wounded, or blind, in the frigates *La Muiron* and *La Carrère*, in which I sailed; but a like number of troops had arrived in *La Justice*, *L'Egyptienne*, and *La Régénérée*. The loss, therefore, was 9,000 men; of whom 4,000 died in 1798 and 1799, and 5,000 in 1800 and 1801, in the hospitals and in the field of battle. When I left the army at the end of August, 1799, the amount of its force was 28,500 Frenchmen, including sick, veterans, persons belonging to the depots, and other non-combatants, following the army.

The English army, in 1801, consisted, at first, of only 18,000 men: but it received, in the months of July and August, 7,000 men from London, Malta, and Port Mahon, and 8,000 from the Indies, who landed at Cosseir, which increased the English force to 32,000, or 34,000. By adding to these 25,000 Turks, it will appear that the allied forces employed against Egypt amounted to nearly 60,000 men. If these had all attacked together, it would, undoubtedly, have been impossible to resist them; but as they came into action only at intervals of several months, victory must infallibly have declared for the French, if Desaix or Kleber had been at the head of the army; or indeed any general but Menou, who, nevertheless, had only to imitate the manoeuvre which I had executed in 1799, when Mustapha-Pacha landed at Aboukir. The religious fanaticism, which had been looked upon as the greatest obstacle to the establishment of the French in Egypt, had been tranquillized; all the ulemas and the great Scheiks were now friendly to the French army.

Saint Louis, in 1250, landed at Damietta with 6,000 men; had he acted as the French did in 1798, he would have triumphed like them, and would have conquered all Egypt; and had I in 1798 conducted myself like the Crusaders of 1250, I would have been defeated. In fact, Saint Louis appeared before Damietta on 5 June; he landed the following day, the Musulmans evacuated the town, which he entered on the 6th; but from 6 June to 6 December he never stirred. On 6 December he began his march, passing up the right bank of the Nile; he arrived on 17 December on the left bank of the Canal of Achmoun, opposite Mausourah, and encamped there two months: this canal was then full of water. On 12 February, 1251, the waters having subsided, he passed this arm of the Nile, and fought a battle, eight months after his debarkation in Egypt. If Saint Louis, on 8 June, 1250, had manoeuvred as the French manoeuvred in 1798, he would have arrived at Mausourah on 12 June; he would have found the canal of Achmoun dry, because at that time the waters of the Nile are at the lowest; he would have crossed it, and arrived on 26 June at Cairo; he would have conquered lower Egypt within a month after his arrival. When the first pigeon carried to Cairo the news of the landing of the infidels at Damietta, the consternation was general; there were no means of resistance: the faithful crowded the mosques, and passed the days and nights in prayer; they were resigned to their fate, and awaited the French army: but in eight months the true believers had time to prepare for resistance. Upper Egypt, Arabia, and Syria, sent their forces; and Saint Louis was defeated, put to flight, and made prisoner. Had I acted in 1798 as Saint Louis did in 1250, had I passed July, August, September, October, November, and December, without stirring from Alexandria, I would have met with insuperable obstacles in January and February. Dumanhour, Rhamaniah, Rosetta, would have been fortified; Girch and Cairo would have been intrenched and defended by cannon and troops; 12,000 Mamelukes, 20,000 Arabs, 50,000 Arabian Janissaries, reinforced by the armies of Arabia, of the Pachalic of Damascus, of Acre, of Jerusalem, and of Tripoli, flocking to the succour of that key of the holy Caba, would have frustrated all the efforts of the French army, which must have re-embarked. In 1250 Egypt was not in a condition to make so good a defence, but Saint Louis knew not how to profit by its weakness: he lost eight months in deliberating with the Pope's legates, and in praying; he had better have employed them in gaining victories.

It was believed that I would not reach France; it had been determined to evacuate Egypt; a justification of this proceeding was wanted. But fortunately for Egypt, a duplicate letter fell into the hands of Admiral Keith, who immediately sent it to London. The English minister instantly wrote to prevent the ratification of any capitulation by which the French army should be allowed to return from Egypt to France, and sent orders, in case the troops had already got to sea, to capture them, and bring them into the Thames.

By a second piece of good fortune, Colonel Latour-Maubourg, who left France at the end of January, with the news of my arrival in France, of 18 Brumaire, and of the Constitution of the year VIII, together with the letter of the Minister of War, dated 12 January, in answer to the foregoing letter of Kleber, arrived at Cairo, on 4 May, ten days before the term fixed for the surrender of that capital to the Grand Vizier. Kleber now comprehended that his business was to conquer or die; but he had only to march.

That rabble which called itself the Grand Vizier's army, was chased beyond the Desert without making any resistance. The French army had not 100 men killed or wounded; but killed 15,000 of the enemy, and took their tents, baggage, and artillery.

An entire change now took place in Kleber; he applied himself seriously to the amelioration of the state of the army and of the country; but on 14 June, 1800, he fell by the dagger of a wretched fanatic.

Had he been living in the following campaign when the English army landed at Aboukir, it would have been destroyed; few of the English would ever have re-embarked, and the French would have possessed Egypt.

Chapter XXXII

THE EIGHTEENTH OF BRUMAIRE
(9 November, 1799)

My arrival in France. Sensation produced by that event. At Paris. The directors, Roger Ducos, Moulins, Gohier, Sieyes. My Conduct. Roederer, Lucien and Joseph, Talleyrand, Fouché, Réal. State of the different parties. They all make proposals to me. Barras. I coalesce with Sieyes. State of feeling among the troops in the Capital. Measures arranged for 18 Brumaire. Proceedings of that day. Decree of the Council of the Ancients, which transfers the seat of the Legislative Body to Saint-Cloud. My speech to the Council of the Ancients. Tumultuous sitting at Saint-Cloud. Adjournment of the Councils for three months.

When lamentable weakness and endless versatility are manifested in the councils of a government; when an administration, yielding by turns to the influence of every opposing party, and going on from day to day without any fixed plan or determined system, has shown its utter insufficiency; and when the most modern citizens in the state are obliged to confess that it is without a government; when rulers, insignificant at home, have shamefully brought on their country the contempt of foreigners—the greatest of injuries in the eyes of a proud people; a vague uneasiness spreads throughout society: agitated by the instinct of self-preservation, it looks into its own resources, and seeks for someone able to save it from destruction.

A populous nation always possesses this tutelary genius in its own bosom, though he may sometimes be tardy in appearing. It is not indeed sufficient for him to exist, he must be known to others, and he must know himself. Until then all endeavours are vain, all schemes ineffectual. The inertness of the multitude is the protection of the nominal government, and in spite of its inexperience and weakness, the efforts of its enemies cannot prevail against it. But let this deliverer, so impatiently expected, suddenly give a proof of his existence, and the nation instinctively acknowledges and calls on him; all obstacles vanish at his approach, and a great people thronging round his steps, seems exultingly to proclaim 'This is the man'.

Such was the state of the public mind in France in the year 1799, when, on 9 October (16 Vendemiaire, year VIII) the frigates *La Muiron* and *La Carrère*, and the zebecks *La Revanche* and *La Fortune*, cast anchor, at the break of day, in the gulf of Frejus.

No sooner were the French frigates recognized, than it was conjectured they came from Egypt. The people ran in crowds to the shore, eager for news from the army. It was soon understood that I was on board; and such was the enthusiasm among the people, that even the wounded soldiers got out of the hospitals, in spite of the guards, and went to the shore. The spectators wept with joy. In a moment the sea was covered with boats. The officers belonging to the fortifications and the Customs, the crews of the ships that were anchored in the road, in short everybody thronged about the frigates. General Pereymont, who commanded on the coast, was the first to go on board. Thus we were enabled to enter, without waiting for the officers of quarantine; for the communication with the shore had been general.

Italy had just been lost; war was about to be recommenced on the Var, and Frejus dreaded an invasion as soon as hostilities should begin. The necessity of having a leader at the head of affairs was too imperious; everyone was too much agitated by my sudden appearance at this juncture, for ordinary considerations to have any weight. The officers of quarantine declared that there was no occasion for subjecting these vessels to it, and grounded their report on the circumstance that communication had taken place at Ajaccio. This argument, however, far from being tenable, only went to prove that Corsica itself ought to have been put under quarantine. The administration at Marseilles made this observation a fortnight afterwards, and with reason. It is true, that during the fifty days which had elapsed from the vessels leaving Egypt, there had been no sickness on board any of them, and indeed the plague had ceased three months before their departure. At six o'clock that evening, I, accompanied by Berthier, set off in a coach for Paris.

The fatigue of my passage, and the effect of the transition from a dry climate to a moist one, determined me to stop six hours at Aix. The inhabitants of the city, and of the neighbouring villages, came in crowds to testify their happiness at seeing me again. The joy was universal. Those who lived too far in the country to present themselves on the road in time, rang the bells, and hoisted flags upon the steeples, which at night blazed with illuminations.

It was not like the return of a citizen to his country, or a general at the head of a victorious army, but like the triumph of a sovereign restored to his people. The enthusiasm of Avignon, Montelimart, Valence, and Vienne, was only surpassed by the rapture of Lyons. That city, in which I rested for twelve hours, was in an universal delirium. The Lyonnese had at all times shown great attachment to me, either from the natural generosity of character by which they are distinguished—or that, considering their city as the capital of the south, they felt peculiarly interested in all that concerned the security of the frontiers on the Italian side—or that the population of Lyons being composed chiefly of natives of Burgundy and Dauphiny, shared the sentiments most prevalent in these provinces. Their imaginations were, moreover, still in a state of exultation at that time, from the accounts which had been spread eight days before of the battle of Aboukir and of the brilliant success of the French arms in Egypt, which formed such a striking contrast to the defeat of their armies in Germany and Italy. 'We are numerous, we are brave,' the people seemed everywhere to say, 'and yet we are conquered. We want a leader to direct us: we now behold him, and our glory will once more shine forth.' In the meantime the news of my return had reached Paris. It was announced at the theatres, and caused an universal sensation—a general delirium, of which the members of the Directory partook. Some of the *Société du Manège* trembled on the occasion; but they dissembled their real feelings so well as to seem to share the general rejoicing. Baudin, the deputy from Ardennes, who was really a worthy man, and sincerely grieved at the unfortunate turn that the affairs of the Republic had taken, died of joy when he heard of my return.

I had already quitted Lyons, when my landing was announced in Paris. With a precaution which was very advisable in my situation, I expressed to my couriers my intention of taking a different road from that which I actually took; so that my wife, my family, and particular friends, went in a wrong direction to meet me, and by that means some days passed before I was able to see them. Having thus arrived in Paris quite unexpectedly, I was in my own house, in the *rue Chantereine,* before anyone knew of my being in the capital. Two hours afterwards, I presented myself to the Directory, and, being recognized by the soldiers on guard, was announced by shouts of gladness. All the members of the Directory appeared to share in the public joy; I had every reason to congratulate myself on the reception I experienced on all sides. The nature of past events sufficiently instructed me as to the situation of France; and the information I had procured on my journey, had made me acquainted with all that was going on. My resolution was taken. What I had been unwilling to attempt on my return from Italy, I was now determined to do immediately. I held the government of the Directory and the leaders of the councils in supreme contempt. Resolved to possess myself of authority, and to restore France to her former glory, by giving a powerful impulse to public affairs, I had left Egypt to execute this project; and all that I had just seen in the interior of France, had confirmed my sentiments and strengthened my resolution.

Of the old Directory only Barras remained. The other members were Roger Ducos, Moulins, Gohier, and Sieyes.

Ducos was a man of narrow mind and easy disposition.

Moulins, a general of division, had never served in war; he was originally in the French guards, and had been advanced in the army of the Interior. He was a worthy man, and a warm and upright patriot.

Gohier was an advocate of considerable reputation, and exalted patriotism; an eminent lawyer, and a man of great integrity and candour.

Sieyes had long been known to me. He was born at Frejus, in Provence. His reputation commenced with the Revolution. He had been called to the constituent assembly by the electors of the third estate, at Paris, after having been repulsed by the assembly of the clergy at Chartres. He was the author of the pamphlet intituled *What is the Third Estate?* which made so much noise. He was not a man of business: knowing but little of men, he knew not how they might be made to act. All his studies having been directed to metaphysics, he had the fault of metaphysicians, of too often despising positive notions; but he was capable of giving useful and luminous advice on matters of importance, or at any momentous crisis. To him France is indebted for the division into departments, which destroyed all provincial prejudices: and though he was never distinguished as an orator, he greatly contributed to the success of the revolution by his advice in the committees. He was nominated as director, when the Directory was first established; but he refused the distinction at that time, and Lareveillere was appointed instead of him. He was afterwards sent ambassador to Berlin, and imbibed a great mistrust of the politics of Prussia in the course of his mission. He had taken a seat in the Directory not long before this time; but he had already been of great service in checking the progress of the *Société du Manège*, which he saw was ready to seize the helm of the state. He was abhorred by that faction; and, fearless of bringing upon himself the enmity of so powerful a party, he courageously resisted the machinations of these men of blood, in order to avert from the Republic the evil with which it was threatened.

At the period of 13 Vendemiaire, the following occurrence had enabled me to form a correct judgment of him. At the most critical moment of that day, when the committee of the Forty seemed quite distracted, Sieyes came to me, and took me into the recess of a window, while the committee was deliberating upon the answer to be given to the summons of the sections. 'You hear them, General,' said he; 'they talk while they should be acting. Bodies of men are wholly unfit to direct armies, for they know not the value of time or opportunity. You have nothing to do here: go, General, consult your genius and the situation of the country: the hope of the Republic rests on you alone.'

I accepted an invitation to dine with each of the directors, on condition that it should be merely a family dinner, and that no stranger should be present. A grand entertainment was given to me by the Directory. The Legislative Body wished to follow the example; but when it was proposed to the general committee, a strong opposition arose: the minority refusing to pay any homage to General Moreau, whom it was proposed to include in the entertainment; he was accused of having misconducted himself on 18 Fructidor. The majority in order to remove every difficulty, had recourse to the expedient of opening a subscription. The festival took place in the church of Saint Sulpice; covers were laid for seven hundred. I remained at table but a short time; I appeared to be uneasy, and much preoccupied. Every one of the ministers wished to give me an entertainment; but I only accepted a dinner with the Minister of Justice, for whom I had a great esteem: I requested that the principal lawyers of the Republic might be there; I was very cheerful at this dinner, conversed at large on the civil and criminal codes, to the great astonishment of Tronchet, Treilhard, Merlin, and Target, and expressed a desire that the persons and the property of the Republic should be governed by a simple code, adapted to the enlightened state of the age.

Constant to my system, I entered but little into these public entertainments, and pursued the same line of conduct that I had followed on my first return from Italy. Always dressed as a member of the Institute, I showed myself in public only with that society: I received at my house none but men of science, the generals of my suite, and a few friends;—such as Regnault-de-Saint-Jean-d'Angely, whom I had employed in Italy in 1797, and subsequently placed at Malta; Volney, the author of excellent Travels in Egypt; Roederer, whom I respected for his probity and noble sentiments; Lucien Bonaparte, one of the most powerful orators of the Council of Five Hundred, who had protected the Republic from the revolutionary *régime,* by opposing the declaration that the country was in danger; and Joseph Bonaparte, who lived in splendour and was highly respected.

I went frequently to the Institute; but never to the theatres, except at times when I was not expected, and then always into the private boxes.

Meanwhile all Europe rang with my arrival; all the troops and friends of the Republic, even the Italians, indulged in the most sanguine hopes: England and Austria were alarmed. The fury of the English was turned against Sir Sidney Smith, and Nelson, who commanded the British naval force in the Mediterranean. A variety of caricatures on this subject were seen in the streets of London. In one of these, Nelson was represented amusing himself with

THE EIGHTEENTH OF BRUMAIRE

dressing Lady Hamilton, while the frigate *La Muiron* was passing between his legs.

Talleyrand was fearful of being ill-received by me. It had been agreed both by the Directory and Talleyrand, that immediately after the departure of the expedition for Egypt, negotiations respecting its object should be opened with the Porte. Talleyrand was even to have been the negotiator, and to have set out for Constantinople twenty-four hours after the sailing of the expedition for Egypt from Toulon. This engagement, which had been formally insisted on and positively consented to, had been immediately consigned to oblivion; not only had Talleyrand remained at Paris, but no sort of negotiation had taken place. Talleyrand did not suppose that I had forgotten this; but the influence of the *Société du Manège* had procured the dismission of this minister; his situation was itself a guarantee. I did not repulse him: Talleyrand, moreover, availed himself of all the resources of a supple and insinuating address, in order to conciliate a person whose suffrage it was important to him to secure.

Fouché had been for several months minister of police; he had, after 13 Vendemiaire, some transactions with me; I was aware of his immoral and versatile disposition. Sieyes had closed the *Manège* without his participation. I effected 18 Brumaire without admitting Fouché into the secret.

Réal, commissioner of the Directory in the department of Paris, gained more of my confidence. Zealous for the revolution, he had been substitute for the attorney of the commune of Paris, at a time of storms and troubles. His disposition was ardent, but he was full of noble and generous sentiments.

All classes of citizens, all the provinces of France, were impatient to see what I would do. From all sides came offers of support, and of entire submission to my will.

I employed myself in listening to the proposals which were submitted to me; in observing all parties; and, in short, in making myself thoroughly master of the true state of affairs. All parties desired a change, and all desired to effect it in concert with me, even the leaders of the *Manège*.

Bernadotte, Augereau, Jourdan, Marbot, etc., who were at the head of the plotters of this society, offered a military dictatorship to me, and proposed to acknowledge me as chief, and to confide the fortunes of the Republic to me, if I would but second the principles of the *Société du Manège*.

Sieyes, who commanded the vote of Roger Ducos in the Directory, swayed the majority of the Council of Ancients, and influenced only a small minority in the Council of Five Hundred, proposed to place me at the head of the government, changing the constitution of the year III, which he deemed defective, and that I should adopt the institutions and the constitution which he had projected, and which he had by him in manuscript.

Regnier, Boulay, a numerous party of the Council of Ancients, and many of the members of that of Five Hundred, were also desirous to place the fate of the Republic in my hands.

This party was composed of the most moderate and wisest men of the legislature: it was the same that joined Lucien Bonaparte in opposing the declaration that the country was in danger.

The directors Barras, Moulins, and Gohier, hinted to me my resuming the command of the army of Italy, my re-establishment of the Cisalpine Republic and the glory of the French arms. Moulins and Gohier had no secret plan in reserve: they were sincere in the scheme they proposed: they trusted that all would go well from the moment that I should lead our armies to new successes. Barras was far from partaking of this security; he knew that everything went wrong, that the Republic was sinking; but whether he had made engagements with the Pretender to the throne, as was asserted at the time (*Biographie des Hommes Vivants, Michand,* 1816, tom. 1, page 214), or whether he deceived himself as to his personal situation—for what errors may not spring from vanity and self-love of an ignorant man?—he imagined he could keep himself at the head of affairs. Barras made the same proposals as were made by Moulins and Gohier.

However, all the factions were in motion. That of the Fructidorisés (who supported the decree of 1795, which had provided for the re-election of two-thirds of the Convention to the new legislature) seemed persuaded of its own influence; but it had no partisans among the existing authorities. I had the choice of several measures, viz.:

To consolidate the existing constitution, and to support the Directory by becoming myself a director. But the constitution was fallen into contempt, and a magistracy in several hands could not lead to any satisfactory result: it would, in fact, have been associating myself with revolutionary prejudices, and with the passions of Barras and of Sieyes, and by the consequent re-action rendering myself obnoxious to the hatred of their enemies.

To change the constitution, and step into power by means of the *Société du Manège*. This society contained a great number of the rankest Jacobins: they commanded the majority in the Council of Five Hundred, and a spirited minority in that of the Ancients. By making use of these men the victory was certain, no resistance would be offered. It was the most certain way to overthrow the existing state of things; but Jacobins do not attach themselves to any leader; they are unbending, and violent in the extreme. It would, therefore, have been necessary, after succeeding by their aid, to get rid of them, and to persecute them. Such treachery would have been unworthy of a noble-minded man.

Barras tendered the support of his friends, but they were men of suspicious morals, and publicly accused of wasting the national wealth. How would it have been possible to govern with such people? for without strict probity it

THE EIGHTEENTH OF BRUMAIRE

would have been impracticable to restore the finances, or to do any real good.

To Sieyes were attached many well-informed men, persons of integrity and republicans upon principle, possessing in general little energy, and much intimidated by the faction *du Manège,* and fearful of popular commotions; but who might be retained after the victory, and be employed with success in an orderly government. No objection could be taken to the character of Sieyes: he could not, in any case, be a dangerous rival. But to side with this party was to declare against Barras and the *Manège,* who abhorred Sieyes.

On 8 Brumaire (30 October) I dined with Barras; only a few persons were there. A conversation took place after dinner: 'The Republic is falling,' said the director, 'things can go no farther; the government is powerless; a change must take place, and Hedouville must be named President of the Republic. As to you, General, you intend to rejoin the army; and for my part, ill as I am, unpopular, and worn out, I am fit only to return to private life.'

I looked steadfastly at him without replying a word. Barras cast down his eyes, and remained silent. Thus the conversation ended. General Hedouville was a man of the most ordinary character. Barras did not give utterance to his thoughts; but his countenance betrayed his secret.

This conversation was decisive. A few minutes afterwards, I called upon Sieyes: I gave him to understand that for ten days all parties had addressed themselves to me, that I was resolved to act with Sieyes and the majority of the Council of Ancients, and that I came for the purpose of giving him a positive assurance of this. It was agreed that the change might be effected between 15 and 20 Brumaire.

On my return to my own house, I found there Talleyrand, Fouché, Roederer, and Réal. I related to them unaffectedly, plainly, and simply, without any indication of countenance which could betray my opinion, what Barras had just said to me. Réal and Fouché, who had a regard to the director, were sensible how ill-timed his dissimulation was. They went to him on purpose to upbraid him with it. The following day, at eight o'clock, Barras came to me. I had not risen: he insisted on seeing me, entered, and told me he feared he had explained himself very imperfectly the preceding evening; that I alone could save the Republic; that he came to place himself at my disposal, to do whatever I wished, and to act whatever part I chose to assign him. He intreated me to give him an assurance that, if I had any project in agitation, I would rely upon him.

But I had already made up my mind: I replied that I had nothing in view; that I was fatigued, indisposed; that I could not accustom myself to the moisture of the atmosphere of the capital, just arrived, as I was, from the dry climate of the sands of Arabia; and I put an end to the interview by similar common-place observations.

THE EIGHTEENTH OF BRUMAIRE

Meanwhile Moulins went daily between eight and nine o'clock to my house, to request my advice on the business of the day. He always had military intelligence, or civil matters, on which he wished for instructions. On what related to military affairs, I replied as I felt; but with respect to civil concerns, thinking that I ought not to disclose my private opinions to him, I only answered in a vague manner.

Gohier came also occasionally to visit me, for the purpose of making proposals to me and asking my advice.

The officers of the garrison, headed by General Moreau, commanding the citadel of Paris, demanded to be presented to me; they could not succeed in their object, and, being put off day to day, they began to complain of my manifesting so little desire to see my old comrades again.

The forty adjutants of the national guard of Paris, who had been appointed by me when I commanded the army of the Interior, had solicited as a favour to see me. I knew almost all of them; but, in order to conceal my designs, I put off the time for receiving them.

The eighth and ninth regiment of dragoons, which were in garrison at Paris, were old regiments of the army of Italy; they longed to muster before their former general. I accepted the offer, and informed them that I would fix the day.

The twenty-first light horse, which had contributed to the success of the day of 13 Vendemiaire was likewise at Paris. Murat came from this corps, and all the officers went daily to him, to ask him on what day I would review it. They were as unsuccessful as the rest.

The citizens of Paris complained of my keeping so close; they went to the theatres, and to the reviews, where it was announced I would be present, but I came not. Nobody could account for this conduct; all were becoming impatient. People began to murmur against me: 'It is now,' they observed, 'a fortnight since his arrival, and he has yet done nothing. Does he mean to behave as he did on his return from Italy, and suffer the Republic to be torn to pieces by these contending factions?'

But the decisive hour approached.

On 15 Brumaire, Sieyes and I had an interview, during which we resolved on the measures for the day of the eighteenth. It was agreed that the Council of Ancients, availing itself of the 102nd article of the Constitution, should decree the removal of the Legislative Body to Saint Cloud, and should appoint me Commander-in-chief of the guard belonging to the Legislative Body, of the troops of the military division of Paris, and of the national guard.

This decree was to be passed on the eighteenth, at seven o'clock in the morning: at eight, I was to go to the Tuileries, where the troops were to be assembled, and there to assume the command of the capital.

On the seventeenth, I informed the officers that I would receive them the

THE EIGHTEENTH OF BRUMAIRE

next day at six in the morning. As that hour might appear to be unseasonable, I feigned being about to set off on a journey: I gave the same invitation to the forty adjutants of the national guard; and I informed the three regiments of cavalry that I would review them in the Champs-Elysées, on the same day, the eighteenth, at seven in the morning. I also intimated to the generals who had returned from Egypt with me, and to all those with whose sentiments I was acquainted, that I should be glad to see them at that hour. Each thought that the invitation was confined to himself alone, and supposed that I had some orders to give him; for it was known that Dubois-Crancé, the minister at war, had taken the reports of the state of the army to me, and had adopted my advice on all that was to be done, as well on the frontiers of the Rhine as in Italy.

Moreau, who had been at the dinner of the Legislative Body, and whom I had there, for the first time, become acquainted with, having learned from public report that a change was in preparation, assured me that he placed himself at my disposal, that he had no wish to be admitted into any secret, and that he required but one hour's notice to prepare himself. Macdonald, who happened then to be at Paris, had made the same tenders of service. At two o'clock in the morning, I let them know that I wished to see them at my house at seven o'clock, and on horseback. I did not apply to Augereau, Bernadotte, etc., however Joseph brought the latter.

General Lefebvre commanded the military division; he was wholly devoted to the Directory. I sent an aide-de-camp to him, at midnight, desiring he would come to me at six.

Everything took place as had been agreed. About seven in the morning, the Council of Ancients assembled under the presidency of Lemercier. Cornudet, Lebrun, and Fargues, depicted in lively colours the miseries of the Republic, the dangers with which it was surrounded, and the obstinate conspiracy of the leaders *du Manège* for the restoration of the reign of terror. Regnier, deputy for La Meurthe, moved that, in pursuance of the 102nd article of the Constitution, the sittings of the Legislative Body should be transferred to Saint Cloud; and that I should be invested with the chief command of the troops of the seventeenth military division, and charged with the execution of this measure. He then spoke in support of his motion. 'The Republic', said he, 'is threatened by anarchists and by the foreign party: measures for the public safety must be taken; we are certain of the support of General Bonaparte: under the shelter of his protecting arm the Councils may discuss the changes which the public interest renders necessary.' As soon as the majority of the Council was satisfied that the motion was in concert with me, the decree passed; but not without strong opposition. It was couched in these terms:

'The Council of Ancients, by virtue of articles 102, 103, and 104, of the Constitution, decrees as follows:

THE EIGHTEENTH OF BRUMAIRE

'Article 1. The Legislative Body is transferred to Saint Cloud; the two Councils shall there sit in the two wings of the palace.

'2. They shall assemble there to-morrow, 19 Brumaire, at noon; all exercise of their functions and all discussions, elsewhere and before that time, is prohibited.

'3. General Bonaparte is charged with the execution of the present decree. He will adopt all measures necessary for the safety of the national representation. The general commanding the seventeenth military division, the guards of the legislative body, the stationary national guards, the troops of the line which are in the commune of Paris, and throughout the whole extent of the seventeenth military division, are placed immediately under his command, and enjoined to recognize him in that capacity; all the citizens are to aid and assist him on his first requisition.

'4. General Bonaparte is summoned to the council-table to receive a copy of the present decree, and to take the oath; he will act in concert with the committees of inspectors of the two Councils.

'5. The present decree shall be immediately transmitted by messengers to the Council of Five Hundred, and to the Executive Directory; it shall be printed, posted, proclaimed, and sent to all the communes of the Republic by couriers extraordinary.'

This decree was made at eight o'clock; and at half-past eight, the state messenger who was the bearer of it arrived at my house. He found the avenues filled with officers of the garrison, adjutants of the national guard, generals, and the three regiments of cavalry. I had the folding-doors opened; and, my house being too small to contain so many persons, I came forward to the steps in front of it, received the compliments of the officers, harangued them, and told them that I relied upon them all for the salvation of France. At the same time I gave them to understand that the Council of Ancients, under the authority of the Constitution, had just conferred on me the command of all the troops; that important measures were in agitation, designed to rescue the country from its alarming situation; that I relied upon their support and good will; and that I was at that moment going to mount my horse to ride to the Tuileries.

Enthusiasm was at its height: all the officers drew their swords, and promised their service and fidelity. I then turned towards Lefebvre, demanding whether he would remain with me or return to the Directory. Lefebvre, powerfully affected, did not hesitate. I instantly mounted, and placed myself at the head of the generals and officers, and of 1,500 horse whom I had halted upon the boulevard, at the corner of the street of *Mont-Blanc*. I gave orders to the adjutants of the national guard to return to their quarters, and beat the generale; to communicate the decree that they had just heard, and to announce that no orders were to be observed but such as should emanate from me.

THE EIGHTEENTH OF BRUMAIRE

I presented myself at the bar of the Council of Ancients, attended by this brilliant escort. 'You are the wisdom of the nation,' said I: 'At this crisis it belongs to you to point out the measures which may save the country: I come, surrounded by all the generals, to promise you their support. I appoint General Lefebvre my lieutenant; I will faithfully fulfil the task with which you have intrusted me: let us not look into the past for examples of what is now going on. Nothing in history resembles the end of the eighteenth century; nothing in the eighteenth century resembles the present moment.'

All the troops were mustered at the Tuileries; I reviewed them, amidst the unanimous acclamations of both citizens and soldiers. I gave the command of the troops intrusted with the protection of the Legislative Body to General Lannes: and to General Murat the command of those sent to Saint Cloud.

I deputed General Moreau to guard the Luxembourg; and, for this purpose, I placed under his orders 500 men of the eighty-sixth regiment. But, at the moment of setting off, these troops refused to obey: they had no confidence in Moreau, who was not, they said, a patriot. I was obliged to harangue them, assuring them that Moreau would act uprightly. Moreau had become suspected through his conduct in *Fructidor*.

The intelligence that I was at the Tuileries, and that I alone was to be obeyed, quickly spread throughout the capital. The people flew to the Tuileries in crowds: some led by mere curiosity to behold so renowned a general, others by patriotic enthusiasm to offer him their support. The following proclamation was everywhere posted.

'Citizens, the Council of Ancients, the depositary of the national wisdom, has just pronounced a decree; for this it has authority from articles 102 and 103 of the Act of the Constitution: it imposes upon me the duty of taking measures for the safety of the national representation. The immediate removal of the representation is necessary; the Legislative Body will then find itself in a condition to rescue the Republic from the imminent danger into which the disorganization of all branches of the administration is conducting us. At this important crisis it requires union and confidence. Rally round it: there is no other method of fixing the Republic upon the basis of civil liberty, internal happiness, victory, and peace.'

To the soldiers I said:

'Soldiers, the special decree of the Council of Ancients is conformable to articles 102 and 103 of the Constitutional Act. It has confided to me the command of the city and of the army. I have accepted that command, in order to second the measures which it is about to adopt, and which are all in favour of the people. Two years has the Republic been ill-governed; you have indulged in the hope that a period would be put to so many evils by my return. This event you have celebrated with an unanimity which imposes obligations upon me that I am about to discharge; you also will discharge yours, and you

THE EIGHTEENTH OF BRUMAIRE

will second your general with the energy, firmness, and fidelity which I have always found in you. Liberty, victory, and peace will reinstate the French Republic in the rank which she held in Europe, and from which imbecility and treachery were alone capable of removing her.'

I now sent an aide-de-camp to the guards of the Directory for the purpose of communicating the decree to them, and enjoining them to receive no order but from me. The guard sounded to horse; the commanding officer consulted his soldiers, they answered by shouts of joy. At this very moment an order from the Directory, contrary to that of my own, arrived; but the soldiers, obeying only my commands, marched to join me. Sieyes and Roger Ducos had been ever since the morning at the Tuileries. It is said that Barras, on seeing Sieyes mount his horse, ridiculed the awkwardness of the unpractised equestrian: he little suspected where they were going. Being shortly after apprised of the decree, he joined Gohier and Moulins: they then learnt that the troops followed me; they saw that even their own guard forsook them. Upon that Moulins went to the Tuileries, and gave in his resignation, as Sieyes and Roger Ducos had already done. Boutot, the secretary of Barras, came to me; I warmly expressed my indignation at the peculations which had ruined the Republic, and insisted that Barras should resign. Talleyrand hastened to the Director, and related this. Barras removed to Gros-Bois, accompanied by a guard of honour of dragoons. From that moment the Directory was dissolved, and I alone was invested with the executive power of the Republic.

In the meanwhile the Council of Five Hundred had met, under the presidency of Lucien. The constitution was explicit; the decree of the Council of Ancients was consistent with its privilege: there was no ground for objection. The members of the council in passing through the streets of Paris, and through the Tuileries, had learnt the occurrences which were taking place, and witnessed the enthusiasm of the public. They were astonished and confounded at the ferment around them. They submitted to necessity, and adjourned their sitting to the next day, the 19th, at Saint Cloud.

Bernadotte had married the sister-in-law of Joseph Bonaparte. He had been two months in the war department of the administration, and was afterwards removed by Sieyes: all he did in office was wrong. He was one of the most furious members of the *Société du Manège*. His political opinions were then very violent, and were censured by all respectable people. Joseph had taken him in the morning to my house, but, when he saw what was going forward, he stole away, and went to inform his friends of the *Manège* of the state of affairs. Jourdan and Augereau came to me at the Tuileries, while the troops were passing in review. I recommended them not to return to Saint Cloud to the sitting of the next day, but to remain quiet, and not to obliterate the memory of the services they had rendered the country; for that no effort could extinguish the flame which had been kindled. Augereau assured me of his devotion, and of his desire to march under my command. He even added, 'What! General, do you not still rely upon your little Augereau?'

Cambaceres, minister of justice, Fouché, minister of police, and all the other ministers, went to the Tuileries, and acknowledged the new authority. Fouché made great professions of attachment and devotion: being in direct opposition to Sieyes, he had not been admitted into the secret of the day. He had given directions for closing the barriers, and preventing the departure of couriers and coaches. 'Why, good God!' said I to him, 'wherefore all these precautions? We go with the nation, and by its strength alone: let no citizen be disturbed, and let the triumph of opinion have nothing in common with the transactions of days in which a factious minority prevailed.'

The members of the majority of the Five Hundred, of the minority of the Ancients, and the leaders of the *Manège*, spent the whole night in factious consultations.

At seven o'clock in the evening I held a council at the Tuileries. Sieyes proposed that the forty principal leaders of the opposite parties should be arrested. The recommendation was a wise one; but I believed I was too strong to need any such precautions. 'I swore in the morning,' said I, 'to protect the national representation; I will not this evening violate my oath: I fear no such weak enemies.' Everybody agreed in opinion with Sieyes, but nothing could overcome this delicacy on my part. It will soon appear that I was in the wrong.

It was at this meeting that the establishment of three Provisional Consuls was agreed on; and Roger Ducos and I were appointed; the adjournment of the councils for three months was also resolved on. The leading members of the two councils came to an understanding on the manner in which they should act at the sitting of Saint Cloud. Lucien, Boulay, Emile Gaudin, Chazal, Cabanis, were the leaders of the Council of Five Hundred; Regnier, Lemercier, Cornudet, Fargues, were those of the Ancients.

General Murat, as has been observed, commanded the public force at Saint Cloud; Pansard commanded the battalion of the guard of the Legislative Body; General Serrurier had under his orders a reserve stationed at Point-du-Jour.

The workmen were actively employed in getting ready the halls of the palace of Saint Cloud. The *orangerie* was allotted to the Council of Five Hundred; and the gallery of Mars, to that of the Ancients; the apartments since designated the Saloon of Princes, and the Emperor's Cabinet, were prepared for me and my staff. The inspectors of the hall occupied the apartments of the Empress. So late as two o'clock in the afternoon, the place assigned to the Council of Five Hundred was not ready. This delay of a few hours was very unfortunate. The deputies who had been on the spot from twelve o'clock, formed groups in the garden: their minds grew heated; they sounded one

THE EIGHTEENTH OF BRUMAIRE

another, interchanged declarations of the state of their feelings, and organized their opposition. They demanded of the Council of Ancients, what was its object? Why had it brought them to Saint Cloud? was it to change the Directory? They generally agreed that Barras was corrupt, and Moulins entitled to no respect; they would name, they said, without hesitation, me and two other citizens to fill up the government. The small number of individuals who were in the secret, then threw out that the object was to regenerate the State, by ameliorating the Constitution, and to adjourn the councils. These hints not being successful, a degree of hesitation shewed itself, even among the members most relied on.

At length the sitting opened. Emile Gaudin ascended the tribune, painted in lively colours the dangers of the country, and proposed thanks to the Council of Ancients, for the measures of public safety which it had set on foot; and that it should be invited, by message, to explain its intentions fully. At the same time, he proposed to appoint a committee of seven persons, to make a report upon the state of the Republic.

The furious rushing forth of the winds inclosed in the caverns of Eolus never raised a more raging storm. The speaker was violently hurled to the bottom of the tribune. The ferment became excessive.

Delbrel desired that the members should swear anew to the Constitution of the year III—Chenier, Lucien, Boulay, trembled. The chamber proceeded to the *Appel Nominal*.

During the *Appel Nominal*, which lasted more than two hours, reports of what was passing were circulated through the capital. The leaders of the assembly *du Manège*, the *tricoteuses*, etc., hastened up. Jourdan and Augereau had kept out of the way; believing me lost, they made all haste to Saint Cloud. Augereau drew near to me, and said, 'Well! here you are, in a pretty situation!' 'Augereau,' I replied, 'remember Arcole: matters appeared much more desperate there. Take my advice, and remain quiet, if you would not fall a victim to this confusion. In half an hour you will see what a turn affairs will have taken.'

The assembly appeared to declare itself with so much unanimity, that no deputy durst refuse to swear to the Constitution: even Lucien himself was compelled to swear. Shouts and cries of 'bravo' were heard throughout the chamber. The moment was critical. Many members, on taking the oath, added observations, and the influence of such speeches might operate upon the troops. All minds were in a state of suspense; the zealous became neuter; the timid had deserted their standard. Not an instant was to be lost. I crossed the saloon of Mars, entered the Council of Ancients, and placed myself opposite to the president. (At the bar.)

'You stand,' said I, 'upon a volcano; the Republic no longer possesses a government; the Directory is dissolved; factions are at work; the hour of

THE EIGHTEENTH OF BRUMAIRE

decision is come. You have called in my arm, and the arms of my comrades, to the support of your wisdom: but the moments are precious; it is necessary to take an ostensible part. I know that Cæsar, and Cromwell, are talked of—as if this day could be conquered with past times. No, I desire nothing but the safety of the Republic, and to maintain the resolutions to which you are about to come.—And you, grenadiers, whose caps I perceive at the doors of this hall—speak—have I ever deceived you? Did I ever forfeit my word, when in camp, in the midst of privations, I promised you victory and plenty; and when, at your head, I led you from conquest to conquest? Now say, was it for my own aggrandisement, or for the interest of the Republic?'

I spoke with energy. The grenadiers, were electrified; and, waving their caps and arms in the air, they all seemed to say, 'Yes, true, true! he always kept his word!'

Upon this a member (Lingley) rose, and said with a loud voice, 'General, we applaud what you say; swear then, with us, obedience to the Constitution of the year III which alone can save the Republic.'

The astonishment caused by these words produced a most profound silence.

I recollected myself for a moment; and then went on again emphatically: 'The Constitution of the year III!—you have it no longer—you violated it on 18 Fructidor, when the Government infringed on the independence of the Legislative Body; you violated it on 30 Prairial, in the year VII, when the Legislative Body struck at the independence of the Government: you violated it on 22 Floreal, when, by a sacrilegious decree, the Government and the Legislative Body invaded the sovereignty of the people, by annulling the elections made by them. The Constitution being violated, there must be a new compact, new guarantees.'

The force of this speech, and my energy, brought over three-fourths of the members of Council, who rose to indicate their approbation. Cornudet and Regnier spoke powerfully to the same effect. A member rose in opposition; he denounced me as the only conspirator against public liberty. I interrupted the orator, and declared that I was in the secret of every party, and that all despised the Constitution of the year III; that the only difference existing between them was, that some desired to have a moderate Republic, in which all the national interests, and all property, should be guaranteed; while, on the other hand, the others wished for a revolutionary government, as warranted by the dangers of the country. At this moment I was informed that the *Appel Nominal* was terminated in the Council of Five Hundred, and that they were endeavouring to force the president Lucien to put the outlawry of his brother to the vote. I immediately hastened to the Five Hundred, entered the chamber with my hat off, and ordered the officers and soldiers who accompanied me, to remain at the doors: I was desirous to present myself at the bar, to rally my party, which was numerous, but which had lost all unity and resolution. But to get to the bar, it was necessary to cross half the chamber, because the President had his seat on one of the wings. When I had advanced alone across one-third of the orangery, two or three hundred suddenly rose, crying, 'Death to the tyrant! down with the dictator!'

Two grenadiers, who, by my order, had remained at the door, and who had reluctantly obeyed, saying to me, 'You do not know them, they are capable of anything!' rushed in, sabre in hand, overthrowing all that opposed their passage, to join me, and cover me with their bodies. All the other grenadiers followed this example, and forced me out of the chamber. In the confusion one of them, named Thomé, was slightly wounded by the thrust of a dagger; and the clothes of another were cut through.

I descended into the courtyard, called the troops into a circle by beat of drum, got on horseback, and harangued them: 'I was about,' said I, 'to point out to them the means of saving the Republic, and restoring our glory. They answered me with their daggers. It was thus they would have accomplished the wishes of the allied kings. What more could England have done? Soldiers, may I rely upon you?'

Unanimous acclamations formed the reply to this speech. I instantly ordered a captain to go with ten men into the chamber of the Five Hundred, and to liberate the President.

Lucien had just thrown off his robe. 'Wretches!' exclaimed he, 'you insist that I should put out of the protection of the laws my brother, the saviour of the country, him whose very name causes kings to tremble! I lay aside the insignia of the popular magistracy; I offer myself in the tribune as the defender of him, whom you command me to immolate unheard.'

Thus saying, he quitted the chair, and darted into the tribune. The officer of grenadiers then presented himself at the door of the chamber, exclaiming, '*Vive la République*'. It was supposed that the troops were sending a deputation to express their devotion to the councils. The captain was received with a joyful expression of feeling. He availed himself of the misapprehension, approached the tribune, and secured the President, saying to him in a low voice, 'It is your brother's order.' The grenadiers at the same time shouted, 'Down with the assassins!'

Upon these exclamations, the joy of the members was converted into sadness; a gloomy silence testified the dejection of the whole assembly. No opposition was offered to the departure of the President, who left the chamber, rushed into the courtyard, mounted a horse, and cried out in his stentorian voice, 'General—and you, soldiers—the President of the Council of Five Hundred proclaims to you that factious men, with drawn daggers, have interrupted the deliberations of that assembly. He calls upon you to employ force against these disturbers. The Council of Five Hundred is dissolved.'

'President,' I replied, 'it shall be done.'

THE EIGHTEENTH OF BRUMAIRE

I then ordered Murat into the chamber, at the head of a detachment in close column. At this crisis General B—— ventured to ask me for fifty men, in order to place himself in ambuscade upon the way, and fire upon the fugitives. I replied to this request only by enjoining the grenadiers to commit no excesses. 'It is my wish,' said I, 'that not one drop of blood may be shed.'

Murat presented himself at the door, and summoned the Council to disperse. The shouts and vociferations continued. Colonel Moulins, aide-de-camp of Brune, who had just arrived from Holland, ordered the charge to be beaten. The drum put an end to the clamour. The soldiers entered the chamber charging bayonets. The deputies leaped out at the windows, and dispersed, leaving their gowns, caps, etc.: in one moment the chamber was empty. Those members of the Council who had shown most pertinacity, fled with the utmost precipitation to Paris.

About one hundred deputies of the Five Hundred rallied at the office and round the inspectors of the hall. They presented themselves in a body to the Council of the Ancients. Lucien represented that the Five Hundred had been dissolved at his instance; that, in the exercise of his functions as President of the Assembly, he had been surrounded by daggers; that he had sent attendants to summon the Council again; that nothing had been done contrary to form, and that the troops had but obeyed his mandate. The Council of the Ancients, which had witnessed with some uneasiness this exercise of military power, was satisfied with the explanation. At eleven at night the two Councils reassembled; they formed large majorities. Two committees were appointed to report upon the state of the Republic. On the report of Beranger, thanks to me and the troops were carried. Boulay de la Meurthe, in the Five Hundred, and Villetard in the Ancients, detailed the situation of the Republic, and the measures necessary to be taken. The law of 19 Brumaire was passed; it adjourned the Councils to 1 Ventose following; it created two committees of twenty-five members each, to represent the Councils provisionally. These committees were also to prepare a civil code. A Provisional Consular Commission, consisting of Sieyes, Roger Ducos, and myself was charged with the executive power.

This law put an end to the Constitution of the year III.

The Provisional Consuls repaired on the 20th, at two in the morning, to the chamber of the Orangery, where the two Councils were assembled. Lucien, the president, addressed them in these words:

'Citizen Consuls, the greatest people on earth intrusts its fate to you. Three months hence, your measures must pass the ordeal of public opinion. The welfare of thirty millions of men, internal quiet, the wants of the armies, peace—such are to be the objects of your cares. Doubtless courage and devotion to your duties are requisite in taking upon you functions so important; but the confidence of our people and warriors is with you, and the Legisla-

THE EIGHTEENTH OF BRUMAIRE

tive Body knows that your hearts are wholly with the country. Citizen Consuls, we have, previously to adjourning, taken the oath which you will repeat in the midst of us: the sacred oath of inviolable fidelity to the sovereignty of the people, to the French Republic, one and indivisible, to liberty, to equality, and to the representative system.'

The assembly separated, and the Consuls returned to Paris, to the palace of the Luxembourg.

Thus was the Revolution of 18 Brumaire crowned with success.

Sieyes, during the most critical moments, had remained in his carriage at the gate of Saint Cloud, ready to follow the march of the troops. His conduct, during the danger, was becoming: he evinced coolness, resolution, and intrepidity.

Chapter XXXIII

PROVISIONAL CONSULS

State of the Capital. My Proclamation. First sitting of the Consuls; myself president. Ministry; changes therein. Maret, Dubois-Crancé, Robert Lindet, Gaudin, Reinhart, Forfait, Laplace. First acts of the Consuls. Funeral honours paid to the Pope. Shipwrecked emigrants at Calais. Nappertandy, Blackwell. Suppression of the Festival of 21 January. Interview of two royalist agents with me. La Vendée, Chatillon, Bernier, D'Autichamp, Georges. Pacification. Discussion on the Constitution. The opinions of Sieyes and myself. Daunou. The Constitution. Nomination of the Consuls Cambaceres and Lebrun.

It would be difficult to describe the anxious suspense of the capital during the Revolution of 18 Brumaire; the most alarming reports were universally circulated; it was said that I was overthrown; the renewal of the Reign of Terror was expected. It was not so much the danger of the Republic that was apprehended, as that which every private family dreaded.

About nine o'clock in the evening, the news from Saint Cloud spread throughout Paris: the public was informed of the events which had taken place; and the liveliest joy succeeded to the most agonizing fears. The following proclamation was read by torchlight:

'Citizens!

'On my return to Paris I found discord pervading every department of government, and only this single truth unanimously agreed on, *that the Constitution was half destroyed, and no longer capable of maintaining our liberty.* Every

PROVISIONAL CONSULS

party applied to me, confided to me its designs, disclosed its secrets, and solicited my support. I refused to become the head of any faction. The Council of Ancients called on me. I answered the appeal. A plan for a general reform had been devised by men in whom the nation is accustomed to behold defenders of liberty, of equality, and of property: this plan demanded calm, free, and impartial examination, unfettered by influence or fear. The Council of Ancients, therefore, determined upon the removal of the Legislative Body to Saint Cloud. It entrusted me with the disposal of the force necessary for the maintenance of its independence. I deemed it due from me to our fellow-citizens, to the soldiers who are laying down their lives in our ranks, to the glory purchased by their blood, to accept the command. The Councils met at Saint Cloud: the troops of the Republic guaranteed safety without; but assassins spread terror within. Several deputies of the Council of Five Hundred, armed with daggers and firearms, dealt threats of death around them. The plans which were to have been brought forward, were withheld, the majority of the assembly was disorganized, the most intrepid orators were disconcerted, and the inutility of any sober proposition became but too evident. Indignant and grieved, I hastened to the Council of Ancients: I intreated it to allow me to carry my designs for the public good into execution. I urged the misfortunes of the country which had suggested them. The Council seconded my views, by new testimonies of its unaltered confidence. I offered myself to the Chamber of Five Hundred, alone, unarmed, my head uncovered, exactly as I had been received by the Ancients with so much approbation. I went to remind the majority of their designs, and to satisfy them of their power. Instantly the daggers which menaced the deputies, were raised against their defender. Twenty assassins rushed upon me, aiming at my breast. The grenadiers of the Legislative Body, whom I had left at the door of the chamber, hastily interposed between the assassins and myself. One of these brave grenadiers (Thomé) received a thrust from a dagger, which pierced his clothes. They carried me off, and at the instant they were doing so, cries were heard to outlaw him who was at that very time the defender of the law. It was the savage yell of murderers against the power destined to crush them. They crowded round the President, threatening him, with arms in their hands; they ordered him to pronounce the outlawry. Apprised of this, I gave directions for rescuing him from their fury, and ten grenadiers of the Legislative Body charged into the chamber and cleared it. The factious parties, intimidated, dispersed and fled. The majority, relieved from their violence, returned freely and peaceably into the chamber, listened to the proposals made to them for the public safety; and on due deliberation, framed the wholesome resolutions which are about to become the new and provisional law of the Republic. Frenchmen! you will, doubtless, recognize in my conduct the zeal of a soldier of liberty, of a citizen devoted to the Republic. The principles of preservation, protection, and liberality, are restored to their due preponderance by the dispersion of those factious men who tyrannized over the Councils, and who, though they have been prevented from becoming the most hateful of mankind, are nevertheless the most wretched.'

On the morning of 11 November, the Consuls held their first sitting. It opened with a discussion respecting the election of a president. The decision of the question depended on the vote of Roger Ducos, whose opinion, in the Directory, had always been governed by that of Sieyes; the latter, therefore, relied upon his observing the same line of conduct in the Consulate. The event proved otherwise. The Consul Roger Ducos had scarcely entered the cabinet, when, turning towards me, he said: 'It is useless to go to the vote on the Presidency; it belongs to you of right.' I then took the chair; and Roger Ducos continued to vote with me. He had some warm discussions with Sieyes on this subject; but he remained firm to his system. This conduct was the result of conviction that I alone was capable of re-establishing and maintaining order. Roger Ducos was not a man of great talent; but he possessed sound commonsense, and his intentions were good.

Lagarde, the Secretary of the Directory, did not enjoy an unblemished reputation. Maret, since Duke of Bassano, was appointed to that office. He was born at Dijon. He was attached to the principles of the Revolution of 1789, and was engaged in the negotiations with England before 10 August; he afterwards treated with Lord Malmesbury at Lisle. Maret is a man of great abilities, of a mild temper, and of great propriety of manners; his probity and delicacy proof against every temptation. He had escaped the Reign of Terror, having been arrested with Semonville as he crossed Lombardy on his way to Venice, intending from thence to go to Naples in the character of Ambassador. After 9 Thermidor he was exchanged for Madame the daughter of Louis XVI then a prisoner in the Temple.

The first sitting of the Consuls lasted several hours. Sieyes had hoped that I would interfere only in military matters, and would leave the regulation of civil affairs to him; but he was much surprised when he observed that I had formed settled opinions on policy, finance, and justice: even on jurisprudence also; and, in a word, on all branches of administration; that I supported my ideas with arguments at once forcible and concise, and that I was not easily convinced. In the evening, on his return home, Sieyes said in the presence of Chazal, Talleyrand, Boulay, Roederer, Cabanis, etc.: 'Gentlemen, you have a master; Napoleon *will* do all, and *can* do all. In our deplorable situation, it is better to submit, than to excite dissensions which would draw down certain ruin.'

The first act of government was the organization of the ministry. Dubois de Crancé was Minister at War. He was incompetent for such a post; a party man, little esteemed, and altogether devoid of habits of business and order.

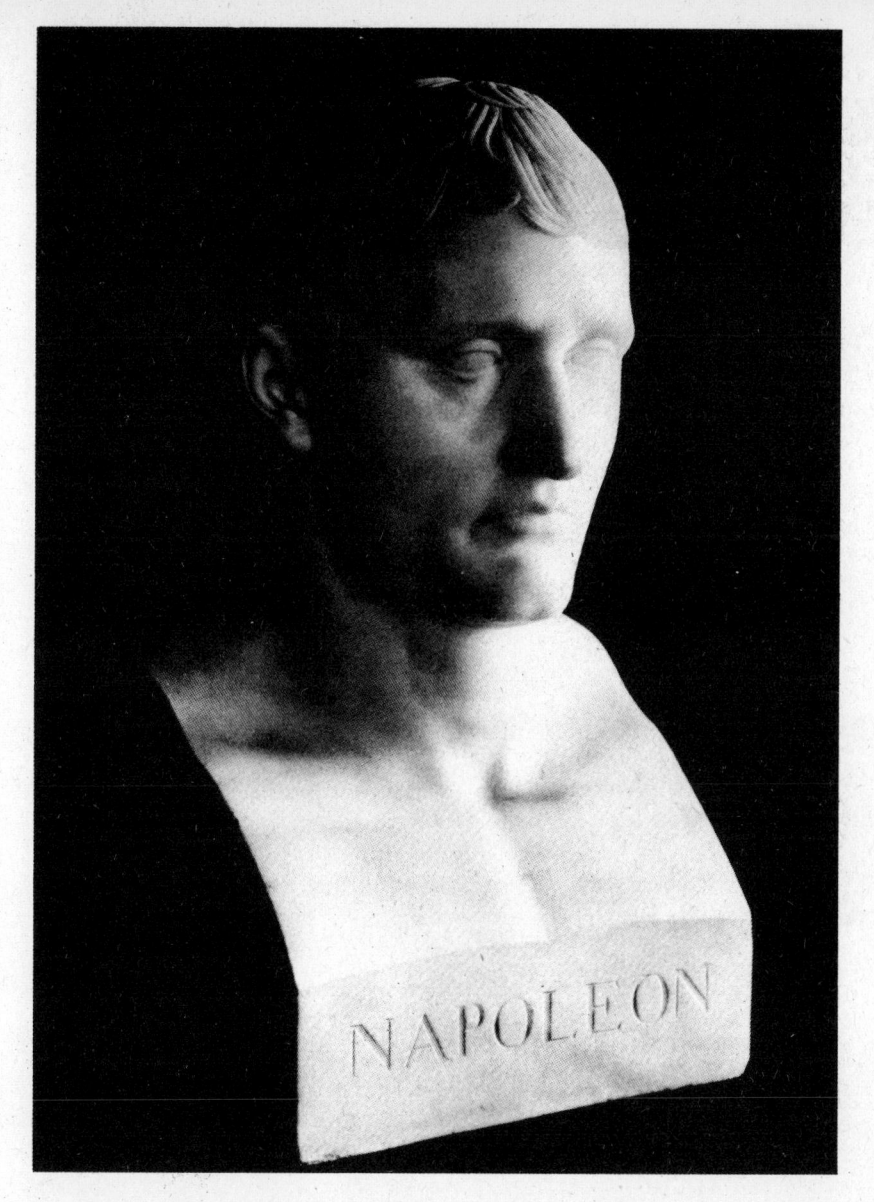

THE EMPEROR NAPOLEON I BY CANOVA

This bust by Canova was brought home after signing The Treaty of Paris by Henry, 3rd Earl Bathurst, K.G., P.C., Secretary of State for War and the Colonies (1812–1827). It has remained at Cirencester Park ever since and is reproduced for the first time by kind permission of the Trustees of Henry, 8th Earl Bathurst.

PROVISIONAL CONSULS

His offices were filled by creatures of faction, who, instead of doing their work, spent their time in discussions; it was a downright chaos. It will hardly be believed that Dubois de Crancé could not furnish me with a single report of the state of the army. Berthier was appointed Minister at War. He was obliged to send a dozen officers, one after another, among the military divisions and regiments, to obtain states of the different corps, their situation, pay, supplies, etc. The ordnance-office was the only one which possessed any returns. A great number of corps had been formed, as well by generals as by the administrations in the different departments; their existence was unknown to the ministry. It was said to Dubois de Crancé: 'You pay the army, you can surely give us a return of the pay.'—'We don't pay it.'—'You victual the army; let us have the returns of the victualling office.'—'We don't victual it.' —'You clothe the army; let us see the statements of the clothing.'—'We don't clothe it.'

The army at home was paid by robbing the public treasury; it was subsisted and clothed by means of requisitions, and the war-office exercised no kind of control. It took General Berthier a month to collect the materials for drawing up a state of the army; and until that had been accomplished, it was impossible to set about its re-organization.

The Army of the North was in Holland; it had just repulsed the English. Its condition was satisfactory. The Dutch, according to the treaty, supplied all its wants.

The Armies of the Rhine and of Helvetia suffered greatly; their state was most disorderly.

The Army of Italy, driven back upon the states of Genoa, was without subsistence, and deprived of everything. Its insubordination had arrived at such a pitch that some corps quitted their position without orders, in presence of the enemy, and betook themselves to places where they hoped to find provisions.

The reform of the war department being effected, discipline was soon restored.

The post of Minister of Finance was held by Robert Lindet, who had been a member of the Committee of Public Safety, in the time of Robespierre. He was a man of integrity, but possessing none of the information necessary for the management of the finances of a great empire. Under the revolutionary government he had, however, obtained the reputation of an able financier; but in those days the true minister of finance was the printer of the assignats.

Lindet was succeeded by Gaudin, subsequently Duke of Gaëta, who had long occupied the place of chief clerk of finance. A man of mild manners, and of inflexible probity.

The treasury was empty; there was not wherewithal to dispatch a courier in it. Nothing came into it but cheques, bills, notes, schedules, and paper of

PROVISIONAL CONSULS

all kinds, on which the receipts of the army had been consumed by anticipation. The contractors, paid in drafts themselves, drew directly on the receivers as fast as anything came into their hands; and yet they did no service. The rate of interest was at 6 per cent. Every source of supply was dried up; credit was annihilated; all was disorder, waste, and destruction. The paymasters, who at the same time exercised the functions of receivers, enriched themselves by a system of jobbing, the more difficult to repress, because every species of the paper-money bore a different real value.

The new minister, Gaudin, adopted measures which checked these abuses and restored confidence. He suppressed the compulsory and progressive loan.

Several citizens offered considerable sums to Government. The trade of Paris supplied a loan of twelve millions; which at that moment was of great importance. The sale of the domains belonging to the House of Orange, which France had reserved to itself by the treaty of the Hague, was effected, and produced twenty-four millions, and cheques, called *bons de rescription,* for the redemption of annuities, were issued to the amount of 150 millions.

The direct impositions were in arrear in consequence of the delay which took place in the completion of the lists. The minister established a commission for the management of the public contributions. The Constituent Assembly, whose principles of administration were defective, because they were the result of an idle theory and not the fruit of experience, had charged the municipal authorities with the formation of lists, which were confirmed and adopted for use on the decision of the councils of departments. This organization was fraught with mischief; yet the evil was but little noticed: in 1792, 93, 94, the assignats provided for everything. When the Constitution of 1795 was formed, 5,000 superintendents were directed to form the lists. At the same time a mixed management was adopted, which cost five millions of livres extra, and effected its object no better than the law of the Constituent Assembly. Gaudin, instructed by experience, confided the formation of these lists to one hundred Directors-general, who had under them one hundred Inspectors and eight hundred and forty Comptrollers, the whole of which cost but three millions of livres. This was, therefore, a saving of two millions of livres.

He created the redemption fund; obliged the receivers of taxes to deposit the amount of a twentieth part of their receipts; and organized the system of the bonds of receivers-general, upon each of which was payable, every month, one twelfth of the amount of the receipts. From that moment all the direct contributions came into the treasury, even before the beginning of the year, and in large sums; so that the minister was enabled to apply them for the service in all parts of France. It was no longer of importance that the levies might be delayed in any degree, or might be effected with more or less activity; that had no influence upon the operations of the treasury. This law was one of the causes of the prosperity and regularity which have since prevailed in the finances.

The Republic had forty millions of livres a year in forest land; but this source of revenue was ill-managed: the registration department appointed to receive this revenue and the stamp duties, as well as to exercise signorial rights, was inadequate to the management of matters which required a particular species of information, and considerable activity. The minister Gaudin appointed a special commission for the management of the woods and forests. This change gave rise to complaints. It was apprehended that the abuses of the ancient administration of the forests and rivers would be revived. 'The Commission', it was said, 'is appointed; it will not be long before its jurisdiction and its special tribunals are renewed; we shall witness the return of all the abuses which excited our complaints in 1789.' These apprehensions were unfounded: the abuses of the ancient administration were gone forever, and the new commissioners bestowed their care on the management of the forests, and the sale and felling of timber; they also paid the minutest attention to the seed-plots and plantations; and recovered to the demesne a large quantity of woodland encroached upon by communes or by private individuals; in short, it produced the most beneficial results, and entirely gained the good opinion of the public.

All that it was possible to effect in a short time, towards rooting out the errors of a vicious and oppressive sway, and restoring the principles of credit and moderation, was accomplished by the minister Gaudin. He was a statesman of integrity and regularity, who knew how to conciliate his subordinate agents; proceeding slowly, but surely. All that he did and proposed in this early period, he supported and perfected throughout fifteen years of able administration. He never had to withdraw any of his measures, because his knowledge was practical and the fruit of long experience.

Cambaceres retained the administration of Justice. A great number of alterations were made among the tribunals.

Talleyrand had been dismissed from the post of Minister of Foreign relations, through the influence of the *Société du Manège*.

Reinhard, who had succeeded him, was a native of Wurtemberg. He was a well-behaved man, of ordinary capacity. The post was properly due to Talleyrand; but, in order to avoid too harsh an opposition to public opinion, which ran strongly against him, especially with regard to American affairs, Reinhard was at first retained in his office; besides, the place was of no great importance, considering the critical situation in which the Republic stood. In fact, it was impossible to enter upon any sort of negotiation without previously re-establishing internal order, re-uniting the nation, and gaining some advantage over our foreign enemies.

Bourdon was succeeded in the Admiralty department by Forfait, and appointed commissioner of marine at Antwerp. Forfait, a native of Normandy, had the reputation of being a naval architect of first-rate talent; but he was a mere projector, and did not answer the expectations formed of him. This department was of the highest importance, because the Republic was under the necessity of sending succours to the army in Egypt, the garrison of Malta, and the colonies.

In the interior, the minister Quinette was removed to make way for Laplace, a geometrician of the first rank; but who soon proved himself below mediocrity as a minister: in his very first essay, the Consuls found that they were deceived: not a question did Laplace seize in its true point of view; he sought for subtleties in everything; had none but problematical ideas, and carried the doctrine of infinite littleness into the business of administration.

The appointments made by the Consuls had been hitherto unanimous; their first difference in opinion arose respecting Fouché, who had been Minister of Police. Sieyes detested him and considered the government insecure, so long as he presided over the police. Fouché was born at Nantes; he had been a public haranguer before the Revolution; he afterwards, filled a subaltern situation in his department, and distinguished himself by the violence of his principles. Deputed to the Convention, he trod in the same path with Collot d'Herbois; and, after the revolution of Thermidor, he was proscribed as a Terrorist. While in the Directory, he had attached himself to Barras, and had commenced his fortune by being a sharer in some contracts to which Government had contrived to recommend a great number of revolutionary characters; a circumstance which had drawn additional odium upon men already rendered unpopular by political events. Fouché, who had now held the administration of the police for several months, had taken a part in opposition to the faction *du Manège,* which still exerted itself, and which it was necessary to destroy: Sieyes, however, ascribed this conduct, not to any fixed principles, but to the absolute hatred which he bore to those societies, wherein incessant declamations were openly held against malversations, and against those who had shared in the public contracts. Sieyes proposed Alquier in the place of Fouché: this alteration did not appear to be indispensably necessary; for, although Fouché was not in the secret of 18 Brumaire, he had conducted himself extremely well. I agreed with Sieyes, that it was impossible to rely in the least on the morality of such a minister or on his versatile disposition; but remarked, at the same time, that after all he had been useful to the Republic. '*We are creating a new era,*' said I, '*of the past we must remember only the good, and forget the evil. Time, habits of business, and experience, have formed many able men, and modified many characters.*' Fouché accordingly retained his place.

The nomination of Gaudin to be minister of finance, left vacant the place of Government commissioner in the department of the Posts, which is one of

PROVISIONAL CONSULS

great trust. It was confided to Laforet, who was then in the treasury at the head of the department of Exterior Relations. He was a clever man, and had been a long time consul-general for France in America.

The Polytechnic-School was then only in its infancy. Monge was charged with that definitive organization of it, which has since received the sanction of experience. This school has become one of the most celebrated in the world. It has furnished a great number of officers, mechanists, and chymists, who have either recruited the scientific departments of the army, or, dispersed throughout our manufactories, have contributed to that perfection in the arts, which have given to French industry the high superiority it possesses.

The new Government was nevertheless surrounded by enemies, who openly carried on their operations. La Vendée, Languedoc and Belgium, were convulsed by disputes and insurrections. The foreign party, which, for many months, had been daily increasing, saw with vexation a change so well adapted to destroy its hopes. The anarchists listened to nothing but their hatred against Sieyes.

Sieyes was often alarmed at the plots of the Jacobins in Paris, and their threats of assassinating the Consuls. He once came in great agitation, and awoke me at three o'clock in the morning, to tell me something of this kind which he had just heard from the police. *'Let them alone,'* I said; *'in war as well as in love we must come to close quarters to make an end of it. Let them come; it may as well be settled one day as another.'* These fears were unfounded. Threats are more easily made than carried into execution, and with anarchists, they precede, by a very long interval, any kind of action.

The law passed on 19 Brumaire at Saint Cloud, had enjoined the Government to take the measures necessary for restoring the tranquillity of the Republic. It had expelled fifty-five deputies from the Legislative Body. A great many others were dissatisfied at the adjournment of the chambers; they persisted in remaining at Paris and assembling there. It was the first time since the Revolution, that the tribune had been silent, and the Legislative Body in recess. Opinions were kept unsettled by the most sinister reports; the Minister of Police, therefore, proposed measures for repressing the audacity of the anarchist party. A decree was passed, by which fifty-nine of the chief disturbers were condemned to deportation; thirty-seven to Guiana, and twenty-two to the island of Oleron; this decree was generally blamed, for public opinion ran against all violent measures; nevertheless it had a salutary effect. The anarchists alarmed in their turn, dispersed. This was all that was desired; shortly afterwards, the decree of deportation was changed for a mere measure of observation—and in a little time the observation itself ceased.

The public claimed the merit of the repeal of this decree. It was thought that the administration had retracted; this was an error, it desired only to terrify, and it had attained its object. The public mind throughout France soon experienced a change. The citizens had assembled, addresses of adhesion poured in from the departments, and the malevolent, of whatever party, ceased to be dangerous. The law of hostages, which had thrown a great number of citizens into prison, was repealed. Intolerant laws had been made by the preceding governments against the priesthood; persecution had been carried as far as the hatred of theophilanthropists would go. Refractory priests, and priests who had submitted to the oaths, were all under the same proscription: some had been sent to the island of Rhé, some to Guiana, some into foreign countries, and others languished in the prisons. It was agreed on, as a principle, that conscience was not amenable to the law, and that the right of the sovereign extended only to the exaction of obedience and fidelity.

If the question had been thus put to the Constituent Assembly, and no oath as to the civil constitution of the clergy, which was, in fact, entering upon theological discussions, had been required, there would not have been any refractory priests. But Talleyrand, and other members of that assembly, imposed that oath, the consequences of which have been so lamentable to France.

The civil constitution of the clergy having become part of the law of the State, it was necessary to protect a great number of priests who had conformed to it, and it is probable that this clergy would have formed the national church; but, when the Legislative Assembly and the Convention shut up the churches, suppressed the observance of the sabbath, and treated with the same contempt the priests who had taken the oaths, and those who refused to take them, they gave the latter a clear advantage.

I, who had meditated much upon religious matters, in Italy and in Egypt, had formed clear ideas on that topic; and I lost no time in putting a stop to persecution. My first step was to order that all priests, married or sworn, who were imprisoned or deported, should be set at liberty. Such had been the indiscriminate violence of the factions, that these two classes had actually been persecuted without distinction. It was decreed that every priest banished, or imprisoned, who would take an oath of fidelity to the established government should be instantly set at liberty. Within a short time after the passing of this law, more than twenty thousand old men returned to their families. A few ignorant priests persisted in their obstinacy, and remained in exile; but in that they condemned themselves, for the precepts of Christianity admit only of one interpretation on this point, and, according to them, an oath of fidelity to the Government cannot be refused without crime.

At this period also, the law of the decades was repealed, the churches were again devoted to public worship, and pensions were granted to persons of both sexes under religious vows, who took the oath of fidelity to the Government. The greater part submitted, and thereby thousands of individuals were snatched from misery; the country churches were re-opened, domestic religious rites were suffered; all forms of worship were protected; and the number of theophilanthropists rapidly diminished.

Pope Pius the sixth died at the age of eighty-two, at Valence, to which place he had retired after the events in Italy. In returning from Egypt, I had conversed a few minutes in that city with Spina, the pope's almoner, whom I subsequently appointed cardinal and archbishop of Genoa; I learnt that no funeral honours had been paid to the Pope, and that his corpse was laid in the sacristy of the cathedral. A decree of the Consuls ordered that the customary honours should be rendered to his remains; and that a monument of marble should be raised upon his tomb. It was an homage paid by the First Consul and the majority of the French people, to an unfortunate sovereign, and the head of religion.

The Consular government by daily acts of justice and generosity, sought to repair the faults and oppressions of the preceding governments. The members of the Constituent Assembly, who had acknowledged the sovereignty of the people, were erased from the list of emigrants, by a decision agreed upon as fundamental: this caused great uneasiness. 'The emigrants will return in crowds,' it was said; 'the royalist party will raise its head, as it did in Fructidor; The Republicans will be massacred.' La Fayette, Latour-Maubourg, and Bureau de Puzy, returned to France, and to the peaceable enjoyment of their property, which had not been alienated.

Meanwhile a few unfortunate wretches were groaning in perpetual apprehension of death. Some years before, a vessel which had left England for La Vendée, having on board nine persons of the most ancient families of France—Talmonts, Montmorencys, and Choiseuils—had been wrecked on the coast of Calais. These passengers were emigrants: they were arrested and from that time had been dragged from prison to prison, from tribunal to tribunal, without having their fate decided. Their arrival in France was not a voluntary act; they were unfortunate castaways; but they were attacked on account of their place of destination. They affirmed, indeed, that they were going to India; but the vessel and its stores testified that they were going to La Vendée. Without entering into that question I saw that the condition of these men rendered them inviolable; they were under the laws of hospitality. To consign to punishment unfortunate men who had preferred committing themselves to the generosity of France, to throwing themselves into the waves, would have been an act of singular barbarity. I decided that the laws against emigrants were political laws, and that their policy would not be violated by the exercise of indulgence towards persons who were so peculiarly situated.

I had already decided a similar question, when, as general of artillery, I was fortifying the coasts of the south. Some members of the Chabrillant family,

PROVISIONAL CONSULS

in the passage from Spain to Italy, had been taken by a corsair and carried into Toulon; they were immediately thrown into prison. The populace, knowing that they were emigrants, would have massacred them. I availed myself of my popularity; and, by means of the cannoneers and workmen of the arsenal, who were foremost in the disturbance, saved this unhappy family; dreading another insurrection of the people, I placed them in empty ammunition-wagons that I was sending to the isles of Hyeres; and thus I preserved them.

The English government did not show equal generosity towards Nappertandy, Blackwell, and other Irishmen, who, after being shipwrecked on the coast of Norway, were crossing the territory of Hamburg to return to Paris. They had been naturalized as Frenchmen, and were officers in the service of the Republic. The British minister at Hamburg compelled the Senate to arrest them on their passage and—who would credit it?—all Europe rose up against these unfortunate people! The Russian and Austrian governments seconded the demands of that of England, to have them given up. The citizens of Hamburg resisted for some time; but, seeing France sinking in importance, and crippled by reverses, in Germany, as well as in Italy, they at last yielded.

France had the greater reason to feel herself offended at this conduct, inasmuch as the city of Hamburg had long been the refuge of 20,000 French emigrants, who had there organized armies, and concerted plots against the Republic; while two unfortunate officers in the service of the Republic, sacred on account of their misfortunes and shipwreck, were delivered up to the executioner.

In consequence of this, the Consuls laid an embargo upon all shipping belonging to Hamburg in the ports of France; recalled from Hamburg the French Agents, both commercial and diplomatic; and dismissed those of Hamburg back to that place.

Shortly after all this, the French arms having been successful, and the happy changes of 18 Brumaire being daily more generally felt, the Senate of Hamburg lost no time in addressing a long letter to me, to testify its repentance to me. I replied thus:

'I have received your letter, gentlemen; it does not justify you. Courage and virtue are the preservers of states: cowardice and crime are their ruin. You have violated the laws of hospitality—a thing which never happened among the most savage hordes of the Desert. Your fellow-citizens will for ever reproach you with it. The two unfortunate men whom you have given up, die with glory; but their blood will bring more evil upon their persecutors than it would be in the power of an army to do.'

A solemn deputation from the Senate arrived at the Tuileries to make public apologies to me. I again testified my indignation: and when the envoys urged their weakness, I said to them, 'Well! and had you not the resource of weak states? Was it not in your power to let them escape?'

The Directory had adopted the plan of supporting the French prisoners in England, so long as England should support its own people who might be prisoners in France: we had more prisoners in England than that power had in France. Provisions were dearer in the former than in the latter country; and, consequently, this state of things was burdensome to France. To this inconvenience was added that of suffering the English government to have, under pretence of keeping accounts, sources of intelligence in the interior of the Republic. The Consular government lost no time in altering this arrangement. Each nation became responsible for the support of the prisoners it detained.

In the existing state of men's minds it became requisite to rally and unite the different parties who had divided the whole nation and laid it open to its external enemies.

The oath of hatred to royalty was suppressed as useless and contrary to the majesty of the Republic, which, acknowledged as it was, on all sides, stood in need of no such support. It was in a similar way resolved that 21 January should be no longer observed.

This anniversary could be viewed only as a day of national calamity. I had already explained myself respecting it, while discussing the subject of 10 August.

'We celebrate a victory,' said I, 'but we weep over its victims, even though our enemies. The festival of 21 January is immoral,' I continued, 'without pronouncing whether the death of Louis XVI, was just or unjust, politic or impolitic, useful or of no use; and even if we decide that it was just, politic, and useful, it was nevertheless a calamity. Under such circumstances, oblivion is, of all things, the best.'

Offices were bestowed upon men of all parties and of all moderate opinions. The effect of this was such, that in a few days there was a general alteration in the temper of the nation. He who a few days before listened to proposals from the foreign powers and the emissaries of the Bourbons, dreading above all things the principles of the *Société du Manège* and the return of the reign of terror, now put confidence in the Government, so truly national, powerful, and generous—which had just established itself, broken former bonds, and once more sided with the nation and the revolution. The foreign faction was for a moment disconcerted at this; it soon recovered, and sought to effect another change in public opinion, by endeavouring to create a persuasion that I was labouring for the Bourbons.

One of the principal agents of the diplomatic body demanded and obtained an interview with me. He confessed to me that he was acquainted with the committee of the agents of the Bourbons, in Paris; that, in despair of the salvation of the country, he had entered into engagements with them, because he preferred anything to the reign of terror: but that, 18 Brumaire having once more formed a national government, he not only renounced that connexion, but came for the purpose of informing me of all he knew; upon condition, nevertheless, that his honour should not be compromised, and that the individuals in question should have liberty to depart in safety.

He even presented to me, Hyde-de-Neuville and Dandigné, two of the agents. I received them at ten at night in one of the small chambers of the Luxembourg. 'A few days ago', said they to me, 'we felt confident of triumph; now everything is altered. But, General, you will never be imprudent enough to rely upon such events? You have it in your power to re-establish the throne, and to restore it to its legitimate master; we are acting in concert with the leaders of La Vendée, we can bring them all here. Disclose to us what you wish to do; how you purpose to conduct yourself; and if your intentions agree with ours, we shall all be at your disposal.'

Hyde-de-Neuville appeared to be a young man of talent; ardent, but not violent. Dandigné seemed an outrageous madman. I answered them 'that it was useless to think of re-establishing the throne of the Bourbons in France: that they could never ascend it but by striding over 500,000 dead bodies; that my intention was to forget the past, and to receive the submission of all who were willing to concur with the nation; that I would willingly treat with Chatillon, Bernier, Bourmont, Suzannet, D'Autichamp, etc.: but upon condition that those chiefs should thenceforward be faithful to the national government, and should break off all communication with the Bourbons, and with foreigners.'

This conference lasted half an hour, and both parties were mutually convinced that there was no possibility of their coming to an understanding upon such a basis.

The new principles adopted by the Consuls and the new functionaries, appeased the troubles of Toulouse, the discontents of the South, and the insurrection of Belgium. My reputation was dear to the Belgians, and had a happy influence upon the public affairs of those departments which the persecution of the priests had so highly exasperated the preceding year.

Nevertheless, La Vendée and the Chouans still disturbed eighteen departments of the Republic. Affairs went on so ill, that Chatillon, chief of the Vendéans, took Nantes: he remained there, indeed, scarcely twenty-four hours. But the Chouans carried their ravages to the very gates of the capital. The leaders replied to the proclamation of Government by counter proclamations, in which they asserted that they fought for the re-establishment of the throne and altar, and that they beheld only usurpers in the Directory and Consuls.

A great number of generals and officers of the army were betraying the Republic, and in league with the heads of the Chouans. The little confidence that the Directory had inspired in them, the disorder that had prevailed in every department of the administration, had tempted these officers to forget their honour and their duty, in order to join a party which they thought on the point of carrying the day. Many were shameless enough to tell this in confidence to me, declaring to me, that they had only yielded to circumstances, and were ready to redeem a moment of irresolution by services which might be the more important, as they were in the secrets of the Chouans and the Vendéans.

Negotiations were entered into with the chiefs in La Vendée, and a considerable force was sent against them at the same time. Everything announced the approaching destruction of their bands; but moral causes acted yet more powerfully; my fame was so great in La Vendée, that the chiefs in that province were fearful of being deserted by public opinion.

On 17 January, Chatillon, Suzannet, D'Autichamp, and the Abbé Bernier, the leaders of the insurrection on the left of the Loire, submitted, at Montluçon.

General Hedouville negotiated the treaty which was signed on 17 January at Montluçon. This treaty of peace had nothing in common with any which had preceded it. It was made with Frenchmen returning to the bosom of their country, and submitting with confidence to the Government. The steps, financial or ecclesiastical, taken by the administration every day contributed more and more to the tranquillity of these departments. These Vendéan chiefs were frequently received at Malmaison: when once peace was made with them, I had every reason to be satisfied with their conduct.

Bernier was rector of Saint Lô. He was short and slender in person. He was a good preacher, and had skill enough to diffuse fanaticism among his flock, without partaking in it himself. He had possessed great influence in La Vendée; his credit had somewhat lessened; but he still retained enough to enable him to be useful to Government. He attached himself to me, and was faithful to his engagements. He was charged with negotiating the concordat with the Court of Rome; and I made him Bishop of Orleans.

Chatillon was an old gentleman of sixty; brave and faithful, without much quickness, but not deficient in vigour. He was lately married, which contributed to keep him true to his promises. He lived alternately at Paris, Nantes, and his own estates. He subsequently obtained many favours of me. Chatillon thought that the war in La Vendée might have been carried on some months longer; but that after 18 Brumaire the chiefs could no longer calculate on the mass of the population. He confessed that towards the conclusion of the campaigns of Italy, the reputation of General Bonaparte had so heated the imaginations of the Vendéan peasantry, that they had been on the point of abandoning the interests of the Bourbons, and sending a deputation to me, offering to submit themselves to my authority.

PROVISIONAL CONSULS

D'Autichamp had served in many campaigns, as a private hussar, in the Republican troops, during the reign of terror. He was a man of limited powers of mind, but possessed the elegance of manners and address, which became his education and acquaintance with the great world.

Georges and La Prevelaye were at the head of the bands in Brittany, on the right of the Loire; Bourmont commanded those of the Maine; Frotté those of Normandy. La Prevelaye and Bourmont submitted, and came to Paris. Georges and Frotté chose to continue the war. It was a state of licentiousness which allowed them, under the colour of political motives, to give themselves up to every species of plunder: to lay the rich under contribution on pretence that they were the purchasers of the national domains; to rob the public coaches, because they carried the revenues of the State; to pillage the bankers, because they were connected with the treasury, etc. They interrupted the communications between Brest and Paris. They kept up an intelligence with all the vilest people in the capital; with men who lived in gaming-houses, and places of the worst description. Thither they brought their plunder; there they gained recruits, and information how to render the snares and ambuscades which they were accustomed to lay on the roads, most profitable.

Generals Chambarlhac and Gardanne entered the department of the Orne, at the head of two moveable columns, to secure Frotté. This chief, young, active, and full of stratagems, was held in dread, and caused many disorders. He was surprised in the house of Guidal, general commandant at Alençon, who had an understanding with him, was admitted into his confidence, and betrayed him. He was tried, and shot.

This prompt proceeding restored tranquillity to this province. There only remained Brulard, and a few chiefs of little consequence, who availed themselves of the facility afforded them by the English cruisers, to land on the coasts, circulate libels, and turn spies in the service of England.

Georges maintained himself in Morbihan with the assistance of the money and arms which the English supplied him with. Attacked, beaten, and hemmed in, at Grand-Champ, by General Brune, he capitulated, gave up his artillery and arms, and promised to live as a good and peaceable subject. He solicited the honour of being presented to the First Consul, and received permission to go to Paris for that purpose. I tried in vain to make the same impression upon him that I had made upon a great number of Vendéans, to awaken a sentiment of French patriotism, the honour of the nation, the love of country; but not one of these chords would vibrate. The war in the West being thus brought to an end, many good regiments were ready to be otherwise disposed of.

Whilst the state of public affairs continued to improve, the labour of re-modelling the Constitution drew towards an end; the two Consuls and the two Committees were incessantly employed in it. The Government con-

PROVISIONAL CONSULS

cerned itself but little with foreign politics. All its proceedings were confined to Prussia, whose sovereign was raising an army just at the time when the Duke of York was landing in Holland, which inspired some distrust. Duroc, my aide-de-camp, was sent to Berlin, with a letter to the King. His object was to sound the cabinet. He succeeded in his mission, and was received with respect, even with kindness, by the Queen.

The people about this court, being themselves all military, listened with great interest to accounts of the wars in Italy and Egypt: they were pleased, also, with the triumph which the military party had obtained in France, by wresting the reins of government out of the hands of the lawyers. There was every reason to be satisfied with the disposition of the Prussian government, which disbanded its army soon after.

The intermediate Legislative Committee of the Five Hundred was successively presided over by Lucien, Boulay de la Meurthe, Daunou, and Jacqueminot: that of the Ancients by Lemercier, Lebrun, and Regnier.

Boulay was afterwards Minister of State, and President of the Legislative Section in the Council of State.

Daunou was an orator, deputed from the Pas-de-Calais, a man of good address, and a good writer. He drew up the Constitutions of the years III and VIII of the Republic. He became keeper of the Imperial records.

Jacqueminot came from Nancy. He was a senator when he died.

Lebrun was third Consul.

Regnier was made Duke of Massa and Chief Judge.

The intermediate Legislative Committees held their meetings privately. Bad effects might have resulted from publishing the debates of an assembly, which often consisted of only fifteen or sixteen members. These two commissions, according to the law of 19 Brumaire, could do nothing but on the proposition of Government, which directed the attention of the Committee of the Five Hundred to any particular point: their resolutions were then drawn up, and carried into a law by the Committee of the Ancients.

The first law of importance passed by this session extraordinary was relative to the constitutional oath; which in fact, could only be taken, as it then stood, to a constitution that no longer existed. It was conceived in these words: 'I swear fidelity to the Republic, one and indivisible, founded on the sovereignty of the people, the representative system, the maintenance of liberty and equality, and the protection of persons and of property.'

According to law the two Councils were to meet on 19 February, 1800; the only method of preventing them was to promulgate a new Constitution, and offer it to the people for acceptance before that epoch. The three Consuls, and the two intermediate Legislative Committees, resolved themselves into a committee for that purpose, during the month of December, in my apartment, from nine in the evening until three in the morning. Daunou acted as clerk. The confidence of the assembly fully rested upon the reputation and experience of Sieyes. The constitution that he had by him, in his portfolio, had long been extolled. He had given some hints respecting it, which were eagerly caught at by his numerous admirers, and from them they found their way to the public, and carried to its height the reputation which Mirabeau was pleased to compliment him on, when he said in the tribunal, *'the silence of Sieyes is a national calamity.'*

He had, indeed, made himself known by many publications, which evinced profound thought. He it was who originally suggested to the Chamber of the Third Estate the grand idea of declaring itself a National Assembly; he likewise proposed the oath of the *jeu de paume,* the suppression of the provinces, and the division of the republican territory into departments. He professed to have composed a theory respecting the representative government, and the sovereignty of the people, full of luminous ideas, which were laid down as fundamental principles. The committee expected to have this long-meditated scheme for the constitution laid before them, and that they should have nothing to do but to revise and modify it; and bring it to perfection by their profound discussions. At the first sitting, however, Sieyes said nothing; he acknowledged that he had a great accumulation of materials in his portfolio, but they were neither classed nor digested. At the following sitting he read a report on lists of notables. The sovereignty resided in the people; it was from the people that every officer, directly or indirectly, received his trust; but the people, however capable of discerning those who deserve its confidence, is not at all capable of allotting the respective duties which its officers are to fulfil. He established three lists of notability; first, the communal; secondly, the departmental; thirdly, the national. The first consisted of a tenth of all the citizens of each commune, selected by the inhabitants themselves; the second, of a tenth of the citizens named in the communal lists of each department; and the third, of a tenth of the individuals whose names appeared in the departmental list: the latter list reduced itself to 6,000 persons, who formed the national notability. This operation was to take place every five years; and all public functionaries, of all orders, were to be selected from the lists. Thus—the government, the ministers, the legislature, the senate or grand jury, the council of state, the tribunal of cassation, and the ambassadors, were to be included in the national list; the prefects, judges, and administrators, in the departmental; and, lastly, the communal administrations, and justices of peace, in the communal list. By this arrangement all public functionaries, even the ministers, would become representatives of the people, and would bear a popular character. These projects had the greatest success: when spread among the public, they gave birth to the most sanguine hopes; they were novel, and the people were weary of all that had been proposed since 1789; they emanated, moreover, from a man of great reputation in the Republican party; they looked like an analysis of something that had existed in all ages. These lists of notability might be described as lists of nobility, not hereditary, but elective. Yet the defect of this system was at once evident to men of sense: they saw that it would cripple the Government, by preventing it from employing many individuals fit for office, merely because they were not to be found on the lists. And still the people would have no direct influence in the nomination of the Legislature; they would possess but a mere illusory and metaphysical participation in it.

Encouraged by his success, Sieyes, in the following sittings, detailed the theory of his constitutional jury, which he agreed to call Conservative Senate. He had conceived it so early as the Constitution of 1795; but it had been rejected by the Convention. 'The Constitution', said he, 'is not endowed with life: it requires a permanent body of judges, to enter into its interests, and interpret it in all doubtful cases. Whatever the social organization may be, it must consist of different parts; one will undertake the care of governing; the other that of discussing and giving sanction to the laws. These assemblies, the attributes of which will be fixed by the constitution, will sometimes clash, and will give different interpretations of the constitution: but the national jury will be at hand to reconcile them, and to confine each body to its proper orbit.' The number of members was settled at eighty, each to be at least forty years of age. These eighty sages, whose political career was terminated, could no longer hold any public office. This idea gave general satisfaction, and was commented upon in various ways; the senators were to be such for life,—this was a novelty since the Revolution, and the public laughed at the very idea of stability; it was tired of the vicissitudes and changes which had succeeded each other for the last ten years.

Shortly afterwards, Sieyes explained his theory of national representation; it was composed of two branches: a Legislative Body of 250 deputies, not intended to enter into discussions, but, like the great chamber of parliament, to vote and determine by scrutiny; and a Tribunal of 100 deputies, which, like an inquest, was to discuss, report, and argue against the resolutions formed by a Council of State, named by the Government, which should have the prerogative of drawing up the laws. Instead, then, of a turbulent Legislative Body, swayed by factions, and its ill-timed motions to order, there would be a solemn assembly to determine on questions, after dispassionately listening to ample discussion respecting them. To the tribunal also, would belong the further duty of denouncing in the senate the unconstitutional acts of the Government, even such laws as had been adopted by the Legislative Body; and to enable them to do this, the Government was to be restrained from proclaiming laws until the expiration of ten days after their adoption by the Legislative Body. These outlines were favourably received by the Committee and the public. The latter was so weary of the empty declamations

PROVISIONAL CONSULS

of the tribunes, and of their untimely motions to order, which had done so much evil and so little good, and whence had sprung so many follies and so few advantages, that they flattered themselves with a prospect of more stability in the legislation, of tranquillity and rest, which were ardently desired.

Several sittings were spent in reducing the plans into form in writing, and in matters of detail relative to the public accounts and the laws. At last the time arrived when Sieyes explained the organization of his government; this was the capital—the most important part of that beautiful piece of architecture, and the influence of which was to be most felt by the people. He proposed a Grand Elector for life, to be chosen by the Conservative Senate, to possess a revenue of six millions of livres, and guard of 3,000 men, and to reside in the palace of Versailles; foreign ambassadors were to be accredited to him; and he was to furnish credentials to the French ambassadors and ministers at foreign courts. All acts of government, all laws, and all judicial proceedings, were to be in his name. He was to be the sole representative of the national glory, power, and dignity; he was to nominate two consuls, one for peace, and the other for war; but to these points his influence upon affairs was to be limited: it is true he was to have the power of removing the consuls, and of replacing them by others; but at the same time the senate was to be allowed, whenever it should deem such an exercise of power arbitrary and opposed to the national interest, *to merge the grand elector*. The effect of this merger was to be equivalent to a removal; the post was to become vacant, but the grand elector was to have a seat in the senate for the rest of his life.

I had said but little in the preceding sittings. I had had no experience in such assemblies; I could only refer on this subject to Sieyes, who had participated in the formation of the Constitutions of 1791, 1793, and 1795; to Daunou, who was accounted one of the principal framers of the latter; and in short, to twenty or thirty members of the Committees, who had all distinguished themselves in legislating, and who took the greater interest in the creation of those bodies which were to make the laws, inasmuch as they were to be themselves a component part of such bodies. But the Government concerned myself. I, therefore, rose to oppose such strange plans. 'The grand elector, if he confines himself strictly to the functions you assign him, will be the shadow, but the mere fleshless shadow, of a *Roi fainéant*. Can you point out a man base enough to humble himself to such mockery? If he abuses his prerogative, you give him an absolute power. If, for example, I became grand elector, when I appointed the consul for war and the consul for peace, I would say, 'If you nominate a single minister, if you sign a single act without my previous approbation, I will remove you.' 'But', you reply, 'the senate in its turn will merge the grand elector:' the remedy is worse than the evil—nobody, according to this scheme, has any guarantee. In another point of

PROVISIONAL CONSULS

view, what will be the situation of these two prime ministers? One will have the ministers of justice, of the interior, of police, of finance, of the treasury under his control; the other, those of the marine, of war, of external relations. The first will be surrounded only by judges, administrators, financiers, men of the long robe; the second only by epaulettes, and military men;—the one will be wanting money and recruits for his armies; the other will not furnish any. Such a government would be a monstrous creation, composed of heterogeneous parts presenting nothing rational. It is a great mistake, to suppose that the shadow of a thing can be of the same use as the thing itself.'

Sieyes answered unsatisfactorily, and was at length reduced to silence; he appeared embarrassed and undecided;—was he concealing some deep design? or was he the dupe of his own theory? These points will never be cleared up; but ultimately, this part of his scheme was found untenable. If he had begun with the development of his whole constitutional project, and described his head of the government first, nothing would have passed, and he would have lost his influence at the outset; but through the confidence which was reposed in him, a partial adoption of the scheme had already taken place.

The adoption of forms purely Republican was proposed; as was also the creation of a President, in the manner of the United States; this President was to hold the government of the Republic for ten years, and was to have the choice of his ministers, of his council of state, and of all the agents of the administration. But circumstances were such that it was thought necessary to disguise the sole magistracy of the President. All opinions were, at length, conciliated by composing a Government of three Consuls, of which one as head of the government was to possess all the authority, since he alone would appoint to all places, and would have a determining voice; and the two others were to be his indispensable counsellors. With a first Consul unity would be gained in the Directory; and with the two other Consuls, who would of course be consulted, and possess the privilege of inscribing their opinions on public documents, unanimity would be preserved, and the spirit of Republicanism conciliated. It was evident that the situation of things and the state of popular feeling could then suggest no better plan. The object of the Revolution which had just been effected, was not the possession of a form of government more or less aristocratical or democratical; but its success depended on the consolidation of all interests, on the triumph of every principle for which the wishes of the nation had been unanimously pronounced in 1789. I was convinced that France could only exist as a monarchy; but the French people being more desirous of equality than of liberty, and the very principle of the Revolution being established on the equalization of all classes, there was of necessity a complete abolition of the aristocracy. If it was difficult to construct a republic on a solid basis without an aristocracy, the difficulty of establishing a monarchy was much greater. To form a constitution in a country without any kind of aristocracy, would be as vain as to attempt to navigate in one element only. The French Revolution undertook a problem as difficult of solution as the direction of a balloon. Sieyes might, if he had chosen it, have obtained the situation of second Consul; but he wished to retire: he was appointed a member of the Senate, contributed to organize that body, and was its first President. In gratitude for his many important services, the Legislative Body, by vote, conferred on him the estate of Crosne as a national recompense. He afterwards observed to me when Emperor, 'I was not aware that you would treat me with so much distinction, or that you would allow an influence to the Consuls which might possibly importune and embarrass you.' Sieyes was the most unfit man in the world for power; but his opinions were very desirable, for his perceptions were often luminous, and of the highest importance. He was fond of money; but of strict integrity: a quality that was extremely agreeable to me, who considered it as of the first importance in a public character.

During the whole of the month of December, my health was much shaken, and threatened to give way entirely.

These nightly sittings and long discussions, in which I was forced to listen to so much nonsense, wasted time that was precious to me, yet were nevertheless interesting to me in a certain degree. I remarked that many men who wrote well and were not without eloquence, were yet entirely devoid of solidity of judgment, had nothing logical in their reasoning, and argued most miserably; the fact is, that there are people who are gifted by nature with the faculty of writing and expressing their thoughts well, as others are with a genius for music, painting, or sculpture. Public affairs either civil or military, require deep thought, profound discrimination, and a power of giving unwearied attention for a great length of time.

I chose Cambaceres as second Consul, and Lebrun for the third. Cambaceres was of an honourable family in Languedoc, he was fifty years of age; he had been a member of the Convention, and had conducted himself with moderation; he was generally esteemed; his political career had not been dishonoured by any excess, and he had a just claim to the reputation which he enjoyed of being one of the ablest lawyers in the Republic. Lebrun was sixty years of age, he came from Normandy; he had been deputed to the Council of Ancients by the department of La Manche. He had been formerly employed in drawing up the decrees of the Chancellor Maupeou, and had distinguished himself by the purity and elegance of his style. He was one of the best writers in France, of inflexible integrity; and approved of the changes of the Revolution only in consideration of the advantages which resulted from them to the mass of the people, for his own family were all of the class of peasantry.

The Constitution of the year VIII, so impatiently expected by all ranks of citizens, was published and submitted to the sanction of the people on 13 Dec-

PROVISIONAL CONSULS

ember, 1799, and proclaimed on the 24th of the same month: thus the Provisional Government lasted forty-three days.

My ideas were fixed; but the aid of time and events was necessary for their realization. The organization of the Consulate had presented nothing in contradiction to them: it taught unanimity, and that was the first step. This point gained, I was quite indifferent as to the forms and denominations of the several constituted bodies; I was a stranger to the Revolution: it was natural that the will of those men who had followed it through all its phases, should prevail in questions as difficult as they were abstract. The wisest plan was to go on from day to day without deviating from one fixed point, the polar star by which I meant to guide the Revolution to the haven I desired.

Chapter XXXIV

OF NEUTRAL POWERS

Of the law of Nations observed by belligerent states in war by land; and of that which is observed by them in maritime war. Of the principles of the maritime rights of neutral powers. Of the armed neutrality of 1780, the principles of which, being those of France, Spain, Holland, Russia, Prussia, Denmark, and Sweden, were in opposition to the claims of the English at that period. New claims of England successively brought forward during the war of the Revolution, from 1793 to 1800. America acknowledges these pretensions; consequent discussions with France. Opposition to these claims on the part of Russia, Sweden, Denmark, and Prussia. Ensuing events. Convention of Copenhagen, in which, notwithstanding the presence of an English Fleet of superior force, Denmark acknowledges none of the pretensions of England, the discussion thereof being adjourned. Treaty of Paris between the French Republic and the United States of America, by which the differences which had arisen between the two powers, in consequence of the submission of the Americans to the claims of England, are terminated. France and America solemnly proclaim the principles of the maritime rights of neutrals. Causes of the Emperor Paul's dissatisfaction with England. Russia, Denmark,

OF NEUTRAL POWERS

Sweden and Prussia, proclaim the principles acknowledged by the treaty of the 30th September between France and America. The Convention, called the Armed Neutrality, signed on the 16th December, 1800. War between England, on one side, and Russia, Denmark, Sweden, and Prussia, on the other; which proves that these powers were as far from acknowledging the claims of the English, as France, Holland, America, or Spain. Battle of Copenhagen, April 2nd, 1801. Assassination of the Emperor Paul I. Russia, Sweden and Denmark desist from the principles of the armed neutrality. New principles of the rights of neutrals acknowledged by these powers. Treaty of June 17, 1801, signed by Lord St. Helens. These new principles binding only on the powers who have acknowledged them by treaty.

The law of nations, in barbarous ages, was the same by land as by sea. Individuals of belligerent nations were made prisoners, whether they were taken in arms, or were private inhabitants; and they could only avoid slavery by paying a ransom. Moveable, and even landed property, was wholly or partly confiscated. Civilisation rapidly developed its effects, and has entirely altered the law of nations in war by land, without having had the same effect in that which is carried on by sea: so that, as if there were two kinds of right and justice, affairs are regulated by two different laws. The law of nations in war by land, no longer allows of the plundering of individuals, or of any alteration in their personal condition. War operates only against governments. Thus property does not change hands; the warehouses of merchants remain untouched, and individuals continue personally free. None are considered prisoners of war, but those who are taken with arms in their hands, and who belong to military bodies. This alteration has greatly diminished the evils of war. It has rendered the conquest of a nation more easy, and made war less sanguinary and less calamitous. A conquered province takes an oath, and, if the victor requires it, gives hostages and delivers up its arms: the public contributions are received by the conqueror for his own profit, who, if he deems it necessary, decrees an extraordinary contribution, either to provide for the

OF NEUTRAL POWERS

support of his army, or to idemnify himself for the expenses to which he has been put by the war. But this contribution, has no reference to the value of goods in store; it is merely a proportionable increase, greater or less in amount, of the ordinary contributions. This contribution seldom amounts to so much as the annual taxes received by the prince of the country, and it is laid on the whole of the state, so that it neither produces the ruin of any individual.

The law of nations, which regulates maritime war, has remained in all its pristine barbarity; the property of individuals is confiscated; persons non-combatant are made prisoners. When two nations are at war, all the ships of both parties, whether at sea or in port, are subject to confiscation, and the individuals on board such ships are made prisoners of war. Thus, by an evident contradiction, an English ship (supposing a war between England and France) being in the port of Nantes, for instance, shall be confiscated the moment war is declared; the men on board shall be prisoners of war, although non-combatant and private citizens: whilst a warehouse of English merchandize, belonging to Englishmen living in the same town, shall neither be sequestrated nor confiscated, and the English merchants travelling in France shall not be made prisoners of war, but shall receive their itinerary and necessary passports to quit the territory. An English vessel at sea, seized by a French ship, shall be confiscated, although its cargo belong to private persons; the individuals found on board this vessel shall be prisoners of war, although non-combatant: and yet a convoy of a hundred waggons of merchandize belonging to English subjects proceeding through France, at the moment of the rupture between the two powers, shall not be seized.

In war by land, not even the territorial property possessed by foreigners is subject to confiscation; it can at most be sequestrated. The laws which regulate war by land are therefore more consistent with civilization and the welfare of individuals; and it is to be wished that a time may come when the same liberal ideas may extend to maritime war, and the naval armies of two powers may fight without occasioning the confiscation of merchant ships, or making merchant seamen and civil passengers prisoners of war. Commerce would then be carried on, at sea, between belligerent nations, as it now is by land, amidst the battles fought by opposing armies.

The sea is the domain of all nations; it extends over three fourths of the globe, and forms a connexion between the different nations. A ship laden with merchandize, sailing on the sea, is subject to the civil and criminal laws of its sovereign, as if it were in the interior of his states. A ship at sea may be considered as a floating colony, in the sense that all nations are equally sovereign at sea. If the merchant vessels of the belligerent powers could sail freely, there could, *à fortiori*, be no inquest to exercise over neutrals. But as it is become a principle that the merchant-ships of belligerent powers are liable to confiscation, a right necessarily resulted hence for all ships of war of belligerent powers to satisfy themselves of the flag of any neutral ship they meet with; for, if it should belong to the enemy, they would have a right to confiscate it. Thence results the right of search which all powers have acknowledged by different treaties; thence the right of belligerent vessels to send their boats on board of neutral merchant-ships, to demand inspection of their papers, and thus satisfy themselves of their flag. In treaties, it has been stipulated that this right should be exercised with all possible consideration, that the armed ship should keep out of the range of cannon, and that only two or three men should board the ship visited, in order that there should be no appearance of force or violence. It has been agreed that a ship belongs to the power whose flag it bears, when it is provided with regular passports and certificates, and when the captain and half the crew are natives of that country. Every power has engaged, by various treaties, to prohibit its neutral subjects from carrying on a contraband trade with belligerent powers; and they have designated as contraband the trade in ammunition of war, as powder, bullets, shells, firelocks, saddles, bridles, cuirasses, etc. Every vessel having these articles on board is considered to have transgressed its sovereign's orders, the latter having engaged to prohibit his subjects from carrying on this trade; and the contraband articles are confiscated accordingly.

Thus the search made by cruisers became no longer a mere visit to satisfy themselves of the flag; and the cruiser exercised, even in the name of the sovereign under whose flag the vessel that was visited sailed, a new right of search, to ascertain whether the ship did not carry contraband goods. The men of the hostile nation, but the military men only, were assimilated to the contraband effects. Thus this inspection did not derogate from the principle that the flag covers the goods.

A third case soon occurred. Neutral vessels presented themselves to enter places besieged and blockaded by hostile squadrons. These neutral vessels did not carry military stores, but provisions, wood, wines, and other goods likely to be of service to the place besieged, and to prolong its defence. After long discussions between the different powers, they agreed, by various treaties, that whenever a place should really be blockaded, so that it would evidently be dangerous for any ship to attempt to enter it, the commander of the blockade might forbid the neutral ship to enter such place; and if, notwithstanding such prohibition, it should employ force or stratagem for the purpose of introducing itself, he should be at liberty to confiscate it.

Thus the maritime laws are founded upon the following principles: 1st, The flag covers the merchandize. 2dly, A neutral ship may be visited by a belligerent vessel, to ascertain its flag and cargo, so far as to be satisfied that it carries no contraband goods. 3dly, Contraband goods are considered to be military stores only. 4thly, Neutral ships may be prevented from entering a place that is besieged, if the blockade be real, and the entrance be evidently

OF NEUTRAL POWERS

dangerous. These principles form the maritime law of neutrals, because the different Governments have, freely, and by treaty, engaged to observe them, and cause them to be observed by their subjects. The different maritime powers, Holland, Portugal, Spain, France, England, Sweden, Denmark, and Russia, have, at different periods successively contracted these engagements with each other, and they have been proclaimed as the general treaties of pacification, such as at those of Westphalia in 1646, and Utrecht in 1712.

England, in the American war of 1778, pretended, 1st, that materials adapted for building ships, such as timber, hemp, tar, etc., were contraband; 2dly, that although a neutral ship had a right to go from a friendly port to an enemy's port, it could not traffic between one hostile port and another; 3dly, that neutral ships could not sail from the enemy's colony to the mother-country; 4thly, that neutral powers had no right to have their merchant-ships convoyed by ships of war; and that, if they did so, this would not exempt them from search.

No independent power would submit to these unjust claims. In fact, the sea being the dominion of all nations, no one has a right to regulate the legislation of what passes there. Ships carrying a neutral flag are only allowed to be searched, because the sovereign himself has permitted it by treaty. Military stores are only contraband, because it has been so determined by treaty. Belligerent powers have a right to seize them, only because the sovereign under whose flag the neutral vessel sails has himself engaged not to allow this kind of commerce. You are not, it was said to the English, to augment the list of contraband goods at your pleasure; and no neutral power has engaged to prohibit the trade in naval stores, such as timber, hemp, tar, etc.

As to the second claim, it was added, it is contrary to received usage. You ought not to interfere in the operations of commerce, except to satisfy yourselves of the flag, and that no contraband articles are carried. You have no right to know what is done in a neutral ship, because that ship, on the high seas, is at home, and by right out of your power. She is not covered by the batteries of her country, but she is so by the moral power of her sovereign.

The third pretension has no better foundation. The state of war can have no influence on neutrals; whatever, therefore, they could do in peace, they may do in war. Now, in time of peace, you would have no right to prevent or object to their carrying on the commerce between the mother-country and its colonies. If foreign ships are prevented from carrying on this commerce, it is not in pursuance of the law of nations, but by a municipal law; and whenever a power has chosen to allow strangers to trade with its colonies, no one has any right to oppose it.

With respect to the fourth claim, it was answered, that, as the right of search only existed for the purpose of ascertaining the flag and searching for contraband goods, an armed ship commissioned by the sovereign was a much better proof of the flag and cargo of the merchant-ships in its convoy, as well as the rules relative to contraband trade decreed by its master, than the search of the paper of a merchant-ship could be; that the result of this claim might be that a convoy, escorted by a fleet of eight or ten seventy-four-gun ships, belonging to a neutral power, might be subjected to search by a single brig or cruiser of a belligerent power.

At the time of the American war, in 1778, M. de Castries, the Minister of the Marine of France, caused a new regulation relating to the commerce of neutrals to be adopted. This regulation was drawn up according to the spirit of the treaty of Utrecht and the rights of neutrals. The four principles above asserted were therein proclaimed; and it was declared that it should be executed for six months, after which it should cease to be in force with respect to those neutral nations which should not have induced England to respect their rights.

This conduct was just and politic; it satisfied all the neutral powers, and threw a new light on this question. The Dutch, who then had the most considerable trade, being annoyed by the English cruisers, and the decisions of the Admiralty of London, had their convoys escorted by ships of war. The English advanced this strange principle, that neutrals cannot escort their own merchant convoys; or, at least, that their doing so does not exempt them from search. A convoy, escorted by several Dutch ships of war, was attacked, taken, and carried into English ports. This event filled Holland with indignation, and she soon afterwards united with France and Spain, and declared war against England.

Catherine, Empress of Russia, took part in these important questions. The dignity of her flag, the interest of her empire, the commerce of which chiefly consisted in articles proper for ship-building, induced her to come to a resolution to form an armed neutrality with Sweden and Denmark. These powers declared they would make war on any belligerent power which should infringe the following principles:—1st, That the flag covers the cargo (except contraband goods);—2dly, That the search of a neutral ship by a vessel of war should be made with all possible respect; 3dly, That military stores only, cannon powder, shot, etc. are contraband articles;—4thly, That every power has a right to convoy its merchant ships, and that in that case the declaration of the commander of the ship of war is sufficient to justify the flag and the cargoes of the ships under convoy;—5thly, and lastly, That a port is only blockaded by a squadron, when it is evidently dangerous to enter it; but that a neutral ship cannot be prevented from entering a port which has been blockaded by a force no longer present before the port, at the moment when the ship presents itself, whatever may be the cause of the removal of the blockading force, whether arising from the state of the wind, or the necessity of obtaining supplies of provisions.

OF NEUTRAL POWERS

This neutrality of the North was signified to the belligerent powers on the 15th of August, 1780. France and Spain, whose principles it solemnly asserted, eagerly adhered to it. England alone testified extreme displeasure; but, not daring to brave the new confederation, she contented herself with relaxing in the execution of all her claims, and did not give room for any complaint on the part of the neutral confederate powers. Thus, by not carrying her principles into execution, she virtually renounced them. Fifteen months after, the peace of 1783 concluded the maritime war.

The war between France and England began in 1793. England soon became the soul of the first coalition. Whilst the Austrian, Prussian, Spanish, and Piedmontese armies were invading our frontiers, she used all possible means to effect the ruin of our colonies. The capture of Toulon, where our squadron was burnt, the insurrection of the provinces of the West, in which so great a number of seamen perished, annihilated our navy. Upon this, England no longer set bounds to her ambition. Thenceforth, preponderating and unrivalled at sea, she thought the moment was come when she might, without danger, proclaim her subjugation of the seas. She resumed the pretentions she had tacitly renounced in 1780, that is to say, 1st, That materials for ship-building are contraband;—2dly, That neutrals have no right to have their trading vessels convoyed; or, at least, that the declaration of the commander of the convoy does not annul the right of search;—3dly, That a place may be blockaded, not only by the presence of a squadron, but even when the squadron is removed from before the port of tempests, or the necessity of taking in water, etc. She went still farther, and brought forward these three new pretensions: 1st, That the flag does not cover the merchandize, but that the merchandize and property of an enemy, in a neutral bottom, are liable to confiscation;—2dly, That a neutral ship has no right to carry on trade between colonies and their mother-country;—3dly, That although a neutral ship may enter an enemy's port, she cannot go from one hostile port to another.

The Government of America, seeing the maritime power of France annihilated, and fearing, on its own account, the influence of the French party, which was composed of the most violent characters, thought it necessary for its own preservation to conciliate England; and submitted to all that was prescribed to it by that power, for the purpose of incumbering and injuring the commerce of France.

The altercations between France and the United States became warm. The envoys of the French Republic, Genest, Adet, and Fauchet, urgently demanded the execution of the treaty of 1778; but they had little success. Various legislative measures analogous to those of the Americans were consequently taken in France; several disputes occurred at sea, and the differences arose to such a pitch of animosity, that France was, in a manner, at war with

OF NEUTRAL POWERS

America. The former of the two nations, however, came triumphantly through the struggle which menaced her existence; anarchy disappeared before order and a regular Government. The Americans then felt the importance of conciliating France. The President himself was sensible how much that power was in the right, in protesting against the treaty which he had concluded with England: and, in his heart, he was ashamed of an act which nothing but the force of circumstances had induced him to sign. Messrs. Pinckney, Marshal, and Gerry, charged with the full powers of the American Government, arrived at Paris at the end of 1797. Every thing encouraged the hope of a speedy reconciliation between the two Republics; but the question remained wholly undecided. The treaty of 1794, and the relinquishment of the rights of neutrality were essentially injurious to the interest of France; and there could be no hope of inducing the United States to return to the execution of the treaty of 1778, or to remember what they owed to France and to themselves, except by effecting a change in their internal organization.

In consequence of the events of the Revolution, the federalist party had gained the ascendancy in that country; but the democratic party was, nevertheless, the most numerous. The Directory thought to strengthen it by refusing to receive two of the American plenipotentiaries, because they were attached to the federalist party, and by acknowledging the third only, who belonged to the opposite party. The Directory farther declared that it could enter into no negotiation until America should have made reparation for the injuries of which the French Republic had to complain; and, on the 18th of January, 1798, solicited a law from the councils, purporting that the neutrality of a ship should not be determined by its flag, but by the nature of its cargo; and that every ship, laden, wholly or in part, with English goods, might be confiscated. The law was just towards America, as being only in reprisal for the treaty which that power had signed with England in 1794; but it was, nevertheless, impolitic and ill timed; it was subversive of all the rights of neutrals. It was declaring that the flag no longer covered the goods; or, in other words, declaring that the seas belonged to the strongest party. It was acting according to the views and interest of England, which power beheld, with secret joy, France proclaiming English principles, and authorizing English usurpation. The Americans were then, undoubtedly, nothing more than the factors of England; but municipal laws, regulating the commerce of France with the Americans, would have destroyed an order of things contrary to the interests of the French; the Republic might have declared, at most, that English goods should be contraband, under those flags which acknowledged the new pretensions of the English. The result of this law was disastrous to the Americans. The French cruisers made numerous prizes; and according to the letter of the law, they were all good. If an American ship had a few tons of English merchandize on board, it was enough to condemn the whole cargo. At the same time, as if there were not already sufficient causes of irritation and disunion between the two countries, the Directory caused an application to be made to the American envoys for a loan of forty-eight millions of francs; grounding their request on the loan formerly made by France to the United States, to enable them to shake off the yoke of England. The intriguing agents, of whom the ministry of exterior relations was full at that period, insinuated that this loan would not be insisted on, provided a sum of twelve hundred thousand francs were paid, which money was to be divided between the Director B—— and the minister T——.

This intelligence was received in America in the month of March; the President communicated it to the Chamber on the 4th of April. Men of all parties rallied around him; the independence of America was even thought to be menaced. All the gazettes and newspapers were full of the preparations which were making in France for the expedition to Egypt; and whether the American Government really apprehended an invasion, or whether it affected to apprehend it, in order to excite the public mind still more powerfully, and to strengthen the federalist party, it caused the command of the army of defence to be intrusted to General Washington. On the 26th of May, an Act of Congress passed, authorizing the President to order the commanders of American ships of war to capture every vessel found near the coast with the intention of committing depredations on shipping belonging to citizens of the United States, and to retake such of the latter ships as might be captured. On the 9th of June, all commercial relations with France were, by a new Bill, suspended. On the 25th, the treaties of 1778, and the Consular Convention of the 4th of November, 1788, were declared void by a new Bill, purporting that the United States were discharged and exonerated from the stipulations of the said treaties. The motives of this Bill were stated to be—1st, That the French Republic had repeatedly violated the treaties concluded with the United States, to the great detriment of the citizens of that country; by confiscating, for instance, merchandize belonging to the enemies of France on board American ships, notwithstanding it was agreed that the vessel saved the cargo; by fitting out privateers, against the rights of neutrality, in the ports of the Union; and by treating American sailors, found on board hostile ships, as pirates, etc.;—2dly, That France, notwithstanding the wish of the United States to set on foot an amicable negotiation, and instead of making reparation for the damage occasioned by such flagrant injustice, had dared, in a haughty manner, to demand a tribute, in the shape of a loan or otherwise. Towards the end of July, the last American plenipotentiary, Mr. Gerry, who had until then remained in Paris, set out for America.

France had just been humbled. The second coalition had gained possession of Italy, and attacked Holland. The French government caused some advances to be made by its minister in Holland, M. Pichon, to the American envoy to the Dutch government. Overtures were made to Mr. Adams, the President of the United States. At the opening of Congress, he stated the attempts which had been made by the French government to renew the negotiations, saying, that although it was the wish of the United States not to come to an absolute rupture with France, it was nevertheless impossible to send the new plenipotentiaries thither without degrading the American nation, until the French government should first give proper assurances that the sacred rights of ambassadors should be respected. He concluded his speech by recommending great preparations for war: but the American nation was far from coinciding in opinion with Mr. Adams, with respect to war with France. The President yielded to the general opinion, and, on the 25th of February, 1799, appointed Messrs. Ellsworth, Henry, and Murray, ministers plenipotentiary to the French Republic, to terminate all differences between the two powers. They landed in France in the beginning of 1800.

The death of Washington, which happened on the 15th of December, 1799, gave me an opportunity of making known my sentiments towards the United States of America. I put on mourning for that great citizen, and directed all my army to wear it likewise, by the following order of the day, dated the 9th February, 1800:—*Washington is dead! That great man fought against tyranny, and established the liberty of his country: his memory will always be dear to the French people, as well as to all freemen in both hemispheres, and especially to French soldiers, who, like him and the soldiers of America, fought for equality and liberty.* I further ordered, that for ten days all the colours and standards of the Republic should be hung with black crape.

On the 9th of February, a ceremony took place at Paris in the *Champ-de-Mars*. The trophies won by the army of the East were carried on this occasion in great pomp; new honours were paid to the American hero, whose funeral oration M. Fontanes pronounced before all the civil and military authorities of the capital. These circumstances banished from the minds of the envoys from the United States all traces of doubt with respect to the success of their negotiation.

The treaty of 1794, between England and America, had been a complete triumph to England; but it had been disapproved of by the neutral powers of Europe. On every occasion, Denmark, Sweden, and Russia, were eager to proclaim the principles of the armed neutrality of 1780.

On the 4th of July, 1798, the Swedish frigate the *Troya,* escorting a convoy, was met by an English squadron, which compelled her to go into Margate with the vessels under her convoy. As soon as the King of Sweden was informed of the circumstance, he gave orders to the commandant of the convoy to proceed to his destination. But a short time afterwards, a second convoy, from the ports of Sweden under the escort of a frigate (the *Hulla Fersen*), commanded by Captain Cederstrom, was treated in the same manner as the former. The King of Sweden had the two commanding officers of the convoy frigates brought before a council of war; Captain Cederstrom was condemned to death.

At the same period an English ship seized a Swedish vessel, and took her into Elsinore; but being soon afterwards blockaded in that port by several Danish frigates, she was compelled to restore her prize. In the course of the two succeeding years, the dispute grew warmer. The destruction of the French squadron at Aboukir, and the misfortunes of France in the campaign of 1799, inflated the pride of the English. About the end of December, 1799, the Danish frigate the *Hanfenen,* Captain Van Dockum, was escorting merchantmen of that nation, when, as she was entering the straits, she fell in with several English frigates. One of them despatched a boat to inform the Danish captain that his convoy was to be searched. The latter replied that the convoy was of his nation, and under his escort, that he would guarantee their flag and cargoes, and would not suffer them to be examined. An English boat immediately made up to one of the ships convoyed, in order to search her. The Danish frigate fired, wounded an Englishman, and seized the boat; which, however, Captain Van Dockum released, on the threat of the English to commence hostilities immediately. The convoy was carried to Gibraltar.

In a note dated the 10th of April, by which Mr. Merry, the English envoy at Copenhagen, demanded the disclaimer, apology, and reparation, which the British government was entitled to receive, he said: 'The right of visiting and searching neutral vessels on the high seas, to whatever nation they may belong, and whatever may be their cargo or destination, is considered by the British government as the incontestable right of every belligerent nation; a right which is founded on the law of nations, and has been generally admitted and acknowledged.' To this note M. Bernstorf, the Danish minister, replied, that the right of searching ships under convoy had never been acknowledged by any independent maritime power, and that they could not submit to it without degrading their own flag; that the conventional right of searching a neutral merchant-ship had only been allowed to belligerent powers to enable them to satisfy themselves of its title to the flag it sails under; that such title is much better established when it is certified by a ship of war of the neutral nation; that were it otherwise, the consequence would be that the greatest squadrons, escorting a convoy, would be liable to the insult of having it searched by a brig, or even by a privateer. He concluded by saying that the Danish captain, who had repelled an act of violence which he had no reason to expect, had only done his duty.

The Danish frigate the *Freya,* escorting a merchant convoy, fell in with four English frigates, at the entrance of the Channel, on the 25th of July, 1800, about eleven o'clock in the morning. One of them sent an officer on board of the Dane to inquire whither she was bound, and to give notice that

OF NEUTRAL POWERS

they should search the convoy. Captain Krapp answered that his convoy was Danish; shewed the English officer the papers and certificates proving his instructions, and declared that he would oppose any search. An English frigate then bore down upon the convoy, which was immediately ordered to rally to the *Freya*. At the same time another frigate approached the latter, and fired on a merchantman. The Dane returned her fire, but in such a manner that the ball passed over the English frigate. About eight o'clock the English commodore arrived with his ship, near the *Freya*, and repeated his demand to search the convoy without opposition. On Captain Krapp's refusal, an English sloop bore down on the nearest merchantman. The Dane gave orders to fire on the sloop; upon which the English commodore, who lay alongside the *Freya*, poured in his whole broadside upon her. The latter returned his fire, and engaged the four English frigates for an hour; but at length, despairing a victory over such superior forces, struck her flag. She had received thirty shot in the hull, and a great number in her masts and rigging. She was taken, with her convoy, into the Downs, where she was anchored alongside the admiral's ship. The English had the Danish flag hoisted on board of the *Freya*, where they placed a guard of English soldiers unarmed.

In the meantime great exasperation prevailed. Denmark, Sweden, and Russia, equipped their squadrons, and loudly declared their determination to maintain their rights by arms. Lord Whitworth was sent to Copenhagen, where he arrived on the 11th of July, with the necessary powers for endeavouring to effect an amicable arrangement. This negotiator was supported by a fleet of twenty-five ships of the line, under the command of Admiral Dickenson, which appeared on the 19th of August, before the Sound. All were in arms on the coast of Denmark; the commencement of hostilities was every moment expected. But the allied fleets of Sweden and Russia were not ready. Those powers had entertained hopes that threats would suffice; and not having expected so sudden attack, they had formed no treaty on the subject. After long conferences Lord Whitworth and Count Bernstorf signed a convention on the 31st of August. It was therein stipulated: 1st, That the right of searching ships sailing without convoy should be considered in a future discussion; 2dly, That his Danish Majesty, to avoid such occurrences as that of the frigate the *Freya*, should dispense with convoying any of his merchant-vessels, until a definitive convention could be effected by means of ulterior explanations on the subject; 3dly, That the *Freya* and her convoy should be released; and that the frigate should be supplied, and his British Majesty's ports, with all things necessary for her repairs, and that according to the custom of friendly and allied powers.

It is evident that England and Denmark were both merely seeking to gain time. Denmark, by means of this convention made under the cannon of a superior English fleet, escaped an imminent danger which threatened her; she acknowledged none of the claims of England, but merely sacrificed her just resentment, and the atonement she had a right to demand, for the insults offered to her flag.

As soon as the Emperor of Russia, Paul I, was informed of the entrance of an English fleet into the Baltic, with hostile intentions, he put a sequestration on all the English ships in his ports, amounting to several hundred. He also caused a declaration to be delivered to the captains of all ships sailing from Russian ports, purporting that the search of any Russian vessel by an English ship would be regarded as a declaration of war.

I appointed the councellors of state Joseph Bonaparte, Roederer, and Fleurieu, to treat with the ministers of the United States. The conference took place successively at Paris and at Morfontaine: many difficulties arose. Had the two Republics been at war or at peace? Neither of them had made any declaration of war; but the American government had, by its Bill of the 7th of July, 1798, declared the United States exonerated from all the rights which France had acquired by the treaty of 6th of February, 1778. The envoys would not consent to repeal this Bill; yet there are only two ways in which a nation can lose rights acquired by treaties, namely, by her own consent, or in consequence of war. The Americans demanded indemnity for all the losses they had sustained from the French privateers, and from the law of the 18th of January, 1798. They agreed, on their part, to indemnify French commerce for the losses it had suffered. But the balance of these indemnities was greatly in favour of America. The French plenipotentiaries proposed the following dilemma to the American envoys: 'We are either at war or at peace. If we are at peace, and our present situation is merely a state of misunderstanding, France ought to make good all the damage her privateers may have done you. You have evidently lost more than we, and it is incumbent on us to pay you the difference. But in that case things ought to be restored to the state they previously stood in, and we ought to enjoy all the rights and privileges we enjoyed before 1778. If, on the contrary, we are at war, you have no right to require indemnity for your losses, and we have no right to insist on privileges granted by treaties which the war has broken off.'

The American ministers were much embarrassed. After long discussions, a middle course was adopted; it was declared that the question, as to which of these two situations the two nations should be considered to stand in, should be decided by an ulterior convention. When once this difficulty was removed it only remained to stipulate for the future; and the principles of the rights of neutrals were fairly entered into. The animosity which existed between the Northern powers and England, the difficult actions which had already taken place, the various causes which had operated on the temper of the Emperor Paul, the victory of Marengo, which had changed the aspect of Europe, in short, everything conspired to prove that a clear and liberal declaration of the

OF NEUTRAL POWERS

principles of maritime rights would be of the greatest importance to the interests of all nations. It was expressly declared, in the new treaty; 1st, That the flag covers the lading: 2dly, That contraband articles can only be understood to be military stores, cannon, firelocks, powder, balls, cuirasses, saddles, etc.: 3dly, That the search of a neutral ship to ascertain its flag, and that it carries no contraband articles, can only be made out of gun-shot of the ship of war that makes the search; that two or three men, at most, should be allowed to go on board the neutral; that in no case should the neutral be obliged to send on board the searching ship; that every ship should carry a certificate to justify its flag; that the mere inspection of this certificate should be sufficient; that a ship carrying contraband goods should only be subject to the confiscation of such contraband articles that no ship under convoy should be subject to search; that the declaration of the commander of the escort of a convoy should be sufficient; that the right of blockade ought only to apply to places really blockaded, into which an entrance could not be effected without evident danger, and not to those considered to be blockaded by cruisers; that the property of an enemy is covered by a neutral flag, just as neutral merchandizes, found on board of enemies' ships, follow the fate of those ships, except always during the first two months after the declaration of war; that the ships and privateers of the two nations should be treated, in the respective ports, as those of the most favoured nation.

This treaty was signed by the ministers plenipotentiary of the two powers, at Paris, on the 30th of September, 1800. On the 3rd of October following, M. Joseph Bonaparte, President of the Commission intrusted with negotiation, gave an entertainment at his estate of Morfontaine, to the American envoys; I was present. The principal events of the war of American independence were commemorated in ingenious emblems and appropriate inscriptions; the arms of the two Republics were seen united on all sides. During dinner I gave the following toast: *'To the names of the French and Americans who fell in the field of battle, fighting for the independence of the New World.'* The Consul Cambaceres gave, *'To the successor of Washington.'* The following was Lebrun's, *'To the union of America with the Northern powers to enforce respect to the freedom of the seas.'* On the next day, the 4th of October, the American ministers took leave of me. The following passages were remarked in their speeches:—That they hoped the Convention signed on the 30th of September would be the foundation of a permanent friendship between France and America, and that the American ministers would take every proper step to make it so. I replied that the differences which had existed were now terminated; that no trace of them ought to be suffered to remain, any more than of a family quarrel; that the liberal principles declared in the Convention of the 30th of September, on the article of navigation, ought to be the basis of the intimate connection of the two Republics, as well as of their interests; and that, under the then existing circumstances, it was become more than ever important to both nations to adhere to them.

The treaty was ratified on the 18th of February, 1801, by the President of the United States, who suppressed Article 2 thereof, which ran in these terms:

'The ministers plenipotentiary of the two powers, being unable, at present, to come to an agreement, with respect to the treaty of alliance of the 6th of February, 1778, the treaty of amity and commerce of the same date, and the Convention dated the 4th of November, 1788; and with respect to the indemnities mutually due or claimed; the parties shall arrange these matters, by ulterior negotiations, at a suitable time; and until they shall be agreed on these points, the said treaties and Convention shall have no effect, and the relations between the two nations shall be regulated in manner following:' etc.

The suppression of this article, at once put an end to the privileges which France had possessed by the treaty of 1778, and annulled the just claims which America might have made for injuries done in time of peace. This was exactly what I had proposed myself in fixing these two points as equiponderating each other. Without this it would have been impossible to satisfy the merchants of the United States, and to banish from their memory the losses they had suffered. My ratification of this treaty was dated July 31st, 1801 and declared that it was to be clearly understood that the suppression of Article 2 annulled all claims for indemnity, etc.

It is not usual to modify ratifications. Nothing can be more inconsistent with the object of every treaty of peace, which is to restore harmony and good understanding. Ratifications ought therefore to be clear and simple; the treaty ought to be transcribed in them without the slightest alteration, in order to avoid entangling the questions in difficulties. If this occurrence could have been foreseen, the plenipotentiaries would have made two copies, and one with Article 2, and the other without it; all would then have proceeded regularly.

The Emperor Paul had succeeded the Empress Catherine. Half frantic with his hostility to the French Revolution, he had performed what his mother had contented herself with promising; and engaged in the second coalition. General Suwarrow, at the head of 60,000 Russians, advanced in Italy, whilst another Russian army entered Switzerland, and a corps of 15,000 men was placed by the Czar at the disposal of the Duke of York for the purpose of conquering Holland. These were all the disposable forces the Russian Empire had. Suwarrow, although victorious at the battles of Cassano, the Trebbia, and Novi, had lost half his army in the Saint-Gothard, and the different valleys of Switzerland, after the battle of Zurich, in which Korsakow had been taken. Paul then became sensible of all the imprudence of his conduct; and in 1800 Suwarrow returned to Russia with scarcely a fourth of his army. The Emperor Paul complained bitterly of having lost the flower of his troops, who had neither been seconded by the Austrians nor by the English. He reproached the Cabinet of Vienna with having refused, after the conquest of Piedmont, to replace the King of Sardinia upon his throne; with being destitute of grand and generous ideas, and wholly governed by calculation and interested views. He also complained that the English when they took Malta, instead of reinstating the order of St. John of Jerusalem, and restoring that island to the Knights, had appropriated it to themselves. I did all in my power to cherish these seeds of discontent, and to make them productive. A little after the battle of Marengo, I found means to flatter the lively and impetutous imagination of the Czar, by sending him the sword which Pope Leo X had given to l'Ile Adam, as a memorial of his satisfaction, for having defended Rhodes against the infidels. From eight to ten thousand Russian soldiers had been made prisoners in Italy, at Zurich, and in Holland: I proposed their exchange to the English and Austrians, both refused; the Austrians, because there were still many of their people prisoners in France; and the English, although they had a great number of French prisoners, because, as they said, this proposal was contrary to their principles. What! it was said to the Cabinet of St. James's, do you refuse to exchange even the Russians, who were taken in Holland, fighting in your own ranks under the Duke of York? And to the Cabinet of Vienna it was observed, How! do you refuse to restore to their country those men of the North to whom you are indebted for the victories of the Trebbia, and Novi, and for your conquest in Italy, and who have left in your hands a multitude of French prisoners taken by them! 'Such injustice excites my indignation,' I said. 'Well! I will restore them to the Czar without exchange; he shall see how I esteem brave men.' The Russian officers who were prisoners immediately received their swords, and the troops of that nation were assembled at Aix-la-Chapelle, where they were soon completely new clothed, and furnished with good arms of French manufacture. A Russian general was instructed to organize them in battalions and regiments. This blow struck at once at London and at Saint-Petersburg. Paul, attacked in so many different directions, gave way to his enthusiastic temper, and attached himself to France with all the ardour of his character. He despatched a letter to me, in which he said, 'Citizen, First Consul, I do not write to you to discuss the rights of men or citizens; every country governs itself as it pleases. Wherever I see at the head of a nation a man who knows how to rule and how to fight, my heart is attracted towards him. I write to acquaint you with my dissatisfaction with England, who violates every article of the law of nations, and who has no guide but her egotism and interest. I wish to unite with you to put an end to the unjust proceedings of that government.'

In the beginning of December, 1800, General Sprengporten, a Finlander, who had entered the Russian service, and who in his heart was attached to

France, arrived at Paris. He brought letters from the Emperor Paul, and was instructed to take the command of the Russian prisoners, and to conduct them back to their country. All the officers of that nation, who returned to Russia, constantly spoke in the highest terms of the kind treatment and attention they had met with in France, particularly after my arrival. The correspondence between the Emperor and myself soon became daily; we treated directly on the most important interests, and on the means of humbling the English power. General Sprengporten was not instructed to make peace; he had no powers for that purpose; neither was he an ambassador; peace did not exist. It was, therefore, an extraordinary mission, which allowed of this general's being treated with every distinction calculated to gratify the sovereign who had sent him, without the possibility of the occurrence of any inconvenience from such attentions.

Admiral Dickenson's expedition, and the foregoing convention of Copenhagen, which had been the consequence thereof, had disconcerted the schemes of the three maritime powers of the North, to oppose the tyranny of the English by a league. The English continued to violate all the rights of neutrals; they said, that since they had been able to attack and take the *Freya* frigate, and carry her into an English port, with her convoy, without Denmark's ceasing to be ally and friend of England, the conduct of the English cruiser must have been lawful, and Denmark had thereby acknowledged the principle that she could not convoy her shipping. Nevertheless, the latter power was far from approving of the insolence and pretensions of England. When taken alone, and unprepared, she had yielded; but she was in hopes that under cover of the ice, which would shortly close the Sound and the Baltic, she should be able, in concert with Sweden and Russia, to compel the observance of the rights of neutral powers. Sweden was offended at the conduct of the Cabinet of Saint James's, and as to Russia, we have already made known her motives for animosity towards the English. The treaty of the 30th of September, between France and America, had now proclaimed anew the principles of the independence of the seas: the winter was come; the Czar openly declared for those principles which, as early as the 15th of August, he had proposed to the Northern powers to recognize.

On the 17th of November, 1800, the Emperor Paul decreed by an ukase, that all the English property and merchandize, which had been attached in his states, in consequence of the embargo which he had laid on English shipping, should be collected in a mass, to liquidate what should be found due to the Russians by the English. He appointed mercantile commissioners to carry this decree into effect. The crews of the ships were considered prisoners of war, and sent into the interior of the empire. At length, on the 16th of December, a convention was signed between Russia, Sweden, and Denmark, to support the rights of neutrality. A short time after, Prussia joined this con-

OF NEUTRAL POWERS

federacy. This convention was called the quadruple alliance. Its principal points were, 1st, The flag covers the goods; 2dly, Every ship under convoy is exempt from search; 3rdly, No articles can be considered contraband, except military stores, such as cannon, etc.; 4thly, The right of blockade can only be applied to a port really blockaded; 5thly, Every neutral ship ought to have its captain and half its crew of the nation whose flag it bears; 6thly, The ships of war, of each of the contracting powers, shall protect and convoy the merchant-ships of the two others; 7thly, A combined squadron shall be assembled in the Baltic, to secure the execution of this convention.

On the 17th of December the English government ordered a cruise against the Russian shipping; and on the 14th of January, 1801, in reprisal of the convention of the 16th of December, 1800, which it called an infringement of its rights, it ordered a general embargo on all the shipping belonging to the three powers who had signed the convention.

As soon as that convention was ratified, the Emperor Paul despatched an officer to me to communicate it to me. This officer was presented to me at Malmaison on the 20th of January, 1801, and delivered his sovereign's letters. On the same day the Consuls published a decree, prohibiting all cruising against Russian ships. There was no occasion to extend this decree to Swedish and Danish vessels, France being at peace with those powers.

On the 12th of February, the Court of Berlin gave notice to the English government of its accession to the convention of the powers of the North, calling upon England to revoke and raise its embargo laid on Danish and Swedish shipping, in opposition to a general principle; distinguishing what related to those two powers from what concerned Russia only.

On the 4th of March, the Swedish minister in England gave in a note to the British Cabinet, in which he communicated the treaty of the 16th of December, 1800. He expresses his astonishment at the assertion of England, that Sweden and the Northern powers were attempting an innovation, when, in fact, they were only supporting the rights established and acknowledged by all powers in preceding treaties, and particularly by England herself in those of 1780, 1783, and 1794. Sweden and Denmark entered into a similar convention; England did not protest, and even looked indifferently on the warlike preparations of those powers to support that treaty. She did not then pretend that such treaty and preparations were an act of hostility; but she was now conducting herself in a different manner: this difference, however, did not arise from any addition made by other powers to their demands; it was only the consequence of a maritime principle which England had adopted, and wished to make other powers adopt in the present war. Thus a power, which had boasted of having taken up arms for the liberty of Europe, was now contriving the subjugation of the seas.

His Swedish Majesty recapitulates the unpunished offences committed by the commanders of English squadrons, even in Swedish ports; the inquisitorial visits to which they had compelled Swedish vessels to submit; the stoppage of the convoys in 1798; the insult offered to the Swedish flag before Barcelona; and the refusal of justice, of which the English tribunals had been guilty. His Swedish Majesty did not seek revenge, but only to secure the respect due to his flag. In the meantime, in reprisal for the embargo laid by the English, he placed one on all the English shipping in his ports, which he would raise whenever the English government would make satisfaction for the stoppage of the convoys in 1798, the affair before Barcelona, and the embargo of the 14th of January, 1801.

The tenor of the convention of the 16th of December, evidently shews that Sweden entered into no other question than that of the rights of neutrals, and intermeddled in no other dispute. The Danish minister concluded by demanding his passports.

Lord Hawkesbury, in reply to this note, stated that his Britannic Majesty had several times made known his invariable right to defend those maritime principles which the experience of several years had shewn to be the best calculated to secure the rights of belligerent powers. To restore the principles of 1780 at this time, was to commit an act of hostility. The embargo on the Swedish vessels would be continued as long as his Swedish Majesty should continue to form part of a confederacy tending to establish a system of public law incompatible with the dignity and independence of the English crown, and the rights and interests of his Britannic Majesty's subjects. It may be seen by this answer of Lord Hawkesbury's that the right claimed by England is posterior to the Treaty of 1780. It was, therefore, incumbent on him to shew the treaties subsequent to that period, by which other powers had acknowledged the new principles of Great Britain with respect to neutrals.

Thus war was declared between England on the one side, and Russia, Sweden, and Denmark on the other. The ice rendered the Baltic innavigable; English expeditions were sent to capture the Danish and Swedish colonies in the West Indies. In the course of March, 1800, the islands of Santa-Cruz, Saint-Thomas, and Saint-Bartholomew, fell into the power of the English.

On the 29th of March, the prince of Hesse, commanding the Danish troops, entered Hamburg, in order to cut off British commerce from the Elbe. In this general's proclamation, Denmark urges the necessity of adopting all means of annoying England, and finally compelling her to respect the rights of nations, and of neutral powers in particular.

The Cabinet of Berlin caused Hanover to be occupied, and thus closed the mouths of the Ems and Weser against the English. The Prussian general, in his manifesto, justifies this measure on the ground of the outrages perpetually committed by England against neutral nations, the losses consequently sustained by the latter, and, in short, on the new maritime laws which England was endeavouring to enforce.

A convention was entered into on the 3rd of April, between the regency and the Prussian ministers, by which the Hanoverian army was disbanded, and the fortresses surrendered to the Prussian troops.

The regency thereby engaged to obey the Prussian authorities. Thus the King of England lost his estates of Hanover; but what was of much more consequence to him, the Baltic, the Elbe, the Weser, and the Ems, were closed against him, as well as France, Holland, and Spain. This was a terrible stroke to the commerce of the English, the effects of which were such, that its continuation alone would have obliged them to renounce their system.

In the meantime the maritime powers of the North were arming with activity. Twelve Russian ships of the line were anchored at Revel, seven belonging to Sweden were ready at Carlscrona; which, added to a like number of Danish ships, would have formed a combined fleet of from twenty-two to twenty-four ships of the line, which would have been successively increased, the three powers being able to augment it to thirty-six, or perhaps forty ships.

Great as were the naval forces of England, a fleet like this was formidable. England was obliged to keep a squadron in the Mediterranean, to prevent France from sending forces to Egypt, and to protect the English trade. The disaster of Aboukir was partly repaired, and there was a squadron of several vessels in Toulon Roads. The English were likewise obliged to keep a squadron before Cadiz, to watch the Spanish ships, and hinder the French divisions from passing the straits. There was a French and Spanish fleet in Brest. England was likewise obliged to have a fleet before the Texel; but in the beginning of April, the Russian, Danish, and Swedish fleets had not joined, although they might have done so in the beginning of March. It was on this delay that the English government founded its plan of operations, for successively attacking the three maritime powers of the Baltic, exerting all its efforts, in the first instance against Denmark, to oblige that power to secede from the convention of the 16th of December, 1800, and to receive English shipping into her ports.

An English fleet of fifty sail, including seventeen ships of the line, under the command of Admiral Parker and Admiral Nelson, sailed from Yarmouth on the 12th of March; it contained 1000 men intended to land. On the 15th it was dispersed by a violent storm. A seventy-four, the *Invincible,* struck on a sand bank, and was totally lost. On the 20th of March signals were made that this fleet was in the Cattegat. On the same day a frigate proceeded to Elsinore, with the commissioner Vansittart, instructed, jointly with Mr. Drummond, to give in the ultimatum of the English government. On the 24th they returned on board of the fleet, bringing intelligence of all that was passing at

OF NEUTRAL POWERS

Copenhagen and in the Baltic. The Russian fleet was still at Revel, and that of Sweden at Carlscrona. The English were fearful of their junction. Their government had instructed Admiral Parker to detach Denmark from her alliance with the two other powers, by means of threats, or, if necessary, by a bombardment. When Denmark should be thus neutralized, the combined fleet would be greatly diminished, and the English would have free entrance to the Baltic. It appears that the Council hesitated whether to enter the Sound, or the Great Belt. The Sound between Cronenberg and the Swedish coast, is 2300 toises wide; its greatest depth is 1500 toises from the batteries of Elsinore, and 800 from the coast of Sweden. If, therefore, the two shores had been equally armed, the English ships would have been under the necessity of passing at the distance of 1100 toises from these batteries. Those of Elsinore and Cronenberg were lined with upwards of one hundred pieces of cannon and mortars. The damage which a squadron must sustain in such a passage, as well by the loss of masts and yards, as by accidents from the bombs, may easily be conceived. At the same time the passage of the Belts was very difficult, and the officers who were against that plan, asserted that it would enable the Danish fleet to sail from Copenhagen, and to join the French and Dutch fleets.

Admiral Parker, however, decided for this passage, and, on the 26th of March, the whole fleet made sail for the Great Belt. But a few light vessels, which acted as scouts, having grounded on the rocks, the fleet resumed its anchorage on the same day. The Admiral then resolved to pass by the Sound; and after having satisfied himself of the intentions of the Commandant of Cronenberg to defend the passage, the fleet, taking advantage of a favourable wind on the 30th, sailed for the Sound. The flotilla of bomb-vessels approached Elsinore, to effect a diversion by bombarding the town and castle; but the fleet having speedily discovered that the Swedish batteries did not fire, neared the shore, and passed the strait out of the reach of the Danish batteries, which threw a shower of balls and shells. All the shot fell above 100 toises from the fleet, which did not lose a single man.

The Swedes, to justify their treacherous conduct, have alleged that during the winter it was not possible to raise batteries, or even to increase that of six guns which they had; and besides, that Denmark had not seemed to wish it, probably fearing lest Sweden should renew her old claims to half the duties which Denmark levies from all ships which pass the strait: their number is from 10 to 12,000 annually; which brings in a yearly revenue of between 2,500,000 and 3,000,000. These reasons are evidently futile. A few days only were requisite for placing a hundred guns in battery, and the preparations which England had for several months been making for this expedition, as well as the presence of the fleet for several days in the Cattegat, had given Sweden much more time than was requisite.

OF NEUTRAL POWERS

On the same day, the 30th March, the fleet anchored between the Isle of Huen and Copenhagen. The English admirals and principal officers immediately embarked in a schooner, for the purpose of reconnoitring the position of the Danes.

After passing the Sound, ships do not immediately enter the Baltic. At a distance of ten leagues from Elsinore stands Copenhagen. On the right of that port is the Isle of Amack, and two leagues from that isle, in front, is the rock of Saltholm. It is necessary to pass into this strait, between Saltholm and Copenhagen, to enter the Baltic. This pass is again divided into two canals, by a bank called the Middle Ground, which is situate opposite Copenhagen; the royal canal is that which passes under the walls of that city. The pass between the Isle of Amack and Saltholm is good only for 74 gun ships; three-deckers cannot easily clear it, and are even obliged to be lightened by taking out part of their artillery. The Danes had placed their line of defence between the bank and the town, in order to oppose the anchoring of the bomb-vessels and gun-boats which might have passed over the bank. The Danes imagined that by these measures they had secured Copenhagen from bombardment.

The night of the 30th was employed by the English in sounding the bank; and, on the 31st, the admirals went on board of a frigate with the artillery officers, in order to reconnoitre the enemy's line again, as well as the anchorage for the bomb-vessels. It was agreed that, in case the enemy's line of defence could be destroyed, bomb-vessels might be placed to bombard the town and port; but that, as long as the line of defence should exist, that measure would be impracticable. The difficulty of attacking this line was very great. The fleet was separated from it by the bank of the Middle Ground, and the shallowness of the water which remained above the bank did not allow of its being cleared by first-rate ships. There was, therefore, no possibility of success, otherwise than by doubling the bank, and afterwards returning, coasting it to starboard, and taking up a station between the bank and the Danish line, —a most hazardous operation. For, 1st, The shape and length of the bank were not perfectly known, and there were none but English pilots on board, who had never sailed in these seas except in merchantmen: it is also well known, that the ablest pilots are guided in such cases only by the buoys, but these the Danes had very properly removed, or purposely misplaced:— 2dly, In doubling the bank, the English ships would be exposed to the whole fire of the Danes, until they should have formed their line of battle:— 3rdly, Every disabled ship would be a ship lost, because it would strike on the bank, and that under the fire of the Danish line and batteries.

The most prudent people thought it not advisable to undertake an attack which might end in the destruction of the fleet. Nelson thought otherwise, and got them to adopt the plan of attacking the line of defence and gaining possession of the crown batteries, by means of 900 soldiers. Supported on these isles, the bombardment of Copenhagen would be easy, and Denmark might thenceforth be considered as subdued. On the 1st of April, the Commander-in-Chief having approved of this plan of attack, detached Nelson, with twelve ships of the line and all the frigates and bomb-vessels. The latter anchored in the evening off Draco Point, near the bank which separated him from the enemy's line and so near it, that the mortars of the Isle of Amack, which made a few discharges, threw their shells into the midst of the squadron at anchor. On the 2nd, the weather being favourable, the English squadron doubled the bank, and, coasting it to starboard, formed in line between the bank and the Danes. One English 74 grounded before it could double the bank, and two others struck after doubling it. These three vessels, in this position, were exposed to the fire of the enemy's line, and received a great number of balls.

The Danish line of defence was supported, on its left, on the crown batteries, artificial islands, 600 toises from Copenhagen, armed with 70 guns, and defended by 1500 picked men; and its right extended on the Isle of Amack. To defend the entrance on the left of the Three Crowns, four ships of the line had been stationed, two of which were completely armed and equipped.

The object of the line of defence was to secure the port and city from bombardment, and to preserve the command of all that part of the roads comprised between the Middle Ground and the Town; this line had been placed as near as possible to the bank. Its right was far advanced before the Isle of Amack; the whole line was upwards of three thousand toises in length, and was formed of twenty ships. They were old vessels cut down, carrying not more than half their artillery, or frigates and other ships formed into floating batteries, carrying a dozen guns. For the effect it was intended to produce, this line was strong enough, and perfectly well placed; no bomb-vessel or gun-boat could approach it. For the reasons above stated, the Danes were not apprehensive of being attacked by first-rate ships. When, therefore, they perceived Nelson's manoeuvre, and comprehended what he was about to attempt, their astonishment was extreme. They then discovered that their line was not sufficiently strong, and that they ought to have formed it, not of hulls of ships, but, on the contrary, of the best vessels in their squadron; that it was too much extended for the number of ships it contained; that the right was not sufficiently supported; that if they had placed this line nearer Copenhagen, it would not have been more than from 1500 to 1800 toises wide; that the right could have been supported by strong batteries, raised on the Isle of Amack, which would have played in advance of the right, and flanked the whole line. It is probable that, in that case, Nelson would have failed in his attack, for it would have been impossible for him to pass between the line and the shore thus lined with cannon. But it was too late; these reflections were unavailing; and the Danes now thought of nothing but making a vigorous defence. The first success that attended them, in the wreck of three of the strongest ships of the enemy, encouraged them to form the most sanguine hopes. But the want of these three vessels compelled Nelson, in order to avoid disseminating his forces too much, to weaken his extreme right. The principal object of his attack, which was the capture of the Three Crowns, was thenceforth abandoned. As soon as Nelson had doubled the bank he approached within 100 toises of the line of defence, and finding four fathoms water, his pilots anchored. The cannonade had commenced with extreme vigour; the Danes displayed the greatest intrepidity, but the English had double their weight of metal.

A line of defence is an immovable force opposed to a force that is movable; and it can only surmount this disadvantage by deriving support from the land batteries, particularly with regard to the flanks. But the Danes, as already remarked, had not flanked their right.

The English, therefore, pressed the right and centre, which were not flanked, silenced their fire, and forced this part of the line, which was not flanked, to strike, after a firm resistance of above four hours. The left of the line, being well supported by the crown batteries, remained unbroken. A division of frigates, in hopes of proving an adequate substitute for the ships which ought to have attacked these batteries, ventured to engage them, as if it had been supported by the fire of the ships. But it suffered considerable loss, and, in spite of all its efforts, was obliged to relinquish this enterprise and sheer off.

Admiral Parker, who had remained with the other part of the fleet without the bank, seeing the active resistance of the Danes, conceived that the greater part of the English ships would be disabled through so obstinate a conflict; that they would be unable to manoeuvre, and would strike on the bank, which expectation was partly fulfilled. He made a signal to desist from the action, and to take up a position in the rear; but even this was become very difficult. Nelson preferred continuing the battle. He was soon convinced of the prudence of the Admiral's signal, and, at length, made up his mind to weigh anchor and retire from the engagement. But, seeing that part of the Danish line was vanquished, he conceived the idea of sending a flag of truce, previously to taking so decisive a step, to propose an arrangement. With this view, he wrote a letter, addressed to the Danes, the brave brothers of the English, in these terms: 'Vice-Admiral Nelson has orders to spare Denmark, if the resistance is not prolonged. The line of defence, which protected its shores, has struck to the English flag; cease then the firing, and allow him to take possession of his prizes, otherwise he will blow them up in the air, with their crews who have so nobly defended them. The brave Danes are the brethren, and will never be the foes of the English.' The Prince of Denmark who was at the seaside, received this note, and in order to obtain explanations respecting it, sent Adjutant-General Lindholm to Nelson, with whom he concluded a suspension of arms. The firing speedily ceased in all directions, and the wounded Danes were carried ashore. Scarce was this armistice concluded, when three English ships, including that in which Nelson himself was, struck on the bank. They were in the jaws of destruction, and could never have escaped if the batteries had continued their fire. They therefore owed their safety to this armistice.

This event saved the English squadron. Nelson went ashore on the 4th of April. He traversed the town, amidst the outcries and threats of the populace; and after several conferences with the Prince Regent, the following convention was signed: 'There shall be an armistice of three months and a half between the English and Denmark; but solely with respect to the city of Copenhagen and the Sound. The English squadron, at liberty to proceed wherever it may be thought expedient, is to keep at the distance of a league from the coast of Denmark, from the capital to the Sound. Notice is to be given of the rupture of the armistice fifteen days before the resumption of hostilities. In all other respects every thing is to remain exactly in *statu quo,* so that there is nothing to prevent Admiral Parker from proceeding to any other point of the Danish possessions, towards the coasts of Jutland, or those of Norway; the English fleet, which is by this time most probably in the Elbe, is to be at liberty to attack the Danish fortress of Gluckstadt; and Denmark is to continue to occupy Hamburg, Lubeck, etc.'

In this battle the English lost 943 men, killed and wounded. Two of their ships were so much injured, that it was impossible to repair them; Admiral Parker was obliged to send them to England. The loss of the Danes was reckoned a little higher than that of the English. The part of the line of defence which fell into the power of the latter was burnt, to the great dissatisfaction of the English officers, whose interest suffered thereby. At the time of the signature of the armistice, the bomb-vessels and gun-boats were in a position to take up a line to bombard the city.

The result of the affair of Copenhagen did not entirely fulfil the intentions of the British government, which had hoped to detach and subdue Denmark, and had only succeeded in getting that power to conclude an armistice by which its forces were paralyzed for fourteen weeks.

The Swedish and Russian squadrons were arming with the greatest activity, and constituted considerable forces. But all military preparations were rendered useless, and the confederation of the northern powers was dissolved, by the death of the Emperor Paul, who was at once the author, the chief, and the soul of that alliance. Paul I was assassinated in the night of the 23rd of March; and the news of his death reached Copenhagen at the time of the signature of the armistice. This monarch had exasperated part of the Russian nobility against himself by an irritable and over-susceptible temper. His hatred of the French Revolution had been the distinguishing feature of his reign. He considered the familiar manners of the French sovereign and princes, and the suppression of etiquette at their court, as one of the causes of that Revolution. He, therefore, established a most strict etiquette at his own court, and exacted tokens of respect by no means conformable to our manners, and which excited general discontent. To be dressed in a frock, wear a round hat, or omit to alight from a carriage when the Czar, or one of the princes of his house, was passing in the streets or public walks, was sufficient to excite his strongest animadversions, and to stamp the offender as a Jacobin, in his opinion. After his reconciliation with me, he had partly given up some of these ideas; and it is probable that had he lived some years longer, he would have regained the alienated esteem and affection of his court. The English, vexed and even extremely irritated at the alteration which had taken place in him in the course of a twelvemonth, took every means of encouraging his domestic enemies. They succeeded in causing a report of his madness to be generally believed, and, at length, a conspiracy was formed against his life.

The evening before his death, Paul, being at supper with his mistress and his favourite, received a despatch, in which all the particulars of the plot against him were disclosed; he put it into his pocket, and deferred the perusal to the next day. In the night he was murdered.

This crime was perpetrated without impediment; P—— had unlimited influence in the palace; he passed for the sovereign's favourite and confidential minister. He presented himself, at two o'clock in the morning at the door of the Emperor's apartment, accompanied by B——, S——, and O——. A faithful Cossack, who was stationed at the door of the chamber, made some difficulty of allowing them to enter; he was instantly massacred. The noise awakened the Emperor, who seized his sword; but the conspirators rushed upon him, threw him down, and strangled him. It was B—— who gave him the last blow, and trampled on his corpse. The Empress, Paul's wife, although she had much reason to complain of her husband's gallantries, testified deep and sincere affliction; and none of those who were engaged in this assassination, were ever restored to her favour. Many years after, General Benigsen still held his command.

This horrible event, however, petrified all Europe with horror; and everyone was particularly shocked at the dreadful openness with which the Russians stated the whole particulars at every court. The situation of England, and the affairs of the whole world, were altered by this circumstance. The difficulties attendant on the commencement of a new reign changed the direction of the policy of the Russian court. On the 5th of April, the English sailors, who had been made prisoners of war, in consequence of the embargo, and sent into the interior of the country, were recalled. The commission, which had been charged with the liquidation of the monies due from the English traders, was dissolved. Count Pahlen, who still remained first minister, informed the English admirals, on the 20th of April, that Russia acceded to all the demands of the English cabinet; that it being the wish of its sovereign to terminate all differences in an amicable manner, according to the proposal of the British government, all hostilities would cease until the arrival of an answer from London. The desire of an immediate peace with England was loudly declared, and everything announced the approaching triumph of that power. After the armistice of Copenhagen, Admiral Parker had proceeded to the Isle of Mona to watch the Russian and Swedish fleets. But Count Pahlen's declaration satisfied him in this respect; and he returned to his moorings at Kioge, after having communicated to the Swedes that he should allow their merchant-ships to pass unmolested.

Denmark, however, continued to put herself in a state of defence. Her fleet remained entire, and had sustained no loss; it consisted of sixteen ships of war. The preparations for its armament, and the works necessary for putting the crown batteries and those of the Isle of Amack in the best possible state of defence, wholly occupied the Prince Royal. But the negotiations were continued with the greatest activity both at London and Berlin, and Lord Saint-Helens left England for St. Petersburg, on the 4th May. The Elbe was soon opened to English commerce. On the 20th of May, Hamburg was evacuated by the Danes, and Hanover by the Prussians.

Nelson, who succeeded Admiral Parker in the command of the squadron, proceeded on the 8th of May to Sweden, and wrote to the Swedish admiral, that if he came out of Carlscrona with his fleet, he would attack him. He then with part of the squadron made for Revel, where he arrived on the 12th. He was in hopes of meeting with the Russian squadron, but it had left that port on the 9th. There is no doubt but that if Nelson had found the Russian fleet in that port, the batteries of which were in a very bad condition, he would have attacked and destroyed it. On the 16th, Nelson left Revel and joined his fleet on the coast of Sweden. That power opened its ports to the English on the 19th of May. The embargo was taken off the British shipping in Russia on the 20th of May. Prussia had been in communication with England from the 16th. Lord St. Helens arrived at St. Petersburg on the 29th of May, and on the 17th of June, signed the famous treaty which put an end to the differences which had arisen between the maritime powers of the North and England. On the 15th, Count Bernstorf, ambassador extraordinary from the Court of Copenhagen, arrived at London, to treat on the part of his sovereign; and on the 17th Denmark raised the embargo laid on the English shipping.

OF NEUTRAL POWERS

Thus, in three months from the death of Paul, the confederacy of the North was dissolved, and the triumph of England secured.

I had sent my aide-de-camp Duroc to Petersburg, where he arrived on the 24th of May; his reception was highly satisfactory, and every protestation of good-will was made to him. He had endeavoured to impress the fatal importance of the least act of weakness to the honour and independence of nations, and the prosperity of the powers of the Baltic; and maintained that no such act would be justified by the state of affairs. England, he said, had the greater part of her land forces in Egypt, and needed several squadrons to cover them, and prevent the fleets of Brest, Cadiz, and Toulon from carrying succours to the French army of the East. England required a squadron of forty or fifty ships to watch Brest, and more than five and twenty ships in the Mediterranean; she was likewise under the necessity of keeping considerable forces before Cadiz and the Texel. He added, that Russia, Sweden, and Denmark, could bring more than thirty-six well-armed ships against the English; that the result of the battle of Copenhagen had only been the destruction of a few hulks, and had in no respect diminished the power of the Danes; that far from changing their sentiments, it had only increased their irritation to the highest pitch; that the ice would soon compel the English to quit the Baltic; that during the winter it would be possible to effect a general pacification; that if the Court of Russia was resolved to conclude peace, as it appeared to be, from the steps already taken, it would at least, be advisable to make only temporary sacrifices, and to avoid making the slightest change in the acknowledged principles of the right of the neutrals and the independence of the seas; that Denmark, when menaced by a numerous squadron, and contending singly against it, had, in the preceding August, consented not to have her ships convoyed, until the subject should have undergone discussion; and that Russia might adopt the same course, gain time by concluding preliminaries, and renouncing the right of convoy, until definite terms of conciliation could be arranged.

These arguments expressed in several notes, seemed, at one time, to have had some effect on the young Emperor. But he was himself under the influence of a party which had been guilty of a great crime, and which, to divert attention from themselves, wished, at any price, to enable the Baltic to enjoy the blessings of peace, in order to cast additional odium on the memory of their victim, and to cheat public opinion.

Europe witnessed with astonishment the ignominious treaty which Russia signed, and which Denmark and Sweden were consequently obliged to adopt. It was equivalent to a declaration of the slavery of the seas, and a proclamation of the sovereignty of the British parliament. This treaty was such, that England had nothing more to wish for, and that a third-rate power would have blushed to sign it. It excited, too, the more surprise, because England

OF NEUTRAL POWERS

was involved in such difficulties that she would have been satisfied with any convention that would have extricated her from them. It was therein declared: 1st, That the flag no longer covered the cargo; that the property of an enemy might be confiscated on board of a neutral vessel: 2dly, That neutral ships under convoy should be subject to search by the cruisers of the belligerents; although not by privateers and letters of marque; which, far from being a concession on the part of England, was wholly for her interest, because the French, being so inferior in strength, had nothing but privateers at sea.

Thus the Emperor Alexander consented to allow one of his squadrons of five or six seventy-fours, escorting a convoy, to be turned from its course, to lose several hours, and to suffer an English brig to carry off part of its convoy. The right of blockade alone was well defined: the English thought it of little importance to prevent neutrals from entering a port, when they were allowed to stop them anywhere, on declaring that the cargo belonged wholly or in part to a merchant of the enemy's country. Russia wished to have it understood as a concession in her favour that naval stores were not comprised among the contraband articles! But the distinction of contraband is a nullity, when everything may be considered so by suspicion of the proprietor; everything is contraband when the flag does not cover the goods.

We have said in this chapter that the principles of the rights of neutrals are: 1st, That the flag covers the cargo: 2dly, That the right of search relates solely to ascertain the flag, and that there is nothing contraband on board: 3dly, That the only contraband articles are military stores: 4thly, That every merchant-ship, convoyed by a ship of war, is exempt from search: 5thly, That the right of blockade relates exclusively to ports really blockaded. We have added that these principles had been defended by all lawyers and all powers, and recognized in all treaties. We have proved that they were in force in 1780, and were respected by the English; that they were still so in 1800, and were the object of the quadruple alliance signed on the 16th of December in that year. It may, at this time, be truly said, that Russia, Sweden, and Denmark, have acknowledged different principles.

We shall see, in the war which succeeded the treaty of Amiens, that England went farther, and disregarded this last principle which she had acknowledged, by establishing the blockade commonly called a blockade upon paper.

Russia, Sweden, and Denmark, declared, by the treaty of the 17th of January, 1801, that the seas belonged to England; and they thereby authorized France, a belligerent power, to acknowledge no principle of neutrality on the seas. Thus at the very time when private property and individuals are respected in warfare by land, private property is seized, in maritime war, not only under the flag of the hostile nation, but even under neutral colours; which affords reason to believe that if England alone had laid down the laws of war by land, she would have established the same principles as she has by sea. Europe would in that case have relapsed into barbarity; and the effects of individuals would have been liable to seizure in the same manner as public property.

Chapter XXXV

ULM. MOREAU

Defects of the plans of the campaigns of 1795, 1796, 1797. Position of the French armies in 1800. Position of the Austrian armies. My plan. My dispositions. Opening of the campaign. Armistice of Pahrsdorf, 15 July, 1800. Critical remarks.

The French Republic had maintained three armies on the Rhine during the campaigns of 1795, 1796, and 1797. That called the Army of the North had its head-quarters at Amsterdam, and was composed of 20,000 Batavians, and as many French troops. By the treaties existing between the two Republics, that of Holland was to maintain a body of 25,000 French to protect the country. This army of from 40 to 45,000 men was to guard the coast of Holland, from the Scheldt to the Ems, and on the land side, the frontiers as far as opposite Wesel. The second army, or that of the Sambre and Meuse, had its head-quarters at Dusseldorf, and blockaded Mentz and Ehrenbreitstein. The head-quarters of the third, called the Army of the Rhine, were at Strasburg; it was supported on Switzerland, and blockaded Philipsburg.

The army of the North was, in reality, only an army of observation, intended to awe the partisans of the house of Orange, and to oppose any attempt the English might make to land troops in Holland. The peace concluded at Basle with Prussia and the houses of Hesse and Saxony, had established tranquillity throughout all the north of Germany.

The army of the Sambre and Meuse, which was necessary as long as Prussia formed part of the coalition, became useless from the moment the French Republic had only to maintain war against Austria, and the southern part of Germany. In the campaign of 1796, this army, commanded by Jourdan, marched upon the Maine, took Wurtzburg, and took up a position on the

ULM. MOREAU

Rednitz; its left supported on the entrance of Bohemia by Egra, whilst its right debouched in the Valley of the Danube. The army of the Rhine, commanded by Moreau, marched from Strasburg, crossed the Black Mountains and Wurtemburg, passed the Lech and entered Bavaria. Whilst these two armies of the Rhine and the Sambre and Meuse were manoeuvring under the command of two generals who acted independently of each other, the Austrian army opposed to them had united under the sole command of the Archduke Charles. Its forces being concentrated on the Danube at Ingoldstadt and Ratisbon, and being placed between the French armies, succeeded in preventing their forming a junction. The Archduke Charles defeated Bernadotte, who commanded the right of the army of the Sambre and Meuse, forced him to retreat towards Wurtzburg, and at length compelled him to repass the Rhine. The army of the Rhine remained spectators of this march of Prince Charles upon the army of the Sambre and Meuse; Moreau, when too late, ordered Desaix to pass over to the left bank of the Danube to the aid of Jourdan; this want of resolution in the general of the army of the Rhine soon obliged that army to retreat. It repassed the Rhine, and took up its first position on the left bank. Thus the Austrian army, which was very inferior to the two French armies, overthrew, without coming to any general engagement, all the plans formed by the French for the campaign, and reconquered the whole of Germany.

The plan of the French was as defective for the defensive as the offensive. From the moment when they had only Austria to contend with, there should have been only one army, having only one line, and directed only by one commander-in-chief.

In 1799, France was mistress of Switzerland. Two armies were formed; the one called the Army of the Rhine, the other the Army of Helvetia. The first, which afterwards took the name of the Army of the Danube, under the command of Jourdan, passed the Rhine, crossed the Black Mountains, and arrived at Stockach, where, being defeated by Prince Charles, it was obliged to repass the Rhine at the very time the army of Helvetia remained in its position, commanding all Switzerland. Thus the French again fell into the error of having two independent armies, when there should have been only one; and when Jourdan was beaten at Stockach, it was upon Switzerland he should have fallen back, and not upon Strasburg and Brisac. The army of the Rhine was afterwards intrusted with the defence of the left bank of the river, opposite Strasburg; and the army of Helvetia, which became the principal army of the Republic, lost part of Switzerland, and remained on the Limath for some time; but at Zurich, under the command of Massena, it took advantage of the error the Allies fell into by dividing themselves likewise into two armies, defeated the Russians, and regained all Switzerland.

In the month of January, 1800, this army of Helvetia cantoned in Switzerland; that of the Lower Rhine, under General Lecourbe, in winter-quarters, on the left bank of the Rhine; that of Holland, under Brune, witnessed the embarkation of the Duke of York's last division. (Generals Massena, Brune, Lecourbe, and Championnet, were personally attached to me, but very inimical to Sieyes; they participated more or less in the opinions of the Jacobins of the *Manège*. It became necessary to break all these connexions, by changing, without delay, the generals-in-chief. If ever the army could give cause for alarm, it could only arise from the influence of the violent party, and not from that of the moderates, which was then greatly in the minority.)

The army of Italy, being defeated at Genoa, rallied in disorder in the passes of the Apennines: Coni capitulated; Genoa was menaced; but Lieutenant-General Saint-Cyr repulsed a corps of the Austrian army beyond the Bocchetta, which gained him a sword of honour; this was the first national reward decreed by me, as head of the state. The two armies went into winter-quarters: the Austrians on the beautiful plains of Piedmont and Mont-Ferrat; the French on the other side of the Apennines, from Genoa to the Var. This country, which had long been blockaded by sea, and without communication with the Valley of the Po, was exhausted. The French administration, which was ill-organized, was intrusted to faithless hands.

The cavalry and other horses were perishing for want; contagious diseases and desertion were disorganizing the army; and the evil rose to such a height, that whole corps abandoned their positions, and, with drums beating and colours flying, repassed the Var. These disorders gave rise to many general orders from me to the soldiers of Italy. I said to them, 'Soldiers, the circumstances which detain me at the head of the Government, prevent my being in the midst of you; your wants are great; every measure is taken to supply them. The first quality of a soldier is patient endurance of fatigue and privation; valour is but a secondary virtue. Several corps have quitted their positions; they have been deaf to the voice of their officers; the seventeenth light demi-brigade is of this number. Are, then, the heroes of Castiglione, of Rivoli, of Neumark, no more? They would rather have perished than have deserted their colours; they would have called their young comrades back to honour and duty. Soldiers, do you complain that your rations have not been regularly distributed? What would you have done, if, like the fourth and twenty-second light demi-brigades, the eighteenth and thirty-second of the line, you had found yourselves in the midst of the Desert, without bread or water, subsisting on horses and camels? *Victory will give us bread, said they;* and you—you desert your colours! Soldiers of Italy, a new general commands you; he was always in the foremost ranks, in the moments of your brightest glory; rest your confidence in him, he will bring back victory to your ranks. I shall cause a daily account to be sent me of the conduct of all the troops, and particularly of that of the seventeenth light demi-brigade and the sixty-third of the line; *they will remember the confidence I once had in them.*'

These magic words put a stop to the evil as by enchantment: the army was reorganized, subsistence was provided, and the deserters returned.

I called Massena from Helvetia, and gave him the command of the army of Italy. This general, who was well acquainted with all the passes of the Apennines, was more fit than any other person for this war of manoeuvres; on 10 February he arrived at his head-quarters at Genoa.

General Brune, who was at first summoned to the Council of State, was some weeks after sent to the Loire to command the army of the West; General Augereau succeeded him in the command in Holland. The following proclamation was issued to the armies:

'Soldiers, in promising peace to the people of France, I spoke to you; I know your valour, you are the same men who conquered in Holland, on the Rhine, in Italy, and who gave peace under the walls of Vienna. Soldiers! it is no longer the frontiers that you are called on to defend, the country of your enemies are to be invaded. There is not one of you who has made a campaign who does not know that the most essential quality of a soldier is the power of bearing hardships with patience: many years of a faulty administration cannot be repaired in a day. As first magistrate of the Republic, it will be gratifying to me to make known to the whole nation those troops, who, by their discipline and valour, shall deserve to be regarded as the supporters of the country. Soldiers! at a fit season I will be in the midst of you, and Europe shall be made to remember that you belong to a valiant race.'

Such was the situation of the armies; I immediately ordered the junction of those of the Rhine and Helvetia into one, under the denomination of the Army of the Rhine; I gave the command to general Moreau, who had shewn himself wholly devoted to me, on 18 Brumaire. Moreau was an enemy to the Directory, and still more so to the *Société du Manège*; although he had met with nothing but losses in the campaign just ended, and was less esteemed than the generals who had lately saved Switzerland at Zurich, and Holland at Alkmaar, by making a son of the King of England capitulate, he was well acquainted with the country which was to be the scene of action for the army of Germany, which determined me to place entire confidence in him, and put him at the head of that army. The French troops were in want of everything, their distress was extreme; all the winter was employed in recruiting, clothing, and paying the arrears of this army. A detachment from the army of Holland was directed towards Mentz, and the army of the Rhine soon became one of the finest the Republic ever had; it amounted to 150,000 men, and was formed of all the old troops.

Paul I was dissatisfied with the policy of Austria and England; the flower of his army had perished in Italy under Suwarrow, in Switzerland under

Korsakow, and in Holland under Hermann. The ancient and new pretensions of the English respecting the navigation of neutral vessels, rendered him daily less favourably disposed towards them; the commerce of neutral vessels, particularly those of the states on the Baltic was interrupted; fleets of merchant ships, convoyed by men of war, were insulted, and subjected to being searched. On the other hand, the changes which had taken place in the principles of the French government, since 18 Brumaire, had lessened, or suspended his hatred to the French Revolution: he admired the firmness which I had shewn in Italy and Egypt, and which I continued every day to display: these circumstances determined his conduct, and if he did not abandon the coalition, he at least ordered his armies to quit the field of battle, and repass the Vistula.

The withdrawing of the Russian army did not discourage Austria. She called forth all her resources, and raised two great armies. The one in Italy consisted of 140,000 men; it was commanded by Field-Marshal Melas, and intended to act on the offensive, and to take Genoa, Nice, and Toulon. It was to be joined under the walls of the latter place by an English army of 18,000 men, who were to assemble at Mahon, and by the Neapolitan army of 20,000 men. Willot was at the head-quarters of Melas, for the purpose of exciting an insurrection in the Southern departments of the Republic, where the Bourbons imagined they had partisans.

The other army, in Germany, commanded by Field-Marshal Kray, was 120,000 strong, including the troops of the Empire, and those in the pay of England. This latter army was intended to remain on the defensive, to protect Germany. The experience of the last campaign had convinced Austria of all the difficulties attached to a war in Switzerland. Field-Marshal Kray had his head-quarters at Donau-Schingen; his principal magazines at Stockach, Engen, Moeskirch, and Biberach. His army was composed of four corps.

The right, commanded by Lieutenant-Field-Marshal Starray, was upon the Maine. The left, under the command of the Prince De Reuss, was in the Tyrol. The two others were on the Danube, with vanguards, one under Lieutenant-General Kienmayer, opposite Kehl; the other under Major-General Giulay, in Brisgaw: a third, under Prince Ferdinand, in the Forest-Towns in the environs of Bâle; a fourth, under the Prince De Vaudemont, opposite Schaffhausen.

Under these circumstances it became necessary for the army of the Rhine to act vigorously on the offensive: its numbers were nearly double those of the enemy, whilst the Austrian army of Italy was more than double the French army, which, consisting of 40,000 men, guarded the Apennines, and the heights of Genoa. An army of reserve, of 35,000 men, was assembled on the Saone, to be in readiness to support the army of Germany, if necessary, to debouch through Switzerland, on the Po, and attack the Austrian army of Italy in the rear.

ULM. MOREAU

The Cabinet of Vienna calculated that its armies would be in the heart of Provence by the middle of summer; and the Cabinet of the Tuileries expected that its army of the Rhine would be on the Inn, before that time.

I ordered General Moreau to act on the offensive, and to enter Germany, in order to arrest the progress of the Austrian army of Italy, which had already reached Genoa. The whole army of the Rhine was to assemble in Switzerland; and pass the Rhine at Schaffhausen: as the movement of the left of the army on its right, was to be screened by the Rhine and to be prepared long beforehand, the enemy would know nothing of it. By throwing four bridges at once across the river at Schaffhausen, all the French army would get over in twenty-four hours, would reach Stockach, overthrow the left of the enemy, and take in the rear all the Austrians placed between the right bank of the Rhine, and the defiles of the Black Forest. In six or seven days from the opening of the campaign the army would be before Ulm; those who could escape from the Austrian army, would retire into Bohemia. Thus the first movement of the campaign would have produced the separation of the Austrian army from Ulm, Philipsburg and Ingolstadt, and placed Wurtemberg and the whole of Suabia and Bavaria in our power. This plan of operation would have produced events more or less decisive, according to the chances of war, and the boldness and rapid movements of the French general. But General Moreau was incapable of executing, or even comprehending such a movement. He sent General Dessolles to Paris, to submit another project to the Minister of War: following the routine of the campaigns of 1796 and 1797, he proposed to pass the Rhine at Mentz, Strasburg, and Bâle. I, much dissatisfied, thought at first of going myself to head the army: I calculated that I should be under the walls of Vienna before the Austrian army of Italy could reach Nice; but the internal agitations of the Republic prevented my leaving the capital and remaining at a great distance for so long a time. Moreau's project was modified, and he was authorised to take a middle course, which consisted in making his left pass the river at Brisach, his centre at Bâle, and his right above Schaffhausen. He was, above all, enjoined to have only one single line of operation; yet this last plan appeared too bold to him when he came to execute it, and he accordingly made some alterations.

The armistice was concluded at Pahrsdorf on 15 July. The three fortresses of Ingolstadt, Ulm, and Philipsburg were to remain blockaded, but to be daily supplied with provisions during the time fixed for the suspension of arms. The whole of the Tyrol remained in the power of Austria, and the line of demarcation passed by the Iser, to the foot of the Tyrolese mountains. From 24 June Field-Marshal Kray had proposed to observe the armistice concluded at Marengo, of which he had just received intelligence. The remainder of the month of July, and during the months of August, September, October, and part of November, the armies remained in presence of each other; and hostilities were not resumed until November.

The Government had directed General Moreau to collect his army behind the lake of Constance, by Switzerland; to conceal his march from the enemy, by precluding all communication from the left to the right bank of the Rhine; towards the close of April to throw four bridges across the river, between Schaffhausen, Stein, and the lake of Constance; to pass upon the right bank of the Danube with his whole army; to advance upon Stockach and Engen; to support his right on the Danube and his left on the lake of Constance; to take in rear all the hostile divisions which should be found in position upon the Black Mountains and in the valley of the Rhine, separate them from their magazines, and afterwards to advance upon Ulm before the enemy. Moreau did not understand this plan. If he had debouched by the lake of Constance with the whole army, he would have surprised, defeated, and taken the half of the Austrian army; the remains of it could only have rallied upon the Neckar: he would have been at Ulm before them! How important would these results have been. The campaign would have been decided within the first fortnight.

The scheme of passing upon the left bank of the Danube, above Ulm, was full of peril and extremely hazardous; if Kray and the Prince of Reuss united, had manoeuvred with the left on the Danube, and the right on the Tyrol, the French army might have been taken *in flagrante delicto,* and greatly endangered. But, since the French general was bent upon this useless and rash operation, he should have executed it resolutely and at once; the passage having been surprised on the 19th, the whole army should have been on the left bank on the 20th, leaving only a few moveable columns in observation upon the right bank, and should have advanced directly upon Ulm and Nordlingen, in order to attack the Austrian army in flank, and to oblige it, if Kray had resolved on retreating, to receive battle; and to seize its intrenched camp, if Kray had determined to pass upon the right bank in order to march against the French army. On this plan Moreau had nothing to fear; his army, superior as it was in strength and confidence, if it had lost the right bank, would have established itself upon the left: all chances were in its favour; having planned the movement it would have marched united to surprise the enemy during his movements, while it would leave nothing exposed to measures which might originate with the enemy. This is the advantage possessed by every army which marches united. What could General Richepanse, who was nearest to Ulm, have done, if Kray and the Prince of Reuss had attacked him with 60,000 men; and what would have become of the army if Richepanse's corps had been defeated, and had lost its line of operation on the right bank, sustaining there so considerable a check before it had gained a footing upon the left bank?

ULM. MOREAU

The armistice did not accomplish the aim of Government, which, in order to secure the position of the armies, was desirous of possessing the four places of Ulm, Philipsburg, Ingolstadt, and Inspruck.

If the Austrian general had availed himself of the advantages he possessed, and of the indecision and erroneous manoeuvres of his adversary, he would, in spite of the successes and superiority of the latter, have driven him back into Switzerland.

Chapter XXXVI

GENOA. MASSENA. 1800

Respective positions of the Armies of Italy. Genoa. Melas intersects the French army. Massena endeavours ineffectually to re-establish his communications with his left. He is invested in Genoa. Blockade of Genoa. Melas marches upon the Var; Suchet abandons Nice. Massena attempts to raise the blockade. Pressed by famine, Massena negotiates. Surrender of Genoa. The Austrians recross the Alps in order to advance to meet the Army of reserve. Suchet pursues them. Consequences of the victory of Marengo. Suchet takes possession of Genoa. Critical remarks.

The principal army of the house of Austria was that of Italy: it was commanded by Field-Marshal Melas; his effective strength amounted to 140,000 men, of which 130,000 were under arms. The whole of Italy was at the command of the Austrians—from Rome to Milan, from the Isonzo to the Alps contiguous to the coast: neither the Grand Duke, nor the King of Sardinia, nor the Pope, had been able to obtain permission to return to their dominions. The minister Thugut retained the first at Vienna, the second at Florence, and the third at Venice.

The operations of the Austrian administration extended over the whole of Italy. Nothing checked it: all the treasures of this beautiful country were devoted to the restoration and improvement of the stores and ammunition of that army, which, proud of the successes it had obtained during the preceding campaign, had now to render itself worthy of fixing the attention of all

GENOA. MASSENA. 1800

Europe, and being called upon to perform the principal part in the campaign about to be opened. Nothing seemed above its reach: its generals flattered themselves with the certainty of entering Genoa and Nice; passing the Var, and joining the English army of Mahon in the port of Toulon; planting the Austrian eagle upon the towers of the ancient city of Marseilles, and taking up their winter quarters upon the Rhône and the Durance.

In the beginning of the month of March, Field-Marshal Melas raised his cantonments, leaving all his cavalry, parks of reserve, and heavy artillery, which would have been useless to him until after passing the Var, in the plains of Italy. He placed 30,000 foot under the command of Generals Wuccassowich, Laudon, Haddich, and Kaim, to guard the fortified places and débouches of the Splugen, Saint-Gothard, the Simplon, Saint-Bernard, Mont Cenis, Mont Genèvre, and Argentiere; and he himself, with from 70 to 80,000 men, approached the Ligurian Apennines. His left, under the command of Lieutenant-Field-Marshal Ott, advanced on Bobbio, whence he pushed a vanguard forward upon Sestri di Levante, to communicate with the English squadron, and draw off the attention of the French general. He marched the centre to Acqui, and fixed his head-quarters there. His right he intrusted to Lieutenant-Field-Marshal Ulsnitz.

The French army beheld with confidence the conqueror of Zurich at its head. It was called on to fight upon ground, every step of which brought some glorious event to its recollection. Four years had not yet elapsed since it had, although scanty in number and in want of everything, but supplying all its deficiencies by courage and undeviating determination, obtained numerous victories, planted its standards upon the banks of the Adige and the confines of the Tyrol within fifty days, and raised to so lofty a pitch the glory of the French name. During the months of January, February, and March, its internal management had been regulated; the pay had been distributed, and considerable supplies of provisions had changed dearth to abundance; the ports of Marseilles, Toulon, and Antibes, were still full of vessels employed in provisioning it. It was beginning to forget the defeats which it had sustained during the year preceding; and it was as well off as the poverty of the country in which it was would admit of. This army amounted to 40,000 men; but it had establishments for 100,000. All the intelligence which it received from the interior of France during the former campaign, had excited the spirit of faction, discussion, and dejection: the Republic seemed at that time writhing in the pangs of death; but now all things concurred to rouse it to emulation, for France was regenerated. Thirty millions of French people, united around their leader and strong in the mutual confidence which they inspired, represented the Hercules of Gaul, armed with his club, and ready to fell the enemies of his liberty and independence, to the earth.

The head-quarters were at Genoa. Brigadier-General Oudinot commanded the staff, and General Lamartelliere the artillery. Massena had confided the left of his army to Lieutenant-General Suchet, who commanded four divisions. The first of these occupied Rocca-Barbena; the second, Settepani and Melagno; the third, Saint-James and Nôtre-Dame de Neves; and the fourth was in reserve at Fiscale, and upon the heights of San Pantaleone: the whole of his force amounted to 12,000 men. Lieutenant-General Soult commanded the centre, which was 12,000 strong, and formed into three divisions. That of General Gardanne defended Cadibona, Vado, Montelegino, and Savona—the flankers defended the heights of Stella; General Gasan defended the debouches in front and rear, and upon the flanks of the Bocchetta; General Marbot commanded the reserve; and Lieutenant-General Miollis the right, 5,000 strong; he covered the eastern coast, occupying Recco by his right, Monte Cornua by his centre, and by his left the Col di Toriglio situated at the beginning of the valley de la Trébia. There was a reserve of 5,000 men in the town; and the whole army amounted to from 34 to 36,000 men. The passes from Argentieres to the sources of the Tanaro were choked up with snow.

Genoa, in the spirit of its government, in its political opinions, and in its devotedness, was thoroughly French.

In the month of March, Vice-Admiral Keith, who commanded the English squadron in the Mediterranean, notified to the consuls of the different nations the blockade of all the ports and coasts of the Republic of Genoa, from Vintimiglia to Sarsana; he forbade neutrals to trade with an extent of coast of sixty leagues, which, however, he could not actually watch: this was, at one stroke of the pen, to declare them out of the protection of their sovereign's flag. At the beginning of April, he was cruising before Genoa, which rendered communications with Provence, and the arrival of the provisions, which were in abundance in the magazines of Marseilles, Toulon, Antibes, Nice, etc., extremely precarious.

The grand operations commenced on 6 April. Field-Marshal Melas, with four divisions, attacked Montelegino and Stella at the same time; Lieutenant-General Soult hastened up with his reserve to the assistance of the left. The action was kept up briskly the whole day; Palfy's division entered Cadibona and Vado; those of Saint-Julien and Lattermann entered Montelegino and Arbizola; Soult rallied his left upon Savona, strengthened the garrison of the citadel, and retired upon Vareggio to cover Genoa; three English ships of war moored in the road of Vado. Melas moved his head-quarters to La Madona di Savona, and invested the fort; he found at Vado several six-and-thirty pounders, and large mortars with which the coast-batteries were lined. The French line was intersected the very first day. Suchet, on the left, was separated from the rest of the army; but he preserved his communication with France.

On the same day, Ott, with the left, debouched in three columns upon

GENOA. MASSENA. 1800

Miollis, the left column along by the sea, the centre by Monte Cornua, and the right by the Col di Toriglio: he was victorious at all points; occupied Monte Faccio and Monte Ratti, invested the three forts of Guezzi, Richelieu, and Santa Tecla; and lighted the fires of his bivouacs a cannon-shot from the latter town. The atmosphere was inflamed by them to the very skies. The Genoese, men, women, old people, and children, ran out upon the walls to gaze on a spectacle so new and so important to them: they waited with impatience for the morning; they were then to become the prey of the Germans, whom their forefathers had, with so much glory, defeated and driven out of their city! Those of the oligarchical party smiled in secret, and with difficulty dissembled their gladness; but the bulk of the people was in consternation. At the first appearance of sunrise, Massena opened the gates and marched out with the division of Miollis and the reserve. He attacked Monte Faccio and Monte Ratti, took them in rear, and precipitated the divisions of the imprudent Ott, who had advanced so inconsiderately alone and so far from the rest of his army, into the ravines and bogs. The victory was complete; Monte Cornua, Recco, and the Col di Toriglio, were retaken. In the evening, 1,500 prisoners, one general, some cannon, and seven colours, the trophies of the day, entered Genoa amidst the acclamations and rejoicings of all its worthy citizens.

The 10th, 11th, 12th, 13th, 14th, and 15th, were spent in marches, manoeuvres, and combats. It often happened that the columns of the two armies were moving, side by side, in opposite directions, separated by torrents or bogs, which prevented their fighting in their marches, though very close to each other. Massena saw the impossibility of restoring his communication: the want of concert between the attacks of Massena and those of Suchet prevented their being simultaneous; but the loss of the enemy, in the various engagements, was double that of the French. On the 21st, Massena evacuated Voltri to approach the ramparts of Genoa, into which town he made 5,000 prisoners file off before him. Colonel Mouton, of the third of the line, since created Count de Lobau, acquired honour in all these attacks; he saved the rearguard at the passage of the bridge of Voltri, by his intrepidity. The people of Genoa, witnessing the bravery of the French soldiers, and the devotion and resolution of the generals, became filled with enthusiasm and affection for the army.

From this day, 21 April, Massena's army no longer bore the character of a campaigning army; it seemed only the strong and brave garrison of a place of the first order. This situation presented him with fresh laurels; few positions were more favourable than that occupied by Massena. Master of so vast an intrenched camp, which bars the whole chain of the Apennines, he was able, by crossing the town, to move from the right to the left in a few hours; which the enemy could not accomplish under several days' march. The Austrian general soon became sensible of all the advantages which such a theatre afforded to his enemy. On the 30th, in a combined attack, he approached the walls of Genoa, while Admiral Keith exchanged a warm cannonade with the batteries of the moles and quays. At first fortune smiled upon all his arrangements. He carried the level of Deux Freres, surrounded fort Diamant, blockaded that of Richelieu, occupied the sides of Monte Ratti, of Monte Faccio, and even of La Madona del Monte, where he was desirous of placing, during the night, upon the position of Albana, a battery of twenty mortars, in order to burn the proud city of Genoa, and to destroy it by conflagration and revolt. But, in the afternoon, Massena, having concentrated all the forces behind his ramparts, intrusted the defence of the town to the National Guard, and debouched upon Monte Faccio, which he surrounded on all sides, and re-took it in spite of the most obstinate resistance: his troops re-entered the fort of Guezzi. Soult then marched upon the level of Deux Freres, and made himself master of it. The enemy lost all the positions they had gained in the morning. In the evening, the General-in-Chief returned to Genoa, with 1,200 prisoners, several flags, and the ladders which the Austrian army had provided for the escalade it had determined to attempt at the uniting point of the two enceintes, on the Bisagno side.

Suchet maintained himself a long time in possession of Saint-Pantaleone and Melagno; but at length he retired into the position of Borghetto, no longer hoping that any efforts of his could re-establish the line of the army.

After the disasters of this day the Austrian generals declined any farther attack upon a place so inauspicious to them. Genoa was without provisions, and could not long avoid a capitulation. According to the principles of warfare in mountainous regions, they occupied strong positions round the place, to prevent the arrival of provisions by land, while the English squadron intercepted them by sea; the French general was, therefore, under the necessity of acting on the offensive and driving them from their posts, if he wished to communicate with the country, and to open the roads in order to procure the necessary forage and victuals.

On the other side, the Court of Vienna was alarmed at the vast superiority of the French army of the Rhine, and at the immense preparations making by me as First Consul to carry the war upon the Danube; it hastened a diversion upon Provence. Melas proceeded to the Var, leaving Lieutenant-Field-Marshal Ott, with 30,000 men, to blockade Genoa in concert with the English squadron.

All the couriers from Paris brought intelligence to Provence of the march of the army of reserve; the vanguard had already appeared at the Saint-Bernard: the result of this manoeuvre was evident alike in soldiers and citizens; the confidence of the troops, like that of the inhabitants, was exalted to the highest pitch of hope. General Willot, who was following the Austrian army, was forming a line of deserters; Pichegru was to put himself at the head of the disaffected of the South. Willot had commanded in Provence, in 1797, before 18 Fructidor: at that moment of reaction, when the enemies of the Republic exerted so much influence in the interior, he corresponded with them; and he had secretly organized a kind of *Chouanerie* in the departments of the Var and of the mouths of the Rhône. In the South the passions are strong; the partisans of the Republic were enthusiastic; they were the most furious anarchists in France: the opposite party was not more moderate; it had raised the standard of revolt and civil war after 31 May, and delivered up Toulon, the principal arsenal of France, to its most mortal enemy. Marseilles subsists only by commerce: the maritime superiority of the English had reduced it to a mere coasting-trade, and this weighed heavily upon it. Of all France, this is the country in which fewest national domains were sold; monks and priests had but few benefices in it, and except in the district of Tarracona, its property experienced but few changes. All the efforts of the partisans of the Bourbons, however, were impotent; the principles of 18 Brumaire had reunited a large majority of the citizens; and at length the movements of the army of reserve suspended all opinions, fixed universal attention, and excited universal interest.

On 11 May, Melas made his entry into Nice; the enthusiasm of the Austrian officers was extreme; they had arrived at last upon the territory of the Republic, after having seen the French armies at the gates of Vienna. An English cruiser moored at the mouth of the Var; it announced the arrival of the army embarked at Mahon, which was to invest the fortress of Toulon. England longed to blow up these superb docks, and utterly destroy that arsenal, whence the army which threatened her Indian empire had issued.

The Var is a torrent which, though generally fordable, occasionally swells in a few hours. Its fords are not to be relied on; and, besides, the line which Suchet defended was short; the left rested upon difficult mountains, and the right upon the sea, at 600 toises distance.

Suchet's corps, if turned would have been obliged to fall back upon Cagnes, and the defiles of the Esterelles. But at length, on the 21st, he received intelligence of the passage of the Saint-Bernard by the army of reserve, and of my arrival at Aosta. Melas set out immediately with two divisions, passed the Col di Tende, and entered Coni on the 23rd; on the 24th he learned, at Savigliano, the taking of Ivrée: he had sent Palfy before him some days previously. He still flattered himself that these pieces of intelligence were exaggerated; that this very formidable army would turn out to be only a body of 15, or at most 20,000 men, which he could easily keep in check with the troops he had brought with him, and those he had concentrated in the plain of Italy, without giving up Genoa, but merely by postponing his plans upon Provence.

As soon as Massena was apprised that he was blockaded by no more than from 30 to 35,000 men, and that Melas had advanced with a part of the army upon the Var, he marched out of Genoa with no ill-founded hope of overthrowing the blockading body of the army, and terminating the campaign. Fifteen thousand Frenchmen in his position were superior to 30,000 Austrians: and, in fact, the enemy were repulsed from all their advanced posts.

On 10 May, Lieutenant-General Soult with 6,000 men, entered the eastern coast, upon the rear of Ott's left, and re-entered Genoa with provisions and prisoners by the way of Monte Faccio; the attacks were renewed on 13 May. Ott concentrated his troops upon Monte Creto: the action was obstinate and bloody; Soult, after having performed prodigies of valour, fell severely wounded, and remained in the power of the enemy.

Massena re-entered Genoa, having lost all hope of raising the blockade; and provisions becoming scarce and extremely dear. The inhabitants were suffering from privation, and the rations of the soldiers were diminished; however, in spite of the vigilance of the English, some vessels from Marseilles, Toulon, and Corsica, succeeded in entering Genoa. This succour would have done very well for the army, but was quite insufficient for a population of 50,000 souls. There was some talk of capitulating, when, on 26 May, arrived the Chief of squadron Franceschi, who, on 24 April, had left Genoa for Paris: having been an eye-witness of the passage of the Saint-Bernard, he announced my approach to the walls of Genoa. This intrepid officer had embarked at Antibes in a light vessel; at the moment he was entering the port, his felucca being on the point of capture, he had, in order to save the despatches, no other resource than to trust to his exertions in swimming. The intelligence which he brought cheered the army and the Genoese; the idea of prompt relief made them endure present evils patiently. The enemies of France were in consternation, their plots confounded, and the people were tracing upon maps, exposed at the shopdoors the advance of an army in which their confidence reposed, and headed by a general beloved by them: they knew from the experience of former campaigns what they might expect from me.

A convoy of corn, announced to be coming from Marseilles, was however expected with the greatest impatience; one of the vessels forming a part of it entered the port on 30 May, and gave intelligence that she was followed by the rest of the convoy: the whole population was to be seen on the quay at the very break of day, to await the arrival of the succour so impatiently looked for. Their hopes were frustrated; no convoy arrived, and in the evening they were informed that it had fallen into the hands of the enemy. This greatly discouraged the people, and the magistrates of the city had recourse to the warehouses of cocoa, a large quantity of which article was in the hands of the merchants. Genoa is the mart which supplies the whole of Italy with it. There were also warehouses of millet, barley, and beans, in the place. On 24 May, the distribution of bread had ceased; and nothing but cocoa was from that time served out. Articles of the strictest necessity were beyond all price: a pound of bad bread cost 30 francs; a pound of meat 6 francs; a fowl 32 francs. During the night of 1 June, at two o'clock, it was supposed that cannon were heard. The soldiers and inhabitants ran out before day upon the ramparts; it was a vain illusion, and hopes thus defeated increased the dejection: desertion, a rare occurrence among French troops, became frequent; but in fact the soldiers had not sufficient food. There were 8,000 Austrian prisoners in the hulks and the bagnios: up to this period they had received rations equally with the soldiers, but now it was impossible to give them any. Massena informed General Ott of this state of things, and requested that provisions might be sent in to the prisoners, giving his word that no part of them should be diverted from the purpose for which they were intended. Ott begged the English Admiral to send in provisions for his prisoners, which the latter refused to do: this was one of the first causes of ill-will between them. The blockading army itself subsisted only by the assistance it received over sea: and depended for that assistance upon the fleet. On 2 June, the patience of the people appeared to be exhausted; the women assembled, tumultuously demanding bread or death. Everything was to be apprehended from the despair of so numerous a population; only ten days had elapsed since the arrival of Colonel Franceschi, but ten days are an age to those who are famishing! 'Since the army of reserve was announced to us,' said they, 'if it were coming at all, it would have been here before now; Napoleon does not march so slowly; he has been stopped in his progress by insurmountable obstacles—he might by this time have marched four times the distance. The Austrian army is too strong, and his too weak; he has been unable to debouch from the mountains; we have no chance, and meanwhile the whole population of our city is contracting diseases which will destroy us all. Have we not manifested sufficient patience, and sufficient attachment to the cause of our allies? Is it not cruel to exact more from so numerous a population, composed of old people, of women and children, and of quiet citizens little accustomed to the horrors of war?'

At length Massena yielded to necessity: he promised the people that if he were not succoured within twenty-four hours, he would treat. He kept his word; on 3 June, he sent Adjutant-General Andrieux to General Ott. Oh, the fatality of human affairs! Andrieux met, in the antichamber of the general, an Austrian staff-officer, who had just arrived post from the general head-quarters of Melas; he was the bearer of an order to raise the blockade, and to move with the utmost expedition upon the Po; and he announced to Ott that I had been at Chivasso ever since the 26th, and was then marching upon Milan. There was not a moment to be lost in providing for the safety of the army.

Andrieux was shewn in, in his turn; he opened the matter, in the usual way, by declaring that his general still had a month's provision for his army;

but that the population was suffering, that his heart was touched at it, and that he would surrender the place, if he were permitted to quit it with his arms, cannon, and baggage, without being made prisoner.

Ott, disguising his surprise and joy, agreed to the proposal with eagerness. The negotiations were begun immediately; they lasted twenty-four hours. Massena attended the conferences on the bridge of Conegliano, in person; he there met Admiral Keith and General Ott; the embarrassment of the latter was extreme; time was exceedingly precious, and he felt all the possible consequences of an hour's delay under such circumstances. On the 4th, during the day, Ott learned that the army of reserve had forced the passage of the Tesino, and entered Milan, occupying Pavia; and that the scouts were already upon the Adda; and yet, if he should accede to Massena's terms, and suffer him to quit Genoa without being a prisoner of war, and retaining his arms and guns, he would have gained nothing. General Massena had still 12,000 men, he would join Suchet, who had as many, and thus united, they would manoeuvre against him, weakened as he would be by the loss of a division, which he must of necessity leave at Genoa. He would therefore be unable to move upon the Po with more than about thirty battalions, which, reduced as they were by the losses of the campaign, would hardly furnish 15,000 men.

Ott proposed that the French army should proceed to Antibes by sea, with their arms and baggage, and without being prisoners. That was rejected, and then it was agreed that 8,500 men of the garrison should quit the place by land, and take the high road to Voltri, and that the rest should be conveyed away by sea. The next day, the 6th, the greater part of the garrison, to the number of 8,500 men, with arms and baggage, but without cannon, marched out and proceeded to Voltri; the General-in-chief with 1,500 men, and twenty field-pieces embarked on board of five French cruisers; the sick and wounded remained in the hospitals, under the care of French medical officers. Ott intrusted Genoa to General Hohenzollern, with whom he left 10,000 men. The English Admiral took possession of the port and maritime establishments; convoys of provisions arrived from all quarters, and in a few days the greatest abundance took place of scarcity. The conduct of the English displeased the people; they laid hands on everything; according to them, it was they who had taken Genoa, since it had yielded only to famine, and it was their cruisers which had stopped all the convoys of provisions.

After the battle of Marengo, Suchet was ordered to march on Genoa: he established his head-quarters at Conegliano, and entered the place on 24 June, conformably to the Convention of Alessandria. On 20 June, however, he signed a particular convention with General Hohenzollern. As soon as the people of Genoa ceased to feel the pangs of famine, they resumed their natural sentiments. The avidity of the English powerfully excited their indignation; the latter wished to carry off everything. They even coveted the merchandize in the open port. Warm discussions and affrays took place between them and the people: several Englishmen were massacred. Suchet, informed of the conduct of the English Admiral, appealed to the clauses of the Convention; which gave rise to a curious correspondence between him and General Hohenzollern, who opposed all the undertakings of the English, and placed guards over the arsenal and at the port, to prevent their taking anything away: he conducted himself honourably.

The first intelligence of the surrender of Genoa was brought to me by some Milanese patriots, who had taken refuge in that city, and afterwards regained their country by crossing the mountains; it was but twenty-four hours later that I received official information of it. When the Genoese heard of the victory of Marengo, their joy was extreme; their country was delivered. They participated sincerely in the glory of their allies. The oligarchical party shrunk again into nothing. The English and Austrians became more and more objects of menace and insult from the populace; blood was shed; and one Austrian regiment was almost entirely destroyed. Hohenzollern was obliged to apply to Suchet for redress, and for his influence with the people to keep them quiet, during the few days he had to remain in the place before the arrival of the moment fixed for its restoration. The entry of Suchet into this great city was a triumph: 400 young ladies dressed in the French and Ligurian colours met the army. General Hohenzollern fulfilled all his engagements; the English squadron stood off; and the Genoese regretted that they had not held out longer. They accused one another of pusillanimity, and of having reposed too little confidence in the fortune of the first magistrate of France; for, had they been certain of not being obliged to suffer for more than five or six days, they would have still found strength to do it.

While these important events were passing, Massena landed at Antibes, and there remained for some time. He arrived afterwards at Milan, before my departure to return to Paris, and assumed the command of the new Army of Italy.

The Austrian army [before Genoa] was more than double that of the French; but the positions which the latter might have occupied were so strong, that it ought to have triumphed. Massena committed a fatal error in his mode of defence.

It was necessary to choose, whether to move the head-quarters to Nice, and defend upon the upper crest from Argentiere to Tende, thence to the Tanarello, the Taggia, or the Roya; or to concentrate the defence round Genoa: it was the latter branch of the alternative which was conformable with my plan of campaign. Genoa is a very large city which presents many resources; it is a strong place; it is, besides, covered by the little fort of Gavi, and had the citadel of Savona upon its left flank. This scheme once adopted, General Massena ought to have acted as if he had been a General of the Ligurian

Republic, and his only object had been to defend the capital. The division of from 3 to 4,000 men which he left at Nice, and for the observation of the passes, was sufficient. General Massena did not know how to decide; he wished to keep up the communications of his army with Nice and Genoa: that was impossible, and he was intersected.

Genoa opened its gates after it was saved. General Massena knew that the succouring army had reached the Po; he was certain that it had experienced no check since, for the enemy would have been eager enough to let him know it. When Cæsar besieged Alesia, he blockaded it with so much care, that the place had no intelligence of what was passing without. The period at which the army of assistance had promised to come up was expired; the Council of the Gauls assembled under the presidency of Vercingetorix; Critognatus rose and said, 'You have no news from your army of assistance; but does not Cæsar give you intelligence of it every day? Can you believe that he would labour so arduously, in raising intrenchments within intrenchments, if he was not apprehensive of the army which the Gauls have collected, and which is approaching? Persevere, then; you will be relieved.' And, in fact, the Gallic army did arrive, 20,000 strong, and attacked Cæsar's legions.

Was not the slightest attention on the part of General Ott and Admiral Keith to the proposal that the garrison should be permitted to quit the city, with their arms, and without being prisoners of war, as indicative as even a letter from me myself, of my near approach? When this basis was agreed to by the enemy, when they insisted that the garrison should proceed to Nice by sea, did they not discover the critical position in which they stood? Massena ought to have broken off, upon the certainty that within four or five days the blockade would be raised; in fact, it would have been raised twelve hours afterwards. The hostile generals knew the extreme dearth which prevailed in the city; they would never have agreed to that condition of the capitulation, that the French army should go out without being prisoners of war, if the army of assistance had not been at hand, and in a situation to raise the siege.

Chapter XXXVII

MARENGO

Army of reserve. My departure. Review at Dijon. Headquarters at Geneva. Lausanne. Passage of the Saint-Bernard. The French army passes the Sesia and the Trebbia. Entry into Milan. Position of the French army at the moment of receiving intelligence of the taking of Genoa. Action of Montebello. Arrival of General Desaix at head-quarters. Battle of Marengo. Armistice of Marengo. Genoa restored to the French. My return to France.

On 7 January, 1800, a decree of the Consuls directed the formation of an Army of Reserve. All the veteran soldiers were called upon to come forward and serve the country, under the command of the First Consul. A levy of 30,000 conscripts was decreed in order to recruit the army. General Berthier, minister at war, set out from Paris, on 2 April, to head the army; for the principles of the Constitution of the year VIII forbade the First Consul to take the command himself. The Consular magistracy was essentially civil; the principle of the division of the powers and responsibility of the ministers, did not permit the First Magistrate of the Republic to command an army immediately in chief; but no provision or principle opposed his being present. In fact, I as First Consul commanded the Army of Reserve, and Berthier, my Major-general, had the title of General-in-chief.

As soon as intelligence was received of the commencement of hostilities in Italy, and of the turn which the operations of the enemy were taking, I judged it indispensable to march at once to the assistance of the Army of Italy; but I preferred debouching by the Great Saint-Bernard, in order to fall upon the rear of the army of Melas, to carry off his magazines, parks, and hospitals, and

MARENGO

at last to give him battle, after having cut him off from Austria. The loss of a single battle would thus occasion the total destruction of the Austrian army, and produce the conquest of all Italy. Such a plan required celerity, profound secrecy, and much boldness: secrecy was the most difficult matter; how was it possible to keep the movements of the army concealed from the numerous spies of England and Austria?—The method deemed eligible by me was to divulge it myself with so much parade that it should become an object of derision to the enemy, and to act in such a manner that the latter should consider all these pompous declarations as merely intended to divert the Austrian army, which was blockading Genoa, from its operations. It was necessary to give the observers and spies a precise point of direction; it was, therefore, declared by messages to the Legislative Body and Senate, and by decrees, by publication in the newspapers, and by intimations of all kinds, that the point of concentration of the Army of reserve was Dijon; that I would review it, etc. All the spies and scouts immediately directed their attention to that city: they there saw, in the beginning of April, a large staff without an army; and in the course of the month, from 5 to 6,000 conscripts and retired soldiers, many of whom were maimed, and were actuated rather by their zeal than their strength. This army soon became an object of ridicule; and, when I myself reviewed it, on 6 May, people were surprised to see there not more than 7 or 8,000 men, the majority of them not even clothed. They were surprised that the Chief Magistrate of the Republic should quit his palace for a review which might have been made by a brigadier-general. These deceitful reports travelled through Brittany, Geneva, Bâle, London, Vienna, and Italy: Europe was full of caricatures: one of them represented a boy twelve years of age, and an invalid with a wooden leg: underneath was written *Bonaparte's Army of Reserve*.

Meantime the real army had been formed, and was ready to march; the divisions were organized on several points of rendezvous. These places were insulated, and had no connexion with each other. The conciliating measures which had been employed by the Consular government, during the winter, coupled with the rapidity of the military operations, had pacified La Vendée, and put an end to the system of the Chouans. A considerable portion of the troops which composed the Army of reserve had been drawn from that country. The Directory had felt the necessity of having several regiments at Paris, for its guard, and to keep down the factions. My government being pre-eminently national, the presence of these troops in the capital became entirely useless; they were despatched to the Army of reserve. Numbers of these regiments had not been in the disastrous campaign of 1799, and had preserved unbroken the sentiment of their superiority and glory. The park of artillery was formed of guns and waggons, sent piecemeal from various arsenals and fortresses. The most difficult thing to conceal was the movement

MARENGO

of the provisions indispensable for an army which was to cross barren mountains, where nothing eatable was to be met with. The Commissary Lambert had prepared two millions of rations of biscuits at Lyons. One hundred thousand were despatched to Toulon, to be sent to Genoa; but 1,800,000 rations were sent to Geneva, embarked upon the lake, and landed at Villeneuve, at the moment when the army arrived there.

At the same time that the formation of the Army of reserve was announced with the greatest ostentation, a number of little manuscript bulletins were prepared, in which, in the midst of many scandalous anecdotes respecting me, it was proved that the Army of reserve did not and could not exist; that from 12 to 15,000 conscripts, at most, were all that could be collected. This was proved by reference to the efforts which had been made during the preceding campaign to form the various armies which had been beaten in Italy, and those which had been made to complete the formidable Army of the Rhine; in a word, said these bulletins, would the Army of Italy be left so weak, if there was power to reinforce it? These various plans for imposing upon the spies were, on the whole, crowned with the most complete success. It was said at Paris, as at Dijon and Vienna, 'There is no Army of reserve.' At the head-quarters of Melas, it was added, 'The Army of reserve, with which we are so much threatened, is a band of from 7 to 8,000 conscripts or invalids, with which they hope to deceive us into raising the siege of Genoa. The French rely too much on our simplicity: they wish to make us realize the fable of the dog who dropped his prey for the shadow.'

On 6 May, 1800, I left Paris; I proceeded to Dijon, in order, as we have just said, to review the insulated soldiers and conscripts who were there. I arrived at Geneva on the 8th. The famous Necker, who was in that city, solicited the honour of being presented to me: he conversed an hour with me, talked much about public credit, and of the morality necessary in a minister of finance; in all he said he suffered it to appear, that he wished and hoped to have the management of the finances of France; yet he did not even know in what manner the public business was conducted with treasury bonds. He praised the military operations going on under his eyes very highly. I was only indifferently pleased with his conversation.

On 13 May, I reviewed the real vanguard of the Army of reserve, at Lausanne; it was commanded by General Lannes: it consisted of six old regiments of chosen troops, perfectly clothed, and completely equipped and appointed. It moved immediately afterwards upon Saint-Pierre; the divisions followed in echelon: the whole formed an army of 36,000 fighting men, in whom confidence might be placed: it had a park of forty guns. Generals Victor, Loison, Vatrin, Boudet, Chambarlhac, Murat, and Monnier, held commands in this army.

I preferred the passage of the Great Saint-Bernard, to that of Mount Cenis:

the one was not more difficult than the other. There is a road practicable for artillery, leading from Lausanne to Saint-Pierre, a village at the foot of the Saint-Bernard; and from the village of Saint-Remi to Aosta, there is likewise a way practicable for carriages. The difficulty then lay only in the ascent and descent of the Saint-Bernard: the same difficulty existed with respect to the passage of Mount Cenis; but the passage of Saint-Bernard offered the advantage of leaving Turin on the right, and acting in a country more covered and less known, and in which the movements of the army could go on more secretly than upon the high road of Savoy, where the enemy would of course have numerous spies. A speedy passage of the artillery appeared impossible. A great number of mules, and a considerable quantity of small cases, to hold the infantry cartridges and the ammunition of the artillery, had been provided. These cases, as well as mountain-forges, were to be carried by the mules, so that the real difficulty which remained to be surmounted, was that of getting the pieces themselves over. But a hundred trunks of trees, hollowed out for the reception of the guns which were fastened into them by their trunnions, had been prepared beforehand: to every piece thus arranged, a hundred soldiers were to be attached; the carriages were to be taken to pieces and placed upon mules. All these arrangements were carried into execution by the Generals of Artillery Gassendi and Marmont, with so much promptness that the march of the artillery caused no delay: the troops themselves made it a point of honour not to leave their artillery in the rear, and undertook to drag it along. Throughout the whole passage the regimental bands were heard; and it was only in difficult spots that the charge was beaten to give fresh vigour to the soldiers. One entire division, rather than leave their artillery, chose to bivouac upon the summit of the mountain in the midst of snow and excessive cold, instead of descending into the plain, though they had time to do so before night. Two half-companies of artillery-artificers had been stationed in the villages of Saint-Pierre and Saint-Remi, with a few field-forges for dismounting and remounting the various artillery-carriages. The army succeeded in getting a hundred waggons over.

On 16 May I slept at the convent of Saint-Maurice, and the whole army passed the Saint-Bernard on 17, 18, 19, and 20 May. I myself crossed on the 20th; in the most difficult places, I rode a mule belonging to one of the inhabitants of Saint-Pierre, pointed out by the Prior of the convent as the most sure-footed in all the country. My guide was a tall robust youth, of twenty-two, who conversed freely with me, with all the confidence becoming his age and the simplicity of the inhabitants of the mountains: he confided all his troubles to me, as well as his dreams of happiness to come. On their arrival at the convent, I, who had till then shewn no intention to do anything for the peasant, wrote a note and gave it to him, desiring him to carry it according to its address. This note was an order for certain arrangements which were made immediately after the passage, and realized all the poor fellow's hopes; such as the building of a house, the purchase of ground, etc. The astonishment of the young mountaineer at seeing, shortly after his return, so many people hurrying to fulfil his wishes, and riches pouring in upon him on all sides, was extreme.

I remained an hour at the convent of the Hospitallers, and performed the descent *à-la-Ramasse*,* down an almost perpendicular glacier. The cold was still sharp; the descent of the Great Saint-Bernard was more difficult for the horses than the ascent had been; there happened, however, but few accidents. The monks of the convent were stored with a great quantity of wine, bread, and cheese; and each soldier, as he passed, received a large ration from the good fathers.

On 16 May, General Lannes with the sixth light half-brigade, the 28th and 44th of the line, the 11th and 12th regiments of hussars, and 21st chasseurs, arrived at Aosta, a town which was a great resource to the army. On the 17th, this vanguard reached Chatillon, where an Austrian corps of from 4 to 5,000 men, which was thought sufficient for the defence of the valley, was in position; it was immediately attacked and routed: on this occasion three guns and some hundreds of prisoners were taken.

The French army fancied every obstacle was overleaped; it was threading a fine valley, in which it found houses, verdure, and spring weather; when all at once its progress was checked by the cannon of fort Bard.

This fort is situated between Aosta and Ivrea, upon a conical hillock, and between two mountains, twenty-five toises distant from each other; at its foot flows the torrent of the Dora, the valley of which it absolutely shuts up; the road passes through the fortifications of the town of Bard, which is walled, and is commanded by the fire of the fort. The engineer officers belonging to the vanguard approached to reconnoitre a passage, and reported that no other than that through the city remained. General Lannes commanded an attack during the night, in order to try the fort; but it was on all sides protected against a *coup de main*. As it always happens under similar circumstances, the panic communicated itself rapidly throughout the army, even to its rear. Orders were even given for stopping the passage of the artillery over the Saint-Bernard: but I, who had already reached Aosta, immediately repaired to Bard: I climbed up the rock Albaredo, upon the left mountain, which rock commands at once both the town and the fort, and

---

* Glissading. By sliding down on a sort of a sledge: This word also occurs in Marbot's *Memoirs*, where he describes the incident of General Massena crawling alone up to an isolated battalion during the Italian campaign and guiding them out of danger by leading them down a precipitous snow-covered slope on his seat and hands. S. de C.

soon perceived the possibility of taking the town. There was not a moment to be lost: on the 25th, at nightfall, the 58th demi-brigade, led by Dufour, scaled the wall, and gained possession of the town, which is only separated from the fort by the stream of the Dora. In vain, during the whole night, the fort showered grape-shot, at half musquet-distance, upon the French within the town; they maintained themselves there, and at last, out of consideration for the inhabitants, the fire of the fort ceased.

The infantry and cavalry passed one by one, up the path of the mountain, which I had climbed, and where no horse had ever stepped: it was a way known to none but goatherds.

On the following nights the artillery officers, with surprising skill, and the gunners, with the greatest intrepidity, took their guns through the town. Every precaution had been taken for concealing the knowledge of this operation from the Commandant of the fort: the road was covered with litter and dung, and the pieces, concealed under branches and straw, were drawn by the men with cords, in the most profound silence. Thus was a space of several hundred toises crossed, within pistol-shot of the batteries of the fort. The garrison, though suspecting nothing, made occasional discharges, which killed or wounded a considerable number of gunners; but that did not in the least check the general zeal. The fort did not surrender until early in June. By that time the French had succeeded, with the utmost difficulty, in mounting several guns upon the Albaredo, whence they thundered upon the batteries of the fort. If they had been forced to delay the passing of the artillery until the capture of this fort, all the hopes of the campaign would have been lost.

This obstacle was more considerable than that of the Great Saint-Bernard itself; yet neither the one nor the other retarded the march of the army a single day. I was well aware of the existence of fort Bard; but all the maps and information which had been obtained upon this subject, induced the belief that it would be easily taken. The Austrian officer, who commanded the fort, despatched letter after letter to Melas, to inform him that he saw more than 30,000 men, 3 or 4,000 horses, and a numerous staff, attempting to pass; that these masses were inclining to his right, by a path of steps in the rock of Albaredo: but he promised that not a single waggon, or piece of artillery, should pass; he said he could hold out for a month, and that therefore, up to that period, it was not probable that the French army would dare to trust itself in the plain, as it would not have received its artillery. After the surrender of the fort, all the officers of the garrison were strangely surprised on learning that all the French artillery had passed by night, at thirty or forty toises from their ramparts.

Supposing it had proved quite impossible to pass the artillery through the town of Bard, would the French army have repassed the Great Saint-

MARENGO

Bernard? No; it would have debouched as far as Ivrea—a movement which would have necessarily recalled Melas from Nice. It had nothing to fear, even without artillery, in the excellent positions presented to it by the entrance of the passes, where it might have awaited the taking of Bard, and in the meanwhile covered the siege of that place. On 1 June, that fort fell, as a matter of course, into the hands of the French; but it is probable that it would have been taken sooner, if it had arrested the passage of the troops, and drawn upon itself all their effort, instead of having to deal only with a brigade of conscripts commanded by General Chabran, who had been left to besiege it. The latter corps had passed by the Little Saint-Bernard.

In the meantime, from 1 May, Melas had been marching troops upon Turin, and reinforcing the divisions which kept the valley of Aosta and that of Mount Cenis; he arrived at Turin, in person, on the 22nd. On the same day General Turreau, who commanded in the Alps, attacked Mount Cenis with 3,000 men, made himself master of it, took some prisoners, and occupied a position between Susa and Turin; the diversion rendered Melas uneasy, and prevented him from directing all his efforts towards the Dora Baltea.

On the 24th, General Lannes, with the vanguard, arrived before Ivrea; he there found a division of from 5 to 6,000 men: the armament of this place and the citadel had been begun eight days before, and fifteen guns were already in battery; but out of this division of 6,000 men, there were 3,000 cavalry, who were not fit for the defence of Ivrea, and the infantry were the same that had been already defeated at Chatillon. The town, attacked with the greatest intrepidity, on one side by General Lannes, and on the other by General Vatrin, was soon carried, as well as the citadel, in which were found numerous magazines of all kinds: the enemy retired behind Chiusella, and took up a position at Romano, to cover Turin, whence he received considerable reinforcements.

On the 26th, General Lannes marched against the enemy, and attacked him in his position; and, after a very warm action, overthrew and drove him in disorder upon Turin. The advanced guard immediately took the position of Chivasso, whence it intercepted the passage of the Po, and seized a great number of vessels laden with provisions and wounded men, and in short, with all that had been sent out of Turin. On the 28th, I reviewed the vanguard at Chivasso, harangued the troops, and bestowed eulogiums upon the corps which composed it.

The vessels taken upon the Po were arranged as if for the construction of a bridge: this threat produced the expected effect; Melas weakened the troops which covered Turin upon the left bank, and sent his principal forces to oppose the construction of the bridge.

This was what I wished for, that I might be left to operate upon Milan unmolested.

MARENGO

General Melas selected one of the officers of the Austrian army, who had the honour of knowing me, and sent him on a parley to the outposts. His surprise at seeing me so near the Austrian army was extreme; the intelligence conveyed by the officer to Melas, overwhelmed him with terror and confusion. The whole Army of reserve, with its artillery, arrived at Ivrea on 26 and 27 May.

The head-quarters of the Austrian army were at Turin; but half the forces of the enemy were before Genoa, and the other half were supposed to be, and in fact were, on their road, by way of the Col di Tende, to reinforce the corps which were at Turin. Under these circumstances, what course was I to pursue? To march upon Turin, repulse Melas, join Turreau, and thus secure my communications with France, and with my arsenals of Grenoble and Briançon? To avail myself of the vessels that fortune had thrown into my power and throw a bridge across at Chivasso—then rapidly push on to Genoa to raise the blockade of that important place? Or to leave Melas behind, pass the Sesia and the Tesino, and proceed upon Milan and the Adda, in order to effect a junction with Moncey's corps, composed of 15,000 men, which came from the army of the Rhine, and had debouched by the Saint-Gothard?

Of these three courses, the first was contrary to the true principles of war, since Melas had considerable forces with him: the French army, therefore, would run the risk of fighting without having a certain retreat, fort Bard not being then taken. Besides, if Melas should abandon Turin and move upon Alessandria, the campaign would be a failure, and each army would find itself in its natural position: the French army resting upon Mont Blanc, and Dauphiny; and that of Melas with its left at Genoa, and in its rear the fortified places of Mantua, Piacenza and Milan.

The second course appeared impracticable: how hazardous would have been the situation of the French in the midst of an army so powerful as that of the Austrians, between the Po and Genoa, without any line of operations, any assured retreat?

The third course, on the other hand, presented every advantage: the French army, once in possession of Milan, would secure all the magazines, depôts, and hospitals, of the enemy's army; it would join the left under General Moncey; and have a safe retreat by the Simplon and Saint-Gothard. The Simplon led to the Valais and Sion, whither all the magazines of provisions for the army had been sent. The Saint-Gothard led into Switzerland, of which we had been in possession for two years, and which was covered by the army of the Rhine, then upon the Iller. In this position I was at liberty to act as I pleased; if Melas should march with his united army from Turin upon the Sesia and the Tesino, the French army could give him battle with this incalculable advantage, that if it should be victorious, Melas, without retreat,

MARENGO

would be pursued and driven into Savoy; and if it should be defeated, it could retreat by the Simplon and the Saint-Gothard. If Melas, as it was natural to suppose, should move towards Alessandria, in order to join the army coming from Genoa, it might be hoped, that by advancing towards him and crossing the Po, he might be intercepted and forced to fight before he could reach Alessandria: the French army having its rear secured by the river, and by Milan, the Simplon and Saint-Gothard; while the Austrian army, having its retreat cut off and having no communication with Mantua and Austria, would be liable to be thrown upon the mountains of the western coast of Genoa, or entirely destroyed or taken at the foot of the Alps, at the Col di Tende and in the county of Nice. Lastly, by adopting the third course, if it should suit me, when once master of Milan, to suffer Melas to pass, and to remain between the Po, the Adda, and the Tesino: I would thus, without a battle, re-conquer Lombardy and Piedmont, the maritime Alps, and the Genoese territory, and raise the blockade of that city: there were flattering results to anticipate.

A corps of 2,000 Italian refugees, commanded by General Lecchi, had, on 21 May, moved from Chatillon upon the Upper Sesia. This corps had an engagement with the legion of Rohan, defeated it, and came to take up a position in the debouches of the Simplon, in the valley of the Domo d'Ossola, in order to secure the communications of the army by the Simplon.

On the 27th, General Murat directed his march upon Vercelli, and passed the Sesia.

On 31 May, I moved rapidly upon the Tesino; the corps of observation which General Melas had left against the debouches of Switzerland, and the divisions of cavalry and artillery which he had not taken with him to the sieges of Genoa, united to defend the passage of the river, and cover Milan. The Tesino is extremely wide and rapid.

Adjutant-General Girard, an officer of the highest merit and most extraordinary intrepidity, was the first to pass the river. The conflict upon the left bank was warm during the whole day. The French army had no bridge; the troops crossed upon four small boats; but as the country is much cut up and very woody, and we were favoured by the position of the Naviglio, or canal of Milan, the enemy's cavalry did not engage upon such ground without reluctance.

On 2 June I entered Milan; I immediately invested the citadel. General Lannes, with the vanguard, had begun a forced march on 30 (May); and, leaving a corps of observation on the left of the Dora Baltea, and a garrison in Ivrea, he marched with all expedition upon Pavia, which he entered on 1 June. He there found considerable magazines and two hundred guns, thirty of which were field-pieces.

In the meantime, on the 4th, the division of Duhesme entered Lodi; on the

MARENGO

5th it invested Pizzighitone, and its light cavalry occupied Cremona: the army soon arrived in Mantua, which had neither provisions nor garrison. Moncey's corps, with 15,000 men of the army of the Rhine, reached Belinzona on 31 May.

It would be difficult to describe the astonishment and enthusiasm of the Milanese on the arrival of the French army: I marched with the vanguard, so that one of the first persons who presented themselves to the eyes of the Milanese whom enthusiasm and curiosity led by all the by-roads to meet the French army, was General Bonaparte. The people of Milan would not believe it: it had been reported that I had died on the Red Sea, and that it was one of my brothers who commanded the French army.

From 2 to 8 June, that is to say, for six days, I was engaged in receiving deputations, and shewing myself to the people who had hastened from all points of Lombardy to see their liberator.

The government of the Cisalpine Republic was re-organized; but a considerable number of the warmest Italian patriots groaned in the prisons of Austria. I addressed the following proclamation to the Army:

ARMY OF RESERVE
Milan, 17 Prairial, year VIII.

THE FIRST CONSUL TO THE ARMY.

'Soldiers!

'One of our departments was in the power of the enemy; consternation reigned over the whole of the South of France.

'The greater part of the territory of the Ligurians, the most faithful friends of the Republic, was invaded.

'The Cisalpine Republic, annihilated by the last campaign, was become the sport of a ridiculous feudal domination.

'Soldiers! you march—and the French territory is already free! Consternation and dread are succeeded by joy and hope in our country.

'You will restore liberty and independence to the people of Genoa; who will be forever delivered from their eternal foes.

'You are in the capital of the Cisalpine!

'The enemy, panic-struck, hope only to regain the frontiers. You have taken from them their stores, their magazines, and their reserve of artillery.

'The first act of the campaign is ended.

'You hear daily millions of men manifest their gratitude to you.

'But shall the violation of the French soil pass unpunished? Will you suffer those soldiers who have carried terror into your families, to return to their fire-sides? You rush to arms!—Well then! march to meet them, oppose their retreat, snatch from them the laurels with which they have decked themselves, and thereby teach the world that a malediction rests upon all madmen who dare to insult the territory of the Great Nation.

'The result of our efforts will be, *Unclouded glory* and *solid peace*.

'THE FIRST CONSUL: (SIGNED) BONAPARTE.'

The 15,000 men, led by General Moncey, came up slowly; they marched only by regiments. This delay was injurious; I reviewed these troops on 6 and 7 June. On the 9th, I set out for Pavia.

General Murat had, on 6 May, advanced before Piacenza, where the enemy had a bridge and a *tête-de-pont*. Murat was fortunate enough to surprise the *tête-de-pont*, and seize almost the whole of the boats.

On the same day he intercepted a despatch from the ministry of Vienna to M. de Melas; it contained some curious information with regard to what it called the pretended Army of Reserve, the existence of which was denied; and Melas was ordered to continue his operations in Provence vigorously. The minister hoped that Genoa would have capitulated, and that the English army would have arrived. He wrote at the same time that success was indispensable; for that the French army of the Rhine was in the heart of Germany, and that any victory would compel its recall to the relief of Provence; that some commotions which had taken place in Paris, had obliged me to return hastily from Geneva to that capital; and that the Court of Vienna placed all its confidence in the talents of General Melas, and in the intrepidity of his victorious army of Italy.

The corps of observation, which we had upon the left bank of the Dora Baltea, was unmolested, as well as the garrison of Ivrea. Fort Bard had been in our possession ever since 1 June, and Ivrea was filling with ammunition of all kinds, provisions, and the baggage of the army. Melas had abandoned Turin, and appeared to direct his march on Alessandria to operate upon the right bank of the Po.

I detached Lapoype's division of General Moncey's corps, to line the Po from Pavia to the Dora Baltea, and to watch the motions of the enemy opposite Piacenza, and determined to move on Stradella, on the right bank of the Po, in order to cut off Melas from the road of Mantua, and oblige him to receive battle with his line of operation intersected, and at once to raise the blockade of Genoa, and drive the enemy to the Alps.

General Lannes, with the vanguard, passed the Po, opposite Pavia at Belgiojoso, during the 6th. On the 7th, General Murat passed the Po at Nocetta, and entered Piacenza, where he found considerable magazines. The next day he defeated an Austrian corps which had come to attack him, and made 2,000 prisoners. General Murat was ordered to proceed to Stradella, there to join the vanguard; the whole army was uniting upon this important point.

MARENGO

But in the midst of such brilliant successes, and while the mind was given up to the fairest hopes, a distressing piece of intelligence was received: Genoa had capitulated on the 4th, and the Austrian troops of the blockade were coming, by forced marches, to join the army of Melas at Alessandria. Some Milanese refugees who had been shut up in Genoa, detailed the operations of the siege. Massena had, after the capitulation, committed the unpardonable error of embarking in a privateer to proceed to Antibes. One part of his army had likewise been embarked for the same place of destination; only one corps of 8,500 men came off by land. The troops had preserved their arms, ammunition, etc. No capitulation could be more honourable, but this fatal arrangement of General Massena, the less excusable because he knew of the arrival of my army upon the Po, annulled all the advantages of the conditions of the capitulation. If, after the surrender, Massena had marched out at the head of all his troops, (and he still had 12,000 disposable men armed and his artillery), and, having reached Voltri, had resumed his operations, he would have kept an equal number of Austrian troops in play: he would have been speedily joined by the troops of General Suchet, which were on their march to Porto Maurizio, and would then have manoeuvred against the enemy with some 20,000 men. But the troops marched out without their general; they directed their course along the coast of Genoa: their movement was not stopped until they were met by General Suchet. Three or four days were thus thrown away; these troops were useless. But the victory of Marengo had remedied everything.

I then saw that I could rely only on my own strength and that I was about to have to manage the whole army. On the evening of the 8th, the enemy's scouts came to observe the French, who had passed the Po, and were in bivouac upon the right bank; they believed them to be not very numerous, and a vanguard of from 4 to 5,000 Austrians came to attack them; but the whole French vanguard, and a part of the main army had already crossed. General Lannes presently routed this vanguard of the enemy; and at night he took up a position before the Austrian army which occupied Montebello and Casteggio.

This army was commanded by General Ott, the same who had commanded the blockade of Genoa; his corps had come up in three marches. The fires of the bivouacs, and the reports of the prisoners and deserters, gave reason to believe that this part of the Austrian army amounted to thirty battalions, or 18,000 men. Ott's grenadiers, the flower of the Austrian army, formed part of it.

General Lannes was in position, and, expecting reinforcements every moment, he had no inducement to attack; but the Austrian general brought on the battle at daybreak. General Lannes had only 8,000 men with him; but Victor's division, which had crossed the river, was not more than three leagues off. The battle was bloody: Lannes covered himself with glory; his troops performed prodigies of intrepidity. About midday Victor's division came up and completely decided the victory. The Austrians fought desperately; they were still proud of the successes they had obtained during the preceding campaign; and they felt that their situation laid them under a necessity to conquer.

On hearing of the enemy's attack upon the French vanguard, I immediately hastened to the field, but, by the time I got there, the victory had been gained: the enemy had lost 3,000 killed, and 6,000 prisoners. The field of battle was entirely strewed with the dead. General Lannes was covered with blood: the troops, conscious that they had behaved well, though worn out with fatigue, were intoxicated with joy.

On the 10th, 11th, and 12th, I remained at the position of Stradella, employing the time in concentrating my army, and in securing its retreat by the construction of two bridges across the Po, fortifying them by two *têtes-de-pont*. Nothing remained to hurry me; Genoa had fallen.

I sent trusty messengers across the mountains with an order to General Suchet to march upon the Scrivia by the debouche of Col di Cadibona.

The enemy's cavalry was formidable, and its artillery very numerous. Neither of those bodies had suffered, while our cavalry and artillery were extremely inferior in point of number: it was, therefore, dangerous to engage in the plain of Marengo. If the enemy desired to re-open his communications and regain Mantua, he must pass by Stradella, and march over the French army. This position of Stradella appeared to have been made expressly for the French army: the enemy's cavalry could do nothing against it, and the vast superiority of their artillery would be felt less there than anywhere else. The right of my army rested upon the Po, and the marshy and impracticable plains in the neighbourhood of that river: the centre, situated upon the high road, was supported on large villages, containing great houses of solid masonry; and the left rested upon fine eminences.

During the battle of the 11th, Desaix, who had returned from Egypt, and had been performing quarantine at Toulon, arrived at the head-quarters, at Montebello, with his aides-de-camp, Rapp and Savary. The whole night was spent in conferences between me and Desaix, on all that had passed in Egypt since the former had quitted that country—the details of the campaign of Upper Egypt—of the negotiations of El-Arisch, and the composition of the Grand Vizier's grand Turkish army—lastly, on the battle of Heliopolis, and the present situation of the French army. 'How', said I, 'could you, Desaix, put your name to the capitulation of El-Arisch?'—'I did it', replied Desaix, 'and I would do it again, because the Commander-in-chief was not willing to remain in Egypt; and because, in any army at a distance from home, and beyond the influence of Government, the inclinations of the Commander-in-chief are equivalent to those of five-sixths of the army. I always had the greatest contempt for the Grand Vizier's army, which I have observed closely. I wrote to Kleber that I would undertake to repulse it with my division alone. If you had left me the command of the army in Egypt, and taken Kleber away with you, I would have preserved that fine province for you, and you should never have heard a word about capitulation; but, however, things turned out well; and Kleber made up at Heliopolis for the mistakes he had been committing for six months'.

Desaix burned to signalize himself. He thirsted to avenge the ill-treatment he had received from Admiral Keith, at Leghorn; this lay at his heart. I immediately gave him the command of the division of Boudet.

Melas's head-quarters were at Alessandria: all his army had been two days assembled there: his position was critical, because he had lost his line of operation. The longer he delayed determining what to do, the worse his position became; for on one side, Suchet's corps was advancing upon his rear, and on the other, the army was daily increasing its fortifications and intrenchments in its position of Stradella.

General Melas, however, made no movement. In the situation in which he was, he had three courses to choose: the first was, to cut his way through my army, the Austrian army being superior to it in number, to gain Piacenza, and resume his line of operation upon Mantua.

The second plan was to cross the Po at Turin, or between that city and the mouth of the Sesia, to advance afterwards, by forced marches, to the Tesino, to cross it; and, reaching Milan before my army, to intersect my line, and force me back behind the Adda.

The third course was, to fall back from Alessandria upon Novi, to rest upon Genoa, and upon Admiral Keith's English squadron; not to assume offensive operations until the arrival of the English army, already collected at Mahon. The Austrian army was certain not to want provisions or ammunition, or even reinforcements, since by its right it could have communicated with Florence and Bologna; in Tuscany it had a Neapolitan division, and, besides, the communications by sea were in its power. From this position General Melas might regain Mantua when he pleased, transporting a great part of his heavy artillery into Tuscany by sea.

General Lapoype, who was on the banks of the Po, was ordered to fall back upon the Tesino, in case the enemy should occupy the left bank; he would there be joined by 5 or 6,000 men, which could be got together by General Moncey, who commanded at Milan. He would then have 10,000 men; more than sufficient to delay the passage, and give me time to return by the two bridges behind the Tesino.

On the 12th, in the afternoon, surprised at the inaction of General Melas, I became uneasy, and began to fear that the Austrian army had moved on

Genoa, or upon the Tesino, or else had marched against Suchet to crush him, with the intention of afterwards returning against me; I determined to quit Stradella, and advance upon the Scrivia, in the form of a strong reconnoitring party, in order to be able to act according to the course adopted by the enemy. In the evening the French army* took up a position upon the Scrivia; Tortona was surrounded; the head-quarters were stationed at Voghera. During this movement, no intelligence of the enemy was obtained; only some few cavalry scouts were perceived, which did not indicate the presence of an army in the plains of Marengo. I no longer doubted that the Austrian army had escaped me.

On the 13th, at daybreak, I passed the Scrivia, and marched to Saint-Juliano, in the midst of the immense plain of Marengo. The light cavalry discovered no enemy; there was no longer room to doubt that he was in full manoeuvre, since, if he had thought proper to wait for the French army, he would not have neglected the fine field of battle presented to him by the plain of Marengo, advantageous as it was for the development of his immense cavalry: it appeared probable that the enemy was marching on Genoa.

Under this impression, with all expedition, I despatched Desaix's corps in the form of a vanguard, upon my extreme left, with orders to observe the high-road leading from Novi to Alessandria; I ordered Victor's division to enter the village of Marengo, and to send scouts upon the Bormida, to ascertain whether the enemy had any bridge there. Victor arrived at Marengo; he there found a rearguard of 3 or 4,000 Austrians, attacked and routed them, and made himself master of the village. His scouts arrived upon the Bormida at night-fall; they gave information that the enemy had no bridge there, and that there was only an ordinary garrison in Alessandria; they gave no intelligence of the army of Melas.

Lannes's corps bivouacked diagonally in the rear of Marengo, upon the right.

I was very uneasy; during the night I determined to visit my head-quarters of the preceding day, in order to meet intelligence from General Moncey, General Lapoype, and the agents who had been sent towards Genoa, and who were to rendezvous upon those head-quarters; but the Scrivia had overflowed its banks. The stream swells considerably in the course of a few hours, and a few hours also are sufficient for its return to its usual state. This circumstance

* French army, 12 and 13 June:
Divisions Vatrin and Mainoni, Lannes: right wing, at Castel-Nuovo di Scrivia.
Divisions Boudet and Monnier, Desaix: centre, Ponte-Curone.
Division Lapoype: order to join Desaix.
The cavalry under Murat, between Ponte-Curone and Tortona, having a van-guard beyond Tortona, under Kellermann.
Divisions Gardanne and Chambarlhac, Victor: left wing, in advance of Tortona, and supporting the van-guard under Kellermann.

MARENGO

determined me to fix my head-quarters at Torre-di-Garafola, between Tortona and Alessandria. In this situation was the night spent.

Meanwhile the most dreadful confusion had prevailed in Alessandria, since the battle of Montebello. The Austrian Council was agitated by the most sinister presentiments: they beheld the Austrian army cut off from its line of operation and depôts, and placed between my army and that of General Suchet, whose advanced posts had passed the mountains, and began to be felt upon the rear of the right flank of the Austrians. The greatest irresolution pervaded their minds.

After much hesitation, Melas, on the 11th, resolved to send a strong detachment against Suchet, the remainder of the Austrian army continuing covered by the Bormida and the citadel of Alessandria; but, during the night of the 11th and 12th, Melas heard of my movement upon the Scrivia. On the 12th, he recalled his detachment, and passed the whole day and night of the 13th in deliberation; at last, after some sharp and stormy discussions, the Council of Melas pronounced that the existence of the Army of reserve had been unknown to him; that the orders and instructions of the Aulic Council had mentioned only the army of Massena; that the unfortunate position in which they found themselves ought, therefore, to be attributed to the ministry, and not to the general; that in this unforeseen situation, brave soldiers ought to do their duty; that they were, then, called upon to cut their way through my army, and thus re-open the communications with Vienna; that, in case of success, everything was gained, since they were masters of Genoa, and, by returning promptly upon Nice, they could execute the plan of operations fixed at Vienna; and, lastly, that if they failed and lost the battle, their position would, no doubt, be dreadful; but that the whole responsibility of it would fall upon the ministry.

This train of reasoning settled all opinions; there was but one cry—To arms! to arms! and everyone began to make his dispositions for the next day's battle.

The chances of victory were wholly in favour of the Austrian army, which was very numerous. It had, at least, three times as many cavalry as the French army. The strength of the latter was not exactly known; but the Austrian army, notwithstanding its losses at the battle of Montebello, and those it had experienced in the neighbourhood of Genoa and Nice, after the retreat, was still very superior to the Army of reserve.

On the 14th, at break of day, the Austrians defiled by the three bridges of the Bormida, and made a furious attack on the village of Marengo. The resistance was obstinately kept up for a long time. Finding, from the briskness of the cannonade, that the Austrians had commenced the attack, I immediately despatched orders to General Desaix to return with his troops upon San-Juliano; he was half a day's march off, to the left. I arrived on the field of

MARENGO

battle at ten o'clock in the morning, between San-Juliano and Marengo. The enemy had at length carried Marengo; and the division under Victor having been forced to give way after a firm resistance, was thrown into the utmost disorder. The plain on the left was covered with our fugitives, who spread alarm wherever they went, and many were even exclaiming in dismay, '*All is lost.*'

The corps of General Lannes, a little in the rear of the right of Marengo, was engaged with the enemy, who, after taking that place, deployed upon its left, and formed its line opposite our right, beyond which it already extended. I immediately despatched my battalion of the cavalry guard, consisting of eight hundred grenadiers, the best troops in the army, to station themselves at five-hundred toises distance from Lannes, on the right, in a good position, in order to keep the enemy in check. I, with the seventy-second demi-brigade, hastened to the support of Lannes, and directed the division of reserve of Cara Saint-Cyr, upon the extreme right, to Castel-Ceriolo, to flank the entire left of the enemy.

In the meantime the army perceived, in the middle of this immense plain, the First Consul, surrounded by his staff, and two hundred horse grenadiers with their fur caps: this sight proved sufficient to inspire the troops with hopes of victory; their confidence revived, and the fugitives rallied upon San-Juliano, in the rear of the left of General Lannes. The latter, though attacked by a large proportion of the enemy's army, was effecting his retreat through the midst of this vast plain, with admirable order and coolness. This corps occupied three hours in retiring three-quarters of a league, entirely exposed to the grape-shot of eighty pieces of cannon; at the same time that by an inverse movement Cara Saint-Cyr advanced upon the extreme right, and turned the left of the enemy.

About three o'clock in the afternoon the corps of Desaix arrived: I made him take a position on the road in advance of San-Juliano. Melas, who believed the victory decided, being overcome with fatigue, repassed the bridges, and entered Alessandria, leaving to General Zach, the head of his staff, the care of pursuing the French army. The latter, thinking that this army was effecting its retreat by the road from Tortona, endeavoured to reach this road behind San-Juliano; but I had altered my line of retreat at the commencement of the action, and had directed it between Sala and Tortona, so that the high-road from Tortona was of no consequence to the French army.

Lannes' corps in its retreat constantly refused its left, thus directing its course towards the new point of retreat; and Cara Saint-Cyr, who was at the extremity of the right, found himself almost upon the line of retreat, at the very time that General Zach imagined the two corps were intersected.

The division of Victor had, in the meantime, rallied, and burnt with impatience to recommence the contest. All the cavalry of the army was concentrated in advance of San-Juliano, on the right of Desaix, and in the rear of the left of General Lannes. Balls and shells fell upon San-Juliano; its left was already gained by a column of 6,000 of Zach's grenadiers. I sent orders to General Desaix to charge with his fresh division this column of the enemy. Desaix immediately prepared to execute these orders accordingly; but, as he advanced at the head of two hundred troopers of the ninth light demi-brigade, he was shot through the heart by a ball, and fell dead at the very moment that he had given the word to charge: by this stroke I was deprived of the man whom I esteemed most worthy of being my lieutenant.

This misfortune by no means disconcerted the movement, and General Boudet easily inspired the soldiers with the same lively desire of instant revenge for so beloved a chief, which actuated his own breast. The ninth light demi-brigade, who did, indeed, on this occasion, deserve the title of *Incomparable,* covered themselves with glory. General Kellermann, with 800 heavy horse, at the same time charged intrepidly the middle of the left flank of the column: in less than half an hour these 6,000 grenadiers were broken, overthrown, dispersed, and put to flight. General Zach and all his staff were made prisoners.

General Lannes immediately charged forward. Cara Saint-Cyr, who was on our right, and *en potence* with the left flank of the enemy, was much nearer than the enemy to the bridges upon the Bormida. The Austrian army was thrown into the most dreadful confusion in a moment. From 8 to 10,000 cavalry, which were spread over the field, fearing that Saint-Cyr's infantry might reach the bridge before them, retreated at full gallop, and overturned all they met with in their way. Victor's division made all imaginable haste to resume its former field of battle, at the village of Marengo. The enemy's army was in the most horrible disorder. No one thought of anything but flight. The pressure and confusion became extreme on the bridges of the Bormida, where the masses of fugitives were obliged to crowd together; and at night, all who remained upon the left bank fell into the power of the Republic.

It would be difficult to describe the confusion and despair of the Austrian army. On one side the French army was on the bank of the Bormida, and was expected to pass it at daybreak. On the other, they had General Suchet with his army on their rear, in the direction of their right.

Which way could they effect their retreat? Behind they would be driven to the Alps, and the frontiers of France: they might have moved towards Genoa on the right, before the battle; but they could not hope to do so after their defeat, and closely followed by the victorious army. In this desperate situation, General Melas resolved to give his troops the whole night to rally and repose themselves, availing himself of the screen of the Bormida and the protection of the citadel of Alessandria for this purpose; and afterwards to repass the Tanaro, if necessary, and thus maintain himself in that position, and

MARENGO

endeavour at any rate, by entering into negotiations, to save his army by capitulating. On the 15th, at daybreak, the Austrians sent a flag of truce with proposals for an armistice, which produced, the same day, the convention, by which Genoa and all the fortified places in Piedmont, Lombardy, and the Legations, were given up to the French army; and by which the Austrian army obtained leave to retire behind Mantua, without being made prisoners of war. Thus was the conquest of all Italy secured.

General Melas acted in conformity to the interests of his sovereign, in saving the Austrian army; and giving up places, which, being ill-provisioned and ill-garrisoned, could not have made any long resistance, or have been of any utility when the army was destroyed.

I, on the other side, considered that 20,000 English had just arrived at Genoa; that with the 10,000 Austrians remaining in that place they formed an army; that not having any place of strength in Italy, the position of the French was precarious; that they had suffered greatly in the battles of Montebello and Marengo; that the French army of Genoa, and that of Suchet, had likewise sustained considerable loss, both before the siege and whilst it lasted, during the movements on Nice, and in the pursuit of the Austrians; that General Melas, having passed the Tanaro, was for several days out of reach of attack; that he would therefore gain time to rally, and put his troops in order once more, and that when the Austrian army should be thus re-organized, a single day's march stolen in advance would be enough to disengage it, either by throwing itself upon Genoa, or reaching Stradella by marching in the night; that the great superiority of the enemy in cavalry gave them many advantages in concealing their movements; and, in short, that if the Austrian army should get clearly away, even with the loss of its artillery and baggage, it would require a great deal of time and abundance of labour to take so many fortified places.

General Suchet, with his corps, marched upon Genoa, and on 24 June entered that city, which was given up to him by Prince Hohenzollern, to the great regret of the English; whose vanguard from Mahon had arrived within sight of the port, with the intention of taking possession of the place. The fortresses of Tortona, Alessandria, Coni, Fenestrelles, Milan, Pizzighetone, Arona, Peschiera, Urbino, and Ferrara, were successively given up to the French, with all their artillery. The army of Melas passed through Stradella and Piacenza, and took up its position behind Mantua.

The joy of the Piedmontese, the Genoese, and the Italians was beyond expression; they saw themselves restored to liberty, without suffering the horrors of a protracted war, which was already removed to their frontiers, and without experiencing any of the inconveniences attendant on sieges of fortified places, always fraught with disastrous consequences to the towns and surrounding country.

MARENGO

In France the intelligence at first appeared incredible. The first courier who arrived at Paris was a commercial express: he brought news that the French army had been defeated. He had set out on the morning of 14 June, between ten and twelve, just as I was coming on the field of battle. This only increased the general joy, when my victory was promulgated, with all its attendant advantages to the Republic. The soldiers of the army of the Rhine were ashamed of having done so little; and a noble emulation impelled them to desire that no armistice should be concluded, until they should be in possession of the whole of Bavaria.

The English troops, crowded together upon the rock of Mahon, became the prey of various maladies, and lost a number of their soldiers. Soon after this celebrated battle of 14 June, all the Italian patriots were released from the dungeons of Austria, and entered the capital of their nation in triumph, amidst the acclamations of their countrymen, and cries of '*Viva il liberatore dell' Italia*'.

I set out on 17 June, from Marengo, for Milan, where I arrived at night: I found the city illuminated, and a scene of the most animated rejoicings: all proclaimed the re-establishment of the Cisalpine Republic; but the Constitution by which it had been regulated being susceptible of improvement, I established a Provisional Government, which left greater facilities for terminating, in a time of peace, the complete and definite organization of this Republic. I charged Petiet, the Commissary-general, who had been Minister of war in France, with the functions of Minister of France to the Cisalpine Republic, instructing him to direct its administration, attend to the wants of the French army, and look into and prevent every species of abuse.

The Ligurian Republic was thus re-organized, and restored to independence. The Austrians had not restored the King of Sardinia, when they made themselves masters of Piedmont, but had appropriated the country to their own profit. In this they differed in opinion with the Russians, who wished the King of Sardinia to be re-established in Piedmont. This monarch, who had landed from Sardinia, was in Tuscany, and had not obtained leave to go to Turin.

I established a Provisional Government in Piedmont, and nominated General Jourdan Minister of the French Republic to this government. He was charged to superintend it, and to reconcile the interests of the people of Piedmont with those of the French Republic. This general, whose conduct had been somewhat suspicious at the time of 18 Brumaire, felt grateful on finding that I had not only entirely forgotten the past, but was also willing to give him so high a proof of confidence. He devoted all his zeal to the public good.

Though General Massena was guilty of an error in embarking his troops at Genoa, instead of conducting them by land, he had always displayed much character and energy. The services he had rendered in the first campaigns, and

MARENGO

latterly at Zurich, testified also in his favour. I appointed him Commander-in-chief of the Army of Italy.

The affairs of the French Republic rendered my presence necessary at Paris. I set out on 5 Messidor (24 June) passed through Turin, staying there only two hours, to visit the Citadel, crossed Mount Cenis, and arrived at Lyons, where I stopped some time to gratify the inhabitants of the city, and lay the first stone for the rebuilding of the *Place Bellecour*. This ceremony was rendered sublime by the immense concourse, and the enthusiasm of the people. I arrived in Paris on 13 Messidor (2 July) unexpectedly, and in the middle of the night; but the next day, as soon as the news was spread through the various quarters of that vast capital, all the city and the suburbs ran to the courts and gardens of the palace of the Tuileries. All the labouring people at once left their occupations; and the populace crowded round the windows in the hope of seeing him to whom France was so much indebted. Acclamations of joy resounded through the gardens, in the courts, and on the quays. In the evening every one, rich or poor, joyfully illuminated his house.

It was a truly glorious day.

PART TWO

WATERLOO CAMPAIGN

MAP TO ILLUSTRATE
NAPOLEON'S MEMOIRS
OF
THE WATERLOO CAMPAIGN

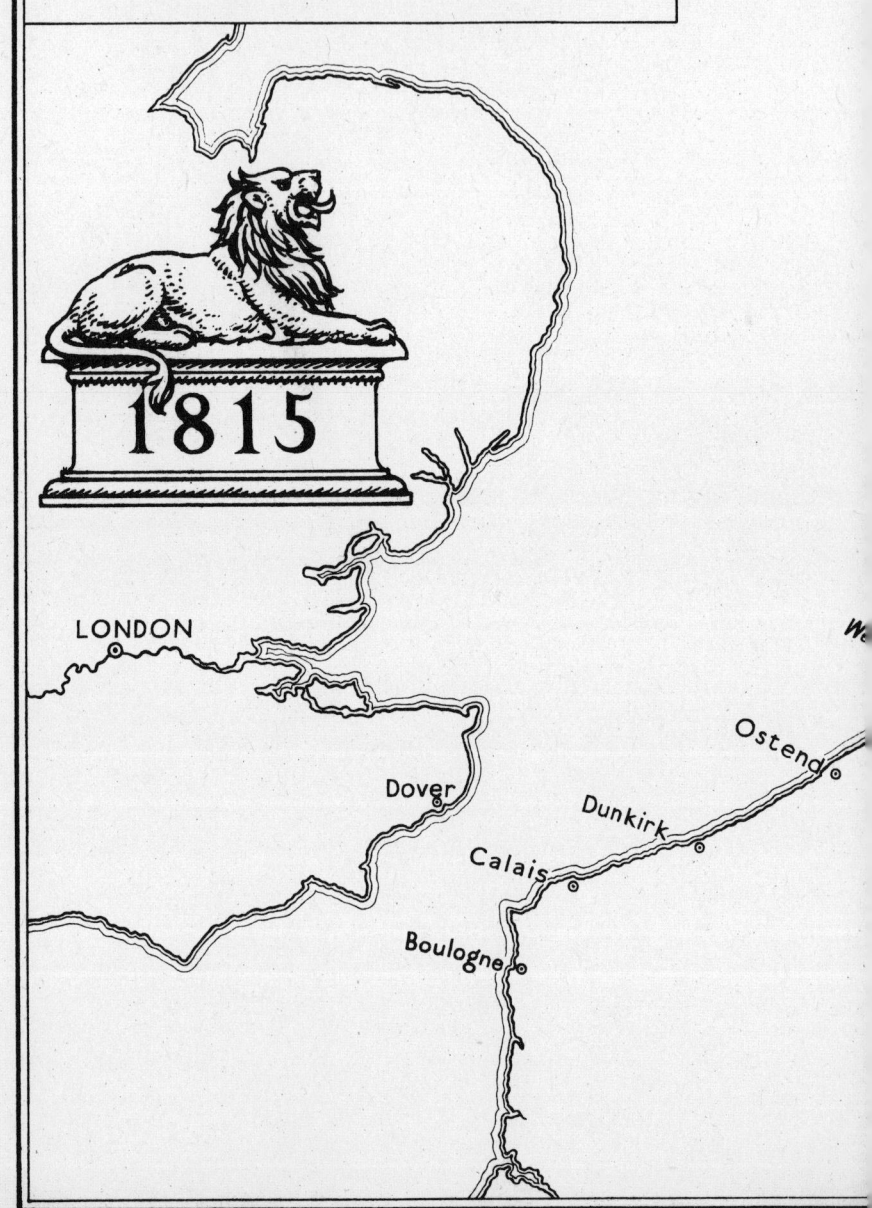

1815

LONDON

Dover

Ostend

Dunkirk

Calais

Boulogne

EDWARD STANFORD LTD, LONDON.

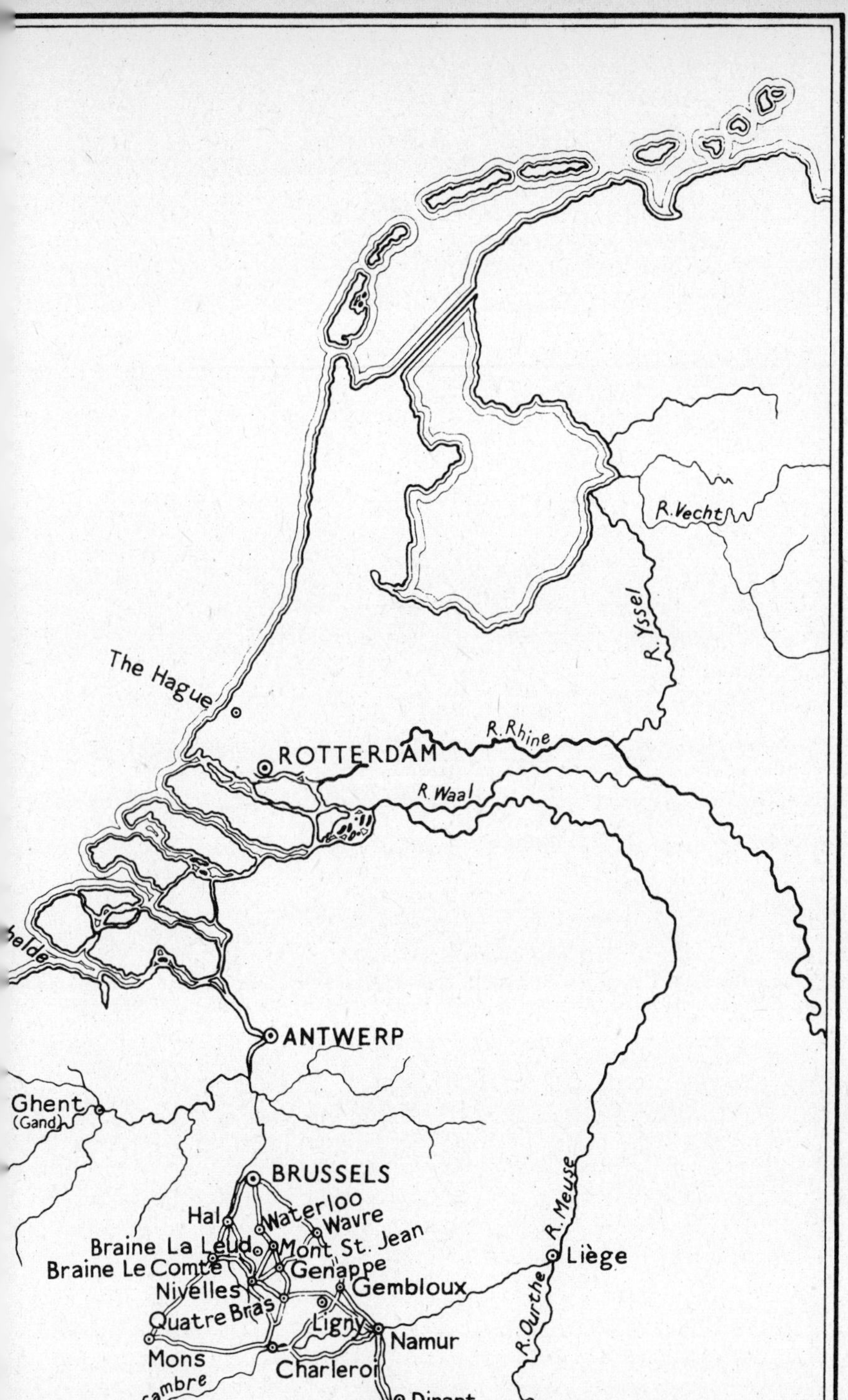

R. Vecht
R. Yssel
The Hague
R. Rhine
ROTTERDAM
R. Waal
helde
ANTWERP
Ghent
(Gand)
BRUSSELS
Hal
Waterloo
Wavre
Braine La Leud
Mont St. Jean
Braine Le Comte
Genappe
Nivelles
Gembloux
Quatre Bras
Ligny
Namur
Mons
Charleroi
Dinant
R. Sambre
R. Meuse
Liège
R. Ourthe

Chapter XXXVIII

RETURN FROM THE ISLAND OF ELBA

The Imperial Eagle flies from steeple to steeple until it reaches the towers of Notre Dame at Paris. The Bourbons leave France. Secret convention concluded at the end of 1814 between Austria, France and England against Russia and Prussia. The King of Naples declares war on Austria on 22 March. The Congress of Vienna in March, 1815.

I

I left the Island of Elba on the 26 February, 1815, at 9 o'clock in the evening. I boarded the brig *Inconstant* which flew the white flag studded with bees throughout the journey. On 1 March at 5 o'clock in the afternoon I landed on the beach of the Gulf of Juan near Cannes.

My little army put on the tricolour cockade. It consisted of 1,100 men, the greater number soldiers of the Old Guard. I passed through Grasse on the 2nd at 9 o'clock in the morning and slept at Sermon, having covered twenty leagues during this first day. On the 3rd I slept at Barrême. On the 4th my advance guard, commanded by General Cambronne, seized the fortress of Sisteron. On the 5th I entered Gap. On the 7th at two o'clock in the afternoon I came face to face, on the heights before Vizille, with the advance guard of the Grenoble garrison which was marching against me.

I approached it alone, harangued it, made it fly the tricolour, put myself at its head, and, at 11 o'clock in the evening, entered Grenoble, having covered eighty leagues in six days across very mountainous country. This is the most prodigious march of which history has any record.

I spent the 8th at Grenoble and left it on the 9th at the head of 8,000 men of

RETURN FROM THE ISLAND OF ELBA

troops of the Line, with thirty guns; and made my entry at ten o'clock in the evening into Lyons, the second city of France. The Count de Fargues, mayor of the city, presented me with the keys. The Count d'Artois, the Duke d'Orleans, and Marshal the Duke of Taranto had escaped from it alone on the 10th. Their arrival unattended at the Tuileries struck stupefaction into the court. At length on 20 March at eight o'clock in the evening, on my son's birthday, I entered Paris. Forty thousand men of the Army of the Line of all arms had successively ranged themselves under my flag. The little army of the Island of Elba arrived the following day, having covered two hundred and forty leagues* in twenty days.

Louis XVIII left Paris during the night of 19/20 March, and France on the 23rd. At his departure from Lille all the fortresses in Flanders were flying the tricolour flag. At the first rumour of my disembarkation the Duke of Bourbon had been sent to Nantes to put himself at the head of la Vendée. The Duke d'Angoulême had been entrusted by the government with the provinces on the left bank of the Loire. All attempts to raise the West were futile: the people of this part of the country remembered all that they owed to me. The Duke of Bourbon embarked at Paimbœuf on 1 April in an English ship. The Duke d'Angoulême sent Baron de Vitrolles, Minister of State, from Bordeaux to set up the head-quarters of his Government at Toulouse; and left the Duchess, his wife, at Bordeaux in the hope of keeping this important city on his side, and of rallying the Spanish army to it. For his own part, at the head of the 10th Regiment of the Infantry of the Line, of the 14th Mounted Chasseurs and some battalions of Royal Volunteers from Languedoc, he conceived the audacious enterprise of marching on Lyons while the men of Marseilles were marching on Grenoble. He crossed the Rhône by the Saint-Esprit bridge, carried the bridge of Drôme which the National Guards of Montelimart were defending, entered Valence on 3 April, and established his advance posts along the left bank of the Isère. At the same time the men of Marseilles, to the number of 2,500, supported by the 83rd and 58th of the Line under the orders of Lieutenant-General Ernouf, entered Gap and marched on Grenoble.

These successes only lasted one day: the Duchess d'Angoulême on 2 April was obliged to leave Bordeaux on the arrival of Lieutenant-General Clausel; she embarked in an English cutter. Vitrolles was arrested on 4 April by Lieutenant-General Laborde and transferred to prison in Paris. General Gilly, profiting by the enthusiasm of the people of Languedoc, put himself at their head: his advance guard, composed of the 10th Mounted Chasseurs and the 6th Light Infantry, got possession of the Saint-Esprit bridge and drove the Royalists off it.

At the rumour of the dangers which were threatening Lyons, the people of

* A league equals approximately three miles. S. de C.

RETURN FROM THE ISLAND OF ELBA

Burgundy and Auvergne rose *en masse* and rushed to Lyons demanding arms in order to march against the princes. In all the communes of Dauphiné the tricolour flag was hoisted, and the tocsin announced the march of the Royalists. The troops of the Line, at the sight of the imperial eagle which Lieutenant-General Chabert displayed to them at the head of a detachment of the National Guard of Grenoble, deserted the Royalist party. The men of Marseilles, hemmed in on all sides, broke rank in disorder, and were glad to return home. At this the Duke d'Angoulême, in deep dismay, realized the foolhardiness of his enterprise. He evacuated Valence in all haste, hoping to reach the Saint-Esprit bridge. General Gilly took him prisoner. I gave him back his liberty, and had him embarked on 16 April at Cette in a Swedish ship. Marshal Massena, by flying the tricolour flag in Provence, put an end to the civil war. On 20 April, a hundred guns from the Invalides announced to the capital, and salvoes from the coast batteries and frontier fortifications announced to foreign nations, that the French people had come into their own again.

History will record with admiration the generosity of the victor in these circumstances. Baron Vitrolles, who had been excluded by a decree of Lyons from the general amnesty, the Duke d'Angoulême, whose sentence was pronounced by the law demanding an eye for an eye and a tooth for a tooth, were alike saved by my clemency. 'I want', I said, 'to be able to pride myself on reconquering my throne without a single drop of blood having been spilt either on the battlefield or the scaffold.'

2

At the end of 1814 and at the beginning of 1815 discord prevailed at the Congress of Vienna. Austria, France and England were bound by a secret convention against Russia and Prussia, who appeared not to want to set any limit to their claims. Prussia wanted to incorporate Dresden within its dominion, which was against the interests of Austria; but France, supported by Spain, demanded that the court of Vienna, in return for the support which she gave it, should agree to the Bourbons of Sicily ascending the throne of Naples again. Austria refused this, as much out of jealousy of the House of Bourbon as in order not to betray King Joachim, who had contributed so much to the success of the Allies in 1814 by making common cause with the enemies of his country against the head of his family and his benefactor.

It was Murat who was the decisive factor. If, with his army of 60,000 men, he had joined the Franco-Italian army which the viceroy commanded, he would have forced the Austrian army to remain on the defensive in Carinthia and the Tyrol. The viceroy's army was superior to that of Field-Marshal Bellegarde, but it was nevertheless held by the Neapolitan army. Thus, the weight

RETURN FROM THE ISLAND OF ELBA

which he put in the balance on this occasion was 120,000 men. With 100,000 men less, the Allies could not have undertaken the invasion of France before the Spring. In 1814, the Neapolitan army was good, because at this period it counted among its ranks 2,000 French officers and N.C.O's, Corsicans or Italians of the kingdom of Italy, who left it as soon as they received the circular by which Count Molé, the High-Judge, recalled the Frenchmen from the service of Naples.

The Austrian ministers at the Congress of Vienna often made it obvious how little importance they attached to the intervention of the court of the Tuileries. Louis XVIII, they said, is not in a position to collect 10,000 men together without fear of seeing the soldiers turn against him. The Prince of Benevento[1] advised the Cabinet of the Tuileries to assemble three camps, one in Franche-Comté, the other in front of Lyons, and the third in the South. These three camps could be expanded to 36,000 or 40,000 men without involving any increase in the military establishment and without being subject to excessive expenditure. They would, however, raise the credit of France abroad. This plan was adopted.

During the course of February, 1815, the troops were set in motion. Ricard, the divisional general, repaired to Vienna and boasted during several conferences of the excellent state of the French army, of its keenness and its attachment to the King. He announced pompously that three camps containing 80,000 men were being formed in the neighbourhood of the Alps. The French plenipotentiaries demanded that this army, supported by a Spanish Division, should be allowed to proceed either by land, by way of Genoa, Florence and Rome, or else by sea, to southern Italy. The King of Naples,[2] for his part, was not asleep. He assembled his army in the Marches. It consisted of 60,000 men. To counterbalance the effect of the negotiations by the Tuileries, he demanded of Austria passage for the troops which he wanted to take over the Alps to enter France, giving as much support thereby as he could to the opinion already widespread that French soldiers were not Bourbon soldiers.

It was at this juncture that I landed. The French regiments, destined to form the three camps in the South, were on the move and were just in the right position to act as my escort from the Gulf of Juan to Paris. Marshal Soult, the Minister of War, was at that time accused of treason; but appearances were deceptive. These troop movements and their disposition, which proved, in the event, to fit in so well with my march, had been carried out by the express order of the King and on the demand of the French plenipotentiaries at Vienna. The foreigners showed that they knew what the secret inclinations of the French army were, better than the Princes and Ministers of the House of Bourbon.

[1] Talleyrand. S. de C. [2] Murat. S. de C.

RETURN FROM THE ISLAND OF ELBA

3

On 16 February, 1815, a few days before leaving the isle of Elba, I sent one of my chamberlains to Naples in order to let the Court there know, *first*, that I was leaving, to re-enter my capital and ascend my throne again; that I was resolved to uphold the Treaty of Paris, which made me hope that the allied powers would take no part in this civil war; that the Russian troops were, moreover, beyond the Niemen, part of the Austrians beyond the Inn, the majority of the Prussians beyond the Oder, and half the English army in America; that the Congress of Vienna had concluded its operations and that the Czar had left for St Petersburg; *secondly*, that I wanted Murat to send a courier to Vienna so that his ambassador could notify this Court that France would continue to carry out the Treaty of Paris, and in particular renounced all claims on Italy; *thirdly*, that in any case hostilities could not begin before the end of July; that France and Naples would have time to act together; that as a preliminary he should reinforce his army, in a good position in front of Ancona, and in all unforeseen circumstances be guided by the principle that it was better to retreat than to advance, and to give battle behind the Garigliano than on the Po; that he could achieve a great deal by way of diversion and when supported by a French army; that he could do nothing without that.

My envoy arrived at Naples on 4 March. The brig *Inconstant*, returning from the Gulf of Juan, arrived on the 12th. A few days afterwards, a courier from Genoa brought the news of my triumphal entry into Grenoble and Lyons. The King did not disguise his feelings. He announced loudly his determination to raise Italy. 'The Emperor', he said, 'will not encounter any obstacle. The whole French nation will fly to his standard. If I delay marching on the Po, if I wait for the month of July, the French armies will have re-established the kingdom of Italy, and seized the Iron Crown again; it is for me to proclaim the independence of Italy.' My envoy and the Queen[1] threw themselves in vain at the King's feet in an effort to make him realize the danger and rashness of this enterprise. Nothing could open his eyes. He left for Ancona, arrived at the head of his army on 22 March, but did not even give himself time to wait for news of my entry into Paris: he crossed the Rubicon, traversed the Romagna and poured his troops into the territory of the Holy See and Tuscany. The Pope retired to Genoa, the Grand-Duke to Leghorn. When he arrived at Bologna, the King of Naples called upon the people of the Kingdom of Italy to rise in revolt. He was asked why he said nothing to them about Napoleon, their legitimate King; and told that without my orders they could not make any move; that it seemed to them, moreover, imprudent to act before the French troops had arrived across the Alps; and that in any

[1] Napoleon's sister, Caroline. S. de C.

RETURN FROM THE ISLAND OF ELBA

case they needed rifles. The province of Bologna alone asked for 40,000. The Neapolitan artillery had not a single one. A few days afterwards the Austrian army, which was concentrated on the left bank of the Po, crossed this river, defeated the Neapolitan army and entered Naples on 12 May. The King, unable to throw himself into the fortress of Gaeta, embarked in a merchant ship and landed in Provence, where he stayed to await his family and gather his supporters together. For her part, the Queen had capitulated to an English commodore, who, following the usual practice of the Allies during this war, as at Danzig and at Dresden, trampled the capitulation underfoot. Instead of transporting this princess to France, he took her to Trieste. During the first days of April Prince Lucien, with one of the Pope's chargé d'affaires in his coach, arrived incognito at Fontainebleau. It was from him that the first news was received in Paris of the King of Naples' invasion. The Pope wrote from Genoa to me that, if I did not guarantee him the possession of Rome, he would go and take refuge in Spain. The Chargé d'Affaires of the Holy See was received at the Tuileries: he left, taking with him the most favourable assurances to the Holy Father. I guaranteed him all that he was assured by the Treaty of Paris, and let him know that I censured the conduct of the King of Naples as contrary to my policy.

4

The news of my landing in France was received at Vienna on 8 March. The Congress had not broken up. On 13 and 25 March the Ministers of the Powers signed acts without parallel in history. They thought I was doomed. 'He will', they said, 'be immediately repulsed and defeated by the faithful subjects of Louis XVIII.' When they learnt later that the Bourbons, without putting up any resistance, had been unable to hold the north, the south, the west, or the east, and that the whole of France had declared for its former sovereign, the *amour propre* of the Allies was compromised. Yet, in spite of that, they hesitated! But, when the Court of Vienna was informed of the opinions of the King of Naples and afterwards of his hostile march, they were no longer in any doubt that he was acting by my orders and that, firm and unswerving in my political methods, I was still the same as I had been at Châtillon, and did not want the crown of France except in conjunction with Belgium, the Rhine, and perhaps even the Iron Crown.

The conference did not hesitate any longer. The Ministers signed a treaty against France by which the four principal powers each undertook to furnish 150,000 men. The ratifications were exchanged on 25 April and it was calculated that 1,000,000 men of all the nations in Europe would be assembled at the end of July on the French frontiers. Sweden and Portugal alone refused to supply their contingent. The Peace between England and the United States

RETURN FROM THE ISLAND OF ELBA

of America had been concluded at Ghent and ratified at the end of February. The English troops, now of no further use in Canada, embarked for the return to Europe. The Duke of Wellington had his head-quarters at Brussels on 15 April, and Prince Blücher at Liége. On the Thames, the Danube, the Spree, the Neva and the Tagus, everything resounded of war. The French frigate *Melpomène*, being on the Neapolitan coast, was seized by the English ship *Rivoli*; but a few days afterwards, orders arrived from London to the Commodore in the Mediterranean to respect the French flag, war not having been declared. Thereafter French ships sailed freely. A French frigate brought Madame* back from Naples to France.

These orders of the English Government were due to the indecision of the sovereigns at Vienna, and to the interest which the Court of London had in gaining time. Its armies in Belgium were in no state to defend that country; and even the Admiralty, experiencing great difficulties in arming its ships, feared that the French squadron at Toulon might be equipped and put to sea before its own. Twice a prey to the most extraordinary aberration, the King of Naples was twice a cause of our misfortune, in 1814 by declaring himself against France, and in 1815 by declaring himself against Austria.

* Napoleon's mother. S. de C.

Chapter XXXIX

MILITARY STATE OF FRANCE

State of the Army on 1 March, 1815. Organization of an Army of 800,000 men. Armament, clothing, re-mounts, finance. State of the Army on 1 June, 1815. Paris. Lyons.

I

During the last six months of 1814, the French Army had been remodelled. In March, 1815, it was composed of a hundred and five regiments of infantry, of which three were in the colonies; three Swiss regiments; four Infantry regiments of the Old Guard, under the name of Grenadiers and Chasseurs of France; fifty-seven regiments of Cavalry of the Line; four regiments of Cavalry of the Old Guard, under the name of Grenadiers, Dragoons, Chasseurs and Lancers of France; eight battalions of the artillery train; two battalions of pontoon builders; three regiments of sappers and pioneers, known as 'the Engineers'.

The Infantry regiments were composed of two battalions, only six of them being of three battalions. The effective strength of each regiment was 900 men, of which 600 were available for war, one battalion reinforcing the other. The Cavalry had an effective strength of 25,000 men and 16,000 horses: it could furnish at the most 11,000 horses to go on campaign.

The Field Artillery battalions were formed of Cadres. They had 2,000 horses at the Depots and 6,000 foraging with the peasants. The total effective strength was 149,000 men, capable of sending on campaign an army of 93,000 men present under arms, a force scarcely sufficient to guard the fortresses of the principal maritime establishments; for all the fleets were disarmed, the crews disbanded, unless one counts a single vessel and three frigates at Toulon and two frigates at Rochefort. Since the only troops which the Navy had on foot were eight battalions of gunners, the land army had to

MILITARY STATE OF FRANCE

provide for the defence of Cherbourg, Brest, Lorient, Rochefort and Toulon.

The artillery equipment, despite the losses suffered through the surrender of the field equipment in the fortified towns of Antwerp, Wesel, Mayence and Alexandria, could furnish the needs of the largest of armies and replace the losses which it might suffer during several campaigns. There were 150,000 new rifles in the magazines and 300,000 rifles in for repairs or replacement of parts, not counting those in the hands of the army. That was very inadequate. All the fortresses were disarmed, the palisades and the siege provisions had been sold, but the artillery equipment would be sufficient as armament for them.

2

Eight hundred thousand men were considered necessary to fight Europe on equal terms. The first cares were those concerned with the morale of the army. The regiments had the numbers which they had borne since 1794 restored to them; they had been rendered illustrious in twenty-five campaigns and a thousand engagements. Cadres were created of the Third, Fourth and Fifth battalions of the Infantry regiments; of the Fourth and Fifth squadrons of the Cavalry regiments; of thirty battalions of Field Artillery; of twenty regiments of the Young Guard; of ten battalions of Military Ordnance; and of twenty Naval regiments: which provided employment for all officers on half-pay of all arms, both of land and sea.

Two hundred picked battalions of the National Guard were called for, each battalion composed of two companies of Grenadiers and two of Voltigeurs, both five hundred and sixty men strong. All the old soldiers were recalled to the Colours. There was no need for any coercive measure to persuade them to obey: they came running and singing. Farm-hands, artisans, tradesmen, etc., all left their work at the end of the week, buckled on their old uniform, and rejoined their former regiments.

This appeal ought to have produced 200,000 men, but only yielded 130,000 for the army of the line; because a great number enrolled in the two hundred picked battalions of the National Guard, which others entered as substitutes in the call-up of the 1815 conscription. The 1815 contingent was called up: it should have yielded 140,000 men, but it only produced 80,000 by the end of May.

The revolt in Vendée caused a shortage of men. Moreover, in several departments, the young men of this call-up had been called in 1814, and they preferred to rejoin their colours under the name of 'old soldiers'. The twenty marine regiments were made up of 30,000 sailors from the old squadrons of Antwerp, Brest, Rochefort and Toulon: the naval Officers and Warrant

MILITARY STATE OF FRANCE

Officers formed the Cadres. A call-up of 250,000 men was to have been proposed to the Chambers during the course of July. This levy would have been finished in September. The number of Officers, N.C.O's and soldiers on the retired list or invalided out came to more than 100,000: 30,000 were capable of serving in the fortresses. They hastened to respond to the appeal which the Minister of War, Marshal the Prince of Eckmühl, made to them. Their experience and their fine spirit were extremely useful in training the new levies, and assured the holding of the fortresses.

The most important subject was firearms. The magazines were supplied with quite enough sabres; and the artillery took several measures in order to double the output of the old factories. First they exempted the workers from military service; secondly they gave the contractors the advances which they needed; and thirdly they relaxed the rigour of their former instructions, authorising their agents to accept various designs with simpler gun-lock plates than those of the 1777 model: they had bronze lock-plates moulded by the thousand, and restored the automatic lock-plate stamping shop. The Imperial factories could supply 20,000 new arms a month. By these extraordinary means they supplied 40,000 which in six months would have meant, 240,000. That was still insufficient. Enough repair shops were established in all the big fortresses to repair all the old rifles which were in the magazines in France within six months, but the principal source of supply was from the workshops which were set up in the capital: they were of three kinds. The first were to mount the spares: the cabinet-makers of the Faubourg Saint-Antoine, at first clumsy at this work, were not slow in making themselves very expert at it. The second were the repair shops for the old rifles. The third were the workshops providing new rifles. The bronze-workers; the clock-maker apprentices; the engravers, who are very numerous in this big city; were all employed. The artillery officers brought so much zeal and intelligence into the running of all these workshops that, from the month of May, they produced 1,500 rifles a day; in June 3,000; and they were to produce 4,000 beginning from 1 July. There was greater activity in the capital than in 1793, but with this difference: that then everything was waste, anarchy and disorder. The arms which the revolutionary workshops made were defective and gave bad service; but in 1815 everything was run with the greatest economy on the principles of good administration. All the arms which left the shops were technically correct. This important service was thus assured.

The cloth factories, for clothing the troops, were numerous in 1812 and 1813; they could provide for all the requirements of the armies, but in 1814 they were entirely deserted. The War Minister did not give any order, and had not made any attempt to clothe the troops, except for the six regiments which bore the name of the King or the Princes. From the month of April the Treasury advanced several millions to the makers of cloth and they got their factories going within a month. The clothing of 800,000 men was certainly a considerable affair; it would have been impossible to have seen to it in time. The Minister adopted the measure of ordering the immobile National Guards, under an article of the law which would provide for the raising of 250,000 men, to furnish 100,000 coats and equipment for the fighting army.

The suppliers had delivered 20,000 cavalry horses before 1 June. Ten thousand horses completely trained had been supplied by the Gendarmerie, which had been dismounted; the cost of these was paid, cash down, to the gendarmes, who re-mounted themselves in a week by buying horses of their own choice.

It was intended to take half their new horses during the course of July, and contracts were agreed on for 14,000 more. Thus at 1 June there were 46,000 cavalry horses at the Depots or in the line, and there would have been 66,000 at the end of July. Five thousand artillery horses were brought back from foraging with the peasants. Contracts for 15,000 horses had been entered into with the suppliers; 12,000 were delivered by 1 June. There were thus at this period 18,000 artillery horses.

The ease with which the Minister of Finance, the Duke of Gaëta, and the Finance Minister, Count Mollien, provided for these enormous expenses was the object of general astonishment. All the services required ready money and most of the suppliers and makers even required advances. However, the Public Debt and the Pensions were served with the greatest exactitude. All the expenses of the Interior, far from being reduced, had been increased; the huge system of public works was resumed throughout France. 'One can easily see', said the workmen, 'that the Great Contractor himself is back again. Everything was dead: now everything comes to life again. We were unemployed: to-day we are all busy.'

The opinion was generally held that I had recovered a hundred millions in gold from my Treasury at the Tuileries. That was wrong: the real treasure that I recovered was the affection of the people, the goodwill not only of the mass of the nation, but also of the French and Dutch capitalists.

The Treasury traded four millions of the Sinking Fund Bonds at fifty per cent for credits on the national forests; this produced, free of all discount, forty millions in cash which came in with incredible speed.

The King had left Paris in such a hurry that he had not been able to carry off either the Royal Plate, valued at six millions, or the coffers of the Treasury, which were scattered throughout France; there were fifty millions in them. Part of this sum was employed by Baron Louis, his Finance Minister, in speculation with the royal bonds. This practice, which was so pernicious, was given up by the Duke of Gaëta, who was empowered to dispose of the shares accumulated in that way. Taxes were not increased, but the people were eager to pay them as quickly as possible. Free gifts were numerous; in some departments these exceeded a million. At every parade, unknown citizens approached me, and handed to me packets of bank bills; several times, on returning to my apartments, I handed over to the Chancellor of the Exchequer eighty or a hundred thousand francs which I had received in this way. These could not yield very considerable sums, but I quote them as evidence of the national enthusiasm.

Thus, by 1 October, France would have a military establishment of 800,000 to 900,000 men completely organized, armed and clothed. The problem of her independence consisted, thereafter, in warding off hostilities until 1 October. The months of May, June, July, August and September were needed for this, but they were sufficient. By this time the frontiers of the Empire would have become frontiers of steel, which no human power could cross with impunity.

4

By 1 June the effective strength of the French troops under arms was 559,000 men. Thus, in two months, the War Ministry had raised 414,000 men, close on 7,000 a day. Of this number, the effective strength of the army of the line amounted to 363,000 men; that of the emergency army to 196,000 men. Of the effective strength of the army of the line, 217,000 men were actually under arms, clothed, armed and trained, ready to go on campaign. They were formed into seven army corps, four corps of Cavalry reserve, four reconnaissance corps, and the army of la Vendée, spread along the frontiers and covering all of them; but the main forces were quartered within reach of Paris and the frontier of Flanders.

On 1 June, all the troops left the fortresses and left the defence of them to the emergency army. The First Corps, commanded by Count d'Erlon, took up its quarters in the neighbourhood of Lille. It was composed of four infantry divisions, each four regiments strong; a division of light cavalry, consisting of four regiments; and six batteries of artillery. The Second Corps, commanded by Count Reille, was quartered around Valenciennes. It was composed in the same way as the First Corps, but was a little stronger, some regiments having three battalions. The Third Corps, commanded by Count Vandamme, was assembled in the neighbourhood of Mézières. It had three divisions of infantry, one of light cavalry, and five batteries. The Fourth Corps, commanded by Count Gérard, was in the neighbourhood of Metz. It had three infantry divisions, one light cavalry division, and five batteries. One of its infantry regiments was detached to la Vendée. The Fifth Corps, commanded by Count Rapp, was in Alsace. It had three infantry divisions, one light cavalry division, and six batteries. The Sixth Corps, commanded by Count de Lobau,

MILITARY STATE OF FRANCE

was assembled at Laon. It was composed of three infantry divisions, a light cavalry division, and six batteries; but each of these infantry divisions had a regiment detached to la Vendée. The Seventh Corps, commanded by Marshal Suchet, was at Chambéry. It was composed of two divisions of infantry of the line, each of four regiments; two divisions of picked National Guards, each of eight battalions; one division of light cavalry; and six batteries.

The strength of the First Reconnaissance Corps, called the 'Jura' Corps, commanded by General Lecourbe, was made up of an infantry division of three regiments; two divisions of picked National Guards, each of eight battalions; a light cavalry division; and five batteries. The Second Reconnaissance Corps, called the 'Var' Corps, commanded by Marshal Brune, was composed of an infantry division, three regiments strong, of which two had three battalions; a regiment of cavalry; and three batteries. These infantry regiments had come from the twenty-third military division, where they had been replaced by Corsican volunteer battalions. The Third Reconnaissance Corps, called the 'East Pyrenees' Corps, commanded by General Decaen, was assembled at Toulouse. It was composed of an infantry division, of three regiments; a cavalry regiment, of sixteen battalions of picked National Guards; and three batteries. The Fourth Reconnaissance Corps, commanded by General Clausel, was at Bordeaux; its composition was the same. These two latter corps were each weakened by a cavalry regiment despatched to la Vendée. La Vendée, after having flown the Imperial Eagle in April, had revolted in May. General Lamarque was Commander-in-Chief there of the Imperial army, consisting of eight regiments of the line; two regiments of the Young Guard; two cavalry regiments; ten squadrons of gendarmerie, each of four hundred men; twelve battalions, or detachments, of the line, destined for the army corps, which had been retained in la Vendée in view of the gravity of the situation.

The four corps of cavalry reserve under the command of Marshal Grouchy, were all quartered between the Aisne and the Sambre. Each cavalry corps had two batteries of light artillery and two divisions, each division being of three regiments. The First Corps, composed of light cavalry, was commanded by Count Pajol. The Second Corps, composed of dragoons, was under the orders of Count Excelmans. The Third Corps, formed of cuirassiers, was commanded by Count Milhaud. The Fourth Corps, likewise composed of cuirassiers, was under the orders of Count Kellermann.

The Imperial Guard was composed of four regiments of Young Guard, four of the Middle Guard, four of the Old Guard, four cavalry regiments, and ninety-six pieces of artillery. The regiments in the army corps, contained, as a general rule, only two battalions: since these battalions numbered 600 men present under arms, they were 240 short of their full complement. This additional manpower was on the way and would have joined them before 1 July.

MILITARY STATE OF FRANCE

The third, fourth, and fifth battalions and the depots were set in motion from all over France, to assemble at Paris, at Lyons, and in the west.

The artillery was preparing a new force of five hundred field guns, personnel, equipment, teams, and double supplies. The two hundred battalions of picked National Guards, forming an effective strength of 112,000 men, was raised in full strength. A hundred and fifty battalions, comprising 85,000 men, were doing garrison duty in the ninety fortresses on the frontiers of the empire. Forty-eight battalions, comprising 26,000 men, were assembled, as I have already said: sixteen with the First 'Jura' Reconnaissance Corps, sixteen with the Seventh Corps, and sixteen forming a reserve on the Loire.

Count Dumas had thrown a tremendous amount of energy into the raising of these troops, and in this matter he deserved well of France. Independently of these two hundred battalions of grenadiers and picked chasseurs, forty-eight battalions of the National Guard were raised during the course of May in Languedoc, Gascony and Dauphiny. Those of Dauphiny were in Provence in June; those of Languedoc brought the Third Reconnaissance Corps up to 15,000 men; those of Gascony brought the Fourth Reconnaissance Corps up to the same strength, which completed the defence of the Pyrenees. These forty-eight battalions were not included at all in the 1 June position, because at this period they had not yet left the chief towns of their departments and because their organization was not completed; but at the end of June they had repaired to their respective destinations.

Of the 30,000 officers, N.C.O's, and ordinary soldiers, brought out of retirement, 20,000 went to strengthen the fortress garrisons, and 10,000 were held in garrison at Marseilles, Bordeaux, and in other towns, where their presence was useful to galvanize public spirit and keep an eye on the ill-disposed. The ninety fortresses were armed, palisaded, provisioned, and commanded by experienced officers.

The first line of the Northern frontiers—Calais, Dunkirk, Saint-Omer, Lille, Condé, Maubeuge, Philippeville—were provisioned for six months and had garrisons up to full strength, but not clothed or trained; they were formed from picked National Guards.

The second line—Ardres, Aire, Béthune, Douai, Valenciennes, le Quesnoy, Avesnes, Rocroy—were provisioned for four months and their garrisons were at half strength.

The third line—Montreuil, Hesdin, Arras, Bouchain, Landrecy, Bapaume, Cambrai, Abbeville, Château d'Amiens, Péronne, château de Ham, Laon—were provisioned for three months and their garrisons were up to quarter strength.

On the Moselle frontier, the first line—Charlemont, Mézières, château de Sédan, château de Bouillon, Longwy, Thionville, Sarre-Louis, Bitche—were provisioned four for months and their garrisons were up to strength.

The second line—Verdun, Metz, Phalsbourg, Toul—were provisioned for four months and their garrisons were half strength.

On the Alsace frontier—Landau, Lauterbourg, Haguenau, Strasbourg, Schelestat, Neubrisach, Huningen—were provisioned for six months and their garrisons were up to strength.

On the Swiss frontier—Béfort, Besançon, Fort Ecluse, Auxonne—were provisioned for four months and had their garrisons.

On the frontier of the Alps—Fort Barraux, Briançon, Mont-Dauphin, Colmars, Entrevaux, Antibes—were provisioned for four months and had their garrisons.

On the Mediterranean frontier—the forts of Sainte-Marguerite, the Castle of Saint-Tropez, the fort of Brigançon. the forts of the Hyères Islands, Toulon, the fort of Bouc, Aigues-Mortes, Cette, and Coilloure—had sufficient garrisons to put these places beyond the reach of a surprise attack and were partially provisioned.

The coastal batteries were rearmed; all the fortresses of the Pyrenees frontier, from Perpignan to Bayonne, both the first and second lines, were armed and provisioned, and had more or less substantial garrisons. Little anxiety was felt from the quarter of Spain.

Finally, all the ocean frontiers—Bayonne, Château-Trompette, the forts of the Island of Aix, of the Island of Oléron, of the Island of Ré, of La Rochelle, the Citadel of Nantes, Île Dieu, Belle-Île, Fort Saint-Malo, Cherbourg, Le Havre, and the Citadel of Dieppe—were armed, had sufficient garrisons to put them beyond reach of a surprise attack, and a start had been made with provisioning them. The Coastguard gunners were raised. All the English troops being employed in Belgium or in America, no serious anxiety was felt from the direction of the sea.

5

If, as was to be feared, hostilities began before the autumn, the armies of Europe, called into being, would far outnumber the French armies, and the destiny of the Empire would then be decided before Paris and Lyons. These two great cities had in former times been fortified, like all the European capitals, and like them, had subsequently ceased to be.

If, however, in 1805 Vienna had been fortified, the battle of Ulm would not have settled the issue of the war: the army corps which General Kutusow commanded would have waited there for the other corps of the Russian army, already arrived at Olmütz, and for the army of Prince Charles coming up from Italy. In 1809, Prince Charles, who had been beaten at Eckmühl and obliged to effect his retreat by way of the left bank of the Danube, would have had time to reach Vienna and join up there with General Hiller's corps and the army of the Archduke John.

MILITARY STATE OF FRANCE

If Berlin had been fortified in 1806, the army, beaten at Jena would have rallied there, and the Russian army have joined it there.

If in 1808 Madrid had been a fortified town, the French army, after the victories of Espinosa, Tudella, Burgos and Sommosierra, would not have marched upon this capital, leaving General Moore's English army and the Spanish army of la Romana behind Salamanca and Valladolid; these two Anglo-Spanish armies would have effected a junction behind the fortifications of Madrid with the army of Aragon and Valencia.

In 1812 I entered Moscow. If the Russians had not taken the course of burning this great city, a course unprecedented in history, and which they alone could carry out, the fall of Moscow would have brought about the submission of Russia; for the victor would have found in this great city, first, everything necessary to make good the clothing and equipment of an army; secondly, the flour, vegetables, wines, brandies, and everything required for the subsistence of a great army; thirdly, re-mounts for the cavalry; and, finally, the support of 30,000 freed men or slaves in possession of great wealth, very impatient of the yoke of the nobility, and who would have imparted ideas of liberty and independence to the slaves: a terrifying prospect, which would have prompted the Czar to make peace, all the more so, as the victor's intentions were moderate. The fire destroyed all the shops, scattered the population. The merchants and the Third Estate were ruined, and this great city was nothing more than a sink of disorder, anarchy, and crime. If it had been fortified, Kutusow would have camped on its ramparts, and the investment of it would have been impossible.

Constantinople, a city much greater than any of our modern capitals, owed its safety solely to its fortifications. Without them, the Empire of Constantine would have come to an end in 700 and would only have lasted three hundred years. The fortunate Muss[elm]en would have set up the standard of the Prophet from that time onwards. They did so in 1453, approximately eight hundred years later. This capital owed to its walls eight centuries of survival. In the interval, it was besieged fifty-three times, fifty-two of which were to no purpose. The French and the Venetians took it, but only after a very vigorous attack.

Paris has owed its safety ten or twelve times to its walls. First in 885, it would have been the prey of the Normans; these barbarians besieged it without success for two years. Secondly in 1358, it was besieged in vain by the Dauphin; and, if a few years afterwards the inhabitants opened the gates to him, it was of their own free will. Thirdly in 1359, Edward, King of England, encamped at Montrouge, ravaged right up to the base of the walls, but fell back before its fortifications and withdrew to Chartres. Fourthly in 1427, King Henry V repulsed Charles VII's attack. Fifthly in 1464, Count de Chalorais surrounded this great city; he failed in all his attacks. Sixthly in

1472, it would have been taken by the Duke of Burgundy, who was obliged to content himself with ravaging its suburbs. Seventhly in 1536, Charles the Fifth, master of Champagne, brought his head-quarters to Meaux; his messengers came right up to the ramparts of the capital, which owed its safety solely to its walls. Eighthly and ninthly in 1588 and 1589, Henry III and Henry IV failed before the fortifications of Paris; and, if, later on, the inhabitants opened their gates, they did it of their own free will, and as a result of the renunciation of Saint-Denis. Tenthly and lastly in 1636, the fortifications of Paris saved its inhabitants for several years. If Paris had still been a fortified town in 1814 and 1815, capable of resisting for only a week, what an influence might that have had on the affairs of the world!

A great capital is the home of the best of the nation. All the great have their homes there, and their families; it is the centre of public opinion, the repository of all. It is the greatest of contradictions and inconsistencies to leave such a place without the means of its own defence. On my return from the Austerlitz campaign, I often discussed various plans for fortifying the heights of Paris, and had them drawn up. The fear of making the inhabitants uneasy, and the events which followed each other with incredible speed, prevented my giving effect to this project. 'What', people will say, 'you hope to fortify towns 12,000 or 15,000 toises* in circumference? You would need eighty or ninety fronts, 50,000 to 60,000 garrison troops, eight hundred or a thousand guns in batteries. But 60,000 soldiers are an army; would it not be better to use them in the line?'

This objection is generally made about fortresses, but it is a fallacy in that it confuses a soldier with a man. Without a doubt, 50,000 to 60,000 men are needed to defend a great capital, but not 50,000 to 60,000 soldiers. At times of misfortune and great calamity, states may lack soldiers, but never lack men for their internal defence. Fifty thousand men, of whom 2,000 to 3,000 are gunners, will defend a capital and deny entry to an army of 300,000 to 400,000 men, whereas 50,000 men, in open country, if they are not trained soldiers and commanded by experienced officers, are put to rout by a charge of 3,000 cavalrymen. Moreover, all the big capitals are capable of covering part of their outer walls by flooding, because they are all situated on big rivers, so that the moats can be filled with water, either by natural means or by fire brigade pumps. Places as extensive as this, which contain such considerable garrisons, have a certain number of dominating positions, without the possession of which it is impossible to risk entering the town.

But, whatever plan of campaign were adopted in 1815; however much trouble were taken over arming, provisioning, and garrisoning the ninety fortresses of the French frontiers; if the enemy began hostilities before autumn, Paris and Lyons were the two important points. So long as they

* A toise equals 2.13 yards or 1.95 metres. S. de C.

MILITARY STATE OF FRANCE

were occupied in strength, the country would not be lost nor obliged to submit to the will of its enemies!

The Engineer General Haxo supervised the system of fortifications of Paris. First of all he had the heights of Montmartre occupied, the lower ones of Moulins, and the plateau from the Chaumont Rise to the heights of Père Lachaise. A few days sufficed to mark out these works and give them a defensive form. He had the Ourcq canal finished, which runs from Saint-Denis to the basin of la Villette. Civil engineer officers were entrusted with this work. They accomplished it with that zeal and patriotism which characterize them.

The earth was thrown up on the left bank to form a rampart. On the right they constructed bays, covering the roads. The little town of Saint-Denis was protected by floodings. From the heights of Père Lachaise to the Seine, the right bank rested on works fixed at the Etoile, under the guns of Vincennes and as far as redoubts in the Bercy park.

A caponier of eight hundred toises joined the Trône gate to the Etoile redoubt. This caponier was already built; the road was raised and trimmed with two good walls. These works were completely finished and armed with six hundred guns by 1 June.

General Haxo had marked out the works on the left bank of the Seine from [a point] opposite Bercy to the gate beyond the Military School: it was completed in a fortnight. This system of fortifications on the two banks was interconnected by following the right bank of the Seine by way of Saint-Cloud, Neuilly and Saint-Denis.

The city being thus protected, a fort had to be constructed surrounding the Arc de Triomphe de l'Etoile, resting its right on the batteries of Montmartre and its left on the works constructed on the heights of the Passy gate. This provided cross fire, with the works set up in the direction of the Military School on the other bank, to the Belleville fronts situated on the topmost crest on the Paris side, in such a way that the troops could rally there, and prevent the enemy, once they had forced the precincts, from exposing Paris on this side.

In a system of permanent fortifications for this city, it would be necessary to extend the inundations over all the low lying parts, and to hold the bridgeheads of Charenton and Neuilly, that is to say the Calvary height, by small forts, so that the army could manoeuvre on the two banks of the Marne and the Seine.

Its artillery parks, for the right and left banks, were divided. The 6, 12 and 18 calibre guns were adopted for the left bank; those of 4, 8, 16 and 24 for the right bank, so as to avoid confusion over calibres. Generals, colonels, and a large number of artillery officers were specifically allocated to the running of this service, as well as two naval gunner battalions, brought from the sea coasts (sixteen hundred men in all), fourteen companies of artillery of the line

MILITARY STATE OF FRANCE

(amounting to fifteen hundred men), and twenty National Guard artillery companies, some volunteers from the Charenton and Polytechnic Schools and from the Lycées—between 5,000 and 6,000 trained gunners, easily capable of manning a thousand guns.

Four hundred steel guns of 24, 18, 12 and 6 calibres had arrived from Le Havre, sent out from the naval arsenals. They were set up in batteries; six hundred bronze field pieces were destined for the same purpose. Twenty harnessed field batteries, forming four reserves of five batteries each, were conveniently distributed so as to be able to go to any point of the line, whether to the Belleville entrenchments, or to the banks of the Seine, if these were threatened. Independently of these 6,000 gunners, 55,000 men sufficed for the defence of the precincts, and Paris presented a strength of more than 100,000 men without weakening the army of the line.

6

The divisional Engineer General Lery supervised the works at Lyons. This place, situated at the junction of the Saône and Rhône, is naturally strong. He constructed a bridgehead at Bretaux, on the left bank of the Rhône, to cover the Morand bridge. He covered the Guillotière bridge with a tambour, and had a drawbridge fixed in the middle arch.

The suburb of la Guillotière is outside the defences of the town, but inhabited by a population full of patriotism and courage. We thought it advisable to protect it by a system of redoubts which would enable it to be defended for a long time. The old precincts, on the right bank of the Saône, runs along the top of hills and along Pierre-Encise; it was then raised in the same way as that between the Saône and Rhône: the true point of attack on Lyons is on the approaches between the two rivers. The engineer provided three positions forward by field forts, which were flanked by the walls and flanked each other.

A hundred naval guns brought from Toulon, and a hundred and fifty bronze field pieces, were set up in batteries. By 25 June all these works were thrown up, palisaded and armed. A battalion of naval gunners six hundred strong, and nine companies of artillery of the line amounting to a thousand men, and nine hundred gunners drawn from the National Guard, from the Veterinary School, and from the Lycées, brought the number of gunners up to 2,500, which was more than was needed to man the guns. A large artillery general-staff had been sent, and considerable stores of provisions had been accumulated there. Fifteen to twenty thousand men were enough to defend Lyons: 30,000 could be counted on without weakening the army of the line.

Chapter XL

PLAN OF CAMPAIGN

Could the French Army begin hostilities on 1 April? Three Plans of Campaign. First project: remain on the defensive and draw the enemy armies upon Paris and Lyons. Second project: take the offensive on 15 June and, in the event of not being successful, draw the enemies on Paris and Lyons. I adopt this plan of operations.

I

On the very night I arrived in Paris, I ordered General Excelmans at the head of 3,000 cavalry to follow the King's military retinue, seize it, break it up, or throw it quickly over the frontier. But this military retinue, composed of such heterogeneous elements, had already broken up of its own accord. The remnants were in part surrounded and disarmed at Béthune, the rest got as far as Neuve-Eglise where Count d'Artois gave it the order to disband. General Excelmans seized all the horses, magazines and baggage of this corps; the officers and guards, hunted down by the peasants, threw away their clothes and disguised themselves in every variety of costume, in order to elude the popular indignation.

A few days later Count Reille made his way to Flanders with 12,000 men to reinforce the troops of Count d'Erlon, who was garrisoning this frontier. I deliberated then whether, with these 35,000 to 36,000 men, I would begin hostilities on 1 April, by marching on Brussels and rallying the Belgian army to my standard. The English and Prussian armies were weak, scattered, without orders, without leaders, and without a plan; some of the officers were away on leave; the Duke of Wellington was in Vienna; Marshal Blücher was in Berlin. The French army could be in Brussels on 2 April.

PLAN OF CAMPAIGN

But, first, hopes of peace were entertained. France wanted it and would severely have blamed a premature offensive movement. Secondly, in order to bring together the 35,000 to 36,000 men, it would have been necessary to throw the twenty-three fortresses from Calais to Philippville, forming the Triple North Line, upon their own resources. If the public spirit of this frontier had been as good as that of Alsace, the Vosges, the Ardennes, or the Alps, this would not have involved any inconvenience. But sentiments were divided in Flanders; it was impossible to abandon the fortresses to local National Guards; a month was required to raise and bring from the neighbouring Departments picked battalions of the National Guard to replace the troops of the line. Thirdly, and finally, the Duke d'Angoulême was marching on Lyons, and the Marseillais on Grenoble. The first news of the commencement of hostilities would have encouraged the malcontents; it was above all essential that the Bourbons should have abandoned the territory, and that all the French should be united; which only came about by 20 April.

2

During the course of May, when France was pacified and when there was no longer any hope of maintaining peace abroad, and the armies of the different powers were on the march to the French frontiers, I meditated on the plan of campaign I had to follow. Three plans presented themselves:

The first plan was to remain on the defensive, letting the allies take upon themselves the odium of aggression, attacking our fortresses, penetrating as far as Paris and Lyons, and to begin around these two bases a lively and decisive war. This project had plenty of advantages.

First, the allies, not being able to start a campaign before 15 July, would not arrive before Paris and Lyons before 15 August. The 1st, 2nd, 3rd, 4th, 5th, 6th Corps, the four corps of heavy cavalry, and the Guard were concentrating about Paris. These corps had, on 15 June, 140,000 men under arms. By 15 August they would have had 240,000. The 1st Reconnaissance, or 'Jura', Corps, and the 7th Corps would concentrate on Lyons. They had, on 15 June 25,000 men under arms and would have, by 15 August, 60,000.

Secondly, the fortifications of Paris and Lyons would be completed and perfected by 15 August.

Thirdly, by this period there would have been time to complete the organization and arming of the forces destined for the defence of Paris and Lyons, to reduce the Paris National Guard to 8,000 men, and to quadruple the sharpshooters of this capital, bringing them up to 60,000 men. These battalions of sharpshooters having officers of the line would give valuable service; and they, joined with 6,000 gunners of the line, of the navy, of the National Guard, and to 40,000 men from the depots of seventy infantry regiments and

PLAN OF CAMPAIGN

from the non-uniformed guard belonging to the corps of the Paris army, would bring up to 116,000 men the force designed to guard the entrenched encampment of Paris. At Lyons the garrison would be comprised of 4,000 National Guards, 12,000 sharpshooters, 2,000 gunners, and 7,000 men from the depots of the eleven infantry regiments of the army based at Lyons—total, 25,000 men.

Fourthly, the enemy armies, which would penetrate to Paris by the north and east, would be obliged to leave 150,000 men before the forty-two fortresses of these two frontiers. Putting the strength of the enemy armies at 600,000 men, they would be reduced to 450,000 men by the time of their arrival in front of Paris. The allied armies which would penetrate to Lyons would be obliged to watch the ten strong-points of the frontier of the Jura and the Alps. Reckoning them at 150,000 men, they would scarcely be 100,000 strong on arriving before Lyons.

Fifthly, on the other hand, the national crisis having reached its peak would produce great activity in Normandy, Brittany, Auvergne, Berry, etc. Numerous battalions would be arriving every day at Paris. The process would be one of continuous increase on the French side and of diminution on the allies' side.

Sixthly, 240,000 men under my command, manoeuvring on the two banks of the Seine and the Marne, protected by the vast entrenched camp of Paris, guarded by 116,000 immobile troops, would emerge victorious in an encounter with 450,000 of the enemy. Sixty thousand men, commanded by Marshal Suchet, manoeuvring on the two banks of the Rhône and the Saône, under the protection of Lyons, guarded by 25,000 immobile men, would overcome the enemy army. The sacred cause of the country would triumph!

3

The second plan was to forestall the allies and begin hostilities before they could be ready. Now, the allies could not begin hostilities before 15 July. It was necessary, therefore, to start the campaign on 15 June; beat the Anglo-Dutch army and the Prusso-Saxon army, which were in Belgium, before the Russian, Austrian, Bavarian and Würtemberg armies, etc., should reach the Rhine. By 15 June it was possible to assemble an army of 140,000 men in Flanders, while leaving a cordon on all the frontiers, and good garrisons in all the fortresses.

First, if the Anglo-Dutch army and the Prusso-Saxon army were beaten, Belgium would rise and its army would become part of the French army. Secondly, the defeat of the English army would bring with it the fall of the English Government, which would be replaced by the friends of peace,

PLAN OF CAMPAIGN

liberty, and the independence of nations. This fact alone would put an end to the war.

Thirdly, if events turned out otherwise, the army, victorious in Belgium, reinforced by the 5th Corps, which remained in Alsace, and the reinforcements which depots would provide during June and July, would move on to the Vosges against the Russian and Austrian army.

Fourthly, the advantages of this project were numerous; it was in keeping with the genius of the nation, the spirit and principles of this war. It would avoid the terrible inconvenience, attached to the first project, of abandoning Flanders, Picardy, Artois, Alsace-Lorraine, Champagne, Burgundy, Franche Comté and Dauphiné, without firing a single shot.

But was it possible, with an army of 140,000 men, to beat the two armies which were covering Belgium, namely, the Anglo-Dutch army comprising 104,000 men under arms, and the Prusso-Saxon army of 120,000 men; that is to say, 224,000 men? It was not right to evaluate the strength of these armies in the ratio of 224,000 to 140,000, because the army of the allies was composed of troops varying in quality. One Englishman, or two Dutchmen, or two Prussians, or two men of the Confederation could be counted as equivalent to one Frenchman. The enemy armies were quartered under the command of two different generals and formed from nations divided in interest and opinion.

4

The month of May was passed in these meditations. The revolt of Vendée weakened the army of Flanders by 12,000 men, and reduced it to 120,000. This was a dire fact which diminished the chances of success. But the war of Vendée might spread. The Allies, masters of several provinces, would be able to rally supporters to the Bourbons; the march of the enemy on Paris and Lyons would favour them. On the other hand, Belgium and the four departments of the Rhine were stretching out their hands, calling for their liberator, and we had good sources of information in the Belgian army, all of which decided me to adopt a third course, which consisted in attacking the Anglo-Dutch and Prusso-Saxon armies on 15 June, in dividing them, beating them, and, if I failed, in withdrawing my army on to Paris and Lyons. Without doubt, after having failed in the attack on Belgium, the army would arrive back on Paris in a weakened condition. The opportunity would be lost of reducing the National Guard of the capital to 8,000 men from the existing 36,000, in order to bring the sharpshooters up to 60,000, because this operation could not be done in my absence and during the war.

It is true to say also that the Allies who, if waited for, would not begin hostilities before 15 July, would be ready by 1 July, if challenged as early as

PLAN OF CAMPAIGN

15 June; that their march on Paris would be all the quicker after victory; and that the army of Flanders, reduced to 120,000 men, was smaller by 90,000 than that of Marshal Blücher and the Duke of Wellington. But in 1814, France, with 40,000 men under arms, had confronted the army commanded by Marshal Blücher and that commanded by the Prince of Schwarzenberg, with the two Emperors and the King of Prussia present. These united armies were 250,000 men strong and yet France had beaten them often! At the battle of Montmirail the corps of Sacken, York and Kleist amounted to 40,000 men; they were attacked, beaten and thrown beyond the Marne by 16,000 Frenchmen, namely, the Foot and Mounted Guard, the Ricard Division of 1,150 men, and a Division of Cuirassiers; while Marshal Blücher, with 20,000 men was held by Marmont's corps of 4,000 men, and the army of Schwarzenberg 100,000 strong was held by the corps of Macdonald, Oudinot and Gérard, comprising, in all, less than 18,000 men.

The Duke of Dalmatia was appointed chief of staff to the army. On 2 June he gave the following order of the day,* and immediately afterwards left Paris to inspect the fortresses in Flanders and the army: 'Our Institutions have just been consecrated by the most august ceremony. The Emperor has received from the People's deputies, and from deputations of all the corps in the army, the expression of the good will of the whole nation on the Supplementary Act to the constitution of the Empire which had been submitted to him for acceptance, and a new oath unites France and the Emperor. Thus destiny fulfils itself, and all the efforts of an impious league are unable any longer to separate the interests of a great people from the hero whose brilliant triumphs have made him the admiration of the universe.

'It is at the moment when the national will expresses itself with so much energy that war-cries are heard. It is at the moment when France is at peace with all Europe that foreign armies advance on our frontiers. What is the hope of this new coalition? Does it want to drive France out of the ranks of the nations? Does it want to plunge 28,000,000 of Frenchmen into servitude? Has it forgotten that the first league that was formed against our independence contributed to our aggrandisement and our glory? A hundred smashing victories, which momentary reverses and unfortunate circumstances have not been able to efface, remind it that a free nation, led by a great man, is invincible.

'Everyone in France is a soldier when the national honour and liberty are at stake; a common interest to-day unites all Frenchmen. The pledges which were wrung from us by force are cancelled by the flight of the Bourbons from French territory, by the appeal which they have made to the foreign armies in order to remount the throne which they have abandoned, and by the unanimous wish of the nation which, in resuming the free exercise of its rights, has solemnly disavowed everything that has been done without its participation.

* Moniteur of 4 June, 1815.

PLAN OF CAMPAIGN

'The French cannot accept laws from abroad. Even those who have gone abroad to beg for assistance in killing their own kith and kin, like their predecessors will not be slow to recognize and feel that contempt and infamy follow their footsteps, and that they cannot wash themselves free of the opprobrium with which they are covered except by re-entering our ranks.

'But a new career of glory opens up before the army; history will consecrate the memory of the military deeds which will render illustrious the defenders of the country and of the national honour. The enemy is numerous, it is said. What does that matter to us? It will be all the more glorious to defeat them and their defeat will be all the more resounding. The struggle which is about to begin is not beyond the genius of Napoleon, nor above our strength. Can not all the Departments be seen vying with each other in enthusiasm and devotion, forming as if by magic five hundred separate battalions of National Guards, who have already come forward to double our ranks, defend our fortifications, and associate themselves with the glory of the army? It is the enthusiasm of a great-hearted people, which no power can conquer, and which posterity will admire. To arms!

'Soon the signal will be given. Let each man do his duty. From the array of the enemies our victorious phalanxes are going to win a new renown. Soldiers! Napoleon guides our steps. We are fighting for the independence of our beautiful country. We are invincible.'

Chapter XLI

OPENING OF THE CAMPAIGN, JUNE, 1815

State and position of the French army on the evening of 14 June. State and position of the Anglo-Dutch and Prusso-Saxon armies. Manoeuvres and fighting during the day of the 15th. Position of the belligerent armies during the night of the 15th to 16th.

I

The Fourth Corps, commanded by Count Gérard, left Metz on 6 June, crossed the Meuse, and reached Philippeville on the 14th. (Lieutenant-General Count *Gérard* commanded the 4th Corps. Lieutenant-General Count *Girard* commanded the 3rd Division of the 2nd Corps. To avoid confusion, I shall give the title of 'Count' to General *Gérard*, and write his name in capital letters. I shall give the title of 'General' to General *Girard* and write his name in ordinary letters.)

Count Belliard took over the command of Metz and the Saar frontier. He was at pains to mask the movement of the 4th Corps, by occupying the frontier with detachments of picked battalions of the National Guard, drawn from the garrison of Metz, Longwy, Sarre-Louis, etc., and by the volunteer corps, all ready clothed and organized, which had been raised in these departments.

The Imperial Guard left Paris on 8 June, and moved on to Avesnes. The 1st Corps left the neighbourhood of Lille, and the 2nd Corps that of Valenciennes, to place themselves between Maubeuge and Avesnes. The garrisons of all the fortresses from Dunkirk masked this movement by occupying the exits with strong detachments, in such a way that, at the moment when the units of this frontier were concentrating, the advance-posts were trebled, and

OPENING OF THE CAMPAIGN, JUNE, 1815

the enemy misled, thinking that the whole army was forming on the left. The 6th Corps left Laon and moved on Avesnes; the four reserve cavalry corps were massed on the Sambre.

I left Paris on the 12th in the morning, lunched at Soissons, slept at Laon, gave my last orders for the armament of this place, and arrived on the 13th at Avesnes. On the evening of the 14th, the army camped in three areas: the left, more than 40,000 strong, composed of the 2nd and 1st Corps, on the right bank of the Sambre at Ham-sur-Eure, and at Solre-sur-Sambre; the centre, of more than 60,000 men, composed of the 3rd and 6th Corps, of the Imperial Guard, and of the cavalry reserves, at Beaumont, where G.H.Q. was set up; the right, of more than 15,000 men, formed by the 4th Corps and a division of Cuirassiers, in front of Philippeville.

The camps were established behind hillocks a league from the frontier, in such a way that the fires were not seen by the enemy, who, indeed, had no knowledge of them. On the evening of the 14th, the roll-calls verified that the strength of the army was 122,000 men, and three hundred and fifty guns, made up as follows:*

Left wing (on the right bank of the Sambre): Infantry, 37,400; Cavalry, 2,800; Artillery, etc., 3,128. Total, 43, 328 men, 92 guns.

Centre (at Beaumont): Infantry, 35,100; Cavalry, 16,000; Artillery, etc., 11,634. Total, 63,734 men, 220 guns.

Right wing (before Philippeville): Infantry, 12,100; Cavalry, 2,800; Artillery, etc., 1,442. Total, 16,342 men, 44 guns.

Grand total, 122,404 men and 350 guns.

On the 14th in the evening, I addressed the army in the following Order of the Day: 'Soldiers, to-day is the anniversary of Marengo and of Friedland, which on two occasions decided the destiny of Europe. Then, as after Austerlitz, as after Wagram, we were too generous! We believed in the protestations and oaths of princes whom we left on their thrones. To-day, however, in a coalition against us, they grudge the independence and the most sacred rights of France. They have started on the most unjust of aggressions. Let us march, therefore, to encounter them. Are not we and they the same men as before?

'Soldiers! At Jena, against these same Prussians, to-day so arrogant, you were one to two, and at Montmirail one to three.

'Let those among you who have been prisoners of the English tell you the story of their galleys and of the fearful wrongs that they have suffered.

'The Saxons, the Belgians, the Hanoverians, the Soldiers of the Confederation of the Rhine, groan at being obliged to support the cause of princes who are enemies of justice and the rights of all peoples. They know that this

* I have omitted the long detailed schedule of corps and other establishments and substituted a brief summary.—S. de C.

OPENING OF THE CAMPAIGN, JUNE, 1815

Coalition is insatiable! After having swallowed up 12,000,000 Poles, 12,000,000 Italians, 1,000,000 Saxons, 6,000,000 Belgians, it will inevitably swallow up the second-class States of Germany.

'The fools! A moment of success blinds them. The ability to oppress and humiliate the French people is beyond their power! If they enter France they will find their graves there.

'Soldiers! we shall have to make some forced marches, fight some battles, run some risks; but with constancy, victory will be ours; the rights, the honour and the happiness of the country will be reconquered.

'For every Frenchman who has courage, the moment has come to conquer or die.'

2

The enemy armies on the evening of the 14th were quite quiet in their billets. The Prusso-Saxon army formed the left, and the Anglo-Dutch army the right. The former, commanded by Marshal Blücher, was 120,000 strong, formed as follows: 85,000 infantrymen, 20,000 cavalry, 15,000 in the artillery, engineers, military stores, 300 guns. It was divided into four corps: the 1st commanded by General Zwietten, resting on the English encampments, lined the Sambre, with its head-quarters at Charleroi, and with Fleurus as its rallying point. The 2nd, under the orders of General Pirch, was quartered on the frontier in the neighbourhood of Namur, which was its rallying point. The 3rd, commanded by General Thielman, lined the Meuse in the neighbourhood of Dinant, and was to concentrate on Ciney. Finally, the 4th Corps, under the orders of General Bülow, was in rear of the three others, with its head-quarters at Liége. Half a day was needed for the assembly of each corps. The army was to assemble in the rear of Fleurus. The 1st Corps was there already; the 2nd from Namur had eight leagues to cover; the 3rd from Ciney fourteen leagues; the 4th at Ham, sixteen. Marshal Blücher's head-quarters were at Namur, separated from the Duke of Wellington's, which were at Brussels, by sixteen leagues.

The Anglo-Dutch army, under the orders of the Duke of Wellington, was formed by twenty-four brigades, of which nine were English, ten German,[1] five Dutch and Belgian; and by eleven cavalry divisions composed of sixteen English regiments, nine German,[2] six Dutch.

Its strength was 104,200 men, made up as follows:

English: Infantry, 22,000; Cavalry, 10,000; Artillery, engineers, storemen and tradesmen, 5,000. Total, 37,000.

[1] Namely: Two Germanic legions in the pay of England, five Hanoverian, one of Nassau, and two of Brunswick.
[2] Namely: Five Germanic legions, three Hanoverian, one of Brunswick.

OPENING OF THE CAMPAIGN, JUNE, 1815

Germans: Infantry (16,000 Hanoverians, 6,000 Germanic League, 4,000 Nassau, 6,000 Brunswick), 32,000; Cavalry (2,000 Hanoverians, 3,000 Germanic League, 1,800 Brunswick), 6,800; Artillery, etc., 3,200. Total, 42,000.

Dutch and Belgians: Infantry, 19,000; Cavalry, 3,200; Artillery, etc., 3,000. Total, 25,200.

Total in each arm: Infantry, 73,000; Cavalry, 20,000; Artillery, etc., 11,200. Grand total, 104,200 men, 250 guns.

This does not include eight English regiments coming from America which had disembarked at Ostend; and, in addition, an English regiment at Nieuport, a battalion of veterans at Ostend, and the 9th, 25th, 29th and 37th English regiments in the fortresses along the Belgian frontier, where considerable bodies of militia had been assembled. The nine English brigades, the five Hanoverian brigades, and the two brigades of the Germanic legion, formed six divisions, called English divisions. The five Dutch brigades and the brigade from Nassau formed three, called Belgian divisions. The troops from Brunswick formed one.

These ten divisions were split up into two large infantry corps: the 1st, under the orders of the Prince of Orange, whose head-quarters were at Braine-le-Comte, was composed of five divisions, of which two were English, the Guards and the 3rd Division, and three Belgian divisions. Their assembly points were Enghien, Soignes, Braine-le-Comte and Nivelles. The 2nd Corps, commanded by Lord Hill, whose head-quarters were at Brussels, was composed of five divisions, four English and the Brunswick troops. Their assembly points were at Brussels, Ath, Hal and Ghent. Lord Uxbridge commanded the cavalry; his assembly point was Grammont. The general park of artillery was dispersed around Ghent.

Half a day was needed for each division to reach its assembly point. The concentration point of the army was at Quatre-Bras in order to be at a point two leagues from the right of the Prussian army. It was six leagues from the head-quarters of the Prince of Orange to Quatre-Bras, from Nivelles two and a half, from Enghien thirteen, from Soignes eleven, from Brussels (G.H.Q. of the army) eight leagues, from Ghent seventeen, from Grammont thirteen, from Ath thirteen. It required, therefore, two whole days for the two armies to effect a junction on a battle-field. Once reunited, they presented a strength of 224,200 men (without counting fourteen English regiments at Ostend or in the fortresses) made up as follows:

Infantry: Anglo-Dutch, 73,000; Prusso-Saxon, 85,000. Total, 158,000.
Cavalry: Anglo-Dutch, 20,000; Prusso-Saxon, 20,000. Total, 40,000.
Artillery: Anglo-Dutch, 11,200; Prusso-Saxon, 15,000. Total, 26,000.
Guns: Anglo-Dutch, 225; Prusso-Saxon, 288. Total, 543.

During the night of the 14th to 15th, secret agents returning to the French head-quarters at Beaumont stated that everything was quiet at Namur,

OPENING OF THE CAMPAIGN, JUNE, 1815

Brussels and Charleroi. This was a happy omen. It was already a great achievement to have succeeded in concealing from the enemy the movements which the French army had been making for two days. The Prussian army found itself already obliged to choose an assembly point further in the rear than Fleurus, or to accept battle in this position without the possibility of assistance from the Anglo-Dutch army.

The characters of the enemy commanders were very different. The hussar habits of Marshal Blücher, his restlessness and dare-devil character contrasted strongly with the cautious character and slow marches of the Duke of Wellington. If the Prusso-Saxon army were not the first to be attacked, it would put more energy and speed into hastening to the help of the Anglo-Dutch army, than would the latter in aiding Marshal Blücher. All my measures had therefore the objective of attacking the Prussians first.

3

On the 15th, at first light, the three French columns began their march. The advance-guard of the left, formed by Prince Jerome's division of the 2nd Corps on leaving its camp ran into the advance-guard of the Prussian corps under General Zwietten, overthrew it, and seized the bridge of Marchiennes, taking five hundred prisoners. The Prussian advance-guard rallied on Charleroi. General Pajol's cavalry corps, forming the advance guard of the centre, moved off at three in the morning. It was to be supported by General Vandamme's infantry corps.

From Beaumont to Charleroi there is no road to facilitate movement on the bad stretches, where defiles were encountered every few yards. The 3rd Corps had been camped a league and a half to the right of Beaumont. At six in the morning, Count Vandamme was still in his camp, although he should have left it at the same time as Pajol's cavalry. Having been apprized of this fact, I took the lead with my Guard and entered Charleroi at noon, being preceded by General Pajol's light cavalry, which was following the enemy with drawn swords. General Vandamme's corps did not get there till three o'clock.

The right, commanded by Count GERARD, took the bridge of Châtelet by surprise, early in the morning; the whole column arrived during the evening. From Charleroi to Brussels is fourteen leagues; a main road connects them, and passes through Gosselies, Frasnes, Quatre-Bras, Gennapes and Waterloo. Five hundred toises from Charleroi, another highway bends away to the right, and leads by way of Gilly to Namur, eight leagues distant from Charleroi.

Zwietten's corps, informed by its hussars of the movements of the French army, evacuated Charleroi in all haste by these two routes. One division withdrew by the Brussels highway, and stopped at Gosselies. Another took

OPENING OF THE CAMPAIGN, JUNE, 1815

the road to Namur and stopped at Gilly. General Pajol followed the enemy along the Namur Road. General Clary with a brigade of Hussars, followed it on the Brussels road. The troops were then skirmishing along these two roads. General Clary, not being strong enough, was supported by General Lefebvre-Desnouettes, with the Light Cavalry of the Guard and its two batteries. The Duhesme division of the Young Foot Guard, placed itself in reserve in the rear of Pajol's cavalry, and detached a regiment to take up its position half-way between Charleroi and Gosselies, acting as reserve to General Lefebvre-Desnouette's cavalry. Count Reille crossed the Sambre by the bridge at Marchiennes, and moved on Gosselies to join the Brussels road there and push on thence to Quatre-Bras. General Count d'Erlon had orders to support General Reille. Marshal Grouchy, as soon as he had debouched on to Charleroi with the cavalry reserves, followed by the 3rd Army Corps, moved on Gilly, which General Zwietten evacuated in order to take up a position between Gilly and Fleurus, with his back to a wood. General Reille obtained possession of Gosselies after slight resistance.

Marshal Ney had just reached the battlefield. I immediately gave him the order to go to Gosselies and take over the command there of the whole of the left composed of the 2nd and 1st Corps, of Lefebvre-Desnouette's cavalry division, and of General Kellermann's corps of heavy cavalry, comprising in all 47,800 men; and to charge like a bull at anything he met on the Gosselies-Brussels road; to take up a position astride this road beyond Quatre-Bras and to hold his position in the military sense, keeping strong advance-guards on the Brussels, Namur and Nivelles roads.

The division of General Zwietten's corps which had defended Gosselies withdrew by a left-wheel on Fleurus. Count Reille sent the 3rd Division, which General Girard commanded, in pursuit, and marched on Quatre-Bras with his cavalry and three other divisions.

Prince Bernard of Saxe commanded a brigade of 4,000 Nassau troops (this was the 2nd Brigade of the 3rd Belgian Division). As soon as he heard gunfire in the Charleroi direction, and was told of General Zwietten's retreat he moved on to Frasnes, and established himself there a thousand toises in advance of Quatre-Bras, astride the Brussels road. General Lefebvre-Desnouettes, after a light cannonade, having threatened to turn his position and cut him off from Quatre-Bras, forced him to withdraw. He took up a position between Quatre-Bras and Gennapes. Count Reille marched with his infantry without encountering any opposition, in order to camp before Quatre-Bras, when he was joined by Marshal Ney, who, having heard the cannonade in the Fleurus direction, and received General Girard's report that there were considerable forces in this direction, thought it wise to take up a position with his advance-guard at Frasnes, with scouts at Quatre-Bras.

The corps of Vandamme and Grouchy were both at Gilly. Misled by false

505

reports they wasted two hours without moving, in the belief that 200,000 Prussians were behind the woods and in front of Fleurus. I made a personal reconnaissance of the enemy and, judging that these woods were only occupied by two divisions of Zwietten's corps, consisting of between 18,000 and 20,000 men, I forthwith gave the order to move forward. The enemy started to withdraw, and was vigorously pursued. A charge by the four squadrons detailed for action, which were led by General Letort, forced two squares and destroyed the 28th Prussian regiment; but the intrepid Letort was fatally wounded. This general was one of the most distinguished cavalry officers. No one was braver. No officer possessed in a higher degree the art of carrying off a charge, and of communicating the electric spark to men and horses alike. At his word, by his example, the most hesitant were transformed into the most intrepid.

When night came, the corps of Vandamme and Grouchy took up positions in the woods of Trichenaye and Lambusart near Fleurus.

4

During the night of the 15th to the 16th, the French G.H.Q. was at Charleroi, Marshal Blücher's at Namur, and the Duke of Wellington's at Brussels. The 1st Corps of the Prusso-Saxon army, commanded by General Zwietten, weakened by 2,000 men whom he had lost during the day, was concentrated on the heights behind Fleurus, occupying this village with a detachment. The 2nd Corps, which had rallied at Namur, marched all night to catch up with the 1st at Sombref. The 3rd Corps had assembled, partly at Namur, partly at Ciney. The first part marched all night and reached Sombref during the morning of the 16th. The second part was not able to arrive until the afternoon of the 16th, during the battle. The 4th Corps, commanded by General Bülow, not having been ordered to muster until very late, in view of the distances, could not begin to move until the 16th; it did not reach Gembloux, two leagues from Sombref, until after the battle was lost, during the night of the 16th to 17th.

On the 15th, at about 7 o'clock in the evening, the Duke of Wellington had received a despatch rider from Marshal Blücher, who informed him that hostilities had begun, that a strong French reconnaissance had sabred some of his advance posts. This did not seem to him to require any action, other than to pass the order all along the line to be on the alert. At eleven o'clock in the evening, a second despatch rider from Marshal Blücher had brought him the news that the French had entered Charleroi at 11 a.m. on the 15th and were marching on a wide front on Brussels; that all the area bounded by Marchiennes, Charleroi, and Châtelet was covered with bridges and troops; that the French army was 150,000 men strong; and that I was at its head. He sent

OPENING OF THE CAMPAÏGN, JUNE, 1815

out orders with all despatch that the troops were to strike camp in all billets, and that each division was to rally at its concentration point and await further orders there. The 3rd Belgian division, which, alone of the Anglo-Dutch army, was quartered within less than six leagues of Quatre-Bras, was the only one which could be got there during the morning of the 16th. Four other divisions, which were within nine leagues, could be got there during the evening of the same day; but the rest of the army, twelve, thirteen, fourteen, seventeen, and nineteen leagues off, could not be assembled there before the night of the 16th to 17th and during the day of the 17th. The artillery and cavalry were in the latter predicament; and, even when assembled at Quatre-Bras, the Anglo-Dutch army would still be two leagues from Fleurus. During the night the alarm was sounded at Brussels. The Brunswick Division and the 5th English Division, who were there, began to march on Quatre-Bras during the morning.

The French army spent the night in three columns; the left, commanded by Marshal Ney, had its head-quarters at Gosselies, with its scouts at Quatre-Bras, and its advance-guard at Frasnes: the 2nd Corps between Frasnes and Gosselies, with General Girard's division as advance-guard on the right along the Fleurus road; the 1st Corps in column from Marchiennes to Gosselies. The centre, composed of the cavalry reserve and the 3rd Corps, was camped in the wood between Fleurus and Charleroi: the Guard was in columns on the road from Charleroi to Gilly and the 6th Corps beyond Charleroi. The 3rd column, forming the right, was in advance of the Châtelet bridge. The whole army was thus united, having crossed the Sambre by three bridges: the left by that at Marchiennes, separated by two thousand toises from that at Charleroi, which the centre had crossed. This was three thousand toises from the Châtelet bridge across which the right had passed.

The French army bivouaced during the night of the 15th to 16th in a square with sides four leagues long. It was equally well placed to press upon the Prusso-Saxon army or the Anglo-Dutch one; it was already placed between them. The two enemy armies were taken by surprise, their communications already considerably embarrassed. All my manoeuvres had succeeded as I wished. I could now take the initiative of attacking the enemy armies, one by one. Their only chance of avoiding this misfortune, the worst of all, was to yield ground and rally on Brussels, or beyond.

Chapter XLII

THE BATTLE OF LIGNY

Marches made by the French army to give battle to the Prusso-Saxon army. Battle of Ligny, 16 June. Engagement at Quatre-Bras, 16 June. Position of the armies during the night of the 16th to 17th. Their manoeuvres during the day of the 17th. Their positions during the night of 17 to 18 June.

I

Marshal Ney received the order, during the night, to move at first light on the 16th beyond Quatre-Bras and to take up a good position astride the Brussels road, guarding the Nivelles and Namur roads with his left and right wings. Count de Flahaut, general aide-de-camp, carried these orders and spent the whole day with the marshal. General Girard's division, the 3rd of the 2nd Corps, which was in a watching position opposite Fleurus, received orders to remain in this position, with the duty of operating under my direct orders. With the centre and right of the army, I marched to fight the Prussian army, before its 4th Corps, under General Bülow, could join it, and before the Anglo-Dutch army was in position on its right.

The sharp-shooters made contact at the village of Fleurus. After a few cannon-shots, the enemy sharp-shooters withdrew on to their army, which was then to be seen in action, with its left at the village of Sombref astride the Namur road, its centre at the village of Ligny, its right at the village of Saint-Amand, and its reserves on the heights of the Bry windmill, occupying a line three thousand toises in length.

The French army halted and formed up: it was ten o'clock in the morning. The 3rd Corps was in front of Fleurus, having the Girard division at a distance

THE BATTLE OF LIGNY

of twelve hundred toises on its left, the 4th Corps in the centre, and Marshal Grouchy with the Cavalry Corps of Pajol and Excelmans on the right. The Guard, cavalry, infantry, artillery, and the corps of Milhaud's cuirassiers, formed up in second line on the curtain of trees which dominates the plain behind Fleurus.

With very few attendants I toured the line of the outposts, climbed heights and windmills, and obtained a perfect reconnaissance of the enemy army. It presented a strength of certainly more than 80,000 men. Its front was covered by a deep ravine, its right was in the air. The battle front was at right angles to the Namur highway, at Quatre-Bras, and in the direction of Sombref to Gosselies. The point of Quatre-Bras was at right angles in rear of the centre of the line. It is clear that Marshal Blücher was not expecting to be attacked on that day. He believed that he had time to complete the assembly of his army and to be supported on his right by the Anglo-Dutch army, which was to debouch on to Quatre-Bras by the Brussels and Nivelles highways during the day of the 17th.

A staff officer on the left reported that Marshal Ney, at the moment when he was getting ready to march to the position in front of Quatre-Bras, had been stopped by the cannonade, which could be heard on his right flank, and by the reports which he had received to the effect that the two Anglo-Dutch and Prusso-Saxon armies had already effected their junction in the Fleurus area; that in this state of affairs, if he proceeded with his movement he would be turned; and, moreover, that he was ready to carry out such orders as I might send him as soon as I was aware of this new factor.

I blamed him for having already wasted eight hours. What he asserted to be a new factor had existed since the previous evening. I repeated the order to him to get in front of Quatre-Bras and, as soon as he should be in position, to detach a column of 8,000 infantrymen, with Lefebvre-Desnouettes' cavalry division and twenty-eight guns, by way of the Quatre-Bras-Namur road. This division should leave this road at the village of Marchais, in order to attack the heights of Bry in rear of the enemy army. With this detachment gone, he would still have 32,000 men and eighty guns, which would be sufficient to hold in check the units of the English army which might arrive during the day of the 16th.

Marshal Ney received this order at half past eleven. He was with his advance-guard near Frasnes. He was to have taken up his position in front of Quatre-Bras by noon. Now, from Quatre-Bras to the heights of Bry is four thousand toises. The column which he was to detach in the rear of Marshal Blücher ought therefore to reach the village of Marchais before two o'clock. The line which the army was holding near Fleurus was not an offensive one. Part of it was screened; the Prussian army must have been without anxiety.

THE BATTLE OF LIGNY

2

But at two o'clock I ordered a change of front facing Fleurus, with the right in advance. This manoeuvre brought the 3rd Corps to within two cannon-shots' distance of Saint-Amand, the 4th to within two cannon-shots of Ligny, the right to within two cannon-shots of Sombref. General Girard with the 3rd Division of the 2nd Corps found himself astride the end of the Prussian army's right. The ravine which covered the front of the enemy's position began between the 3rd Corps and Girard's division, in such a way that this division was on the left bank of this ravine. The Guard and Milhaud's cavalry carried out the same manoeuvre and found themselves in the second line at six hundred toises behind the 3rd and 4th Corps. The 6th Corps, which was on the way from Charleroi, received orders to speed up its march and to take up a position in front of Fleurus, as general reserve. Everything pointed to the destruction of the Prussian army. Count GERARD, having come up to me to ask for some instructions about attacking the village of Ligny, I told him 'It is possible that in three hours the issue of the war will be decided. If Ney carries out my orders well, not a single gun of the Prussian army will escape; it is caught red handed.' The French army at Ligny was 71,000 strong with two hundred and forty guns.

At three o'clock in the afternoon, the 3rd Corps assaulted the village of Saint-Amand. A quarter of an hour later, the 4th Corps assaulted the village of Ligny, and Marshal Grouchy bent back the left of the Prussian army. All the positions and houses situated on the right of the ravine were taken, and the enemy army thrown back on to the left bank.

The remainder of the 3rd Corps of the Prussian army arrived during the battle by way of the village of Sombref, which brought the strength of the enemy army up to 90,000 men. The French army, including the 6th Corps, which remained throughout in reserve, was 70,000 men: less than 60,000 deployed.

The village of Ligny was taken and retaken four times. Count GERARD covered himself with glory there and displayed as much bravery as talent. The attack was weak at the village of Saint-Amand, which was also taken and retaken; but it was carried by General Girard, who, having received the order to advance by the left of the ravine with his division, the 3rd of the 2nd Corps, brought into play there that intrepidity of which he had shown so many examples during his military career. He overthrew at the point of the bayonet all who thought to oppose his advance, and took possession of half the village; but he fell, fatally wounded. The 5th Corps maintained themselves in the other half of this village.

It was half-past five, and I was having several manoeuvres carried out by the infantry and by my Guard, in order to bring it to bear on Ligny, when

THE BATTLE OF LIGNY

General Vandamme reported that a column of 30,000 men, infantry, cavalry and artillery was advancing on Fleurus, and that it had at first been mistaken for the column detached from the left; but, apart from the fact that it was much stronger, it was coming by a different route; that General Girard's men, having recognized it as enemy, had in consequence abandoned the end of the village and taken up a position at the wood, in order to cover Fleurus; that his 3rd Corps, itself, had been shaken by it, and that, if the reserve did not come up to check this column, he would be obliged to evacuate Saint-Amand and to beat a retreat.

The manoeuvre of this column appeared inexplicable. It had apparently passed between Marshal Ney and Marshal Blücher, or perhaps between Quatre-Bras and Charleroi. However, the information being repeated, I halted the march of the Guard and sent my aide-de-camp, General Dejean, a reliable officer, in all haste to reconnoitre the number, the strength, and the intentions of this column.

An hour later, it was known that this column, supposed to be English, was the 1st Corps commanded by Count d'Erlon, who, having been left in reserve two and a half leagues from Quatre-Bras, was hastening up to support the attack on Saint-Amand, and that General Girard's division, having been undeceived, had recovered its position again and the 3rd Corps its equanimity.

The Guard thereupon resumed its march on Ligny. General Pecheux, at the head of his division, crossed the ravine; Count GERARD, the whole of the Guard, infantry, cavalry, artillery and cuirassiers, and Milhaud's division supported his movement. All the enemy reserves were overwhelmed at the point of the bayonet; the centre of his line was pierced. Forty guns, eight flags or standards, and a good number of prisoners were the trophies of this day. Marshal Grouchy and Generals Excelmans and Pajol attracted notice by their intrepidity.

Lieutenant-General Monthion was given the task, during the night, of pursuing the Prussian left. The enemy, in his official reports, reckoned his losses at 25,000 men killed, wounded or missing; without counting 20,000 men who deserted and ravaged the banks of the Meuse as far as Liége. The Guard and the 6th Corps suffered no losses. These were heavy in the 4th Corps, and in the Cavalry Corps of Excelmans and Pajol, but much less so in the 3rd. Girard's division, of the 2nd Corps, lost more. The total losses were in the neighbourhood of 6,950 men, killed or wounded. Several enemy generals were killed or wounded. Marshal Blücher was overthrown by a charge of cuirassiers and trampled under the horses' feet; but the French cuirassiers continued their charge without seeing him; it was already night. This marshal managed to save himself, bruised and half maimed.

The disparity to be observed between the losses of the Prussian and French armies arises from the fact that the reserves of the French army were held,

THE BATTLE OF LIGNY

throughout the battle, beyond cannon range, and that the 3rd and 4th Corps which were in the front line, were masked by the folds in the ground, whereas the Prussian army was massed altogether on the amphitheatre which runs from Saint-Amand and Ligny to the heights of Bry. All the cannon-balls of the French army which missed the front lines, hit the reserves: not a shot was lost.

General Girard had distinguished himself at the crossing of the Tessino in 1800; he had made an important contribution to the winning of the battle of Lutzen in 1813; he was one of the most intrepid officers in the French army: he had, in a marked degree, the sacred spark.

I was so satisfied with Count GERARD, commanding the 4th Corps, that I intended to give him the baton of a Marshal of the Empire. I regarded him as one of the hopes of France.

3

The Prince of Orange whose head-quarters were at Braine-le-Comte, did not receive the Duke of Wellington's order to concentrate his troops till first light on the 16th. He proceeded with the 2nd Brigade of the 3rd Belgian Division to Quatre-Bras, in order to support one of the brigades which Prince Bernard of Saxony was commanding and which, since the 15th, had taken up a position between Quatre-Bras and Gennapes, after having defended Frasnes. The Prince of Orange remained all morning with 8,000 or 9,000 Belgian or Nassau troops, infantry, cavalry and artillery, in this important position.

He knew that the Anglo-Dutch army had struck camp and was moving on Quatre-Bras by the Brussels and Nivelles roads. He grasped the vital importance of this position, for, if the allies lost it, they could only effect their junction across country and behind Gennapes, since all their units came along the Nivelles highway. If, therefore, Marshal Ney had carried out his orders, and had gone, with his 43,000 men, at first light on the 16th to Quatre-Bras, he would have got possession of this position, and, with his numerous cavalry and light artillery, he would have routed and scattered this division. More than that, he would have been able to attack the divisions of the English army, on the march, which were isolated on the Nivelles and Brussels highways.

At noon this Marshal, having received the new orders which I sent him from Fleurus, marched with the three Infantry divisions of the 2nd Corps, a division of light cavalry, and a division of Kellermann's cuirassiers, in all 16,000 infantrymen, 3,000 cavalrymen and 45 guns (21,000 or 22,000 men).

He left the 1st Corps in reserve in front of Gosselies, to watch Fleurus and assure his line of retreat: 16,000 strong in infantry, with General Lefebvre-Desnouette's light cavalry division of the Guard and a cuirassier division of

THE BATTLE OF LIGNY

Kellermann's; a total of 16,000 infantrymen, 4,500 cavalrymen, and 64 guns.

His sharp-shooters were engaged at two o'clock, but it was not till three o'clock, when the cannonade of the battle at Ligny could be heard in all its ferocity, that he really got to grips with the enemy. The Prince of Orange and his division were soon overthrown; but it was supported by the Prince of Brunswick's Division, and the 5th English Division, which arrived helter-skelter. These two divisions had left Brussels at ten o'clock in the morning and had covered eight leagues; they had neither artillery nor cavalry.

The fight was renewed with vigour; the enemy had the superiority in numbers, since Marshal Ney's 2nd Line was three leagues in the rear, but the French artillery and cavalry were in much greater numbers. The Brunswick troops, repulsed, like those from Nassau, left plenty of dead, among whom was the reigning prince of Brunswick. The 42nd Highland Regiment of Picton's division, having formed itself into a square in order to withstand a charge by the cuirassiers, was smashed in and cut to pieces; its colonel was killed; its colours taken. The French sharp-shooters were already arriving at the farm of Quatre-Bras when the 1st English Guards Division and Alten's 3rd Division came up at the double on the Nivelles road; they too were without artillery and cavalry.*

At this juncture, Marshal Ney felt the need of his second line. He sent for it, but too late, for it was six o'clock; it could not arrive on the battle field before about eight o'clock. The Marshal, however, fought with his usual intrepidity; the French troops covered themselves with glory; and the enemy, although twice as strong in infantry, remaining much weaker in artillery and cavalry, could not make any headway; but he took advantage of the wood which flanked his position and held on to it until nightfall. Marshal Ney set up his head-quarters at Frasnes, a thousand toises from Quatre-Bras, with his line two cannon-shots from the enemy army. He was joined by the 1st Corps commanded by Count d'Erlon, whose movement by way of Saint-Amand had only delayed his arrival by half an hour.

The losses of the Anglo-Dutch army are reckoned at 9,000 men in the official reports. The losses of the French army were 3,400 men.

The reason for this disparity in losses can easily be appreciated when one reflects that the Anglo-Dutch army, deprived of artillery and cavalry, had to

---

* Summary of table given by Napoleon as a footnote: The Anglo-Dutch army at Quatre-Bras from 3 p.m. to 6 p.m. consisted of 25,200 infantry, 1,500 cavalry, and twelve pieces of artillery. Between 6 p.m. and 9 p.m. the arrival of General Cook's 1st Guards Division and General Alten's 3rd Division brought the infantry strength up to 37,500. The remainder of the army, the artillery and the cavalry arrived during the night of the 17th to 18th. S. de C.

THE BATTLE OF LIGNY

remain massed under the hail of grape-shot from fifty guns, which did not cease firing from three in the afternoon, till eight in the evening.

4

The 3rd Corps of the French army bivouaced on the battlefield before Saint-Amand, the 4th Corps in front of Ligny, Marshal Grouchy at Sombref, the Imperial Guard on the heights of Bry, the light cavalry having its advance posts as far forward as the Namur road, the 6th Corps in reserve behind Ligny.

Blücher beat a retreat on Wavres in two columns, one by way of Tilly, the other by Gembloux where the 4th Corps, commanded by General Bülow, coming from Liége, arrived at eleven p.m. The Prussian fugitives swarmed over the whole countryside and perpetrated the most horrible atrocities there. Namur, and the country between the Sambre and Meuse, were the victims of this. The defeat of these oppressors of Belgium and of the right bank of the Rhine filled the inhabitants of these thirteen departments, who already saw themselves restored to the great family of their affections, with hope and joy.

The Duke of Wellington spent the night at Quatre-Bras. The English troops continued to come up by the two roads. They were worn out. They had been on the march all the night of the 15th to 16th, the day of the 16th, and the night of the 16th to 17th.

5

At daylight on the 17th, General Pajol, with a division of his light cavalry corps and Teste's infantry division of the 6th Corps, set out in pursuit of the Prussian army, in the direction of Wavres, along the Tilly and Gembloux roads, and took a great number of wagons and numerous parks of limbers. Marshal Ney had received the order to go to Quatre-Bras at first light, and to attack the English vanguard briskly. Count de Lobau, with two infantry divisions of his corps, his light cavalry and Milhaud's cuirassiers, moved on Quatre-Bras by the Namur highway, in order to improve the chances of Marshal Ney's attack by taking the English army in flank.

Marshal Grouchy left with Excelman's cavalry corps and the 3rd and 4th infantry Corps, so as to support General Pajol, tread on Blücher's heels and prevent him from rallying. He had a definite order to remain throughout between the road from Charleroi to Brussels and Blücher, so as to keep continuously in touch with, and be in a position to join up with, the army. It was probable that Marshal Blücher would retire on Wavres: this order directed him to be there at the same time. If the enemy continued to march on Brussels, and spent the night covered by the forest of Soignes, he should have him fol-

THE BATTLE OF LIGNY

lowed right up to the edge of the forest. If he retired on the Meuse, in order to cover his communications with Germany, he should have him watched by General Pajol's advance-guard, and should occupy Wavres with Excelman's cavalry, the 3rd and 4th infantry Corps, in order to keep in touch with the head-quarters, which was marching on Brussels along the Charleroi road. The 3rd Division of the 2nd Corps, which had suffered heavily at the Battle of Ligny, remained to hold the battlefield and bring help to the wounded. Thus the French Army was marching on Brussels in two columns, one 69,000 strong and the other 34,000.

I visited the battlefield, and saw that assistance was given to the wounded. The Prussian losses were enormous; six of their corpses could be seen for every French corpse. A large number of wounded who had not received any assistance were attended to. All the pages* and several officers remained to watch over them. Young Gudin, the son of the brave general of this name, who was killed in Russia at the engagement of Valontina, distinguished himself by his active sympathy. This sacred duty fulfilled, I galloped on to reach Quatre-Bras at the same time as Count de Lobau's cavalry.

I came up with him at the village of Marchais; but on coming within sight of Quatre-Bras farm, I saw that it was still occupied by a corps of English cavalry. A moment later, a reconnaissance party of a hundred French hussars, streamed back, vigorously pressed by an English cavalry regiment. The French cavalry took up position, with Milhaud's cuirassiers on the right and the light cavalry on the left. The infantry ranged itself as a second line, and the batteries got into position. A party of five hundred horse was sent to communicate with Frasnes and to get news of the left. How did it come to be in camp still, since it should have been on the march since six in the morning? When they had arrived at the edge of the forest, the hussars began to shoot, but they did not take long in recognizing the red lancers of the Guard, which they had mistaken for Englishmen. Officers were sent to Ney to urge him on to debouch on Quatre-Bras, and immediately afterwards, Count de Lobau reformed and marched forward.

An English vivandière who was brought in as a prisoner, gave information about the movements of her army. The Duke of Wellington had only learnt of the disaster of Ligny very late in the night. He had immediately given orders to beat a retreat in the direction of Brussels, leaving General Uxbridge with a cavalry corps and some light artillery batteries as rear guard. General [Lord] Uxbridge withdrew as soon as he saw Count de Lobau's army corps.

On arriving at the farm of Quatre-Bras, I had twelve pieces of light artillery formed into a battery, which took on two English batteries. The rain was

---

* Napoleon had reinstituted the system of pages: young men of the nobility who were thus given an opportunity of learning the art of war in the entourage of a martial prince. S. de C.

THE BATTLE OF LIGNY

falling in torrents. However, the troops of the left were still not debouching, and, my patience being exhausted, orders were sent direct to the corps commanders. At length Count d'Erlon appeared. He went to the front of the column and took on the task of pressing the enemy rear-guard vigorously. General Reille with the 2nd Corps followed him.

When Ney appeared, I showed him my annoyance for all his hesitation and slowness which had just lost me three precious hours. The Marshal stammered out his excuses, that he had thought Wellington was still at Quatre-Bras with his whole army.

Count de Lobau's corps followed the 2nd Corps, the Guard marching next. Milhaud's cuirassiers, guided by a light cavalry division of General Pajol's, commanded by General Subervic, formed an intermediate column.

I went to the front of the army. The weather was frightful. On the roadway the soldiers were halfway up to their knees in water. On the surrounding ground they sank up to their knees. The artillery could not get through, and the cavalry could only get along with difficulty. This made the retreat of the enemy's cavalry difficult, and enabled the French artillery to give it some punishment.

At six in the evening the enemy, who had up till then only supported the retreat with a few guns, unmasked fifteen of them. The weather was foggy. It was impossible to gauge the strength of his rear-guard. It was clear that it had been reinforced within the last few minutes and, as we were not far from the forest of Soignes, it was probable that it wanted to hold this position during the night. In order to make sure about this, Milhaud's cuirassiers deployed and, under the protection of the fire of four batteries of light artillery, made as if to charge them. The enemy then unmasked fifty or sixty guns: the whole army was there. It would have required two more hours of daylight to be able to attack it. The French army took up position in front of Planchenoit. The head-quarters were fixed at the farm of Caillou, two thousand four hundred toises from the village of Mont-Saint-Jean.

During this retreat, several English cavalry officers were taken and brought to me; several were wounded. I had their wounds dressed by my surgeon before interrogating them, after which I cross-examined them on the state of their army, using General Flahaut as interpreter. Among these officers was Captain Elphinstone. In covering the road from Brussels to Quatre-Bras, it was easy to judge how great had been the English losses, in spite of the fact that they had already buried the greater part of their dead.

Marshal Grouchy had pursued Blücher along the Mont-Guibert and Gembloux roads, but, reports having made him think that the greater part of the Prussian army had withdrawn by way of Gembloux, he moved on to this point with his principal units. He arrived there on the 16th at four in the evening; there he discovered that Bülow's corps had reached it during the night, and had not taken part in the battle; that the disorder was considerable in several corps of the Prussian army, that all the surrounding villages were full of wounded and fugitives, that desertion was already rife among the Saxon and Westphalian troops, and even among the Prussians themselves.

He sent out reconnaissance parties in the two directions of Wavres and Liége on the tail of the two enemy rear-guards, which had retired that way. This done, Grouchy made his troops take up their position. He had, however, only covered two leagues. Towards evening he received definite information to the effect that the principal units of the enemy were making for Wavres, but it was after six o'clock, and the men were just making their soup. He thought he would be in time next day to follow the enemy, who were thus found to have gained three hours on him. This disastrous resolve is the principal cause of the loss of the battle of Waterloo.

During the night, the rain continued to fall, which made all the flat country more or less impassable for artillery, cavalry, and even infantry. During the day of the 17th and even the night of the 17th to 18th, the right flank of the French army reported that they were in touch with Marshal Grouchy's troops, who had been pursuing Marshal Blücher all day without anything of importance happening. At nine in the evening, General Milhaud, who had marched with his corps to maintain the communications with Marshal Grouchy, reported that he had received information of a column of enemy cavalry which had fallen back on Wavres in all haste from Tilly. A corps of 2,000 horse was making for Hal, threatening to turn the right of the forest of Soignes and to move on Brussels. The Duke of Wellington, alarmed, sent the 4th Infantry Division there. During the night the French cavalry returned to camp. The English division remained in observation and was pinned down during the battle.

6

I was camped in front of Planchenoit, astride the main Brussels highway, and four and a half leagues from this great town, with the 1st, 2nd and 6th infantry Corps, the Guard, a light cavalry division of Pajol's, and the two cuirassier corps of Milhaud and Kellermann, in all 68,900 men and 242 guns, with the Anglo-Dutch army in front of me, 90,000 men strong, with 250 guns, and with its head-quarters at Waterloo. Marshal Grouchy, with 34,000 men and a hundred and eight guns, ought to have been at Wavres; but he was in fact in front of Gembloux, having lost sight of the Prussian army, which was at Wavres. Its four corps were assembled there, 75,000 strong.

At ten o'clock in the evening, I sent an officer to Marshal Grouchy whom I supposed to be at Wavres, in order to let him know that there would be a big battle next day; that the Anglo-Dutch army was in position in front of the

THE BATTLE OF LIGNY

forest of Soignes, with its left resting on the village of La Haye; that I ordered him to detach from his camp at Wavres a division of 7,000 men of all arms and sixteen guns, before daylight, to go to Saint-Lambert to join the right of the Grand Army and co-operate with it; that, as soon as he was satisfied that Marshal Blücher had evacuated Wavres, whether to continue his retreat on Brussels or to go in any other direction, he was to march with the bulk of his troops to support the detachment which he had sent to Saint-Lambert.

At eleven o'clock in the evening, an hour after this despatch had been sent off, a report came in from Marshal Grouchy, dated from Gembloux at 5 p.m. It reported that he was at Gembloux with his army, unaware as to which direction Marshal Blücher had taken, whether he had gone towards Brussels or Liége; that he had accordingly set up two advance-guards, one between Gembloux and Wavres, and the other a league from Gembloux in the direction of Liège. Thus Marshal Blücher had given him the slip and was three leagues from him! Marshal Grouchy had only covered two leagues during the day of the 17th.

A second officer was sent to him at four in the morning to repeat the order which had been sent to him at ten in the evening. An hour later, at five o'clock, a new report came in, dated from Gembloux at 2 a.m.; the Marshal reported that he had learnt at 6 p.m. that Blücher had moved with all units on Wavres; that, in view of this, he had wanted to follow him then and there, but that, the troops having already made camp, and prepared their meal, he would only be starting at daylight, in order to arrive early in front of Wavres, which would come to the same thing, and that the men would be well rested and full of dash.

Chapter XLIII

BATTLE OF MONT-SAINT-JEAN (WATERLOO)

The Anglo-Dutch army's line of battle. The French army's line of battle. My aims; attack on Hougoumont. General Bülow arrives on the battlefield with 30,000 men, which brings the Duke of Wellington's army up to 120,000 men. Attack on la Haie-Sainte by the First Corps. General Bülow is repulsed. Cavalry charge on the plateau. Marshal Grouchy's movements. Marshal Blücher's movements, which brought the enemy on the battlefield to 150,000 men. Movements of the Imperial Guard.

I

During the night, I gave all the orders necessary for the battle next day, although everything seemed to show that it would not take place. During the four days since hostilities had begun, I had, by the most skilful manoeuvres, surprised my enemies, won a smashing victory, and divided the two armies. It added considerably to my glory, but had not yet sufficiently improved my position. The three hours delay which the left had suffered, during its movement, had prevented my attacking the Anglo-Dutch army, as I had intended, during the afternoon of the 17th, which would have crowned the campaign with success! It was, in fact, probable that the Duke of Wellington and Marshal Blücher were taking advantage of this very night to cross the forest of Soignes and join up in front of Brussels. After that junction, which would

BATTLE OF MONT-SAINT-JEAN (WATERLOO)

be effected before nine in the morning, the position of the French army would become extremely delicate. The two armies would be reinforced with everything that they had in their rear. Six thousand English had disembarked at Ostend within the last few days: they were troops returning from America. It would be impossible for the French army to risk crossing the forest of Soignes in order to encounter, on emerging, forces more than twice as strong, joined up and in position; and yet, in less than a few weeks, the Russian, Austrian, and Bavarian armies, etc., would cross the Rhine and move towards the Marne. The 5th Corps, on the look-out in Alsace, was only 20,000 strong.

At one o'clock in the morning, much preoccupied with these weighty thoughts, I went out on foot, accompanied only by my Grand Marshal. My intention was to follow the English army in its retreat and to attempt to engage it, in spite of the darkness of the night, as soon as it was on the march. I went along the line of the main defences. The forest of Soignes looked as if it were on fire. The horizon between this forest, Braine-la-Leud, the farms of the Belle-Alliance and La Haye, was aglow with the fires of bivouacs. The most complete silence prevailed. The Anglo-Dutch army was wrapped in a profound slumber, following on the fatigues which it had experienced during the preceding days. On arriving near the woods of the Château of Hougoumont, I heard the noise of a column on the march; it was half past two. Now, at this hour, the rear-guard would be leaving its position, if the enemy were in retreat; but this illusion was short-lived.

The noise stopped; the rain fell in torrents. Various officers sent out on reconnaissance and some secret agents, returning at half past three, confirmed that the Anglo-Dutch were showing no signs of movement. At four o'clock, the despatch riders brought me a peasant who had acted as guide to an English cavalry brigade which had gone to take up a position on the extreme left at the village of Ohain. Two Belgian deserters, who had just quitted their regiment, told me that their army was preparing for battle, and that no retreating movement had taken place; that Belgium was offering prayers for my success; and that the English and the Prussians were both equally hated there.

The enemy general could do nothing more at variance with the interests of his cause and his country, to the whole spirit of this campaign, and even to the most elementary rules of war, than to remain in the position which he occupied. He had behind him the defiles of the forest of Soignes. If he were beaten any retreat was impossible.

The French troops were bivouacked in the middle of the mud. The officers considered it impossible to give battle during the day. The artillery and cavalry could not manoeuvre on the ground, so drenched was it. They calculated that it would require twelve hours of fine weather to dry it up.

The day began to dawn. I returned to my head-quarters thoroughly satisfied with the great mistake which the enemy general was making and very anxious

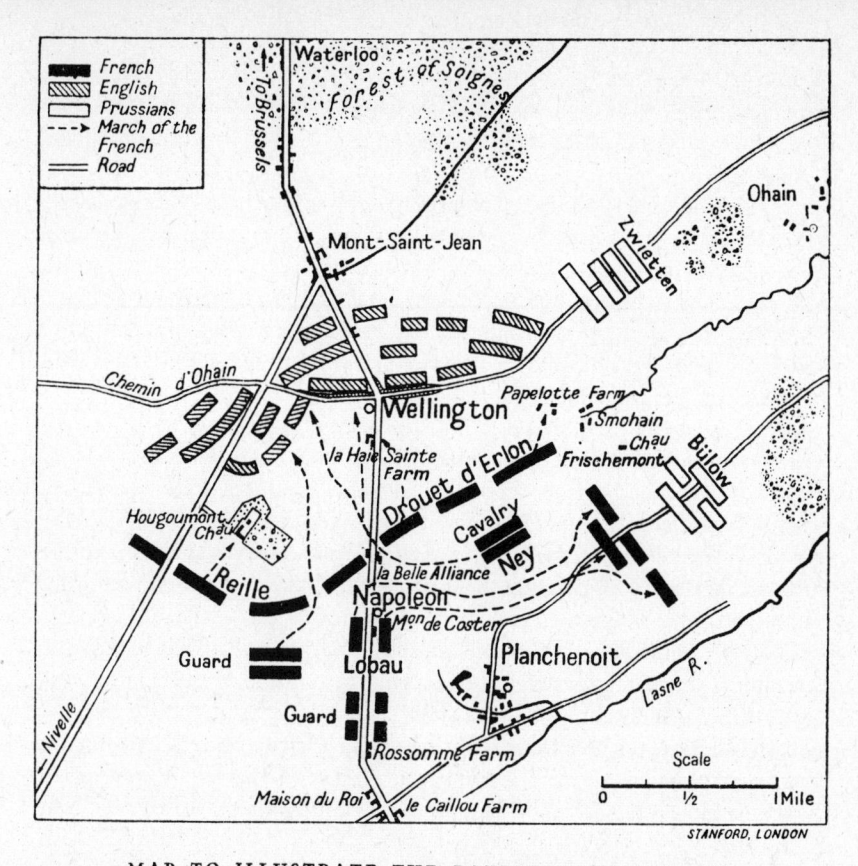

MAP TO ILLUSTRATE THE BATTLE OF WATERLOO

BATTLE OF MONT-SAINT-JEAN (WATERLOO)

lest the bad weather should prevent my taking advantage of it. But already the sky was clearing. At five o'clock I perceived a few rays of that sun which should, before going down, light up the defeat of the English army: the British oligarchy would be overthrown by it! France was going to rise, that day, more glorious, more powerful and greater than ever!

The Anglo-Dutch army was in battle position on the road from Charleroi to Brussels, in front of the forest of Soignes, standing on a fairly good plateau. The right, composed of the 1st and 2nd English Divisions and the Brunswick Division, commanded by Generals Cook and Clinton, rested on a ravine beyond the Nivelles road. It occupied the Château of Hougoumont, in advance of its front, with a detachment. The centre, composed of the 3rd English Division and the 1st and 2nd Belgian Divisions, commanded by Generals Alten, Collaert and Chassé, were in front of Mont-Saint-Jean. The left rested on the Charleroi road, and occupied the farm of la Haie-Sainte with one of its brigades. The left, made up of the 5th and 6th English Divisions and the 3rd Belgian Division, under the command of Generals Picton, Lambert and Perponcher, had its right resting on the Charleroi road and its left behind the village of La Haye, which it occupied with a strong detachment. The reserve was at Mont-Saint-Jean, at the intersection of the roads from Charleroi and Nivelles to Brussels. The cavalry, drawn up in three rows on the heights of Mont-Saint-Jean, lined the whole rear of the army's battle front which covered a distance of 2,500 toises.

The enemy's front was protected by a natural obstacle. The plateau was slightly hollow at its centre and the ground sloped away gently to a deep ravine. The 4th English Division, commanded by General Colville, occupied, as right flank, all the exits from Hal to Braine-la-Leud. An English cavalry brigade occupied, as left flank, all the exits from the village of Ohain. The units which the enemy revealed were of varying strength; but the most experienced officers estimated them at 90,000 men, including the flanking corps, which tallied with the general information received. The French army numbered only 69,000 men, but victory appeared no less certain on that account. These 69,000 men were good troops; and, in the enemy army, only the English, who numbered 40,000 men at most, could be counted as such.

At eight o'clock, breakfast was brought to me, in which I was joined by several generals. I said, 'The enemy army exceeds ours by nearly a quarter; but the odds are nine to one in our favour.'

'No doubt,' said Marshal Ney, who came in at this moment, 'if the Duke of Wellington were simple enough to wait for Your Majesty; but I come to inform you that, already, his columns are in full retreat. They are disappearing into the forest.'

'You have not seen right,' I replied. 'There is no longer time, he will

BATTLE OF MONT-SAINT-JEAN (WATERLOO)

expose himself to a certain defeat. He has thrown the dice, and our number has turned up!'

At this moment some artillery officers, who had been all over the plain, announced that the artillery could manoeuvre, although with some difficulty, which, in an hour's time, would be considerably lessened. I mounted my horse at once and went to the sharpshooters opposite la Haie-Sainte; reconnoitred the enemy line again; and told the sapper General Haxo, a reliable officer, to get nearer to it, in order to satisfy himself as to whether they had erected some redoubts or entrenchments. This general returned promptly to report that he had seen no trace of fortifications.

I reflected for a quarter of an hour, dictated the battle orders, which two generals, seated on the ground, wrote down. The aides-de-camp carried them to the different army corps, who were standing to arms, full of impatience and ardour. The army moved off and began to march forward in eleven columns.

2

It had been arranged that, of these eleven columns, four were to form the first line, four the second line, and three the third.

The four columns of the first line were: the first, that on the left, formed by the cavalry of the 2nd Corps; [the next, by three infantry divisions of the 2nd Corps;] the [third], by three infantry divisions of the 1st Corps; the fourth, by the light cavalry of the 1st Corps.

The four columns of the second line were: that of the left formed by Kellermann's corps of cuirassiers; the second, by the two infantry divisions of the 6th Corps; the third, by two light cavalry divisions, one of the 6th Corps, commanded by the divisional general Daumont, the other detached from Pajol's corps and commanded by the divisional general Subervic; the fourth, by Milhaud's corps of cuirassiers.

The three columns of the third line were: that of the left, formed by the division of mounted grenadiers and the dragoons of the Guard, commanded by General Guyot; the second, by the three divisions of the Old, Middle and Young Guard, commanded by Lieutenant-Generals Friant, Morand and Duhesme; the third by the mounted Chasseurs and the lancers of the Guard, under Lieutenant-General Lefebvre-Desnouettes. The artillery marched on the flanks of the columns; the parks and the ambulances at the tail.

At nine o'clock, the heads of the four columns forming the first line, arrived at the point where they were to deploy. At the same time the other seven columns could be seen not very far off debouching from the heights. They were on the march, the trumpets and drums summoning them to battle. The music resounded with airs which brought back to the soldiers the memories of a

BATTLE OF MONT-SAINT-JEAN (WATERLOO)

hundred victories. The very soil seemed proud to support so many brave men. This was a magnificent spectacle; and the enemy, who were situated in such a way that every man was visible, must have been struck by it. The army must have seemed to them twice as big as it really was.

These eleven columns deployed with such precision that there was no confusion; and each man took up exactly the place which had been planned for him in the very mind of his leader. Never had such huge masses moved about with such ease.

The light cavalry of the 2nd Corps, which formed the first column of the left in the front line, deployed in three lines astride the road from Nivelles to Brussels, more or less on a level with the first woods of Hougoumont park, with a view, on the left, of the whole plain with large numbers of Guards at Braine-la-Leud and its light artillery battery on the Nivelles highway.

The 2nd Corps, under the orders of General Reille, occupied the area between the Nivelles and Charleroi roads, a stretch of between 900 and 1,000 toises; Prince Jérôme's division, holding the left near the Nivelles highway and the Hougoumont wood, General Foy the centre; and General Bachelu the right, which reached the Charleroi road near the farm of la Belle-Alliance. Each infantry division was in two lines, the 2nd thirty toises from the first, with its artillery in front and its parks in the rear near the Nivelles road.

The third column, formed by the first corps, and commanded by Lieutenant-General Count d'Erlon, rested its left on la Belle-Alliance, on the right of the Charleroi road, and its right opposite the farm of La Haye where the enemy's left were. Each infantry division was in two lines; the artillery in the gap between the brigades.

Its light cavalry, which formed the fourth column, deployed on its right in three lines, watching La Haye, Frischermont, and throwing out posts at Ohain, in order to observe the enemy's flank. Its light artillery was on its right.

The front line was scarcely formed up before the heads of the four columns of the second line reached the point where they were to deploy. Kellermann's cuirassiers established themselves in two lines thirty toises from each other, resting their left on the Nivelles road, a hundred toises from the 2nd Corps, and their right on the Charleroi road. They covered an area of eleven hundred toises. One of their batteries took up position on the left, near the Nivelles road; the other on the right, near the Charleroi road.

The second column, under Lieutenant-General Count de Lobau, moved up to fifty toises behind the second line of the 2nd Corps; it remained in columns, drawn up by divisions, occupying a depth of about a hundred toises, along and on the left of the Charleroi road, with a distance of ten toises between the two divisional columns, and its artillery on its right flank.

The third column, its light cavalry, under the divisional general Daumont,

BATTLE OF MONT-SAINT-JEAN (WATERLOO)

followed by General Subervic's, placed itself in column drawn up by squadrons, with the left resting on the Charleroi road, opposite its infantry, from which it was only separated by the roadway; its light artillery was on its right flank.

The fourth column, Milhaud's corps of Cuirassiers, deployed in two lines thirty toises apart and a hundred toises behind the second line of the 1st Corps, the left resting on the Charleroi road, the right in the direction of Frischermont; it covered about nine hundred toises, its batteries were on its left, near the Charleroi road, and in its centre.

Before this second line had formed up, the heads of the three reserve columns arrived at their deploying points. The heavy cavalry of the Guard placed itself a hundred toises behind Kellermann, ready for action in two lines, thirty toises apart, the left on the side of Charleroi, with the artillery in the centre.

The central column, composed of the infantry of the Guard, deployed in six lines, each of four battalions, ten toises from each other, astride the Charleroi road and a little in front of the farm of Rossomme. The artillery batteries belonging to the different regiments placed themselves on the left and right, those of the reserve, both on foot and mounted, behind the lines.

The third column, the mounted chasseurs and the lancers of the Guard, deployed in two lines thirty toises apart, a hundred toises behind General Milhaud, the left on the Charleroi road, and the right in the Frischermont direction, with its light artillery at its centre. At half past ten, which seemed incredible, the whole manoeuvre was complete, all the troops were in their positions. The most complete silence reigned over the field of battle.

The army was drawn up in six lines, forming the figure of six V's: the first two, of infantry, having the light cavalry on the wings; the third and fourth, cuirassiers; the fifth and sixth, cavalry of the Guard, with six lines of infantry of the Guard, placed at right angles at the head of the six V's, and the 6th Corps, drawn up in columns, at right angles to the lines taken up by the Guard. The infantry was on the left of the road, its cavalry on the right. The Charleroi and Nivelles roads were clear, being the means of communication whereby the artillery of the reserve could reach the different points of the line quickly.

I passed along the ranks; it would be difficult to express the enthusiasm which animated all the soldiers: the infantry raised their shakos on the ends of their bayonets; the cuirassiers, dragoons and light cavalry, their helmets or shakos on the ends of their sabres. Victory seemed certain; the old soldiers who had been present at so many engagements admired this new order of battle. They sought to divine what aims their general had in mind; they argued about the point at which, and the manner in which, the attack would take place. During this time, I gave my final orders and went at the head of

BATTLE OF MONT-SAINT-JEAN (WATERLOO)

my Guard to the apex of the six V's on the heights of Rossomme, and dismounted; from there I could see both armies; the view extended far into the distance to right and left of the battlefield.

A battle is a dramatic action, which has its beginning, its middle, and its end. The order of battle which the two armies take up, the opening moves to come to grips, are the exposition; the counter-moves, which the attacked army makes, form the crux which imposes new dispositions and brings on the crisis; from which springs the result, or dénouement. As soon as the attack by the centre of the French army was revealed, the enemy general would make counter-moves, either with his wings, or behind his line, in order to provide a diversion, or rush to the support of the point attacked; none of these movements could escape my experienced eye in the central position which I had taken up, and I had all my reserves under control to send them according to my will or wherever the pressure of circumstances should demand their presence.

3

Ten artillery divisions, including three divisions of twelve, came together, the left resting on the Charleroi road on the hillock beyond La Belle-Alliance and in front of the left-hand division of the 1st Corps. They were intended to support the attack on la Haie-Sainte, which two divisions of the 1st Corps and the two divisions of the 6th were to make, at the same time as the two other divisions of the 1st Corps were moving on La Haye. By this means, the whole left of the enemy would be turned. The light cavalry division of the 6th Corps, drawn up in close formation, and that of the 1st Corps on its wings, were to take part in this attack, which the 2nd and 3rd lines of cavalry would support, as well as the whole Guard, both on foot and mounted. The French army, master of La Haye and Mont-Saint-Jean, would cut the Brussels road along the whole right of the English army where its principal forces were.

I had preferred to turn the enemy's left, rather than his right, first, in order to cut it off from the Prussians who were at Wavres, and to oppose their joining up again, if they had intended doing so; and, even if they had not intended doing so, if the attack had been made on the right, the English army, on being repulsed, would have fallen back on to the Prussian army; whereas, if made on the left, it would be separated therefrom and thrown back in the direction of the sea; secondly, because the left appeared to be much weaker; thirdly and finally, because I was expecting every moment the arrival of a detachment from Marshal Grouchy on my right, and did not want to run the risks of finding myself separated from it.

While everything was going forward for this decisive attack, Prince Jérôme's division, on the left, exchanged shots at the Hougoumont wood.

BATTLE OF MONT-SAINT-JEAN (WATERLOO)

Soon the firing became very brisk. The enemy having unmasked close on forty guns, General Reille moved forward the artillery battery of his 2nd Division, and I sent orders to General Kellermann to have his twelve light guns moved up. Soon the cannonade became really hot. Prince Jérôme carried the Hougoumont wood several times, and was several times turned out of it. This was defended by an English Guards division, the enemy's best troops, which I was glad to see on his right, which made the attack on the left all the easier. Foy's division supported Prince Jérôme's, and both sides performed prodigies of valour. The English Guards covered the woods and avenues of the Château with their dead, but not without selling their lives dearly. After various vicissitudes, which took up several hours of the day, the whole wood remained in French hands; but the château, where several hundred stout fellows were embattled, put up an unbreakable resistance. I gave orders to assemble a battery of eight field howitzers which set fire to the barns and roofs, and made the French masters of this position.

Marshal Ney received the honour of commanding the big attack in the centre. It could not be entrusted to a braver man, nor to one more accustomed to this kind of thing. He sent one of his aides-de-camp to announce that everything was ready and that he waited only for the signal. Before giving it, I wanted to cast a final look over the whole battlefield, and perceived in the direction of Saint-Lambert a cloud which looked to me like troops. I said to my chief of staff, 'Marshal, what do you see towards Saint-Lambert? I think I can see five to six thousand men there; that is probably a detachment of Grouchy's.'

All the glasses of the general-staff were fixed on this point. The weather was rather misty. Some maintained, as often happens on such occasions, that they were not troops, but trees; others that they were columns in position; some others that they were troops on the march. In this uncertainty, without further deliberation, I sent for Lieutenant-General Daumont, and ordered him to go with his division of light cavalry and General Subervic's to reconnoitre the right, get into touch speedily with the troops which were arriving at Saint-Lambert, effect a junction with them if they belonged to Marshal Grouchy, hold them if they belonged to the enemy. These 3,000 cavalrymen only had to do a right wheel in fours to get outside the lines of the army; they moved quickly and without confusion for three thousand toises, and there drew themselves up in battle array, as a cross-piece to the whole right of the army.

4

A quarter of an hour later, a Chasseur officer brought in a Prussian Black Hussar who had just been taken prisoner by the despatch-riders of a flying

BATTLE OF MONT-SAINT-JEAN (WATERLOO)

column of three hundred chasseurs, who were out scouting between Wavres and Planchenoit. This hussar was the bearer of a letter. He was extremely intelligent and gave by word of mouth all the information that could be desired. The column which was to be seen at Saint-Lambert was the advance-guard of the Prussian General Bülow, who was arriving with 30,000 men; it was the 4th Prussian Corps which had not been engaged at Ligny.

The letter was in fact the announcement of the arrival of this corps; the general was asking the Duke of Wellington for further orders. The hussar said that he had been at Wavres that morning, that the three other corps of the Prussian army were camped there, that they had spent the night of the 17th to 18th there, that there were no Frenchmen in front of them, that he presumed the French to have marched on Planchenoit, that one patrol of his regiment had been as far as two leagues from Wavres during the night without encountering any French body. The Duke of Dalmatia immediately sent the intercepted letter and the hussar's report to Marshal Grouchy, to whom he repeated the order to march, without halting, on Saint-Lambert, and to take General Bülow's corps in the rear.

It was eleven o'clock; the officer had at most only five leagues to cover, on good roads all the way, to reach Marshal Grouchy; he promised to be there at one o'clock. From the most recent news received of this marshal, it was known that he was to move, at daylight, on Wavres. Now, from Gembloux to Wavres is only three leagues: whether or not he had received the orders sent from the imperial head-quarters during the night, he must without doubt be engaged at that moment before Wavres. The glasses turned in that direction picked up nothing; no gunfire could be heard. Soon after, General Daumont sent word that some well-mounted despatch-riders who were going ahead of him, had run into some enemy patrols in the direction of Saint-Lambert; that it could be taken as certain that the troops to be seen there were enemy troops; that he had sent out picked patrols in several directions to communicate with Marshal Grouchy, and take information and orders to him.

I immediately gave orders to Count de Lobau to cross the Charleroi road, by a change of direction to his right by divisions, and to go towards Saint-Lambert to support the light cavalry; to choose a good intermediate position where he could, with 10,000 men, hold up 30,000, if that became necessary; to attack the Prussians vigorously, as soon as he should hear the first cannon shots from the troops which Marshal Grouchy had detached in their rear.

These dispositions were carried out at once. It was of the utmost importance that Count de Lobau's movement should take place without delay. Marshal Grouchy must have detached from Wavres 6,000 to 7,000 men to search in the direction of Saint-Lambert, and these would find themselves compromised, since General Bülow's corps amounted to 30,000 men. In exactly

BATTLE OF MONT-SAINT-JEAN (WATERLOO)

the same way General Bülow's corps would be compromised and lost, if, at the moment when he was attacked in the rear by 6,000 to 7,000 men, he were attacked in front by a man of Count de Lobau's calibre.

Seventeen to eighteen thousand Frenchmen, disposed and commanded in this fashion, were worth a great deal more than 30,000 Prussians; but these events involved a change in my original plan. I found myself weakened on the battlefield by 10,000 men, whom I was obliged to send against General Bülow. I only had 59,000 men against 90,000; moreover, the enemy army, which I was to attack, had just been increased by 30,000 men, already on the battlefield. It was 120,000 strong against 69,000—two to one.

'This morning the odds were nine to one in our favour,' I said to the Duke of Dalmatia. 'Bülow's arrival deprives us of three; but that still leaves us with six to four in our favour, and, if Grouchy retrieves the horrible blunder he made yesterday of twiddling his thumbs at Gembloux, and sends his detachment with speed, victory will be all the more decisive, because Bülow's corps will be entirely destroyed.'

No anxieties were felt as to Marshal Grouchy's safety. After dispensing with the detachment to Saint-Lambert, he still retained 27,000 to 28,000 men. Now the three corps which Marshal Blücher had at Wavres, and which, prior to Ligny, were 90,000 strong, were reduced to 40,000, not merely by the loss of 30,000, which he had suffered in the battle, but also by that of 20,000 who had fled in disorder and were ravaging the banks of the Meuse, and by that of some detachments, which the Marshal had been obliged to use to make good their loss, as well as by that of the baggage trains which were in the Namur and Liége areas. Now, 40,000 or 45,000 Prussians, beaten and disheartened, could not impose their will on 28,000 Frenchmen well placed and victorious.

5

It was noon, and the sharp-shooters were engaged all along the line; but the battle had only really begun on the left, in the wood and around the Château of Hougoumont. On the extreme right General Bülow's troops were still stationary. They appeared to be forming up and to be waiting for their artillery to come through the defile.

I sent orders to Marshal Ney to open fire with his batteries, to get hold of the farm of la Haie-Sainte and to put an infantry division in position there; also to get hold of the village of La Haye and turn the enemy out of it, in order to cut all communication between the Anglo-Dutch army and General Bülow's corps. Eighty pieces of artillery soon belched forth death upon the whole left of the English line; one of their divisions was entirely wiped out by the cannon-balls and grape-shot.

BATTLE OF MONT-SAINT-JEAN (WATERLOO)

While this attack was being unmasked, I watched closely to see what would be the movement of the enemy's general. He made none on his right; but I saw that on his left he was preparing for a big cavalry charge; I dashed there at the gallop. The charge had taken place; it had repulsed a column of infantry which was advancing on the plateau, had taken two eagles from it, and put seven guns out of action.

I ordered a brigade of General Milhaud's cuirassiers, of the second line, to charge this cavalry. It went off with shouts of 'Vive l'Empereur'; the English cavalry was broken, most of the men were left behind on the battlefield; the guns were retaken; the infantry protected.

Various infantry and cavalry charges took place; the detailed narration of them belongs rather to the history of each regiment than to the general history of the battle, into which these accounts, if multiplied, would only bring confusion. It is enough to say that, after three hours fighting, the farm of la Haie-Sainte, despite the resistance of the Scots regiments, was occupied by the French infantry; and the objective which I had set myself realized. The 6th and 7th English Divisions were destroyed, and General Picton was left dead on the battlefield.

During this engagement I went along the line of the infantry of the 1st Corps, the cavalry of Milhaud's cuirassiers, and the Guard in the third line, in the midst of the cannon-balls, grape-shot and shells; they ricocheted between the lines. Brave General Devaux, commanding the artillery of the Guard, who was beside me, was killed by a cannon-ball. This loss was keenly felt, especially at that moment, for he knew better than anyone the positions occupied by the artillery reserves of the Guard, ninety-six pieces strong. Brigadier-General Lallemand succeeded him, and was wounded soon afterwards.

Confusion reigned in the English army. The baggage trains, the transport, and the wounded, seeing the French approaching the Brussels highway and the principal exit of the forest, scrambled *en masse* to effect their retreat. All the English, Belgian and German fugitives, who had received sabre wounds from the cavalry, rushed towards Brussels. It was four o'clock. Victory ought from then on to have been assured; but General Bülow's corps carried out its powerful diversion at this moment. From two o'clock in the afternoon onwards General Daumont had reported that General Bülow was debouching in three columns, and that the French Chasseurs were keeping up their fire all the while they were retiring before the enemy, which seemed to him very numerous. He estimated them at more than 40,000 men. He said, moreover, that his despatch riders, well mounted, had gone several leagues in different directions and had not reported any news of Marshal Grouchy; and that, therefore, he could not be counted on.

At this very juncture, I received extremely annoying news from Gembloux. Marshal Grouchy, instead of leaving Gembloux at first light, as he had

BATTLE OF MONT-SAINT-JEAN (WATERLOO)

announced in his despatch of two in the morning, had still not left this camp at 10 a.m. The officer attributed this fact to the horrible weather—a ridiculous reason. This inexcusable inertia, in circumstances of such delicacy, on the part of such a zealous officer, was inexplicable.

6

However, the exchange of artillery fire between General Bülow and Count de Lobau broke out with little delay. The Prussian army was marching in échelons, with the centre in front. Its line of battle was at right angles to the right flank of the army, parallel to the road from la Haie-Sainte to Planchenoit. The centre échelon unmasked about thirty pieces of artillery. Our artillery opposed an equal number to it.

After an hour's cannonade, Count de Lobau, seeing that the first échelon was not supported, marched up to it, broke into it, and pushed it back a long way; but the two other lines, which appeared to have been delayed by the bad roads, rallied to the first échelon, and, without trying to breach the French line, sought to outflank it by a left wheel in battle. Count de Lobau, fearing that he might be turned, carried out his retreat, chequerwise, approaching the army. The fire of the Prussian batteries redoubled; up to sixty pieces of artillery could be counted. The cannon-balls were falling on the roadway before and behind La Belle-Alliance, where I was with my Guard: it was the fighting zone of the army.

At the most critical moment the enemy got so close that his grape-shot raked this road. I thereupon ordered General Duhesme, commanding my Young Guard, to go to the right of the 6th Corps with his two infantry brigades and twenty-four pieces of artillery, belonging to the Guard. A quarter of an hour later, this formidable battery opened up; the French artillery did not take long to gain the advantage: it was better manned and placed. As soon as the Young Guard were in action, the movement of the Prussians seemed to be halted; one could see signs of wavering in their line; however, they still continued to extend it to their left, outflanking the French right and reaching as far as the heights of Planchenoit.

Lieutenant-General Morand thereupon proceeded with four battalions of the Old Guard and sixteen guns to the right of the Young Guard. Two regiments of the Old Guard took up positions in front of Planchenoit. The Prussian line was outflanked, General Bülow was repulsed, his left moved backwards, closed in, and imperceptibly his whole line fell back. Count de Lobau, General Duhesme and Marshal Morand marched forward; they soon occupied the positions which General Bülow's artillery had held. Not only had this general exhausted his attack, and brought into play all his reserves, but, held at first, he was now in retreat. The Prussian cannon-balls not only

BATTLE OF MONT-SAINT-JEAN (WATERLOO)

fell short of the Charleroi road, but did not even reach the positions which Count de Lobau had occupied; it was seven p.m.

7

It was two hours since Count d'Erlon had got possession of La Haye, had outflanked the whole English left and General Bülow's right. The light cavalry of the 1st Corps, pursuing the enemy infantry on the plateau of La Haye, had been brought back by a superior force of cavalry. Count Milhaud thereupon climbed the height with his cuirassiers and warned General Lefebvre-Desnouettes, who started at once at the trot to back him up.

It was five o'clock, the moment when General Bülow's attack was at its worst, when, far from being held, he kept on throwing in new troops, which extended his line to the right. The English cavalry was repulsed by the bold cuirassiers and chasseurs of the Guard. The English abandoned all the battlefield between la Haie-Sainte and Mont-Saint-Jean, which their left had occupied, and were brought to bay on their right. At the sight of these brilliant charges, shouts of victory were heard on the battlefield. I said 'It is an hour too soon; nevertheless what has been done must be followed up.'

I sent an order to Kellermann's cuirassiers, who were still in position on the left, to go at full trot to support the cavalry on the plateau. General Bülow was at this moment threatening the flank and rear of the army; it was important not to fall back at any point, and to hold the present position which the cavalry had taken, although it was premature. This move at full trot by 3,000 cuirassiers who passed by with shouts of 'Vive l'Empereur', and under the gunfire of the Prussians, created a fortunate diversion at this critical moment. The cavalry were marching on as if to pursue the English army, and General Bülow's army was still making progress on the flank and in the rear. To know whether we were victorious or in danger the soldiers, even the officers, sought to divine the answer from the expression on my face; but it radiated only confidence. It was the fiftieth pitched battle that I had conducted in twenty years.

However, the heavy cavalry division of the Guard, under the orders of General Guyot, who was in second line behind Kellermann's cuirassiers, followed at full trot and proceeded to the plateau. I noticed this, and sent Count Bertrand to recall it; it was my reserve. When this general got there, it was already committed and any movement of withdrawal would have been dangerous. From five p.m. onwards, I was thus deprived of my cavalry reserve, of that reserve which, skilfully employed, had so often brought me victory.

However, these 12,000 picked cavalrymen performed miracles; they overwhelmed all the more numerous enemy cavalry which sought to oppose

BATTLE OF MONT-SAINT-JEAN (WATERLOO)

them, drove in several infantry squares, broke them up, seized sixty pieces of artillery, and, in the middle of the squares, captured ten standards, which three Chasseurs of the Guard and three cuirassiers presented to me in front of La Belle-Alliance. The enemy, for the second time that day, thought the battle lost, and saw with apprehension to what extent the bad battle-site which he had selected was going to add to his difficulties in his retreat. Ponsonby's brigade, charged by the red lancers of the Guard under General Colbert, was broken into. Its general was pierced by seven lance thrusts, and fell dead. The Prince of Orange, on the point of being seized, was severely wounded; but, not being backed up by a strong mass of infantry, which was still contained by General Bülow's attack, this gallant cavalry had to confine itself to holding the battlefield which it had conquered.

At length, at seven o'clock, when General Bülow's attack had been repulsed and the cavalry was still holding its own on the plateau which it had carried, the victory was won; 69,000 Frenchmen had beaten 120,000 men. Joy was visible on every face and hearts were lifted high. This feeling followed on the shock that had been experienced during the flank attack, launched by an entire army, which, for an hour, had even threatened to bring about the retreat of the army. At this juncture Marshal Grouchy's gunfire could be heard distinctly. It had passed beyond Wavres at the most distant point and at the nearest point; it was behind Saint-Lambert.

8

Marshal Grouchy had only left his camp at Gembloux at ten in the morning, and was half way to Wavres between noon and one o'clock. He heard the dreadful cannonade of Waterloo. No experienced man could have mistaken it: it was the sound of several hundred guns, and from that moment two armies were hurling death at each other. General Excelmans, commanding the cavalry, was profoundly moved by it. He went up to the Marshal and said to him: 'The Emperor is at grips with the English army; there can be no doubt about it, such a furious fire can be no skirmish. Monsieur le Maréchal, we must march towards the sound of the guns. I am an old soldier of the Army of Italy; I have heard General Bonaparte preach this principle a hundred times. If we turn to the left we shall be on the battlefield in two hours.'

'I believe', the Marshal said to him, 'that you are right; but if Blücher debouches from Wavres on to me, and takes me in the flank, I shall be compromised for not having obeyed my orders, which are to march against Blücher.'

Count GERARD joined the Marshal at this moment, and gave him the same advice as General Excelmans. 'Your orders', he said to him, 'were to be at Wavres yesterday and not to-day; the safest thing is to go straight to the

BATTLE OF MONT-SAINT-JEAN (WATERLOO)

battlefield. You cannot conceal from yourself the fact that General Blücher has gained a march on you; he was at Wavres yesterday and you were at Gembloux, and goodness knows where he is now! If he has joined up with Wellington we shall find him on the battlefield, and from then on your orders will have been fulfilled to the letter! If he is not there, your arrival will decide the battle! In two hours we can take part in the firing, and, if we have destroyed the English army, what is it to us that Blücher is as good as beaten!'

The Marshal appeared to be convinced; but at this moment he received the report that his light cavalry had arrived at Wavres and was at grips with the Prussians; that all their units were assembled there; and that they amounted to at least 80,000 men. At this news, he continued his move on Wavres: he reached there at four in the afternoon. Believing that he had in front of him the whole Prussian army, he took two hours to take up battle stations and make his dispositions. It was then that he received the officer sent from the battlefield at ten in the morning. He detached General Pajol with 12,000 men to go to Limate, a bridge on the Dyle, a league in the rear of Saint-Lambert. This general arrived there at seven p.m. and crossed the river. Meanwhile Grouchy attacked Wavres.

9

Marshal Blücher had spent the night of the 17th to 18th at Wavres with the four corps of his army, amounting to 75,000 men. Being told that the Duke of Wellington had decided to accept battle in front of the Forest of Soignes, if he could count on his co-operation, he detached his fourth Corps during the morning, which crossed the Dyle at Limate, and assembled at Saint-Lambert. This corps was complete; it was the one which had not been engaged at Ligny. Marshal Blücher's light cavalry, which was out scouting two leagues from his camp at Wavres, still had no news of Marshal Grouchy; at 7 a.m., it could only see a few pickets of despatch riders. Blücher concluded from this that the whole army was together in front of Mont-Saint-Jean; he set the 2nd Corps, commanded by General Pirch, in motion. This corps was reduced to 18,000 men. He himself marched with General Zwietten's 1st Corps, reduced to 13,000 men, and left General Thielman with the 3rd Corps in position at Wavres.

General Pirch's 2nd Corps marched by way of Lasne, and Blücher with the 1st Corps marched on Ohain, where he joined the English cavalry brigade, which was on the flank, at 6 o'clock in the evening. There he received the report that Marshal Grouchy had appeared before Wavres in considerable strength at 4 o'clock; that he was making his dispositions for attack, and that the 3rd Corps was not in a position to resist it.

Marshal Blücher saw that there was only one thing to do. He brought his

BATTLE OF MONT-SAINT-JEAN (WATERLOO)

main strength to the side of General Bülow and the English, and sent orders to General Thielman to hold on as long as possible, and to fall back on him if he was obliged to. Anyhow, he was no longer in a position to turn back towards Wavres; he would only have arrived there after dark, and, if the Anglo-Dutch army was beaten, he would find himself between two fires, whereas, if he continued towards the Anglo-Dutch army and it won the victory, he would still have time to turn round and face Marshal Grouchy.

His progress was extremely slow, his troops were very tired, and the roads completely broken down and full of defiles. These two columns, together 31,000 strong, opened up communication between General Bülow and the English. The former, who was in full retreat, halted. Wellington, who was in despair and had before him only the prospect of certain defeat, saw his salvation. The English cavalry brigade, which was at Ohain, joined him, as well as a part of the 4th Division from the right flank.

If Marshal Grouchy had slept in front of Wavres, as he ought to have done and had orders to do, on the evening of the 17th, Marshal Blücher would have remained in observation there with all his troops, believing himself to be pursued by the whole French army. If Marshal Grouchy, as he had written at two in the morning from his camp at Gembloux, had taken up arms at first light, that is to say at 4 a.m., he would not have arrived at Wavres in time to intercept General Bülow's detachment; but he would have stopped Marshal Blücher's three other corps; and victory would still have been certain. But Marshal Grouchy only arrived in front of Wavres at half past four and did not attack until six o'clock; it was no longer the time for it!

The French army, 69,000 strong, which at 7 p.m. had gained a victory over an army of 120,000 men, held half the Anglo-Dutch battlefield, and had repulsed General Bülow's corps, saw victory snatched from it by the arrival of General Blücher with 30,000 fresh troops, a reinforcement which brought the allied army in the line up to nearly 150,000 men, that is two and a half to one.

10

As soon as General Bülow's attack had been repulsed, I gave orders to General Drouot, who was doing the duties of aide Major-General of the Guard, to rally his whole guard in front of the farm of La Belle-Alliance, where I was with eight battalions drawn up in two lines; the other eight had marched on to support the Young Guard and defend Planchenoit. However, the cavalry, which continued to hold the position on the plateau from which it dominated the whole battlefield, saw General Bülow's move but, deriving confidence from the reserves of the Guard, which it saw there to hold them, did not feel any anxiety as a result, and gave vent to cries of victory when they saw this

BATTLE OF MONT-SAINT-JEAN (WATERLOO)

corps repulsed. They were only waiting for the arrival of the infantry of the Guard to decide the victory; but they were staggered when they perceived the arrival of the numerous columns of Marshal Blücher.

Some regiments drew back. I noticed this. It was of the highest importance to put the cavalry in countenance again; and, realizing that I still needed another quarter of an hour to rally my whole Guard, I put myself at the head of four battalions, and advanced to the left in front of la Haie-Sainte, sending aides-de-camp along the line to announce the arrival of Marshal Grouchy, and to say that, with a little determination, the victory was soon to be decided.

General Reille assembled his whole corps on the left, in front of the Château of Hougoumont, and prepared his attack. It was important that the Guard should be in action all at once, but the eight other battalions were still in the rear. Being at the mercy of events, and seeing the cavalry put out of countenance, and realizing that a reserve of infantry was needed to support it, I ordered General Friant to go with these four battalions of the Middle Guard to meet the enemy's attack; the cavalry pulled itself together again and marched forward with its accustomed dash. The four battalions of the Guard repulsed everybody that they encountered; cavalry charges struck terror into the English ranks. Ten minutes later, the other battalions of the Guard arrived. I drew them up in brigades, two battalions in battle array and two in columns on the right and the left; the 2nd Brigade in échelons, which combined the advantage of the two types of formation.

The sun had gone down; General Friant, who had been wounded, and was passing by at this moment, said that everything was going well, that the enemy appeared to be forming up his rear-guard to support his retreat, but that he would be completely broken, as soon as the rest of the Guard debouched. A quarter of an hour was needed!

It was at this moment that Marshal Blücher arrived at la Haie* and overthrew the French unit defending it; this was the 4th Division of the 1st Corps; it fell back, routed, and only offered slight resistance. Although it was attacked by forces four times as strong, if only it had shown a little resolution, or had barricaded itself up in the houses, since night had already fallen, Marshal Blücher would not have had the time to carry the village. It is there that the cry of 'Sauve qui peut' is said to have been heard.

The breach effected, the line having been broken owing to the lack of vigour of the troops at la Haie, the enemy cavalry swept over the battlefield. General Bülow marched forward; Count de Lobau put on a bold front. The rout became such that it was necessary to give orders to the Guard, which was formed up to go forward, to change direction. This move was carried out in good order; the Guard faced about, with its left on the side of la Haie-Sainte

* A cluster of buildings east of Papelotte usually spelt la Haye by Napoleon, probably to avoid confusion with la Haie-Sainte. S. de C.

BATTLE OF MONT-SAINT-JEAN (WATERLOO)

and its right on the side of La Belle-Alliance, confronting the Prussians and the attack on la Haie. Immediately afterwards, each battalion formed itself into a square. The four squadrons detailed for action charged the Prussians. At this moment the English cavalry brigade, which arrived from Ohain, marched forward. These 2,000 horse got in between General Reille and the Guard.

The disorder became appalling over the whole battlefield; I only just had time to place myself under the protection of one of the squares of the Guard. If General Guyot's cavalry division of the reserve had not committed itself, without orders, to following up Kellermann's cuirassiers, it would have repulsed this charge, prevented the English cavalry from penetrating into the battlefield, and the Foot Guard would then have been able to hold all the enemy's efforts. General Bülow marched on his left, still outflanking the whole battlefield.

Night added to the confusion and obstructed everything; if it had been daylight, and the troops had been able to see me, they would have rallied: nothing was possible in the darkness. The Guard began to retreat, the enemy's fire was already a hundred toises behind and the roads were cut. I remained for a long time, with my general staff, with the regiments of the Guard on a hillock. Four guns which were there, fired briskly into the plain; the last charge wounded Lord Paget, the English cavalry general. At last, there was not a moment to lose. I could only effect my retreat across country; cavalry, artillery, infantry, were all mingled pell mell.

The general staff reached the little village of Gennapes; it hoped to be able to rally a rear-guard corps there; but the disorder was appalling, all efforts were in vain. It was eleven p.m. Finding it impossible to organize a defence, I pinned my hope on Girard's division, the 3rd of the 2nd Corps, which I had left on the battlefield at Ligny, and to which I had sent orders to move on to Quatre-Bras to support the retreat.

Never had the French army fought better than on this day; it performed prodigies of valour; and the superiority of the French troops over the enemy was such that, but for the arrival of the 1st and 2nd Prussian Corps, victory would have been won, and would have been complete over the Anglo-Dutch army and General Bülow's corps, that is to say one against two (69,000 men against 120,000).

The losses of the Anglo-Dutch army and that of General Bülow during the battle were far higher than those of the French; and the losses which the French suffered in the retreat, although considerable, since there were 6,000 prisoners, still do not balance the losses of the allies during those four days. These losses they admit to be 60,000 men; viz: 11,000 English, 3,500 Hanoverians, 8,000 Belgian, Nassau and Brunswick troops; total, 22,800 for the Anglo-Dutch army: Prussians, 38,000; grand total 60,800 men. The losses of

BATTLE OF MONT-SAINT-JEAN (WATERLOO)

the French army, even including those suffered during the rout and up to the gates of Paris, were 41,000 men.

The Imperial Guard upheld its former reputation; but it was engaged in unfortunate circumstances. It was outflanked on the right and the left, swamped by fugitives and by the enemy, just when it was joining in the fray; for, if this Guard had been able to fight, supported on the flanks, it would have repulsed the efforts of the two enemy armies combined. For more than four hours 12,000 French cavalrymen had been masters of a part of the enemy's side of the battlefield, had fought against the whole infantry and against 18,000 of the Anglo-Dutch cavalry, who were again and again repulsed in all their charges. Lieutenant-General Duhesme, an old soldier covered with wounds and of the utmost bravery, was taken prisoner as he tried to rally a rearguard. Count de Lobau was likewise taken. Cambronne, the General of the Guard, remained on the battlefield, severely wounded. Out of twenty-four English generals, twelve were killed or severely wounded. The Dutch lost three generals. The French general Duhesme was assassinated on the 19th by a Brunswick hussar, in spite of being a prisoner; this crime went unpunished. He was a brave soldier and a consummate general, who was always steadfast and unshakable in good as in bad fortune.

Chapter XLIV

THE RALLYING

Rallying of the army at Laon. Marshal Grouchy's retreat. Resources remaining to France. Effects of my abdication.

I

The Charleroi road is very wide; it was enough for the retreat of the army. The bridge of Gennapes is of similar width; five or six files of vehicles can cross abreast there. But from the moment that the first fugitives arrived, the men in the artillery parks which were there thought it advisable to barricade themselves, by placing upturned vehicles on the road in such a way as to leave a passage of only three toises. The confusion was soon appalling. Gennapes is, moreover, in a hollow; the first Prussian troops who were pursuing the army, having arrived on the heights, which dominate it, at eleven p.m., easily succeeded in disorganizing a handful of good men whom the brave General Duhesme had rallied, and entered the town. Among the vehicles which they took was my post-chaise, in which I had not ridden since Avesnes. The general practice was that on the battlefield it followed behind the reserves of the Guard. It always carried a dressing-case, a change of clothing, a sword, a great-coat and an iron bed.

At one o'clock in the morning I arrived at Quatre-Bras, dismounted at a bivouac, and sent several officers to Marshal Grouchy to inform him of the loss of the battle and to order him to retreat on to Namur. The officers whom I had sent from the battle field to take Girard's division to Ligny and place it in position at Quatre-Bras, or advance it as far as Gennapes, if there were time, reported to me the infuriating news that they had been unable to find this division.

The artillery General Nègre, a most meritorious officer, was at Quatre-Bras with the reserve parks, but he only had a weak escort; a few hundred

THE RALLYING

horsemen rallied, Count de Lobau placed himself at their head, and took all possible measures to organize a rearguard. The soldiers of the 1st and 2nd Corps, who had crossed the Sambre by the Marchiennes bridge, went towards this bridge, and left the road at Quatre-Bras or at Gosselies to take a short cut. The troops of the Guard and of the 6th Corps withdrew on to Charleroi. I sent Prince Jérôme to Marchiennes with orders to rally the army between Avesnes and Maubeuge, and betook myself to Charleroi.

When I arrived, at six in the morning, a large number of men and especially of cavalry had already crossed the Sambre, marching towards Beaumont. I stopped for an hour on the left bank, sent off some orders, and headed for Philippeville in order to be in a better position to communicate with Marshal Grouchy and to send my orders to the Rhine frontiers. After having stopped for four hours in this town, I took post to get to Laon, where I arrived on the 20th at four in the afternoon. I conferred with the prefect, entrusted my aide-de-camp, Count de Bussy, with the task of seeing to the defence of this important place, sent Count de Dejean to Guise, and Count de Flahaut to Avesnes.

I waited for Prince Jérôme's despatches, which informed me that he had rallied more than 25,000 men behind Avesnes and about fifty guns; that General Morand was commanding the Foot Guard, and General Colbert the cavalry of the Guard; that the army appeared to be increasing visibly; that most of the generals had arrived; that my losses were not as high as might be thought: more than half the artillery equipment had been saved; a hundred and seventy pieces of artillery were lost, but the men and horses had arrived at Avesnes. I gave orders for them to proceed to la Fère to collect guns there, and entrusted reliable officers with the task of reorganising a new field force there.

Marshal Soult had orders to place himself at Laon with the G.H.Q. The prefect took all measures to fill the magazines of the town and to assure supplies for an army of 80,000 to 90,000 men, who would be assembled within a few days around this town. I expected that the enemy generals, profiting by their victory, would push their army forward as far as the Somme. I ordered Prince Jérôme to leave Avesnes on the 22nd with the army and lead it to Laon, the assembly point given to Marshal Grouchy and General Rapp. Not being more than twelve hours march from Paris, I considered it necessary to go there. There was no need for my presence with the army during the days of the 21st, 22nd, 23rd and 24th. I counted on being back at Laon on the 25th. I employed these six days in the capital, in organizing the national emergency measures, in completing the preparations for the defence of Paris, and in speeding up all the help which the depots and the provinces could provide. It was easy then to judge that, should Marshal Grouchy's corps arrive intact, of which there was little doubt, the losses of the French army would be smaller than those which the enemy armies had suffered at the battles of Ligny

THE RALLYING

and Waterloo, and at the engagement of Quatre-Bras. It has since actually been calculated that the Allies' losses amounted to 63,000 men, and that those of the French did not exceed 41,000 men, including the prisoners which were taken from them during the retreat.

2

On the 18th, Marshal Grouchy had attacked Wavres at six p.m. General Thielman offered a vigorous resistance, but he was beaten. Count GERARD, at the head of the 4th Corps, forced the passage of the Dyle. Lieutenant-General Pajol, with 12,000 men, had been detached to march on Limate. There he repulsed General Bülow's rear-guard, crossed the Dyle and got to the top of the opposing heights; but the night was so dark by 10 p.m. that he could not then continue his march; and, moreover, since he could no longer hear the cannonade of Mont-Saint-Jean, he took up his position. Count GERARD was severely wounded in the attack on Wavres; a bullet passed through his chest, but luckily the wound was not fatal.

On the 19th, at dawn, General Thielman attacked Marshal Grouchy, and was vigorously repulsed. The village of Bielau and all the heights beyond Wavres were carried by the French. Brigadier-General Peine, a distinguished officer, was fatally wounded in this engagement. Marshal Grouchy was giving orders to pursue the enemy and to march in the direction of Brussels, when he received the news of the loss of the battle and my order to make his retreat on Namur. He began this at once. The Prussians followed him cautiously; but getting too far ahead, they were repulsed and lost some guns and a few hundred prisoners. General Vandamme took up his position at Namur, Marshal Grouchy at Dinant. General Thielman failed in all the attacks which he attempted. On the 24th, the whole of Marshal Grouchy's corps was at Rethel; on the 26th, it joined the army of Laon. It numbered 32,000, among which were 6,500 cavalry and 108 guns, apart from about 1,000 men crippled and little groups of cavalry who were following.

3

The position of France was critical after the battle of Waterloo, but not desperate. Everything had been prepared on the hypothesis that the attack on Belgium would fail. Seventy thousand men were rallied on the 27th between Paris and Laon; 25,000 to 30,000 men, including those of the Guard who had been left in garrison, were on the march from Paris and the depots. General Rapp, with 25,000 picked troops, was due to arrive on the Marne during the first days of July; all the losses in artillery material were made good. Paris alone contained 500 field guns, and only seventy had been lost. Thus, an army of 120,000 men, equal to that which had crossed the Sambre on the 15th, and

THE RALLYING

having an artillery train of three hundred and fifty pieces of artillery, would cover Paris on 1 July. Apart from this, the capital had, for its defence, 36,000 men of the National Guard, 30,000 sharpshooters, 6,000 gunners, six hundred pieces of artillery in batteries, formidable entrenchments on the right bank of the Seine, and, within a few days, those on the left bank would have been completely finished.

However, the Anglo-Dutch and Prusso-Saxon armies, weakened by more than 80,000 men, and now more than 140,000 in number, could not pass beyond the Somme with more than 90,000 men. There they would await the co-operation of the Austrian and Russian armies which could not be on the Marne before 15 July. Paris thus had twenty-five days to prepare its defence, complete its armament, its supplies, its fortifications, and draw troops from all over France. Even by 15 July, only 30,000 or 40,000 men could have arrived on the Rhine; the bulk of the Russian and Austrian armies could not go into action until later. Neither the arms, nor the munitions, nor the officers were lacking in the capital; the sharpshooters could easily be raised to 80,000 men, and the field artillery increased to 600 pieces.

Marshal Suchet, joined up with General Lecourbe, would, by the same period, have more than 30,000 men in front of Lyons independently of the garrison of this town, which would be well armed, well provisioned, and entrenched. The defence of all the fortresses was assured; they were commanded by picked officers, and defended by loyal troops. Everything could be put right; but character, energy, and firmness were needed on the part of officers, of the government, of the Chambers and of the whole nation! It was necessary that it should be animated by the feeling of honour, of glory, of national independence, and that it should have in mind the example of Rome after the battle of Cannae, and not of Carthage after Zama! If France attained this level, she was invincible; her people contained more martial elements than any other nation in the world. War material existed in abundance and could meet all requirements.

4

On 21 June, Marshal Blücher and the Duke of Wellington entered French territory in two columns. On the 22nd, the powder magazines at Avesnes took fire; the place surrendered. On the 24th the Prussians entered Guise and the Duke of Wellington Cambrai; on the 26th, he was at Péronne. During all this time, the fortresses of the 1st, 2nd and 3rd lines in Flanders were invested. However, these two generals learnt on the 25th of my abdication, which had taken place on the 22nd; of the revolt of the Chambers; of the despondency into which these circumstances had plunged the army, and of the hopes which our enemies within our midst derived from them.

THE RALLYING

From that moment, their one thought was to march on the capital, under the walls of which they arrived during the last days of June, with less than 90,000 men; a proceeding which would have been disastrous for them, and would have brought about their complete ruin, if they had risked it in opposition to me. But I had abdicated! The troops of the line who were at Paris, more than 6,000 men of the depots of the Guard, the sharpshooters of the National Guard, chosen from among the population of this great capital, were all devoted to me; I could strike down the enemies within! But in order to follow the motives which determined my conduct at this momentous juncture, which has had such disastrous consequences for myself and for France, we must take up the tale further back, and that is what we shall do in the next book.

Chapter XLV

OBSERVATIONS

FIRST OBSERVATION. I have been reproached, first, with having given up the dictatorship at the moment when France needed a dictator most; secondly, with having changed the constitution of the Empire at a moment when my one concern should have been to preserve it from invasion; thirdly, with having allowed the Vendéens to be stirred up, when they had first refused to take up arms against the imperial regime; fourthly, with having reassembled the Chambers when I should only have assembled the armies; fifthly, with having abdicated and left France at the mercy of a divided and inexperienced assembly; for, if it is true that it was impossible for me to save the country without the nation's confidence, it was equally impossible, in these critical circumstances, for the country to save either its honour or its independence without me.

We will not express any opinions on these matters which are dealt with thoroughly and at length in Book X.*

SECOND OBSERVATION. The skill with which the movements of the different army corps were concealed from the enemy's knowledge at the beginning of the campaign, cannot be too carefully noted. Marshal Blücher and the Duke of Wellington were taken by surprise. They saw nothing, knew nothing of all the moves which were going on close to their advance posts.

To attack the two enemy armies, the French could outflank their right, their left, or pierce their centre. In the first case, they would debouch by way of Lille and would meet the Anglo-Dutch army: in the second, they would debouch by Givet and Charlemont, and would meet the Prussian army. These two armies remained together since they would be pressed close together, with the left to the right, and vice versa. I adopted the course of covering my movements by the Sambre and of piercing the line of the two armies at Charleroi, the hinge of their junction, manoeuvring with speed and skill. Thus I found, in the secrets of the art, additional resources which served

* If so, the book has not so far come to light. S. de C.

OBSERVATIONS

me in lieu of the 100,000 men of which I was short. This plan was conceived and carried out with boldness and wisdom.

THIRD OBSERVATION. The character of several generals had been softened by the events of 1814. They had lost something of that dash, that resolution and that self-confidence which had won so much glory for them and had contributed so much to the success of former campaigns.

1. On 15 June, the 3rd Corps was supposed to take up arms at three a.m. and arrive before Charleroi at ten o'clock; it only arrived at three in the afternoon.

2. On the same day, the attack on the woods in front of Fleurus, which had been ordered for 4 p.m., did not take place until seven o'clock. Night supervened before Fleurus could be entered, where it had been my intention to place my headquarters that same day. This loss of seven hours was extremely disconcerting at the beginning of a campaign.

3. Ney received the order to get in front of Quatre-Bras on the 16th, with 43,000 men who comprised the left which he commanded, to take up position there at first light, and even to dig in there. He wavered and lost eight hours. The Prince of Orange, with only 9,000 men, held on to this important position on the 16th until three o'clock in the afternoon. When finally, at midday, the Marshal received the order dated from Fleurus, and saw that I was going to close with the Prussians, he moved on Quatre-Bras, but only with half his force. He left the other half two leagues behind to cover his line of retreat. He forgot it until six o'clock in the evening, when he felt the need of it for his own defence. In the other campaigns, this general would have occupied the position before Quatre-Bras at six a.m., would have defeated and taken the whole Belgian division; and would either have turned the Prussian army by sending a detachment by the Namur road which would have fallen upon the rear of the line of battle, or, by moving quickly on the Gennapes road, he would have surprised the Brunswick Division and the 5th English Division on the march, as they were coming from Brussels, and from there marched to meet the 1st and 3rd English Divisions, which were coming up by the Nivelles road, both without cavalry or artillery, and worn out with fatigue. Always the first under fire, Ney forgot the troops who were not under his eye. The bravery which a General-in-chief ought to display is different from that which a divisional general must have, just as the latter's ought not to be the same as that of a captain of grenadiers.

4. The advance-guard of the French army only arrived in front of Waterloo at 6 p.m. But for vexatious hesitations, it would have arrived there at 3 p.m. I revealed myself much put out by this. I said, pointing to the sun: 'What would I not give to-day to have Joshua's power and delay its progress by two hours!'

OBSERVATIONS

FOURTH OBSERVATION. Never has the French soldier shown more courage, good will, and enthusiasm. He was full of the consciousness of his superiority over all the soldiers of Europe. His confidence in me was complete, and had perhaps grown greater; but he was touchy with his other chiefs and mistrustful of them. The treacheries of 1814 were always present in his mind; every move which he did not understand worried him; he believed himself betrayed. At the moment when the first cannon were being fired near Saint-Amand, an old Corporal came up to me and said: 'Sire, don't trust Marshal Soult. You may be certain that he will betray us.'

'You need not worry,' I replied to him, 'I can answer for him as for myself.'

In the middle of the battle, an officer reported to Marshal Soult that General Vandamme had gone over to the enemy, and that his men were crying out that I should be notified of it. Towards the end of the battle, a dragoon, with his sabre all dripping with blood ran up crying, 'Sire, come quickly to the division. General d'Henin is haranguing the dragoons and telling them to go over to the enemy.'

'Did you hear him?'

'No, Sire; but an officer who is looking for you saw it, and ordered me to tell you about it.'

Meanwhile the worthy General d'Henin was hit by a cannon-ball, which shot away one of his thighs, after he had repulsed an enemy charge.

On the 14th, in the evening, Lieutenant-General Bourmont, Colonel Clouet, and the general staff-officer Villontrey, had deserted from the 4th Corps and gone over to the enemy. Their names will be held in execration so long as the French people constitute a nation. This desertion had considerably increased the soldiers' uneasiness. It seems to be more or less established that the cry of 'sauve qui peut' was raised in the 3rd Division* of the 1st Corps, on the evening of the battle of Waterloo, when Marshal Blücher was attacking the village of la Haie. This village was not defended as it ought to have been. It is equally probable that several officers, bearing orders, disappeared. But, if some officers deserted, not a single common soldier was guilty of this crime. Several killed themselves on the battlefield where they had remained wounded, when they learnt of the army's rout.

FIFTH OBSERVATION. During the day of the 17th, the French army was divided into three parts: 69,000 men, under my orders, marched on Brussels by the Charleroi road; 34,000, under the orders of Marshal Grouchy, went towards this capital by the Wavres road in the wake of the Prussians; 7,000 or 8,000 men remained on the battlefield of Ligny, namely: 3,000 men of

---

*Napoleon refers on page 535 to the 4th Division giving way at la Haie where 'the cry of "sauve qui peut" is said to have been heard.' The two divisions may have been adjoining.

S. de C.

OBSERVATIONS

Girard's division, to succour the wounded and provide a reserve at Quatre-Bras against any unforeseen contingency; 4,000 to 5,000 men forming the reserve artillery parks, remained at Fleurus and Charleroi.

Marshal Grouchy's 34,000 men, having 108 guns, were sufficient to overthrow the Prussian rear-guard in any positions they might take up, press on the retreat of the defeated army, and contain it. It was a splendid result of the battle of Ligny, thus to be able to oppose an army, which had been 120,000 strong, with 34,000 men. The 69,000 men under my orders, were sufficient for defeating the Anglo-Dutch army of 90,000 men. The disproportion which existed on the 15th between the two belligerent masses, which was then in the ratio of one to two, was satisfactorily changed; it was now only in the ratio of three to four.

If the Anglo-Dutch army had defeated the 69,000 men marching against them, I could have been reproached with having miscalculated; but it is established, even by the enemy's own admission, that, but for the arrival of General Blücher, the Anglo-Dutch army would have been driven off the battlefield between eight and nine in the evening. But for the arrival of Marshal Blücher at eight o'clock in the evening with his 1st and 2nd Corps, the march on Brussels, in two columns, during the day of the 13th, had several advantages; the left pressed the Anglo-Dutch army hard, and held it; the right, under the orders of Marshal Grouchy, pursued the Prusso-Saxon army and held it, and by evening the whole French army was to be reunited on a line of under five leagues from Mont-Saint-Jean to Wavres, with its advance posts at the edge of the forest. But the mistake made by Marshal Grouchy of stopping on the 17th at Gembloux, when he had only covered under two leagues during the day, instead of marching on until he was opposite Wavres, that is, instead of doing another three leagues, was aggravated and rendered irretrievable by the one which he made on the following day, the 18th, in wasting twelve hours, and only arriving at four in the afternoon before Wavres, instead of getting there at six a.m.

1. Though he had been entrusted with the task of pursuing Marshal Blücher, Grouchy lost sight of him for twenty-four hours, from 4 p.m. on the 17th to 4 p.m. on the 18th.

2. The movement of cavalry on the plateau, while General Bülow's attack was not yet repulsed, was a grievous accident; my intention was to order this move—but an hour later—and to have it backed up by the sixteen infantry battalions of the Guard and a hundred guns.

3. The mounted grenadiers and the dragoons of the Guard, under General Guyot, committed themselves without orders. Thus at 5 in the afternoon, the army found itself without a cavalry reserve. If, at eight-thirty, this reserve had existed, the storm which overwhelmed the battlefield would have been averted. With the enemy cavalry charges repulsed, the two armies would

OBSERVATIONS

have slept on the battlefield, notwithstanding the arrival of General Bülow and Marshal Blücher, one after the other. The balance would still have been in favour of the French army, for Marshal Grouchy's 34,000 men, with eight hundred guns, were fresh and would have bivouaced on the battlefield; the two enemy armies would have taken cover during the night in the Forest of Soignes.

It was the invariable practice, in all battles, that the division of Grenadiers and dragoons of the Guard should not lose sight of me, or charge without a verbal order given by me to the general commanding it.

Marshal Mortier, who was Commander-in-Chief of the Guard, gave up this command at Beaumont, on the 15th, just as hostilities were beginning. He was not replaced, [an omission] which had several disadvantages.

SIXTH OBSERVATION. 1. The French army manoeuvred on the right of the Sambre on the 13th and 14th. It camped, on the night of the 14th to 15th, half a league from the Prussian advance posts; and, in spite of this, Marshal Blücher was in complete ignorance of it all. When, during the morning of the 15th, he learnt at his head-quarters in Namur that I was entering Charleroi, the Prusso-Saxon army was still quartered over an area of thirty leagues, and requiring two days to be assembled. He ought, since 15 May, to have moved his head-quarters up to Fleurus; to have concentrated his army's billets within a radius of eight leagues, with advance guards watching the crossings of the Meuse and the Sambre. His army could then have assembled at Ligny on the 15th at noon, and have awaited there the attack of the French army, or could have marched against it during the evening of the 15th, and thrown it into the Sambre.

2. However, although taken by surprise, Marshal Blücher went on with his plan of assembling his army on the heights of Ligny behind Fleurus, taking the risk of being attacked there before his army had come up. On the morning of the 16th, he had only, so far, got together two army corps, and already the French army was at Fleurus. The 3rd Corps came up during the day, but the 4th, commanded by General Bülow, could not reach the battle. As soon as he knew that the French were at Charleroi, that is to say, during the evening of the 15th, Marshal Blücher ought to have given, as rallying point for his army, not Fleurus, nor Ligny (which was already under his enemy's gunfire) but Wavres, where the French could not arrive until the 17th. He would have had, in addition, the whole day of the 16th and the night of the 16th to 17th to carry out the complete assembly of his army.

3. After having lost the battle of Ligny, the Prussian general, instead of retreating on to Wavres, ought to have manoeuvred back on to the Duke of Wellington's army, either at Quatre-Bras, since the latter had held his position there, or else on to Waterloo. The whole of Marshal Blücher's retreat

OBSERVATIONS

during the morning of the 17th, was in the wrong direction, since the two armies which were only three thousand toises from each other on the evening of the 16th, with a good road connecting them, so that they could fairly be considered to be together, found themselves, on the evening of the 17th, separated by more than ten thousand toises and divided by defiles and impracticable roads.

The Prussian General violated the three great rules of war: first, to keep one's billets close together; secondly, to give a rallying point which all can reach before the enemy; thirdly, to carry out one's retreat towards reinforcements.

SEVENTH OBSERVATION: 1. The Duke of Wellington was surprised in his quarters. He ought on 15 May to have concentrated them within a radius of eight leagues from Brussels with advance-guards watching the exits from Flanders. The French army had been manoeuvring for three days within range of his advance-posts; for the last twenty-four hours it had been engaged in hostilities; its head-quarters had been at Charleroi for twelve hours; and yet the English general at Brussels still knew nothing about it, and his whole army was still comfortably ensconced in its quarters, extending over an area of more than twenty leagues.

2. The Prince of Saxe-Weimar, who was acting as part of the Anglo-Dutch army, was in position beyond Frasnes at 4 p.m. on the 15th and knew that the French army was at Charleroi; if he had sent an aide-de-camp straight to Brussels, he would have arrived there at six o'clock in the evening; and yet it was not until 11 p.m. that the Duke of Wellington was informed that the French army was at Charleroi. Thus he lost five hours in a situation and against a man where the loss of a single hour was a matter of great importance.

3. The infantry, the cavalry and the artillery of this army were quartered separately, in such a way that the infantry went into action, at Quatre-Bras, without cavalry or artillery; and this caused it to suffer considerable losses, since it was obliged to remain drawn up in columns, in close formation, under a hail of shot from fifty pieces of artillery, in order to face the charges of cuirassiers. These fine men were sacrificed like lambs led to the slaughter, without cavalry to protect them and artillery to avenge them. As the three arms cannot get on for a moment without each other, they ought always to be quartered and placed in such a way as to be able at all times to help one another.

4. The English general, although taken by surprise, gave, as a rallying point to his army, Quatre-Bras, which had been in the hands of the French for twenty-four hours. He exposed his troops to being defeated piecemeal as they arrived. The danger to which he exposed them was even greater, since he made them come up without artillery and cavalry. He delivered his infantry

OBSERVATIONS

into the enemy's hands in small groups, and without the support of the other two arms. His rallying point should have been Waterloo. He would then have had the whole day of the 16th and the night of the 16th to 17th, which was enough to bring the whole of his army, infantry, cavalry and artillery, together there. The French could not be there before the 17th and would have found the whole of his army in position.

EIGHTH OBSERVATION. The English general gave battle at Waterloo on the 18th. This course was contrary to the interests of his country, and to the general plan of campaign adopted by the Allies; it violated all the rules of war. It was not in the interests of England, who needs so many men to recruit her armies for India, her American colonies, and her vast establishments, to expose herself, wantonly, to a murderous struggle, which could lose her the only army she had, and, at the least, cost her the flower of her manhood. The Allies' plan of campaign consisted in acting *en masse* and in not getting engaged in detail. Nothing was more contrary to their interests and their plan than to risk the success of their cause in a hazardous battle, with more or less equal forces, where the odds were against them. If the Anglo-Dutch army had been destroyed at Waterloo, of what avail would have been the large number of armies which were preparing to cross the Rhine, the Alps, and the Pyrenees?

The English general, in deciding to accept battle at Waterloo, only based his decision on the co-operation of the Prussians; but this co-operation could not come about until the afternoon; he therefore remained exposed and alone, from four in the morning until five in the afternoon, that is to say, for thirteen hours. Ordinarily a battle only lasts six hours. So this co-operation was illusory.

But, in relying on the co-operation of the Prussians, he assumed that the whole French army was facing him; and, if that were so, he was counting on defending his ground, for thirteen hours, with 90,000 troops, of diverse nationality, against an army of 104,000 Frenchmen. This calculation was manifestly unsound; he could not have maintained his position for three hours; everything would have been over by eight in the morning, and the Prussians would have arrived only to be taken in the rear. Within a single day both the armies would have been destroyed. If he relied on the fact that part of the French army would follow up the Prussian army, in accordance with the rules of war, it must then have been evident to him that he could expect no assistance from it, and that the Prussians, defeated at Ligny, having lost between 25,000 and 30,000 men on the battlefield, and having had 20,000 scattered, pursued by 35,000 to 40,000 victorious Frenchmen, would not have parted with a man, and would have considered themselves scarcely strong enough to hold their own. In that case, the Anglo-Dutch army would have had to bear alone the impact of 69,000 Frenchmen throughout the day of the

OBSERVATIONS

18th, and there is not an Englishman who would not concede that the outcome of such a struggle could be in no doubt—their army was not constituted to withstand the shock of the imperial army for four hours.

Throughout the night of the 17th to 18th, the weather was horrible, which rendered the ground impassable until nine o'clock in the morning. The loss of these six hours, since dawn, was all to the enemy's advantage, but could its general let the issue of such a conflict depend upon the probable state of the weather during the night of the 17th to 18th? Marshal Grouchy, with 34,000 men and 108 guns, accomplished the impossible, by being, neither on the field of battle at Mont-Saint-Jean, nor at Wavres during the day of the 18th. But had the English general the personal assurance of this Marshal that he would blunder about in such a peculiar manner? Marshal Grouchy's conduct was just as unpredictable as if his army had experienced an earthquake on the way which had swallowed it up.

To sum up, if Marshal Grouchy had been on the battlefield of Mont-Saint-Jean, as the English General and the Prussian General expected throughout the night of the 17th to 18th, and, if the weather had allowed the French army to get into position for battle at four in the morning, the Anglo-Dutch army would have been cut up and scattered before seven o'clock; it would have been totally defeated. And, if the weather had not allowed the French army to take up its battle stations until ten o'clock, by one o'clock in the afternoon the Anglo-Dutch army would have met its fate; the remnants of it would have been hurled beyond the Forest or in the direction of Hal, and there would have been plenty of time, in the evening, to march on to meet Marshal Blücher, and make him suffer a similar fate. If Marshal Grouchy had camped before Wavres on the night of the 17th to 18th, the Prussian army would not have been able to detach any force to save the English army, and the latter would have been completely defeated by the 69,000 Frenchmen opposing it.

The Mont-Saint-Jean position was ill chosen. The first essential of a battlefield is not to have any defiles in its rear. During the battle, the English general did not know how to use his numerous cavalry to advantage; he did not judge that he should and would be attacked on his left; he believed that it would come on his right. In spite of the diversion effected in his favour by General Bülow's 30,000 Prussians, he would twice during the day have carried out his retreat, if he had been able to do so. So, in the event—oh, strange irony of human affairs!—the bad choice of his battlefield, which made all retreat impossible, was the cause of his success!

NINTH OBSERVATION. It will be asked: what ought the English general to have done after the Battle of Ligny and the engagement at Quatre-Bras? Posterity will not be in any doubt. He ought to have crossed the Forest of Soignes in the night of 17th to 18th, by the Charleroi road; the Prussian army

OBSERVATIONS

ought similarly to have crossed it by the Wavres road; the two armies ought to have effected their junction on Brussels at first light and have left rearguards to defend the forest. He should have gained a few days to give time to the Prussians, dispersed by the Battle of Ligny, to rejoin their army; reinforced himself by fourteen English regiments, which were in garrison in the fortresses of Belgium or had just disembarked at Ostend on returning from America, and have let me manoeuvre as I liked.

Would I, with an army of 100,000 men, have crossed the Forest of Soignes, in order to attack, on issuing from it, the two armies joined together, more than 200,000 strong and in position? That would certainly have been the most advantageous thing that could have happened to the allies. Would I have been content to take up a position myself? My inaction could not have lasted long, for 300,000 Russians, Austrians, and Bavarians, etc., had arrived on the Rhine. They would be on the Marne within a few weeks, which would force me to hasten to the rescue of my capital.

It was then that the Anglo-Prussian army should have marched and joined up with the allies before Paris. It would have been running no risk, would have suffered no losses, would have acted in conformity with the interests of the English nation, the general war plans adopted by the Allies, and the rules of the art of war. From the 15th to the 18th the Duke of Wellington manoeuvred continuously as I wanted him to; he did nothing that I feared he might. The English infantry was firm and sound. The cavalry could have done better. The Anglo-Dutch army was saved twice during the day by the Prussians; the first time, before three o'clock, by the arrival of General Bülow, with 30,000 men; and the second time, by the arrival of Marshal Blücher, with 31,000 men. During that day, 69,000 Frenchmen defeated 120,000 men. Victory was snatched from them between eight and nine o'clock, by 150,000 men.

One can imagine the attitude of the people of London at the moment when they learnt of the catastrophe which had befallen their army, and that their best blood had been shed in the cause of Kings against peoples, of privilege against equality, of oligarchs against liberals, of the principles of the Holy Alliance against the Sovereignty of the People!

APPENDIX A

TABLE A

Military Situation of France in March 1815

	Effective Army		Ready to take the Field		Observations
	Men	Horses	Men	Horses	
102 regiments of infantry of the line - - -	91,000	—	61,200	,,	These regiments were dismissed on the 20th March, which is the reason why they are noted here.
4 regiments of foreign infantry (Swiss) - -	4,000	—	—	—	
4 regiments of infantry of the Old Guard -	4,000	—	3,300	,,	Produced only 11,000 men, owing to the deficiency in the number of horses.
57 regiments of cavalry of the line - - -	25,000	16,000	11,000	11,000	
4 regiments of cavalry of the Old Guard -	3,200	3,000	2,800	2,800	
12 regiments of artillery of the line - - -	16,000	—	12,000	—	These 12,000 men are in proportion to the army.
Artillery of the Old Guard	,,	,,	,,	,,	
Engineers of the line -	5,000	—	3,000	,,	
Engineers of the Old Guard	,,	,,	,,	,,	
Waggon corps of the line -	1,000	,,	600	,,	
Waggon corps of the Old Guard - - - -	,,	,,	,,	,,	
Totals - - -	149,200	19,000	93,900	13,800	

N.B. Besides 12,000 gendarmes (or military police) and 10,000 veterans.

TABLE B

Organization of the French Army to 800,000 men, 1st of September, 1815

Sub-divisions		Soldiers	
102 regiments of the line, forming 510 battalions of 880 men	428,400	1st These sub-sections were to be completed by— 145,000 men, effective on 1st of March, deducting from the effective number the 4 Swiss regiments which were dismissed at the end of May	145,200
12 foreign battalions	10,800		
52 battalions of the Imperial Guard	31,200	473,400	
10 squadrons of select gendarmerie	3,000		
57 regiments of cavalry	57,000	61,000	2nd The enrolment of the military on half-pay	130,000
4 regiments of cavalry of the guard	4,000		3rd From the Conscript of 1815, received in June	80,000
Horse and foot artillery, waggon train, pontoon corps, pioneers, workmen, drivers of military stores, including the guard	50,000	50,000	4th From do. to be received in July and August	20,000
			5th The summons to 250,000 men, which was to be made in July	250,000
Extraordinary Army			6th The 200 select battalions of national guards	112,000
200 batts. selected from the national guard			7th The 48 ditto of the South of France	26,000
48 battalions of ditto from Dauphiny, Languedoc, and La Gironde	26,800	112,200	8th The battalions of marine artillery	
10 battalions of marine artillery	10,000		9th The summons of 4,000 marine artillerymen on half-pay	4,000
20 regiments of seamen	30,000	224,800	10th 30,000 seamen of the former fleets	30,000
10 regiments of veterans	10,000		11th Battalions of veterans existing in March	10,000
Coast-guards	6,000		12th Summons to 30,000 men on half-pay	30,000
Battalion of non-commissioned officers			13th Foreign regiments, Piedmontese, Italians, Spaniards, Irish, Flemings, etc.	14,000
Soldiers on half-pay	30,000			
	Total	809,200	Total	888,000

TABLE C

Arms

Arms in possession of the soldiers in March 1815	150,000
In the magazines	150,000
Additional supplies from the munitions factories, during April, May, June, July, August, and September	240,000
Extra from munitions factories established in Paris, and in all the fortified towns, whether for repairing muskets, new stocked, spare arms, or for new guns, for April and May	60,000
For June	120,000
For July, August, and September	450,000
Total	1,170,000

TABLE D

Military Situation of France on the 1st of June, 1815

Army of the Line	Under Arms.	Depots	Effective	Extraordinary Army — Employed in guarding the fortresses and coasts.	
Each of the regiments of the line has furnished 2 battalions of 600 men to the army in the field, leaving in depot its 3rd, 4th and 5th battalions	126,000	85,000	211,000	200 battalions of select national guards, of 560 men each	112,000
Regiment of foreign infantry	—	8,000	8,000	20 regiments of seamen	30,000
Infantry of the Guard	14,000	10,000	24,000	10 battalions of marine artillerymen	8,000
10 squadrons of gendarmerie serving in the army of La Vendée, count as infantry	3,000	—	3,000	Coast-guards	6,000
As cavalry	1,500	—	1,500	Veterans	10,000
57 regiments of cavalry of the line	28,500	17,000	45,500	Military on half-pay and reduced, placed in garrison	30,000
Cavalry of the Guard	4,000	2,000	6,000		
Artillery of the line	22,000	12,000	34,000		
Artillery of the Guard	400				
Waggon train of the line	6,000				
Waggon train of the Guard	2,000				
Totals	217,400	146,100	363,500	Total	196,000

Summary. Effective of the army of the line - - - - - 363,500
Effective of the extraordinary army - - - - - 196,000
General effective military strength of France, on the 1st June, 1815 - 559,500

N.B. In this statement the 12,000 men of the gendarmerie, in the margin, and employed in the police of the interior are not included. In June there were therefore 146,000 men at the depots. In July there were 200,000 to be raised. By supposing that on the 15th of August, 100,000 of them should have arrived at the depots, that would increase them to 246,000 men. At that period, 100,000 men were necessary for recruiting the army near Paris, 18,000 men, for that near Lyons. Total 118,000 men. Further and not equipped, 40,000 men for the garrison at Paris, and 10,000 men for that of Lyons. Total 50,000 men. General total 168,000 men. There would therefore remain at the depots for the divisions, the sick, etc., 73,000 men, who would be augmented with 100,000 men in September, by the completion of the levy of the 200,000 men.

TABLE E

Detail of the Situation of the Army of the Line, on the 1st of June, 1815

	On the 1st March, 1815			On the 1st June, 1815				
	In arms disposable	Depots organizing	Effective on 1st March	Summons of retired Military	Conscription of 1815	In arms disposable	Depots organizing	Effective on 1st June
102 regiments of infantry of the line	61,200	29,800	91,000	70,000	50,000	126,000	85,000	211,000
Foreign regiments	—	—	4,000	—	—	—	8,000	8,000
Regiments of infantry of the Guard	3,300	700	4,000	10,000	10,000	14,000	10,000	24,000
Regiments of cavalry of the line	11,000	14,000	25,000	15,000	5,500	28,500	17,000	45,000
4 regiments of cavalry of the Guard	2,800	400	3,200	2,800	—	4,000	2,000	6,000
Artillery of the line	12,000	4,000	16,000	14,000	4,000	22,000	12,000	34,000
Artillery of the Guard	—	—	—	5,000	2,000	4,000	3,000	7,000
Engineers of the line	3,000	2,000	5,000	5,000	2,000	6,000	6,000	12,000
Ditto of the Guard	—	—	—	500	—	400	100	500
Waggon corps	600	400	1,000	4,000	3,000	6,000	2,000	8,000
Ditto of the Guard	—	—	—	2,000	1,000	2,000	1,000	3,000
Gendarmerie of the Guard on service	—	—	—	—	—	4,500	—	4,500
Totals	93,900	51,300	149,200	128,300	77,500	217,400	146,100	363,500

Besides 12,000 gendarmes for the police of the interior of the Empire, and 10,000 veterans

TABLE G

Statement of the Strength of the Anglo-Dutch Army Assembled in Flanders, on 15th June, 1815.

Corps	Description of Forces	Divisions	Troops Composing the Divisions	Numbers of Regiments	Strength in Brigades	Strength in Divisions	Strength in Armies	Strength in Corps
1st Corps H.S.H. the Prince of Orange	INFANTRY	1st Gen. Cooke	1st Brig. of Brit. Guards / 2nd do. do.	1 & 3 / 2 & 3	1,800 / 1,700	3,500	41,300	73,000
		3rd Bar. Alten	5th Brigade of British / 1st do. Ger. light inf. / 3rd do. Hanoverian	30 33 67 73 / 581 & 2 leg. / 4 battalions	2,600 / 3,000 / 3,200	8,800		
		7th Lieut.-Gen. Collaert	Dutch, Flemings	12 do.	.. ..	7,500		
		8th Lieut.-Gen. Chassé	Dutch, Flemings	12 do.	.. ..	7,500		
		9th Lieut.-Gen. Perponcher	Dutch, Flemings, Nassau	12 do.	.. ..	8,000		
		10th H.S.H. the Duke of Brunswick	Brunswickers	8 do.	.. ..	6,000		
2nd Corps Lord Hill	INFANTRY	2nd Sir H. Clinton	3rd Brigade of British / 2nd do. German Legion / 3rd do. Hanoverians	52 71 95 / 1 2 3 4 /	2,700 / 3,000 / 3,200	8,900	31,700	
		4th General C. Colville	4th Brigade of British / 6th do. do. / 6th do. Hanoverians	14 26 51 / 35 54 59 91 /	1,900 / 2,000 / 3,200	7,100		
		5th Sir T. Picton	8th Brigade of British / 9th do. do. / 5th do. Hanoverians	28 32 79 91 / 1 42 44 92 /	3,000 / 3,000 / 3,200	9,200		
		6th Sir J. Lambert	10th Brigade of British / 4th do. Hanoverians	4 27 40 81 /	3,300 / 3,200	6,500		
Lord Uxbridge	CAVALRY	1st Lord E. Somerset	1st & 2nd Life Guards / Royal Horse Guards blue. 1st Dragoon Guards	.. .. /	1,250 / 1,250	2,500	20,000	
		2nd Sir W. Ponsonby	1st, 2nd, & 6th Dragoons.. ..	.. ..	..	1,875		
		3rd Sir W. Dornberg	1st & 2nd Light dragoons of Mtd. German legion / 23rd Dragoons..	.. ..	1,200 / 625	1,825		
		4th Sir Ormsby Vandeleur	11th, 12th, & 16th Light Dragoons	.. ..	..	1,875		
		5th Sir C. Grant	2nd Hussars of German legion / 7th Light Dragoons, 5th Hussars	.. ..	600 / 1,250	1,850		
		6th Sir R. H. Vivian	1st Hussars of German Legion / 18th Light dragoons & 10th Hussars	..	600 / 1,250	1,850		
		7th Sir F. d'Arentschild	3rd Hussars of German Legion / 13th Light Dragoons / Prince Regent's Bremen Verdan.	.. / .. .. / ..	600 / 625 / —	—		
		8th Col. Astorf.	Cumberland, Hanoverian Hussars..	.. ..	..	2,000		
		9th	Dutch and Flemish Cavalry	.. ..	..	3,200		
		10th	Brunswick Cavalry	.. ..	..	1,800		
	Artil. Engin. Waggon-Train, having 250 guns.		British / Dutch / Flemish	.. .. / .. .. /	5,000 / 3,200 / 3,000			11,200

Total Strength of the Anglo-Dutch Army, 104,200 men, 250 pieces of cannon.

N.B. Besides 14 regiments of infantry recently landed at Ostend, or in garrison at fortresses in Flanders.

APPENDIX B

SUPPER AT BEAUCAIRE

by
NAPOLEON
BONAPARTE

Translated by
SOMERSET DE CHAIR

A CONVERSATION

between a Soldier of the army of Carteaux, a Marseillais, a Nîmois, and a Manufacturer of Montpellier, on the events which have taken place in the above district upon the arrival of the men of Marseilles.

I was in Beaucaire on the last day of the fair. Chance gave me for companions at supper two business men from Marseilles, a man from Nîmes, and a manufacturer of Montpellier.

After several minutes taken up with introducing ourselves, it transpired that I was from Avignon and was a soldier. The attention of my companions, which had all the week been directed towards the affairs of business and the getting of money, was now turned to the probable outcome of current events, and the conversation ran on these lines. They were anxious to know my opinion, so that by comparing it with their own, they might revise or acquire suppositions as to the future which would affect each member of the company in a different way.

The two Marseillais seemed especially subdued. The evacuation of Avignon had led them to have misgivings about everything. Nothing was left to them but a considerable anxiety as to the lot in store for them. Mutual confidence, however, soon rendered all members of the party talkative, and they began a discussion, more or less in the following terms:

THE NÎMOIS: Is the army of Carteaux strong? I am told that it suffered considerable loss in the attack; but if it is true that it was repulsed, why have the Marseillais evacuated Avignon?

THE SOLDIER: The army was four thousand strong when it attacked Avignon. It is six thousand strong to-day. Within four days' time it will be ten thousand strong. It has lost five men killed and four wounded. It has not in any way been repulsed, for it has not made a single attack in battle formation. It cantered around the place, made some attempts to force in the gates by setting mines up against them; it has fired a few cannon balls to test the strength of the garrison. It then retired within its quarters in order to concert

A CONVERSATION

its plan of attack for the following night. The Marseillais were three thousand six hundred strong. They had more artillery and guns of larger calibre. Yet they have been obliged to recross the Durance. That astonishes you, does it? The reason is that only veteran troops can stand up to the uncertainties of a siege. As it was we were masters of the Rhône, of Villeneuve and of the surrounding country. We would have been able to cut all their communications. Therefore they had to evacuate the town. The cavalry pursued their retreat, and have taken many prisoners, while only losing two guns.

THE MARSEILLAIS: That is not the account I heard. I do not wish to question the truth of your statements, seeing that you were present. Nevertheless you must admit that what you have just recounted does not mean a thing. Our army is at Aix. Three good generals have arrived to replace the former ones. Fresh battalions are being raised at Marseilles. We have a new train of artillery, including several 24-pounders. In no time we will be in a position to retake Avignon, or at the very worst we shall remain masters of the Durance.

THE SOLDIER: There you are. That is exactly what they tell you to drag you into the precipice which deepens at every instant, and which perhaps will swallow up the most beautiful town in France, the town which has deserved more than any other the praise of patriots. They told you that you would sweep across France and call the tune for the Republic to dance to. Yet your first stages have been reverses. They told you that Avignon could hold out a long time against twenty thousand men, yet a single column of the army, without siege artillery, was master of the place within twenty-four hours. They told you that the South had risen to a man, and yet you stand alone. They told you that the Nîmois cavalry would crush the Allobroges, while these were already at the Saint-Esprit and at Villeneuve. They told you that four thousand Lyons men were on the march to reinforce you. At that moment the Lyonnais were negotiating their terms for peace.

Admit then that you are being deceived. Consider the incompetence of your leaders and mistrust their calculations. The most dangerous counsellor is self-esteem. You are by nature of quick intelligence. You are being led to your destruction by the same process which has ruined so many peoples: by flattering their vanity. You have riches and a considerable population, but you are told that they are greater than they are. You have rendered striking services to the cause of Liberty. They remind you of them without drawing attention to the fact that the Genius of the Republic was then on your side, whereas it abandons you to-day.

Your army, you say, is at Aix with a great train of artillery and good generals. Well, I can only tell you that whatever it does it will be beaten. You had three thousand six hundred men; a good half have slunk away. Marseilles and a few refugees of the department can furnish you with four thousand men. That is a lot. You will therefore have five to six thousand men, lacking cohesion, lacking unity, without war-experience.

You have good generals. I have never heard of them. I am not in a position to contest their ability, but their whole attention will be taken up with details. They will not be backed up by their subordinates. Whatever reputation they may have acquired, they will be able to do nothing to maintain it, because they would need two months to organise their army decently, and within four days Carteaux will be over the Durance, and with what soldiers!—with the excellent light troop of the Allobroges, the veteran regiment of Bourgogne, a good regiment of cavalry, the fine battalion of the Côte-d'Or, which has a hundred times seen victory go before it into battle, and six or seven other corps, all of veteran soldiers, fortified by their successes on the frontiers and over your army.

You have some 24- and 18-pounders and you believe it impossible that you should be dislodged. Your authority is popular opinion, but the trained soldier will tell you, and a disastrous experience is going to show you, that good 4- and 8-pounder cannon are as effective for field work as pieces of larger calibre, and are in many respects preferable to them. You have gunners freshly recruited and your antagonists have artillerymen from regiments of the line, who are the masters of Europe in their profession.

What will your army do if it concentrates on Aix? It will be beaten. It is an axiom in the military art that to remain in one's entrenchments is to be defeated. Practice and theory are in agreement on this point, and the walls of Aix are not worth the worst trench in open country if attention is paid to their extended length and to the houses that cluster round them within pistol range. Rest assured then that this course of action, which seems to you to be the best, is the worst. Besides, how will you be able to provision the town in so short a time, with all that it will need?

Will your army advance to attack the enemy? Why, it is smaller in numbers; why, its artillery is less adapted for open country. It will be broken in pieces. After that: complete rout; for the cavalry will prevent it from rallying.

Suppose then that you wait to fight it out in the Marseilles territory: one party of considerable strength there is in favour of the Republic. It will be just the opportunity they want. They will effect a junction; and this city, the centre of the commerce of the Levant, the trading centre for the South of Europe, will be overthrown.

Remember the recent example of Lisle and consider the barbarous rules of war. Why, what madness has all of a sudden taken possession of your people? What fatal blindness is it that leads them on to ruin? How can you hope to hold out against the entire Republic? Even if you should force this army to fall back before Avignon, can you doubt that within a few days, new combatants will come to replace the first? Do you suppose that the Republic, which gives the law to Europe, is going to take it from Marseilles?

In conjunction with Bordeaux, Lyons, Montpellier, Nîmes, Grenoble, the Jura, the Eure, and the Calvados, you undertook a revolution. You had a fair chance of success. The people who started it may have been wrongly actuated, but at least you had an imposing array. To-day, on the other hand, when Lyons, Nîmes, Montpellier, Bordeaux, the Jura, the Eure, Grenoble and Caen have adopted the Constitution; to-day when Avignon, Tarascon and Arles have given way, admit that there is folly in your obstinacy in holding out. The reason for it is that you are under the influence of men who, no longer having anything to lose, are dragging you with them in their ruin.

Your army will be composed of the most comfortably off elements of the wealthy of your city, because the sans-culottes are only too likely to turn against you. You are, therefore, going to endanger the flower of your youth, who are accustomed to sway the commercial balance of the Mediterranean and enrich you by their business methods and their speculations; you are going to pit them against veteran soldiers who have been spattered a hundred times with the blood of the aristocrats mad with rage or of the ferocious Prussian.

Leave it to poor countries to fight to the bitter end. The inhabitant of the Vivarais, of the Cevennes, or of Corsica, can expose himself without fear to the issue of a fight. If he wins, he has fulfilled his aim. If he loses, he finds himself where he was before, in a position to make peace. He is no worse off.

But you! ... Lose one battle, and the fruit of a thousand years of effort, pain, sacrifice and happiness, becomes the prey of the soldier.

Those are the risks that you are being made to run with so little heed.

THE MARSEILLAIS: You move quickly and you alarm me. I agree with you that the situation is critical. It may even be true that not enough heed is being paid to the position we are in.

But admit that we still have immense resources with which to oppose you.

You have persuaded me that we cannot hold out at Aix. Your remark upon the lack of subsistence for a long siege is perhaps unanswerable; but do you really believe that the whole of Provence will stand by for long impassive while Aix is blockaded? The South will rise spontaneously and your army, shut in on all sides, will be lucky if it can get back over the Durance.

THE SOLDIER: That shows how little you understand the temper of men or of the moment. Everywhere there are two parties. From the moment you are besieged, the secession party will be worsted in all the provinces. The example of Tarascon, Orgon and Arles ought to convince you of that. Twenty dragoons sufficed to restore the former administrators and set the others to rout. From now on any great movement in your favour is impossible in your department. There might have been a chance when the army was beyond the Durance and you were united. At Toulon, now, feelings are very divided, and the separatists have not the same ascendancy as at Marseilles. They will therefore have to remain inside the town in order to hold their enemies.

As for the department of the Lower Alps, you know that the Constitution has been accepted there almost unanimously.

THE MARSEILLAIS: We will attack Carteaux in our mountainous country where his cavalry will not be able to help him.

THE SOLDIER: As if an army guarding a town were master of the point of attack! In any case it is not true that there are mountains near Marseilles sufficiently precipitous to discount the services of cavalry. On the other hand, your olive groves are sufficiently steep to make the attack from artillery more formidable and to give your enemies a great advantage; for it is in this cut up country that the speed and certainty of movement, and the accuracy of range-finding, give the good artilleryman the superiority.

THE MARSEILLAIS: You consider us stripped of all resources then. Can it be possible that it was written in the destiny of this town which resisted the Romans, and maintained a part of its own laws under the despots who succeeded them, that it should become the prey of a few brigands? What! Is the Allobroge, loaded with the spoils of Lisle, to give the law in Marseilles! What! Are Dubois de Crancé and Albitte to go unchallenged! Are these men, athirst for blood, whom chance misfortunes of circumstance have placed at the helm of affairs, to be the absolute masters? What a melancholy prospect you offer. Our properties, on one pretext or another, would be invaded. From hour to hour we should be the victims of brutal troopers whom the prospect of pillage has alone drawn together under the colours. Our best citizens would be imprisoned and would be criminally put to death. The Club would raise its monstrous head again to carry out its infamous projects! Nothing can be worse than so horrible a picture. Better to risk oneself with the possibility of victory than to become a victim without hope.

THE SOLDIER: That is just the trouble with civil war. We tear each other to pieces, we hate each other, and we kill each other without knowing what our opponents are like. . . . The Allobroges—what do you suppose they are? Africans, or the inhabitants of Siberia? Well! No they are not. They are your compatriots, men of Provence, of Dauphiny, of Savoy. They are considered barbarians because their name is foreign. If your phalanx happened to be called the Phocian phalanx, the most fabulous reports would be believed, on the strength of it.

Admittedly you have reminded me of one instance, namely that of Lisle. I am not trying to justify it, but I will explain it. The people of Lisle killed the negotiator who had been sent to them under a flag of truce. They resisted without a hope of success. They were taken by assault. The soldier entered the city under fire in the midst of dead and dying. It was no longer possible to hold him in. Exasperation did the rest. These soldiers whom you call brigands are our best troops, our most disciplined battalions, their reputation above calumny.

Dubois-Crancé and Albitte, long-standing friends of the people, have never deviated from the straight path. They are criminals in the eyes of the wicked. But Condorcet, Brissot, and Barbaroux were also regarded as criminals when they were pure. It is the prerogative of good people to have evil thought of them by the bad. You seem to think that they are ruthless with you; whereas in point of fact they treat you as erring children. Do you suppose that, if they had wished to prevent it, Marseilles would have been allowed to withdraw the goods which it had at Beaucaire? They could have confiscated them until the issue of the war was decided! They did not choose to do it, and thanks to them you can return in peace to your homes.

You call Carteaux an assassin. Indeed! Perhaps you do not know that this general worries himself to death over order and discipline. Witness his conduct at Saint-Esprit and at Avignon. Not a pin was plundered. He had a sergeant imprisoned for violating the sanctuary of a citizen's home without a specific order. The sergeant's only crime was that he had arrested one Marseillais of your army who had stayed behind in the house. Some people in Avignon were penalised for going so far as to point out a house as that of an aristocrat. I could recite the case of a writ issued against a common soldier on the accusation of theft. . . . Your army, on the other hand, has killed or murdered more than thirty people, has broken into the sanctuary of families, and has filled the prisons with citizens on the vague pretext that they were brigands. Do not get alarmed about the army. It respects Marseilles, because it knows that no city has done as much for the public weal. You have eighteen thousand men away at the front, and you have not spared yourselves in any circumstances. Shake off the yoke of the small number of aristocrats who are leading you; adopt once again more reasonable counsels and you will have no truer friend than the soldier.

THE MARSEILLAIS: Oh! but your soldiers have degenerated far below what they were in the army of 1789. That army would not take arms against the nation. Your soldiers ought to emulate so fine an example and not turn their weapons against their fellow citizens.

THE SOLDIER: On those lines Vendée would by now have planted the Bourbon flag above the walls of a rebuilt Bastille, and the camp of Jalès would rule over Marseilles!

THE MARSEILLAIS: Vendée wants a king, wants a counter-revolution. The war of Vendée and of the camp of Jalès is a war of fanaticism. Ours, on the contrary, is one of true republicans, enemies of anarchy and scoundrels. Do

A CONVERSATION

we not fly the tricolour flag? And what interest should we have in wanting slavery?

THE SOLDIER: I know well that the people of Marseilles are poles apart from those of Vendée in the matter of a counter-revolution. The people of Vendée are robust and healthy, those of Marseilles are weak and ill. The pill has to be sugared; and to establish the new doctrine they have to be deceived. But after four years of revolution, after so many plots, plans and conspiracies, human perversity has been stretched to its utmost limits in all directions. Men have sharpened their natural faculties to perfection.

This is so true that, in spite of the departmental coalition, despite the skill of the leaders, and the great variety of tricks to which the enemies of the revolution have resorted, the common people have everywhere woken up, just when they were believed to be completely bewitched.

You have the tricolour flag, you say?

Paoli flew it in Corsica too, in order to gain time to deceive the people, to crush the true friends of liberty, and to drag his countrymen into his ambitious and criminal projects. He flew the tricolour flag and he had the buildings belonging to the Republic fired upon, and he had our troops driven out of the fortresses, and he disarmed those who were in them. He mobilized in order to drive out the Republicans in the island, and he pillaged the magazines, selling everything they contained, at any price he could get, in order to obtain money to keep up his rebellion, and he violated and confiscated the properties of the most well-to-do families just because they supported the unity of the Republic, and he had himself appointed generalissimo so as to declare all who remained in our armies enemies of the country. He had already made the expedition (to the Maddalena islands) against Sardinia fail; and yet he had the impudence to call himself the friend of France and a good republican, and tricked the Convention which decreed his dismissal. Finally he behaved so cleverly that, when he had been found out through his own letters found at Calvi, it was too late. The enemy fleets were able to intercept all communications and stop any information reaching the mainland.

It is no use bothering with words. It is necessary to analyse actions; and you must admit that in sizing yours up it is easy to prove you counter-revolutionaries.

What effect has the movement you set on foot produced in the Republic? You have led her to the brink of ruin. You have delayed the operations of our armies. I do not know if you are in the pay of the Spaniard and the Austrian; certainly they could not wish for a better diversion of our strength. What more could you do if you were in their pay?

Your success is day and night the object of the greatest concern of the best known aristocrats. You have placed avowed aristocrats at the head of your

A CONVERSATION

organisations and your armies, such as Latourette, an ex-colonel, and Soumise, an ex-lieutenant-colonel of Engineers, men who deserted their regiments in the hour of war so as not to have to fight for the liberty of peoples. Your battalions are full of such men and your cause would not be theirs if it were that of the Republic.

THE MARSEILLAIS: But are Brissot, Barbaroux, Condorcet, Buzot, Vergniaux also aristocrats? Who then established the Republic? Who overthrew the tyrant? Who, finally, kept up the fight during the most critical phase of the last campaign?

THE SOLDIER: I am not concerned with whether these men, who have done such wonderful services for the people on so many occasions, have conspired against the people. It is enough for me to know that, since 'The Mountain', either by public spirit or party spirit, have gone to the extent of taking extreme measures against them and have carried to the last extremity of hostility to them, decreed them prisoners and—I will even allow you this—calumniated them, the Brissot party were done for, if there had been no civil war giving them the opportunity to lay down the law to their enemies.

Thus your war was especially wasted on them. If they had been worthy of their former reputation, they would have thrown down their arms in support of the Constitution, they would have sacrificed their own interests to the public good. But it is easier to quote Decius than to imitate him; and to-day they stand convicted of the worst of all crimes. By their own actions they have justified the decree of execution against them. The blood that they have spilled has wiped out the services which they once rendered.

THE MANUFACTURER OF MONTPELLIER: You have considered this matter from the point of view most favourable to these gentlemen in the most convincing light; for it seems to have been proved that the Brissot party were really guilty: but, guilty or not, we are no longer in the times when one went to war over the life of a few individuals.

England spilt torrents of blood for the families of Lancaster and York, and France for the Lorrains and the Bourbons. Are we still in those barbarous times?

THE NÎMOIS: Yes, that is why we abandoned the people of Marseilles as soon as we realised that they were out for a counter-revolution, and that they were fighting over private quarrels. They were unmasked from the moment they refused to publish the Constitution. Then we forgave 'The Mountain' a few irregularities. We forgot Rabaud and his Jeremiads and saw only the newborn Republic, surrounded by the most terrible of coalitions, threatening to stifle it in its cradle; we saw only the joy with which the aristocrats and all Europe wished to conquer it.

THE MARSEILLAIS: You deserted us in cowardly fashion, after having roused us with ephemeral deputations.

A CONVERSATION

THE NÎMOIS: We acted in good faith, while you had the fox under your cloak all the time. We wanted the Republic, consequently we accepted a republican constitution.

You were dissatisfied with 'The Mountain' and the events of 31 May. You ought therefore to have accepted the constitution in order to overthrow 'The Mountain' legally and put an end to its mission.

THE MARSEILLAIS: We want the Republic too, but we want our constitution to be formed by representatives who are free in their actions. We want liberty, but we want to be given it by representatives whom we respect. We do not want our constitution to uphold pillage and anarchy. Our first conditions are: no Club, none of these interminable primary assemblies, and lastly, respect of private property.

THE MANUFACTURER OF MONTPELLIER: It is patent to whoever cares to reflect on the matter, that a part of Marseilles wants the counter-revolution. They pretend to want the Republic, but that is a veil which would become more transparent every day. You would soon see the counter-revolution in all its nakedness and would take it for granted. For a long time the veil which covered it was only made of gauze. Your people were good, but, if it were not for the Genius of the Revolution which watches over them, they would have been perverted.

Our troops have done a great service to the country, in having taken the field against you with such energy. There was no reason for them to imitate the army of 1789, for you are not the nation. The centre of unity is the Convention, which is the true sovereign, above all when the people are divided.

You have overthrown all the laws and all the conventions. By what right did you strip your department of its constitutional authority? As if Marseilles had created it in the first place! By what right does the battalion of your city over-run the surrounding districts? By what right did your national guards presume to enter Avignon? The department as such being dissolved, the district of this town was of longer standing than yours. By what right did you presume to trespass on the territory of Drôme? And why should you imagine that this department has not the right to call the public arm to its defence? Thus you have cut across every established right. You have set up anarchy, and since you choose to justify your actions by the right of force, I presume you must be brigands and anarchists.

You have set up a popular government. Marseilles alone has elected it. It is in defiance of all the laws and can only be a tribunal of blood, because it is the tribunal of a single faction. You have subjected the whole of your department to this tribunal, by force. By what right? Are you not therefore usurping the very authority which you censure in Paris? Your sectional committee has acknowledged that it has affiliations. There, then, you have an amalgamation comparable to that of the Clubs against which you protest. Your committee

A CONVERSATION

has executed administrative acts among the communes of Var. There, then, is an instance of the abuse of territorial divisions.

At Avignon you have imprisoned whole administrative bodies without authority, without decree, without warrant. You have violated the sanctuary of families, and abused the liberty of the individual. You have assassinated in cold blood in the public squares. You have renewed the very scenes which sullied the origin of the revolution, and whose horror you exaggerated, without information, without legal procedure, without even knowing the victims, merely on the accusation of their enemies. You have seized them, snatched them from beside their children, and dragged them through the streets; and sabred them to death.

The number you have sacrificed in this manner is reckoned as high as thirty. You have dragged the statue of Liberty in the mud. You have given her a public execution. It has been the victim of every degree of violence among an unbridled youth. You slashed at it with swords, You cannot deny that. It was in broad daylight, and more than two hundred of your people witnessed this criminal outrage. The procession passed through several streets and arrived at the Clock Square.

I will check my reminiscences and my indignation.

Is this, however, what you want the Republic to be? You have slowed up the progress of our armies (at the front) by stopping the convoys. How can you deny the evidence of so many facts, and evade the title of enemies of the country?

THE SOLDIER: There is no doubt about the Marseillais having hindered the operations of our armies, and having wished to destroy liberty. That is not the point at this moment. The question is to know whether they have any hope and what course of action remains for them to adopt?

THE MARSEILLAIS: We certainly seem to be worse off than I thought; but one is very strong when one is resolved to die, and we are prepared to die rather than assume once more the yoke of the men governing the State.

You know that a drowning man will clutch at any straw, and indeed so will we, rather than let ourselves be murdered.

Yes, we have all taken a hand in this new revolution; we shall be sacrificed as the victims of revenge. Two months ago there was a conspiracy to slaughter four thousand of our best citizens. Imagine to what excesses they would go to-day. One can never forget that monster, who, nevertheless, was one of the leading men of the Club. He had a citizen hanged, plundered his house, and raped his wife, after making her drink a glass of her husband's blood.

THE SOLDIER: How horrible! But is this instance true? I doubt it because you know that no one believes in rape now....

THE MARSEILLAIS: Anyway, rather than submit to such men, we will go to any length. We will hand ourselves over to the nation's enemies. We will

A CONVERSATION

call in the Spaniards, and there does not exist a people whose character is as little compatible with our own as theirs is; there is no people more hateful to us. By the sacrifice that we are prepared to make, judge for yourself the dastardliness of the men whom we fear.

THE SOLDIER: Surrender to the Spaniards! We will not give you the time.

THE MARSEILLAIS: They are reported every day to be outside our harbours.

THE NÎMOIS: This sole threat would be sufficient for me to see whether it was the Confederates or 'The Mountain' who were the real republicans. 'The Mountain' was at one moment in the weakest possible position. The disorder appeared to be universal. But did it ever speak of calling in the enemy? Don't you realise that the struggle between the patriots and the despots of Europe is a fight to the death?

If therefore you expect help from them, it means that your leaders have good reasons for being accepted by them. But I still have too high an opinion of your people to believe that you, at Marseilles, would be the foremost in so cowardly a project.

THE SOLDIER: Do you even think that you would be inflicting any damage on the Republic, and that your threat is at all alarming? Consider it.

The Spaniards have no landing troops. Their ships cannot enter your harbour. If you called in the Spaniards, that would be a useful ruse for your leaders to get away with some part of their fortune. But indignation would be general throughout the Republic. You would have sixty thousand men on top of you within a week. The Spaniards would carry off what they could from Marseilles, and there would still be enough left to enrich the victors.

If the Spaniards had thirty or forty thousand men in their fleet ready to disembark, your threat would be frightening; but to-day it is only silly, and will only hasten your end.

THE MANUFACTURER OF MONTPELLIER: If you were really capable of such a vile action, not a single stone ought to be left standing in your superb city. It ought to be so dealt with that in a month from now, the traveller, crossing through your ruins, would believe that you had been destroyed a hundred years ago.

THE SOLDIER: Listen to me, my friends from Marseilles, shake off the yoke of the small number of criminals who are leading you into the counter-revolution. Re-establish your constitutional authorities. Accept the Constitution. Restore to the deputies their liberty. Let them go to Paris to plead for you. You have been led astray. It is nothing new for the people to be so led by a small number of conspirators and intriguers. In all ages the gullibility and ignorance of the mob have been the cause of most civil wars.

THE MARSEILLAIS: Ah, sir! Who can do any good in Marseilles? Is it to be the refugees who arrive among us from all sides of the department? Their only interest is to act like desperadoes. Is it to be those who govern us? Are

A CONVERSATION

they not in the same predicament? Is it to be the people? One half does not know its own plight, being blinded and fanatic. The other half is disarmed, suspected, trampled down. In direst sorrow, then, I see only misfortunes without remedy.

THE SOLDIER: There, you see reason at last. Why should not a similar change of heart be accomplished among a large number of your fellow citizens who have been deceived and who are still of good intentions! Then Albitte, who can only want to spare French blood, will send you some man who is loyal and capable. Our disputes will be at an end, and without halting for another instant, the army will march to the walls of Perpignan and make the Spaniard, who is puffed up with some slight success, dance the Carmagnole; while Marseilles will continue to be the centre of gravity for liberty. It will only be necessary for her to tear a few pages out of her history.

This happy forecast put the company in good humour once more. The Marseillais willingly paid for several bottles of Champagne, which entirely dissipated cares and anxieties alike. We went to bed at two o'clock in the morning, arranging to meet again at breakfast the next day, when the Marseillais had several more doubts to put forward, and I plenty of interesting truths to bring home to him.   29 July, 1793.

INDEX

Abbeville, 488
Abdalla, 333
Abercrombie, General Sir Ralph, in Egypt, 350, 353, 357
Aboukir, 292, 293, 298, 355, 360; artillery landed at, 281, 283, 287; Brueys anchors off, 282–3, 284; naval action off, 284–8, 290, 333, 350, 354–5, 359, 412, 421; Turks land at, 333, 343, 344; fort captured, 344; French converge on, 344–6; battle of, 347–9, 352, 354, 358, 359, 363; Abercrombie at, 350
Abou-Neshabe, 306
Abyssinia, 295, 297
Acqui, 30, 54, 55, 57, 183, 441
Acre, 325, 331, 332, 334, 360; siege of, 6, 287–8, 335, 340, 343, 349, 352, 354, 358; three phases of, 335 *et seq.*; French artillery at, 335, 337; counterscarp mined, 336, 337; tower blown up, 337, 338; French assault on, 338–9; siege raised, 339
Adams, John, and France, 410, 411; and Franco-American Convention (1799), 416
Adda, river, 60, 65, 66, 68, 69, 183, 231, 232, 448, 458, 459, 464; demanded as Austrian boundary, 258–9
Adet, Pierre Auguste, 408
Adige, river, 47, 49, 60, 61, 62, 74, 87, 94, 95, 102, 123, 125, 126, 131, 134, 142, 152, 160, 161, 182, 184, 186 *et seq.*, 194 *et seq.*, 200, 201, 202, 206, 208, 229, 255, 260; and siege of Mantua, 80, 83, 84; French arrive on, 92; Austrians advance down, 93; French return to, 98; French defence of, 103, 105, 107; Wurmser crosses, 107; Vaubois's retreat on, 113; Alvinzi's attempts to cross, 114 *et seq.*; Provera checked on lower, 139, 140–1; Provera crosses, 143; French reserves left on, 160; Joubert's drive up, 167–8; as Austrian frontier, 252, 259
Aigues-Mortes, 489
Aiquadieh, 316
Aire, 488
Aisne, river, 487
Aix, 568; N.'s reception in, 362–3; Marseillais army at, 566, 567
Aix, Island of, 489
Aix-la-Chapelle, 417
Ajaccio, 4, 6, 7, 362; French occupy (1768), 5

Alba, 57, 62, 64, 183
Albani, Cardinal, 130, 148, 227; Busca's letter to, 147–8
Albania, 282, 304
Albaredo, 107, 114, 117, 118, 119, 188, 195
Albenga, 52, 58
Albenza, 180
Albitte, Antoine Louis de, 15, 29, 569, 570, 576
Alceste, the, 358
Aleppo, 316, 330, 331, 332
Aleria, 5, 6
Alessandri, ———, 230
Alessandria, 58, 71, 92, 183, 458, 459, 465, 468; surrendered to French, 59, 63, 64; Convention of, 448; Austrians march on, 461, 462, 464; Austrians at, 466; surrender of, 469
Alexander, the, 286
Alexander I, Tsar, 429, 479, 498
Alexander the Great, 288, 292, 293, 298
Alexandretta, 280, 298, 330; Gulf of, 331
Alexandria, 197, 283–5, 313, 328, 331–7, 350, 351, 353, 355, 356–60, 483; Nelson at, 280; Brueys ordered to enter, 281–2; Nelson leaves, 287; description of, 292–3; N. fortifies, 293; commercial importance, 298, 302; library burnt, 316
Algiers, 297
Ali, Caliph, 319, 332
Alkam, 305, 344
Alkmaar, battle of, 435
Alla, 98, 103
Allobroges, 566, 567, 569
Alpon, river, 114, 117, 118, 119, 121, 195
Alps, geography of, 46; difficulties of passing, 47–8; N. passes, 453–5
Alps, Army of, 32, 60
Alquier, Charles Marie Jean, 386
Alsace, 91, 495, 497; French troops in, 486, 520
Alten, Sir Charles, Count von, 560; at Quatre Bras, 513 *and n.*; at Waterloo, 521
Altenkirchen, 178
Alvinzi (Alvintzy), Baron Joseph von Barberek, Austrian Field-Marshal, 125, 130, 131, 132, 133, 158, 207; ordered to relieve Mantua, 111; plans of, 112; near the Brenta, 112–3; his northern army advances to Rivoli, 113, 115; on the Adige, 114; battle of Arcole, 115 *et seq.*; retreats, 121; losses at Arcole, 122;

INDEX

Alvinzi (Alvintzy), Baron Joseph—*cont.* reinforced, 138; strength of (Jan. 1797), 138; again plans to relieve Mantua, 139; operates on the lower Adige, 140-1; at Rivoli, 141-3; retreats across the Piave, 144; losses of (January), 144; N.'s observations on actions against, 191-7
Aly Bey, youth of, 318
Amack, Isle of, 423, 424, 428
Amasia, 316, 331
America, War of Independence, 406, 407; strained relations with France, 408-11; negotiates Convention with France, 411, 414-6; English troops in, 479, 489, 503, 520, 551
Amiens, 488; Peace of, 430
Amsterdam, 432
Ancients, Council of, 37, 242, 267, 366, 368, 374, 395, 400; Directory arrests members of, 245; decrees removal to St Cloud, 369, 370-1, 372, 381; N. addresses, 372, 375-6; at St Cloud, 375 *et seq.*
Ancona, 49, 153, 154, 156, 228, 355, 479; French garrison in, 86; French occupy, 151; weeping Madonna at, 151-2; to remain in French hands, 155; garrisoned by French, 157
Andreossy, General, 65, 89, 117, 165, 269, 327
Andrieux, Colonel, 216, 447-8
Angely, Reynault de Saint Jean de, 37
Anghiari, 143, 194
Angoulême, Louis Antoine de Bourbon, Duc de, 476, 477, 495
Angoulême, Marie Thérèse Charlotte, Duchesse de, 476
Ante-Lebanon, 331
Antibes, 27, 52, 441, 446, 448, 449, 462, 489
Antilles, 332
Antioch, 331; Gulf of, 330
Antonelle, ——, 43
Antwerp, 386, 483; N. at, 270
Aosta, 47; Duke of, 51; N. at, 445, 455
Apennines, 50, 84, 85, 86, 87, 131, 157, 161, 180, 435-6, 441, 443; geography of, 46; French pass the, 153, 154
Aquilea, 254
Aquilon, the 286
Arabia, 296, 297, 302, 304, 332, 333, 351, 360; description of, 330
Arabs, 298, 360; power and character of, 299-300; wandering, 301; fear of Mamelukes, 301-2; Egyptian government intrusted to, 303; at battle of Pyramids, 306 *et seq.*; spread Islam, 315-6; and art and science, 317, 324, 325; dress of, 323; horses of, 326; revolt of, 341-2
Aragon, 490
Arbizola, 442
Architecture of Egypt, 323-4
Arcole, 132, 191, 194, 269; N. at, 107; terrain near, 114, 117; Alvinzi at, 115; battle of, 117 *et seq.,* 130, 138, 144, 158, 195-

6, 375; French occupy, 119-20; Austrians take, 120; the general engagement, 121-2; Austrians retreat, 122
Arçon, General de, 16
Ardennes, 495
Ardres, 488
Argau, 271
Argenteau, Lt.-General de, 51, 53-4
Argentieres, 52, 441, 442, 449
Arles, 568
Armed Neutrality, the first (1780), 407-8, 411; the second (1800), 418-9, 429; England's efforts to break, 421 *et seq.*
Arno, river, 87
Arona, surrender of, 469
Arosoia, river, 180
Arquata, 84
Arras, 488
Artois, 497
Artois, Charles Philippe, Comte de, 476, 494
Arts and sciences of Egypt, 324-5
Asolo, 163
Astore, Colonel, 560
Ath, 503
Aubry, François, N.'s interview with, 34
Augereau, Pierre François Charles, Duke of Castiglione, Marshal of France, 51, 53, 56, 57, 75, 79, 161, 190 ; at Millesimo, 54-5; on the Scrivia, 64; at Pavia, 69; career of, 73; at Mantua, 81; in Bologna and Ferrara, 84-5; at Legnago, 92; at Borghetto, 94, 95; marches on Brescia, 95; at Lonato, 96; at Castiglione, 97, 98; crosses the Mincio, 98; Castiglione bestowed on, 101; marches to Trent, 103-4; marches to Bassano, 105; at Padua, 106; sent to Legnago, 107; at Verona, 110, 112; on the Brenta, 113; at Arcole, 118, 119; marches on Dolce, 123; at Legnago, 138; defends Adige river against Provera, 141; near Mantua, 143, 144; at Treviso, 144; and Eighteenth Fructidor, 244, 245; political opinions of, 255; in command of combined Rhine-Moselle and Sambre-Meuse Armies, 262; and Brumaire, 366, 370, 373-4, 375; commands Army of North, 435
Augsburg, 202
Aulic Council, 159, 162, 193, 268, 466
Austerlitz, 501
Austria, and Cherasco armistice, 61-2, 127; Papal alliance with, 129-31, 147-8; French descent into, 159 *et seq.*; French enter, 166; armistice with France, 174 *et seq.*; French march into, 198-201; and Venetian neutrality, 205 *et seq.*; and Russia, 260; territory ceded to, 252, 255, 257-8, 258-60; refuses to support Sardinia, 417, 470; and Russian prisoners, 417; at Vienna Congress, 477, 478; *see also* Francis II
Austrian Army, 74, 77; strength of (1796), 51; separated from Sardinian Army, 55, 60, 126; after Mondovi, 58; strength on the Adda, 68; behind the Mincio, 78; Neapolitan

578

INDEX

cavalry quits, 82; under Wurmser (*q.v.*), 89, 91 *et seq.*; losses (29 July-12 August), 99; attempts to relieve Mantua (Sept.), 102 *et seq.*; losses (1 June-18 Sept.), 109; under Alvinzi (*q.v.*), 111 *et seq.*; losses at Arcole, 122; strength (Jan. 1797), 138; last attempt to relieve Mantua, 138 *et seq.*; losses (Jan.), 144; under Archduke Charles (*q.v.*), 159 *et seq.*; N.'s observations on operations against, under Beaulieu, 180-4; under Wurmser, 184, 186-91; under Alvinzi, 191-7; under Prince Charles, 198-201; occupies whole of Tyrol, 210; on the Drave and in Carniola, 259; strength on the Rhine (1796), 268; defeats Rhine armies, 433; defeats Army of Italy (1799), 434; campaign of 1800, 436 *et seq.*; dispositions of, 436; defeated in Germany, 436-9, 444; strength in Italy, 436, 440; in possession of entire country, 440-1; dispositions, 441; intersects French army, 442; invests Genoa, 443 *et seq.*, 458, 462; concentrates near Turin, 457-8; marches on Alessandria, 461, 462, 464; battle of Montebello, 462-3, 466; inactivity of, 464-5; battle of Marengo, 466-8; retreat of, 468-9; defeats Murat, 479
Autichamp, Charles de Beaumont, Count de, 392, 393, 394
Auvergne, 477, 496
Auxonne, 7, 489
Avesnes, 488, 538, 539; French march to, 500, 501; surrenders to Allies, 541
Avignon, 51, 363; Marseillais in, 10, 573, 574; N.'s mission to, 11; Carteaux takes, 15, 565-6, 567, 568, 570; ceded to France, 155
Avisio, river, 188, 198, 199; French arrive at, 104, 105; Vaubois on, 110, 112; Vaubois forced from, 113; French reoccupy, 144; Joubert on, 167; Serviez on, 168; French leave, 210
Ayer, Sheik of, 334, 343
Aza, Cape, 280
Azara, Chevalier J. N. de, 86

Bab-el-Mandeb, 330
Baboeuf, François Noël, 43, 73
Baboust, 297
Bachelu, General, 523
Badouville, Brig.-General, 246-7
Bahar-el-Margi, 331
Bahire, 284, 296, 301, 346; revolt in, 341-2
Bairout, 331
Balagnier, 17, 21, 22
Balastreno, 30
Balbec, 331
Balland, General, 167, 211
Baltic Sea, 355, 357, 358, 414, 420, 421, 422
Bapaume, 488
Baradee, river, 331
Barbaroux, C. J. M., 570, 572
Barbé-Marbois, Marquis de, 250
Barcelona, naval incident at, 420

Barcelonetta, 47
Bard, 47, 63; the town captured, 455-6; artillery taken through, 456; siege of fort, 456, 457, 458, 461
Bardinetto, 30, 180
Barras, P. F. J. N., 15, 236, 240, 364, 375, 386; and siege of Toulon, 19-20, 21; and Thirteenth Vendémiaire, 39-40, 42; N.'s rejection of, 367-8; resigns from Directory, 373
Barré, Captain, 281, 282
Barrème, 475
Barthelemy, François, Marquis de, 232, 248, 356; in Directory, 240; arrested, 245; Moreau's letter to, 246-7; N.'s view of, 247; a senator, 250
Basel, 437; Treaty of, 432
Bassano, 102, 139, 187, 188, 191, 207, 216, 269; battle of, 82, 106-7, 109, 110, 191; Austrians march to, 103; Wurmser at, 104-5; French march to, 105-6; Massena occupies, 110, 112, 144; N. near, 113, 162
Basseville, ——, 156
Bastia, 5; siege of, 8, 9
Batavian Republic, *see* Holland
Battaglia, Proveditore, on Venetian aid to France, 205-6; and Brescian revolt, 207; arrested, 209-10; and fall of Venice, 215-6
Baudin, P. C. L., 363
Bavaria, 257, 433, 437
Bayalitsch, General, 93, 194, 200; at Lonato, 96; at Caldiero, 139; ordered to Tarwis, 164; defeated at Chiusa, 165-6
Bayonne, 489
Beaucaire, N. at, 565 *et seq.*
Beauharnais, Eugene de, 43, 258, 322
Beauharnais, Josephine de, *see* Josephine, Empress of the French
Beaulieu, Baron Jean Pierre de, 71, 112, 116, 132, 204, 207; forces under, 51; and battle of Montenotte, 53-4; at Acqui, 55; retreats to river Po, 57; at Valenza, 64; marches to Fombio, 65-6; positions on the Mincio, 78; recalled, 82; remnants of his army added to Wurmser's, 9, 91, 99; N.'s observations on operations against, 180 *et seq.*
Beaumont, 503, 504, 539, 547; French forces at, 501
Beaumont, General, 68
Beausset, 15, 16
Béfort, 489
Belbeis, 345
Belbo, river, 56, 183
Belgiojoso, 461
Belgium, 133, 134, 256, 257, 270, 280; Austrian cession of, 177, 248, 258-9; Archduke Charles's property in, 261; insurrection in, 387, 392; *see also* Waterloo campaign
Belinzona, 460
Bellegarde, Comte Henri de, 173, 477
Belle Ile, 489
Bellerophon, the, 285, 286
Belleville, ——, 87

579

INDEX

Belliard, Count Augustin Daniel, 119, 353, 358, 500
Belluno, French capture, 163
Belmonte, Prince of, 82
Belus, river, 335
Benezech, Pierre, 240, 250, 356
Benigsen, L. A. T., Comte de, 427
Benisouf, 296
Beragno, 124
Beranger, Pierre Jean de, 378
Berenice, 296, 297
Berg, Duchy of, 258
Bergamo, 116, 138, 208, 216, 269; French occupy, 137; revolt of, 207, 209
Berlin, Sieyes in, 364; Duroc in, 395; in 1806 campaign, 490; Blücher in, 494
Bernadotte, General Jean Baptiste Jules, 199, 200, 216, 218; arrives in Italy, 158; on the Piave, 161; at Conegliano, 163; at Gradisca, 165; at Leoben, 174; as Ambassador to Venice, 273; and Brumaire, 366, 370, 373; in Germany, 433
Berne, 232, 234, 251, 271; congress at, 176, 251, 253; N. in, 264
Bernier, Abbé E. A. J. B. M., 392, 393
Bernstorf, Count Andreas Peter von, 412, 413, 428
Berri, Charles, Duc de, 476
Berruyer, General, 40
Berry, 496
Berthier, Louis Alexandre, Marshal of France, 58, 74, 77, 85, 173, 174, 178, 218, 244, 268, 356, 362; takes Laharpe's command, 66; an account of, 72; sent to Paris, 262; marches on Rome, 273; appointed Minster at War, 383; and Reserve Army command, 451
Berthollet, Claude Louis, 268, 327
Besançon, 489
Bessieres, Jean Baptiste, Duke of Istria, Marshal of France, 79–80, 144
Bethlehem, 332
Béthune, 488, 494
Bevilacqua, 138, 139
Beyrand, General, at Lugo, 88; killed, 96
Beys, Egyptian, 299
Biberach, 436
Bielau, 540
Biestro, 54, 55
Binasco, pillaged, 75, 184
Bionde, 117
Birketh, 346, 347
Bisagno, river, 222, 444
Bitche, 488
Black Forest, 437
Black Mountains, 433, 438
Blackwell, ——, 390–1
Blücher, Gebhard Lebrecht, Prince von, 519; at Liége, 481; forces under, 489, 497, 498; in Berlin, 494; N.'s plans of campaign against, 495 et seq.; dispositions and strength of (June 14), 502; character of, 504; withdraws before French, 504–5, 506; at nightfall (June 15), 506, 507; N. prepares to attack, 508–9; battle of Ligny, 510–2; injured, 511; retreats on Wavres, 514–5, 516–7, 517–8, 527, 528, 545–6; Bülow's forces engaged, 527–8, 529, 530–1, 532, 534, 535, 536, 546, 550; Grouchy attacks, 532–3, 533–4, 540, 546; reinforces Wellington, 533–4, 546, 551; defeats French forces, 535–7; losses of, 536; pursues the French, 538; enters France, 541–2; N.'s observations on, 543 et seq.; taken by surprise, 543, 547; mistakes of, 547–8; Wellington's reliance on, 549–50
Bobbio, 441
Bochetta Pass, 46, 53, 54, 124, 180, 434, 442
Bohemia, 433, 437
Boissy d'Angla's Comte François Antoine de, 247, 250
Bologna, 47, 61, 62, 89, 116, 127, 129, 131, 134, 160, 201, 209, 229, 258, 260, 269, 270, 464, 480; N. in, 3–4, 88, 130, 137, 140, 145, 224; French entry of, 84, 85; conditions in, 85–6; loyalty of, 100, 112; joins Cispadan Republic, 135–6; Franco-Papal armistice signed at, 148–9; ceded to France, 155, 156, 157; ceded to Venice, 176; French re-enter, 184
Bolzano, 168, 198, 202
Bon, General L. A., 109, 309, 310, 339, 344
Bonaparte, Charles, 4–5, 6
Bonaparte, Jerome, King of Westphalia, crosses the Sambre, 504; at Waterloo, 523, 525, 526; at Marchiennes, 539
Bonaparte, Joseph, King of Spain, 6, 272, 365, 370, 373, 414, 415
Bonaparte, Letitia (née Ramolino), 5, 481
Bonaparte, Lucien, 365, 367, 374, 381, 395; takes the oath, 375; opposes outlaw motion, 376–7; addresses provisional Consuls, 378–9; at Fontainebleu, 480
Bonaparte family, genealogy, 3–5; spelling of name, 4; leaves Corsica, 10
Bonara, Cape, 279, 280
Bonifacio, 5, 7
Bonnel, General, 55
Bonnier-d'Arco, Ange E. L. A., 249, 264, 265
Borda, Jean Charles, 268
Bordeaux, 14, 476, 568; troops at, 487, 488
Borghetto, 96, 98, 269; capture of, 78–9; battle of, 184
Borghetto, defensive position of, 35, 72, 444
Borgo-forte, 81, 84, 85, 99, 129, 148
Borgo-Val-Sugagno, 105, 191
Borgues, Chevalier, 89
Bormida, river, 29, 30, 46, 51, 54, 183, 465, 466, 468
Bormio, river, 231, 233, 234, 269
Borromean Islands, 217
Bosco, 64
Bouc, 27, 489
Bouchain, 488
Boudet, General, 453, 464, 465n., 468
Bouillon, 488
Boulac, 310, 311, 325

INDEX

Boulay de la Meurthe, A. J. C. J., Comte, 374, 378, 382, 395
Bouquet, ——, 216
Bourdon de la Crosnière, L. J. J., 385
Bourgogne, 568
Bourlos, Lake, 298, 327
Bourmont, L. A. V., Comte de Chaisne de, 392, 394, 545
Boutot, ——, 373
Bra, 58
Braine le Comte, 503, 512
Braine le Leud (Braine l'Alleud), 520, 521, 523
Braschi, Duke of, 154, 157
Brenner Pass, 47, 160, 199; Kerpen's retreat to, 167, 168
Brenta, river, 47, 60, 103, 139, 194, 196, 203, 218; Mezaros crosses, 105; French movements along, 105-6, 107; Alvinzi's reverses on, 112-3, 115; French retreat from, 114; French return to, 191
Brescia, 92, 94, 99, 103, 116, 137, 138, 149, 182, 187, 190, 191, 196, 204, 208, 210, 216, 269; French occupy, 77-8; pro-French attitude of, 85; Austrians take, 93; French re-occupy, 95; Mattei at, 100; Austrians take, 189; N. at, 206; insurrection of, 207, 209
Brest, 14, 23, 278, 279, 355, 356, 421, 429, 483
Bretagne, 278
Briançon, 47, 458, 489
Brie, Jean de, 34
Brienne military school, 6, 242
Brig, 47
Brigançon, 489
Brindisi, 151, 355
Brisac, 433, 437
Brisgaw, 260, 436
Brissot de Warville, Jean Pierre, 570, 572
Brittany, 394, 452, 496
Brixen (Bressanone), 160, 174, 199
Brottier, Abbé, 242
Brouis, 30
Bruck an der Mur, 160, 161, 174, 175
Brueys d'Aigalliers, Admiral François Paul, 221, 350, 355; forces under, 280-1; ordered to enter Alexandria, 281-2; anchors off Aboukir, 282-3; dispositions of, 283; battle of the Nile, 284-7; death of, 287
Brulard (Bruslart), Louis Guérin de, 394
Brulé, Brigadier-General, 32
Brumaire *coup d'état*, 43, 244, 270, 353, 355, 360, 378, 386, 387, 393, 395, 435, 436, 445, 470; N. surveys the factions, 364-8; decides to act with Sieyes, 368; plans made for, 369-70; decree of the Ancients, 370-1; parade at the Tuileries, 371-4; Directors resign, 373; events at St Cloud, 374-9; N.'s proclamation on, 380-2
Brune, Guillaume Marie Anne, Marshal of France, 378; at Tarwis, 164; defeats Cadoudal, 394; in Holland, 434; commands Army of West, 435; forces under, 487
Brune, the, 214

Brunet, General, 28
Brunswick-Oels, Friedrich Wilhelm, Duke of, 513, 560
Brussels, 494, 503, 504-9, 512-9, 521, 523, 540, 544, 548, 551; Wellington at, 481, 502; Anglo-Dutch retreats towards, 529, 546
Bry (Brye), 512, 514; French near, 508; Ney ordered to attack, 509
Buhar, Admiral, 278
Bülow, Friedrich Wilhelm, Count von Dennewitz, 506, 508, 540, 547; at Liége, 502; at Gembloux, 514, 516; at St Lambert, 527-8; attacks at Waterloo, 529-31, 532, 534, 535, 536, 546, 547, 550
Burgos, battle of, 490
Burgundy, 363, 477, 497
Busca, Cardinal, 197, 227; intercepted letter of, 147-8; on the Senio, 149, 150; dismissed, 153
Bussolengo, 92, 138; Vaubois at, 120; Austrians take, 123
Bussy, Comte de, 539
Buzot, F. L. N., 572

Cabanis, Jean Pierre Georges, 374, 382
Cacault, François, 130, 148, 149
Cadibona, 51, 180, 181, 442
Cadiz, 278, 279, 421, 429
Cadore, 163
Cadoudal, Georges, 394
Caen, 568
Cæsarea, 316, 331
Caffarelli Dufalga, General L. M. J. M., 268, 293, 307, 328, 337
Cagliari, French attempt on, 7, 14
Cagnes, 445
Caiffa (Haifa), 335
Caillou, 516
Cairo, 89, 294, 324, 325, 335, 342, 343-5, 351, 353, 358-60; French capture, 282, 284, 311; caravans to, 297; Old, 310, 311, 312; French march on, 305 *et seq.*; description of, 311-2, 313; artisans of, 325; transport in, 326; Institute established in, 327-8; French construction in, 329
Cairo, Italy, 29, 30, 54, 180
Caisrum, river, 335
Calais, 270, 488, 495; emigrants shipwrecked at, 389
Calder, Admiral, 357
Caldiero, 122, 191, 192, 193, 196; battle of, 114-5, 116, 269; Alvinzi at, 117, 118, 119, 120; Bayalitsch at, 139
Calliano, 103, 104, 113, 188
Calvados, 568
Calvi, 5, 571; siege of, 8, 9
Camaldolites, general of, 153
Cambacérès, Jean Jacques Régis de, 415; entertains N., 365; and Brumaire, 374; Minister of Justice, 385; appointed second Consul, 400; career of, 400
Cambon, Joseph, 33
Cambra, 167

581

INDEX

Cambrai, 488, 541
Cambronne, General, 475, 537
Camerino, 155
Campo Formio Treaty, 131, 175n., 223, 226, 228, 249, 262, 265, 269, 270, 271; terms of, 229, 251-2, 255, 258-60; preliminaries signed, 251; signature of, 256, 260
Canaam, battle of, 337
Canada, 257, 481
Candia, 280, 356
Cannes, 475
Caporetto, 161, 164, 165, 166, 199, 200
Caprara, Count, 4, 85
Carcari, 50, 51, 54
Carinthia, 168-9, 199, 200, 201, 211, 257, 259, 477; N.'s proclamation in, 166-7; French evacuate, 176
Carinthian road to Vienna, 160; connexions with Carniolan and Tyrolese roads, 160-1; closed to Austrian forces, 164-5
Carniola, 168, 200, 259; N.'s proclamation in, 166-7; French forces leave, 174-5, 176
Carniolan road to Vienna, 160-1
Carlscrona, Swedish fleet at, 421, 422, 428
Carmignano, 112
Carnic Alps, 160, 166
Carnot, L. N. M., 236, 240, 248, 252, 274, 356; and royalist conspiracy, 241; escapes to Geneva, 245; N.'s view of, 247; appointed minister, 250
Caroline, Queen of Naples, 479, 480
Carrère, Colonel, 173
Carrère, the, 359, 362
Carteaux, General Jean François, operates against Marseillais, 15, 19, 565 *et seq.*; relieved of Toulon command, 18-19
Casabianca, Louis, 287
Casal Maggiore, 100
Casal-Pusterlengo, 67
Cassano, 67, 68, 69, 416
Cassario, 93
Casteggio, 462
Castel-Bolognese, 149
Castel Franco, 144
Castellazzo, 54
Castel Nuovo, 79, 92, 93, 120, 140, 196
Castel-Nuovo di Scrivia, 465n.
Castel-Sainte-Joane, 65
Castiglione, 78, 95, 194, 269; battle of, 82, 96-8, 100, 103, 218, 434
Castiglione di Mori, 214
Castries, C. E. G. de la Croix, Marquis de, 407
Catherine II, Tsarina, 260; and Armed Neutrality, 407-8, 411; death of, 416
Cathieh, 345
Cattegot, 421, 422
Causse, General, 55
Causse, the, 287
Cederstrom, Captain, 411, 412
Cephalonia, 215, 228, 261
Cerea, 108, 182

Ceresa, 80, 81, 109
Cerigo, 215, 260
Cervoni, General, 22-3, 53, 54
Cesena, 151, 154
Cette, 477, 489
Ceva, 53, 55, 56, 59, 60, 64, 71, 181, 183
Chabart, Lt.-General, 477
Chabot, General, 143
Chabran, General, 212, 457
Chambarlhac, General, 453, 465n.
Chambéry, 487
Champagne, 497
Championnet, General Jean Etienne, 178, 434
Champy, ——, 354
Charlemont, 488, 543
Charleroi, 505-7, 510, 511, 514, 515, 521, 523-5, 527, 531, 543-5, 550; Zwietten at, 502; French take, 504, 547, 548; French retreat on, 538-9
Charles, Archduke of Austria, 73, 88, 207, 208, 209, 210, 216, 218, 260, 268; in Germany, 111, 132, 133; takes command of Austrian Army in Italy, 159; strength of (March 1797), 161; dispositions of, 162; on the Tagliamento, 163-4; at Tarwis, 164; his Tyrolese forces defeated, 167-8; losses in twenty days, 168-9; strength of, 169; correspondence with N., 171-2, 173, 198; at Neumarck, 172-3; stratagem to gain time, 173; state of forces under, 177; N.'s observations on operations against, 198-200; property in Belgium, 261; defeats Rhine armies, 433; during 1805, 489
Charles IV, King of Spain, 127, 240
Charles Emmanuel IV, King of Sardinia, 50, 58, 133, 134, 164, 263, 265, 269, 475; armistice with, 59-60, 61-2, 63, 125, 126; unreliability of, 60; relations with France, 89-90; and treaty with France, 127-8, 224-6; forces with Army of Italy, 159, 160; insecurity of, 227; Austria refuses to support, 417, 470, at Florence, 440
Charton, General, 108
Chassé, General, 521, 560
Chasseloup, General, 81, 82, 89, 158
Chateaubriand, François Auguste, Vicomte de, genius of, 253
Châtelet, 504, 506, 507
Chatillon, Austrians defeated at, 455, 457, 459
Chatillon, ——, Vendéan chief, 392, 393
Châtillon-sur-Seine, 34, 480
Chazal, Jean Pierre, 374, 382
Chefamer (Shafa 'Amr), 332, 335
Chenier, Marie Joseph de, 375
Cherasco, 71, 126; capture of, 57, 58; N.'s speech at, 59; Treaty of, 58, 59-60, 64, 74, 126
Cherbourg, 483, 489
Cherkaoui, Sheik, 351
Chevalier, General, 212
Chiaramonte, *see* Pius VII
Chiavenna, 231, 232, 234, 269

582

INDEX

Chiesa, river, 103, 139, 182, 187, 189, 191, 196; French forces on, 92; Austrian attacks on, 93, 95
Chitisa, 192, 211
Chiusa di Pletz, 161, 164-5
Chiusella, 457
Chivasso, 447, 457, 458
Choiseul, E. F., Duc de, 10
Chouans, 392-3, 445, 452
Christianity, rise of, 314-5; compared with Islam, 315, 351; in Syria, 332
Christina, Archduchess, 261
Cilli, 200
Ciney, 502, 506
Circassians, see Mamelukes
Cisalpine Republic, 218, 259, 271, 272, 367; influence of, 134; under Leoben preliminaries, 176; and Papal States, 227; formation of, 229-30, 256, 260; declaration of independence, 230; change of manners in, 231; Valteline unites with, 231-4; N.'s farewell address to, 262-3; re-established, 460-1, 470
Cismone, 106
Cispadan Republic, 154, 162, 216, 219; and Lombardy, 135, 136; formation of, 136; discontent in, 228-9; merged into Cisalpine Republic, 229
City of the Dead, 309, 312-3
Cividale, 164, 165, 198, 199, 200
Civita-Vecchia, 278
Clarke, H. J. G., Comte d'Hunebourg, Marshal of France, 127, 133, 218, 249; and Leoben preliminaries, 175, 178; and Franco-Sardinian treaty, 224, 226; career and character of, 252; at Udine, 253; recalled, 254
Clairfait (Clerfayt), F. S. C. Joseph de Croix, 242
Clary, General, 505
Clausel, Bertrand, Comte, Marshal of France, 476, 487
Clausen, 168
Clichy party, 221, 241, 243
Clinton, General Sir Henry, 521, 560
Clouet, Colonel, 545
Cobentzel, Count John Philip, 261; at Udine, 253, 254, 259-60; character of, 254; demands of, 258-9; at Rastadt, 264
Cochon de l'Apparent, Comte Charles, 240, 250
Codogno, 65, 66
Codroipo, 164, 198
Cogna, river, 64
Coilloure, 489
Coire, 231, 233
Col Ardente, 28
Colbert, General, 532, 539
Col di Cadibona, 46, 53, 54, 463
Col di Tende, 28, 30, 32, 47, 82, 180, 445, 449, 458, 459
Col di Toriglio, 442, 443
Collaert, General, 521, 560
Colli-Ricci, Baron L. L. G. Venance de, 51, 53, 67, 68, 78, 181; and battle of Millesimo, 54-5; at Ceva, 55; at Mondovi, 57; in command of Papal army, 148, 151
Colmar, 32
Colmars, 489
Colognola, 115
Colonna, ——, 9
Colville, General Sir Charles, 521, 560
Comeyras, ——, 233
Committee of Forty, 39, 40-1
Committee of Public Safety, 16, 18, 19, 25, 32, 39, 197, 241, 252, 383; and N.'s appointment to Army of Italy, 34-5
Como, Lake, 69, 138, 217, 231
Condé, 488
Condé, Louis Joseph de Bourbon, Prince de, 178, 245, 246
Condorcet, M. J. A. N. Caritat, Marquis de, 570, 572
Conegliano, 112, 163, 198, 448
Coni, 47, 59, 71, 83, 92, 445; French take, 59, 60, 63, 64; Austrians take, 434; capture of, 469
Conquerant, the, 283, 285, 286
Constance, Lake, 438
Constantinople, 281, 296, 302, 304, 316, 329, 333, 334; Patriarch of, 300; fortifications of, 490
Constituent Assembly, see National Assembly
Constitution of 1791, 37
Constitution of Year III (1795), 37, 179, 235, 248, 366, 375, 376, 378, 384, 395
Constitution of Year VIII (1800), 360, 451; work on, 394, 395-6; Sieyes' proposals, 396-9; form adopted, 399-401
Consulate, 250, 270; formation of, 399-400
Containi, ——, 230
Conté, Nicholas Jacques, 324, 327, 354
Cook (Cooke), Lt.-General Sir George, at Quatre Bras, 513n.; at Waterloo, 521, 560
Cool (Coote), General Sir Eyre, 358
Copenhagen, 412; Anglo-Danish Convention signed at, 413, 418; Danish fleet destroyed at, 421 *et seq.*, 429
Copts, 293, 300, 312, 351; as tax collectors, 303; N.'s attitude to, 304; in French army, 354
Corfu, 228, 281, 282, 284, 332; French occupy, 215; ceded to France, 261
Corniche road, 46, 53
Cornudet des Chomettes, Joseph, Comte, 370, 374, 376
Corsaglia, river, 56
Corsica, 45, 48, 49, 131, 215, 219, 221, 279, 362, 446, 568, 571; description of, 5-6; breaks with France, 8-9; under English rule, 9-10; troops in Sardinia, 14; English troops in, 84; refugees at Leghorn, 86, 87; French retake, 131, 132, 162
Corte, 5
Cossaria, 54-5, 195
Cosseir (Kosseir), 297; British land at, 350, 359

583

INDEX

Costaz, ——, 327
Costumes of Egypt, 323
Côte d'Or, 567
Council of State, 395, 435
Courageuse, the, 358
Covolo, 106
Crema, 68
Cremona, 77, 80, 93, 116, 183; French take, 69; pro-Austrian feeling in, 100; Duhesme takes, 460
Cretin, Colonel, 293, 344, 346, 348, 349
Culloden, the, 285, 286
Cuto, Prince de, 79

Daifih, 296
Dallemagne, Claude, Baron, 65, 97; at Mantua, 89; at Verona, 92; at Lonato, 94; at Borgo-forte, 99
Dalmatia, Duke of, *see* Soult
Damanhour, 306, 310, 342, 360
Damascus, 316, 331, 332, 360
Damian, Clement, 224, 226
Damietta, 283, 294, 296, 298, 309, 328, 345, 355, 357, 359, 360
Dammartin, General Elzéard Auguste, 82, 92, 104
Dandalo, ——, 215
Dandigné, ——, 392
Danican, General Auguste, 41
Danton, Georges Jacques, 36
Danube, river, 160, 161, 433, 438
Danzig, 480
D'Arentschild, Sir F., 560
Darfur, 354, 355
Daumont, General, 522, 523-4, 527, 529
Daunau, Pierre C. F., 395, 398
Dauphiné, 268, 363, 458, 477, 488, 497, 556, 569
Davidowich, Baron Paul, 186-8, 191, 195, 199; intentions of, 93; defends the Tyrol, 102, 103, 109; at Calliano, 104; forces under, 112; threatens Verona, 113; advances to Rivoli, 120, 121; French attack on, 122, 123
Davout, Louis Nicholas, Prince of Eckmühl, Marshal of France, 484, 485
Dead Sea, 331
Decaen, Comte, forces under, 487
Defence, the, 285
Dego, 30, 54, 181, 183; battle of, 55-6
Dejean, Jean François Aimé, Comte, 511, 539
De La Haye, ——, 241
Delbrel, Pierre, 375
Delmas, General, 158, 161, 167
Demasis, ——, 6
Demonte, 47, 89
Denmark, and Armed Neutrality, 407-8, 411, 412-3, 418-9, 420; signs Convention with England, 413-4, 418; enters second Armed Neutrality League, 418; at war with England, 420 *et seq.*; signs armistice, 426, 428, 429, 430
Desaix de Veygoux, General L. C. A., 178, 247, 255, 268, 274, 345, 346, 354, 356, 359; on Pichegru, 261; visits N., 261; at battle of Pyramids, 307-9; in Germany, 433; arrives at Montebello, 463; on Egyptian campaign, 463-4; at Ponte-Curone, 465n.; ordered to San-Juliano, 466; at Marengo, 467-8; death of, 468
Despinois (Despinoy), Comte Hyacinthe F. J., 71, 74, 92, 95
Dessolles, J. J. P. A., Marquis, 176, 437
Destaing, General J. Zacharie, 347, 348
Devaux, General, 337, 529
Devaux, Marshal, 5
Devins, General, 35
Dezenzano, 78, 94, 95, 138, 140, 142, 187
Diane, the, 286, 358
Dickenson (Dixon), Admiral, 413, 418
Dieppe, 489
Dijon, mock Reserve Army at, 452, 453
Dinant, 502, 540
Directory, 37, 43, 44, 60, 73, 82, 162, 353, 382, 435, 452; attempts to split Italian command, 71, 171, 184, 255; and reinforcement of Army of Italy, 92, 112, 158, 256; and Genoa, 125; and Sardinia, 127, 160, 225, 226, 227, 256; and Pius VI, 129, 130; and Naples, 132; and Francis II, 132-4; and exiled priests, 153; and N.'s negotiations with Rome, 153; and movements of Rhine armies, 170-1, 178, 179, 200; and Leoben preliminaries, 176, 178; friction in, 177; and Wurmser's surrender, 196; and war with Venice, 208, 213; and Cisalpine Republic, 230; members set up courts, 235-6; opposition to, 236-7, 240, 241, 242, 250, 274; policy of, 237; petty legislation by, 237-8, 240; members of, 240, 248, 364, 366; and the Press, 241; N. invited to overthrow, 244, 274-5; conspiracy against, 245 *et seq.*; punitive measures by, 245, 247-8; and negotiations with England, 248, 249; and public debt, 249-50; Clarke the secret agent of, 252; and Campo Formio Treaty, 254-5, 262; and Congress of Rastadt, 265; opposes gifts of property to N., 267; ceremonial reception of N. by, 268-9; jealousy of N., 270, 275-6; and Switzerland, 271; and the Bernadotte incident, 275; and Egyptian expedition, 273-4, 307, 356; countermands Irish expedition, 333; rejoices at N.'s return from Egypt, 363; N. determines to overthrow, 363-4; entertains N., 365; N.'s plans concerning, 367-8; dissolved, 373, 375, 382; and America, 409, 410
Djezzar (Ahmed Pasha), and Mutualis, 332; commands Syrian army, 333; at Acre, 336; and Emir of Hadji, 340; decline of, 343
Dockum, Captain van, 412
Dolce, 93, 123, 140, 141, 192
Dombrowski, General John Henry, 135
Domo d'Ossola, 459
Donau-Schingen (Donaueschingen), 436
Doppet, General F. Amédée, 19, 25
Dora Baltea, river, 455, 456, 457, 459, 461

584

INDEX

Doria, Cardinal, 153
Dornberg, Sir W., 560
Douai, 7, 488
Doulcet, A. T. Louis, 34
Drave, river, 160, 161, 164, 166, 167, 199, 200, 259
Dresden, 480; Prussia claims, 477
Drôme, 476, 573
Drouot, General, 534
Drummond, Sir William, 421
Druses, 332, 334, 343
Dubois, General, 104
Dubois, the, 287
Dubois-Crancé, E. L. Alexis, 569, 570; seeks N.'s advice, 370; incompetence of, 382-3
Ducos, Roger, 366; character of, 364; resigns directorship, 373; appointed provisional Consul, 374, 378; supports N., 382
Due-Castelli, 108, 109
Dufour, Galbo, 7, 456
Dugear, General, 10, 11
Dugommier, General J. F. Coquille, 26, 72; at Toulon, 18 *et seq.*, 25; praises N., 25
Dugua, General Charles F. J., in Italy, 164, 165; in Egypt, 308, 309, 340, 341
Duhesme, Comte Philippe Guillaume, 459, 505, 521, 538; at Waterloo, 530, 537
Dujard, General, 82
Dumas, Comte Matthieu, 161, 168, 250, 356, 488
Dumerbion, General Pierre Jadar, 28, 29, 31, 72
Dumolard, Joseph Vincent, 247, 274
Dumouriez, General Charles François, 57, 270
Dundas, General Sir David, 9
Dunkirk, 488, 500
Du Petit-Thouard, ——, 287
Duphot, General Léonard, 139, 140; on the Tagliamento, 163; in Genoa, 222-3; murdered in Rome, 271-2
Duplantier, ——, 250
Dupont de l'Etang, Comte Pierre, 89
Dupuy, General Dominique, 311
Durance, river, 20, 441, 566-9
Duroc, G. C. M., Duke of Friuli, 395, 428
Dusseldorf, 160, 178, 432
Dutertre, Jean Baptiste, 327
Duverne de Presle, T. L. M., 240, 242, 245
Duvivier, ——, 349
Dyle, river, 533, 540
Dyrmonk, 316

Eckmühl, battle of, 489; Prince of, *see* Davout
Edessa, bishop of, 88
Egra, 433
Eguillette, 17, 21, 22
Egypt, 262, 362, 366, 370, 388, 395, 436; expedition to, 270, 273-4, 275, 279 *et seq.*; population of, 294-5, 296, 298 *et seq.*, 332; area of, 296; products of, 296; trade of, 297-8; ports of, 298; deserts of, 301; banditry in, 302; under Roman rule, 302; under Selim I, 302-3; N.'s administrative policy in, 303-4;

French march on Cairo, 305 *et seq.*; women of, 321-3; marriage in, 322-3; costumes of, 323; architecture of, 323-4; arts and sciences in, 324-5; modes of transportation in, 325-6; Institute established, 326-8; health services in, 328-9; objects of expedition to, 332-3, 350; revolt in, 341-3; Turks land in, 344-6; battle of Aboukir, 347-9; events following N.'s departure from, 353 *et seq.*, 386, 429; resumé of N.'s achievements in, 358; St Louis' campaign in, 359-60; Desaix on, 463-4
Egypt, Army of, provisioning of, 305, 306; marches to Cairo, 305 *et seq.*; discontent in, 306-7; pack animals of, 326; health of, 328, 339; in Syria, 332 *et seq.*; actions against insurgents, 340-3; converges on Aboukir, 344-6; at Aboukir, 347-9; and conversion to Islam, 351-2; achievements of, 352, 358; its condition on N.'s departure from Egypt, 352-3; Anglo-Turkish defeats of, 353, 358-9; attempts to reinforce, 354-8, 421
Egyptienne, the, 355, 359
Ehrenbreistein, 160, 432
El-Arisch, 296, 298, 345; Turkish forces at, 333; Convention of, 350, 353, 358, 360, 463-4
Elba, N. leaves, 475, 479
El Baratoun, 357
Elbe, river, 420, 421, 426, 428
El Bekir, Sheik, entertains N., 320
El Bekra, Sheik, 300
Elephantina, Isle of, 294
El-Fayoum, Sheik, 320, 325
Elizabeth, Princess (Madame), 382
El-Kanones, 296
Elliot, aide-de-camp, 121
Elliott, General Sir Gilbert, 9, 87
Ellsworth, Oliver, 411
Elmodi, Sheik, 302
Elmody, the 'angel', 341-2
El-Mondi, Sheik, 329
Elphi Bey, 311, 329, 343
Elphinstone, Captain, 516
El Sadda, Sheik, 300, 320
Elsinore, 412, 421, 422, 423
Embabeh, 307, 309
Emetri, 65
Emili, Proveditore, 211
Emilian Republic, 229
Ems, river, 420, 421, 432
Engelmann, Baron, 254
Engen, 436, 438
Enghien, 503
England, 171, 224, 254, 273, 365; occupies Corsica, 9-10; domestic affairs of, 61; factory at Leghorn, 84, 86, 87, 131, 162; withdraws from Mediterranean, 128, 132; gainer in the war, 166; goods in Trieste siezed, 167; Press in, 241-2; negotiations with France, 248-9, 267; and Venice, 253, 257; blockade of, 258; and Belgium, 259; proposed expedition to, 269, 270, 278-9; and French occupation of Egypt, 297-8, 350; and Syrian

585

INDEX

England—*cont.*
   expedition, 332-3; forces at Acre, 335, 337; at Aboukir, 344, 345, 346, 349; defeats French in Egypt, 350, 353, 357, 358, 359, 360; as potential threat to Egypt, 354; prisoners of war in, 391; and Chouans, 394; signs Convention with Denmark, 413-4; Paul I's grievances against, 417, 435-6; Russian action against, 418; and second Armed Neutrality League, 418-20; at war with Russia, Denmark and Sweden, 420 *et seq.*; signs armistice with Denmark, 426, 428; changed Russian attitude to, 427-8; obtains Treaty of St Petersburg, 428-30; at Vienna Congress, 477; troops in America, 479, 480-1; in Belgium, *see* Wellington; and Waterloo, 549, 551; *see also* Royal Navy
Ens, river, 160, 161
Entraigues, Comte de, 218-9, 242, 243, 245
Entrevaux, 26, 489
Ercole III, Duke of Modena, 71, 84, 128, 269
Erlon, Jean Baptiste, Comte de, Marshal of France, 516; forces under, 486, 494; supports Reille, 505; at Ligny, 511; recalled to Quatre Bras, 513; at Waterloo, 523, 531
Ernouf, Lt.-General, 476
Espinosa, battle of, 490
Euphrates, river, 330, 331, 333, 334
Excelmans, R. J. T., Comte, Marshal of France, forces under, 487; disperses royal retinue, 494; near Fleurus, 509; pursues Prussians, 514, 515; and Grouchy, 532
Exilles, 47, 68, 89

Faenza, 150, 153
Fano, 156
Fargues, Count de, 476
Fargues, Henri, 370, 374
Fauchet, ——, 408
Fayoum, 296
Faypoult, Guillaume Charles, 84; character of, 219; and Genoese rising, 220, 221, 222
Feltre, 163
Fenestrelles, 47, 469
Ferdinand III, Grand Duke of Tuscany, 86, 131, 137, 436, 440, 479; N.'s visit to, 87-8
Ferrara, 47, 61, 138, 140, 196, 228, 229, 258, 260, 269; French in, 84, 85, 86, 88, 92, 184, 469; loyalty of, 100; N. at, 130; joins Cispadan Republic, 135-6; ceded to France, 155, 156, 157; ceded to Venice, 176
Fersen, Baron, 265
Fez, 297
Fiévé, Joseph, 356
Finale, 53, 181
Fioravanti, General, 201, 210
Fiorella, General Pascal Antoine, 97-8
Firenzuola, 86
Fiscale, 442
Fiume, 132, 168, 174-5
Fiumorbo, 87

Five Hundred, Council of, 37, 223, 240, 242, 365, 366, 367, 395; and Hoche, 244; Directory arrests members of, 245; and Brumaire, 371 *et seq.*; at St Cloud, 374 *et seq.*; troops used against, 377-8, 381
Flahaut, Comte de, 508, 516, 539, 541
Flanders, 495-8; Allies enter, 541
Fleurieu, Comte de, 44
Fleurus, 507, 509-12, 544, 545, 546; Prussians concentrate near, 502; Zwietten retreats to, 504-6; Vandamme and Grouchy near, 506; Girard at, 508
Florence, 3, 129, 137, 148, 272, 274, 440, 464, 478; N. at, 87-8
Fombio, 65, 66, 68, 183
Fontainebleu, 480
Fontana, ——, 77, 88
Fontana-Bona, 60, 124
Fontana Viva, 269
Fontanes, Louis, Marquis de, 247, 356, 411
Fonte Niva, Alvinzi at, 112
Forfait, ——, 385, 386
Forli, 151
Fort Bard, *see* Bard
Fort Barraux, 489
Fort Ecluse, 489
Fort la Malgue, 15, 22
Fort Malbosquet, 17-18, 19, 22
Fort Pharaon, 15, 22
Fort Poné, 22
Fort Saint-James, 29
Fort Saint-Nicholas, 29
Fortune, the, 362
Foscarelli, Proveditore, 80, 206
Foscarini, Proveditore, 211
Fossano, 57
Fouché, Joseph, Duke of Otranto, and Brumaire, 366, 368, 374; career of, 386
Fouquier-Tinville, A. Quentin, 247
Fourches, 30
Fourrier, Jean Baptiste Joseph, 327
Foy, General Maximilien Sébastien, 523, 526
France, state of parties in (1793), 12-14; naval losses at Toulon, 23; state of parties in (1795), 36-7; frontiers with Italy, 47; alliance with Spain, 128, 132; diplomatic relations (1796), with Genoa, 124-6; with Sardinia, 126-8; with Parma, 128; with Modena, 128-9; with Pius VI, 129-31; with Tuscany, 131; with Naples, 131-2; with Austria, 132-4; with Lombardy, 134-6; finance in, 134, 177, 179, 268, 383 *et seq.*, 485-6; armistice with Rome broken, 147-9; exiled priests of, 152-3; sum paid by Rome to, 155; and Leoben preliminaries, 175-6; Austrian recognition of Republic, 175 *and n.*, 260; and expulsion of nobles, 223-4, 250; diplomatic relations (1797), with Genoa, 219-24; with Sardinia, 224-7; with Naples, 227-8; Cisalpine Republic formed, 228-31; Valteline-Grisons dispute, 231-4; dissatisfaction with Directory (*q.v.*), 235 *et seq.*; parties in (1797),

INDEX

236–7, 241; religion in, 237, 388–9; weights and measures of, 238–40; alleged royalist conspiracy in, 241, 242 *et seq.*; public debt of, 249–50; civil war in, 253 (*see also* La Vendeé); corruption in, 256, 268; anxious for peace, 257, 495; territory gained by Campo Formio Treaty, 260–1; Turkey declares war on, 288; navy compared with British, 290–1; compared with Egypt, 295; value of Egypt to, 297–8; N.'s return from Egypt, 352, 356, 360, 362 *et seq.*; negotiations with Turkey, 360; Brumaire *coup d'état*, 368 *et seq.*; new Ministry formed, 382–3, 385–7; strained relations with America, 408–11; negotiates Convention with America (1799), 411, 414–5, 416; N.'s return from Elba, 475 *et seq.*, 480; at Vienna Congress, 477, 478; armies of (1815), 478, 482–3; N. reorganizes, 483–6 (*see also* Waterloo campaign); fortified centres of, 488–9, 491–3; military position after Waterloo, 540–1; military situation (March 1815), 555; army of 800,000 planned, 556–7; military situation (1 June, 1815), 558–9

Franceschi, Colonel, 446, 447
Franche-Comté, 242, 271, 478, 497
Francis II, Emperor (later Francis I, Emperor of Austria), 162, 198, 212, 224, 267–9, 273, 365, 498; and peace negotiations, 132–3, 134, 175–6, 177–8, 217, 221, 223, 248, 251 *et seq.*, 256–61; instructions to Wurmser, 139; requests an armistice, 173–4; and Venetian neutrality, 182; and Congress of Rastadt, 264, 265
Frankfort, 178
Franklin, the, 283, 285, 286
Frasnes, 504, 505, 507, 509, 512, 513, 515, 548
Frederick VI, Prince Royal of Denmark, 425–6, 428
Frederick William II, King of Prussia, 127
Frederick William III, King of Prussia, 240, 395, 498
Freisach, 172
Fréjus, 27, 364; N. lands at, 362
Fréron, L. Stanislas, 15, 19–20, 21, 42
Freya, the, 412–3, 418
Friant, Comte Louis, 174–5, 357, 522, 535
Friburg, 271
Friedberg, 178
Friedland, 501
Frioul (Friuli), 83, 104, 109, 138, 159, 161, 162, 167, 207, 211
Frischermont, 523, 524
Frontin, General, 65
Frotté, Comte Louis de, 394
Fructidor, Eighteenth, 37, 73, 244 *et seq.*, 249, 252–6, 267, 269, 274, 276, 365, 445
Fuentes, 138

Gaeta, 480; duke of, *see* Gaudin
Galeazzi, ——, 9
Galeppi, I., 129, 154, 157

Gallo, Marzio Mastrilli, Marchese di, 229; at Leoben, 175; at Gratz, 176; and peace negotiations, 251, 253; character of, 254; at Passeriano, 260
Gambione, 117
Gantheaume, Admiral Honoré J. A., attempts to reinforce Army of Egypt, 355–8
Gap, 475, 476
Garat, D. Joseph, 280
Garbich, 296
Garchi coffee-house murders, 276
Garda, Lake, 80, 92–5, 103, 138, 140, 141, 144, 182, 187, 189, 192
Gardanne, General Antoine, 79, 442, 465*n*.
Garessio, 53, 56, 183
Garigliano, river, 479
Gasan, General, 442
Gasparin, T. Augustin de, 15, 16
Gascony, 488
Gassendi, General, 16, 454
Gau, ——, 250
Gaudaloupe, 357
Gaudin, Emile, 374, 375
Gaudin, Martin Michel Charles, Duke of Gaeta, as Minister of Finance, 383–5, 485
Gavardo, 93, 94, 97, 182
Gavi, 53
Gaza, 298, 331, 333, 334, 335, 345
Gembloux, 514, 516; Grouchy at, 517, 518, 527, 528, 529–30, 532, 533, 534, 546
Gemil-Azar, *see* Jemil-Azar
Genereux, the, 283, 286
Genest, Edmond, 408
Geneva, 453, 461; N. at, 264
Gennapes, 504, 505, 512, 544; French retreat to, 536, 538
Genoa, 46, 48, 49, 52, 53, 54, 58, 83, 87, 127, 133, 134, 135, 180, 181, 243, 258, 268, 269, 278, 383, 436, 437, 441, 459, 464, 465, 468, 478, 479; defences of, 28, 124, 449–50; neutrality of, 31–2, 62, 124–5; French invasion of, 53; government in, 60; French communications through, 83–4, 125; negotiations with France (1796), 125–6; rising in, 219–20; N.'s ultimatum to, 221; democracy established in, 222; N.'s letter to, 223–4, 250; Austrians menace, 434; Massena's headquarters, 435; Austrians advance to, 442; siege of, 443 *et seq.*, 452, 453, 458, 460, 461; conditions in, 446–7; surrender of, 447–8, 449, 450, 462, 463, 466, 470; French re-enter, 449, 469; and Reserve Army, 462; restored to independence, 470
Gentili, ——, 9, 87
Geoffroy Saint-Hilaire, Etienne, 327
George III, King of England, accepts Corsican crown, 9; loses Hanover, 421
Gérard, Comte Etienne Maurice, Marshal of France, 327, 498, 540; forces under, 486; at Philippeville, 500; crosses the Sambre, 504; at Ligny, 510, 511, 512; advises Grouchy, 532–3

INDEX

Germany, 131, 132, 133, 153; Austrian successes in, 138, 159; Austrian claims in, 257, 261, 264; Moreau's advance into, 432-3, 436-9, 461; hostilities cease in, 437-8
Gerola, ——, 83, 84, 125, 126
Gerry, Elbridge, 409, 410
Gesch, 358
Gezzar Pasha, *see* Djezzar
Ghent, 503; Peace of, 481; Chateaubriand at, 253
Gibraltar, 357, 412
Gillette, 26
Gilly, 504, 505, 507
Gilly, General, 476, 477
Giraldi, ——, 133
Girard, Baron Jean Baptiste, crosses the Ticino, 459, 512; forces under, 500; pursues Zwietten, 505; near Fleurus, 507, 508; at Ligny, 510, 511; career of, 512; as reserve, 536, 538, 545
Girch, 360
Girgeh, 296
Girondins, the, 13-14
Giulay, Major-General, 436
Givet, 543
Gizeh (Ghizeh), 296, 297, 306-11, 343, 344
Gluckstadt, 426
Gohier, L. Jerome, character of, 364; attitude to N., 367; asks advice of N., 369; and Brumaire, 373
Goito, 78
Goliath, the, 285
Golo, river, 5
Goritz, 159, 161, 165-8, 170, 200, 210
Gosselies, 504, 505, 507, 509, 512, 539
Gouvion, Captain, 7
Governolo, 80, 81, 99, 109, 119
Gradisca, 160, 164, 165, 198, 200, 218
Grafignana road, 46
Grammont, 503
Grand-Champ, 394
Grant, Sir Colquhoun, 560
Grasse, 475
Gratz, 174, 175, 176, 177, 213
Great Belt, the, 422
Great Oasis, 296, 343
Great St Bernard Pass, 47, 451, 456-7; Austrian forces at, 441; Reserve Army crosses, 445, 446, 454-5
Greece, 303, 314
Gregorian calendar, 238
Grenelle, 43
Grenoble, 7, 47, 458, 477, 479, 495, 568; N. gathers adherents at, 475-6
Grison League, and Valteline, 231-4, 243
Groetz, 200
Grouchy, Emmanuel, Marquis de, Marshal of France, 535, 539; forces under, 487; at Gilly, 505; at Fleurus, 506, 509; at Ligny, 510, 511; pursues Prussians, 514-5, 516-7, 517-8, 545-6; N.'s orders to, 518, 525, 526, 527, 529-30, 534, 546; attacks Wavres, 532-3, 533-4, 540,
546, 550; ordered to Namur, 538, 540; retreats to Laon, 540
Guastella, Duchy of, 67
Guerrier, the, 283, 285, 286
Guibert, aide-de-camp, 349
Guides, formation of the, 79, 80
Guieux, General Jean Joseph, 119, 161, 199, 200; defends Salo, 94; at Conegliano, 163; at Chiusa, 165; at Neumarck, 172
Guillaume, General, 92, 98
Guillaume Tell, the, 283, 286
Guinguené, ——, 263
Guise, 539, 541
Gustavus IV Adolphus, King of Sweden, 412
Guyot, General, 522, 531, 536, 546

Haddich, General, 441
Hadji, revolt of, 341
Haguenau, 489
Hal, 517, 521, 550
Hamburg, and Irish prisoners, 390-1; Denmark occupies, 420, 426; Danes leave, 428
Hamilton, Emma Lyon, Lady, 366
Ham-sur-Eure, 488, 501, 502
Hanfenen, the, 412
Hanover, Prussia occupies, 420-1; Prussians leave, 428
Haquin, General, 76
Harem, description of, 324
Hatry, General, 44
Hawkesbury, Lord, 420
Haxo, General, 522
Hedersdorf, 178
Hedouville, Comte G. M. T. de, 368, 393
Heliopolis, battle of, 353, 463, 464
Helvetia, Army of, 383, 433-4, 435
Henin, General de, 545
Henry, ——, 411
Herbin, General, 95, 97
Herbois, Collot de, 386
Hercule, Major, 122
Hermann, General, 436
Hesdin, 488
Heureux, the, 286
Hill, General Sir Rowland, Viscount, 503, 560
Hiller, Johann, Baron von, 489
Hilliers, General Baraguay de, 137, 161, 167, 215
Hoche, General Lazare, account of, 178, 261-2; marches near Paris, 244, 262
Hohenzollern, General, 112, 113, 139, 143-4, 448-9, 469
Holland, 258, 383, 421; French conquest of, 240, 242; English forces in, 395, 416, 417, 434, 435; and rights of neutrals, 407; Russians in, 417, 436; French army in, 432, 434, 435
Hood, Admiral Sir Samuel, Viscount, 9, 21-2
Hougoumont, 520, 521, 523, 528, 535; French take, 525-6
Huen, Isle of, 423
Hulla Fersen, the, 411

588

INDEX

Hungary, 257, 259
Huningen, 160, 489; siege of, 132, 133, 159
Hutchinson, General J. H., 358
Hyde-de-Neuville, Jean Guillaume, Baron, 392
Hyères, 22, 23, 24, 26, 34, 390, 489

Ibrahim Bey, 311, 325, 328, 334, 343
Idria, 200
Idro, Lake, 92, 98, 182, 189
Île Dieu (d'Yeu), 489
Iller, river, 458
Imbert-Colomes, Jacques, 241, 247, 250
Imola, N.'s proclamation at, 149; bishop of, see Pius VII
Incanale, 141, 187, 192
Inconstant, the, 475, 479
India, 315, 356; trade with Egypt, 297, 298, 301; and Syrian campaign, 332–3; and Egyptian expedition, 333, 350
Indus, river, 334, 350
Ingoldstadt, 433, 437, 439
Inn, river, 160, 437, 479
Inquisition, N.'s desire to suppress, 157
Inspruck, 159, 161, 168, 439
Institute of Egypt, members and activities of, 326–8
Interior, Army of, 369; N. commands, 42–3, 44
Invincible, the, 421
Ionian Islands, 215, 228, 261
Ireland, 257, 279; expedition to, 244, 262, 333; French connexions with, 278
Irles, General Canto de, 88–9
Iser, river, 437
Isère, river, 476
Islam, tenets and spread of, 314 *et seq.*, 332; project to convert French to, 351–2
Isonzo, river, 47, 49, 60, 112, 160, 161, 164, 167, 168, 177, 198, 200, 210, 256, 259; French crossings of, 165, 218
Istac, 27
Istria, 168; N.'s proclamation in, 166–7
Italy, 332, 351, 353–6, 365, 370, 388–90, 395, 436; Bonaparte connexions with, 3–5; geography of, 45 *et seq.*; population of, 45; ancient divisions of, 45–6; invasions of, 48; capital of, 48–9; in the event of French withdrawal, 134; desire for unity in, 135, 229, 258; in 1812, 258; N.'s achievements in, 267; Egyptian campaign and, 306, 307; Russians in, 435; Murat's precipitate action in, 479–80
Italy, Army of, 10, 11, 25; and Sardinian expedition, 14–15; campaign of 1794, 26 *et seq.*; Kellermann commands, 34, 35; N. rejoins, 35; N. takes command of, 44; campaign of 1796, 50 *et seq.*; state of, 50–2; at Montenotte, 53–4; advances to Dego, 54–6; to Cherasco, 56–8; condition after Mondovi, 58; N. harangues, 59; crosses the Po, 64–5, 66; N.'s Milan speech to, 69–70; Directory attempts to divide, 71, 171, 184, 367; leaves Lombardy, 74–5; provisioning of, 77; enters Republic of Venice, 77; operates south of the Po, 84 *et seq.*, 87, 88; dispositions (July 1796), 92; counter-attacks against Wurmser, 94 *et seq.*; losses (29 July–12 August), 99; operations in the Tyrol, 103–5; on the Brenta, 105–6; pursues Wurmser to Mantua, 106 *et seq.*; losses (1 June–18 Sept.), 109; reinforced, 112; Italian confidence in, 112; dispositions (October), 112; Austrian successes against, 113–4, 115–6, 120; unrest in, 116; battle of Arcole, 117 *et seq.*; the price of victory, 123; enters Bologna, 137; strength and dispositions (Jan. 1797), 138; checks Austrians on the Adige, 139, 140–1; battle of Rivoli, 141–3; action of La Favorite, 144; surrender of Mantua, 145–6; occupies Papal States, 148 *et seq.*, 208; crosses the Senio, 149–50; passes the Apennines, 153, 154; at Tolentino, 154; reinforced, 158; strength of (March), 159–60; dispositions of, 161; achievements to date, 162; crosses the Tagliamento, 163–4; enters Austria, 166; victories during twenty days, 168–9; reaches Leoben, 173; evacuates Styria, Carniola and Carinthia, 176; state of (April), 173; reinforcements desert, 177; N.'s observations on operations against Beaulieu, 180–4; against Wurmser, 184, 186–91; against Alvinzi, 191–7; against Prince Charles, 198–201; and Venetian insurrection, 211–2; leaves Cisalpine Republic, 231; N.'s address on royalist conspiracy to, 243–4; refused reinforcements, 255–6; on the Isonzo, 259; N.'s Order of the Day on leaving, 264; effects of victories of, 267–8; finances of, 268; achievements under N., 269; reverses and condition of (1799), 352, 362, 363, 383, 416, 417, 434–5; N.'s resumption of command hinted at, 367; conditions and dispositions of (1800), 441–2; Austrians intersect, 442; Genoa invested, 443 *et seq.*; attacks on the Var, 444, 445; reinforcement of, see Reserve, Army of; surrender of Genoa, 447–50, 462
Ivrea, 455, 457, 459, 461
Ivrée, 445

Jacobins, 33, 38, 43; punitive measures against, 387–8; see also 'Société du Manège'
Jacqueminot, Jean Ignace, 395
Jaffa, 331, 332, 335, 343, 346; Turkish forces at, 333, 334, 336; description of, 334; French wounded at, 339
Jalès, federation of, 570
Janissaries, 298, 299, 303, 317, 360; disaffection of, 304; at battle of Pyramids, 306 *et seq.*; surrender of, 311
Jemil-Azar (el-Azhar), mosque, 300, 312, 324
Jena, 501; battle of, 490
Jerusalem, 316, 331, 332, 343, 360
Jews, and slavery, 318; in Syria, 332
John, Archduke of Austria, 489
Jordan, river, 330, 331, 334

589

INDEX

Josephine, Empress of the French, 217, 363
Joubert, General Barthélemy Catharine, 55, 92, 199, 201, 210, 269; retreats from La Corona, 93, 113, 140; at Montebaldo, 138; at Rivoli, 141, 143, 192–3; enters Trent, 144; account of, 146; in the Tyrol, 161–2; N.'s orders to, 167; at St Michael, 167–8; joins main army, 168; at Spittal, 174; marches from the Tyrol, 210, 211, 212
Jourdon, Comte Jean Baptiste, Marshal of France, 268, 353; on Stockach, 186; and Brumaire, 366, 373–4, 375, 470; commands Sambre-Meuse Army, 432–3; accredited to Piedmont, 470
Juan, Gulf of, 27, 475, 478, 479
Judenburg, 161, 173, 175, 200, 212
Juidiconni, ——, 232
Julian Alps, 136, 159, 160, 166, 168, 170, 177, 199, 210
Julien, aide-de-camp, 284
Junon, the, 358
Junot, Jean Andoche, Duc d'Abrantès, 62, 157, 212–3
Justice, the, 280, 286, 355, 358, 359
Jutland, 426

Kaim, General, 166, 172, 441
Kehl, 160, 436; siege of, 132, 133, 159; French take, 178
Keith, George Keith Elphinstone, Viscount, Admiral, 357, 358, 360; at Genoa, 442, 444, 447, 448, 449, 450, 464
Kelioubieh, 296
Kellermann, François Christophe, Duke of Valmy, Marshal of France, commands Army of Italy, 34, 35, 72; proposed for northern Italian command, 71, 184
Kellermann, François Etienne, Duke of Valmy, 465n., 505, 517; at Marengo, 468; forces under, 487; at Quatre Bras, 512, 513; at Waterloo, 522, 523, 524, 526, 531, 536
Kerpen, General, 173, 198; at St Michael, 167–8; retreats to the Brenner, 168; leaves the Tyrol, 210
Kiaschefs, 299
Kienmayer, Baron Michel de, 436
Kilmaine, General Charles Joseph, 51, 92, 107, 108, 167, 176, 188, 195, 201; ordered to defend the Adige, 103; blockades Mantua, 109, 110; account of, 110; at Verona, 117, 123; and Veronese rebellion, 211–2
Kilstett, 178
Kintzig, river, 178
Kioge, 428
Klagenfurth, 160, 161, 163, 170, 171, 172, 173, 174, 177, 199; Prince Charles at, 164; French enter, 166
Kleber, General Jean Baptiste, 268, 274, 345, 359; capitulates at El-Arisch, 350, 353, 358, 360; murdered, 351, 353, 356, 360; career of, 353–4; given Egyptian command, 354; N.'s instructions to, 355; Desaix on, 464

Kleist von Nollendorf, Emilius Friedrich, Count, 498
Klenau, aide-de-camp, 145
Klinglin, General, 178, 246, 247, 261
Knittelfeld, French take, 173
Koblos, General, at Rivoli, 141, 142
Koich, river, 334
Koik, river, 331
Korsakow, General A. M., 416, 436
Kounscheric, 305
Krapp, Captain, 413
Kray de Krajof, Baron Paul von, 178, 436–9
Kutusow, M. L. G., Prince of Smolensk, 489, 490

La Belle Alliance, 520, 523, 525, 535; N. at, 530, 532, 534
La Bicoque, 57
Laborde, Lt.-General, 476
La Brunette, 47, 63
La Chaise, ——, 221
Lacken mansion, N. buys, 261
La Combe, ——, 9
La Corona, 92, 93, 113, 120, 138, 144, 192, 196
Lacoste, Colonel, 59
Lacretelle the younger, 37
Lacroix, Charles, 126, 248
Ladrone, 103
La Favorite, 80, 81, 82, 109, 195, 269; battle of, 133, 144, 158, 190
Lafayette, Marquis de, 389
Lafond, ——, 41, 42
Lafôret, ——, 387
La Fossa Maestra, 81
La Fère regiment, 6–7
Lagarde, Baron Joseph Jean, 382
La Gironde, 556
Lagrange, Brig.-General, 343
Lagrange, Comte Joseph Louis, 268, 270
La Haie Sainte, 521, 522, 530, 531; French attack, 525, 528; capture of, 529; N. near, 535
Laharpe, General Amédée Emmanuel, 51, 53, 64, 69; at Montenotte, 54; at Dego, 55; at Emetri, 65; death of, 66
La Harpe, Jean François de, 37
La Haye, 518, 520, 521, 523; French attack, 525, 528; capture of, 531; Prussians take, 535, 545
Lahoz, General, 89, 183, 201, 210, 212; in Papal States, 148, 150
Lallemand, Brig.-General, 529
Lallemand, Captain, 92
Lallemant, ——, 201, 213
La Madonna della Neva, 181
La Madonna del Monte, 444
La Madonna di Savona, 50, 53, 442
La Madonna di Vico, 56, 57
Lamartelliere, General, 442
Lambert, ——, 453
Lambert, Major, 335
Lambert, General Sir John, 521, 560

INDEX

Lambusart, 506
La Mezzola, 147, 156
Landau, 25, 489
Landon, General, 113
Landrecy, 488
Languedoc, 387, 476, 488, 556
Lannes, Jean, Duke of Montebello, Marshal of France, 65, 75, 84, 344, 465n.; at Dego, 56; saves N. at Arcole, 119; in Papal States, 150; at Acre, 338–9; at Aboukir, 347, 348; and Brumaire, 372; commands vanguard of Reserve Army, 453; at Bard, 455; captures Ivrea, 457; enters Pavia, 459; marches to Stradella, 461; defeats Ott at Montebello, 462–3; at Marengo, 465, 467, 468
La Novalese, 47
Lanslebourg, 47
Lanusse, General, 65; at Dego, 55; defeats Elmody, 342; qualities of, 356
Laon, 488; Lobau at, 487; N. at, 501; French forces assemble at, 539, 540
Laplace, Pierre Simon, Marquis de, 6, 268, 270, 386
Lapoype, General, 15, 22, 461, 464, 465n.
La Prevelaye, ——, 394
La Reveillere (Revellière)—Lepeaux, Louis Marie de, 236, 237, 240, 274, 364; and Rome, 273
La Rocca, 87
La Rochelle, 489
Lasalle, Major, 142
La Scaliera, 143, 144
Lasne, 533
Latour, Count Maximilian Baillet von, 51, 59
Latourette, Colonel, 572
Latour-Maubourg, Marie Victor de Fay, Marquis de, 358, 360, 389
Lattermann, General, 442
Laudon, Baron Gideon Ernst von, 441; in the Tyrol, 167, 168, 210–11; occupies Trent, 210; calls for Italian insurrection, 210–11
Laugier, Adjutant-commander, 336
Laugier, Lt., 212, 214
Laumont (Laumond), ——, 250, 356
Launay, Brig.-General, 115
Lausanne, 453, 454
Lauterbourg, 489
Lavalette, Antoine M. C., Comte de, 174, 221, 222, 250
La Vendée, 72, 73, 452; revolt in, 25, 197, 262, 356, 387, 392–3, 452, 476, 483, 487, 497, 543, 570–1; N. refuses a command in, 34; Army of, 486, 487
Lavis, 103, 162, 167
Laybach, 160, 161, 165, 166, 170, 174, 200
Leander, the, 286
Lebrun, Charles François, Duke of Piacenza, 370, 395, 415; appointed third Consul, 400; career of, 400
Lecchi, General, 459
Lech, river, 102, 268, 433

Leclerc, General Victor Emmanuel, 142, 172
Lecourbe, Claude Joseph, Comte, 287, 434, 541
Ledro, 99
Lefebvre, François Joseph, Duke of Danzig, Marshal of France, 268, 342; and Brumaire, 370, 372
Lefebvre-Desnouettes, Comte Charles, 509; supports Clary, 505; at Quatre Bras, 512; at Waterloo, 522, 531
Leghorn, 23, 84, 268, 464, 479; French descent on, 86–7, 92, 131, 162, 184
Legislative Body, 240, 248, 250, 269, 365, 400, 452; moved to St Cloud, 369 et seq., 381–2; adjourned for three months, 374, 378, 387; intermediate committees of, 394, 395–6, 398
Legnago, 80, 92, 94, 103, 121, 122, 139, 140, 143, 191, 197, 204; Austrians occupy, 107; Wurmser leaves, 108; French recapture, 109; Augereau at, 138; French evacuation of, 188, 190
Le Havre, 489
Lemarrois, Comte, 104, 176
Lemercier, Louis Nicholas, Comte, 370, 374, 395
Lenova, 113
Leoben, 73, 161; peace preliminaries of, 134, 175–6, 177–8, 200, 201, 212, 248, 251, 259, 269; French assemble at, 174, 175; and Rhine armies, 178–9
Leopold II, Emperor, 88
Lepelletier, Section of, 38–9, 40, 41, 42
Lepeyre, ——, 327
Leroy, ——, 282
Lespinasse, General, 82
Letort, General, 506
Letourneur, C. L. F. Honoré, 34, 240, 248
Lezegno, 56, 57
Lherbach, Count, 264
Liamone, river, 5
Libérateur d'Italie, the, 214, 243
Liége, 133, 481, 502, 511, 514, 517, 518, 528
Lienz, 160, 174, 199
Ligny, 514, 536, 538, 545, 547; French dispositions near, 508–9; battle of, 510–2, 515, 527, 528, 533, 539, 546, 549, 551
Lille, 476, 486, 488, 500, 543, 567, 569–70; Malmesbury at, 248, 249
Lille, Comte de, 204
Limate, 533, 540
Limath, river, 433
Lindet, Robert, 383
Lindholm, Adjutant-General, 426
Linz, 161
Liptay, Baron Anton, 51, 65, 78, 93, 112, 113; at Lonato, 96; at Rivoli, 141, 142
Lisle, *see* Lille
Little Gibraltar, Toulon, 17, 19, 20–1
Little St Bernard Pass, 47, 180, 457
Livenza, river, 47, 203
Loano, 30, 53; action at, 35, 44, 125

591

INDEX

Lobau, Georges Mouton, Comte de, Marshal of France, 514, 515, 516, 539; at Voltri, 443; forces under, 487; at Waterloo, 523, 527, 528, 530–1, 535, 537
Lodi, 65, 66, 69, 71, 75, 79, 116, 194, 268, 269; battle of, 67–8, 183; bridge of, 106; Duhesme takes, 459
Lodrone, 98, 103, 189, 190
Loire, river, 435, 476, 488
Loison, General, 453
Lombardy, 46, 60, 61, 69, 70, 71, 74, 76, 127, 129, 183, 256–8, 260, 269, 306, 459, 460, 469; French security in, 89–90; pro-French, 100; secret arrangements about, 134; and Cispadan Republic, 135, 136; French achievements in, 184; and Transpadan Republic, 228
Lonato, 95, 99, 187, 269; Austrian defeat at, 94, 96, 97, 98, 101, 103
Longwy, 488, 500
Loretto, 151, 153; *Casa Santa* at, 152
Lorient, 483
Lorset, Adjutant-General, 121
Louvet de Couvray, Jean Baptiste, 42
Louis IX, King of France (St Louis), campaign in Egypt, 359–60
Louis XIV, King of France, 185
Louis XVI, King of France, 8, 12, 236, 244, 249, 382; anniversary of his execution, 275–6, 391
Louis XVIII, King of France, leaves Paris, 476; armies of, 478; flees from France, 480, 494; plate left by, 485
Louis, Louis Dominique, Baron, 485
Louisa, Queen of Prussia, 395
Lowendahl, Comte Ulrich de, 270
Lubeck, 426
Lucca, 46, 69
Lugano, Lake, 138
Lugo, 88
Lutzen, battle of, 512
Luxembourg, 133, 134
Luzignan, General, 141, 142, 143, 163, 193
Lyons, 13, 268, 453, 477, 478, 479, 488, 497; revolt of, 6–7, 15, 24, 566, 568; Gulf of, 27; N. in, 363, 471, 476; defences of, 489, 490, 493, 495, 496, 541, 558

Maadieh, Lake, 197, 344, 345, 346, 347
Maar, river, 334
Macdonald, Etienne J. J. A., Duke of Taranto, 370, 476, 498
Macerata, 153, 154, 156, 157, 228
Madrid, in 1808 campaign, 490
Magano, 103
Maggiore, Lake, 138, 217
Mahomet, tenets and conquests of, 315 *et seq.*
Mahon, *see* Port Mahon
Mailly, ——, 336
Maine, river, 178, 432, 436
Mainoni, General, 465*n*.
Mainz (Mayence, Mentz), 134, 160, 257, 258, 259, 353, 432, 435, 437; Pichegru and, 242, 261; surrendered to France, 260, 264, 265
Maire, 357
Majestic, the, 285
Malleo, 65
Malmesbury, James Harris, Earl of, 248–9, 382
Malta, 332, 356, 359, 365, 386; French capture, 279, 280; English retake, 417
Mamelukes, 281, 351, 352, 360; power and character of, 298–9; Arab fear of, 301–2; their tax collectors, 303; N.'s war against, 303–4, 305 *et seq.*, 343; the Porte's wars against, 304; at battle of Pyramids, 306 *et seq.*; losses of, 310; and slavery, 318; wives of, 322; defeat of, 343
Manfredini, Federigo, 86, 131, 137; character of, 88
Manheim (Mannheim), 160
Manini (Manin), Lodovico, 216
Mansoura, 296
Mantua, 61, 81, 93, 97, 125, 126, 127, 129, 131, 134, 158, 196, 201, 206, 214, 228, 259, 269, 458, 459, 461, 464, 469; siege of, 71, 73, 80 *et seq.*; defences of, 74, 78, 80–1; dispositions necessary for siege of, 80; circumvallation of, 82; besieging train for, 83, 85, 94, 95, 99; defenders of, 88–9; French attempt to cross lower lake at, 89; French losses from sickness, 92, 100, 110; siege raised, 94, 100; Wurmser at, 95, 96, 98; Liptay retreats to, 96; French re-impose blockade on, 99–100; Wurmser's efforts to relieve, 102 *et seq.*; Wurmser trapped in, 109, 110; Alvinzi's efforts to relieve, 111 *et seq.*; sorties from, 115; N. on, 116; expected to surrender, 123, 137; Austro-French negotiations over, 132–3; forces in (Jan. 1797), 138; Austrian defeats before, 143–4; surrender of, 145–6, 162, 218; N. at, 157–8; refortified, 158; retained by Austria, 176; during campaign against Beaulieu, 182, 183; against Wurmser, 187, 188, 190, 191, 193; against Alvinzi, 194–5; ceded to Cisalpine Republic, 252; Reserve Army takes, 460
Marbot, General Antoine, 366, 442
Marburg (Maribor), 160, 161
Marcaria, 96, 97
Marchais, 509, 515
Marchiennes, 504, 505, 506, 507, 539
Marengo, battle of, 355, 417, 437, 448, 449, 462, 501; dispositions before, 465 *and n.*; Austrians attack, 466–7; arrival of Desaix, 467–8; Austrians routed, 468–9; Convention of, 469; Paris rejoices at, 470, 471
Mareotis, Lake, 197, 292
Marescalchi, Ferdinand, 4, 85
Marescot, ——, 16
Maret, Hugues Bernard, Duke of Bassano, 248–9, 382
Margate, 411
Maria Louisa, Empress of the French, 170
Mariana, 6

592

INDEX

Maria Teresa, Empress, 175
Mariette, ——, 33, 39
Marigny, Admiral, 278
Maritime Alps, 180
Marmont, Auguste F. L. Viesse de, Duke of Ragusa, Marshal of France, 34, 344, 454, 498; at Castiglione, 98; an account of, 109-10
Marne, river, 496, 498, 540, 541, 551
Marseilles, 13, 34, 51, 87, 353, 362, 441, 442, 445, 446, 476, 477, 495; N.'s mission to, 10-11; troops in Sardinia, 14; revolt of, 15, 19, 565 *et seq.*; fortification of, 27, 29-30; Jacobin excesses in, 33; troops at, 488
Marshal, John, 409
Marsin, Comte Ferdinand de, Marshal of France, 185, 186
Martin, Admiral Pierre, 290
Massa di Carara, 126, 269
Massena, André, Duke of Rivoli, Prince d'Essling, Marshal of France, 31, 51, 53, 54, 57, 79, 94, 108, 143, 161, 176-7, 189, 190, 455n., 466; takes Saorgio, 28-9; at Mt Tanardo, 33; at Dego, 55; at Alessandria, 64; crosses the Po, 66; at Bussolengo, 92; account of, 72-3; at or near Verona, 80, 138, 140, 193; at Rivoli, 93, 123, 142; marches on Brescia, 95; at Castiglione, 98; retakes La Corona, 98; marches to Trent, 103; marches to Bassano, 105; at Bassano, 106, 110, 144; marches on Vicenza, 106; crosses the Adige, 107; at Due-Castelli, 109; on the Brenta, 112-3; at Caldiero, 115; at Arcole, 119, 121, 195; at St Michel, 139; made Duke of Rivoli, 145; crosses the Piave, 162-3; takes Ponteba, 164; at Tarwis, 164-5, 198, 200; at Neumarck, 172, 177; at Bruck, 175; at Mondovi, 183; in Switzerland, 433, 435; commands Army of Italy, 435; dispositions of, 441-2; separated from Suchet, 442; besieged in Genoa, 443 *et seq.*; attempts to break out, 446; surrenders Genoa, 447, 448, 450, 462, 470; travels to Milan, 449; in command of augmented Army of Italy, 449, 471; and N.'s return from Elba, 477
Massimi, Marquis, 154, 157
Materia, Friant at, 175
Mattei, Cardinal Alessandro, 149, 154; N. confers with, 130, 131; an account of, 100-1
Maubeuge, 488, 500
Mayence, *see* Mainz
Mecca, 297, 316, 341
Medina, 316
Mediterranean Sea, coastal fortifications of, 26-8, 32-3; English withdraw from, 128; French control of, 268
Medole, 98
Melagno, 30, 442, 444
Melas, General Michael F. Benedict, 51, 78, 82, 93; forces under, 436, 440; dispositions of, 441; intersects French forces, 442; invests Genoa, 443 *et seq.*; enters Nice, 445; and approach of Reserve Army, 447, 453, 456, 458, 461, 466; N.'s plans of campaign against, 451-2, 458-9, 463; reinforces Turin area, 457; Thugut's dispatch to, 461; marches on Alessandria, 461, 462, 464; courses open to, 464; inactivity of, 464-5; decides to attack, 466; leaves Marengo battlefield, 467; retreat of, 468-9
Melpomène, the, 481
Melzi d'Eril, Francis, Duke of Lodi, 69
Memphis, 297
Menard, General Philippe Romain, 55, 221
Menou, Baron Jacques François de, 38-9, 40, 42, 309, 310; converted to Islam, 323, 352; as commander in Egypt, 351, 353, 356, 358, 359
Menouf, 296, 305
Menton, 28
Mentz, *see* Mainz
Menzaleh, Lake, 298, 327
Mercantin, General, 166, 172
Mercure, the, 286
Merfeld (Merveldt), Maximilian, Count von, 173, 175, 253-4
Merlin, Comte Philippe Antoine, 240-1, 245, 248, 365
Merry, ——, 412
Messina, 280
Metric system, 239-40
Metrouski, General, 93, 112, 118
Metternich-Winneburg, Clement W. N. L., Prince of, 264
Metz, 486, 489, 500
Meuse, river, 500, 502, 511, 514, 515, 528, 547
Mezaros de Szoboszlo, General Johann, 93, 103-7, 188
Mézières, 486, 488
Migliazetto, 89
Milan, 49, 51, 53, 58, 62, 64, 67, 76, 77, 80, 92, 112, 116, 119, 133, 135, 137, 181, 204, 213, 217, 218, 219, 223, 230, 250, 252, 440, 448, 449, 464; and battle of Millesimo, 54; submission of, 69; conditions of, 70-1; citadel invested, 74, 83, 84; unrest in, 75; archbishop of, 75, 76; citadel taken, 88; N. at, 89, 158, 253, 262, 460, 470; Austrian attempt to cut communications with, 93; N. on loyalty of, 100; Bergamo unites with, 209; capital of Cisalpine Republic, 229, 231; N. decides to attack, 457-8; capture of, 459, 469
Milhaud, General, 106, 509, 510, 511, 514-7, 521; forces under, 487; at Waterloo, 522, 524, 529, 531
Millesimo, 181, 269; battle of, 54-5, 56, 195
Mincio, river, 60, 80, 81, 94, 95, 109, 134, 186, 187, 189, 196, 201, 204, 228; Austrian positions on, 78; French crossings of, 79, 98; Austrians cross, 95, 96; Austrians retreat to, 98; Beaulieu's defence of, 182-3; Austrians claim as frontier, 259
Minotaur, the, 285
Miollis, General S. A. F., 143, 144, 442, 443
Mirandola, 71, 109, 260

INDEX

Mittenwald, Kerpen at, 168
Mocenigo, Proveditore (of Brescia), 206
Mocenigo, Proveditore (of Friuli), 211
Modena, 46, 61, 69, 80, 134, 182, 229, 258, 260, 269; armistice with, 71; N. in, 84; attitude to French, 88, 100, 112; provisions Mantua, 110; French occupy, 129; joins Cispadan Republic, 135-6; duke of, *see* Ercole III
Modeste, the, 31, 125
Moeskirch, 436
Molé, Louis Mathieu, Comte de, 478
Molinella, river, 107, 108, 143, 144, 191, 196, 197
Mollien, Nicolas François, Comte, 485
Mona, Isle of, 428
Monaco, 52
Moncey, Bon Adrien Jeannot de, Duke of Conegliano, Marshal of France, 458, 460, 461, 464, 465
Mondovi, 73, 151, 269; battle of, 57, 183, 218
Monge, Gaspard, Comte de Péluse, 151, 268, 327, 387; character of, 262
Monnier, Jean Charles, Comte, 453, 465*n*.
Montagnana, 107, 139
Mont Blanc, 32, 50, 458
Mont Cenis, 47, 264, 441; Pass, 453, 454, 457, 471
Mont Dauphin, 489
Montebaldo, 80, 92, 93, 98, 113, 114, 191-4; Joubert at, 138; Austrian main forces at, 139, 140, 141; French retreat to, 210
Montebello, 106, 122, 228, 229, 232, 233; Convention of, 126, 222; N.'s court at, 217; Franco-Austrian conferences at, 253, 254, 255; battle of, 462-3, 466, 469
Monte Cherigio, 129
Montechiaro, 78, 95
Monte Cornua, 442, 443
Monte Faccio, 443, 444, 446
Montefaiale, 180
Montefalcone, 165
Monte Grande, 32, 180
Montelegino, 53, 54, 180, 181, 442
Montelimart, 363, 476
Monte Magnone, 140, 141, 142, 192, 193
Montenotte, 30, 181, 268, 269; battle of, 33, 53-4, 56
Montepopoli, 193
Monte Ratti, 443, 444
Montezemoto, 56
Montferrat, 46, 51, 181, 434
Mont Genèvre, 47, 441
Mont Guibert, 516
Monthion, Lt.-General, 511
Montluçon, Treaty of, 393
Montmirail, battle of, 498, 501
Montpellier, 14; the manufacturer from, 566 *et seq.*
Montreuil, 488
Mont St Jean, 516, 521, 525, 531, 533, 540, 550

Moore, General Sir John, 490
Morand, C. A. L. A., Comte, 522, 530, 539
Morandi club, 220, 221, 224
Morbihan, 394
Moreau, General Jean Victor, 171, 177, 178, 268, 365; and siege of Kehl, 132, 133; and Pichegru, 245-7, 261; relieved of his command, 255, 262; and Brumaire, 369, 370, 372, 435; repulsed by Archduke Charles, 433; commands Army of Rhine, 435; advances into Germany, 436-9, 461
Morfontaine, American envoys at, 414, 415
Mori, 103, 104, 162, 188, 190
Morocco, 297, 304
Morosini, ——, 216
Mortier, E. A. C. J., Duke of Treviso, Marshal of France, 547
Moscati, ——, 230
Moscow, destruction of, 490
Moulins, Colonel, 378
Moulins, Jean F. Auguste, Baron, 375; character of, 364; attitude to N., 367; asks advice of N., 369; resigns 373
Mountain party, 13-14, 19, 33, 572, 573, 575
Mount Ariol, 46
Mount Carmel, 334-5, 357, 358
Mount Cassins, 357
Mount Cimone, 46
Mount Lebanon, 330, 331, 332, 334
Mount Olivetto, 115
Mount Saint-Pellegrino, 46
Mount Tabor, 331; battle of, 337, 341, 354
Mount Velino, 48
Mouton, Colonel, *see* Lobau
Muer, river, 160, 161, 173, 174, 210
Muiron, Captain, 21, 119
Muiron, the, 359, 362, 366
Mulback (Mulnbach), 174
Munich, 202
Murad Bey, 334; military qualities of, 308; at battle of Pyramids, 308, 309, 310; country house of, 310; youth of, 318; wife of, 334; defeat of, 343
Muraire, ——, 247, 250, 274
Murat, Joachim, King of Naples, Marshal of France, 40, 108, 143, 344, 369, 465*n*.; at Mondovi, 57; sent to Paris, 62; at Borghetto, 78; account of, 79-80; at Genoa, 84; at Leghorn, 86; at Mantua, 89; at Rivoli, 144; on the Tagliamento, 163; receives Berg, 258; defeats Murad Bey, 343; at Aboukir, 348, 349; and Brumaire, 372, 374, 378; with Reserve Army, 453; crosses Sesia river, 459; takes Piacenza, 461; conduct during 1814, 477-8, 481; demands passage to France, 478; N. sends envoy to, 479; invades Papal States, 479, 481; Austrians defeat, 480
Murau, 173, 198
Murray, William Vans, 411
Mustapha Pasha, at Aboukir, 344, 345-6, 348, 349, 359
Mutualis, 319, 332, 334, 343

INDEX

Namur, 503–6, 508, 509, 514, 528, 544, 547; Pirch near, 502; Grouchy ordered to, 538, 540

Nantes, 476, 489; Vendéans capture, 392

Naples, 48, 49, 71, 82, 134, 152, 162, 184, 194, 201, 210, 255, 258, 382, 481; armistice with, 82, 131–2; offers aid to Rome, 130; hostile attitude of, 132, 154, 227–8, 272; and Tolentino Treaty, 157; treaty with France, 227, 228; Nelson at, 279–80, 287; Austrians enter, 480; *see also* Murat

Naples, Maria Carolina, Queen of, 227, 228, 254

Napoleon I, Emperor of the French, genealogy of, 3–5; early military career, 6–7, 10–11; and Paoli, 7; his *Souper de Beaucaire*, 11, 565 *et seq.*; at Toulon, 15 *et seq.*, 33–4, 389–90; fortifies Mediterranean coasts, 26–8, 32–3; general of artillery in Italy, 28 *et seq.*; and fortification of Marseilles, 29–30; value of 1794 campaign to, 33; removed from active list, 34; joins topographical service of Army of Italy, 35; and Vendémiaire, 39 *et seq.*; commands Army of Interior, 42–3; meets Josephine, 43; commands Army of Italy, 44 *et seq.*; campaign of 1796, 50 *et seq.*; speeches and proclamations to troops, 52–3, 59, 69–70, 114, 162, 243–4, 264, 309, 434–5, 460–1, 501–2; at Cherasco, 57 *et seq.*; on military and political situation after Cherasco armistice, 60–2; at Piacenza, 65, 66; crosses the Adda, 68; in Milan, 69; Directory's attempt to interfere with, 71, 171, 184; on insurrection, 77, 184; personal escape at Valeggio, 79; enters the Papal States, 85 *et seq.*; returns to Mantua, 88; on inadequacy of his forces, 92; counter-measures against Wurmser's offensive, 94 *et seq.*; at Lonato, 94, 96, 97; pursues Wurmser to Mantua, 104 *et seq.*; narrow escape at Cerea, 108; manoeuvres against Alvinzi, 112 *et seq.*; tactics at Arcole, 116 *et seq.*; narrow escape at Arcole, 119; and French wounded at St Boniface, 122; exerts pressure on Genoa, 126–7; negotiates treaty with Sardinia, 127–8; relations with Modena, 128–9; negotiates with Rome, 130–1; and armistice with Austria, 132–4; and Lombardy and Cispadan Republic, 134–6; his use of Italian patriotism, 135; feints towards Rome, 137–8; returns to Roverbella, 140; at Rivoli, 141–3; at Mantua, 143–4; and surrender of Mantua, 145–6; plot to poison, 145; marches on Rome, 145, 148 *et seq.*, 227; letter to Cacault, 148; manifesto on Franco-Papal armistice, 148–9; treatment of Italian prisoners by, 150–1, 152; and exiled French priests, 152–3; negotiates Treaty of Tolentino, 154 *et seq.*; returns to Mantua and Milan, 157–8; prepares to invade Austria, 159–61; at Bassano, 162; crosses the Isonzo, 165; his proclamation to conquered provinces, 166–7; on co-operation of Rhine armies, 170–1, 177, 178–9, 200; corresponds with Prince Charles, 171–2, 173, 198; and Leoben preliminaries, 173 *et seq.*, 251; and Austrian recognition of French Republic, 175 *and n.*, 260; offered a German sovereignty, 176; observations on campaigns against Beaulieu, 180–4; against Wurmser, 184–91; against Alvinzi, 191–7; against the Pope, 197; against Prince Charles, 198–201; his principles of war, 181, 187, 192, 193, 194, 199; on obeying orders, 184–6, 255; attitude to Wurmser, 196; and Venetian neutrality, 206–10; and Venetian insurrection, 211–5; occupies Venice, 215–6; his court at Montebello, 217; praises Serrurier, 218; creates Ligurian Republic, 221–4; and Franco-Sardinian treaty, 224–6; Neapolitan attitude to, 227–8; creates Cisalpine Republic, 228–31, 262; settles Grison-Valteline dispute, 231–4; criticisms of Directory, 235 *et seq.*; supports Directory (Fructidor), 244–5; deplores consequent deportations, 247–8, 274; on public debt, 249–50; peace conferences at Montebello, Udine and Passeriano, 251 *et seq.*; attitude to Clarke, 252; decides to sign Campo-Formio Treaty, 255–6; proclamation to Cisalpine Republic, 262–3; at Rastadt, 264–6; returns to Paris, 267 *et seq.*; commands Army of England, 270, 278; on policy towards Rome, 272; and Egyptian campaign, 273–4, 275; and celebration of Louis XVI's death, 275–6, 391; sails for Egypt, 279; in Egypt, 280 *et seq.*; and naval battle of Aboukir, 281 *et seq.*; fortifies Alexandria, 293; marches on Cairo, 305 *et seq.*; hardships during, 307; at Embabeh, 307–9; in Gizeh, 309–10; in Cairo, 311 *et seq.*; and Mohammedanism, 320, 351–2; Arabic name of, 321; establishes Institute of Egypt, 326–8; reasons for Syrian expedition, 332–4; at Acre, 335 *et seq.*; returns to Egypt, 342, 343; and Turkish landings at Aboukir, 344–5, 346; attacks at Aboukir, 347–9; motives for Egyptian campaign, 350; reasons for returning to France, 352 *et seq.*; resumé of events in Egypt, 358–9, 360; arrives in France, 362 *et seq.*; in Paris, 363 *et seq.*; determines to overthrow Directory, 363–4; and Sieyes, 364–5, 366, 382; surveys the factions, 366–9; plans for Brumaire *coup*, 369 *et seq.*; addresses Council of Ancients, 372, 375–6; his proclamations on Brumaire, 372–3, 380–2; forces resignation of Directors, 373; provisional Consuls appointed, 374; at St Cloud, 375 *et seq.*; in Council of Five Hundred, 376–7; defends Fouché, 386; on Jacobin plots, 387; laws repealed by, 387–9; and Hamburg incident, 390–1; and Bourbon agents, 392–4; works on Constitution of Year VIII, 394 *et seq.*; and death of Washington, 411; and Franco-American negotiations, 414–6; alienates Paul I from England, 417–8; attempts to

595

INDEX

Napoleon I, Emperor of the French—*cont.*
win over Alexander I, 429; summarizes neutral rights, 430; reorganizes French armies, 434–5; plans to reconquer Italy, 436–7; on Moreau's drive into Germany, 437–9; hears of surrender of Genoa, 449, 462; forms Army of Reserve, 451–3; crosses the Alps, 453–5; at Bard, 455–7; decides to take Milan, 457–8; enters Milan, 459–60; at Stradella, 461–3; Desaix discusses Egypt with, 463–4; uneasy at inaction of Melas, 464–5; at battle of Marengo, 466–8; after Marengo, 469–71; returns to Paris, 471; leaves Elba, 475; marches to Paris, 475–6; and Murat, 479–80, 481; reaction of Vienna Congress to his return, 480–1; remodels French armies, 483 *et seq.*; dispositions of (1 June), 486–9; on value of fortified cities, 489–93; plans Belgian campaign, 494 *et seq.*; dispositions of (14 June), 500–1; crosses the Sambre, 504–5; near Fleurus, 506; in Charleroi, 506; gains the initiative, 507; attacks Prussian army, 508 *et seq.*; at Ligny, 510–1, 515; at Quatre Bras, 515–6; near Planchenoit, 516 *et seq.*; attacks Anglo-Dutch army, 519 *et seq.*, 528 *et seq.*; Bülow arrives, 527 *et seq.*; deprived of cavalry reserve, 531; Blücher defeats, 533 *et seq.*; at La Haie Sainte, 535; escapes from battlefield, 536; retreats to Laon, 539; in Paris, 539; abdicates, 541, 542, 543; criticisms of Waterloo campaign, 543–51

Nappertandy, James, 390–1
National Assembly, 8, 37, 218, 265, 276, 384, 388, 389, 396; errors and parties of, 12–13
National Convention, 8, 20, 22, 23, 25, 236, 241, 386; summons Marseilles artillery commandant, 29–30; and Genoa, 31–2; after fall of revolutionary government, 36–7; decrees of Fructidor (1795), 37; and revolt of Paris Sections, 38 *et seq.*
National Guards, Parisian revolt against Convention, 37 *et seq.*; N. reforms, 42–3; during 1815, 483, 485, 487, 488, 495, 496, 497, 499, 500, 541, 542
Natron lakes, 296, 327, 343
Naval and land warfare compared, 288–9, 430–1
Navarre, 128
Nazareth, 332, 334; battle of, 337
Neckar, river, 438
Necker, Jacques, meets N., 453
Nègre, General, 538
Negroni, ——, 9
Nelson, Horatio Nelson, Viscount, 9, 54, 358; seeks French fleet, 279–80; forces under, 280, 281; and battle of the Nile, 284–7; returns to Naples, 287; caricature of, 365–6; destroys Danish fleet, 421 *et seq.*; demands Danish surrender, 425; signs armistice in Copenhagen, 426
Nervia, river, 28, 29
Neubrisach (Neubreisach), 489

Neufchâteau, François de, 245, 248
Neumarck (Austria), 172, 177, 269, 434
Neumarck (Italy), 168
Neutrals, rights of, 404 *et seq.*, 418 *et seq.*, 430–1, 436; *see also* Visit and Search
Neuve-Eglise, 494
Neuwied, 178
Ney, Michel, Duke of Elchingen, Prince de La Moskowa, Marshal of France, 511; advances on Quartre Bras, 505; at Gosselies, 507; ordered to move beyond Quatre Bras, 508–10, 512, 514–6; forced from Quatre Bras, 513; at Waterloo, 521, 526, 528; mistakes of, 544
Nice, 10, 15, 27, 28, 32, 34, 35, 46, 47, 58, 83, 180, 436, 437, 441, 442, 449, 450, 457, 459, 466, 469; N. at, 52; ceded to France, 227, 256, 258; Austrians enter, 445
Nidda, river, 178
Niemen, river, 479
Nieperg, General, 211
Nieuport, 503
Nile, river, 292, 293, 306, 307, 343, 346, 350; battle of, 284–8, 333, 350, 354–5, 359, 412, 421; course of, 294, 296, 301; inundations of, 294, 295; canals of, 297, 298, 325; Mamelukes drowned in, 309, 310; at Cairo, 310–3; navigation of, 325
Nîmes, 14; the man from, 565 *et seq.*
Nivelles, 503, 505, 508, 509, 512, 513, 523, 524, 544
Nizza della Paglia, 57, 64, 183
Nocetta, 461
Noel, ——, 327
Nomi, 113
Nordlingen, 438
Noric Alps, 159
Normandy, 270, 278, 496
North, Army of, 383, 432, 435
Norway, 426
Notre-Dame de Neves, 442
Nourris, ——, 327
Novi, 53, 84, 464, 465; battle of, 146, 416, 417
Nubia, 294, 343
Nuremberg, 202

Oasis of Jupiter Ammon, 296
Ocskay, General, 93, 163, 164; at Lonato, 94; at Rivoli, 141, 142
Oder, river, 479
Oglio, river, 60, 61, 67, 69, 76, 77, 182; boundary of Austria and Cisalpine Republic, 176
Ohain, 520, 521, 523, 533, 534, 536
O'Hara, General Charles, 18
Ollioules, passes of, 15, 16
Olmütz, 489
Omar, Caliph, 316
Omedinar, 306
Oneglia, 14, 29, 31, 180, 204; French capture, 32
Orange, 13

INDEX

Orange, Prince Frederick of, 172; at Braine le Comte, 503; at Quatre Bras, 512, 544; at Waterloo, 532; forces under, 560
Orient, the, 282, 283, 285, 286, 287
Orion, the, 285
Oristagni, Gulf of, 279
Orleans, Louis Philippe, Duke of, 476
Orleans, Philippe II, Duke of, 185–6
Ormea, 183
Orontes, river, 330–1
Orza, 142
Osman Bey, 343
Osopo, 164, 211
Ospedaletto, 163
Ostend, 503, 520, 551
Osteria della Dugana, 141, 192
Ott von Batorkez, Baron P. C. von, 441, 444, 447; attacks Genoa, 442–3; Massena attacks, 446; negotiates surrender of Genoa, 448, 450; defeated at Montebello, 462–3
Oudinot, Charles Nicholas, Duke of Reggio, Marshal of France, 441–2, 498

Padua, 88, 163, 189, 207, 216; Augereau at, 106, 107; Provera at, 139, 140; insurrection in, 213, 214
Pahlen, Count Peter, 427, 428
Pahrsdorf, Treaty of, 437, 439
Paimboeuf, 476
Pajol, Count, 516, 517, 540; forces under, 487; enters Charleroi, 504; pursues Prussians, 505, 514, 515; near Fleurus, 509; at Ligny, 511; at Waterloo, 521; crosses the Dyle, 533
Palestine, 331 *et seq.*, 334 *et seq.*
Palfy, General, 442, 445
Palma-Nuova, 164, 165, 174, 177, 198, 200, 207, 210, 211, 213, 264
Palmyra, 330, 331
Pansard, General, 374
Pantheon, Society of the, 43
Paoli, General Pascal, 14; revolts against the French, 5, 7, 8–9, 571; leaves Corsica (1769), 5; and N., 7; leaves Corsica (1795), 10
Papal Army, 140, 197; French operate against, 84–6; Austrians plan to join with, 139; efforts to form, 147; defeated on the Senio, 149–50, 151; disbanded, 201; Provera and, 227, 271, 272
Papal States, 62, 134; French invasions of, 84 *et seq.*, 184, 197, 208, 227–8; and Cispadan Republic, 136; French priests in, 152–3; Cisalpine claims on, 227; French occupation of, 272, 273, 274; Murat invades, 479; *see also* Pius VI *and* VII
Papelotte, 535n.
Paradisi, ——, 230
Paribelli, ——, 232
Paris, 132, 174, 176, 178, 488, 497, 498; Charles Bonaparte at, 6; Paoli's reception in, 8; insurrection of Vendémiaire, 37 *et seq.*; captured colours presented at, 62, 109, 144, 176–7, 216, 218, 262; works of art sent to, 67, 86, 88, 152, 162, 268, 269; N. in, 92; Franco-Genoese treaty signed in, 126; Hoche marches near, 262, 268; N. returns from Italy, 265, 267; N. returns from Egypt, 362 *et seq.*; N. commands troops of, 369 *et seq.*; N.'s proclamation on Brumaire, 380–2; American envoys in, 409, 410, 414, 415; mourns Washington, 411; troops withdrawn from, 452; celebrates Marengo, 470, 471; N.'s return after Marengo, 476; munitions made in, 484; defences of, 489, 490–3, 495–6, 540–1, 542, 558; N.'s return from Elba, 494; N. leaves for Belgium, 501; French retreat on, 536 *et seq.*; N. arrives after Waterloo, 539
Parker, Admiral Sir Hyde, 428; destroys Danish fleet, 421 *et seq.*
Parma, 46, 61, 69, 70, 71, 84, 134, 135, 258; armistice with, 66–7; loyalty of, 100; treaty with, 128
Parma, Ferdinand, Duke of, 128, 162, 269
Pas de Calais, 278
Pas de Suze, 47
Passeriano, 228; conferences at, 254–6, 259, 260, 261
Pastoret, Claude E. J. P., Marquis de, 250, 356
Paul I, Tsar, and Egypt, 354; and Armed Neutrality, 411, 413; seizes English ships, 414; military defeats of, 416–7; and Russian prisoners, 417; corresponds with N., 417–8; enters second Armed Neutrality, 418–9; at war with England, 420 *et seq.*; murdered, 426–7, 429; grievances against England, 435–6
Pavia, 65, 66, 69, 116, 461; revolt of, 75–7, 150, 184; pro-Austrian feeling in, 100; Reserve Army takes, 448, 459
Pazzone, 144
Pecaduc, Major, 6
Pecheux, General, 511
Peine, Brig.-General, 540
Pelusium, 294, 296, 297, 298
Peninsular War, 490
Pereymont, General, 362
Péronne, 488, 541
Perpignan, 489, 576
Perponcher, General, 521, 560
Perré (Perée), Rear-Admiral, 311, 337, 338, 339, 358
Persia, 316, 317
Persian Gulf, 330
Perugino, 154, 155
Pesaro, ——, 210, 211; N.'s interviews with, 209, 210; escapes to Vienna, 215
Peschiera, 78, 79, 80, 92, 96, 117, 138, 140, 182, 183, 187, 192, 196, 201, 204; Austrians near, 95, 98; Austrians occupy, 204, 206, 207; surrender of, 469
Petiet, Claude, 240, 470
Petrarchi, Mgr., 129
Peuple Souverain, the, 285, 286
Pezaro, 151

597

INDEX

Phalsbourg, 489
Phelippeaux, Antoine Le Picard de, 6, 338
Philipsburg, 160, 432, 437
Phillipville, 488, 495, 500, 501, 539
Piacenza, 65, 66, 67, 84, 183, 458, 461, 464, 469
Piave, river, 47, 60, 106, 110, 113, 114, 130, 134, 139, 167, 170, 188, 198, 203, 208; Alvinzi crosses, 112; Austrians retreat across, 144; Prince Charles behind, 161; French crossings of, 162–3, 209, 259
Picardy, 270, 497
Pichegru, General Charles, 36, 250, 253, 445; treachery of, 178, 242 *et seq.*; President of Five Hundred, 240, 242; royalist partisan, 241; career of, 242; in Holland, 243; arrested, 245; Moreau on, 245–7; N.'s view of, 247; Desaix on, 261
Picton, General Sir Thomas, 521, 529, 560; at Quatre Bras, 513; at Waterloo, 521
Piedmont, 46, 47, 61, 62, 69, 70, 83, 126, 256, 258, 417, 434, 459, 469, 470; defences of, 50–1; French invade, 54; and Cherasco armistice, 58, 59–60; N.'s observations on manoeuvres in, 180 *et seq.*
Piedmontese Army, attempts invasion of Provence, 26; loses Saorgio, 29; on Genoese territory, 31; advantages of, 32; troops for Army of Italy, 127, 128; *see also* Colli-Ricci *and* Sardinian Army
Pietoli, 81, 89, 158, 182
Pieva, 180
Pigeon, General, 95, 96, 103–4, 108
Pignatelli, François, Prince of Strongoli, 131, 157
Pinckney, Charles Cotesworth, 409
Pipolo, 142
Pirch, General, 502, 533
Pisa, 5, 87
Pistoia, 86
Pitt, William, 241, 248, 249
Pittony (Pittone), Philip, Baron, 78
Pius VI (Giovanni Angelo Braschi), Pope, 134, 135, 162, 201, 228, 229, 269; armistice with, 86, 129; death of, 100, 389; supports Austria, 129–31; and Treaty of Tolentino, 131, 136, 153 *et seq.*; and N.'s feint towards Rome, 137–8; armistice with France broken, 147–9; and the Inquisition, 157; declining temporal power of, 227; fall of, 272, 274; *see also* Papal Army
Pius VII (Gregorio Bernabo Chiaramonti), Pope, 149; and revolt of Lugo, 88; election of, 101; temporal power of, 258; at Venice, 440; in Genoa, 479; N. reassures, 480
Pizzighettone, 65, 68, 69, 92, 138, 460, 469
Planchenoit, 527, 530, 534; French advance to, 515–6; French dispositions near, 517
Planta, Gaudenzio, 232, 233
Pleville-le-Peley, Georges René, 248
Po, river, 48, 49, 64, 69, 71, 76, 80, 81, 82, 129, 134, 136, 189, 191, 194, 196, 201, 202, 228,

434, 436, 450, 459, 462, 463, 464, 479, 480; description of, 46–7; French crossings of, 65, 87, 88, 140, 181–2, 183; French operations south of, 83, 84–6, 137–8, 145, 148 *et seq.*, 184; Melas orders Austrians to, 447, 448; Reserve Army reaches, 457
Point, General, 144
Pola (Polo), 103, 190
Polcevera, 124, 222
Polygamy, 317–8, 319
Polytechnic School, 387
Ponsonby, Major-General Sir William, 532, 560
Ponteba, 160, 162, 163, 164, 198, 199
Pontécoulant, L. G. Doubet de, 34
Ponte-Curone, 465*n*.
Ponte di Lagoscuro, 140
Ponte-di-Nave, 58
Ponte di San Marco, 93, 95, 96, 97
Ponte-Lechio, 10
Ponte-Vecchio, 80
Porcil, 117, 118, 120, 195
Porquerolles, 23, 25
Portalis, Jean Etienne Marie, 247, 250, 274, 356
Porteros, 25
Port Mahon, 345, 359; English army at, 436, 441, 445, 461, 464, 469, 470
Porto Ferrajo, 25
Porto Maurizio, 462
Porto Vecchio, 5
Portugal, 357, 480
Pourailles, Colonel, 96
Poussielgues, ——, 127
Pozzo di Borgo, Count Carlo Andrea, 9
Pozzuolo, 78
Pradella, 80, 81, 109, 158, 182
Primolana, battle of, 105–6
Priuli, Proveditore, 213
Prony, Gaspard de, Baron, 268
Provence, 51, 268, 279, 358, 364, 442, 444, 445, 461, 477, 480, 568, 569; coastal fortifications of, 26–7
Provera, Giovanni, Marquis de, 51, 55, 194, 197; on the Brenta, 112–3; at Arcole, 118; checked on the Adige, 139, 140–1; approaches Mantua, 143–4; defeated, 144; N.'s praise of, 195; in Papal State, 227, 271, 272
Provisional Consuls, appointed, 374, 378; first sitting of, 382; form new ministry, 382–3, 385–7; pass decree against anarchists, 387–8; laws repealed by, 388, 389; and Hamburg, 390; and prisoners of war, 391; and insurgents, 391–4; discuss new Constitution, 395 *et seq.*; time in office, 401
Pruneken (Brunico), 168
Prussia, 256, 265, 364, 395, 432, 479; joins second Armed Neutrality, 418–9; occupies Hanover, 420–1; at peace with England, 477; at peace with England, 477; at Vienna Congress, 477; *see also* Blücher
Ptolemais, 332
Pusterthal, the, 167, 168, 199, 201, 211

598

INDEX

Puzy, Bureau de, 389
Pyramids, 297, 306, 343; battle of, 283, 284, 304, 307 *et seq.*, 333, 351, 354
Pyrenees, 35, 549; defences of, 487, 488, 489

Quasdanowich (Quosdanovich), General Peter Vitus von, 142, 186, 187, 189, 192–3; on the Chiesa, 93; French attacks on, 94, 95, 96, 98; at Lavis, 103; at Bassano, 105; in the Friuli, 106, 109; on the Brenta, 112–3
Quatre Bras, 504, 511, 536, 546; Anglo-Dutch army concentrates at, 503, 507; French assemble before, 505–7; Ney's orders concerning, 508, 509, 512, 514, 515, 516; battle of, 512–3, 540, 547, 548, 550; French retreat from, 513; losses at, 513–4; English retreat from, 515–6; French retreat to, 538–9; Ney's mistakes at, 544
Quesnoy, 488
Quinette, ——, 386
Quinze-Vingts, Section of, 42

Raffa, 330
Rambaut (Rambeaud), General, 338
Ramel de Nogaret, Jacques, 240–1
Rampon, Comte Antoine Guillaume, 53, 54, 308
Rapp, Comte Jean de, 463, 539, 540; forces under, 486
Rastadt, 161, 353; Congress of, 251, 260, 261, 262, 264–6, 273; N. leaves, 267
Ratisbon, 433
Raus, 30
Razelgate, 330
Ré, Island of, 489
Réal, Comte Pierre François, 366, 368
Recco, 442, 443
Rednitz, river, 102, 433
Red Sea, 296, 297, 330, 343
Refah, 296
Régénérée, the, 355, 357, 359
Reggio, 71, 84, 88, 229, 260; loyalty of, 110, 112; capture of Austrians in, 129; joins Cispadan Republic, 135–6
Regnault, Jean Baptiste, Baron, 365
Regnier, Claude Ambrose, Duke of Massa, 366, 370, 374, 376, 396
Regnier (Reynier), Jean L. Ebenezer, Comte, 247, 261, 308, 309, 345; military qualities of, 356
Reille, Comte Honoré C. M. J., Marshal of France, 516; forces under, 487, 494; before Quatre Bras, 505; at Waterloo, 523, 526, 535, 536
Reinhard, Charles Frederic, Count, 385
Reno, river, 85
Reserve, Army of, 436; enters Italy, 445, 446, 454 *et seq.*; surrender of Genoa and, 446–50; formation of, 451, 452–3; commands of, 451, 453; by-passes Fort Bard, 455–7; secures Milan, 458–9; N.'s proclamation to, 460–1;

converges on Stradella, 461, 463; battle of Montebello, 462–3; takes Marengo, 465; dispositions of, 465*n*.; battle of Marengo, 466–8
Rethel, 540
Reuss, Henry, Prince of, 93, 103, 436, 438
Revanche, the, 362
Revel, Count, 63
Revel, Russian ships at, 421, 422, 428
Rewbell, Jean François, 240, 271
Rey, General, 138, 145
Rhamanieh, 284, 342, 344, 345, 346, 360
Rhine, river, 232, 355, 480; French crossings of, 102, 132, 178–9; French forces on, 111–2, 432 *et seq.*; and French frontiers, 133, 134, 176, 260, 261; Austrian divisions sent from, 159, 161, 162, 166, 167, 168, 169, 198; and Campo-Formio Treaty, 251–2; French reverses on (1799), 352, 363; Allied armies march on, 496, 520, 541, 549, 551
Rhine-Moselle Army, 25, 159, 169, 211, 212, 244, 255–6, 268, 444, 470; reverses of, 91, 92, 383, 433; troops in Italy, 158, 172 (*see also* Moncey); N. expects co-operation of, 160, 168, 170–1, 177, 178–9, 200; Pichegru commands, 242; Sambre-Meuse Army united with, 262; Moreau's drive into Germany with, 435, 461
Rhodes, 280, 358; Turkish army of, 333, 334, 339, 354
Rhône, river, 27, 50, 51, 441, 496, 566
Ricard, General, 478
Richelieu, Armand E. S. S. du Plessis, Duc de, 253
Richepanse, General Antoine, 438
Ricors (Ricord), Jean François, 28
Rigolo, ——, 327
Rimini, 151
Riva, 98, 190
Rivoli, 92, 93, 113, 117, 144, 182, 187, 189, 195, 196, 244, 269; N. addresses troops at, 114; Austrians take, 120; battle of, 131, 133, 140–3, 158, 192–3, 194, 434
Rivoli, the, 282, 481
Robert, General, 119
Robespierre, Augustin, 28
Robespierre, Maximilien Marie Isidore, 36
Rocca, Cesari, 9
Rocca Barbena, 180, 442
Rocca d'Anfo, 93, 98, 103, 189, 196
Roccavina, General, 89, 98
Rochefort, 23, 355, 357, 482, 483
Rocroi, 488
Rodah, Isle of, 309, 310, 328, 329
Roederer, Comte Pierre Louis, 365, 368, 414
Rogers, Admiral, 279
Rohan-Guemené, C. A. G., Duke of Montbazon, 459
Romagna, 47, 201, 229, 258, 269, 479; joins Cispadan Republic, 136; Papal Army in, 139; French enter, 145, 149, 197; ceded to France, 155, 156–7; ceded to Venice, 176

599

INDEX

Romano, 457
Roman Republic, 72, 272, 274
Rome, 3, 5, 48, 50, 71, 72, 82, 184, 194, 210, 258, 440, 478; as capital of Italy, 49; march on, impracticable, 86; French insulted in, 100; N. threatens, 130, 137–8; French march on, 145, 148 *et seq.*, 197; French occupy, 272, 274; and Egypt, 296, 302; and Greek culture, 314
Ronco, 107, 108, 118, 119, 120, 121, 191; bridge at, 117, 195
Rosas, 330
Roselmini, General, 67, 89
Rosetta, 282, 293, 294, 296, 298, 309, 313, 323, 328, 344, 346, 360
Rossomme, N. at, 524–5
Rostino, convent of, 7
Rotenmann, 161, 210
Roverbella, 80, 81, 89, 120, 143, 145, 191, 195
Rovere, J. S. François Xavier, 241
Roveredo, 99, 103, 139, 187, 188, 189, 190, 269; Austrian retreat to, 98; battle of, 104, 107, 109, 110, 191
Rovigo, 103
Roya, river, 28, 32, 449
Royal Navy, compared with French navy, 290–1; commitments of, 357, 421, 428; arrests neutral shipping, 411–3, 418; in the Baltic, 414, 422 *et seq.*; *see also* Visit and Search *and* Nelson
Rubicon, river, Murat crosses, 479
Rusca, Brigadier-General, 31
Russia, 256, 355, 356, 357, 358, 479; Austria and, 253, 254, 260; and Venice, 257; not an European power, 265; and Egypt, 354; in Second Coalition, 416–7; at war with England, 418 *et seq.*; Treaty of St Petersburg, 428, 429–31; at Vienna Congress, 477; N.'s invasion of, 479; *see also* Catherine II, Paul I *and* Alexander I

Sablons, 40
Sacile, 163
Sacken, F. G. von der Osten, Prince de, 498
Saffet, battle of, 337
Sahuguet, General, 107, 108; at Mantua, 99–100, 103, 109
Saide, 296
St Amand, 508, 512, 513, 514, 545; French take, 510–1
St Bartholomew, 420
St Boniface, French wounded at, 122
Saint Cloud, Legislature moved to, 369, 370, 372, 373; events at, 374 *et seq.*; N.'s proclamation on events at, 380–2
Saint-Cyr, Marquis Laurent Gouvion de, 434, 467, 468
St Domingo, *see* San Domingo
Ste Marguerite, 489
St Esprit, 566, 570
St Felix, 208

St George, 80, 81, 82, 89, 108, 143–4, 182, 190, 269; battle of, 109, 110, 188, 194–5
Saint Gothard Pass, 48, 458, 459
St Helens, Alleyne Fitzherbert, Baron, 428
Saint-Hilaire, General, 96, 97, 98, 103, 190
St Jacques, 34, 46, 50, 180, 181
St James, 30, 442
St Jean d'Acre, *see* Acre
St John, Knights of, 279, 417
Saint-Julien, General, 442
Saint-Just, Antoine L. Léon, 242
St Lambert, 532, 533; Prussians at, 526–7, 528; Grouchy ordered to, 518, 527
St Malo, 489
St Mark, *see* San Marco
Saint-Marsan, Comte de, 89, 127
St Maurice, 454
St Michel (on the Avisio), 113, 115; battle of, 167–8
Saint-Michel, ——, 9
St Michel (on the Adige), 138, 139, 140
St Michel (on the Corsaglia), 56–7
St Omer, 488
St Ozetto, 93, 95, 97, 182
St Peter, 208
St Petersburg, 479; Treaty of, 428–31
St Peter's Isles, 279
St Pierre, 453, 454
St Polten, 161
St Quentin, 270
St Remi, 454
St Thomas, 420
St Tropez, 27, 489
St Veit, 172
St Vincent, John Jervis, Earl of, 279
Salahieh, 345, 351
Salamanca, 490
Salicetti, Christophe, 15, 29
Salmatoris, ——, 59
Salo, 92, 95, 187, 189, 210; Austrians attack, 93, 94; French capture, 96
Saltholm, 423
Salzburg, 160, 161, 210
Sambre, river, 487, 501, 502, 514, 540, 543; French cross, 504, 505, 507, 539, 547
Sambre-Meuse Army, 158, 159, 169, 200, 211, 242, 244, 255–6, 261, 268, 353, 354, 432–3 N. expects co-operation of, 160, 170–1, 177, 178–9; united with Rhine-Moselle Army, 262
Samson, General, 335
San Bartolomeo, 180
San Benedetto, 56, 81, 183
San Daniele, 160, 164, 198
San Domingo, 297, 332, 350, 357
San Fiorenzo, 5, 9, 10
San Giovanni di Murialto, 56
Sanguinetto, 108
San Juliano, 465, 466, 467, 468
San Marco, 103, 104, 188, 190, 196; chapel of, 141–2, 192
San Miniato, 3, 4

600

INDEX

San Pantaleone, 442, 444
Santa-Cruz, 420
Santa Maura, 215, 228; ceded to France, 261
Saône river, 436, 496
Saorgio, 28, 29, 32, 52
Sarca, river, 103, 190
Sardinia, 45, 48, 49, 252, 258, 279, 357; French attack island of, 7, 14–15, 571; armistice with, 125, 126; treaty with France, 127–8, 224–6, 256; *see also* Charles Emmanuel IV
Sardinian Army, strength and dispositions of, 51; separated from Austrian Army, 55, 60; after Mondovi, 58; N.'s observations on operations against, 181, 183; *see also* Piedmontese Army
Sarre-Louis (Saarlauten), 488, 500
Sarzana, 3, 442
Sassello, 53, 55, 181
Saulnier, 15
Savary, A. J. M., Duke of Rovigo, 463
Save, river, 161, 174
Savigliano, 445
Savona, 30, 46, 50, 53, 58, 83, 124, 181, 442
Savoy, 47, 271, 569; ceded to France, 227, 256, 258
Saxe-Teschen, Albert Casimir, Duke of, 261
Saxe-Weimar, Prince Bernard of, 505, 512, 548
Saxony, 432
Scez, 47
Schaffhausen, 436, 437, 438
Scheifling, 161, 172–3, 198, 210
Scheldt, river, 278, 290, 432
Schelestat, 489
Scherer, General Barthelmy, L. J., 35, 44, 52, 72
Schwarzenberg, Karl Philipp, Prince von, 498
Scrivia, river, 64, 463, 465, 466
Sea Without Water, 296
Sebaiar, Oasis of, 343
Sebottendorf van der Rose, Baron Karl Philipp, 51, 67, 78, 79, 93; at Rovigo, 103; at Bassano, 104–5
Second Coalition, formation of, 352
Sédan, 488
Segonzano, 113, 167
Seigny, Colonel, 29–30
Seine, 20
Seine, river, 496
Selim I, administration of Egypt, 302–3
Seltz, conferences of, 273
Senegal, 297
Sennaar, 354, 355
Septipani (Settepani), 30, 442
Seraglio, the, 78, 81, 99, 139, 182, 187, 188
Serbelloni, Duke of, 69, 230
Serea, 103
Serizi, ——, 37
Sermon, 475
Serravalle, 103, 104, 190
Serrurier, Jean M. Philibert, Marshal of France, 51, 53, 55, 58, 69, 79, 161, 199, 200; at St Michel, 56–7; at Tortona, 64; an account of, 73; at Mantua, 81, 92, 94, 138, 144, 145; at Roverbella, 89; at Marcaria, 96, 97; his command taken by Fiorella, 97–8; at Verona, 98; at Conegliano, 163; crosses the Tagliamento, 164; takes Gradisca, 165; at Neumarck, 172; at Gratz, 175; at Mondovi, 183; N.'s praise of, 218; and Brumaire, 374
Serviez, General, 168, 210
Sesia, river, 64, 458, 459, 464
Sestri di Levante, 441
Shabur, 305, 344
Sharkieh, 296, 345; revolt of, 341, 343, 344
Shebreis, 305, 307
Sicily, 45, 48, 49, 356, 477
Sieyes, Comte Emmanuel Joseph, 34, 42, 223, 230, 367; qualities of, 364, 368, 400; at Vendémiaire, 364–5; proposals for new Constitution, 366, 396–9; N. resolves to act with, 368; agrees on measures for Brumaire, 369; resigns directorship, 373; proposes arrest of opponents, 374; appointed provisional Consul, 378; conduct during Brumaire, 379; loses Ducos' vote, 382; on N.'s mastery, 382; detestation of Fouché, 386; and Jacobin plots, 387; appointed to Senate, 400
Simeon, Comte Joseph Jerome, 250
Simering (Semmering) Pass, 160, 167, 171, 174, 175, 177, 200
Simplon Pass, 48, 441, 458, 459
Sinigaglia, 151
Siout, 296
Sisteron, 475
Slavery, Eastern and Western attitude to, 318–9
Smith, Admiral Sir William Sidney, 352, 365; at Toulon, 23; and siege of Acre, 335, 358; suggests surrender of French, 340; at Aboukir, 344, 349
Société du Manège, 364, 370, 373–5, 385, 386, 434, 435; and N.'s return to Paris, 363; and Talleyrand, 366; offers dictatorship to N., 366; N.'s rejection of, 367; and Sieyes, 368
Soignies, Forest of, 503, 514, 516 *et seq.*, 533, 547, 550, 551
Soissons, 501
Soleure, 271
Solre-sur-Sambre, 501
Sombref, 506, 508, 509, 510, 514
Somerset, Lord Edward, 560
Sommosierra, battle of, 490
Soncino, 77
Songis, General, 82
Sophia Dorothea, Tsarina, 427
Soret, General, 92, 94, 95, 96, 97, 189
Sotin de la Coindière, Pierre J. M., 276
Soult, Jean Nicholas de Dieu, Duke of Dalmatia, Marshal of France, 442; captured, 446; and N.'s return from Elba, 478; proclamation issued by, 498–9; at Waterloo, 526, 527, 528; at Laon, 539; French distrust of, 545
Soumise, Colonel, 572
Souper de Beaucaire, Le (Napoleon), 11, 565 *et seq.*

601

INDEX

Spain, 127, 279, 357, 390, 407, 421; alliance with France, 128, 132; and Armed Neutrality, 421; at Vienna Congress, 477; and safety of France, 489; Marseilles and, 571, 575, 576
Spanocchi, ——, 87
Spartiate, the, 285, 286
Spigno, 55
Spinola, Marquis de, 84
Spinola, Vincente, 126
Spital, 161
Spittal, 160, 167, 174, 199
Splügen Pass, 48, 441
Sporck, General, 168, 198
Sprengporten, General, 417-8
Starray (Sztarray), Lt.-Field-Marshal, 178, 436
States of the Church, *see* Papal States
Stein, 438
Stella, 180, 442
Stengel, General, 51, 56, 57
Sterzing (Sterzen), 168
Stockach, 186, 433, 436, 437, 438
Stradella, 182, 461, 463, 465, 469
Strasbourg, 160, 178, 245, 432, 433, 437, 489
Stura, river, 47, 53, 57, 58
Styria, 176, 257, 259
Suabia, 437
Subervic, General, 516, 521; at Waterloo, 522, 524, 526
Suchet, Louis Gabriel, Duke of Albufera, Marshal of France, 98; 465, 466, 468, 541; separated from Massena, 442; defends the Var, 444, 445; marches to Genoa, 448, 449; after surrender of Genoa, 462, 463; re-enters Genoa, 469; forces under (1815), 487, 496
Suez, 296, 312, 330; canal, 297, 298, 329
Sugny, General, 82
Sukolski, Colonel, 328
Suwarrow (Suvaroff), Alexander Vassilievitch, Count, 416, 435
Suza (Susa), 63, 89, 457
Suzannet, ——, 392, 393
Sweden, mediatrix at Rastadt, 264-5; and Armed Neutrality, 407-8, 411, 413, 418, 419-20; England arrests ships of, 411-2; at war with England, 420 *et seq.*; fails to attack Nelson, 422; at peace with England, 429-30; at Vienna Congress, 480
Swiftsure, the, 286
Switzerland, 354, 355, 432, 437, 438; and Grisons-Valteline dispute, 231-4; N. in, 264; French invade, 271, 273, 433; Russian forces in, 416, 435-6
Syracuse, 280
Syria, 287-8, 296, 297, 315, 316, 317, 350, 354, 355, 360; Christians of, 300, 312, 332, 334, 343, 351; description of, 330-2; objects of French expedition into, 332-4; capture of Jaffa, 334-5; siege of Acre, 335-9; N. returns from, 342-3

Taggia (Taggio), river, 28, 29, 32, 449

Tagliamento, river, 47, 60, 160, 161, 167, 198, 254; French cross, 162, 163-4, 218; battle of, 165, 166, 167, 170, 171, 198, 199, 201, 209, 210, 269
Tagliamone, roads of, 279
Tagoast, 297
Talleyrand-Périgord, Charles Maurice de, Prince of Benevento, 382, 385; entertains N., 269; and negotiations with Turkey, 281, 304, 366; and N.'s return to Paris, 366; and Brumaire, 368, 373; and French armies, 478
Tanarello, river, 180, 449
Tanaro, river, 29, 32, 53, 56, 57, 180, 442, 468, 469
Tarascon, 568
Tarentaise road, 47
Tarento, 49
Tarentum, 355
Target, G. J. B., 365
Tarracona, 445
Tartaro, river, 191, 196
Tarwis, 160, 161, 166, 198, 200, 210, 269; battle for, 164-5, 170
Tavignano, river, 5
Teramea, 284
Tesino, river, *see* Ticino
Teschen, Treaty of, 265
Teste, General, 514
Texel, 421, 429
Thebes, 296, 297
Thermard, ——, 287
Thermidor, Ninth of, 33, 37, 72, 236, 237, 241, 382, 386
Theseus, the, 358
Thielman, General J. A., near Dinant, 502; defends Wavres, 533, 534, 540
Thionville, 488
Thomé, Thomas, 377, 381
Thugut, Baron Franz von, 253, 254, 461
Tiber, river, 49
Ticino, river, 60, 61, 62, 64, 66, 69, 75, 76, 77, 182, 228, 229, 448, 458, 459, 464, 465, 512
Tiger, the, 335, 358
Tilly, 514, 517
Timolean, the, 286
Tintura (Tantura), 337, 339
Tolbach (Toblaco), 168
Tolentino, 100, 127, 207; Treaty of, 131, 136, 153-7, 201, 229, 271
Tonnant, the, 283, 285, 286
Torbole, 113, 162
Torre, 57
Torre-di-Garafola, 466
Tortona, 58, 59, 60, 64, 66, 71, 83, 84, 92, 125, 221, 222, 224, 465 *and n.*, 469
Toul, 489
Toulon, 14, 51, 215, 221, 268, 278, 281, 284, 290, 298, 353, 355, 357, 421, 429, 436, 442, 446, 463, 481, 482, 483, 489, 569; English capture, 9, 11, 445; siege of, 15 *et seq.*; executions in, 22, 24; fortification of, 27; N. saves emigrants in, 33-4, 390; N. sails from, 279, 280

INDEX

Toulouse, 476, 487
Tourville, Admiral, 184
Tramin, 168
Transpadan Republic, 162, 216, 219; formation of, 228; merged into Cisalpine Republic, 229
Trebbia, river, 66, 442; battle of, 416, 417
Treilhard, Comte Jean Baptiste, 249, 264, 265, 365
Trent, 77, 80, 92, 123, 160, 188, 190, 191, 192, 199; Austrians at, 93, 98, 103; French capture, 103–4; Vaubois at, 110, 112; Austrians occupy, 113, 210
Treviso, 3, 144, 163, 212
Trichenaye, 506
Trieste, 132, 163, 166, 167, 175, 198, 200, 480; French take, 165, 168
Triola, 28
Tripoli, 297, 331, 360
Tronchet, François Denis, 365
Tronçon-Ducoudray, Guillaume Alexandre, 247
Tronto, river, 157
Troya, the, 411
Truguet, Admiral Laurent Jean François, 7, 14, 240
Tudella, battle of, 490
Tunis, 297, 298
Turin, 28, 49, 51, 54, 55, 60, 63, 126, 127, 175, 181, 202, 210, 454, 464, 470, 471; fortifications of, 58; Orleans at, 185–6; Franco-Sardinian treaty signed at, 224–6; N. at, 263–4; Austrians march on, 457, 458
Turkey, 356; N.'s hopes of conciliating, 281, 304, 366; declares war on France, 333 *et seq.*, 359; forces at Acre, 335 *et seq.*; forces at Aboukir, 344–9; defeats of, 354, 358, 360
Turreau de Linières, Baron Louis Marie, 457, 458
Tuscany, 48, 82, 129, 134, 258, 279, 464, 470; Murat invades, 479; *see also* Ferdinand III, Grand Duke of
Two Sicilies, *see* Naples
Tyre, 331
Tyrol, 80, 83, 103–5, 115, 116, 120, 122, 123, 125, 130, 138, 139, 144, 174, 175, 187, 188, 191, 195, 196, 198, 199, 201, 436, 437, 438, 477; Austrian forces in, 89, 91, 92, 93, 102, 109, 112, 159, 161–2, 210; road to Vienna from, 160–1; Austrian withdrawal from, 167–8

Uckerath, 178
Udine, 164, 165, 216, 228; Franco-Austrian conferences at, 253, 259–60
Ulm, 202; Moreau strikes towards, 436–9, 489
Ulsnitz (Elsnitz), Lt.-Field-Marshal, 441
Umbria, 155
Unzmarkt, action of, 173
Urbino, 138, 154, 156, 157, 228; French enter, 84–5, 88, 184, 469
Ushant, action off, 290

Utrecht, Treaty of, 407
Uxbridge, Henry William Paget, second Earl of, 536; near Grammont, 503; withdraws from Quatre Bras, 515; forces under, 560

Vado, 30, 32, 33, 181, 442; fortifications of, 27–8
Valais road, 47
Valeggio, 64, 78, 79, 182
Valence, 6, 7, 363, 389, 476, 477
Valencia, 490
Valenciennes, 486, 488, 500
Valenza, 60, 64
Valette, General, 96
Valladolid, 490
Valteline, 260, 269; added to Cisalpine Republic, 229, 231–4, 243
Valvasone, French cross the Tagliamento at, 163–4
Vandamme, Dominique René, Comte d'Unebourg, 540; forces under, 486; reaches Charleroi, 504; at Gilly, 505; near Fleurus, 506; at Ligny, 511
Vandeleur, Sir John Ormsby, 560
Vanguard, the, 285
Vansittart, Nicholas, 421
Var, river, 26, 28, 32, 47, 51, 180, 362, 434, 441; Suchet defends, 444, 445, 446
Vareggio, 442
Varennes, flight to, 12
Vatican, French plunder, 272
Vatrin, General, 453, 457, 465*n*.
Vaublanc, Comte Vincent M. Viénot de, 37, 42, 250
Vaubois, Claude Henri Belgrand, Comte de, 7, 84, 86, 189, 190, 195; at Leghorn, 87; marches to the Avisio, 103–4; on the Avisio, 110, 112; retreats, 113; N. reproaches troops of, 114; losses of, 115; at Bussolengo, 120, 121; at Castel-Nuovo, 123; Joubert succeeds, 146
Vaudemont, Prince of, 436
Venasque, ceded to France, 155
Vendée, *see* La Vendée
Vendémiaire, insurrection of, 35, 36 *et seq.*, 369; N.'s part in, 39 *et seq.*; Sieyes and, 364–5
Venice, 47, 77, 80, 84, 128, 151, 196, 218, 228, 243; as capital of Italy, 48–9; neutrality of, 61, 182–3, 204–6, 210; French enter, 77–8; and democracy, 134; hostility of, 137, 160; forces left to watch, 160, 161; insurrection in, 175, 176, 200–1, 207, 209–12, 216; and Leoben preliminaries, 176, 177–8; description of, 202–3; armed forces of, 203, 208, 215, 268; N. considers war against, 208; N. offers an alliance to, 209, 210; Junot's mission to, 212–3; war declared against, 213–5; democracy established in, 215, 219; votes for Italian Republic, 229; and Treaty of Campo-Formio, 229, 252, 260, 261; ceded to Austria, 252, 254, 257–8, 261, 264
Vercelli, 459
Verdier, General, 98, 114

INDEX

Verdun, 489
Vergniaux, Pierre Victorin, 572
Verona, 62, 92, 94, 99, 114, 121, 137, 139, 142, 143, 160, 167, 182, 188, 191, 192, 193, 194, 195, 196, 199, 204, 205, 207, 208, 210, 269; French capture, 80; Austrians approach, 93; French recapture, 98; fortifications of, 103; Mezaros before, 104, 106, 107; Augereau at, 110, 112; Austrian threat to, 113, 115, 118, 120; road from Vicenza to, 114; N. at, 115, 140, 206; French march to Ronco from, 116-7; French return to, 122-3; Massena at, 138; revolt in, 201, 211-2, 213, 214, 218, 243; looting in, 216
Versailles, Peace of (1783), 408
Vial, General Honoré, 31, 141, 310
Vicenza, 106, 107, 112, 114, 121, 122, 133, 196, 207, 211, 213, 216
Victor, Claude Perrin, Duke of Belluna, 161, 212, 453; at La Favorite, 144; in Papal States, 148, 151, 157; and Venetian insurrection, 201; at Montebello, 462-3; at Marengo, 465, 467, 468
Vienna, 138, 176, 437, 440; French march on, 127, 136, 154, 158, 159 et seq., 170 et seq., 198-201, 207, 208, 210, 256, 435, 445, 466; roads to, 160-1; Imperial Court leaves, 170; Bernadotte causes trouble at, 273; in 1805 campaign, 489; Wellington in, 494
Vienna, Congress of, discord in, 477-8; and N.'s return from Elba, 480
Vienne, 363
Vigevano, 61
Vignolles (Vignoles), Colonel, 85, 113, 119
Villach, 159, 160, 161, 164, 165, 166, 174, 199, 201, 212
Villa Franca, 49, 52, 78, 79
Villa-Impenta, action of, 108
Villa-Nuova, 114, 118, 119, 121, 122, 196
Villaret-Joyeuse, Comte Louis Thomas, 250, 290
Villeneuve, Admiral Pierre C. J. B. Silvestre, 453, 567; at Aboukir, 286, 287, 290
Villetard, Alexandre E. P., Comte, 378
Villontrey, ——, 545
Vincent, Freiherr Karl von, 133, 175
Vintimiglia, 28, 32, 442
Visit and Search, principles of, 404 et seq., 418-20, 430-1; and contraband, 405, 406, 409-10, 415, 419, 430; English attitude to, 406, 407, 408, 412, 418, 419, 420, 430-1, 436; Anglo-American agreement on, 408, 409, 411; Franco-American agreement on, 414-5, 418; St Petersburg Treaty and, 430-1
Vistula, river, 436
Vitrolles, E. F. A. d'Arnaud, Baron de, 476, 477
Vivian, Sir Richard Hussey, Baron, 560
Vizille, 475
Voghera, 465
Volney, C. F. C., Comte de, 365
Voltri, 53, 54, 55, 181, 443, 448, 462

Vosges, 495, 497
Vostanieh, 296

Wagram, 501
Wardan, 306, 344
Warfare, N.'s principles of, 181, 187, 192, 193, 194, 199, 532, 548; comparison between land and sea, 288-9, 404, 430-1; the phases of battle, 525; *see also* Neutrals
Warren, Admiral Sir John, 357
Washington, George, 409, 415; death of, 411
Waterloo, 504, 517, 544, 547, 548
Waterloo campaign: disposition of French forces (June 1), 486-9; N.'s plans for, 494 *et seq.*; French positions (June 14), 500; Allied positions (June 14), 502-3; fighting during June 15, 504-6; positions at nightfall, 506-7; French advance to Fleurus, 508-9; battle of Ligny, 510-11; Quatre Bras battle, 512-4; positions at nightfall (June 16), 514; French advance to Planchenoit, 514-6; Grouchy marches to Gembloux, 516-8; battle of Mont St Jean, 519 *et seq.*; Anglo-Dutch positions, 521; French line of battle, 522-5; French take Hougoumont, 525-6; Bülow's arrival, 526-8; Anglo-Dutch left attacked, 528-30, 531-2; Bülow attacks, 530-1, 532, 534; action of Wavres, 533, 534, 540; Blücher reinforces Allies, 533-4; French routed, 535-7; losses, 536; French converge on Laon, 539-40; Allies invade France, 541; N.'s observations on, 543-51
Wavres, 547; Prussian retreat on, 514, 515, 516-8, 545-6; Prussian forces at, 525, 527, 528; Grouchy attacks, 532-3, 533-4, 540, 550, 551
Weights and measures, 238-40
Weissemburg, lines of, 25, 242, 261
Wellington, Arthur Wellesley, Duke of, 481, 519, 533; forces under, 489, 494, 497, 498, 517, 521, 560; N.'s plans of campaign against, 495 *et seq.*, 520-1; dispositions and strength of (June 14), 502-3; character of, 504; during June 15, 506-7; and Quatre Bras, 512-4; retreats towards Brussels, 515-6; takes up battle position, 520-1; French attacks on his left, 525-6, 528-9, 531-2, 534; Blücher reinforces, 533 *et seq.*, 546; losses of, 536; enters France, 541-2; N.'s observations on operations against, 543 *et seq.*; taken by surprise, 543; mistakes of, 548-51; strength of (June 15), 560
Wesel, 432, 483
Weser, river, 420, 421
West, Army of, 435
West Indies, 257, 420
Westphalia, Treaty of, 265
Wetzlar, river, 178
What is the Third Estate? (Sieyes), 364
Whitworth, Charles, Baron (later Earl) Whitworth, 413
William V, Prince of Orange, 133

604

INDEX

Willot, Comte Amédée de, 241, 245, 247, 250, 436, 444–5

Wukassowich (Vukassovich), Baron Joseph Philip von, 51, 55, 67, 68, 98, 192, 441; at Mantua, 89; at San Marco, 103; at Serravalle, 104; at Rivoli, 141, 142

Wurmser, Dagobert L., Count von, 73, 112, 116, 117, 120, 125, 132, 133, 193, 207, 268; succeeds Beaulieu, 82; marches into Italy, 84, 91, 92, 93; dispositions and plans of, 93, 94; his right defeated at Lonato, 94; passes the Adige, 94–5; at Mantua, 95, 96; battle of Lonato, 96; reforms his forces, 96–7; battle of Castiglione, 97–8; retreats to Trent, 98; mistakes of, 99; plans and dispositions of (Sept. 1796), 102–3; marches to Bassano, 103, 104–5; in despair after battle there, 106–7; crosses the Adige, 107; marches to Mantua, 108; trapped in Mantua, 109; Alvinzi's efforts to relieve, 111 *et seq.*; Emperor's orders to, 139; at La Favorite, 144; surrender of, 145–6, 196; N.'s observations on operations against, 184, 186–91, 194, 196

Wurtemberg, 433, 437

Wurtzburg, 432, 433

York, Frederick Augustus, Duke of, 395; in Holland, 416, 434, 435

York von Wartenburg, H. D. L., Count, 498

Zach, General, 467, 468

Zajonczek, General Joseph, 135, 174, 305

Zante, 215, 228, 261

Zealous, the, 285

Zelada, Cardinal, 147

Zurich, battle of, 416, 417, 433, 435, 441

Zwietten (Ziethen), H. E. K., Count von, on the Sambre, 502; retreats to Fleurus, 504–6; at Waterloo, 533

Also published by The Soho Book Company:

THE DEAD SEAGULL, by GEORGE BARKER

George Barker was born in Essex in 1913 of an English father and an Irish mother. At an early age he came to London, where he set up a printing press in Shepherd's Bush (The Phoenix Press). His first poems were printed there. He was soon noticed as an extravagant figure around town and his work attracted the practical encouragement of T. S. Eliot and the admiration of W. B. Yeats. *Thirty Preliminary Poems* were published in 1933, followed by *A Vision of Beasts and Gods*, *Eros in Dogma* (1944), *News of the World* (1950), *The True Confession of George Barker* (1950), *Calamiterror* and other works. His *Collected Poems* were first published by Faber & Faber in 1957. His more recent works include *In Memory of David Archer* (1973), *Villa Stellar*, and *Anno Domini* (1983). Apart from verse, George Barker has written three books for children. He has lived in the United States, Japan and Italy, and now lives in Norfolk.

His novel, *The Dead Seagull*, was first published in 1950. It is recognisably the work of a poet being short, lyrical and strong. It is the closely-observed story of a love affair, sometimes brutally scathing, sometimes almost pornographical; above all it is an unparalleled description of the power of sexual love.

'I warn you that as you lie in your bed and feel the determination of your lover slipping its blade between your ribs, this is the real consummation. "Kill me, Kill me," you murmur. But it always surprises you when you die.'

ISBN 0948166 00 2 £4.95

Please ask for these books at your local bookshop. If unavailable they can be ordered direct from The Soho Book Company, Orders Department, 1/3 Brewer Street, London W1R 3FN. Please enclose £1 extra for each complete order to cover postage and packing.

Also published by The Soho Book Company:

MY HEART LAID BARE,
by CHARLES BAUDELAIRE

Charles Baudelaire was born in Paris in 1821. His passionate and almost unnatural love for his young widowed mother was shattered when she married General Aupick in 1828. He came to see Aupick as a symbol of the respectability and authority he loathed, and his loss of the love of his mother as a symbol of his destiny in the world. His parents opposed his determination to become a poet and embarked him for India but Baudelaire left the ship at Reunion and returned to Paris. He set up an apartment on the Ile Saint-Louis, which he furnished in decadent style, filling it with gilt and damasks and paintings by Delacroix. Here he set out to embody his ideal of the Dandy. He contracted dangerous debts and his life of desperate excess soon became depraved and sordid when he began the disastrous liasion with the mulatto actress Jeanne Duval, the *Venus Noire* of his poems. In 1857 he published *Les Fleurs du Mal*. He was prosecuted and fined for offences to public morals and a ban was imposed on the more obscene poems in the work which was not lifted until 1949. By 1864, Baudelaire's resources were exhausted and he fled to Brussels where his ruined constitution finally gave way. He was brought back to Paris in 1866 suffering from general paralysis and lingered on until 31 August 1867, when he died.

A characteristic theme of Baudelaire's is "l'horreur et l'extase de la vie." He found inspiration in the streets and the mysterious hidden life of Paris, and also in the spirit of evil itself. A sense of damnation provoked him to blasphemy; "*Enfer ou Ciel, qu'importe?*" he wrote. Beauty, to him, already contained the elements of its own corruption. *My Heart Laid Bare* and the other prose works published in this volume exhibit all Baudelaire's characteristic themes and are written with a disturbing blend of intellectual precision and romantic beauty, and with a sarcasm which merges into squalid decadence.

ISBN 0948166 07 X   £5.95

Please ask for these books at your local bookshop. If unavailable they can be ordered direct from The Soho Book Company, Orders Department, 1/3 Brewer Street, London W1R 3FN. Please enclose £1 extra for each complete order to cover postage and packing.

Also published by The Soho Book Company:

DOMINIQUE, by EUGENE FROMENTIN

Eugene Fromentin was born at La Rochelle, on the Atlantic coast of France, in 1820. His family owned considerable properties in the area and his father was the superintendent of a mental hospital. He was sent to Paris to read for the bar but gave up law for painting. He was a successful artist of the school of Delacroix, and was highly esteemed by his contemporaries for his paintings of North Africa, which he visited several times during the 1840's and 1850's. *A Summer in the Sahara* (1857) and *A Year in the Sahel* (1859) are accounts of his wanderings there which at once established him as a literary artist of the first order. After the publication of *Dominique* he felt unable to satisfy his high literary standards and returned to painting. Shortly before his death he published *The Old Masters of Belgium and Holland* (1876), essays on the Dutch and Flemish painters. He died prematurely of an anthrax infection in 1876.

Dominique, his masterpiece, first appeared in 1862. The touching freshness of its landscapes would alone render it valuable, but it is remarkable as a sober analysis of delirious passion. While still at school M. Dominique de Bray falls in love with Madeleine d'Orsel, who is a few years older than him. She discovers this only after her marriage, and elects to cure him, but falls in love herself. Their moral distress rises to a climax when by accident, Dominique discovers this. The book offers a vision of chastity and pain which hints at the dark side of life, suggesting that there are other ends to existence besides mere happiness.

ISBN 0948166 06 1 £4.95

Please ask for these books at your local bookshop. If unavailable they can be ordered direct from The Soho Book Company, Orders Department, 1/3 Brewer Street, London W1R 3FN. Please enclose £1 extra for each complete order to cover postage and packing.

Also published by The Soho Book Company:

SELECTED LETTERS of FRIEDRICH NIETZSCHE

Friedrich Wilhelm Nietzsche was born near Leipzig in 1844, the son of a Lutheran pastor. His upbringing was very pious. He went to the famous grammar school of Pforta, and then to the universities of Bonn and Leipzig where he was powerfully influenced by his reading of Schopenhauer. His brilliance as a philologist was such that he was appointed to the chair of classical philology at the University of Basel at the age of 24, before he had taken his degree. While at Basel he made and broke his passionate friendship with the composer Richard Wagner and took part as an ambulance orderly in the Franco-Prussian war. Plagued by ill health, he was obliged to retire from the University in 1879. After this he lived a reclusive life in Switzerland, France and Italy, until in 1889 he became paralysed and went mad. He died in 1900.

Nietzsche became famous with *The Birth of Tragedy* (1872) which was of revolutionary importance, challenging the accepted tradition of classical scholarship. He achieved lasting fame with *Thus Spake Zarathustra*, mostly written between 1883 and 1885. His other works include *Untimely Meditations* (1873–6); *Human, All Too Human* (1878–9); *The Wanderer and his Shadow* (1880); *The Dawn* (1881); *The Gay Science* (1882 & 1887); *Beyond Good and Evil* (1886); *Towards a Genealogy of Morals* (1887); and, at the end of his working life, *The Twilight of the Idols*, *The Anti-Christ* and *Ecce Homo*. In seeking to analyse and redefine morality, Nietzsche was led to reject Christian ethics and affirm the "Superman" and the doctrine of power. His influence on modern German literature has been enormous.

This selection of his letters by Oscar Levy, the Nietzschean scholar, contains the essence of a vast correspondence spanning Nietzsche's life and work. It includes confessional letters to his mother and sister, alongside impassioned correspondence with great figures of the time, such as Strindberg, Burckhardt and Taine. In it we see "a writer of the most forbidding aspect, a prophet of almost superhuman inspiration, a hermit inabiting a desert of icy glaciers, coming down, so to say, to the inhabited valley, to the familiar plain, where he assumes a human form and a human speech." (O. Levy)

Translated by A. N. Ludovici. Edited with an introduction by O. Levy.

ISBN 0948166 01 0 £6.95

Please ask for these books at your local bookshop. If unavailable they can be ordered direct from The Soho Book Company, Orders Department, 1/3 Brewer Street, London WIR 3FN. Please enclose £1 extra for each complete order to cover postage and packing.

Also published by The Soho Book Company:

MARIUS THE EPICUREAN, by WALTER PATER

Walter Horatio Pater was born in 1839 into a family of Dutch descent. He spent his entire working life at Oxford, where he received his B.A. from Queen's College in 1862. In 1864 he became a fellow of Brasenose College. He became associated with the Pre-Raphaelites, particularly Swinburne, in 1869. A volume of collected essays entitled *Studies in the History of the Renaissance* (1873) first brought Pater fame. It was followed by other collections: *Imaginary Portraits* (1887); *Appreciations* (1889), containing his judgements of Shakespeare, Wordsworth and other English writers; *Plato and Platonism* (1893); and two posthumous collections issued in 1895. *Gaston de LaTour* (1896), a story of the France of Charles IX, was left unfinished at Pater's death in 1894. It was as a critic and a humanist that he became a powerful influence on his own and succeeding generations, claiming disciples as diverse as Virginia Woolf and Ezra Pound.

Marius the Epicurean stands apart from the rest of his work, enshrining its values and presenting them in a more rounded and complete form. It has been described as "the most highly finished of all his works and the expression of his deepest thought." He gave up a considerable period, between 1880 and 1885, to its composition. It is the story of the life, at the time of the Antonines, of a grave and thoughtful man. Pater traces the reactions of Marius to the spiritual and philosophical influences to which he is subjected. These range from the *Golden Book* of Lucius Apuleius to the stoicism of Marcus Aurelius, and from the tranquil beauties of the old Roman religion to the lurid horrors of the Christian persecution. An excuse for the detailed examination of a series of human ideals, the book was written to illustrate the highest aim of the aesthetic life.

ISBN 0948166 02 9 £7.95

Please ask for these books at your local bookshop. If unavailable they can be ordered direct from The Soho Book Company, Orders Department, 1/3 Brewer Street, London W1R 3FN. Please enclose £1 extra for each complete order to cover postage and packing.

Also published by The Soho Book Company:

ARMANCE, by STENDHAL

Stendhal was one of the many pen-names used by Henri Beyle. He was born at Grenoble in 1783, and educated there. His mother died when he was seven; he detested his father and the rest of his family, and the devout, Royalist atmosphere in which they lived. In Paris by 1799, he procured an army commission in 1800 which took him to Milan. In Italy, he fell in love and discovered his spiritual home. Between 1806 and 1813 the victualling of Napoleon's armies in Germany, Russia and Austria constituted much of his work. He left the army at the end of this period, his health impaired largely through his own excesses. He refused office under the Bourbons and spent seven years in Italy, absorbed by a shattering unrequited passion which was the main event of his life. Unjustly accused of spying, he was forced to leave and from 1821 to 1830 he was mostly in Paris, living frugally, writing, and frequenting literary *salons*. He published *Of Love* (1822) and *The Red and the Black* (1830) during this period. Under the July monarchy he was appointed French consul at Trieste, but was soon transferred to Civitavecchia, a dreary, unhealthy port, 45 miles outside Rome. He held this office until his sudden death from apoplexy, in a Paris street in 1842. His masterpiece *The Charterhouse of Parma*, which he wrote in 52 days, appeared in 1839. Stendhal was not a conscious stylist, and was prepared to sacrifice harmony and rhythm to the lucidity with which he expressed his often complicated ideas. He had an ironical attitude to life, and the behaviour of his characters, and even their virtue, springs from their passions. His ideal was what he called Beylism; a worship of magnificent, all-conquering energy in the pursuit of happiness.

Armance, his earliest novel, appeared in 1827. It exemplifies Stendhal's style and attitude to life. Set in contemporary Paris, this charming love story conceals a powerful study of nobility of spirit. Armance and Octave are secretly in love: as clouds of passionate tension gather we are compelled to ask whether destiny will allow them to meet, and honour allow them to be happy.

Translated by C. K. Scott Moncrieff.

ISBN 0948166 03 7 £5.95

Please ask for these books at your local bookshop. If unavailable they can be ordered direct from The Soho Book Company, Orders Department, 1/3 Brewer Street, London W1R 3FN. Please enclose £1 extra for each complete order to cover postage and packing.

Also published by The Soho Book Company:

TO THE HAPPY FEW
SELECTED LETTERS OF STENDHAL

Stendhal was one of the many pen-names used by Henri Beyle. He was born at Grenoble in 1783, and educated there. His mother died when he was seven; he detested his father and the rest of his family, and the devout, Royalist atmosphere in which they lived. In Paris by 1799, he procured an army commission in 1800 which took him to Milan. In Italy, he fell in love and discovered his spiritual home. Between 1806 and 1813 the victualling of Napoleon's armies in Germany, Russia and Austria constituted much of his work. He left the army at the end of this period, his health impaired largely through his own excesses. He refused office under the Bourbons and spent seven years in Italy, absorbed by a shattering unrequited passion which was the main event of his life. Unjustly accused of spying, he was forced to leave and from 1821 to 1830 he was mostly in Paris, living frugally, writing, and frequenting literary *salons*. He published *Of Love* (1822) and *The Red and the Black* (1830) during this period. Under the July monarchy he was appointed French consul at Trieste, but was soon transferred to Civitavecchia, a dreary, unhealthy port, 45 miles outside Rome. He held this office until his sudden death from apoplexy, in a Paris street in 1842. His masterpiece *The Charterhouse of Parma*, which he wrote in 52 days, appeared in 1839. Stendhal was not a conscious stylist, and was prepared to sacrifice harmony and rhythm to the lucidity with which he expressed his often complicated ideas. He had an ironical attitude to life, and the behaviour of his characters, and even their virtue, springs from their passions. His ideal was what he called Beylism; a worship of magnificent, all-conquering energy in the pursuit of happiness.

Stendhal's life resembled that of his novels. If his heroes were on the whole younger and better looking than he was, they were less mature; in many of these letters it is the poet who did not die young who writes, in a poetry of ideas. The three persistent themes of the novels, the love affairs, the life of action, and the precise analysis of the various forms of passion he distilled from these, are also the persistent themes of his correspondence. Here Stendhal courts Metilde, delineates the anatomy of love and struggles through the snow, retreating from Russia.

ISBN 0948166 09 6   £6.95

Please ask for these books at your local bookshop. If unavailable they can be ordered direct from The Soho Book Company, Orders Department, 1/3 Brewer Street, London W1R 3FN. Please enclose £1 extra for each complete order to cover postage and packing.

Also published by The Soho Book Company:

AXEL, by VILLIERS de l'ISLE-ADAM

Philippe-Auguste, Comte de Villiers de l'Isle-Adam was born at St Brieuc, Britanny, in 1838. He came of an ancient, impoverished and eccentric family, fervently Catholic and steeped in chivalric tradition. He lived mostly in Paris, making literature the sole object of a vagabond existence, and suffered atrocious poverty until his death in 1889. His writing has a powerful poetic quality, concealing a mystical philosophy beneath an ornate and extravagantly decadent romantic style.

Axel is the epitome of symbolist drama, and gave its name to the definitive work on decadence and symbolism, Edmund Wilson's *Axel's Castle*. "Count Villiers de l'Isle-Adam," wrote W. B. Yeats, "swept together words behind which glimmered a spiritual and passionate mood, as the flame glimmers behind the dusky blue and red glass in an Eastern lamp." Villiers started Axel at about the time he became acquainted with Wagner, in 1869, and worked on it during nearly two decades. Over this period his own metaphysical enthusiasms moved from occultism, through more orthodox idealisms and back to Catholicism, which he had never ceased to practice. Each of these positions is examined in turn by Axel, Count of Auersperg and by Sara, an escaped nun of heartbreaking beauty whom he discovers in the vaults of his storm-swept castle. Each is rejected and it is with the dramatic discovery of the highest ideal, amidst tumbling cascades of gold and jewels, that the work ends.

ISBN 0948166 05 3 £4.95

Please ask for these books at your local bookshop. If unavailable they can be ordered direct from The Soho Book Company, Orders Department, 1/3 Brewer Street, London W1R 3FN. Please enclose £1 extra for each complete order to cover postage and packing.

THE SOHO BOOK COMPANY

NAPOLEON'S MEMOIRS
A classic of military
and political autobiography.
(Observer)

ISBN 0948166 10 X/£7.95

STENDHAL'S LETTERS
You can read your way out
of anything with this. It
is another world and a better.
(Cyril Connolly)

ISBN 0948166 09 6/£6.95

**THE ENCHANTED
WANDERER,
by NICOLAI LYESKOV**
He deserves the privilege of
standing with Tolstoy. (M. Gorky)

ISBN 0948166 04 5/£5.95

**SELECTED LETTERS
OF FRIEDRICH NIETZSCHE**
Visions have appeared on my
horizon the like of which I have
never seen.

ISBN 0948166 01 0/£6.95

**DOMINIQUE,
by EUGENE FROMENTIN**
I feel myself a child before
a man who has reflected so much.
(George Sand)

ISBN 0948166 06 1/£4.95

**THE DEAD SEAGULL,
by GEORGE BARKER**
I warn you that as you lie in your
bed and feel the determination of
your lover slipping its blade
between your ribs, this is the real
consummation. "Kill me, Kill me,"
you murmer, but it always surprises
you when you die.

ISBN 0948166 00 2/£4.95

**MARIUS THE EPICUREAN,
by WALTER PATER**
The only great prose in
modern English. (W. B. Yeats)

ISBN 0948166 02 9/£7.95

ARMANCE, by STENDHAL
A neglected masterpiece. (A. Gide)

ISBN 0948166 03 7/£5.95

**AXEL, by VILLIERS de
l'ISLE ADAM**
Admirable, but mad. (J. P. Sartre)

ISBN 0948166 05 3/£4.95

**MY HEART LAID BARE,
by CHARLES BAUDELAIRE**
Enfer ou Ciel,
qu'importe?

ISBN 0948166 07 x/£5.95

Please ask for these books at your local bookshop. If unavailable they can be ordered direct from The Soho Book Company, Orders Department, 1/3 Brewer Street, London W1R 3FN. Please add £1 extra for each complete order to cover postage and packing.